Revolutionizing the Family

Revolutionizing the Family

Politics, Love, and Divorce
in Urban and Rural China, 1949–1968

Neil J. Diamant

UNIVERSITY OF CALIFORNIA PRESS
Berkeley · Los Angeles · London

University of California Press
Berkeley and Los Angeles, California

University of California Press, Ltd.
London, England

© 2000 by the Regents of the University of California

Library of Congress Cataloging-in-Publication Data
Diamant, Neil Jeffrey, 1964–
    Revolutionizing the family : politics, love, and divorce in urban and rural China,
1949–1968 / Neil J. Diamant.
        p.   cm.
    Includes bibliographical references and index.
    ISBN 0-520-21720-9 (alk. paper)
    1. Family—China   2. Family policy—China.   3. China—Social conditions—
1949–1976   I. Title: Politics, love, and divorce in urban and rural China,
1949–1968.   II. Title.
HQ684. D53   2000
306.85′0951—dc21   99-032304

Manufactured in the United States of America

08 07 06 05 04 03 02 01 00 99   10 9 8 7 6 5 4 3 2 1

The paper used in this publication meets the minimum requirements of ANSI/NISO
Z39.48-1992 (R 1997) (*Permanence of Paper*). ♾

For D.T., Lani, and Eli

CONTENTS

MAPS, TABLES, AND FIGURES

MAPS

TABLES

FIGURES

PREFACE

This book is about one of the most dramatic and far-reaching attempts by a state to reshape "traditional" marriage and family structures and relations into those seen as more compatible with the "modern" world and with a specific political ideology. Its point of departure is the promulgation and enforcement of the People's Republic of China's (PRC) "Marriage Law" of 1950 and its impact on the Chinese family and conceptualizations of "proper" family and marital relations. Like many other family laws enacted by modern states, the PRC's Marriage Law inserted the state into private and/or community decisions concerning courtship, engagement, marriage, divorce, property arrangements, and even with whom it was appropriate and legitimate to have sexual intercourse. Whom to marry, whom to love, and with whom to have sex, in addition to questions concerning when and under what conditions a couple should divorce, came under the scrutiny of state authorities. But whereas the enforcement of laws and regulations concerning the family is our beginning point, how people—ranging from high-level political officials in Beijing to fruit and tofu peddlers in a Shanghai shantytown—dealt with the new regulations and expectations constitutes the core of this book. In the following chapters, we will see how, contrary to expectations, those whom we would consider the most traditional members of society were the most eager, aggressive, and in the end also very successful in taking advantage of the "modern" provisions of the law (such as making it easier to divorce and choosing a partner of one's individual liking) and new state institutions, while those often described as the most cosmopolitan were the most conciliatory when dealing with family disputes and timid when dealing with the state. We will see the unintended outcomes of trying to use political ideology and language to guide people's intimate decisions in the family, as well as many forms of "unorthodox" behavior on the part of people said to be the most conservative members of society. These unanticipated or unintended outcomes challenge previously held ideas concerning modernity and tradition, the politicization of everyday life in China, the way in which different classes of citizens interact with state institutions, and the nature of peasant and urban society.

It was not long after arriving in China to begin my fieldwork that I realized that my own assumptions and scholarly baggage failed to explain even casual observations of the urban and rural population. When I was in Shanghai in 1993 I met a woman—call her Miss Z—who was in her early forties, well educated, a scholar, and a Communist Party member whose father had been a high-ranking official. Although she and her family had suffered during the Cultural Revolution, Miss Z fervently believed in the ideals of the Communist revolution. She also considered herself an avid supporter of "women's liberation." After we came to know each other better, Miss Z entrusted me with information she considered very personal, but only under the condition that I not tell anyone else in the *danwei*—her "work unit." Miss Z's secret was that she had been divorced several years earlier. After this revelation, she invited me into her small study, where, along with many papers, she also kept her photo albums. Among the tattered black-and-white photos were shots of her as a youthful, proud-looking Red Guard during the Cultural Revolution, of her at university in the southwestern province of Yunnan, and finally, of her ex-husband. The pictures of her husband, she said, had never been shown to her close friends.

During my time in Shanghai, I found that others shared Miss Z's hesitation to expose their private lives. This hesitation also seemed to involve certain notions of privacy concerning space. Although both my wife (who worked as an occupational therapist at an orphanage in the city) and I were considered "friends of China," it took several months for us to receive an invitation to a meal or tea in our intellectual friends' homes. Frustrated, I asked my research assistant why she thought this was the case. She replied that although she couldn't be sure, it was probably because scholars at our institute feared that they and the Communist Party would "lose face" if Westerners saw the size of their apartments after forty-five years of Communist Party–led "progress and development." She did not mention the possibility that our friends might get in trouble with the party branch in the work unit should the latter find out about such unauthorized visits. Given that this was in 1993–1994, memories of the 1989 political crackdown after the Tiananmen Square protests were still fresh.

This sense of privacy, fear, and face also seemed to be at the heart of trouble I encountered in arranging a donation for senior-citizen homes in Shanghai. The U.S.-based firm Johnson & Johnson gave me some money to spend on whatever I thought would improve the lives of the elderly in

Shanghai. A contact arranged for me to meet the director and some residents of Shanghai's premier senior facility, where many top bureaucrats and intellectuals were now spending their retirement. Finding out what the seniors themselves wanted proved difficult, however, as most of the people we were introduced to were "model residents" or "model couples," handpicked by the authorities to impress visitors. "Everything is fine," the model seniors replied. "The party and government give us everything we need." Maybe this was true: the Number One Senior Home was indeed the premier facility in Shanghai. But if this was the case, why bother to provide us with "model" residents as escorts during our visit?

As my research shifted from urban to suburban and then rural areas, I noticed important differences in how people defined public and private, and in the way in which they interacted with state institutions more generally. In Qingpu, a suburban county just west of Shanghai, for instance, I happened upon a young woman in a small restaurant near the archives where I was working. After some chitchat, I told her about my research and some of my findings. Without any prompting, she told me that she was recently divorced: "My husband was too poor, so I divorced him. I can find someone better." Since we had met only that night, I was taken aback both by the speed with which she revealed this to me and by the frank way in which she explained its cause. But then again, perhaps this did not mean anything; after all, she knew that we would not see each other again. This occasion, however, was not the only one upon which I was impressed by suburbanites' frankness. Unlike the senior citizens' home in Shanghai, where it was difficult to prod the residents to advise me as to how to use the Johnson & Johnson contribution, in the suburban townships of Qingpu it was easy to find out what people wanted. In the presence of the county's director of civil affairs, the seniors rattled off a list of requests: Could we purchase a color television? How about a VCR? A satellite dish? "The reception we get isn't too good from this old set," they complained. The seniors, it seemed, were concerned neither about the party losing face nor about retribution from the director of civil affairs, who could have easily interpreted these requests as criticism of his own failures.

As my attention shifted to even more remote rural areas, I noticed that frankness in discussing matters of marriage, divorce, and politics was not limited to residents of suburban areas. When I was in Yunnan Province I took a walk one evening with my local host, Mr. Yang, a university-educated member of the Yi ethnic minority group. On the side of a small street we saw a fairly large crowd gathered. After maneuvering to the front row we saw three people—an older man and a woman and someone playing a Chinese *erhu*, a two-stringed musical instrument. Accompanied by the high-pitched tones of the instrument, the couple were singing to each other, using a dialect I couldn't decipher. Looking slightly embarrassed, my host told me that the couple, both of the Yi minority, were singing a courting song. To rousing whoops and hollers from the audience, the man told the woman something like "The moment I saw you I wanted you," to which she replied, "I saw you and thought you were uglier than a mule." On and on this banter went, until finally the story ended when the couple were married. Moving on, I told my host that this was the first time I had heard such public story-telling in China. He wasn't surprised. Such stories, especially about love, would likely be considered backward and uncivilized in "modern" cities such as Shanghai. Other differences between Shanghai and Yunnan were also immediately noticeable. Whereas in Shanghai we were rarely invited to people's homes, in Yunnan I was invited for daily meals at my host's home, which was quite small even by Chinese standards and much more shabby than those of friends in Shanghai; unlike Shanghai, where I was unsuccessful in drawing my intellectual friends into political conversations, in Yunnan, at one of the dilapidated homes I visited, I had the frankest political conversation of my entire time in China, with a peasant who was in the city visiting my friend. Our conversation centered on how U.S. policies during the Vietnam War had affected China's Southwest, and to my surprise, this peasant was as critical of China's policies at the time as she was of U.S. "imperialism." Yet, here again, maybe it was only the circumstances of research that led to the revealing of political views: this peasant woman knew that I was leaving in a couple of days.

Nonetheless, something strange seemed to be happening here. In Shanghai, a woman who called herself a feminist and Maoist, and who considered herself quite cosmopolitan, was reluctant to divulge that she had divorced her husband. Intellectuals, whom I had expected to be the most liberal and cosmopolitan, turned out to be very concerned with the face of the Communist Party and how a Westerner would look upon the size of their apartments. At the seniors' home in Shanghai, it was hard to get a frank answer even about whether some extra blankets would help. Frankness in dealing with matters that in modern Shanghai were considered private (such as love and divorce) seemed to be less of a problem in the "backward" courtship song in Yunnan, however. Nor was frankness a problem in dealing with the state; suburban residents of Qingpu clearly shared their urban counterparts' quest for modernity, but were interacting with state officials in a way quite different from that of the most "modern" of Shanghai's residents.

At the end of the year, I left with many questions: What was the relationship between "Chinese" modernity and tradition, and between perceptions of public and private? What were the sources of the variations I was observing? Were differences in conceptions of public and private the result of ethnic differences, as the Yi courting song might indicate, or perhaps of social class or living in an urban and rural locale, a possibility suggested by the contrast between Miss Z and the woman in Qingpu? Was it possible to speak of "the" Chinese state acting upon "society" when there were clear differences in how different sorts of political institutions interacted with different types of citizens? Finally, what did all of this have to do with my dissertation, which concerned the impact of the 1950 Marriage Law?

Only in hindsight did I recognize that these causal observations dovetailed nicely with the many archival documents I had been plumbing through. Concern with face and privacy appeared to be more prevalent in some places than others well before the post-Mao reform period. Moreover, state efforts to change family relations were sometimes rebuffed and at other times aided by an unwillingness or willingness to "go public" with matters of the heart. In this sense, how people interacted with the state, the culture of private and public, and perhaps even the very meaning of marriage and divorce shaped the way in which people dealt with the state's efforts to change the family and played an important role in the unanticipated outcomes I was trying to explain. In the process of figuring out these differences, I realized that I would have to rethink much of what I had assumed about intellectuals, peasants, cities, rural areas, and state-society relations during the Maoist period.

Much of the newfound knowledge I gained in this study was the result of a methodology that emphasized comparisons—between regions, classes, and levels of the state and party apparatus itself. J. H. Hexter wrote that historians can generally be divided into "lumpers," or those who "want to put the past into boxes . . . and then to tie all the boxes together into one nice shapely bundle," and "splitters," who would rather "point out divergences . . . perceive differences [and] . . . draw distinctions."[1] During most of my research, I was a committed "splitter." Moving from Shanghai to Beijing to Qingpu and Kunming was a splitter's strategy. As I developed the topic, however, it soon became clear that an even finer slice would be necessary to make sense of some of the patterns I was discerning. Even within "the" city there were differences in upper- and working-class districts, while Qingpu seemed neither wholly urban nor completely rural. An up-close look at the state in each of these areas also made it difficult to become more of a "lumper": village, township, district, county, and court officials acted in different, and sometimes contradictory, ways, suggesting that "the party" was far from a monolithic entity; peasants, moreover, afforded different amounts of legitimacy to different sorts of political institutions. Yet, despite all of these differences, and sometimes despite myself, some commonalties poked through the surface of a sea of local variations: whether in the suburbs of Shanghai or in the mountains of Yunnan, peasants seemed to have similar ways of interacting with courts; courts in all areas made "rash" decisions in divorce cases; and many village mediators experienced difficulties in handling family disputes.

The conversion to becoming something of a "lumper" was not limited to pointing out similarities within China. The more I delved into the secondary literature, the more it became clear that debates about the role of law and the state in family life were not limited to China, to revolutionary states more generally, or even to the twentieth century. In their respective revolutions, the French and the Russians also engaged in heated arguments about whether and how the state should and could use law to change and regulate private life and family relations. In the second half of the twentieth century, questions that French, Russian, and Chinese revolutionaries tried to answer still remain the subject of vigorous debate in legislatures, religious and social organizations, and families. In Ireland, for instance, the legislature and church are at loggerheads about whether even to allow divorce,[2] and in the United States, state legislatures are now attacking as harmful to women and children no-fault divorce laws enacted during the heyday of the civil rights and feminist movements in the 1960s and 1970s.[3] In India, where religious and secular laws concerning the family coexist in a fragile partnership, a Muslim woman's demand for alimony after her well-to-do husband divorced her after forty-three years of marriage resulted in heightened tensions between Muslim and Hindu communities, shaping the outcome of the national elections.[4] In Iran, where Islamic law is not challenged by secular models, women have also been pressing the government and courts for more equitable property settlements in divorce cases after it became apparent that husbands who climbed the social ladder were abandoning their wives for younger women.[5] But such conflicts are not limited to cases where there is a clear conflict between religious laws and demands for greater equality and better treatment in the family. In the Ivory Coast, for instance, some women are crusading against polygamy, targeting men who take multiple wives and women who agree to participate in such relationships.[6] Even as the nature and tone of these debates differ from country to country, what seems clear is that, in a world undergoing rapid political and economic changes, contestations about the state, law, and the role of each in shaping family relations are unlikely to subside. This study, which draws on both past and present cases of state attempts to grapple with and change family relations, intends to contribute to this debate.

In all stages of designing and carrying out this project, I was privileged to be the beneficiary of expert advice, wisdom, criticism, guidance, encouragement, and friendship from my dissertation advisor, Elizabeth Perry. Those who are familiar with her work will immediately notice her influence on this study. Other members of the dissertation committee, Laura Stoker, Hong Yung Lee, Peter Evans, and especially Joe Esherick, also provided much-needed advice at various stages of the dissertation. Joel Migdal was an early supporter of the ideas that eventually germinated into this project, and his counsel and support over the years have been wise and generous. Colleagues at the Department of Political Science at Tel Aviv University, Israel, and especially its chairman, Yossi Shain, provided me with a warm academic home, and were a constant source of good advice, encouragement, and thoughtful comments as I struggled to combine teaching with revising my dissertation for publication. I am also indebted to other institutions, scholars, and friends who took from their valuable time to suggest sources, read chapters, and provide much-needed critical comments. As a student at Berkeley, I was the happy beneficiary of the amazing resourcefulness and expertise of the librarians of the Center for Chinese Studies, Annie Chang, Jeff Kapellas, and Allison Alstatt, all of whom consistently brought new sources to my attention as I was writing my dissertation. The chairs of the Center during those years, Thomas Gold and Yeh Wen-hsin, and Joan Kask of the Institute of East Asian Studies, facilitated and supported my research and participation in conferences and other forums where I could float my ideas. Other scholars whose wise comments and advice have helped shaped this book include Pam Burdman, David Collier, Nara Dillon, Robyn Eckhardt, Kathleen Irwin, Mark Frazier, Dennis Galvan, Stevan Harrell, Gail Hershatter, Philip Huang, William Kirby, Daniel Lev, Susan Mann, Greg Noble, Vivienne Shue, G. William Skinner, Richard Snyder, Tim Weston, and Lynn White. David Strand, Kenneth Pomeranz, and another scholar who remains anonymous, as readers for the University of California Press, provided the sort of thoughtful, conscientious, and balanced criticism that every author hopes for. At the Press, Senior Editor Sheila Levine supported the project while it was still in the dissertation stage, and I will be forever grateful for her wise and insightful selection of readers for the manuscript. Jan Spauschus Johnson helped move the manuscript through the production process with a polite and firm hand, and Carl Walesa, as copy editor, gave the book more stylistic grace and grammatical cohesion than I was capable of giving it. Barry Bristman deserves much praise for the index. It is my hope that this book has justified their time and effort. Any remaining errors, of course, are my sole responsibility. I would also like to thank my mother, Arline Diamant-Gold, and grandmother, Sylvia Rothenberg, who were always there to read a chapter and to offer needed encouragement and support. The incredible generosity of my in-laws, Patricia and Irving Altman, helped us get through more than one financial drought. Finally, my wife, Debbey Altman-Diamant, not only supported a tenuous, nomadic, and protracted career path and agreed to go to China with me, but also, with her professional skills, made the life of some orphans a bit happier for a while.

In China, I was also the beneficiary of many institutions and individuals. During my year of research there I was graciously hosted and given much assistance by the law institutes and foreign affairs departments at the Shanghai Academy of Social Sciences (SASS), the Chinese Academy of Social Sciences (CASS), and the Jiangsu Academy of Social Sciences (JASS). Archivists in Shanghai, Beijing, Kunming, and Nanjing, in Qingpu and Tong Counties, and in Chuxiong Prefecture in Yunnan made available the documents (many of them recently declassified) that made this research possible and interesting. I am also grateful to numerous individuals who helped me gain my footing and remain grounded: in Shanghai, to Shen Guoming, Fei Chengkang, Lin Zhe, Shen Xueheng, Tang Xiaobo, Ma Jianjun, Xu Anqi, Zhang Jishun, and Xiao Guanhong; in Nanjing, to Pan Aizheng and Cai Shaoqing; in Beijing, to Wang Shaoling and An Xiuhua; in Yunnan, to Yang Hesen as well as his family and friends.

Financial support for this study was provided by fellowships from the Committee for Scholarly Communication with China (United States), the Pacific Cultural Foundation (Taiwan), and the Alon Memorial Scholarship (Israel), and the faculty of Social Science, Tel Aviv University.

Neil J. Diamant
Tel Aviv, Israel

CHAPTER ONE

Introduction

THE STATE AND THE FAMILY

Immediately after the Republican Party took control of both houses of Congress in the United States in 1994 there was a great deal of talk about "revolution," the role of family in society, and the relationship between the state and the family. Led by the man who would soon become Speaker of the House of Representatives—Representative Newt Gingrich—political debate focused on the extent to which the "decline" of "family values" led to a comparable decline in America's ability to compete in a rapidly changing world economy. "American civilization," prominent Republicans argued, was at risk due to the nefarious influence of counterculture values, the bloated, bureaucratic welfare system, and, of course, Hollywood—all of which undermined more "traditional" family values, such as morality, monogamy, discipline, and hard work. "What troubles this country," Representative John Kasich of Ohio claimed, "are issues of the soul . . . We need to restore the institution of the family and the institution of faith." In his attack on the welfare system, Mr. Gingrich noted its effect on sexuality and the family: "It is impossible to maintain civilization with twelve-year-olds having babies."[1]

Even though Speaker Gingrich and other Republicans were soon confronted with their own not-quite-so-traditional family ethics (divorce, adultery), it has become a staple of the American political scene for politicians, particularly those of the Republican Party, to use the family as a metaphor for both the good and ethical society on the one hand, and a society lacking in basic morality on the other. According to the cognitive scientist and linguist George Lakoff, American "conservatives know that politics is not just about policy and interest groups and issue-by-issue debate. They have learned that *politics is about family and morality,* about myth and metaphor and emotional identification. They have . . . managed to forge conceptual links in the voters' minds between morality and public policy." Liberals, he argues, have largely ignored the familial metaphors of politics, and have suffered at the ballot box as a consequence.[2] By casting the Republican victory in highly moral terms, Gingrich and other Republican spokesmen were tapping into a very rich emotional vein that had served their party well in the past, so there was little that was surprising in the content of Gingrich's speeches in the postelection euphoria. What was more surprising was that Gingrich, who holds a doctorate in history, failed to offer historical examples of other "revolutionary" states' attempts to reshape family values along lines more in tune with a particular political ideology. Had he looked even into the writings of his fellow revolutionaries and political philosophers, he would have found a gold mine of references that would have placed his ideas into historical and political context, perhaps making them a bit more palatable to a skeptical public.

This book deals with a question that is indeed close to the heart of present-day American politicians and self-appointed moralists and guardians of public ethics: To what extent can states change family structure, family relations, and conceptions of "proper" family behavior? This question, as Lakoff makes clear, is neither very new nor restricted to policy prescriptions: long before Republicans began touting "family values" in their speeches and campaigns, philosophers and social critics—not unlike Gingrich—debated the appropriate relationship between the state and the family, and used the family as both model and metaphor for the good and ethical society. In Plato's *Laws,* for instance, the state was conceptualized as a union of households and families, and his proposed legislation concerning marriage (marriage should be compulsory), property, and inheritance all spoke to the crucial role the family played in his analysis of the "good" state. Aristotle, by contrast, defined the family in direct *opposition* to the state; men could become moral and rational only by leaving the feminine sphere of the family (*oikos*) and participating in the public-cum-male sphere of the *polis*. In his *Persian Letters,* Montesquieu condemned Louis XIV by comparing his management of state affairs with the way an "Oriental" master of a harem controls his women and slaves. In this conceptual vein, the historian Lynn Hunt has argued that the French Revolution was in and of itself a form of collective emancipation from authoritarian "national parents" and a replacement of them with new ones, whose children—the French people—would now be able to act as individuals. Likewise, after the Chinese revolution of 1911, scholars such as Wu Yu (1872–1949), echoing Montesquieu's critique of Louis XIV, argued that the traditional family system was "intimately bound up" with state despotism. "Traditional" (i.e., Confucian) Chinese family values, such as the hierarchical relationship between ruler and subjects and filiality toward family elders, he argued in a 1916 essay entitled "The Family System Is the Foundation of Authoritarianism," were the pillars of a state system that crushed individuality and freedom.[3] For Chinese intellectuals such as Wu, it was obvious that a strong Chinese state could and should contribute a great deal to individual happiness by destroying the traditional Chinese family.

But unlike philosophers who limited themselves to the question of whether states should change family relations, modern state rulers have both envisioned a new family order and devoted considerable resources to remolding family structure and relations according to this vision. Among these rulers, none have tried harder than those who rose to power claiming to represent new social, political, legal, and moral orders, rulers whose regimes we now associate with the term "revolution." Echoing Gingrich's call for a renewal of American civilization by reforming family values, many of these states have heeded the nineteenth-century German social theorist Ferdinand Lassalle's call to reconstruct their societies from the ground up, by "stag[ing] a revolution with regard to love, sexual life and morality."[4] Frequently manifested in the enactment of radical changes in the family law of the regime they replaced, such changes were seen as necessary to transform the values and morality of society, as well as to empower previously disadvantaged social groups, women in particular. Since values were inculcated in the family, remolding subjects into "modern" citizens required the restructuring of this basic "unit" of society. Soon after the French Revolution, for example, the National Assembly liberalized the requirements for marriage and divorce in the hope that these changes would weaken the influence of the clergy and change relationships within the family.[5] Leaders of the (1776) American Revolution raised similar demands, arguing that Republicanism demanded not only a political transformation but a *moral* reformation of the American people as well.[6] Moving closer to the contemporary period, the Soviet Union promulgated a new family law only eleven months after the Bolshevik Revolution. These laws and regulations—the very first of the new Soviet state—were a crucial step toward fulfilling Marx and Engels' promise to reconstitute society along more egalitarian lines, a reconstitution that would eventually end with the demise of the family as an institution in the new communist society.[7]

As one of the twentieth century's most revolutionary states, China was not an exception to the pattern of active state intervention in the family.[8] Family reform was on the agenda of intellectuals after the 1911 revolution, and the Nationalist Party, or Guomindang (GMD), which was in power in China between 1928 and 1949, legislated a family code in 1931 that called for women's equality, easier access to divorce, more equitable property rights for women, and the abolishment of concubinage and bigamy.[9] Due to growing anomie and withdrawal among the student population, the GMD's embrace of more traditional cultural values in the New Life Movement, and political and military distractions such as the Japanese invasion of Manchuria and growing Communist strength, however, the code's impact was limited to urban areas, but even there the impact was marginal. Divorce rates were almost as low as during the Imperial period, when it was virtually impossible for a woman to seek out a divorce of her own accord. In rural areas the law had virtually no impact, and divorce was also extremely rare.[10]

The Chinese Communist Party (CCP), for its part, promoted its own version of a family law based in part upon Marx and Engels' notion that the family was an oppressive institution at odds with individual freedom and happiness, enslaving women in particular. Engels and Marx viewed the family in the evolutionary terms commonly used in the late nineteenth century: "primitive" families shared communal property without splitting off into husband-and-wife units; sexual promiscuity was common. As society became more "civilized" and property was privatized, monogamy became the accepted norm. With monogamy and men's control over private property, Engels argued, came the sexual oppression of women by men. Emancipation could come only by destroying the basis of monogamous, repressive relationships—private property.[11] The Chinese Communists, however, did not advocate the destruction of the institution of the family, but instead followed the Republican Code and called only for the end of what were deemed "feudal" or "traditional" marriages (based upon extensive intervention of parents and communities in their children's marriage affairs, the exchange of money or gifts in marriage, concubinage, bigamy, and taking in "child brides" who would later wed a son) and their replacement with more "modern" ones based on the principles of monogamy, love, free choice in marriage partners, easier access to divorce, and extensive courtship between two individuals. In these laws we can see a clear modernizing impulse, one that was common to other late-developing states in the late nineteenth and twentieth centuries. As in China, social reformers in Thailand and Turkey also believed that becoming a "civilized" nation required laws establishing monogamy as the legal requirement for marriage and rules permitting people to leave unsatisfactory relationships; only in such relationships could "love" flourish and women become productive members of society.[12]

Many of these ideas became embedded in the CCP's first legal effort to change family relations. Its 1931 "Marriage Regulations," promulgated in the party's embattled "soviet" in the rural province of Jiangxi, provided in Article 1 a totalistic condemnation of the "feudal" Chinese family: "The principle of freedom of marriage between a man and a woman is established, and the entire feudal system of marriage arranged by persons other than the parties themselves, forced upon the parties, and contracted by purchase and sale is abolished." The definition of a feudal relationship was broad, including not only marriages arranged by parents and based on material exchanges, but also those involving concubines, blood relations within the fifth generation, bigamy, and polygamy. The granting of an expansive right to divorce was a powerful weapon in destroying such marriages. According to the 1931 "Marriage Regulations" and the subsequent 1934 "Marriage Law," divorce would have "immediate effect . . . whenever both the man and the woman agree to the divorce," or when "one party, either the man or the woman, is determined to claim a divorce."[13] The freedom to divorce, however, was juxtaposed with strict limitations on how new relationships were to be formed. People suffering from venereal disease, leprosy, tuberculosis, and "suchlike dangerous contagious diseases" were not permitted to marry unless they received special permission from a physician. To date, very little is known about how these laws were implemented and how people reacted to them, although there is some evidence suggesting that implementation tended to be radical and many rural women were quick to take advantage of the law to seek divorce and pursue love affairs. However, since the CCP in 1934 was isolated and increasingly threatened with political extinction by Nationalist forces, social reforms that distracted from the main task of recruiting young men into militias and the army were not given high priority during those years.[14]

Later on, as many of the top CCP leaders settled into base areas in Shaanxi Province in the rural North, the 1934 Marriage Law again was employed as a means to mobilize women to support the revolutionary cause. The basic idea of abolishing the "feudal" family system remained unchanged, as did many of the prohibitions on marriage. There were, however, some modifications in the requirements for divorce. Unlike the 1934 law, which allowed divorce upon mutual consent and if one party was "determined" to do so, the laws regulating divorce in the border regions required a specific reason. Still, the grounds for divorce were actually quite exhaustive: divorce could be granted in cases where there was sufficient evidence of bigamy, adultery, cruelty, desertion in bad faith, attempts to injure the other spouse, impotence, or incurable or contagious mental or venereal disease. Moreover, in another important break from the 1934 law, divorce might also be granted in cases where spouses could find no way to "continue living together" owing to the absence of affection or "love," described legally as "disharmony in sentiments" (*ganqing bu he*). As one legal guidebook from the period stated:

> Marriage must be based on profound love, only then can it work well. Fundamental conflicts in sentiments will cause great pain to both parties. However, the expression "disharmony in sentiments" only refers to cases where it is impossible to continue living together. Therefore, in applying this Article you must not grant divorce simply because of an occasional quarrel between husband and wife.[15]

As in Jiangxi during the early 1930s, marriage and divorce in the northern border regions were contentious issues. Scholars who have written about this period tend to emphasize the large cultural and political gulf separating progressive female marriage reformers, who were mostly urban, educated, and resolutely antifeudal, from "the party," which was staffed by more conservative peasant men who were more interested in mobilization for war than gender equality for women.[16] Moreover, wartime conditions in the base areas made it difficult to enforce laws that granted divorce on fairly wide grounds. Peasant males who joined the military would be understandably upset should their wives petition for divorce while they were away fighting. Moreover, party officials were more concerned with agricultural production to support the war than with enforcing a law whose ultimate effect might be to weaken the family unit. As one author admitted in 1950, "The Marriage Law was not pursued with great force in the Border Areas."[17]

It was only when the Communists took over state power in 1949 that they had the opportunity to implement their new vision of family structure and relationships nationwide. In 1950 the CCP promulgated a revised version of the Marriage Law that had been used in Jiangxi Soviet and the northern border regions. This law—one of the first legislated by the new state—initiated one of the largest-scale and most radical experiments in the history of social reform programs. Like its 1934 predecessor, Article 1 of the 1950 Marriage Law called for the "abolishment" of the "feudal marriage system," a system that was said to be based on "arbitrary" and "compulsory" arrangements. The new, "democratic" marriage system would instead be predicated upon the "complete willingness of the two parties to marry," "monogamy," and "equal rights" for both sexes. Other forms of family relationship, such as bigamy, concubinage, and child betrothal, as well as the exchange of gifts in connection to marriage, were now banned, and violators would be "punished." In Article 4, the law also established the minimum "legal" age for marriage at twenty for men and eighteen for women. Relations between husband and wife, and parents and children, were also subject to legislation. Husband and wife, according to Article 7, were "duty bound to love, respect, assist, and look after each other, to live in harmony, to engage in productive work, to care for the children, and to strive jointly for the welfare of the family and for the building up of the new society." Parents, for their part, were responsible for raising and educating their children, while children "have the duty to support and assist their parents." Desertion or maltreatment either by parents or children was banned, as were "infanticide by drowning and similar criminal acts."

By promoting the idea of marriage as a contract between two individuals and attacking any sort of parental or community arrangements made on behalf of young couples, the Marriage Law invoked important principles of the Western liberal tradition—namely, that "freedom" (here in the case of marriage) is rooted in individualism, and that "free" choice is more likely to bring about personal happiness than a constrained one. These ideas were imported into China by intellectuals during the two decades prior to the May 4th Movement of 1919, and represented a dramatic departure from past marriage practices, even those prevailing in many intellectuals' own families.[18]

Yet, alongside this May 4th–inspired notion of "free choice" individualist marriages was a second, contradictory impulse oriented toward molding people's choices according to the state's ideology. The Communists, who often claimed their allegiance to the spirit of May 4th, had not only an egalitarian conception of the "good" family (seen in the inclusion of gender equality as a legal mandate), but also a Marxist *class-based* understanding of moral and ethical worthiness. As in the Soviet Union, a mainstay of CCP policies in urban and rural areas was to divide the population into good and bad classes, classes that were "exploitative" and those that were "exploited." While the definition of who might be included in these classes changed according to political and military circumstances, the basic idea that a person's class status determined his or her ideas about morality, politics, and even behavior in the family was rarely questioned. So it was important to have a marriage that not only was not "feudal," but also, it was hoped, would account for one's spouse's stance toward the regime and politics more generally. "Proper" family relationship should include political considerations. "Real love," according to one newspaper article, "cannot exist between a feudalistic [person] and a progressive person."[19] In practice, this meant that people who were given politically "progressive" class status, such as poor and middle peasants, workers, cadres, soldiers, and wives of revolutionary martyrs, should try to avoid fraternization with, and marriage to, people assigned to "bad" class categories, such as former landlords, capitalists, counterrevolutionaries, "bad elements," and "rightists." According to many scholars, these designations of class became, despite Mao's frequent emphasis on the malleability of human nature, somewhat similar to Hindu castes: people of "good" class status became reluctant to befriend, marry, or have intimate relations with those of "bad" class status, either because of fear of punishment or out of a belief that bad class status meant that one actually had bad or even evil character. It is said that by the time the Cultural Revolution began in 1966, the hostility resulting from such political labeling had led to the formation of antagonistic groups of Red Guards.[20]

But probably the most crucial article of the Marriage Law concerned divorce. Even though the name of the law was the "Marriage Law," for many it became known as the "Divorce Law" because of its Article 17. In comparison with the very liberal divorce provision of the Jiangxi period, which granted divorces on the basis of one party being "determined" to do so, the 1950 law was more conservative. It allowed divorce in uncontested cases, but only after mediation by a government registrar; in cases in which only one spouse pressed for divorce, it would be granted "only when mediation by the district people's government and the judicial organ has failed to bring about a reconciliation." Only if mediation failed would the local government "refer the case to the county or municipal people's court for decision." Nevertheless, it was still easier to divorce than in the Republican period, primarily because there were no charges or fees assessed when filing a claim in court. In addition to establishing mediation as a barrier to divorce for ordinary Chinese, special provisions were inserted to help officials deal with cases of spouses of soldiers in the People's Liberation Army (PLA). According to Article 19, a PLA spouse would be required to obtain the "consent" of her husband in order to apply for divorce. Only if the soldier did not maintain correspondence with his wife for two years from the date of promulgation of the Marriage Law would a court agree to grant a divorce.[21]

What was the impact of this law on the family? According to most of the secondary literature on the subject, it was very limited and short-lived. Almost without exception, scholars who have written either about the law, Chinese family relations and structure more generally, or about CCP policies in the early 1950s, have either ignored the Marriage Law altogether or argued that it failed to render significant, long-lasting changes in "traditional" family structure and relations, particularly in rural areas, and that it was only in the more cosmopolitan, industrialized cities that the law's promise of liberation through easier access to divorce and freer marriage found more fertile soil. Unlike urban areas, where there were women who had an independent income from factory work or who were exposed to Western notions of freedom, love, and individualism, in rural areas the law is said to have threatened the interests of the poor, sexually puritanical peasant men who were the regime's primary supporters. "Divorce," Kay Johnson argues, "threatened to disrupt the exchange of women upon which patrilineal families and rural communities were based. When a woman got a divorce, she was divorcing a family as much as a husband and the family was threatened with the loss of its bride price investment."[22] Local officials, most of whom were themselves peasants, supported the interests of poor men and violently resisted implementation of the law. The party, soon realizing the difficulty of changing family structure and behavior through law, capitulated to these forces of cultural and political conservatism and "placed marriage reform on a back burner" after the second Marriage Law campaign ended in 1953. As a consequence, women who were subjected to violence and rape had no ability to get justice in male-dominated, "macho" state institutions and remained helpless victims of their husbands, in-laws, and communities; marriages continued to be arranged by parents, and divorce was "almost nonexistent" in rural areas (except in cases where politics made it impossible for a couple to remain together). Despite some changes in the distribution of power between generations, the rural marriage remained basically "stable": writing in the late 1970s, William Parish and Martin Whyte found that "[i]ndividuals expect, *as in the past,* to stay married for life, and both the local kinship structures and government policy favor such stability." "The outcome of nearly a century of upheaval and revolution," Kay Johnson argues, "has done more to restore the traditional role and structure of the family than to fundamentally reform it." Family reform remains the CCP's "uncompleted task." Margery Wolf calls the Marriage Law "ill-fated" and decries the "failure of the family and the feminist revolution in China."[23]

In this study I take a dramatically new look at the impact of the Marriage Law (and, in a larger sense, the state) on family structure and relations after the CCP took over power in China. In the process I will challenge much of the conventional wisdom concerning family and gender politics in urban and rural areas, the role of class in Maoist China, the inner workings of the Chinese state, the meaning of marriage and divorce among different populations, the role of community in social change, and the sources of conflict manifested during the Cultural Revolution. I will be arguing not only that the Marriage Law continued to shape family dynamics well after the early 1950s, but also that throughout the 1950s and 1960s it was in *rural* areas and among "rural-educated" people in cities that its effects—intended and *unintended*—were felt most intensely. It what follows we will see that rural family relations were not nearly as stable as suggested in the literature and that there were significant power shifts between generations and between men and women; we will see that many people did not view marriage as a lifetime proposition and that many couples informally separated and formally divorced (sometimes with surprising ease) in rural areas throughout the 1950s and 1960s; we will see that rural community fostered both legal strategies and cultures that facilitated taking advantage of the Marriage Law and of Communist political and legal institutions. Such changes in state-family relations challenge both an underlying assumption in many feminist studies of women in the PRC—that there is an all-pervasive Chinese cultural and political reality oppressive to all women—and our understanding of the "sexual" identity of the Chinese state. How can we explain significant and long-lasting changes in the rural family if "patriarchy" was the primary "cultural lens through which Mao and his confederates viewed their work," and rural women were so "inexperienced" and "illiterate," as Margery Wolf argues?[24] When new evidence reveals cases of young rural women telling their in-laws, "Even if this food was shit, I still wouldn't give it to you," calling in-laws and officials who opposed their divorce "landlords," and divorcing on multiple occasions only to marry men considered enemies of the regime, all during the same years when divorce is said to have been virtually nonexistent, we have sufficient evidentiary grounds to revisit the question of just who benefited and suffered from the Communist revolution in China. Unable to explain these findings using concepts such as "patriarchy," "modernization," and others prevalent in the literature, I have tried to use different approaches and develop new concepts to better account for the impact, or lack thereof, of the Marriage Law on urban and rural society.[25]

First, rather than emphasize *the* party or "state" as if either were a unified entity separate from society, this study takes a disaggregated, "bottom-up" approach to them, one that looks at the actions of a variety of state institutions and actors in terms of their social background and experiences, spatial location (what I will call the "political geography" of the state), relationship to the state center, and degree of legitimacy among different social strata in different areas. In this study I will show the difficulty of posing "the state" or "the party" as an entity culturally or sociologically distinct from the peasantry or Chinese society. The Chinese revolution brought to power millions of peasants who did not stop thinking and acting in rural ways once they became "the state." Such officials, while still "the state," did not have a great deal in common with those who joined the party-state from an intellectual background, and who often served in capacities requiring greater knowledge of the written word (especially in the ministries of education and propaganda). Both sorts of officials were all "the state," but their different backgrounds ensured a different approach to politics and morality; the state, this study suggests, is a composite creature best understood by not setting up a priori, artificial, or theory-driven boundaries between it and society.[26] This sociological perspective on the state will be crucial in explaining how it happened that many officials did not consider adultery by military wives a political offense (even though military divorces were virtually forbidden by the law) and why state officials' sexual practices were subject to Red Guard attacks during the Cultural Revolution. Looking at the state as a highly variegated institution in terms of space, behavior, and legitimacy will also help explain why peasants preferred to go to certain — often fairly remote — state institutions to petition for divorce, shunning others even though they were much more convenient to use, as well as why state institutions even in the same county might be in conflict over whether to grant a divorce. Legitimacy, I will suggest, should not be seen as something that "the" state has or does not have, gains or loses; even within a three-mile radius in rural China different institutions enjoyed different degrees of legitimacy. Comparing legitimacy in urban and rural areas reveals even greater contrasts.[27]

Second, rather than focus on the party-state whose decisions regarding the family were not necessarily implemented or even important, I often stress the *unintended* consequences of policies and their "billiard" nature; the party-state may have "broken the (social) rack" by legislating and enforcing the Marriage Law, but how the balls would actually scatter and how subsequent shots would be taken were far more ad hoc, resulting in a state whose modus operandi could best be described as bumbling and whose actions vis-à-vis social forces often had a catching-up quality to them. Changes unleashed by the law and the new tools provided by it—new institutions and a new political vocabulary in particular—proved very difficult to manage. Looking at consequences both intended and unintended allows us to see gender relations in the PRC in a very different light than in previous scholarship. Poor peasant men, not peasant women, were often those most victimized by the politics of family reform in the PRC. This did not happen because state officials in Beijing were "pro-women" or supported "gender equality," but because administrative bumbling and incompetence, coupled with new opportunities, provided a good deal of space for women to change their status in the absence of feminist-minded officials. Central state intentions and policy prescriptions regarding women, which were probably suspect, are not always good barometers for determining actual change, given the often-large discrepancy between what is said, proclaimed, and legislated in Beijing and what actually happens "on the ground." Equally important, women's own lack of Western-liberal-inspired feminist ideals of gender equality (which have been based on criteria such as the extent to which women can engage in wage labor or participate in politics) were also not barriers to political or legal action. The rural and working-class women who were most aggressive in suing their relatives and husbands in court often had highly "traditional" views toward the division of labor in the family, believing that men should work outside the home and women inside, and that society was better off by having men rather than women serving in public roles. This sort of inequality did *not*, however, preclude an aggressive pursuit of rights. In some cases, gender inequality actually facilitated change.

Third, rather than stress people's (particularly women's) virtual dependence on the law (read: state) to change their family situation, this study emphasizes *agency* vis-à-vis the state—the creative use of laws and institutions (or what I will call "legal culture"), and other resources such as community, land, time, space, and political language, to secure changes in the family. The extant literature has been wrong in assuming that once "the" state or "the" party retreated from family reform, this would automatically and necessarily disempower women to the extent that they would no longer be capable of taking advantage of the Marriage Law. According to Margery Wolf, women who sought to divorce found that "the official to whom they must first apply was a local cadre and as such either a relative or friend of several generations to their husbands' families. The mechanisms for getting around such a roadblock were usually too complex for illiterate, inexperienced women who often had not left their husbands' villages since the day they were delivered there in the bridal chair." In China, she asserts, "a woman's life is still determined by her relationship to a man, be he father or husband, *not by her own efforts or failures.*[28] Such an interpretation, which reflects Western feminists' disappointment both with the Chinese "patriarchal" regime and with Chinese women's own failure to mount a gender-based, highly public social movement, grossly underestimates women's agency and overestimates the cohesiveness and internal integrity of the state. We will see many instances in which different layers of the state acted in ways sympathetic to women—there was more to "the state" than "local cadres"—as well as examples showing that rights once granted are not easily taken away or forgotten, and that language once learned, even among illiterates, could become part of a repertoire of skills used, either individually or collectively, as a weapon against recalcitrant husbands, in-laws, or officials. Whether women got together to collectively petition for divorce or protest injustice, trade land for freedom, or run home from their husband's village and from there petition for divorce, their capacity to demand change and receive positive responses was not squashed by the party's refusal to mount another campaign to enforce the Marriage Law after 1953.

Finally, rather than emphasize the lasting power of conservative Confucian sexual morality on both rural society and the state, this study will argue that peasants' "sexual culture"—which was also reflected in the behavior of many state officials and the practices of political institutions—was actually quite Rabelaisian, and that it was intellectuals whose prudishness and concern for social order often got in the way of taking advantage of the law. In villages there was no such thing as "privacy," and this created a culture of openness about sexuality and sex-related problems that allowed peasants to divulge domestic problems to state authorities in a frank and feisty fashion. This open sexual culture was congruent with the new demands of the Marriage Law, which turned marriage and divorce from family or community concerns into state affairs requiring public disclosure (in state forums) of domestic problems. In short, rather than seeing peasant community only as an obstacle to divorce, I see many elements in rural community life that facilitated the sort of the change envisioned by this "modernist" law. Among more "cultured" urbanites, however, the traditional concern with face and the more modern concern with privacy came together to produce the opposite result: higher social standing required that "private" problems remain private and not become subject to public discussion. Differences of this sort in dealing with the state in divorce matters can also be seen when looking at marriage. In contrast to studies that emphasize the success of the state in promoting and creating new identities on the basis of political categories, my evidence suggests that, with the exception of intellectuals, political class was *not* very important either in selecting or divorcing marriage partners, in friendship, or in sex. Other, more prosaic factors, such as love, desire, beauty, money, face, the pursuit of entertainment and leisure, and whether one lived in a rural or urban setting, were often more important than statist notions of good and bad political classes. To the extent that political class was taken into account in these matters, it often occurred in ways completely *unanticipated* by the state and diametrically opposed to the state's original intention of promoting "good class" marriages.

WHY WOULD A POLITICAL SCIENTIST STUDY FAMILY RELATIONS?

Given the academic division of labor, my choice of topics is odd, and I have been reminded of this on many occasions. Feminist scholars, sociologists, and anthropologists, far more than students of politics, have taken the family as a subject of inquiry as their own. Feminists' efforts to recover the history of women have produced hundreds of valuable works devoted to women's role in the family, society, and politics, but this has led both to the isolation of "women's studies" in the academe in "Women's Studies" or "Gender Studies" programs, and to the claim, sometimes justified and sometimes not, that "women's history is about sex and the family and should be done separately from political and economic history."[29] Much like feminist scholars studying the history of women or gender relations, many of the major journals in sociology frequently include articles about divorce and marriage, and there are journals specifically devoted to these topics whose contributors are sociologists or scholars in fields such as psychology and social work. These scholars and journals analyze the family as an institution primarily through its foundations and internal dynamics (how does age of marriage affect the longevity of marriage? how does the two-career family affect divorce?), but less so in direct reference to the way state policies affect the family. These latter questions have been largely left to legal scholars, since the modern state has sought to change family relations primarily through legal means. Books and articles in law review journals have been written about how changes in family law have affected women's status, the legal history of divorce law, and how courts have dealt with custody issues (among others). In these studies, in contrast to the more sociologically oriented ones, the main emphasis is placed on how various courts have interpreted statutes and applied them to specific cases. The court, rather than the interaction between court officials and people, is the main "unit of analysis." The same is true in many studies of law in China (by Chinese and Western scholars), which, as the Chinese legal scholar William Alford points out, "generally slight both the processes through which . . . rules are formed and the ways in which these rules operate in society."[30] Political scientists, for their part, by and large have ignored the family, with the notable exception of students of political theory who have studied "family metaphors" of major philosophers. Recent years have witnessed the emergence of important studies of the state and of the way in which the state interacts with various social classes and interest groups, as well as studies in political economy and rational choice, yet that institution that all of us are a part of—the family—has not been seen as sufficiently "political" to warrant much attention. This being the case, why would I, as a student of politics, concern myself with matters of marriage and divorce? What is "political" about these subjects?

Allow me to briefly state three reasons. First, I am convinced that studying marriage and divorce opens a wide window onto what might be called the "interface" between state and society, allowing us to peek in on not only the interests, values, and circumstances that brought people together and pulled them apart, but also how the state dealt with its citizens and the problems that shaped their daily lives. In historical time, people's tendency to couple off and create families is quite old. But much more recent has been the drive of states to keep close tabs on how relationships are formed or dissolved. In England, for instance, marriage, birth, and death registration began in 1538, after Henry VIII broke from the pope. In 1603 James I established parish registrars, and in 1653 the British Parliament adopted an act that treated marriage as a civil contract, solemnized by a justice of the peace rather than a clergy member. There was also a financial stake in registering birth, marriage, and death. If every birth, marriage, and death in the nation were registered and each person or couple paid a small fee, state revenue could be quite substantial. Not surprisingly, according to the registration clause in the act, state tax collectors were allowed "free access" to records in each parish.[31] All this was new in the seventeenth century, but by the twentieth we have all become accustomed to registering our marriages, filling in forms, going to court for divorce, and even undergoing blood tests. A 1966 pamphlet concerning marriage and divorce registration in the United States could thus state, without any controversy whatsoever, that "we need to know . . . about the effects of marriage and divorce on the family, the community, and the Nation."[32]

State-building in China, not unlike Europe, also witnessed massive attempts to make society more "legible" by keeping records of milestone events in people's lives.[33] In the 1930s, Western-trained statisticians flocked to the countryside in an effort to register births, deaths, and marriages, but soon encountered peasant resistance. One researcher in the early Republican years had this to say about his experiences:

> The people were full of fears and ignorance. They feared that following the work of vital statistics a poll tax would be levied and compulsory military service would be required of the people. When the census was taken in 1932, there was a rumor in the county that the government was going to tax every person five cents and was going to use the census as a basis for the selection of soldiers. Nobody liked to pay more taxes and nobody wanted to be a soldier.[34]

Of course, it did not help any that researchers told peasants that their survey was authorized by "the city and local governments," nor that they were accompanied by militiamen! Not surprisingly, many peasants lied. The Chinese Communists, for their part, were also determined to insert the state into matters of marriage and divorce. As one commentator put it:

> The parties and their families look to the short-term advantages, but do not, indeed cannot, take into account the real long term interests of every man and woman who are about to marry, not to mention the interests of society and the State. The concern and the responsibility of the People's Government and its registration agencies are very different from theirs. On the basis of the definite principles of modern sociology and modern science, it earnestly takes care of the general interest of the people who marry . . . The People's Government does not regard the problem of people's marriage as a private affair that does not concern the public interest of society and the State.[35]

The way I see it, modern citizens' (whether in Europe, the United States, or China) loss of autonomy in handling their family affairs has been the political scientist's gain: owing to state intervention in the family, we have records of people interacting with a great number of state agencies; in documents of court hearings and mediation sessions and in registrars' reports we can get a glimpse of the way in which people framed the circumstances that resulted in their relationship, why they are divorcing, and, most importantly from the political scientist's perspective, how state officials responded to the problem at hand. With these sorts of documents we can ask questions that have long interested political scientists: To what extent did people view the state as "legitimate"? To what extent did state intervention affect power relations in society? Were there class differences in the way people interacted with the state? In short, mining the interface of state and society by looking at family law can give us important insights into the sort of everyday interactions between citizen and state that are often obscured in sociologically oriented studies of marriage and divorce and statute-centered studies of law. We can find out a great deal about marriage and divorce while at the same time exploring how state institutions worked in practice *and* how people dealt with state institutions.

While the methodological focus on divorce and marriage as a revealing interface between state and society can be (and has been) applied to a number of countries, the nature of the Chinese revolution makes the topic of marriage and divorce even more appealing to a political scientist. The Chinese revolution, unlike the other major nineteenth- and twentieth-century ones, was based primarily in rural areas, and its supporters were predominantly peasants. Because of the success of the revolution, poor men were supposed to be its primary beneficiaries. Yet here we have a law that *attacked* the traditional shame attached to divorce *and* the very real property, financial, and patrilineal-related interests of men, but at the same time required that these very men enforce it.[36] As state agents, these male political officials—who were constantly reminded that they were liberated and now powerful thanks to the Communist Party—were placed in a position in which enforcing the law might threaten their own and their villages' interests and values, as granting women divorces might cause village men and their families to lose their wives. Moreover, in traditional Chinese culture the private sphere of the family, which included marriage, was associated with the feminine, whereas affairs of state and law (the "public" sphere) were masculine. The "Marriage Law," in its very name, forced many male officials to deal with issues for which they had little preparation in their socialization and background. Most of the literature on family change in the PRC suggests that such men either were apathetic to laws and regulations intended to improve the lot women or else resisted, sometimes violently, calls to enforce the new law in order to uphold patriarchal community interests. But if this was the rule, how can we explain evidence of local officials implementing the Marriage Law in ways the central state deemed *too radical?* In the end, what sort of "hat" or identity shaped the behavior of state officials enforcing the law: the one based on their gender, or that based on their politics? At issue here are two very "political" questions: Just who benefited from the Communist revolution?; and, What forces caused state officials to behave in certain ways?

The statement cited above that "The People's Government cannot keep aloof from that great event of marriage in the life of a man and a woman" also raises interesting questions about the relationship between state and society in the People's Republic and further justifies my choice of topics. The Nationalists and the Communists both saw divorce as a method of freeing women from the oppression of the traditional marriage, but the Communists were especially interested in how new relationships would be formed. Requiring medical exams and forbidding marriage in cases of mental retardation were just two manifestations of this concern. Another, equally important, one was politics. Prior to marriage, citizens were requested to fill out forms and undergo questioning regarding their choice of spouse; registrars were expected to conduct ideological education prior to approving a marriage. As noted earlier, the CCP had a clear notion of which classes were politically trustworthy and which were not, and tried to inculcate a sense of class consciousness among its favored classes. From the political science perspective, marriage in the PRC becomes a "political" subject because Chinese citizens were expected to consider potential partners' political stance vis-à-vis the regime when considering friendship, marriage, and even sex. Documents dealing with marriage allow us to ask: To what extent was the state successful in creating a new version of the "proper" family structure and relationships? What sort of people thought about politics in matters of marriage and intimacy? Did ordinary people's conception of "good" and "bad" political classes match those of the state? Given the many characterizations of the Chinese state in the 1950s and 1960s as "authoritarian," "strong," and "penetrating" (in contrast to the 1980s and 1990s, when the state is often depicted as having retreated from society), the connection, or absence thereof, between state-sponsored notions of the proper or "politically correct" relationship and the actual character of such relationships might be particularly interesting. What might we conclude about the Chinese state should there be a high degree of non-fit between state orthodoxy and popular practices, even in this highly politicized period?

In the PRC, therefore, marriage and divorce were political. They were political in the sense that the state tried to use new family regulations and other incentives to mold a new sort of citizen and relationship between the family and the state, and also because people were instructed to consider politics in their decisions regarding marriage and the family. In this study I have mined sources that bring to life what happened to society, and to the state apparatus itself, when the top leadership of the Communist Party tried to promote a new vision of the family through the Marriage Law. In the chapters that follow, I will present new evidence structured mainly around the following questions: First, in what ways did the Marriage Law's divorce clause have impact on family dynamics? Second, which groups were more willing and able to use, and successful in using, new laws and institutions to change their family situation? Third, to what extent does the evidence show that people considered political categories in selecting spouses, friends, and lovers?

This study is organized chronologically and geographically. In this chapter I focus on some theoretical and methodological issues, particularly those related to case selection. Why study the impact of the Marriage Law in different neighborhoods in cities, suburbs, and more remote rural areas? The next three chapters trace the impact of the Marriage Law in, respectively, urban, suburban, and rural areas between 1950 and 1953, with one eye cast back to the original hypothesis that formed the basis of the study (to be discussed shortly) and one eye cast forward toward the development of the argument and concepts discussed above. Chapters 5 and 6 deal with state-family relations in urban and then rural areas from 1954 to 1966 (with less emphasis on the differences between types of urban or rural areas than in the first three chapters), a period that encompassed many political and economic changes but from the perspective of the Marriage Law saw little change: unlike the early years, the state between 1954 and 1966 did *not* actively enforce the law through political campaigns. These chapters serve as a sort of test to see if the arguments proposed in the earlier chapters hold water under a different set of social and political circumstances. The material in chapter 6 dealing with marriage and divorce in the People's Liberation Army (PLA) is a test case study of arguments in the secondary literature regarding the impact of the law, since a key argument in this literature is that the party (in the pre-1949 period) could not afford to risk alienating PLA soldiers whose wives might take advantage of a liberalized Marriage Law. After 1949, such fears also existed. Chapter 7 builds on the findings of previous chapters to posit a new hypothesis concerning the forms of violence and political critique manifested during the Cultural Revolution, as well as how people reacted to these.

CASE SELECTION: FOUR APPROACHES, ONE HYPOTHESIS

The main question of this study—to what extent can states change family relations, family structure, and conceptions of "proper" family behavior?—shares common ground with four literatures. At the risk of oversimplification, I will categorize them as "academic feminist," "modernization," "law and social change," and "strong state." Among these four, only the feminist literature on Communist China has dealt specifically with the implementation of the Marriage Law, yet all of them overlap in hypothesizing that the relationship between law or state policy and family change can largely be understood by focusing on *where* state law is implemented. Whether we focus on people's willingness to use state law, on their actual capacity for doing so, or on their success in securing a positive outcome, the guiding hypothesis will be identical: law's impact on society is largely contingent upon whether the law or policy is enforced in an "urban" or "rural" setting. Without exception in the social science literature, scholars have argued that urbanites, not peasants, are those most likely to be more interested in changing family relationships, better able to realize those interests, and most likely to receive state approval. In short, state law will have greater impact on urban than rural families. It was this hypothesis that guided my choice of research sites.

The academic feminist literature dealing with state and social change is extensive and, as is to be expected, far from unified in theory, definition of concepts, method, or conclusions. But what distinguishes this theory from those other literatures is the insight that the state and its laws have a *gendered* quality, and that this quality shapes women's capacity to use law to improve their legal status in society. Catherine MacKinnon argues that "[t]he state is male jurisprudentially, meaning that it adopts the standpoint of male power on the relation between law and society."[37] Because laws are legislated by men, women find them of little relevance. "To most women," MacKinnon claims with her characteristic bluntness, "the law is a foreign country with an unintelligible tongue, alien mores, obscure but rigid dogmas, barbaric and draconian rituals, and consequences as scary as they are incomprehensible . . . in their [women's] view . . . if you try to use the law, it is as likely to blow up in your face as to help."[38] In less colorful prose, even if women seek out legal remedies to improve their situation or to protect themselves, the law will not give them the means to do so. This view of the state and law, of course, is not shared by all those who consider themselves feminists. Nevertheless, feminism, particularly its academic variant, had its theoretical basis in the writings of Marx and Engels, and as such gave rise to a worldview focusing on questions of exploitation, power, domination, and victimization of women by men; feminist consciousness, Sandra Bartky concludes, is "a consciousness of victimization."[39] Unfortunately, feminist theory also inherited from Marx a simplistic, functionalist view of the state and an even less sophisticated view of the relationship between social class and the state.[40] MacKinnon's "theory" of the state simply assumes that all state officials act the way they do because of their sexual identity, without actually providing us with information about how state institutions work in practice, or how different classes interact with the state institutions. Her analysis is based upon a close reading of a number of legal cases, but we are not told if these cases are in any way representative of the universe of cases available for analysis. As a result, the gap between her evidence and her theoretical aspirations and claims is extremely wide.[41]

Much like MacKinnon and others working at the intersection of law, the state, and social change, feminist scholars of Communist China have also focused on the gendered nature of the state. But whereas MacKinnon writes more generally about "the state" or, at times, the "liberal state," these scholars have focused on the nature of law and social change in a socialist state that was expected to have actively worked for gender equality and raising the status of women. Nevertheless, despite their different interests, the conclusions are largely similar. Writing mostly in the 1980s, scholars such as Kay Johnson, Emily Honig, Gail Hershatter, Margery Wolf, Phyllis Andors, and Judith Stacey have all emphasized the weakness and short-lived quality of the CCP's commitment to family reform, and the subsequent difficulty women have had in using state institutions to either protect their interests and rights or improve their situation in the family; hopes generated by the Communist revolution were ultimately dashed by the forces of peasant conservatism. Johnson's argument in *Women, the Family, and Peasant Revolution in China* (1983), which has since become the "conventional wisdom" about the Marriage Law despite the passing of many years since the book's publication, has been that once the party retreated from a full-blown commitment to family reform through law, rural Chinese women were not in a position to question or resist the new Communist/patriarchal order. At issue here is an argument about the nature of the Chinese state: because the

Chinese revolution was peasant-based, the regime at no point could afford to alienate poor peasant men, local officials, or soldiers, all of whom were threatened by the prospect of losing village women who married into their communities. In other words, central state officials acted in the interest of peasant men, and this was enough to stop in its tracks the movement toward progressive change in the family. After 1953, she argues, "the Party . . . quickly retreated in the face of the inevitable conflict and traditionalist resistance that arose." Johnson, however, is not the only scholar of women in the PRC to emphasize the weakness of the party-state's commitment to marriage and family reform and the subsequent lack of change. Such a view can also be seen in Margery Wolf's *Revolution Postponed* (1985) and in Judith Stacey's *Patriarchy and Socialist Revolution in China* (1983), a book that suggests that the Communists *intentionally* reinstated rural "patriarchy" during the 1950s and that Communist Party puritanism is rooted in peasant culture.[42]

By reaffirming the difficulty of state-led legal change on behalf of women, these scholars have in a sense confirmed MacKinnon's argument concerning the nature of law in liberal states. However, by focusing on the *peasant* nature of the Chinese state and looking at different levels of the state (reformers in the central state and local officials, for instance), they have raised some good questions. First, what is it about *peasant* society, as opposed to industrial society, that would make law-inspired change particularly difficult? MacKinnon and other feminist legal scholars often point out that laws support men as a sex with uniform interests, but perhaps there are differences in the interests of rural and urban men that might, in turn, affect how laws are implemented and used. In rural areas, for instance, men might object to women filing for divorce because they are partially dependent on their labor at home or in the fields, or are dependent on them in order to bear male children to continue the family line. In urban areas, by contrast, men might be less dependent on women for their direct participation in labor, and thus perhaps more willing to have them go their separate way. Moreover, even those feminist scholars of China who criticize CCP policies toward women after 1953 still admit that, in comparative perspective, the Communist Party has done more to improve the lot of women than other Chinese and Western regimes. Second, their perspective on the state can be methodologically helpful. By pointing to village-level officials as the main obstacle to divorce, this literature highlights the possibility of *conflict* between different levels of the state; the state, these scholars suggest, can be divided against itself—a perspective not found in MacKinnon's work. Indeed, my research confirms Johnson's argument that there was a great deal of resistance among local officials. The problem with these studies, however, was their failure to analyze other levels of the state beyond the village: in rural China "the state" also included (in hierarchical order) townships, districts, and counties and provinces, as well as courts and mobile legal units. Furthermore, it was unquestionably assumed that village-level resistance was enough to stop women who wanted to take advantage of the law; despite Johnson's, Stacey's, and Wolf's commitment to feminism, Chinese women's *agency* vis-à-vis the state was downplayed.[43] Nonetheless, by highlighting differences between states, between urban and rural areas, and between men, rather than assuming or deducing the existence of uniform interests and values based on sex, these books have made a significant contribution to the study of women in Communist China.

Differences between urban and rural areas have also drawn attention from scholars working within the modernization paradigm, which dominated U.S. social science scholarship after World War II until the mid-1970s or so. Central to theories of family change in the modernization literature has been the extent to which people "become modern" in terms of their identity and structural position vis-à-vis community. According to Edward Shorter, for instance, the "modern" family parted ways from the "traditional" one mainly in its emphasis on "sentiment" in relationships and on "individual self-realization," and in its "cutting of family ties to the community." Rural communities, in contrast, are characterized by strong interpersonal ties, "surveillance" of personal and interpersonal behavior, "instrumental" rather than affective values in marriage and family life, and "massive stability." Because Shorter views demand for divorce as the end product of a long process of individualization, he claims that it was "virtually non-existent" in "traditional" society, where identity is communal. Change in rural values, he notes, occurs only when peasants move from villages to the more liberal and modern cities.[44] In short, Shorter and others view the rural community only as an obstacle to change, either because people do not see themselves as individuals or because their structural position in society does not provide an avenue for escape. Scholars of family change in China have largely concurred with this position: rural Chinese women were not the vaunted "individuals" that modernization theorists have credited with liberal social change, but rather members of families, lineages, secret societies, and, in some areas, tight-knit ethnic groups that made leaving extremely costly. As the anthropologists Sulamith Heins Potter and Jack Potter have written, "In the new society as in the old society, women fell between two stools . . . They literally had nowhere to go after a divorce . . . In spite of the fact that the right [to divorce] existed in theory, *the social structure made it a practical impossibility.*"[45] Even though China scholars disagree with modernization theory's premise that change cannot take place without the weakening or abandonment of rural ties by pointing to the role of the politics of the Chinese revolution, few have contested the basic idea that, in relative terms, family change is still *more likely* to occur in urban areas because communities' ties are much weaker there than in rural areas.[46]

There are other reasons why I expected state laws to have a different impact in urban and rural areas. Scholars of law and social change have also noted the difficulties of enforcing state laws in rural areas, and the relative ease in urban ones, albeit for different reasons than in the other literatures. Unlike feminist scholars or modernization theorists, scholars of the "law and social change" school focus much more on what can be called the "nitty-gritty" of the legal process, such as historical case studies of law enforcement, how cases are brought to court, class differences in people's willingness to file suits, and the nature of the dispute process.[47] However, a common denominator of these literatures is their focus on the particular composition of the *setting* where laws are being implemented. For laws to be successfully implemented, legal scholars have argued, people first need to understand the law and, in geographical terms, have easy access to legal forums. All these factors strongly favor urban areas, since most educational institutions are located there, courts are accessible, and communication through the mass media is convenient.[48] Rural areas enjoy none of these advantages: illiteracy rates are often high, courts are (geographically speaking) few and far between, and the vast distances in the countryside make it difficult for the state to teach people about what laws are about. Making state law and courts even less important to the lives of disputing villagers is the accessibility of community mediators or close relatives whom the parties trust. In small communities, William Felstiner argues, the trust that develops between people makes mediation much more likely than adjudication because mediators "share the social and cultural experience of the disputants they serve." In contrast, larger cities are more anonymous, making it difficult to find a trusted mediator, and this, in turn, leads people to seek out the assistance of the state's legal apparatus.[49] Studies of the disputing process in other agrarian societies have found that mediation is in fact preferred over adjudication. In Thailand, for instance, the use of courts increases as the geographic distance between the litigants becomes greater; people who know each other, in other words, rarely sue one another.[50] Since divorce in modern times is a legal process dominated by state rather than community institutions such as mediation committees, divorce is said to be largely an urban phenomenon.

The "law and social change" and modernization literature's concern with the relationship between access to legal forums (whether as a result of close geographical distances or urbanization and industrialization) and the extent of change is also reflected in the literature concerning *policy-led* change. Reacting to what they perceived as economically or psychosocially deterministic accounts of change in the Marxist and Freudian-inspired literature, scholars such as Theda Skocpol, Charles Tilly, Joel Migdal, and Peter Evans have emphasized change's highly *political* nature. Social change, they note, results not only from transformations in the economy and culture but also from the administrative ability of the state to organize and implement its policies. Where the state cannot carry out its preferences due to the presence of "local strongmen," tight-knit communities, or insufficiently trained personnel, state-led social change will be difficult to enforce. Prescriptively, some of the state-building literature called for developing educated state elites and autonomous bureaucracies, or, in more general terms, strengthening state administrative capacities. According to Migdal, Maoist China stands out as an example of a state that became "strong" by doing just this.[51]

Scholars in the China field were not very active in the effort to "bring the state back in" mainly because in China, unlike Latin America, Africa, or the United States, the state was rarely "out." Scholars differed on the methods or modes through which the state exercised influence, but did not really question the basic assumption that the Chinese state wields considerable power. For the period of time this study is concerned with—the 1950s and 1960s—there seems to be a consensus that the state was at the apotheosis of its power over society, a power wielded in political campaigns, the work-unit system, bureaucracy, surveillance, and prisons, and which was also reflected in the state's ability to shape patterns of marriage and friendship.[52]

Although few of the scholars who have emphasized the power of the state in the 1950s and 1960s discuss the enforcement of the Marriage Law specifically, their analysis leads to a hypothesis similar to the one suggested in the literatures above: that change will be deepest where and when the state is best able to "penetrate" society. According to what we know about Maoist China, both of these dimensions point to urban China in the 1950s as a "most likely" case. For instance, the "dense" quality of state institutions (or "political geography," defined as the number of political institutions in a given area) in cities—institutions such as courts, registration bureaus, mediation committees, women's committees, residence committees, the Women's Federation, and unions—allowed for convenient access to those institutions for those who wanted to extricate themselves from unsatisfactory personal relationships; in urban areas the state was easy to find. But quite a different situation existed in rural areas, particularly those far away from urban centers. In rural areas the implementation of state law might be hindered by the resistance of village leaders and by the difficulty ordinary villagers would encounter just in finding and going to widely scattered and distant state institutions; unlike dense cities, where residents could bump into three institutions within a three-block radius, in the countryside the political geography was "thin" or "scattered." This meant that it might require a walk of a couple of miles just for a petitioner to get to a state institution, and an even longer walk to get to a second and third. Thus, a plausible hypothesis according to both the modernization and state-led notions of change would be that wherever "traditional" social and political ties are weakened, the impact of state-led change will be greater. Where the "modernization" and "strong state" schools differ is not so much in the *location* of this rupturing of tradition, but rather in its *causes*. The former school emphasizes economic or technological causes, and the latter, the impact of the state. Neither school, however, would disagree that state policy will have its greatest impact *wherever* "traditional" ties are weakened, *whatever* the cause. (To my knowledge there are no theories in the social science literature predicting greater demand for divorce or an easier time getting one in remote rural areas.) In China, both of these causes point to cities as the location where state law will have its greatest impact, as they were the loci of political control, industry, education, and communications, and boasted a dense political infrastructure that allowed for more thorough law enforcement and easier access to courts. These factors, in combination with the relative weakness of their community ties, make cities a far more hospitable environment than rural areas for a law with decidedly "modernist" premises (individual choice, love, courtship, etc.).

The following three chapters put this hypothesis to a test by examining the impact of the Marriage Law on family structure and relations in three types of areas, each chosen according to degree of urbanization: a major industrialized city, Shanghai, and the Chinese Communists' political center, Beijing; the suburban areas of these two cities; and a highly rural frontier area in the Southwest. My choice of these areas was based on the hypotheses that the impact of the state would decrease the farther one moves away from urban centers, and that those most likely and better able to take advantage of new opportunities for family change would have close ties to cities. Given my reading of these literatures, I expected literate urbanites to be the pioneers in demanding changes in the family and certainly better able to act upon these demands, and that they would be followed by urban factory workers and lastly by peasants in highly rural areas; I expected officials in urban areas to be more likely to be sympathetic to divorce than their rural counterparts.

AREAS

The following three chapters each include a moderately detailed description of the respective cities, suburbs, and rural areas I researched (see map 1), so here I will provide only a brief summary of what is to follow. In this study, the "most likely" loci for cases of state laws and policies reshaping family relations were Shanghai and Beijing, the focus of the next chapter. Shanghai was a key industrial city where the Communists were determined to establish centralized control. Beijing, though lacking Shanghai's industrial importance to the state, was the national capital, and thus also an example of a city where the state's presence was both strongly felt (in mass rallies, in the reorganization of space—such as Tiananmen Square—to allow room for

Map 1. Research Areas

political spectacles) and institutionally dense. As the capital, it suffered no shortage of bureaucrats.

"Intermediate" cases of state-led family change (and the subject of chapter 3) include the suburbs of Shanghai and Beijing and their slightly more rural counties: respectively, Qingpu County in the Yangzi Delta, and Tong County in the North China plain. Although scholars have usually analyzed North and South China as distinct ecological and political regions, in this study Qingpu and Tong are grouped under the common heading of "suburb" (*jiaoqu* in Chinese) largely because of their close relationship to the city.[53] Some villagers in these areas commuted to day jobs in the city but returned home in the evenings; others were farther away and did not commute, but still might go to the city for a good time, to sightsee, or to market their produce. Politically, Chinese suburbs were often governed by rural political leadership—that is, village chiefs, peasant associations, and the like—but their proximity to the city allowed city-based officials some control over the political scene there. Thus, the suburbs rank lower on the "state-control" scale than do cities, but still relatively high on the industrialization/modernization scale.

The third area and the subject of chapter 4, the Chuxiong Yi Minority Autonomous Prefecture, located in the southwestern province of Yunnan, was chosen as the "least likely" case of the state being able to affect family relations.[54] Very remote both from Beijing and from the nearest city, Kunming, Chuxiong is a prefecture in a province located on the Chinese rural frontier. Yunnan, owing to its location, was very poor and never under firm control of any government in either the Imperial or the Republican period. Power was usually in the hands of the same "local strongmen" Migdal views as impediments to the implementation of state law. Prior to 1949, Chuxiong (as well as other areas of Yunnan) had very few of the facilities (such as roads, trains, and telephones) that would enhance its citizens' ability to take advantage of new laws: mountains would have to be climbed to get to a district government, and even more walking would be necessary to get to the county seat; peasants in the area were only rarely employed as temporary workers in urban factories like their counterparts in the Shanghai countryside. Moreover, I hypothesized that the *ethnic* history of the area would not bode well for the new Communist state's effort to change "traditional" family relations. Unlike cities and the suburbs, which were predominantly Han Chinese, in Yunnan and the Southwest there were a wide variety of ethnic minority groups, many of whom historically had antagonistic and often openly conflictual relationships with Chinese and with each other. Prior to my field research, I guessed that members of the Yi, Dai, and Miao would feel more comfortable dealing with a Yi elder who lived in the community and spoke their language than with spending three days on the road to go to a court whose officials were Han Chinese and spoke in a foreign tongue.

SOURCES

Before we begin, I should say a word or two about the sources used in this study, since they are new in the China field (post-1949) and will thus likely provoke a good number of questions as to their origin and nature. This study is based almost entirely on archival sources in the People's Republic of China. Until very recently, it was almost impossible to gain access to such sources, and when access was given, the selection of readable materials was often limited. Fortunately, during my time in China (1993–1994, 1997) I was able to visit a wide range of archives, in urban, suburban, and rural areas. In cities, for instance, I gathered information from archives in districts considered "elite" (such as the Jing'an Archives in Shanghai) and in more "working class" ones, in addition to the better-known Shanghai Municipal Archives. In the suburbs of Shanghai and Beijing I collected many confidential reports from party and Women's Federation archives, but I was particularly fortunate to have visited an archive in Yunnan where I was given all relevant indices to the archival material and then permitted to photocopy any and every report I considered relevant to the study. As readers will discover in the forthcoming chapters, these materials provide us with a magnifying glass with which we can almost visualize what happened in the urban and rural Chinese family. We will be able to listen in to conversations between officials and citizens, husbands and wives and lovers (heterosexual and homosexual) in factories, apartments, villages, and government offices to an extent that has not been possible in the past. Such materials assure that even those who disagree with my conclusions and arguments will probably find this book a good read.

A brief introduction to these new sources would perhaps be helpful. Usually organized by government department, files were packed with a wide range of information. For instance, the Women's Federation files included investigation reports concerning marriage and divorce, various plans for state holidays, personnel issues, and studies of women's participation in labor, child care, "physiological" problems (such as homosexuality), health, and the like; Bureau of Civil Affairs records detailed problems among discharged military personnel, marriage and divorce registration, and ethnic conflicts between Han and minority groups in the Southwest; trade-union reports frequently dealt with problems of labor discipline among workers, as well as their family and domestic problems; court materials included year-by-year summaries of types of cases heard, as well as "special reports" investigating a particular problem, such as those entitled "The Causes of Rash Marriage and Divorce" and "Special Report on Military Marriages in 1956." Many of these reports were in handwritten Chinese (with not a few misstroked characters), but even those that were typed often had "confidential" stamped on the top (especially those dealing with military and party officials) and were read only by members of that particular unit or other government or party institutions dealing with that particular issue. For the most part, these materials are similar to ones we might discover in state archives in many other countries, and I have treated them as such. That is, I think that they do reveal much about the society and state, but they also tell us something their "authors," since the people investigating, writing, summarizing, and criticizing approached the topic with certain values, ideas, and stereotypes. It would be wrong to say, on the one hand, that the reports referred to in this study represent 100 percent confirmable "facts"; on the other hand, it would be equally wrong to take a deconstructionist position, arguing that the reports are "merely" a "construction" of the state for the purposes of imposing certain ideas on the populace; after all, a very minuscule proportion of the Chinese population even read these reports, and the authors themselves often seemed surprised at their own findings.

Because of the candid nature of these materials, I have largely avoided corroborating them with newspaper accounts (although I do refer to some local newspapers, legal journals, memoirs, and the secondary literature) or national and provincial-level statistical information. The former, unlike many of the archival reports, go through many levels of editing and approval before they become available to readers, and, as anyone who is familiar with Chinese newspapers will attest, they are frequently used to support a particular political standpoint rather than objectively reporting facts. As for the latter, I am of the view that much of what is published by national and provincial statistical bureaus in China needs to be evaluated with a great deal of caution. Although many in the social sciences are of the view that quantitative data are far more "objective" and "true" than qualitative, in China there are many reasons to be skeptical of any numbers cited by statistical agencies. Among them, we might point to the near absence of trained statisticians given China's size and population (Yasheng Huang, for instance, notes that in 1988, some ten years *after* the economic reforms began, the headquarters of the State Statistical Bureau employed only 580 people, far fewer than its counterpart in the Soviet Union;[55] surely in the 1950s and 1960s, when many statisticians were hauled off to be "re-educated" through labor in remote areas of the country, there were far fewer), heavy-handed political interference in the data-collection process, political campaigns targeting intellectuals, the weak connection between local governments and various statistical bureaus, public distrust of official surveys, the near absence of enforceable sanctions for fabricating figures, and the general mismanagement and incompetence that characterize Chinese governance. To remedy this, I have cobbled together a rough estimate of the number of divorcing couples in a given year by looking at village, township, and street committee reports scattered in the archives (whose numbers rarely reached higher levels) and then comparing these numbers to demographic data on those units (using the number of households as the common unit). These data are certainly not the best that a researcher would hope for, but I believe that their reliability is far greater than that of the numbers that meander into the national statistical yearbooks, particularly those that appeared during the revolutionary 1950s and 1960s.

Finally, I should also be up-front about the issue of possible selection bias. That is, by focusing on divorce, am I not describing a very circumscribed social world inhabited by people who marriages were highly likely to give way under pressure in the first place because of their weak foundation? Am I, in other words, building a case upon the small percentage of "deviants" who wound up in courts or other state institutions? Here I offer a three-pronged response. First, I do not think that divorcing couples are *necessarily* an extreme representation of an already weak marriage. Surely readers who know divorced couples would admit that most are not "aberrant" and did not start marriage on the wrong foot; a sudden crisis caused by adultery, for example, could result in divorce as easily as a marriage "rashly" entered into, and even marriages that appear to include all the "right ingredients" by modern standards (love, courtship, individual choice) fail. By the same token, not a few couples who fall in love and marry a short time afterward might remain together a lifetime. Second, the sources I have used go beyond divorce cases in courts. I have read a wide variety of reports written by several state organizations concerning marriage, divorce, and ordinary problems among several social strata in different areas of the country. Some of these organizations were more likely to notice "ideological" and other "deviations" from what they considered the "proper" marriage (particularly the Women's Federation), but others were far more "bureaucratic" and much less concerned with this (such as the Bureau of Civil Affairs and unions). Had I found a wide discrepancy in these reports either by organization or by area I would have been suspicious that there was a systematic bias. But when I found a large area of overlap in the findings of different types of reports in different areas and among different organizations, I became convinced that I was onto something. Third, we should recognize at the outset that most married people do not divorce (even in the United States). This, however, does not mean that they are all happy and monogamous. Many couples stay together for the sake of children, out of an inability to find another spouse, or because of simple inertia; "getting by" can often be less painful than breaking up, and it is often much less of a hassle. In other words, the behavior that I will be describing among workers and peasants could easily have existed *without* a correspondingly high divorce rate.

But even given these potential biases, these sources are among the most candid to emerge in the China field in recent years. As such, they provide a look at the dynamics between the state and the Chinese family and community that is extremely rich.

CHAPTER TWO

The State and the Family in Urban China: Beijing and Shanghai, 1950–1953

The demand and capacity for, and success at, using state laws to sue for divorce have by most accounts been a function of urban status, in China and in other parts of the world; one of the reasons I have yet to come across a systematic analysis of rural divorce is that divorce is generally assumed to be an urban phenomenon. In this chapter, I suggest that in China this correlation may not be true: fragmentary quantitative and substantial qualitative evidence points to the possibility that demand, capacity, and actual divorce outcomes were all *inversely* related to urban status, and to the hypothesis that the features that facilitated divorce claims in urban areas actually stemmed from petitioners' *rural* background. This chapter challenges the notion that state-led family change in urban China can be explained by the theories discussed in the previous chapter. Instead, I begin to develop a different set of variables to explain why divorce might be more common among those *least* "urban" in urban areas.

A PUZZLE

In the 1930s and 1940s, sociologists in the United States attributed the rising demand for divorce, greater capacity to leave unsatisfactory relationships, and higher divorce rates in cities mainly to urbanization and modernization.[1] As people migrated from rural areas to cities, according to these accounts, they left behind close-knit families, strong communities, religious prohibitions (as in France), and other attachments to "tradition." Absent these ties, it was easier to approach the appropriate state institution and demand a divorce, as community or kinship structures that might otherwise have intervened to prevent the breakup of relationships were no longer available, or were much less influential than before. Forces of modernization accelerated these trends. As city dwellers became more educated, individualistic, and economically independent, they became increasingly dissatisfied with arranged or "institutional" marriages and demanded divorce to pursue relationships that were more romantic, fulfilling, and in tune with their own personalities; this is said to be true of both sexes, but particularly of women, who suffered more than men in rural communities. Advances in urban infrastructure facilitated new claims for freedom from family and community ties. In the West, city hotels, apartments, and private homes gave people seeking divorce temporary refuge from spouses and families. Urban density and increasingly convenient transportation also ensured that courts were accessible.[2]

As noted in the previous chapter, the increase in demand for divorce, people's capability of getting one, and actual divorce rates in the urban West have been a response not only to secular changes such as urbanization, increased literacy, and urban development. States have sometimes taken an active stance in changing family structure, such as legislating new family laws and creating new institutions specifically designed to weaken or break the power of the family, community, or religious leaders in matters concerning marriage and divorce.[3] The historical record shows that such laws and institutions have all had greater impact in cities than in the countryside; after the Russian and French revolutions, divorces directly inspired by new state laws occurred primarily in urban areas, but decreased the farther way one moved from the city.[4] Given the way we ordinarily think about political control and modernization, many will find this not the least bit surprising. With few exceptions, states have always been able to enforce new legislation more effectively in cities than in rural areas. The same density and infrastructure that make it convenient for people to walk or take a bus to the modern university or courthouse also allow state officials to investigate living conditions, collect taxes, police communities, publicize the state's goals, enforce sanitation laws, and otherwise "intrude" into people's everyday lives.[5]

With the secondary literature showing cities as a far more hospitable environment to family change (whether in response to urbanization or to state policies) than rural areas, there were many reasons to hypothesize initially that residents of Chinese cities would also have been quite responsive to the PRC's 1950 Marriage Law. As in Europe, Chinese cities (while differing from their European counterparts in their role in the national economy) had historically been the locus of political, financial, and administrative control. As new regimes consolidated power and reorganized administratively, prominent cities that had served primarily as trading centers were often turned into political capitals.[6]

While China and Europe shared some structural and functional features in the early modern period, they differed in the extent of state, or municipal, intrusiveness into private affairs. Evidence shows that, overall, Chinese administrators were less involved in citizens' everyday lives than nascent European city-builders and public administrators.[7] Traditionally, as I noted in the previous chapter, there was a commonsense understanding in China that some matters were "public" (*gong*) and others "private" (*si*); affairs of state, charity, and public works were all considered *gong,* but family matters largely belonged to the private sphere.[8] While family law included both civil and criminal provisions, state law basically upheld male authority in the family and village and did not allow much scope for popular challenges, challenges that would presumably come from women. Concern for what happened to the family, however, rarely translated into active intervention *inside* the family: so long as there was domestic peace, the Imperial Chinese state was usually content to allow informal, community-based mechanisms of justice to continue unimpeded. When such mechanisms failed, however, magistrates did not see dealing with family matters as beneath themselves and frequently rendered unequivocal verdicts for one of the parties to the case.[9]

Even toward the end of the nineteenth and the beginning of the twentieth centuries, when the late Qing and Republican states (largely inspired by Western and Japanese models) adopted a more proactive stance toward policing, taxation, and public health, the state still adopted a rather passive stance toward the private realm.[10] Prasenjit Duara, who has probably made the strongest case to date for state strengthening during the late Qing period (1644–1911) and Republican years, nevertheless points out that community mediation was performed *not* by state officials, but by middlemen with resources or face in their communities by virtue of their leading position in kinship groups or community, in age, in education, or in reputation for trustworthiness.[11] In most areas of China, moreover, the Nationalists' family code, ostensibly their most determined effort to change family relations, was not actively enforced.[12] Even native-place associations, common community organizations in Chinese cities, rarely dealt with family-related matters.[13]

Studies of the role of the state in family change in China during the early 1950s have also reflected the "urban thesis" posited by Western sociologists and historians. As noted in the previous chapter, scholars focused on the urban features of industrialization, infrastructural development, and "cosmopolitanism" as the main causal forces leading to the rupture of the "traditional" family. Kay Johnson suggests that

> one of the main points at which the complex of modernizing-urbanizing-industrializing factors is thought to induce family change is where such factors begin to disrupt traditional kin patterns and to deprive the family's patriarchal elders of the ability to provide or control the economic and social role opportunities of its members. At the same time, [in cities] new economically viable alternatives for individual family members become available outside of

the family . . . urban areas, far more than most rural areas, contained the seeds of the cultural family change which marriage reformers sought to encourage. This was particularly true among the relatively small numbers of women workers . . . and among students and intellectuals who had inherited the legacy of family reform ideas of the May Fourth generation.[14]

According to Johnson, urban *spatial* features made it relatively easy for the state to teach the urban population about the new Marriage Law and facilitated filing divorce claims. Because communication in cities was more developed, and the legal apparatus "more accessible to women and young people," groups favoring change were "more likely to learn about and to be able to use the Marriage Law than women in more remote rural areas." These groups, unlike peasants, were also not "preoccupied with land reform"—allowing them the time to take advantage of state institutions.[15] Johnson's analysis uses similar terms and concepts of scholars of urban family change in the West, and, perhaps not surprisingly, reaches similar conclusions concerning which social groups will form the vanguard of social change: full-time factory workers, "enlightenment" intellectuals, and students (who congregate in urban universities).

A Tale of Two Cities: Urban Core Elites and Working-Class Peripheral Urbanites

To the extent that the interest in taking advantage of liberalized marriage and divorce laws and the ability to do so hinge upon "urbanization" and "modernization," it would not be unreasonable to anticipate that changes in the family would be most common among those who, according to socioeconomic indicators, were the *most* "urban" and "modern." There is no need to cite scholarly sources to argue that most people think about cities, not the countryside, as places where people can pursue individualistic goals and interests without extensive intervention by the community; it is extremely rare to find a farmer or peasant described as "worldly," "liberal," or "open-minded." Not coincidentally, the word "cosmopolitanism" itself, with all of its positive connotations, is etymologically related to the Latin *polis,* "city" (as in "polite," "police," etc.). Certainly in Europe aspirants to high status knew that "cosmopolitanism" depended on attaining full "urban" status. Thomas J. Schlereth, writing on the typical Enlightenment cosmopolitan, argues that "he was eminently, almost incurably, an urban man."[16]

The distinction between "urban" as modern, cosmopolitan, civil, and progressive, and "rural" as barbarous and backward, has been analytically convenient but empirically false for the simple reason that cities worldwide have always been places where people from a wide variety of backgrounds congregate. Speaking of *"the* city" as if it were one place with a singular cultural identity is very problematic. As many urbanites know, cities have different neighborhoods, each with its localistic identity: Upper East-Siders in New York claim an urban identity quite distinct from residents of the Upper West Side, even though the only thing separating them is the narrow width of Central Park. It certainly was the case that Enlightenment intellectuals were more comfortable in the city than in the countryside, and in this sense we can speak of "the city" as a distinct identity, but *within* the city they still congregated in areas frequented and inhabited by people of like mind, background, dress, wealth, and education, or, in a larger sense, *class*. Usually, these neighborhoods were located in the urban core, where businesses, theaters, and coffeehouses were concentrated.[17] In contrast, recent migrants to cities who occupied the lower strata of urban society were often forced by circumstances to live in leftover, poorer, and usually more crime-ridden areas on the urban periphery. For such urbanites, the initial urban experience was "peripheral" not only in terms of their spatial location in the city, but also on a scale of "urbanity." Earning the much-coveted status of full-fledged urbanite required passing through multiple gateways: of dress, speech, cultural activities, and wealth.[18] Guarding these gates were the city elites, who frequently looked with disdain upon new city residents as "green" or "yokels" who were less urban(e) than themselves.[19] To include these different urban experiences, the concept of "city" cannot be a dichotomous either/or category, but instead a fluid one that includes both location and identity vis-à-vis the dominant social group.

In the development of urban China we can also witness the fluid quality of urbanity within the geographically "urban" area. Historians of early Chinese cities have argued that among the urban elite there was no notion of an autonomous urban identity distinct from rural values, and scholars of Chinese cities in the nineteenth and twentieth centuries have also downplayed the development of a singular, distinct urban identity, even in the most developed and "modern" city—Shanghai.[20] For some scholars, Shanghai, at least until the late 1920s, was still a city of "sojourners," full of people whose primary attachment was to their native rural home rather than to the city.[21]

By the 1930s and 1940s, however, there were signs of birth of an urban upper class comparable to Europe in the nineteenth century. Spatially, some cities became divided into "core" elite and peripheral working-class districts reflecting growing class differences. In Shanghai, for example, the burgeoning Western-oriented, educated middle and upper classes worked, shopped, dined, and danced in the French Quarter and the elite Jing'an and Xincheng Districts.[22] Nanjing Road—with its department stores, shops, theaters, cinemas, and restaurants—sliced through the densely populated urban core, its sidewalks providing space for members of this class to strut and show off their urban refinements.[23] Above the bustling street were the commercial offices where Chinese trained in law and business worked. Upon their return, they were likely met by servants, by wives who usually came from a prominent and well-connected family, and, in some cases, by one or two maids. Even though such men sometimes considered their lives to be quite boring and dominated by routine, they were, according to Yeh Wen-hsin, "a worthy target of pursuit in the marriage market."[24] A man who could afford it would also maintain a concubine in addition to his wife. Like wearing imported clothes and wearing a watch, maintaining a concubine was a marker of high status in Chinese society.[25]

In Shanghai, urban status might also depend on native place. Those hailing from the relatively well-off Jiangnan region (southern Jiangsu Province) and Zhejiang Province tended to occupy the higher ranks in urban society as well-paid skilled workers, bankers, and shopkeepers. Those who migrated to the city from the poorer regions of North China occupied the bottom rungs of the urban hierarchy, working as rickshaw pullers, peddlers, tailors, bathhouse workers, temporary and contract workers—all positions that would be considered inappropriate for urbanites with any claim to culture and civility.[26] Peripheral working-class urbanites differed from their middle- and upper-class (or "core urbanite") neighbors most importantly in the fragility of their economic and personal stake in the city. Western-educated urbanites such as those who worked at the Bank of China were attached to the countryside primarily through their Jeffersonian longing for an escape from the daily office grind; only a few actually left the city to live as villagers.[27] Peripheral working-class urbanites, in contrast, were both more closely attached to their rural homes and more mobile, moving between city and countryside depending on personal and family circumstances.[28]

For many working-class urbanites, but especially those with marginal status in the city, travel between city and countryside could be a family or individual enterprise. Rural families, particularly those from very poor or flood-ravaged areas, sold daughters and adopted daughters-in-law (*tong-yangxi*) to labor contractors in cities, where they would work until their parents or bosses arranged a marriage with someone in their village. (A *tongyangxi* was usually a girl from a poor family who was sold or given to a family of more means in the hope that she would marry their son when the children matured.) Single life in the city may have encouraged unconventional private behavior: in the Shanghai press there were many reports about these women's "scandalous" relationships.[29] Precarious attachment to the city was also reflected in housing arrangements. Unlike urban-educated commercial elites who found housing in relatively private Western-style apartments, peripheral urbanites lived in more communal and poorer settings—the *shikumen* (a row house originally designed for one family but often home to extended families prior to 1949, and to several unrelated families after 1949) or, worst of all, the bare-bones, hastily erected shack settlements sprinkled along rivers and near factories.[30] One's home was an

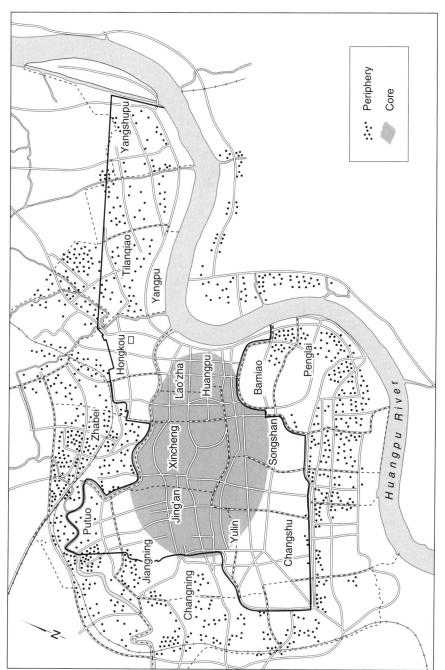

Map 2. "Core" and "Peripheral" Shanghai, Early 1950s. Adapted from Shanghai Academy of Social Sciences, *Shanghai penghu qu de bianqian* (Shanghai: Shanghai Renmin Chubanshe, 1962).

TABLE 1   Jing'an and Changning Districts,
Population by Occupation (1950)

District	Population	Health	Education/ Culture/ Students	Industry	Merchants	Agri- culture	Service
Jing'an	187, 821	1, 559	14, 361	14, 963	22, 330	195	12, 310
Changning	163, 154	498	6, 156	6, 035	3, 829	881	4, 656

SOURCE: Zou Yiren, *Jiu Shanghai renkou bianqian de yanjiu* (Shanghai: People's Publishing House, 1980), 109. Figures concerning students, merchants, and service are from 1946. "Education" refers to schools and universities, "culture" to publishing houses, newspapers, theater, and so forth, and "health" to hospitals and health stations (clinics).

TABLE 2   Jing'an and Changning Districts,
Population by Native Place (1950)

District	Population	Zhejiang	%	Jiangsu	%	Shandong	%	Shanghai	%
Jing'an	187, 821	56, 808	30	78, 526	41	3, 070	1	20, 803	11
Changning	163, 154	33, 497	20	91, 731	56	4, 666	2	18,000	11

SOURCE: Zou Yiren, *Jiu Shanghai renkou bianqian de yanjiu* (Shanghai: People's Publishing House, 1980), 116–17. The percentages do not add up to 100 because I have not included people who hailed from other provinces such as Anhui, Fujian, Hunan, Hubei, Guangdong, and so on.

important marker of status in the city: moving from a shack into a *shikumen* meant that one had "made it" and gave people the right to look down upon those who remained in the shacks as "peasants."[31] (See map 2 for the distribution of core and peripheral populations in Shanghai.)

Tables 1 and 2, comparing two districts in Shanghai—Jing'an in the "core" and Changning in the urban periphery—illustrate these class differences. As these tables show, Jing'an has far more of the characteristics we would tend to associate with the most "cosmopolitan" and "urban" sections of a city: students, teachers, artists, nurses and physicians, stores, and service industries were heavily congregated there, whereas peasants and factories were largely in Changning. Migrants from Zhejiang, who tended to be better off than their counterparts from Jiangsu and Shandong, were also based in Jing'an.

Class differences, as measured by such indicators, still do not reveal the complexity of class relations in urban areas, however. Even though elite and peripheral urbanites lived separately and had different degrees of attachment and stake in urban living, urban density allowed them to witness how one another lived. Among the poor, such comparisons naturally led to aspirations for the life they associated with their more urban neighbors. Even as peripheral urbanites continued to practice rural customs, from participation in secret societies and violent feuds to selling daughters-in-law, many still tried to *differentiate* themselves from recently arrived counterparts by adopting noticeably "urban" practices. In the Shanghai silk-weaving industry, for instance, even minimally literate migrants from eastern Zhejiang Province "prided themselves on being sophisticated urbanites, fully attuned to the ways of the big city," Elizabeth Perry has found. "When they had saved up some money, they spent it on the accouterments of a 'modern' life-style: Western clothing, leather shoes, trolley rides, movie tickets, foreign food."[32]

In sum, on a rough scale of urbanity and modernity there were clear and substantial differences between different populations within an urban area. If demand for divorce and a person's capacity to translate this desire into action are said to represent the combination of an individualistic quest for independence (contingent upon education, elite status), well-developed housing, the relative lack of rural-like communal ties, and convenient access to local government institutions, we should expect to find more divorce cases in core districts such as Jing'an than in urban neighborhoods and districts with closer connections to rural areas.

Some quantitative evidence from Shanghai and Beijing archives, however, shows that this may not be the case. In Shanghai's Jing'an District, home to the city's premier education and cultural institutions, there were apparently *fewer* divorce cases than in Changning District, the peripheral, semirural area, even though its population was higher (see table 1). During the height of the PRC's 1953 Marriage Law campaign, Changning District Court handled 500 cases of marriage disputes, of which 75 percent, or 387, were divorce cases.[33] In contrast, of Jing'an District Court's 468 marriage dispute cases, only 159, or 33 percent, involved divorce.[34] Incomplete statistics from 1950 hint that divorce in cities was more common among temporary workers and the unemployed than among wage-earning workers in large factories, contrary to predictions in the secondary literature.[35] Divorce in China, these figures show, may be inversely related to urban status. If these figures are even partially reliable, and even if we admit that there may have been more demand than actual people who showed up in court, there is still something puzzling about the twofold difference between the two districts, particularly since it was in Jing'an that we would have expected to find the majority of cases. Clearly there is something happening here that is at odds with the European, Russian, and American cases, where it really does seem to be the case that urbanization and industrialization led to more demand for divorce. This in itself is a good reason for reexamining the Chinese experience in a different light.

Much as it is difficult to argue for a singular urban identity, so too is it difficult to suggest that "the city" means the same thing to different states. Since states have not been content to allow economic forces alone to shape family dynamics by legislating new family laws and policies, we also have to consider the way in which different Chinese regimes conceptualized "the city." The Marriage Law, after all, was implemented in urban areas by a regime largely alien to the urban population, and whose primary orientation and experience were *rural*. How the Communists viewed "the city," we will see, was as important as the way in which different classes of urbanites viewed themselves in relationship to it. It is here, I believe, that we can find the first clue to why there were more divorce cases in Changning than in Jing'an.

States and Cities

State leaders and their administrations have always had close ties to cities. In the development of the European state, aspirants to political power forged close ties with urban-based merchants in order to extract sufficient resources to build armies and bureaucracies. The need to ensure a stable tax base later led to the development of rationalized bureaucracies, with a concomitant lengthening of the state's reach into people's everyday lives. In China, as noted earlier, dynastic leaders also established themselves in large cities, and this did not change much with the advent of Republican government between 1911 and 1949. The Guomindang was headquartered in the city of Nanjing between 1928 and 1937, and there it developed close ties with major industrialists in Shanghai.[36] The GMD also had close ties with other, less savory but nonetheless profit-making enterprises in Shanghai, such as the Green Gang. In the 1920s the CCP, for its part, forged alliances with gangs to mobilize workers and undermine Nationalist control of the city and its labor force.[37]

The CCP and GMD's agreement over the political and economic significance of cities was not always matched by a shared *image* of them. Initially, both parties shared Marx and Lenin's top-down view of political change: change would emanate first from the progressive cities, where most intellectuals and workers were congregated, and would later spread to the vast and politically backward countryside. During the period between the founding of the Communist Party in 1921 and the CCP's split with the GMD in 1927, both parties attempted to recruit workers and capitalists. But after the Nationalists' routing of both the Communists and the provincial warlords during the Northern Expedition in 1927, and the subsequent consolidation of Nationalist control in urban areas and Communists' flight to the countryside, the city assumed different meanings to each party. This divergence would have important consequences for the way in which the Communists exercised control after conquering urban China in 1949.

The most obvious difference between the two parties stemmed from the city's significance in revolutionary strategy. Because the Nationalists established their political base in cities after Chiang Kai-shek's April 1927 coup,

Communists increasingly came to see cities as "enemy territory," even though party cells were active in many industries and other urban institutions. According to CCP military strategy, cities were to be surrounded and then conquered from rural bases. Second, cities were the "home base" of the GMD, bourgeoisie, capitalists, and absentee landlords, and as such embodied values and culture antithetical to the spirit of sacrifice, mutual aid, resistance, and martyrdom that Mao and others associated with the CCP's revolutionary work among the peasants.[38]

The extent to which Mao's view of cities was shared among PLA officers and soldiers (most of whom came from peasant stock) is not known. Although Western scholars have sometimes pointed to a supposed antiurban bias among the peasantry,[39] the comparative historical record suggests that the official party line regarding the "decadence" of cities would not have been automatically accepted. Despite urban elites' criticism of cities as bastions of decadence, cities worldwide have offered refuge, opportunities for upward mobility, and a more exciting life, even if peasants ended up struggling to make ends meet.

The manner in which the party-state entered cities in 1949 was also crucial in shaping state-city relations. The CCP's formative political experiences were in the countryside, where it developed mobilization methods that exploited cleavages in rural society to mobilize peasants.[40] Mobilization methods were frequently extraordinarily violent: landlords, village "bullies," and low-level GMD functionaries were often executed after being fingered by peasants seeking revenge.[41] During "rectification" and "anti-traitor" campaigns, the CCP purged erring cadres in its own ranks. By the time the CCP arrived in cities in 1949, it had already developed a well-honed repertoire of mobilization tactics for rural areas, but very few suitable methods or institutions capable of administering cities and the urban population. After 1949, many positions of authority in urban China were transferred to people who had little experience in cities, but who had participated in rural military campaigns against the Japanese or violent campaigns against rural landlords, had been active in the Communist underground in cities, or simply had good political status because of their pre-1949 position vis-à-vis the means of production. During this process, urban community organizations, such as native-place organizations and guilds, were dismantled or placed under Communist authority.

This configuration of state-urban relations in early 1950s China proved critical in shaping how people responded to the early 1950s Marriage Law campaigns. To take advantage of laws that allowed divorce and promised freedom to marry a spouse of one's choice, people were forced to confront a state official and present a claim concerning personal and/or family problems. In other words, people had to make public and official an issue that, at least in the "Great Tradition" of Confucianism, purportedly belonged to the private (*si*), nonstate sphere.[42] How people felt about such exposure and the level of legitimacy they accorded to the state officials responsible for enforcing the new law shaped the outcome of the campaigns to enforce the Marriage Law.

In what follows in this chapter I contrast how elite core and working-class peripheral urbanites dealt with the new state intrusion into family affairs represented by the Marriage Law. Based on the quantitative evidence above and many archival reports detailing how different urban populations dealt with the state, I begin to develop a set of working hypotheses that might explain the differences in divorce and marriage patterns among various urban types, as well as in the countryside—the subject of chapters 3 and 4. Specifically, peripheral working-class urbanites' higher propensity to demand divorce and greater capability of translating demand into action can largely be explained by the resources they were able to employ to support their divorce claims, by what I call their legal and sexual cultures, and by their desire to become urban. These resources, cultures, and desires can be attributed primarily to their experience of *rural life*. Chapters 3 and 4, which move geographically westward toward suburban and rural areas, trace the origins of these features.

Since the argument of this chapter is that there were significant political, economic, and cultural differences in how urban types reacted to the Marriage Law, I have organized this chapter according to political and social strata. In the first part, I examine the behavior of the state officials called upon to enforce the Marriage Law. Cadres in factories and unions and on street and mediation committees were the central state's trench soldiers in the campaigns to enforce the law in 1951 and 1953. How officials and institutions responded to the promulgation of the law, how they handled legal claims, and their degree of legitimacy among different social strata were important factors shaping people's willingness to take advantage of the law's provisions. The second and third parts of the chapter deal with elite "core" urbanites such as businessmen, bankers, post office and telegraph workers, teachers, and students, and then with those with less stake in and previous attachment to the city, such as pedicab drivers, nursemaids, tailors, and newly arrived state officials in Beijing.

THE STATE

Prior to the Marriage Law: Urban Political Repression

In a recent article, Tiejun Cheng and Mark Selden refer to the early 1950s as the "honeymoon years of the People's Republic."[43] While this was certainly true in some respects—the CCP managed to regain control of the economy, restore domestic peace after years of civil war, and give some people a greater sense of national pride—we should also keep in mind that, for many people, Communist control also ushered in a period of harsh political repression. During those years, urban areas were racked with successive, violent political campaigns targeting various political "enemies": gangsters, former GMD officials, secret-society members, intellectuals, businessmen, and many members of the middle class. The Marriage Law campaigns began amid these politically repressive ones.

Political campaigns prior to the Marriage Law campaign remain sensitive topics in the PRC. As a result, in the secondary literature there are only a few accounts of the impact of these campaigns on urban society, all based on official sources. Kenneth Lieberthal's *Revolution and Tradition in Tientsin, 1949–1952* and John Gardner's 1971 essay on the "Five Antis" campaign (which targeted bribery, tax evasion, theft of state property, cheating on government contracts, and stealing state economic information) in Shanghai emphasize their transformative impact on urban society. According to both Lieberthal and Gardner, early PRC efforts in urban areas were motivated by the need to extract financial resources from urban business interests, warn enemies of the regime that dissent would not be tolerated, and begin the process of building Communist-controlled political institutions. These campaigns were also the logical outgrowth of pre-1949 CCP images of cities as places whose values were antagonistic to the Communists.[44]

Scholars who have emphasized the powerful impact of early 1950s campaigns are right to argue that these campaigns consolidated political control. The Communists' success in establishing "control," however, contradicted another state goal—generating legitimacy. Mass arrests, fines, and suicides of "class enemies" during these campaigns tell a story of repression and political terror. In Shanghai, for example, CCP hostility to foreigners resulted in mass dismissals of staff who worked with foreign businesses. Many laid-off employees committed suicide soon afterward.[45] During the "Five Antis" movement in Beijing's commercial Dongcheng District, 13 percent of business households in the district were forced to pay special fines,[46] and in the "Suppress Counter-Revolutionaries" campaign of early 1951, the Dongcheng District's Public Security Bureau arrested "forty-eight GMD spies, eighty-two landlords and murderers" in a three-month period.[47] These arrests undoubtedly had what the legal scholar Marc Galanter calls a "radiating effect," since word of mouth ensured that neighbors, friends, and family heard of these events.[48]

The extent to which establishing political order complicated efforts to establish popular legitimacy in urban areas is evident in ordinary people's reactions to these campaigns. As John Gardner rightly noted, "The campaign to suppress counter-revolutionaries was important in that it introduced the populace to the processes of institutionalized violence, both physical and mental."[49] Forced participation in mass rallies held in public squares (the very same squares built and used during the late Qing and Republican period as loci of an emerging "public sphere") and house-to-house investigations (facilitated by urban density) all reinforced the regime's message that it would not tolerate subversion. The political tactics developed during the CCP's tenure in rural areas and later transplanted to urban areas during campaigns against counterrevolutionaries were then employed by inexperienced cadres to enforce a civil law during the Marriage Law campaign.

The State in the Trenches: Propagandizing the Marriage Law

To propagandize the Marriage Law, state and party officials took full advantage of "modern" urban infrastructure. Open public spaces such as parks, theaters, and public squares—hallmarks of urban cosmopolitanism and pride—were used for mass struggle sessions against offenders of the new law. During the 1951 campaign in Beijing, for instance, the Municipal Marriage Law Office organized 211 show trials, which were, according to one report, attended by 103,800 people gathered together from *hutongs* (or "lanes").[50] In most cases, those who were brought before the assembled masses for summary judgment were men accused of spousal abuse that resulted in death. Often, offenders were executed. Audiences were then informed that spousal abuse was "illegal" in the new family order, heard the confession of the accused, and were told that his behavior was a remnant of the "feudal" marriage system. In a typical trial in Shanghai in 1951 that was attended by many residents and officials, a man surnamed Ma was sentenced to death for killing his wife. After Ma was taken away, another man was sentenced in a public trial to four years for murder.[51] At some trials, urban residents were told to be "wary and vigilant."[52] In Shanghai, a public trial attended by eighteen hundred people at the Hengfeng Cotton Mill was held for cases involving "rape," "seducing women," "abuse," and the somewhat bizarre charge of "messing around with women" (*wannong funü*). People convicted of these crimes were summarily sentenced to two to four years in prison or labor camp.[53]

If the goal of these campaigns was to communicate the new regime's commitment to the protection of women's legal rights, there is some evidence of success. People learned about the new law, but the lessons probably resulted more in fear of it than admiration for the state's new ideology. According to one report, one member of a struggle-session audience commented, "Strike down one and intimidate a hundred (*dadao yi ge, xia yi bai ge*)! Men who beat their daughters-in-law won't dare do it again."[54] Someone else in the audience pointed directly to the radiating effect of these trials: "Not only does it [the public trial] educate a thousand people in the square, but when people go home the effectiveness of the propaganda will be even greater!"[55]

In addition to taking advantage of urban public spaces, officials also capitalized on urban density to investigate urban dwellers. Largely locked out of urban areas during the preceding years, upon assuming power the CCP and state agencies were quite interested in "digging" under the modern facades of urban society in almost voyeurlike fashion, to figure out exactly what they had inherited from the GMD and the imperialists. Indicative of this interest is the word state agencies used to describe their findings: instead of using words such as "found" or "saw," the most frequently used term in investigation reports was "discovered" (*faxian*).[56] Using *faxian* seems to convey surprise at having unraveled a mystery, or a sense of having unlocked a box whose contents were not precisely known but whose outer wrapping was tempting to the eye.

Investigative methods were borrowed from previous political campaigns. As in campaigns against counterrevolutionaries and later during the Five Antis, "work teams" comprising officials from the police, district government, and Women's Federation fanned out into preselected "key point" or "experimental" lanes to analyze residents' social and political problems. The teams conducted house-to-house interviews, asking whether residents knew of serious cases of abuse, infanticide, or couples being forced into an arranged marriage. Teams were also expected to classify residents according to the normative elements of the law, such as whether a couple had a "harmonious" (*hemu*), "ordinary" (*yi ban*), or "bad" (*bu hao*) relationship.[57]

After descending into factories, *lilong,* and *hutongs,* work teams gathered residents together and then separated them into social and political groupings. In Shanghai's Changshu District, marriage registration bureau officials investigated a lane along the old Avenue Joffre (now renamed Huaihai Road) and "discovered" 100 capitalist households among the lane's residents, of which 11 had more than one wife. Among the "middling sorts" (*zhongdeng*) of the lane, the family situation was said to be "very complicated." One alley in the lane, they found, had 250 households. Of those, 16 had short- and long-term common-law marriages (*pingju*), 6 had adopted daughters-in-law (*tongyangxi*), and 14 had polygamous relationships.[58] Marriage Law investigations also focused on the issue of political affiliations and ordinary behavior. In Hongxing Alley in Shanghai's working-class Yulin District, investigators found that over one hundred residents as well as some local cadres participated in secret societies such as the Yiguandao.[59] Other workers were "local hoodlums and gangsters" and simply described as "backward": "They like to eat, drink, gamble, whore, chat, and gossip," the report complained.[60]

Thus divided, urbanites were encouraged to "confess yourself, expose others," as well as to "speak bitterness" about previous personal and family misfortunes caused by the "feudal" marriage system. For many urbanites, this was an entirely new and frightening experience: How could they know how the new regime would treat the new information it had at its disposal? If some were hauled off for "fooling around with women," who could be assured that their own private behavior in the past would not also be dragged out and used against them? The safest strategy was to expose others, and hope that a self-confession could be avoided. During forty-two meetings in Beijing's working-class Xuanwu District and fifty-seven meetings in Chongwen District, 194 cases were thus "exposed," most involving accusations of abuse. In Beijing's sixth district, officials arranged for 1,584 meetings, reports, and public trials, involving some 53,200 propaganda workers, or 42 percent of the district's population.[61]

Although the campaigns against political enemies foreshadowed the tactics employed during the Marriage Law campaigns in 1951 and 1953, the initiation of investigations of urban residents' *private* family behavior was historically unprecedented. Justifying this breach thus required a redefinition of "public" and "private." In the early stages of the 1951 Marriage Law campaign in Shanghai, officials from the Women's Federation argued,

> [t]here was a saying: "Even upright officials cannot adjudicate family affairs." Today, there are still those who regard marriage problems as "personal affairs." This viewpoint is mistaken. In the past, one man would have two or three women. They would quarrel all the time. The neighbors could not sleep, but no one would come by and ask. Even if someone told an official, he would say, "Aiya! Even upright officials cannot deal well with these matters," in order to dismiss the case in a perfunctory manner. This was because the official himself had three or four wives . . . When people were finally motivated to tell him, he would say, "This is a personal matter. It's none of your business" . . . Now we have to publicize the Marriage Law and have public trials to convince people that marriage problems are not just personal matters and everyone should care.[62]

For some state agents, redefining family matters as "public" was a new departure. Some welcomed the opportunity to "discover" urban society, or to use the state repressive apparatus to avenge past grievances (what I will call "drawing in the state"); others, however, hunkered down by withdrawing into the private sphere and hoping that the winds of the campaign would soon blow over.

Despite the state's ability to congregate people into rooms and meeting halls, propaganda work did not always proceed smoothly. Because the CCP's earlier efforts at family reform had all taken place in the countryside, propaganda departments often lacked materials suitable for the urban areas they had only recently conquered. Urbanites who considered themselves "modern" took umbrage when they were shown cartoons depicting valiant peasants struggling against the "feudal" marriage system and exploiting landlords. The Marriage Law, according to one junior high school student, was a "peasant affair" (*xiang xia ren de shi*).[63] Even some cadres suggested that the national guidelines for implementing the Marriage Law were ill suited to Shanghai because of the prevalence there of "bourgeois customs," such as polygamous families and "illicit sexual relations," rather than problems with landlords and adopted daughters-in-law.[64] A Women's Federation report sought to refute the notion that "Shanghai isn't feudal" by arguing that "because the city and the countryside are so closely connected here, the city has the same evil customs as in the countryside."[65]

Problems stemming from the lack of appropriate propaganda materials were complicated further by language barriers. As Elizabeth Perry and Emily Honig have shown, migrants to Shanghai lived in native-place enclaves where they spoke their native dialect with others from their home region.[66] For cadres who hailed from the North, exercising leadership in this linguistic mosaic often proved impossible. Many workers at Shanghai's Jiangnan Shipyard, for example, migrated from Canton and Fujian in southern China, where many of them had acquired skills as boatmen. When shipyard union officials from North China began to tell them about the Marriage Law, workers did not understand their dialect. Nor could they understand various propaganda films.[67]

The close temporal proximity between the Communist takeover of cities and the Marriage Law complicated matters further. In neighborhoods and factories, political methods that were the hallmark of the CCP's revolutionary tactics in rural areas, such as struggle sessions (including direct verbal or physical confrontation between an accuser and his oppressor) and mutual recriminations, infused the campaigns, blurring the boundaries between state and society, and urban and rural. CCP mobilization methods that found their way into urban areas were not suddenly "discovered" by the party's top leaders; instead, it was the genius of Mao and the Communist leadership that turned *native* sources of peasant violence toward revolutionary goals. Peasants "struggled" their enemies long before the Communists arrived on the scene. "Struggle," however, did not always have an exclusively political content. Like peasants in many areas of the world, Chinese peasants employed community sanctions, sometime violent ones, against offenders of village *sexual* codes as well, particularly those whose promiscuity could confuse rightful paternity. These practices included lying in ambush for an adulterer, condemning women who had affairs, or jeering at men whose wives slept around or beat them.[68] Since many new cadres and the urban working classes hailed from villages, it is likely that they brought to the city some of these practices. The Marriage Law said nothing *explicitly* about adultery, but did deal with matters of marriage and divorce, and these, in turn, were *implicitly* conceived by local official as relating to sexual practices. Two unintended consequences of the implementation of the Marriage Law, therefore, were that local state officials involved themselves in ordinary people's sex lives, and that they did so in ways that appear to be very similar to village practices, despite the "urban" milieu in which they operated. In cities, this mix—often referred to as "leftist deviations"—could be particularly lethal for those urban bourgeoisie who had more than one wife and were generally seen as frequently involved in extramarital affairs. Their class and family status made them doubly suspect.

Instances of "leftism" were common in both Shanghai and Beijing. In Shanghai's working-class Changning District, for instance, a female union cadre wanted to "punish" those who abused women and to "solve" the problem of bigamous relationships, in addition to dealing with illicit affairs.[69] Targeting those "guilty" of adultery, even though the Marriage Law was completely silent on the issue of illicit sexual relations, forced Shanghai municipal authorities to call upon neighborhood cadres to "rectify their past practices of trying to catch red-handed people committing adultery (*ding xiao*)" in addition to "other unorganized and undisciplined activities."[70] And in the adjacent and exclusive Xincheng District, the district chief himself wanted to use the movement to "catch people having illicit affairs."[71]

There were similar problems in factories. In Shanghai, for example, work teams reported that many factory cadres had "feudal thinking: they think that men and women courting is *luan* (chaos), and that widows' affairs with unmarried men were also *luan*," even for couples who had been living together for years but were not formally married.[72] Similar events were reported in Beijing's Xinhua Press Printing Factory, where the union, with the factory administration's support, convened a meeting of female employees to roundly criticize a female worker who had an affair.[73]

The Bumbling State: New Communist Institutions

The CCP's entrance into urban centers not only blurred the long-standing divide between public and private affairs, but also initiated the demise of social and political institutions that, prior to 1949, occupied the middle ground between state and society, such as native-place associations, guilds, and student associations. In contrast to postrevolutionary France, where local leadership, mediation, and administrative roles were often assigned to lawyers and professionals active during the prerevolutionary regime, the Communists disbanded all extrastate urban organizations whose membership created an alternative source of social identification and political solidarity and replaced them with institutions embedded in the regime's power structure and whose class composition reflected the new state's idea of political virtue.[74] Building new political institutions on the basis of politics rather than competence had profound implications for those seeking di-

vorce because these new institutions frequently stood between the petitioner and the court or district government, the two places where a divorce
could be obtained. How these low-level institutions dealt with the state's
new effort to penetrate the private sphere, and the degree of legitimacy afforded these new institutions, helps explain patterns of state-family interaction during 1950–1953.

In pre-1949 China, an important element determining whether a dispute could be resolved outside of the state court system was the extent to
which the disputants trusted the mediator. Trust, in turn, hinged on the
mediator's face, or reputation—an asset often correlated with a certain
level of wealth, education, or experience.[75] The Communists, however, rejected such indicators of social status. Instead, they attempted to construct,
from the ground up, new institutions that represented the regime's favored
groups—workers, and those classified as "poor" and "middle" peasants—
regardless of their level of cultural face or of administrative experience and
competence. One Shanghai residence committee, for example, consisted of
thirteen cadres (twelve men and one woman), among whom were workers
from the tobacco industry and transport services, the self-employed (peddlers, rickshaw men, fruit-stand owners), unemployed workers, and one relative of a worker (*gongren jiashu*). The women's committee consisted of nine
cadres whose occupations ranged from unemployed workers (three) and
relatives of workers (three) to a local merchant (*gongshang*), an unemployed
intellectual, and a member of a teacher's family. Similarly, the mediation
committee comprised eight cadres—four workers and four relatives of
workers, among whom none had any formal education or high status in
pre–1949 Shanghai.[76]

In theory, this arrangement had potential benefits. Representatives
would be held somewhat accountable for their actions through a system of
local elections, and by making local organizations more "like" the people,
there was a chance they could become organizations "of" the people. In
practice, however, the attempt to install these neighborhood organizations
encountered many difficulties, as evidence from Beijing demonstrates. One
vexing problem was the sex of some of the committee members. To promote the participation of women in the political process, the Women's Federation tried to enlist female residents with good class status to join the
nascent organizations. These efforts were often resisted by other female residents, who refused to accept the regime's new measure of political virtue.
A report on local elections in Beijing's working-class Qianmen District
showed that women residents did not want to elect a fellow woman as their
representative, thinking that women "would not be able get anything done"
because they "have no culture and little experience." But even when the
Woman's Federation identified a good candidate, it found that many were
unwilling to serve on local committees because the job was both unreward-

ing and a strain on their time. One elderly woman said, "To be a representative you have to attend a lot of meetings. We'll only go if someone will prepare our meals for us."[77]

In addition to the gendered composition of new urban committees, another problem was that neither the state nor local residents had any experience with democratic procedure. During local elections in Beijing, for instance, Women's Federation officials made sure that a woman was elected even if the residents did not want one by demanding that they choose a woman and nullifying the votes for other candidates.[78] In another case, a resident, on a lark, blurted out, "Let's elect someone whose name we don't know!" The group then elected an insane man to be their representative.[79]

But even when saner candidates were elected, there were no guarantees that they would work well on behalf of city residents. Lacking experience and residents' trust, many new officials were at a complete loss when it came to handling family and other disputes. Confusion, evasion of responsibility, and administrative bumbling were the hallmarks of low-level political administration in the early years of the PRC. According to one report,

> women's representatives in Qianmen District have the attitude, "If there's a problem, organize a meeting; if there is no problem, why bother?"; others don't know how to go about doing their work . . . They don't have an effective way of handling problems, and can't handle problems quickly. Sometimes problems pile up (*yiya*) for a long time. Work isn't routinized, and sometimes the propaganda is very poor.[80]

Instead of mediating, neighborhood committees frequently sent cases involving what was deemed "ordinary conflict"—often family and neighborhood squabbles—to court. As a result, the courts' heavy caseload (from prosecution of criminal cases left over from previous campaigns) grew even heavier.[81] According to a Beijing Marriage Law Office report,

> the Women's Federation pushes cases to court because it says it can only mediate, while courts can actually decide things, but courts will take women's cases seriously only if there is a threat of committing suicide. [As a result] cases are shifted between courts, the Women's Federation, and the local police station, and then back to court. In the meantime, they still have to live with abusive relatives. They then think the only way out is to commit suicide.[82]

Similar difficulties were encountered in the establishment of low-level factory institutions, such as the women workers' departments (*fugongbu*) and women's representative committees. Like many neighborhood cadres, low-level cadres in factories were frequently illiterate, very young, and only recently promoted from among the relatives of ordinary factory workers. As such, they tended to be either committed but completely incompetent at handling domestic difficulties, or not committed and incompetent.[83]

Furthermore, as organizations composed of women, the women workers' departments met with the derision of male-dominated administrations and unions. Because the authority of women workers' departments was not taken seriously by the factory administration, an August 1951 report found, party work among women workers was "completely chaotic" (*shifen hunluan*).[84]

Local-level officials in factories shared their neighborhood counterparts' discomfort with the electoral process. When factories held elections for low-level posts, those who lost the elections refused to cooperate with victors. One woman said, upon her defeat, "I'm the veteran committee member! I won't follow the orders of the new committee member."[85]

The tight schedules of factory production and political work were also severe impediments to the proper functioning of institutions assigned to implement the Marriage Law. Factory management was under severe pressure to meet production quotas and satisfy new political demands for study sessions amid several intense campaigns, and as a result had little time to conduct Marriage Law propaganda work in a proper fashion. As one factory cadre in Beijing groused, "There are so many important documents to study, when is there time to study the Marriage Law?"[86] Complaints such as these sometimes filtered up to the Municipal Federation of Trade Unions. In Beijing, the secretary of the union, Liang Keping, penned a letter to the deputy mayor complaining that some factory managers spent only fourteen hours training cadres to implement the Marriage Law—not enough time to carry the movement through successfully.[87]

There were similar difficulties lower down the administrative hierarchy. Female cadres in women workers' departments also had little time to study the law, let alone conduct marriage and family mediation for troubled workers. Many of these cadres were holding down their regular factory positions in addition to doing their committee work.[88] When they were approached for advice, workers found that department officials were frequently too busy to be bothered. To save time, women workers' departments and union cadres simply told arguing couples to "get a divorce." This led to a crisis of confidence in these organizations' ability to solve marital disputes. Many workers, reports noted, did not trust these officials and refused to seek out their assistance to discuss their marital problems.[89]

The legitimacy of low-level state institutions in urban areas was further compromised by urban geographic density and the intimate knowledge generated by living and working in close quarters. Ironically, the same urban density that facilitated political communication concomitantly *delegitimized* the carriers of the political message because not a few officials had marriage problems of their own that violated the Marriage Law and that were well known to their neighbors. Such local knowledge about people's private behavior made it difficult for the state to find irreproachable local agents in urban areas to enforce the law. To ensure at least minimal compliance, state agents' own behavior had to be either exemplary or simply not known to other residents. Had the Chinese state relied exclusively on family courts that were geographically distant from local residents, the latter scenario might have been feasible, but the creation of grassroots political institutions embedded in tight-knit urban enclaves precluded this. In Beijing, for instance, many political workers in neighborhoods refused to allow their wives to work, let alone attend political meetings. When the Marriage Law campaign began, these very same officials instructed residents to attend a meeting about the new law. As they walked from door to door telling people to come out, Beijingers grumbled: "There are some basic-level cadres who themselves don't allow their wives to go outside, but are telling us to tell our wives to go to meetings!"[90]

The contrast between private behavior and political responsibilities and expectations made female officials particularly vulnerable targets for popular ridicule. Since they were assigned a key role in enforcing the law, female cadres were stage-front in this new public political theater. Such exposure was difficult; many female cadres in *hutongs* and *lilong* were themselves involved in the types of relationships deemed feudal and banned by the Marriage Law. One cadre, for instance, had been living as a concubine for seven years. Fearful that the Marriage Law would break up her family, she convened group meetings for residents but made a prior arrangement with her daughter to come to the meeting and (falsely) tell everyone that the mother had to leave because she was needed at home.[91] Other cadres were in the midst of extramarital affairs that were known to other residents. Thin apartment walls and close living quarters (especially in poorer areas of the city), after all, made it difficult to keep affairs secret. As a result, some cadres did not dare propagandize the Marriage Law because they feared ridicule.[92]

Not only were low-level cadres delegitimized by a discrepancy between private behavior and public posturing; some were also paralyzed by fear of how the Marriage Law would affect their families. In Shanghai's Lao'zha District, cadres in Changji Lane "panicked" because they feared investigation and being singled out for political struggle. This fear of investigation and struggle sometimes resulted in ad hoc defensive pacts or alliances (*tongmeng*) among cadres' family members. For instance, a cadre involved in a bigamous relationship feared he would be sent to labor reform, so he pleaded to his older wife, "I already left my younger wife, so do you have to say anything about my having had a second wife during the Marriage Law campaign?" Women often shared their husbands' reluctance to "speak bitterness" about past relationships and abuses, lest these confessions land the latter in jail.[93] Husbands were well aware of their wives' economic dependence, and used the possibility of a jail term to deter their wives from speaking up. In Shanghai's Xuhui District, a cadre told his wife: "You want to divorce, go ahead. Just don't saying anything bad about me. My going to jail won't be good for you, either."[94]

Even in the upper-class Jing'an District in Shanghai, where modernization theorists would have predicted a relatively positive response to the law, local women's representatives were conspicuously silent. Many feared for their futures in their families should they expose experiences of injustice. A Municipal Women's Federation document captured these fears:

> [E]ven if women are suffering [they] still don't dare say anything because they're afraid that if they do their situation will get worse. Some protect their husband because they're afraid something bad will happen to him during the course of the movement. Because of this, they say their marriage problems are caused by their own bad disposition.[95]

There are also reasons to believe that elite urban status itself made it difficult to expose matters hitherto considered "private." To the extent that social status is at least partially gained by maintaining a positive public posture (Hollywood stars' public affairs seem to be an exception!), the possibility of publicly airing dirty laundry represented a threat to some status-conscious individuals.[96] As one report from Jing'an noted:

> Some [cadres] love face (*ai mianzi*). They are not willing to admit to problems for fear of being laughed at. Male cadres think that if they speak up, everyone will lose face, so they don't say anything.[97]

Yet, despite the new intrusiveness of the state and the bumbling quality of many grassroots institutions, there were nonetheless instances of divorce in both Shanghai and Beijing. In the following, I contrast the response of two types of urban populations—elite "core urbanites" and working-class "peripheral urbanites"—according to variables I suggested earlier: the extent to which people saw the regime's agents as legitimate, their resources, and sexual and legal cultures. This comparative analysis suggests that, although core and peripheral urbanites shared many of the same fears of the state and did not view local political institutions as legitimate, the latter sought out divorce more aggressively because of a contentious "legal culture";[98] a different way of approaching marriage, divorce, and sex; and better material resources. These features allowed them to circumvent obstructionist state institutions and to present their claims in a very forceful manner. At the same time, like many peasants worldwide, recent migrants to cities were also aggressive in pursuing upward mobility through marriage to those in the urban core. Core elite urbanites—for reasons of fear, attachment to and stake in the city, lack of resources, a status-conscious culture of marriage, divorce, and sex, and a cultural propensity militating against public conflict—were more reluctant to use state institutions to change their relationship in the family.

URBAN SOCIETY

Upper-Class Urbanites during Marriage Reform

To date, Chinese urban elites' view of the early 1950s has been colored in romantic, but ultimately distorted, shades of red. According to Yue Daiyun, Chinese intellectuals of the 1950s saw in the Communist Party China's savior—a pure, powerful, and incorruptible political party. "Full of confidence and enthusiasm for the Communist Party," she writes, intellectuals had a love for the party that "permeate[d] every aspect of the way they conduct[ed] themselves and the way they treat[ed] others."[99] Looking back at the early 1950s after the Anti-Rightist campaign, Liu Binyan and other intellectuals also paint a rosy picture of the era: "Most people," Liu recalls, "felt nostalgic for 1956 and regarded it as the best period in the history of the People's Republic . . . Some thought if it had not been for the anti-rightist campaign of the following year, Chinese society would have developed in a far more humane way."[100] New evidence, however, shows that urban intellectuals could be blinded by these romanticizations. Full of new hope and belief in a reified "party," they did not notice political repression happening under their very noses. Businessmen and their wives and concubines and people in white-collar offices, we can see below, had a different sort of experience with the state. Moreover, other intellectuals, such as teachers and students, were not as enthusiastic about some CCP politics as these accounts suggest. Many urban elites were particularly wary of the Marriage Law owing to their previous political experiences, status consciousness, lack of economic independence, and a certain elitism and prudishness about sex and marriage.

True to its notion of cities as decadent and reactionary, the new regime signaled early on that it would show little tolerance for the urban upper crust. One of the first urban campaigns was the Five Antis, which was directed primarily at the urban middle and upper classes. In this campaign (which Liu Binyan ignores in his fond recollections of the period), activists gathered capitalists and other wealthy urbanites into small rooms, where they were instructed to "confess" to embezzling money, cheating workers, and colluding with foreigners. After this campaign, few had reason to feel confident that they would receive a sympathetic hearing in nonbusiness matters, such as knotty divorce and related property issues. Intellectuals, had they not been so eager to commit themselves to the incorruptible party, might have taken more seriously the implications of "thought reform" campaigns in urban universities, instead of thinking that they actually deserved "ideological remolding" given their problematic "class standpoint."[101] When the Marriage Law campaigns began in 1951 and 1953, local officials once again rounded up businessmen, teachers, and their families and put them together in small rooms. There the latter were instructed to confess to various types of wrongdoing in the family and to read various articles on the new law.

Because many upper-class urbanites had been involved in bigamous relationships, there was great concern that the Marriage Law's monogamy requirement suddenly illegalized their relationships. Local officials, themselves barely literate, were unable to explain that the law actually did *not* prohibit polygamous affairs dating *before* 1949, only those that started *after* the Marriage Law was promulgated. As a result, businessmen either were convinced that, like the Five Antis, the Marriage Law campaign specifically targeted them, or were simply very confused about the law's provisions.

For businessmen and their families one word "fused" the Five Antis and Marriage Law campaigns: *qingsuan,* to "confiscate" or "liquidate." In one meeting in Shanghai, Liu Mingzhen, a daughter of a well-known Shanghai capitalist, said, "Some people say the real purpose of the Five Antis movement was to confiscate businesspeople's money; the Marriage Law campaign's real objective is to confiscate the capitalist class's concubines" (known as "wife number two," "wife number three," etc.).[102] In Beijing, a merchant who was rounded up by local officials said, "During the Five Antis, my money was confiscated; now, with the Marriage Law, one of my wives will be taken away too!"[103]

Interpreting the Marriage Law through the prism of their previous political experiences had important consequences for how merchants and businessmen dealt with state officials assigned to teaching them about the law. Looking back at their travails during 1951–1952, many could not but wonder whether everything they held dear in the pre-1949 period— namely, their money, property, and status—would be lost during the course of these early political campaigns. In this atmosphere, the Marriage Law only added sorrow to hardship. The prospect of losing a valued member of their family, in addition to their assets, was terrifying. Avoiding state institutions seemed to be the best way of avoiding further danger to themselves and their families.

Several quotes from Women's Federation reports are enough to give some sense of these efforts to withdraw from the state. In Beijing, for instance, cadres assigned to implement the Marriage Law among businessmen found them "very worried, unwilling to talk," and "panicked." One businessman, who was over sixty years old and had two wives, contended that all his wives "get along well, don't argue," and that "all are relatively old and do not want to divorce." Other participants, they found, were unhappy with their marriages, but did not request divorces because they were worried about how CCP courts would handle property, housing, and custody arrangements.[104] Elsewhere in the city, work team officials forced businessmen to confess and would not let them leave until they did. Finally, one meekly pleaded, "Elder brother, elder brother (*laoge, laoge*), please lift your hand and let me leave."[105] In Shanghai, one capitalist emphasized how harmonious his family life was prior to 1949, most probably in order to persuade officials that there was no need for state intervention. "Before the Marriage Law," he stressed, "my wives got along fine. There were no conflicts."[106]

Fearful of how the Communist regime would deal with their family affairs and understandably distrustful of the often bumbling new urban cadres, such families typically resolved marriage difficulties through mediation leading to reconciliation, rather than through the same courts that had handled political accusations during the previous movements. Statistics from Xincheng District in Shanghai's elite core are somewhat revealing here. An investigation by the district's Women's Federation branch found that most of the residents in the district were "petit bourgeois," and as a result, "most problems are those of bigamy, cohabiting, and adultery." Between July and December 1951, the Women's Federation's mediation section handled 256 "marriage cases," the majority relating to nonmonogamous relationships. Of these, 71 percent were reported to have been "successfully mediated" and only 14 percent sent to court. Others were still being processed by the federation.[107]

Many other relationships among the Chinese business elite were never brought to state mediation. Why, many probably asked themselves, should they, with their high urban status, entrust a solution to their problems to young, inexperienced, and often illiterate working-class or peasant-bred officials? This, together with the high risk involved in drawing the state into private affairs, prompted many elites to adopt evasive strategies. These tactics included deceit, intrafamily pacts, and sudden changes in public behavior. In Shanghai, for instance, investigation reports found that families with more than one wife "are very afraid, and do not want to go out to participate in meetings," while men who had abused their older wives now treat them well "on the surface." Others planned to send their concubines to Hong Kong, to the countryside, or to their natal homes.[108] A Bureau of Civil Affairs investigation report in Beijing's Dongdan District lucidly conveys elite urbanites' fears and strategies:

> Those who have had more than one wife or have had illicit affairs are very worried. Some people want to accuse (*gao*) these people. As a result, some divorce in public but secretly stay together (*ming li, an bu li*). Some are making arrangements to hide their younger wives before the movement comes . . . Residents tell those with more than one wife: "Why haven't you let your younger wife leave? The government will be enforcing the Marriage Law soon."[109]

This evasive strategy was abetted by people's knowledge that campaigns did not last forever, and that if they could only manage to hold out a little bit longer, the political winds would soon change. In one report, businessmen were said to be "biding their time" until the movement passed.[110] As a result, many nonmonogamous relationships continued well beyond the Marriage Law campaigns.

Women's economic considerations often lay at the heart of these strategies. In addition to the risks of bringing the state into one's family affairs and court investigations, women married to elite men feared the Marriage Law, especially its monogamy and divorce provisions, largely owing to their lack of independent income. In Shanghai, for instance, an article written by a Women's Federation cadre concluded that older wives frequently objected to the monogamy clause, convinced that if the husband were to divorce anyone, it would be her and not the younger wife, who was seen as more desirable. Such fears, together with the feeling of having no political or social recourse, resulted in many suicides; suicides, investigation reports make clear, were not necessarily the result of a denial of divorce or resistance to an arranged marriage, as suggested in the feminist literature on the Marriage Law, but rather the result of some women's unwillingness or inability to give public expression to their problems or even contemplate life *without* a husband and family.[111] In Shanghai's elite Xincheng District, the local Women's Federation branch reported in late 1951 that in the year since the promulgation of the Marriage Law the number of people seeking advice had risen fivefold, but that in general women in the district remained "silent" about marriage difficulties and reluctant to go to court "even if they have suffered bitterly."[112] A Women's Federation mediator wrote the following in an article in the local press:

> A frequently encountered problem during mediation is that the number-one wife always wants to accuse the younger wife, even though she knows fault lies with the husband. They're afraid to criticize the husband, afraid to hurt his feelings. Even if the husband has committed a serious offense and has been detained by the court, she will come weeping to court and request his release. She says that otherwise he'll be even worse toward her when he's released, and that this is the only way they'll be able to reconcile.[113]

While much of this behavior can probably be attributed to elite women's fear of losing the source of their livelihood, status consciousness was also an underlying issue. Women who married elite urban men had risen a notch on the social ladder because they did not have to work; compared with women forced to work in grimy factories—or, even worse, fields—they were pretty well off. In China during these years, it appears that few women shared the notion common in Western feminism that emancipation from family oppression is gained primarily through wage-earning labor. To change these women's negative stance toward manual labor, the CCP attempted to teach women rudimentary skills, so as to allow them to join the labor force. But such efforts had only partial success: an investigation of the relatively well-off West Kusi Lane in Beijing's Dongdan District found that the only women who wanted to work were those whose lives were "difficult" (*shenghuo kunnan*). Out of fifty-seven households in the lane, thirty-eight were relatively affluent, but of these, only nine women sought employment. By contrast, in the households with economic difficulties, *every* adult member wished to participate in the employment drive.[114] The desire to maintain high urban status, therefore, made such women highly dependent on their husband's families, and less capable of sustaining a livelihood after divorce.

Difficulties stemming from the lack of independent economic resources and concern for social status were compounded further by state efforts to reduce urban overcrowding by sending city dwellers back to their home villages. Many urban residents balked at the prospect of leaving the bright city lights to return to an uncertain future in the countryside.[115] Concubines in elite families thus felt the dual pressure of expulsion from the city and the Marriage Law's monogamy clause. As one Shanghai report found, "Some concubines who are also prostitutes and dancing girls say: 'In the old society we were discriminated against and oppressed, but in the new society we still cannot emancipate (*fanshen*). Instead, our suffering has gotten worse.'"[116] Making matters worse was the lack of urban housing, particularly in the core districts. In contrast to cities such as Paris, which offered women seeking divorce temporary refuge in pensions, hostels, and apartments, in early 1950s Shanghai, municipal agencies were slow to designate spaces of refuge for women.[117] Seeing the city rather than the countryside as their permanent home, many were reluctant to move back to the countryside after divorce. Caught between dependence on their husband's family, the lack of refuge, and unwillingness to return to the countryside, many concubines despaired. As one Women's Federation report noted:

> Some [concubines] are willing to divorce, but are worried they will not be able to get by, and that no matter where they turn, their lives will be very difficult. They do not think the Women's Federation can help them.[118]

Similar responses to the Marriage Law were found in Hangzhou—an important silk-reeling center in eastern Zhejiang Province. One 1953 report compiled by a Marriage Law investigation small group noted that

> most managers' concubines, either because they want to continue to live a carefree and comfortable life (*anyi*), or because they have no economic independence, still do not dare ask for a divorce."[119]

Even if we dismiss the content of this report because of its condemning tone (not surprising given these women's "capitalist" lifestyle), we should keep in mind that many cases involving the urban middle and upper class that ended up in courts and other institutions were handled in such a way as to substantiate the concubines' fears. Take as an example the case of Chuan Naiwen, a staff member of the Bank of China in Shanghai, an urban institution par excellence. Chuan met his wife, Wang Shou, during school and married her in 1950. Before long, he had an affair with Guo Shulan, who worked for him. During the affair, however, Chuan and Wang's marriage deteriorated. In September 1950 he left home and went to live in the bank's dormitory, where he stayed until May 1951, when he petitioned for divorce. The court, following the Marriage Law's requirement that divorce cases be mediated before the state grant a divorce, told him to reconsider and tried to mediate the case. After mediation failed, the court proceeded to "analyze" Chuan's reasons for seeking divorce by dispatching an investigation team to collect his personal correspondence and work-related items. This investigation resulted in the formation of an ad hoc "small group" at the bank to discuss the matter. Fellow bank employees supported his claim because he was a good worker and active in the Democratic Youth Organization, and because his girlfriend, Guo, had already left Shanghai to work in Beijing. Moreover, Guo sent a letter to her work unit indicating she was no longer interested in continuing the relationship. The court, however, believed otherwise. It argued that the heart of the issue was the "face problem (*mianzi wenti*) of petits bourgeoises" such as Chuan. After plumbing through Chuan and Wang's personal documents, the court found conclusive "evidence" that the couple still had feelings for one another. The problem, the court argued without much elaboration, was impossible to solve unless Chuan "broke the hold of his petit bourgeois feelings." In the verdict the court wrote: "The claim is denied. No reasonable cause."[120]

The case of Lu Zhuyin, thirty-two, an unmarried female operator at another very urban institution, the Shanghai Telephone Company, also exemplifies the collision between the state's penetration into the family and the most urbanized sectors of Shanghai society. In this case, the postrevolutionary transplant of rural-derived political methods into urban areas resulted in a fatal outcome. For some urbanites, the sudden exposure of their "private" problems to harsh, public political light was too much to bear.

In the winter of 1952, Lu Zhuyin entered a hospital to recuperate from an illness. There she met a man, Gu Yunfa, who also worked for the telephone company. Even though Gu was married, the two patients grew close during their stay at the hospital. After their discharge, Gu invited Lu to stay at his house while his wife was away. The two then had sex, but it was not long before Gu's wife discovered the affair. Lu, however, did not seek state intervention. Instead, the three lived together. For both women, it seems, marriage to a white-collar worker in the city as part of a threesome was preferable to living with a poor man in an urban shantytown or rural village.

Moreover, with the exception of their natal homes, there were few places women with strong urban attachments could live outside of marriage.

In the case of Lu and the Gu, state invention soon put an end to the new living arrangement. Gu Yunfa's mother-in-law trotted over to the company's union and reported their affair, "raising a racket" in the process. Acting on the complaint, the union ordered Lu to make a self-criticism, but even after Lu acceded to this demand, union officials claimed that her confession was not "deep enough," and that the "roots" of her *sixiang* (thoughts) had not yet been "exposed." Lu told her brother, "The union is insisting I confess and write another self-criticism. They are also watching my movements and saying I am a 'loose' woman and using money to seduce men. My mind is reeling." Lu also heard rumors that the district government was making special preparations to use her case as an exemplar of how to handle these problems when the March 1953 Marriage Law campaign began. On February 16, 1953, Lu leaped from a tall building to her death.[121]

In Chuan and Lu's cases we can see how features identified in the state-building and sociolegal literature as facilitating social change could actually hinder such change in China. Advances in urban infrastructure that made courts more accessible to the urban population also made the urban population more accessible, and thus also more vulnerable, to the state's investigative apparatus. Because better transportation shortened the traveling time between courts and plaintiffs' home, courts, in conjunction with unions, workers' committees, and street committees, could conduct relatively thorough and time-consuming investigations if they so desired.[122] Moreover, the state and party institutions responsible for such cases were capable of contacting each other with regard to a particular case, which most likely increased the amount of bureaucratic red tape. These two factors—urban density on the one hand and the "thick" or "dense" state apparatus on the other—probably explain why courts accumulated a large backlog of cases. According to one report, in a two-month period the Shanghai Municipal Court handled only two cases out of one hundred introduced by the Marriage Law reception office.[123]

An example of how urban policy and density made divorce highly problematic for white-collar workers is the case of Zhang Jinfeng, who migrated to Shanghai from the poor province of Henan. After living in the city for a while, Zhang married a man named Ren Changming, a white-collar staff worker at a Shanghai bank. Ren filed for divorce in the Huangpu District Court because the couple's "feelings were not compatible" (*ganqing bu he*). Unlike the case of Chuan Naiwen seen earlier, in this case the court agreed, but during the proceedings Zhang refused to go back to her village, insisting that Ren help her find work in Shanghai. Undaunted by this decision, Zhang appealed to the Shanghai Municipal Court. Eventually the Women's Federation and the court "persuaded" her to return to her village.[124] In other cases, women who were forced out of their homes by their husbands after filing for divorce found themselves sleeping outside for several days. When cases such as these reached the court, court officials would usually instruct the women to return to their villages. If they refused, the court did little to assist them, even as the women remained homeless.[125]

At the same time that urban density made it difficult for core elite urban women to divorce, it also made it easy for state institutions (usually staffed by men) to fob off responsibility for helping women in distress. Sometimes this had fatal results, as the following case demonstrates. A woman in Shanghai's wealthy Xincheng District, Ye Xiaonü, was married to one Luo Hongsheng. According to their neighbors, Ye and Luo had a very bad relationship; Luo constantly beat her. Afraid for her life, Ye asked the local mediation committee to help her petition for divorce. The mediation committee, however, felt that there was "no need to report a case of domestic quarreling to the higher authorities" and advised her to go to the nearby police station on Beijing Road—a reasonable request given the proximity of the two places. But male officials at the police station did not want to deal with her, and told her to return to the mediation committee. The mediation committee, in turn, told her to go to court. For two days, Ye failed to return home, her whereabouts unknown. When she finally returned, Luo slashed her face, chopped off her hand, and then stabbed her more than forty times. According to the report, Luo murdered her because he was convinced she was having an affair during the time she was away. After the murder, he surrendered himself to the Xincheng District government.[126]

Lacking urban refuge, reluctant to return to rural areas, and fearful of the state, many women in the urban core remained silent about their family problems. Another contributing factor to this silence, however, was class-related divisions in the meaning of public and private, sex, marriage, and the family, or what I will call "sexual culture." In China, aspirants to, or those with, high cultural status were extremely concerned that "private" problems not be aired publicly, as the resulting revelations would result in loss of face and reputation among one's close friends and relatives. This rather thick line between "public" and "private," I believe, prevented many middle- and upper-class urban women from even discussing their difficulties with friends or state agencies. Without such recourse, some committed suicide to escape their predicament and to protest injustice.[127] In one case in Hangzhou, for instance, the wife of the manager of a barbershop was having an affair. After her husband discovered her and her lover in bed, she threw herself in a river, committing suicide. According to the investigation report, no one knew about her difficulties. "In order to save face," the report noted, "family conflicts such as these are usually not spoken of. The women don't tell fellow employees, relatives, or friends, nor do they go to court to ask for assistance." In another case in Hangzhou, the Marriage Law investigation report complained that the wife of a silk-factory owner refused to divorce her husband even though he was sleeping with her sister. In order to divorce, the team argued, the wife would first need to "get rid of her concern with face" (*qudiao mianzi guannian*)."[128]

Officials in Shanghai and Beijing reported similar experiences. In Shanghai's Xuhui District, a district Women's Federation report from 1951 found that, "among the bourgeoisie the women suffer largely from psychological abuse; *on the outside everything is tranquil,* but inside they are suffering . . . they are quite vain and concerned with face."[129] In a meeting with female teachers in Shanghai's Songshan District, Women's Federation officials complained that it was difficult to help the teachers because they "kept their problems to themselves." In Beijing, reports noted similar silences. One report discussed a female intellectual working in a district health bureau who was abused by her husband, a university professor. According to the brief case report, this woman believed that "people would look down upon her" if she divulged her situation, and as a result did not "dare talk about it to anyone." When her husband beat her black and blue, she left her apartment and rode her bike around the neighborhood, aimlessly and silently. According to the report, she was suicidal.[130] Another report from Beijing commented that women in elite families "think that children of great families should not be like working-class families. If they handle their problems on the basis of the Marriage Law, it will harm their ancestors' moral influence."[131]

The same concerns with respect to class and "culture" that limited divorce among urban elites can also be seen in their marriage preferences. As might be expected given their high status, marriage was a very serious matter for them, requiring consideration of the potential spouse's (and his or her family's) education, background, politics, skills, prospects, and status. One could not enter marriage lightly, thinking that one could simply divorce if it did not work out: family reputations were at stake. According to a Women's Federation report on the marriage situation of teachers in Shanghai's Songshan and Beijing's Dongcheng Districts, for instance, female teachers there demanded that their husbands have a special skill, like engineering; money; good manners; a cultural and "theoretical level" (*lilun shuiping*) higher than their own; good looks; vigor; and, last but not least, considerable height (he should be tall). Unwilling to settle for less, in one vocational primary school in Shanghai's Songshan District, seventeen of the twenty-four teachers in the school were not married by the age of twenty-five, an age that was already considered late; in another middle school, six out of eight teachers had not married by their mid-twenties. Castigated by CCP officials for their vanity, some admitted (or perhaps confessed) that their demands were either too high or "not appropriate."[132]

Limited spatial, temporal, and financial resources also contributed to these teachers' lack of choice in family matters. Many such women worried they would not be able to find an apartment after they married, and complained that between their jobs and political meetings they had no time to look for a spouse. Anxious about their marriage prospects, some of the teachers thought it best that their parents decide for them. As one teacher said, "No one has given me an introduction. How can I look for myself?"[133] Although there is no hard evidence for this, it seems likely that, to the extent that such women depended on family introductions to find an appropriate spouse, the social *cost* of divorce increased. Moreover, the more effort they put into finding "Mr. Right," the less likely it was that they would later divorce him: given their age and past effort, there were simply too many "sunk costs." For instance, if she married only after the age of twenty-five, a woman's chances of finding another high-status husband willing to accept an older, educated divorcée were very slim. This most likely increased women's dependence on both their families and future husbands.

Not all teachers wanted to marry, however. In meetings in Shanghai and Beijing, female teachers and university students expressed their fear of marriage, sex, men, and especially their future mothers-in-law. Others were conflicted by their ambition to advance professionally and the social pressure to raise children. In Shanghai, the Songshan District teachers told interviewers that children were "a burden" and "hassle" that limited one's freedom, and at a Beijing college, work team officials found that female students were completely apathetic to the Marriage Law because they were not interested in marriage at all, except with a handsome man or a university student at Qinghua or Yanjing. "All other men," they said, "are bad." For them, marriage meant having children and staying at home. As one female student argued, "Get married, have kids, and then what?" Youth, in their opinion, was better spent on patriotic goals, such as "rebuilding the motherland." This commitment, which dovetailed with party ideologues' effort to transfer family loyalty to the new state, meant that such women would have to defer more self-oriented activities, such as romance, courtship, and marriage, which were at the heart of the Marriage Law.[134] This "statism"—the idea that individual liberation is not to be "wasted" on the pursuit of individual happiness but rather used to serve the state—together with their fear of marriage and selectivity in marriage choice, resulted in very little interest in the Marriage Law on the part of female students.

But even if students answered the state's clarion call and demanded to take advantage of the law by ending arranged marriages, few actually had the resources with which to accomplish this. Many Chinese students, like students elsewhere in the world, depended on their parents to pay tuition and living stipends (such dependence might be even greater in China because of the traditional disdain for manual labor and the more restricted labor markets; few students would consider selling tofu to help pay for their tuition). By providing subsidies, parents gained a good deal of leverage over their children's choice of spouse. In Beijing, for instance, when university students expressed little interest in "free"-choice marriage, they explained their position by noting that if they chose their own mate against their parents' wishes, the latter would likely withdraw tuition money.[135] Perhaps this helps explain why even one of the most famous "liberals" among the early twentieth-century Chinese intelligentsia—Hu Shi—agreed to marry the woman his parents arranged for him and also defended the system of arranged marriages;[136] some of Hu's contemporaries also admitted that they agreed to marry the woman picked out for them by their parents because of their "fear of overt confrontation," and "addiction to dignity, honor, and status" (i.e., face).[137] As a result, there was often a large discrepancy bordering on hypocrisy between what they prescribed for society ("free marriage") and how they actually handled their own marital arrangements.[138]

Teachers' and students' indifference to the Marriage Law was also rooted in a certain reverence and respect for Chinese "tradition," even though intellectuals, at least according to Marxism-Leninism, were expected to be in the vanguard of breaking old ways of thought. In family matters, respect for tradition meant listening to parents' opinions and not making individualist-cum-"selfish" choices. Elite culture, together with students' financial dependence on their parents, militated against the aggressive pursuit of new rights. In Beijing, for instance, students at Datong University said, "Marriages arranged by parents or matchmakers are very good; it's the Chinese tradition. One's personal problems shouldn't be the cause of parents' suicide."[139] Some students even resisted some of the milder propaganda efforts, such as articles in the newspapers *Qingnianbao* and *Xinminbao* about marriage problems, calling such articles "pornography." Often these reports included stories about "model" citizens who resisted their arranged marriages but committed suicide after encountering parental resistance. Rather than evincing sympathy, some students condemned the woman who dared to resist, saying, "That woman deserved to die."[140]

Of course, there were some students who were bold enough to support the idea of marriage freedom, but even when they did, they found the road toward free-choice marriages littered with obstacles. One report found that some students "see friends making their own matches and think it's 'very interesting,' and are jealous. Others want to, but don't dare do anything about it. Students who do court openly are rebuked by their teachers because it interferes with their studies."[141] Education, which gave entrée into good jobs and high status in Chinese society, was clearly at odds with the demand for free-choice marriages or divorce, contrary to the expectations of modernization theory.

A Comparative Perspective

Is the reluctance of Chinese intellectuals to take advantage of the Marriage Law very surprising? The secondary literature tends to emphasize their commitment to Enlightenment values, particularly during and after the May 4th Movement of 1919, when student protests erupted all over the country in response to China's treatment at the peace talks in Versailles.[142] It was this literature that shaped some of my initial hypotheses. New research on Beijing University by Timothy Weston, however, found that students there were far more status-conscious and oriented toward state service than previous studies have suggested.[143] In a similar vein, scholars of early twentieth-century Chinese literature have recently argued that "mainstream" intellectuals defended arranged marriages as the only way for a couple to develop long-lasting love.[144] The view that the "proper" place for passion to develop was in a larger social or political framework is echoed in Colleen She's study of the Beijing intelligentsia in the 1920s and 1930s. She argues: "The Peking intelligentsia could not accept romantic love as something which existed for the sake of individual pleasure, but instead made love, in general, into a matter of social concern . . . they always maintained that social stability and the interests of society should come before individual satisfaction."[145] For some, sex outside of the context of "love" bordered on immorality and divorce was a matter of last resort, and should never be too messy. As Wen-hsin Yeh notes of the journalist Zou Taofen,

> Zou Taofen's understanding of love was straightforward enough: true love entails a serious moral commitment; it must never be confused with either sexual licentiousness or emotional blackmail . . . in case of disputes, always try gentle persuasion before confrontation . . . Men should always recognize their responsibility to their dependents, and not speak lightly of divorce.[146]

Zou's advocacy of persuasion rather than confrontation seems consistent with elite Confucian legal culture. As Jerome Cohen has pointed out, "According to Confucianists, the legal process was . . . a regrettable necessity. Indeed, it was considered disreputable to become involved in the law courts . . . A lawsuit symbolized disruption of the natural harmony that was thought to exist in human affairs."[147]

Similar notions of law are also at work in modern Japan, another country heavily influenced by Confucian ethics. There judges, who invariably come from a narrow section of the educated upper classes, view divorce in ways very similar to those of Zou Taofen. Divorce, they believe, disrupts social stability. Frank Upham writes:

> Family court judges, who not only frown on no-fault contested divorce but sometimes also deny divorce even with clear evidence of fault on the respondent's side, and the family court mediators, who at times consciously and ex-

plicitly attempt to represent "social values," are from a very narrow range of the elite in Japan. Whether or not this antipathy toward divorce is shared by most Japanese, it is certainly not reflected in the legal norms.[148]

Evidence from other countries on upper- and middle-class urbanites reveals concerns about divorce and sexuality similar to those we have seen in China. In England, Lawrence Stone has argued, middle- and upper-class women in the nineteenth century were a powerful lobby *against* any relaxation of a strict divorce law, fearing that this would "encourage their husbands to desert them" and that they would suffer serious property loss; the poor, by contrast, could not afford to hire a lawyer anyway and so "contrived their own quasi-legal or illegal means of self-divorce."[149] In the United States during the nineteenth century, class formation was partially based on one's success in keeping one's sexual appetite under a tight lid and limited to certain prescribed places—the parlor for courtship and the bedroom for sex. These restrictions marked one's attainment of elite status and one's differentiation from the urban working class, whose sexuality was much more often publicly displayed and discussed. Many workers, however, actually hailed from rural areas of Europe, suggesting that brazen displays of sexuality in urban areas among the working class may have had rural origins.[150] Of course, this "openness" may not have been by choice or even shaped by rural culture but may perhaps have been simply the result of cramped housing. Given their own sense of private space and sublimation of public displays of affection, it is not surprising to find middle-class reformers condemning the social conditions in working-class neighborhoods:

> Families crowded into tiny apartments, with adolescent boys and girls sharing the same sleeping quarters, parents' beds in sight of their young children, and male boarders mingling with familiarity among wives and daughters. To college-educated social workers, this sort of family life did not recall the simplicity of the colonial or frontier experience, but instead seemed a source of "moral contamination," with the presence of boarders "always evil" . . . Accustomed to ideals of purity, reticence, and conjugal intimacy that rested on privacy, the middle class could see in these districts nothing but an alien, anarchic sexuality.[151]

These class distinctions seem to have persisted well into the twentieth century. According to Sally Engle Merry, middle-class urbanites view with disdain people who bring family disputes to court because "taking these intimate, domestic problems to court allows everyone to see one's personal affairs and to talk about them. Instead, respectable people should put up with their problems."[152] Elite discourse in the United States suggesting "the end of civilization as we know it" because of talk shows in which the usually working-class participants talk openly about sex is yet another manifestation of this phenomenon.

Elite urbanites in nineteenth-century Russia were likewise concerned with maintaining the sanctity of the private sphere. In her discussion of sexuality and law in Russia in the late nineteenth century, Laura Engelstein cites one observer of the Russian urban scene who noted: "An educated person does not like and tries not to permit outside eyes to penetrate his strictly individual life."[153] As in China, educated Russian urbanites of the period sought individual sexual freedom, but only in the context of state and social goals. Barbara Alpern Engel writes: "Progressives agreed that personal happiness and family happiness were not worthwhile goals in themselves." Instead, the largely middle- and upper-class progressives were concerned with the way "improved family relationships would benefit public life."[154] Concern with the public good at the expense of private happiness often resulted in the radical ascetic notion that celibacy should be obligatory for all women, women's willingness to become martyrs for a higher cause, and the belief in statist solutions for solving marriage and personal problems.

Peripheral, Working-Class Urbanites: Pioneers in Social Change

Workers on the periphery of urban life shared their elite core counterparts' fear of the new state's sudden entry into the private sphere and were doubtful that local state agents could handle their family problems. Many tried to evade the state's deepening reach by promising to change their behavior; others took advantage of their ties to the countryside by temporarily taking leave of the city. While this intrusion into people's domestic affairs created much resentment, however, other state policies created more opportunities for poorer urbanites to extract themselves from family relationships. What explains peripheral urbanites' willingness to use state law in their family affairs, I suggest, lies not in dramatically different experiences with state power or the extent to which they viewed the new state as legitimate, but with their feisty legal culture, the different meanings attributed to marriage, divorce, and sex, and the resources with which they were able to support their claims. These cultural and economic features made it easier for them to take advantage of new opportunities created by the Communists. In this section I begin to develop the argument that cultural and economic ties to *rural areas,* and the simultaneous desire to break them, account for the statistical clue I pointed out earlier regarding the higher number of divorce cases received in the working-class Changning District, and the anecdotal evidence presented below suggesting important differences in the way urban elites and the working classes dealt with the Marriage Law.

Panic in the Urban Periphery

The enforcement of a campaign targeting the "feudal" family provoked strong reactions among working-class and elite urbanites alike. As with businessmen and other elites, political experiences prior to the Marriage Law undoubtedly resulted in a heightened wariness of state policy among the urban working class. During campaigns against gangs, secret societies, and GMD organizations, and during the Five Antis campaign, urbanites of all classes were required to submit political histories, participate in struggle sessions, and in some cases inform on fellow workers and neighbors. Not surprisingly, the rhetoric of investigation (*diaocha*) and struggle (*douzheng*) from these earlier campaigns carried over to the Marriage Law, even though the central state never really intended for this to happen. As a resident of Beijing said, "Aiya! The Marriage Law is being enforced. Who knows which family will get into trouble?" Some complained that "the Communist Party struggles here, then struggles there. Now it's come inside the family!"[155] An old woman in Shanghai asked, "Will there be an investigation of whether a couple sleeps on the same bed?" and another rhetorically asked work team cadres: "My husband's already in the coffin. Do you want me to take him out to struggle against him?!"[156] In Shanghai's Yong'an Cotton Mill, workers, having learned the CCP modus operandi, took the initiative and classified themselves into two groups as soon as the campaign began: those with marriage "problems" formed one line, and those whose marriages were "harmonious" formed the other.[157]

The state's efforts to promote a new vision of the family also encountered resistance. Certainly a big part of the problem was that officials without much authority or legitimacy were enforcing a law with an unfamiliar language and a very vague ideological agenda. One man from Shanghai's Xinxin Alley responded to an activist's attempt to "educate" him by saying, "What's it your business if I beat my wife? I'm unemployed. Why haven't you solved that?"[158] At Shanghai's Number Seven Cotton Mill, some women were seriously abused and therefore encouraged by work team members to "speak bitterness," but the workers demurred: "After I speak up, will you be able to solve the problem?"; "Will someone back me up?"; "Won't things get even worse?"[159] Likewise, a Beijing woman complained, "I'm willing to take a beating. The government is meddling in everything these days, but will you be there if I have nothing to eat?"[160] And a female worker at Shanghai's Number Six Cotton Mill suggested that family affairs were not likely to be handled well by local authorities. Because she could not have children, this woman had found a concubine for her husband. When she was rebuked by union officials, she returned fire with fire: "When I die, will you union fellows arrange for the funeral? Hah!"[161]

State intervention in cases of domestic violence were also met with derision, particularly by men. For many, such violence belonged in the family sphere, and was so common it was seen as normal. While the state simplistically condemned domestic violence as the "remnants of the feudal marriage system," local residents offered more complex reasons. In Shanghai's

Xuhui District, men claimed that they fought over money, over their wives' disobedience, and because their wives made them lose face in front of their buddies by barging into gambling sessions and "ordering them home." When criticized, few showed remorse: in Xuhui District, one worker from Anhui Province said, "What the hell is this Marriage Law? Women emancipating? I don't give a damn. Go ahead and take me out to Longhua District to execute me. See if I care!"[162] In Beijing's Dongcheng District, a man bluntly told an official, "The government is meddling in trivial matters (*duo guan xian shi*). Every family quarrels. When you cook, doesn't the spoon hit the side of the pot?"[163] And old men in Shanghai's lanes and alleys said, "The government is meddling in trivial affairs. Husbands and wives always fight. A Buddhist monk trying to stop a couple quarreling is meddlesome."[164]

Panic and resentment toward the state also reflected generational anxieties. While some older men and women hoped the law would save them money and free them from the trouble of arranging their children's marriages,[165] others were afraid the state would unduly empower the younger generation. One report noted that elderly women in Shanghai feared having no control over daughters-in-law who entered the family through a free marriage. Such daughters-in-law, they worried, would not look after the household or them. Elderly and poor working-class urbanites were also concerned that their poverty would pose an insurmountable obstacle to their sons' marriage prospects. Some pointed the finger of blame directly at Mao: "Chairman Mao only cares about the second generation. He doesn't want our first generation."[166] Others were resentful that the state condemned them for "feudal" behavior when all they were trying to do by arranging their children's marriage was to "love and protect" them; without their guidance, they argued, their children might get into serious trouble with a nefarious character.[167] Not everyone panicked, however. The association of the campaign with "marriage" also meant that older people might be exempted because they were *already* married or old. As some elderly women remarked, "I'm old. The Marriage Law has nothing to do with me"; "I'm old and will die soon anyway. What's the point of studying the Marriage Law and confessing?"[168]

Younger working-class males also had grounds to object to the Marriage Law. In particular, many resented the power the state granted to women by liberalizing divorce and promising them legal protection. One young man said, "Okay, from here on in women can play mah-jongg and we can't do anything about it; otherwise, they'll divorce us." A noodle-factory worker likewise groused, "Chairman Mao's good; it's just the Marriage Law that's bad. If we workers become unemployed, our wives will divorce us." Female sexuality was also threatening to them. Believing that the Marriage Law granted protection to women who had extramarital affairs, some Shanghai men said, "The Marriage Law has arrived! Now women will run around having sex and men will be cuckolded!"[169]

Rather than promoting change within the family, the state's strong-arm tactics sometimes resulted in the formation of family compacts against the state similar to those forged by state officials. One report noted that some women who were beaten "do not dare actively participate in the movement because they're afraid their husbands and/or mothers-in-law will be locked up, or that families will be broken up." Such fears were not limited to abused daughters-in-law. Because mother and son often collaborated in the abuse of his *tongyangxi* or wife, both were "terrified." One such mother-in-law said, "From here on in I won't have anything to do with her. I'll spend more time burning joss sticks, less time talking."[170]

Even as many workers in Shanghai and Beijing feared and resented the state's new intrusion into the family, other state policies were more welcomed. Among the most important changes the Communists implemented upon their entrance into cities was to make it easier to file court cases by reducing and sometimes eliminating court fees. For those urban poor who felt that the expense of filing suit and a bias toward the rich made Republican-era courts impenetrable, the CCP's ideal of a more egalitarian court was a welcome change in policy. A Women's Federation report from Xuhui District, for instance, noted that "some people" praised the CCP because "in the past if you didn't have any money, you couldn't go to court; if you filed suit against a rich man, he would always win. Now we can all file suits."[171]

The many similarities between elite and working-class urbanites' reactions to the Marriage Law, even if workers' welcomed their new access to courts, suggests to me that the explanation for the high proportion of divorce cases in Changning (in relation to Jing'an) cannot be attributed only to political factors—an explanation that might make sense given the fact that the CCP supposedly "represented" the interests of the working class. CCP rhetoric maintaining that 1949 was the year of "liberation" notwithstanding, in scores of documents I have not found much evidence suggesting that workers afforded local state officials a great deal of legitimacy. While many appreciated some CCP policies, such as curbing the runaway inflation and disorder that prevailed in the last years of the Guomindang, other policies made the urban political experience a negative one for many urban dwellers, regardless of their status in the city. That said, we also have to point out that there still were important differences in how core and peripheral urbanites dealt with the state apparatus for enforcing the law; in general, working-class urbanites were more willing to draw the state into their private affairs, more aggressive in pursuing their rights, and more willing to reveal family problems in state institutions than those whose lives were more intimately connected to the "civilized" city. I am going to argue in this and subsequent chapters that these two aspects of working-class culture—one relating to law and the other to openness about family problems and sexuality—explain working-class urbanites' higher propensity to sue for divorce.

Legal Culture

State officials investigating working-class families in the urban periphery encountered problems fundamentally different than those among the bourgeoisie in urban cores. Among the latter, if we recall, officials pointed to problems of *jingshen nüedai,* or "psychological abuse"; when they investigated a relatively posh lane in Xuhui District, they found that "on the outside, everything is tranquil." In contrast, among peddlers, tailors, and pedicab drivers in the periphery, there was no tranquillity to be found: physical violence against women was both common and, importantly, *well known* to everyone in the neighborhood. One resident of such a district in Shanghai gave Marriage Law work team members a "tour" of his neighborhood:

> As soon as I open my window I hear people fighting and screaming. On the left is Old Chen's wife. She was abandoned by him and left alone with the kids. Now she depends on a small sock stand to support them. Whenever she gets angry, she takes it out on the kids. On the right is Cai Linfeng, a rickshaw puller. He comes home, and as soon as he opens up his mouth, they start fighting. He smacks her around once or twice and it's over.[172]

When the state gave workers the opportunity to air grievances under the rubric of "protected speech" during the Marriage Law campaign, officials soon heard an earful of complaints. In Beijing's Suianbo Lane (*hutong*), for instance, residents demanded that work team members "punish" a man who abused his stepdaughter.[173] In another *hutong,* the work team found people a bit *too* anxious to tell them about their neighbors' problems, especially about their fights.[174] On some occasions, charges of abuse were spurious, motivated by vengefulness and what reports called "everyday prejudices" against particularly difficult individuals.[175]

Willingness to draw the state into family and community affairs was not limited to cases of neighbors demanding that the state punish residents against whom there were long-standing grievances. Women's Federation officials in Beijing were forced to deal with women who had illegitimate children because of affairs or rape. Many of these women did not hesitate to "speak truth to power" to get their problem solved. One report commented: "Not a few women with illegitimate children come to the Women's Federation to talk, and there are also those who go directly to court to force the man to admit that the child is his and make him give money for the child's education. They think they [the children] are guaranteed the state's protection."[176]

Requests for state intervention were also common in marriage and divorce-related disputes. Working-class urbanites frequently pounded on the state's door requesting assistance. A lane and alley committee reported, "Every day, there are two to three incidents of marriage conflict where the parties ask the residence committee to mediate. Most family conflicts are among ordinary laborers."[177] The Women's Federation in Beijing reported similar findings. In a 1951 report, it found that the number of marriage cases had increased by one-third since the promulgation of the Marriage Law in late 1950, and that "most are of the laboring classes, and 80 percent are divorce cases."[178]

Peripheral working-class urbanites' relative openness about family conflicts can be clearly seen in two Shanghai cases. The first involved a twenty-year-old female plaintiff named Hai Dingxiu, who hailed from He County in Anhui. Hai and her husband, Wang Defu, shared the same native place. Their marriage had been arranged in 1948 by their fathers, who were related, when Hai was sixteen. In 1951 she was "tricked" by her parents into coming to Shanghai, and lived in the home of Wang's aunt to help with the housework. Although she had been a member of the Communist Youth League in He County, she was not able to hook up with the CYL during her stay in Shanghai. Hai and Wang were married in 1952, and lived on Hunan Road.

Hai and Wang's relationship was never good; they frequently were involved in loud arguments. According to the Women's Federation report, Hai sought to participate in CYL activities, but her husband prevented her. As an activist during the Five Antis campaign, she reported her husband's alleged theft to the authorities and tried to get his elder brother, Wang Dequan, to confirm her accusations. However, Dequan told his brother about the Five Antis materials she had collected. The men's parents, in turn, began spreading rumors about Hai, saying she had been having an illicit affair with a fellow worker.

Not long after this, Hai, much like the women seeking alimony from deadbeat fathers above, went to court to file for divorce, bypassing the residence committee. She pointed out that her marriage had been arranged, her husband was preventing her participation in social activities, they did not have the same political standpoint, and their marriage had no basis in *ganqing* (love). Her case then came before the court, the lane and alley committee, the mediation small group, the union, and the CYL. All of these organizations confirmed her account but still tried, unsuccessfully, to mediate. The court, following the "mass line" in legal work, dispatched some officials to their residence and asked local residents their opinion of the case. Residents from nearby alleys, as well as his family members, also came to this court session.[179]

During this meeting, Hai and Wang's family tensions came into public view. Wang's parents raised a racket, vehemently cursing residents and mediators. After they were removed, this ad hoc court calmed down. Hai then repeated her reasons for seeking a divorce, and the residents "supported" her claim. Court officials later gave their oral approval of the divorce. Wang, however, refused to accept the verdict, and his parents, coming to his aid, once again raised a commotion. The meeting was unable to continue, so the settlement of property issues was deferred back to the regular court.

When the case was finally heard, the parties appeared together with representatives from the Women's Federation, the CYL Party Committee, the neighborhood mediator, and a lawyer for the defendants. In court, Wang continued his family's practice of fearlessly cursing state officials, but upon seeing that this would not help him win property, he apologized. Already trying to deal with a large backlog of cases, the court suggested that Hai and Wang settle the property issue themselves.[180] She demurred, asking for the court's assistance. Apparently, right after the oral verdict was handed down, Wang returned home and destroyed all of her clothes, shoes, and possessions. She then requested that court officials accompany her home to enforce the decision, as she heard that her husband had a gun. Accompanied by representatives of the Women's Federation, a mediator, and court policemen, she returned home. Having secured the court's cooperation, Hai requested that they pay Wang a monthly visit to collect alimony. Wang's subsequent appeal was rejected.[181]

Wang's propensity to resort to violence seems to have been common among Shanghai residents who hailed from Anhui, according to party report. Unlike Hai Dingxiu, who was eventually able to hook up with the Shanghai CYL for help in getting the state to intervene in her family dispute (and for this reason her case might not be typical of all women), many women did not take the initiative. The case described below shows how brutal domestic violence forced women into the arms of the state to seek protection. In both scenarios, however, the outcome was similar: even if they were not immediately resolved, private problems became public.

Sun Zengyi, fifty-two, hailed from Anhui's Huaiying County and worked in a Shanghai tobacco factory. According to a Women's Federation report, Sun frequently abused his wife, Huang Aliu. Although formally married to Huang, Sun had been living with a female coworker, Yu Aying, who also was from Anhui's Huaiyang County, for six to seven years. Like Huang, Yu was also abused by Sun. After a political campaign in their factory, Yu went to court seeking a separation.[182] While the case was in court, Sun was forced by the factory administration to return to his former wife. At home, he accused Huang of instigating the separation case. Apparently believing that killing her would put an end to his problems, he purchased a knife and hid it under his pillow. His plan to murder Huang, however, was foiled by his daughter, who found the knife and ran to the local police station.

After hearing the complaint, the police promptly sent Sun and Huang back home, informing the local mediation committee about the situation. When the couple's fighting and Sun's threats continued, the mediation committee tried to intervene. Sun, however, was unrepentant, and boasted, "The police station is like my aunt's home, and the courthouse is like my mother's: I go in and out of each just as I please." He brashly told the police, "I have a knife and am going to kill Huang." The police, however, did not make a preemptive arrest, and released him after an hour. Huang then went to the Woman's Federation to complain: "You say women have been emancipated (*fanshen*), but I don't see it. You can't even protect my life. Are you waiting for me to die before you do anything?" The Women's Federation decided to encourage the couple to divorce and told Sun that "getting arrested won't solve your problem." The federation also decided to meet with court officials regarding the children's custody and expenses.[183]

The legal culture that emboldened Wang and Sun to berate mediators and court officials frequently appears in documents detailing life in urban factories and working-class neighborhoods. In factory reports, I have found no instances of workers pleading with work teams using the honorific "elder brother, elder brother," as among some businessmen. Overt confrontation seemed to be more the norm. In Beijing, for instance, a female worker who was forced to attend one too many meetings publicly threatened to "barrel over" whoever came to demand that she go to yet another one.[184] Pedicab drivers were reported to have been especially contentious with local state officials, openly mocking them when they tried to convince the drivers to register their marriages with the local government.[185] In one factory, workers called union officials they disliked or resented "capitalist running dogs."[186] At another factory in the capital, a female worker was revealed as a prostitute. She was "educated" by the union, but workers, who were apparently excited to have a prostitute in their midst, screamed out during lunch hour, "Wild chicken" (i.e., a prostitute)! When union officials objected to the ruckus, a worker correctly said, "The government has no regulation forbidding sex with wild chickens!"[187] In another case, workers in a wool factory conducted a struggle session against cadres who were caught having illicit affairs but went unpunished by the union. Probably upset that these supposed models of exemplary political behavior were violating their own rules and regulations about behavior in the workplace, workers conducted a struggle session against them and then "expelled" them from the Communist Party.[188]

This culture of public confrontation was also manifested in the way in which intrafamily disputes were handled in working-class communities. Officials often complained that arguments quickly turned into fights and fights into lawsuits. In Shanghai's working-class Bamiao District, for instance, Women's Federation officials found that some couples "have a little argument that immediately turns into a ruckus (*danao*)." Such couples, the federation complained,

> do not want to make a self-confession, only divorce. They go to court, insisting that they can't get along and want a divorce. Because mediation was not completed, the court sends them home. By the time they get home, they have calmed down and no longer want a divorce. The next day they go to court and seek to cancel the suit. This makes it difficult for the court to get anything done.[189]

In Beijing, reports pointed to a similar pattern. One report noted that "some residents, as soon as they have a quarrel, go to court and request a divorce,"[190] and a Bureau of Civil Affairs report on the causes of divorce in Beijing found that in the working-class Xuanwu District, 32 percent of divorces between January and April 1954 were caused by "fighting over small matters and rashly filing for divorce . . . this problem occurs predominantly among workers and demobilized soldiers."[191]

Of course, not all such cases resulted in divorce, as the above quotation indicates, nor should we necessarily believe that divorce cases were filed "rashly," since this might reflect educated officials' bias against the uneducated. But perhaps the conviction that workers and others who were not educated were incapable of using the sort of "gentle persuasion before confrontation" advocated by the 1930s journalist Zou Taofen led the state to set up numerous obstacles to people (usually women) who wanted to divorce. Even though plaintiffs sometimes went directly to courts, courts might send such cases back to lane and alley committees, unions, and work units. Each unit, in turn, was required to submit official documentation of the parties' reasons for divorce, as well as testimony from neighbors, friends, and superiors—a long process that increased the risk of close scrutiny of one's family affairs. This meant that if an investigation revealed that one had extramarital affairs, for example, this would likely become part of one's official record. In some cases, men decided not to file for divorce in the first place because they feared that if their real motives were revealed, their file would receive a permanent stain and the court would not agree to the divorce.[192] For many urban residents, the state's "thick" "political geography" was sometimes sufficient to stifle litigious tendencies. Still, the degree of "thickness" varied in different districts and institutions: the state was particularly "thick" in white-collar firms and offices and in large, state-run factories that had an established party presence, but appears to have "thinned out" in smaller factories and private firms, and among the unemployed, independent peddlers, tailors, and pedicab drivers—a population concentrated in the urban periphery. Such workers' location in the state's political geography is probably part of the explanation for their ability to sue for divorce.

All these examples suggest important cultural features that likely contributed to the differences in the way working-class and elite urbanites dealt with the state in the context of the Marriage Law. First, workers, whether employed in factories or selling odds and ends, on the whole appeared to be less cowed or enthralled by the state than upper-class urbanites. Second, working-class urbanites seem to have been less concerned than elites about exposing family dirty laundry; the Wang family feud, we should recall, happened in full public view, and the dispute between Huang and Sun likewise involved several levels of state institutions. Because the Marriage Law made divorce a public, official process in which "private" conflicts between plaintiff and defendant had to be exposed to state institutions, the willingness to be frank, aggressive, defiant, and stubborn in pursuit of a claim could be a critical factor in shaping the outcome of cases. Third, in some of these cases we can see another facet of working-class legal culture: Hai Dingxiu and others went *directly* to court.

How might we explain this working-class litigiousness and the upper classes' tendency to hold the state at arm's length? I can think of at least four possible explanations, all of which will be explored in the coming chapters. The first is that Hai and others were willing to go to court because they were conscious of, and felt empowered by, their favored "proletarian" status, and as a result dared to challenge both family members and state officials in ways unimaginable for those of the higher classes. The second explanation is that people such as Hai, by going directly to court to complain about family members, consciously sought to bypass local institutions because they were untrustworthy, incompetent, or obstructionist. The third is that direct appeal to court was a reflexive reaction, or a habit, whose origins can be traced to their *rural* native place. Finally, it is also plausible that seeking recourse in courts was more or less typical of the *urban* working class.

Which explanations are supported by the evidence? The first—attributing to workers a high degree of class consciousness—is not well supported by party investigations on workers and factories from the early 1950s; I have seen only a couple of statements by workers indicating that they were highly aware of their good class status in this period, let alone of the possible benefits this status conferred on them in their dealings with residence committees, courts, and other state institutions. However, since Hai Dingxiu *was* a member of the Communist Youth League, it is still too early to rule out this explanation. The second explanation is supported by evidence presented earlier concerning the way in which local officials frequently bungled the handling of family cases. Given the surfeit of local knowledge about officials' private lives and the mistrust this fostered, going to court would appear to be a reasonable way to get a hearing in front of a relatively objective official. The latter two explanations also seem plausible, and are supported both by the historical record and by comparative evidence. Elizabeth Perry, in her study of social movements in Anhui, for instance, has found that going to court to redress grievances was a common peasant practice in the nineteenth and early twentieth centuries.[193] Hai Dingxiu also hailed from Anhui. Comparative evidence, however, might also suggest that petitioners such as Hai behaved in a way typical of working-class *urbanites* elsewhere in the world, and that Hai's rural background might be irrelevant to her willingness to invoke courts. In his study of a U.S. suburb, for instance, M. P. Baumgarten found that working-class suburbanites "experience a greater amount of open and substantive third-party intervention in their domestic conflicts than middle class people. Middle class people, when they involve outsiders at all, are more likely to turn to therapists for 'problems' not defined as conflicts."[194] In Egypt as well, Enid Hill has found that workers to go to court more regularly than the more "modern" middle and upper classes.[195] In Turkey, most divorces occur in urban areas, but if we look at the issue of class, divorce rates mostly *decline* with increasing levels of education; those most likely to sue for divorce are people who are "just literate."[196] Class differences in the extent of willingness to expose "private" problems in courts and aggressively confront abusive family members were also found in India.[197] Are the differences between Hai and upper-class urbanites, then, the result of class differences *within* urban society—differences that might, for instance, be attributed to the fact that poor folks live in simple, crowded housing and have little conception of "privacy"—or alternatively, was Hai's and other working-class urbanites' willingness to go to court and expose private problems the product of their *rural* background?

Resources

Decisions to sue for divorce are shaped not only by people's willingness to reveal personal and family affairs in state forums; material and livelihood considerations are often at issue. According to Kay Johnson, urban factory workers were in a better position to divorce than peasants precisely because their "remunerative work roles enhanced their potential for independence, self-determination, and family power."[198] New evidence, however, suggests that wage earnings did not necessarily guarantee such independence and power. In Beijing, for instance, a trade union investigation found that factory women often did not control what happened to their wages after they were distributed. In many cases, women workers were forced to fork over their salaries to their in-laws; in others, husbands took their money out of their hands the day they received it.[199]

During the early 1950s, marshaling resources for divorce seems to have been easier for those urbanites who retained close ties to *rural* areas, rather than those most tightly enmeshed in urban life and institutions. Because the state did not consider sojourners full-fledged urbanites worthy of urban household registration, many were forced to leave the city to alleviate congestion. While many of these peripheral urban workers resisted these efforts, others took advantage of their designation as "peasant" by claiming the land that was distributed to poor and middle peasants during the 1951–1952 land reform. In a random sample of one hundred uncontested divorce cases from 1951 to 1953 in Shanghai's Xuhui District's Bureau of Civil Affairs, over 75 percent of plaintiffs were self-employed—mostly servants, unemployed workers, fruit and tofu peddlers, barbers, vegetable sellers, and tailors.[200] According to the 1946 population census for Changshu District (later incorporated into Xuhui), those with occupations categorized as "agriculture," "transport," "independent," and "household" accounted for only 41 percent of the district's residents.[201] This suggests that in this district, those with peripheral urban status sued for divorce in proportions much higher than their number in the overall population. This reason for this, I suggest in the three cases described below, was their ability to use a rural resource—land—to bargain with state officials and their husbands, which facilitated settlements.

One case involved a Zhejiang woman named Zhu Qin, twenty-eight, who was married to Cha Zulian, thirty-six. The two were married when she was sixteen, and she had her first child when she was nineteen. After her child died, she left the village and went to the city of Hangzhou to work as a nursemaid. Soon after that she moved again, this time to Shanghai. In 1951 she met another man, married him, and had another child. When Cha heard through the grapevine that his wife was living with another man, he came to Shanghai and tried to force her to return to the village. Moreover, he demanded compensation for the debt he incurred in coming to Shanghai. Zhu then went to court to petition for divorce. In the court's first mediation session, Cha did not agree to the divorce, but during the second mediation session she paid him fifty thousand cash for his travel expenses, and told him to return to the village and wait for the court to handle the case. During this time the court investigated. They found that Zhu and her new husband ran a small vending stand selling odds and ends, and had just enough to cover their own living expenses. Moreover, their daughter was in the hospital. In the final mediation session, the court granted the divorce after Zhu agreed to forgo all of her material possessions and land in the village, and Cha dropped his demand for compensation.

Peripheral urban status was also an advantage for Sun Qilong in her divorce proceedings. Sun, twenty-five, married at the age of twenty to Chen Zhilong, a twenty-five-year-old cobbler, and had a four-year-old child. Sun's marriage to Chen was arranged: she had been an adopted daughter-in-law (*tongyangxi*) in his family since she was sixteen years old. Employed as a servant in Shanghai several years prior the Communist Revolution, in May 1950 Sun was dismissed from her job, forcing her to move out of her apartment and find someplace else to live. Soon after this, she became pregnant again. For reasons that are not quite clear, she went to the district mediation committee to register for divorce and request mediation. The mediation committee, however, convinced her to drop the case. In October 1953, Sun once again knocked on the district registration office's door requesting a divorce. This time she was more determined, having a new card to play. Having received land during land reform, she demanded that her husband drop all claims for compensation for wedding expenses in return for the five *mu* of land she had received during land reform. (One standard *mu* equals one-sixth of an acre, or one-fifteenth of a hectare.) She also demanded that he pay their child's living expenses. Chen refused, but the court approved Sun's request, citing her "determination" to divorce and Article 17 of the Marriage Law, which allowed divorces if a marriage was arranged and mediation was unsuccessful. She was awarded custody of her child as well as alimony. The court further determined that the land would be registered in her, Chen's, and their daughter's name. Income from Chen's portion of the land would pay for their daughter's educational expenses.[202]

Having some land also gave peripheral working-class women more bargaining power in cases that underwent extensive mediation at the lane and alley level, allowing them to refuse state-mandated mediated settlements. For instance, an Anhui woman living in Changshu District named Tong Xiuhua filed for divorce. Only seventeen years old, Tong lived in a shack settlement. Her husband, Tang Xiancheng, twenty-five, was also from Anhui, and made his living selling old goods. Tong had been his *tongyangxi* from the time she was three until they married when she was sixteen. Because their incessant and loud fighting disturbed their neighbors, the case was mediated by the district's Women's Federation and lane and alley committee. Unwilling to reconcile after seven sessions, Tong went to court to petition for divorce and claim some of her property, 1.2 *mu* of land, five hundred thousand yuan, and travel expenses to return to her village. Tang refused, arguing that at the time he was in tough economic straits, with heavy debts accumulated during the marriage. He further claimed that they only had 3 *mu* of land, which would not be enough to sustain his family if it were divided. After investigation, the court decided to grant the divorce, as well as grant her property rights.[203]

As these cases suggest, continued ties to rural areas did not lead to conservative notions toward divorce. On the contrary, the attachment of peripheral urbanites to the countryside allowed them to pursue a "modernist" goal, divorce—an option that elite core urbanites were often unwilling or unable to pursue precisely because of their attachment to and stake in the city. In the next two chapters we will see how having land, rather than the status and security of urban residents in work units, also worked to the advantage of rural Chinese seeking to divorce.

Working-Class "Sexual Culture"

Divorce cannot be considered independent of marriage. Before the modern era, divorce was often inhibited by community pressure, as young couples married not as "individuals" but as members of kin groups. If a couple was having problems, communities might step in to prevent the breakup of the relationship. Laws also made it difficult for women to sue for divorce, and there were often numerous religious and ethical injunctions for a couple to remain together, even in difficult times. Community involvement and legal and religious injunctions meant that there was less chance that the couple would be able to divorce solely on the basis of whimsical desires, passion, and changing fancies.[204]

The Marriage Law of 1950, as I pointed out in the last chapter, intended to change traditional family structure by changing both legal rights and the institutional basis of marriage. In addition to granting people a more expansive right to divorce, the law also prohibited marriages arranged by parents or matchmakers. Freed from such constraints, the state believed, people would take advantage of their new rights to pursue "love-based" marriages, which were assumed, of course, to be happier than those based on community arrangements. Optimally, marriage choices would be based on political criteria as well: people from good classes should fall in love with and marry other good-class people.

The CCP's advocacy of love-based marriages revealed its commitment to family reform as well as its utopian vision of social change. Notably absent from the law and propaganda campaigns was any mention of exactly *how* men and women would find spouses without parental or community involvement. How would youth working long days in factories and offices find the time to seek an appropriate spouse without family assistance?

"Rash" Marriages   In urban China, the regime's hopes of promoting love-based and political marriages were often dashed by the time and spatial constraints of urban life. In Beijing, residents recognized the utility of arranged marriages even as they admitted to their contribution to a couple's unhappiness. "Even though arranged marriages were bad," one male said, "at least you were able to get a wife. Where am I supposed to go to find one by myself?"[205] At Shanghai's Shenxin Number Two Mill, some workers faced a similar dilemma:

> Before the Marriage Law, young workers complained that there was no place
> to find a partner. They said their routine consisted of working long hours and

then returning to the factory dorms. This problem still exists after the Marriage Law campaign, and requires factory leaders' assistance to solve . . . At the Jiangnan Shipyard, male workers . . . are worried they will not have the time, or the ability, to find a wife by themselves.[206]

Despite these objective difficulties, there is no evidence suggesting that the state took an active role in promoting the realization of new socialist marriages. Among teachers, as we have seen above, a similar predicament led young women to request family intervention in finding a marriage partner. For the urban working class, however, the post–Marriage Law predicament led to a different outcome. State officials writing about marriage and relationships among urban workers habitually pointed to the "rushed" and "careless" way in which workers handled their marriage and family problems — the opposite of the complaint about teachers, who were seen as too picky and snobbish. Although the contrast in these two views might be attributed to literate critics' cultural bias against workers, evidence does point to a rather "fluid" family structure among the urban working class, one that might be attributed not only to lack of time or space. The fluidity of relationships may indicate something deeper: that the actual meaning of "marriage" and "divorce" was understood differently among the elite and the working classes. Most important, it seems that the latter paid more attention to pure economic considerations than to class, cultural, or political compatibility, and (related to the first, most likely) were also more willing to "trade in" failed spouses for potentially better ones. Take, for instance, the situation of ex-prostitutes and "female entertainers" in Beijing. One report noted that such women were heavily concentrated in one area of the city — "Big Ditch Head" (*da gou tou*). During several months of 1951, many of these women married workers from nearby factories, but not one of these relationships lasted: one couple stayed together for a year before divorcing, but all the others divorced after far less time — some after only three days, others after three months. The frequent changing of partners in the area led to a popular saying — "Marry in May and June, divorce in July and August"[207] — and to criticism of legal and Bureau of Civil Affairs cadres who did "careless work" by granting speedy divorces to residents who, "as soon as they quarrel, go to the court and request a divorce . . . but two days after the divorce come again and want to remarry."[208] Another Beijing report commented that workers "casually" marry and divorce (*qing jie, qing li,* or *qingyi jiehun lihun*),[209] and in Shanghai, officials in the Changshu District marriage registration bureau and the Xuhui District Women's Federation remarked that among the local populace there was a tendency to "fall in love at first sight, argue for three days afterward, and then divorce," as well as to "select a spouse without principle."[210] Concurring with these assessments was a report from the Shanghai Trade Union, which griped that factory workers "are not clear about the distinction between 'friend' (*pengyou*), 'comrade' (*tongzhi*), and 'lover' (*airen*). Couples go to one or two movies, and then decide to marry. The man sees someone else and forgets about the first woman."[211]

Many of these "rash" marriages and divorces were often accompanied by a certain willingness to "go public" with one's marriage and family matters, something we did not really see too much of among the Shanghai teachers discussed earlier, who often kept silent about their problems. What's more, few women in this population expressed the same reservations or fears of men or marriage, another feature that stood out among the teachers. Documents from Beijing, which, given their handwritten, sloppy prose, I do not think were purposely sensationalized as a warning of what constituted "aberrant" behavior, tell a story of relationships—marriages, live-in lovers, one-night stands—quite different than among elite women. In Beijing's Hengdecheng Cotton Weaving Factory, for example, two female workers became somewhat notorious for their ability to find boyfriends along a local street. Meeting a man for the first time, they asked for a watch; the next day, they requested clothes. If they were not interested in continuing the relationship, they would call it off. The men would then ask for their gifts back, in addition to an introduction to other female friends.[212] Other Beijing workers went on dates to Tianqiao, a public area long the center of traveling theater in the city, to listen to local opera performances. After the opera, they went to the movies or the sports arena and then returned home to have sex.[213] The nature of sexual relations among this population is also evident in a 1951 report from a Shanghai tobacco factory: "The year 1951 was the most chaotic of years: unmarried women were getting pregnant all over and casually shacking up with men."[214] In some instances, the frequency of casually "marrying" and "divorcing" shocked officials. A report circulated in Shanghai cited a case of a woman in a shack district who worked as a fish seller. The woman was only twenty-two years old, but had already been "married and divorced sixteen times." This woman's explanation succinctly captures what was at the heart of these seemingly "rash" marriages and divorces. When officials asked her about her recurrent divorces, she replied, "I marry to eat; if I have nothing to eat, I divorce."[215]

When examined comparatively, Chinese workers' frank attitude toward sex and very pragmatic view of relationships seem less surprising, or the product of some state project to construct new, modernist sexual norms. According to the historian Diane Koenker, Russian workers were also quite frank regarding sex and relationships, frequently embarrassing and frustrating more literate urbanites. Among women, she writes, "[t]he laughter starts with general questions and ends with intimate details of family life—but all are devoted to sexual questions: who is sleeping with whom, paternity, and prostitution." When a newspaper correspondent wove his way through the crowd of bantering women, he reportedly "blushed" upon hearing their sexual banter.[216] Given the commonalty of these attitudes toward sexuality, the interesting question concerns the origins of this "culture." As in China, Russian workers in the early part of the twentieth century hailed mostly from villages.

Becoming Urban   Hastily arranged, economically motivated marriages are probably another reason for the greater proportion of divorce cases in peripheral Changning District and the surfeit of anecdotal evidence supporting these numbers. But what seems to me just as crucial as a willingness to leave a poor husband is the ambition to marry *up* the urban ladder. Like many workers worldwide, workers in China, especially women, wanted to marry someone more urban, and thus more cultured and economically better off, than themselves and their current spouses. Core urbanites, such as intellectuals, businessmen, reporters, and factory staff, commanded higher salaries and better housing than spouses only one step removed from rural areas, and were thus a target for seduction and sexual favor.

A case of a female worker at a rubber factory illustrates how the pursuit of urbanity contributed to "rash" divorces among the working-class urban population. Sometime during her off hours, this woman had sex with another worker and became pregnant. Later, seeking to escape the factory confines, she took what would soon be a fateful trolley-car ride. Riding in the trolley car, she met a reporter. After this chance meeting, she moved into his apartment, even though he was already married. According to the report, she was willing to become his mistress and live in an apartment that was probably much larger than her dorm room. After she became pregnant and gave birth, another worker and the reporter's wife raised objections to their relationship. Even though her situation was exposed, this woman, having moved up a notch on the urban social ladder by "marrying" an elite urbanite, was reluctant to climb down. After finally moving out of the reporter's home, she took up with a colleague of the reporter, got pregnant again, and had another child. She never formally married any of these three men. Workers, the report lamented, have the attitude of "causally marry, casually divorce" (*suibian jiehun, suibian lihun*),[217] which in this worker's case is probably better rendered as "casually shack up, casually separate," since there is no indication that any of these liaisons involved a formal marriage or divorce.

Preference for upper-class urbanites is also revealed in frequent complaints by the Chinese Women's Federation that politics did not play any role in workers' marriage choices. Seeking to promote marriages between people of good political status, the Women's Federation was understandably upset when women with good political class, such as workers, scorned other good-class workers in favor of men whose political standing was shaky but whose wealth or cultural status would allow them to enjoy the cultural possibilities the city offered. In Shenxin Number Two Mill in Shanghai, for instance, a woman was married to a peasant who still lived in a village. During the 1953 Marriage Law campaign, she requested a divorce, claiming that her husband was a peasant and thus "backward" (*luohuo*).[218] A report from Beijing complained that women workers completely misunderstand the Marriage Law because "they are not willing to marry other workers." Their reasons for refusing to consider such marriages reflected widespread urban disdain for rural people: workers were deemed by factory women, who themselves might have been recently relocated from the countryside, as "impolite," "not cultivated," and "loud." As one report lamented, women workers "do not want to marry other workers, only office staff . . . They think other workers are good-for-nothings (*mei you chuxi*). They say, 'When you get married you should have fun, not work.'"[219] As one Beijing report disdainfully commented: "These women only want to have a good time. They have an 'I want to be a *tai tai* (madam)' dependency thinking."[220] And in Shanghai, a report complained that women workers "slept with whoever could give them a lot of money" and that they told men flat out, "So long as you treat me well, I'll have sex with you."[221] Interestingly, Soviet officials trying to mobilize women in factories in the 1920s encountered similar difficulties: "Young women," state officials lamented, "cared mainly about dressing well and dancing."[222]

Fluid marriage and family relations were also caused by what official critics called a "misunderstanding" of Marriage Law propaganda. Often illiterate, workers heard about the Marriage Law only through verbal communication; none read the preamble or its articles. As a result, many had a rather expansive, and unintended, interpretation of the law's advocacy of marriage "freedom" that, in the end, undermined the state's goals for political relationships. At a Shanghai tobacco factory, the union reported:

> Women workers think that "freedom" means you can "casually marry and casually divorce." They frequently change boyfriends, always looking for someone with more money. They see someone with a new boyfriend and the first question they ask is: "Is he good-looking?" The second question is: "Does he have money?" After that they ask questions about the shape of his head, feet, eyes, nose, and whether he is tall or short. They do not ask whether his thinking is progressive, or whether he is active in production.[223]

Workers were not alone in denigrating politics as a factor in marriage selection. Despite the politically charged atmosphere of early 1950s China, parents still preferred their daughters to marry capitalists rather than other workers. One report found that mothers who interfered with marriage freedom did so to try to get their daughters to marry someone with money. In this way, both parents and daughter could avoid work for the rest of their lives.[224]

The desire to "become urban" by using the Marriage Law was particularly prevalent among the most recent rural arrivals in cities—the high-ranking male CCP officials who made up the new Chinese "patriarchy." The rash of divorces among high-level cadres was yet another unintended consequence of the Marriage Law. The Marriage Law's rationale, as was seen in the last chapter, was based on a black-and-white view of oppression: women were oppressed, and men were the oppressors. As a result of this view, Mao and the party gave little thought to how to handle *male* demands for divorce after 1950.

Despite the CCP's attempt to raise the status of women by prohibiting arranged marriages and by allowing divorces in cases of such marriages, men also proved willing to take advantage of the new provisions in the Marriage Law. Men who joined the Red Army during the Anti-Japanese War came largely from peasant families in North China. Many (including Mao) had had their marriages arranged by their families when they were children. As soldiers, they spent years away from their villages and experienced the deprivation common to a wartime existence. Rising through the ranks during the war in the hinterland, high-ranked party and army officials saw cities as a welcome destination. Having finally arrived, officials were immediately struck by the disparity between city and village women. These new "urban" men saw rural women as drab and uncultured, and urban women as the "spoils" of the city to which they, as "conquerors," were now entitled. Often uneducated, new urban cadres sought an educated and beautiful wife to complement their already high political status with high cultural status. As one report put it:

> Cadres who come into the city want to divorce their village wives, even though they have feelings for one another (*ganqing*). They see them as clumsy and awkward, and without culture. They see young, beautiful, cultured, and brightly colored (*huahua lülü de*) city women and want to marry them. They then request divorces from their wives. Others do not petition for divorce; instead they abuse them to force them to petition for divorce.[225]

Another Women's Federation report noted that veteran cadres (*lao ganbu*) are "politically progressive" (*jinbu*), and as a result "look down upon their wives in the village, and because of this seek divorce." Cases such as these led the chief judge of the Dongcheng District Court, Shi Lei, to criticize cadres' "capitalist and corrupt thinking."[226] The Women's Federation similarly complained that cadres are "Marxist-Leninist in their work, but feudal in their own relationships."[227]

Discarding peasant wives for urban sophisticates was common in Shanghai as well. The city's Women's Federation complained about men who called their peasant wives "old hags" (*huang lianpo*) and claimed that their marriage was arranged in order to get a divorce and marry a city woman. An article in the Shanghai press expressed concern that such men were "secretly happy" at the promulgation of the Marriage Law because the law would allow them to leave their *huang lianpo* and then "seek a young, beautiful, and educated woman." The article criticized this attitude as "very selfish."[228]

Huang lianpo was only one of many expressions used to convey these "urban" men's disdain for rural women. Veteran cadres sometimes used gastronomic metaphors to describe the difference between urban and rural women. For them, city women were analogized as *mantou*—a steamed bun made out of wheat flour; rural women, in contrast, were called *wowotou*, a dry, shriveled-looking piece of bread made of cornmeal and usually eaten by the poor, who could not afford to eat *mantou*. According to a Women's Federation official who dealt with such cases, male cadres would say that "they do not want to eat *wowotou*; they want to eat *mantou*."[229]

Divorce and marriage, of course, require two people, so explaining the desire of urban male cadres to marry female *mantou* reveals only half the picture. The "young and beautiful" women referred to in the Women's Federation report were often willing accomplices to new urban cadre divorces, much to the consternation of the Women's Federation. Seeking to improve their status by marrying a male high up on the political ladder, both single and married Beijing women sometimes sought to marry cadres, but only those with a car, a bodyguard, and high rank. A Women's Federation report complained that these women were "building their happiness on the foundation of someone else's sorrow."[230]

An important dimension of high-ranking cadres' quest for high cultural status through marriage was their desire to gain face by appearing as urban or "urbane" as possible. In Chinese cities, this often meant strolling around public places with beautiful urban women on their arms—the same public spaces where mass trials had been held earlier. According to some reports, cadres who sought to divorce their peasant wives often did so because they did not want to be seen in public with women who were not "cultured." Shi Lei, the district court chief, complained that cadres ask for divorce because their wives "do not know how to have fun (*wan*) or speak well . . . when strolling through the park they want someone who is young and beautiful. They think this is 'glorious' (*guangrong*) and 'increases face' (*ti mian*) . . . They do not ask about their political status." This quest for face led to not a few rash, "politically incorrect" marriages. Court and Women's Federation reports complained that newly arrived cadres married dancing girls, female hoodlums, secretaries, staff, typists, students, nurses, and even people with serious "political problems."[231]

On occasion, higher-up party officials tried to prevent marriage alliances between "good"-class cadres in their units and "bad"-class hoodlums, prostitutes, dancers, and the like. When they did so, they met with furious resistance. The Women's Federation found that if party branches did not agree to a divorce claim, male cadres would "threaten their unit by saying they'll leave the party, send someone else to do their job, or commit suicide."[232] Other cadres said, "I'd rather have a wife than party discipline" and "Marxism-Leninism cannot control people's private lives; the party cannot interfere with marriage freedom,"[233] an ironic statement given that it was the party itself that granted "marriage freedom" in the first place.

CONCLUSION

The conclusions of this chapter are tentative ones. Rather than establishing a clear trend or argument, I have tried to develop concepts and arguments that might explain the initial puzzle presented at the beginning of the chapter: Why does it appear that divorce cases were more heavily concentrated in working-class than elite districts of the city?

Let us consider two explanations, one derived from the secondary literature, the other from the data presented in this chapter. The first would center on the "urbanness" of working-class and peripheral urbanites. According to theories of modernization, it *is* possible that working-class urbanites were able to take advantage of the Marriage Law because of their rather fluid social structure, having moved from a rural to an urban area. That is, their propensity to divorce is explainable by the severance ties to "traditional" villages. Less restricted by "conservative" peasant norms, the city gave people (and women in particular) more opportunities to divorce. In this sense, urban divorce in China can be seen as a confirmation of the predictions of modernization theory, the result of the individualization and "liberation" one achieves by leaving a small community to live in a city. Generally, this explanation seems a bit less convincing given what we have seen in this chapter on Chinese urban elites and new scholarship on elites in the pre-1949 period. Elites, supposedly the most "urban" and the most "modern" of the urban population, demonstrated a tendency to avoid state institutions and keep their family problems private rather than divorce. This evidence in itself demonstrates that there are sufficient grounds to question the applicability of modernization theory to family change in China, even at this early stage in the study.[234] Chapter 5, which looks at cities between 1954 and 1966, will put us in a better position to assess this question more definitively.

A second plausible explanation can also be extracted from the data in this chapter: that divorce among the working-class population, and in particular their willingness to seek out the state, can be explained by their *rural* background, and their continued ties *to* the countryside. Since most workers, peddlers, janitors, and rickshaw men hailed from villages, it is impossible to ignore their rural background as a potential explanation of their divorce in urban settings. In this chapter I have focused on three important features of this background as "candidate" solutions to the puzzle: how "peripheral urbanites" interacted with state institutions or their "legal culture," how they dealt with issues concerning marriage, sex, and privacy ("sexual culture"), and the material resources they were able to bring to state forums. The next chapter, which takes us a bit farther out into the countryside, will I hope move us closer toward one end of the "urban" or "rural" continuum for explanation.

CHAPTER THREE

Between "Urban" and "Rural": Family Reform in the Beijing and Shanghai Suburbs, 1950–1953

A MATTER OF DEATH AND DIVORCE

In 1953, a fifty-four-year-old man named Jin Xiangsheng committed suicide by hanging himself in his room. His body was found by his mother, dangling. Jin's suicide prompted a state investigation, which attributed his suicide to his difficult economic situation, as well as to recent changes that had transformed politics in the area.

Investigators found that, until 1938, Jin, a resident of Lianhe Township in the Shanghai suburbs, had worked in an electricity plant in Shanghai's working-class Zhabei District. Though ostensibly a member of the working class, Jin was clearly among the elite of Shanghai workers. His salary, for instance, enabled him to have two wives. According to the report, he also gambled frequently and smoked opium. Neighbors told investigators that Jin was often embroiled in loud arguments with his family. In 1938, Jin's fortunes took a dramatic turn for the worse when his leg was crushed in an accident at the factory. Unable to work, he returned to his village, where he lived together with his mother, wives, two sons, daughter, and grandchildren.

Economically, the sources of Jin's family income reflected the proximity of Lianhe Township to metropolitan Shanghai. Jin's family owned six *mu* of land and rented some land to poorer peasants. One son, Jin Binying, did not work in the fields, but at a restaurant in Shanghai. With this income, Binying was able to pay off some of his father's gambling debts. Jin was also supported by other family members. When he was forced to leave the factory, he introduced his cousin to his foreman, who hired him. To repay his debt, the cousin gave Jin a portion of his monthly salary.

Jin's political and economic situation deteriorated when, in April 1953, his cousin informed him he could no longer pay him a monthly subsidy because his factory salary had been drastically reduced. Jin then asked his wife for some money, but she claimed she had none to give him. Jin then yelled at her. When he finished and stormed out of the house, she went to the township (*xiang*) government and requested that they "educate" him. Unluckily for Jin, this spat with his wife occurred just as the township was convening a mass meeting to teach residents about the new Marriage Law. Jin did not attend the meeting, claiming he was too busy. His son Binying, however, did attend, and upon his return told his father, "We've been liberated. You're not allowed to beat anybody anymore. If you have a problem, we can talk about it." Jin replied that he would continue in his old ways, and would rather die than not be able to beat his family if he so pleased. Faced with his father's intransigence, Binying too went to the township government to seek its intervention.

Several days later, investigators found, a Marriage Law instructor named Wang and a policeman named Wu went to Jin's home to talk with him about these events. Jin showed no remorse, telling them, "She's mine; it's none of your business if I beat her." Jin told the officials that he wanted to separate from his family, and that he "could bear to eat cold rice and congee, but could not bear cold talk." Policeman Wu then asked him what he would eat if the family separated. Jin replied, "I can go out to beg for food, but I can't go out to raise a family." He also explained, "We fight because we're poor." Wu then got to the point and asked, "From now on are you going to beat anyone? If you do, the law will come after you." This meeting was followed up by a visit from the township chief, a man surnamed Zhou. Upon further questioning, Jin again tried to excuse his behavior by claiming that his abuse was the result of poverty. "We fight because we're poor," he argued. Township chief Zhou grew inpatient: "Hitting is against the law!" he shouted, and told Jin to go to the police station, where the police admonished him to desist from beating his family.

That evening Jin returned home and told his family, "This evening, they're holding a confession session. I'm going to confess. You should all come participate." When they refused, Jin threatened them by invoking Confucian notions of the responsibility of the young to their elders: "The three of you [wife, son, and daughter-in-law] should go accuse me. Accuse me and let yourselves live! Go ahead! Do it and you'll be left without any descendants!" Toward his daughter-in-law, who once told him, "After liberation you still hit people; you're an old feudal!" he said, "Whatever Chairman Mao says is very popular now. You women have all been emancipated (*fanshen*)! You've already *fanshen*'ed up to the eaves of the house; now you want to *fanshen* to the top of the trees! Now you think you're a 'cadre' and can order me around."

Several days after this incident, Jin was found dead. In their report, investigators blamed the suicide on economic and political factors. Jin, they noted, was economically hard-pressed. In the past he had a substantial income, which, since his accident, was drastically reduced. In addition, he had recently lost the supplemental income provided by his cousin at the electricity plant. Politically, investigators attributed his death to women's new-found willingness to stand up to him. His wife's "daring to report what he did at home to the township government" and his daughter-in-law's "daring to tell him he couldn't beat them anymore" sparked the ultimately fatal chain of events. Inept handling by local officials was also a contributing factor. Township officials' methods for handling this family were said to be "shallow, crude, and bureaucratic." Those officials' first impression of Jin was that "he wasn't good," and their methods reflected that impression. Their telling him that "the court will take care of you" and that "if you hit again the law will come after you," and asking him, "If you separate how will you eat?" apparently frightened Jin and left him confused about state policy. Feeling he had nowhere to turn, he committed suicide.[1]

At roughly the same time that Jin Xiangsheng committed suicide, a woman from suburban Qingpu County named Shen Ayuan knocked on the door of a government office to request a divorce. Like Jin, Shen had spent some time in Shanghai's working-class Zhabei District. It was in Zhabei that the district government penned a letter to the Qingpu County government requesting help in solving a particularly vexing divorce suit. In their letter, the Zhabei District government requested that Qingpu dispatch an official there to accompany Shen back to her village. At the district government, Shen told the assembled Zhabei officials that her sister in Shanghai refused to subsidize her stay in the city. She also informed them that she had divorced her husband, Qian Ada, in 1952, and had left the village for Shanghai soon afterward. Shen also claimed that, prior to the divorce, she was "abused" by her husband, and that in their divorce settlement she had received six *mu* of land. She also charged that her husband and in-laws "threatened her, and did not allow her to return to the village." The Zhabei District government sought Qingpu's help in returning Shen to her village and making "arrangements that would guarantee the protection of women's personal freedom and property rights."[2]

Upon receipt of this letter, Qingpu's Bureau of Civil Affairs (BCA) began its investigation. Officials from the county government contacted the Zhujiajiao District government and asked for any relevant information about her case. Their research found "many inconsistencies" between Shen's testimony and their own investigation. In the "corrected" version of the story, Shen went to Shanghai's Songshan District Court in March 1951 seeking to divorce her husband. Her husband, Qian Ada, was the local village chief. At that time, Qian Ada refused to divorce. In May 1951, Shen resurfaced at a district government in Qingpu County, once again seeking a divorce, but again Qian refused. During the divorce negotiations Shen voluntarily gave up four *mu* of her land, and requested only some articles of clothing and twenty thousand yuan (approximately one day's wage of a Shanghai worker at the time). Shen also claimed that an aunt in Shanghai would be able to find a job for her in the city. In the end, Shen and Qian divorced. In return for giving up her land, she received fifty thousand yuan, more than twice the amount of cash she originally requested. Thus, the BCA investigation concluded, "the part about not allowing her to return to the *xiang* (township) never occurred. She was abused, however, but this abuse was of the 'ordinary' sort (*yibanxing*). It is true that in Shanghai Shen has no place to return to and has economic difficulties."[3]

With this transaction, officials breathed a sigh of relief that the case was finally settled. To their dismay, in March 1952 Shen once again appeared in Qingpu, this time at the county court to file for a *restoration* of her relationship with Qian Ada. The court sent the case to the district government's mediation section, where Shen and Qian reconciled and remarried.

Relief at the second conclusion of a difficult case proved premature, however. During the same month, Shen once again requested a divorce at the district government. This time, the divorce was immediately granted. Shen then left for Shanghai, but upon arrival discovered that her relatives were not willing to provide for her after all. Nine days later she returned to Qingpu, this time to the county court, and again requested a reconciliation with her husband. A court official went to the district government, and from there proceeded to Qian Ada's village to persuade him to remarry Shen. Qian agreed, and was greeted by laudatory comments from the district officials: "This Qian Ada's *sixiang* (thinking/attitude) is pretty good; he's willing to listen to what the government says."

Qian Ada's willingness to reconcile notwithstanding, in March 1953, during the Marriage Law campaign, Shen again appeared at the gates of the district government seeking a divorce. This time, however, Qian refused, arguing that he had already acceded to her demands on several occasions. Nonetheless, Shen was determined to separate. Qian finally concurred, but told her and the district officials that he would no longer take her in should she decide to return to the village. The district government then wrote a letter to the court and told Shen and Qian to finalize the agreement at the county court. Before leaving, they told Qian to "let her divorce" (*rang ta li*) even though she was "lazy" and had "lied."[4]

THE SUBURBS AS A TRANSITIONAL CASE

Taken together, the circumstances surrounding Jin Xiangsheng's suicide and Shen Ayuan's multiple divorces raise several crucial methodological and analytical issues. First, neither of these cases comfortably fits into the "urban" and "rural" categories commonly used in explanations of social change. Jin, for instance, worked in urban Shanghai, but maintained a home in a nearby village. His cousin worked in a Shanghai restaurant, but his wife and daughter requested intervention at a *rural* township government, not an urban one. Shen Ayuan likewise came from a village, but spent time in Shanghai. Seeking to divorce, she walked up and down the paths of urban *and* rural governments. Jin and Shen's cases thus raise the question, How shall we define and study agricultural areas with many industries, and peasants who visit and have relatives in cities but who still might work the land (part-time) and live in villages, not urban neighborhoods? Here, the boundaries between "urban" and "rural" features will probably complicate any attempted generalization about "urban" and "rural" areas. The literature on the Marriage Law, for instance, argues that were important differences between "urban" and "rural" China, and emphasizes the difficulties the party encountered when trying to use law to change social structure in the latter case.[5] But in their blend of urban and rural living and employment arrangements and overlapping urban and rural state institutions, Jin and Shen's cases clearly fit somewhere between the "peripheral" urban boundary (such as Shanghai's working-class Zhabei District) and an area we would consider more typical of a purely "rural" community.[6]

Second, Jin Xiangsheng's suicide and Shen Ayuan's multiple divorces and reconciliations may challenge the prevailing wisdom about "urban" and "rural" differences in divorce in the secondary literature. States that have attempted to change family structure through liberalized divorce laws have generally been more "successful" in "urban" rather than "rural" areas; the more "urban" an area, the greater the number of people seeking divorce. "Divorce," Roderick Philips argues for the postrevolutionary French case, "was primarily an urban phenomenon" owing to the freedoms enjoyed by urbanites who were no longer bound by rural conservatism and patriarchal values.[7] Kay Johnson, discussing the Marriage Law in China, explains the failure of the law in "rural areas" by emphasizing the resistance of young male cadres as well as older men and women, peasants' preoccupation with land reform, and the administrative weakness of the state in rural areas. Yet these cases show that local cadre resistance was not uniform and that the purported peasant "patriarch" committed suicide owing in part to other male officials' bullying; moreover, a young, uneducated, and *unemployed* woman (in contrast to female factory workers, who are said to have been more capable of requesting divorce) divorced *several* times, land was used as a bargaining chip, and local officials proved surprisingly willing to grant her requests, even though she was found to be a "liar" and "lazy," two not very socialist values. Are these phenomena in any way related? Why were higher-level rural and urban political institutions such as districts, counties, and courts (and sometimes townships), rather than villages, the focus of peasant women's legal strategies, and what resources enabled them to be as "determined" as Shen? Was her experience the result of her exposure to city life and access to urban political institutions, as modernization, state-building, and law and social-change theories would suggest, or rather the result of her partial integration into rural life—the argument I began to develop in the previous chapter? Were Shen's multiple divorces the *intended* consequence of state policies, or do they show how the state's breaking the social rack led to unintended consequences. Statistical evidence from other agricultural areas near Shanghai further whets the appetite for a conclusive answer: In Chongming County (an island county to the immediate north-east of Shanghai) court officials granted divorces in *96 percent* of divorce cases, and the Shanghai Women's Federation officials commented on the "ease" (*rongyi*) of divorce in agricultural areas near the city.[8]

In this chapter I take a look at how the Marriage Law shaped family dynamics between 1950 and 1953 in two mixed industrial and agricultural areas near Shanghai and Beijing. As areas that occupy the intermediate ground between "urban" and "rural," they will be referred to here as "suburbs," largely because this is the best translation of the original Chinese term, *jiaoqu*. And although I call these areas "suburbs," I ask readers not to think of U.S.-style shopping malls and bedroom communities; in the Chinese context, "suburbs" are often agricultural, with many peasant residents, but also sprinkled with small and large-scale industries. To help situate the two areas discussed below— Qingpu and Tong Counties—on the Chinese political and geographic map and in term of the urban/rural continuum, a brief introduction is necessary.

The suburbs of Beijing and Shanghai belong to two very different ecosystems. The area surrounding Beijing is part of the North China plain, or to use G. William Skinner's concept, the "North China macroregion," an arid area dominated by dry, low-yield farming, few navigable rivers, poverty, overpopulation, and recurrent natural disasters due to flooding from the Yellow River.[9] Historically, these conditions were often the breeding grounds for social protest: the Boxer Uprising (1900–1901) began in Shandong, and the Communists found many recruits among landless peasants in the area. In contrast, Qingpu and the communities surrounding Shanghai are part of the Yangzi Delta, a lush, fertile area with irrigated agriculture and crisscrossing waterways, conditions that allowed for a highly commercialized economy. The infrequency of major natural disasters (compared with the North China plain) and relatively mild climates allowed for multiple cropping seasons and high output per *mu* of land.[10]

These differences, however, should not obscure important commonalties. According to Skinner, many areas of Qingpu and Tong Counties are located within their respective macroregions' "cores," those areas that are more densely populated, fertile, commercialized, and served by better transportation networks (to other rural areas and to cities) than the "peripheries" of those macroregions.[11] The Tong County seat at Tongzhou, for instance, was linked to Beijing by rail in 1937, and two major highways (one constructed in the early years of the Republic, the other in the 1930s) crossed the county, eventually feeding into Beijing.[12] Qingpu County and Shanghai's surrounding districts were even more densely linked to modern cities, as we can see on map 3. Three rivers served as major arteries in the county, and, together with their tributaries, allowed for convenient transportation to Shanghai, as well as to surrounding provinces. Telephones also helped link Qingpu to the urban core.[13]

Qingpu and Tong's blend of urban and rural characteristics is also reflected in the occupational diversity of their populations. In Tong County, for instance, Chengguan, a town several miles north of the county seat and situated on the railway connecting Shunyi County to Beijing, had over nine hundred families engaged in commerce. Even some inhabitants of towns not located on a railroad line and farther away from the county engaged in commerce. Businesses were of a mixed sort: a 1941 survey found people working in hotels, tobacco factories, bathhouses, restaurants, small stalls, and the like.[14] A CCP investigation of a mining district (Datai) in Beijing's western hills included forty-eight natural villages and fifteen townships (*xiang*). According to the report, "this district is vast and mountainous. Most of the population relies on part-time farming and part-time employment (*bannong, bangong*) in the mines." Such employment was necessary because land was not sufficiently fertile to support a family year-round. Other Datai residents raised bees, sheep, pigs, cows, donkeys, and mules, or hauled cargo from one village to the next or to market the produce in Beijing.[15] In Qingpu, as might be expected given its proximity to lakes and rivers, residents engaged in fishing and transport, usually on a family basis.[16] In districts closer to Shanghai than Qingpu, the division between agricultural and industrial work was even less pronounced. Factories built after Shanghai became a major treaty port employed peasants such as Jin, his cousin, and Shen Ayuan's aunt, who came from nearby villages. One of these districts, Jiangwan, had close to two hundred factories as well as two universities by the early 1950s. Comprising twenty-one townships (*xiang*) and one town (*zhen*), the district had a population that was a mixture of peasants, handicraft workers, and small businesses.[17]

Family structure also reflected proximity to cities. Industrial development in and around Beijing and Shanghai, like many industrializing areas, attracted peasants seeking employment from other, often poorer, parts of the country. In Jiangwan District near Shanghai, for instance, residents

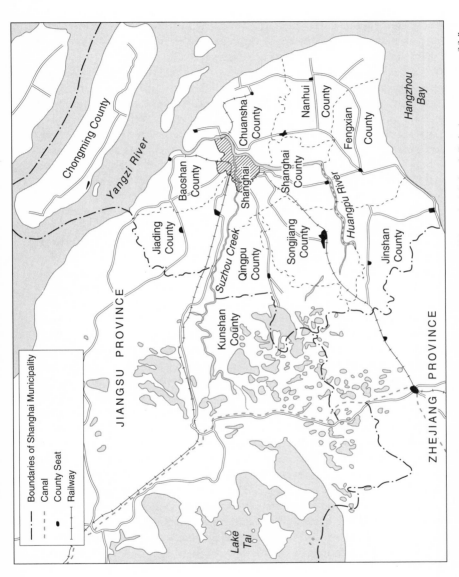

Map 3. Suburban Shanghai. Adapted from Lynn T. White III, "Shanghai-Suburb Relations, 1949–1966," in Christopher Howe, ed., *Shanghai: Revolution and Development in an Asian Metropolis* (Cambridge: Cambridge University Press, 1981), 240.

hailed from Jiangsu, Zhejiang, Fujian, Guangdong, Henan, and Jiangxi Provinces.[18] We do know that migration to cities sometimes, but not always, broke up rural marriages, resulting in de facto separations.[19] Migrants from the poor areas of Jiangsu Province often came with their entire families, but in other cases women (and probably men as well) left for the city by themselves after hearing of job opportunities there.

Despite the presence of industry, shops, banks, and relatively convenient transportation in these areas, industrialization and urbanization did not completely change rural ways. While some suburbanites were organized into unions in nearby factories or mines, others belonged to those "traditional" community-based organizations that are often the nemesis of modernizing and expanding states. The Qingpu County gazetteer notes that in 1950 there were fifteen "reactionary" secret societies, with the Yiguandao holding the longest membership lists. In one village, almost every household had a member of the society. During early political campaigns after the Communist revolution, the state suppressed their activities by executing leaders and forcing others to register with the government. After these measures, reports found that close to forty-seven hundred people left these associations.[20]

Yet, despite the state's determination to wipe out this sort of "traditional" community because of its purported threat to the implementation of "modern" state goals, we will see in this chapter that community, rather than being the nemesis of state-led social change, actually worked to facilitate it. What's more, this chapter also develops the argument that other key factors identified in the secondary literature as militating *against* family change in fact led to significant social transformations, even if many of these changes were entirely unintended. In the suburbs, evidence shows, marriage disputes in many instances reached courts and other government institutions; my evidence shows that in the early 1950s there were villages where 4 percent of households experienced divorce, and in other villages the figure was closer to 10 percent,[21] a higher rate than previously estimated (according to Meijer, 0.05 percent nationwide) for the Marriage Law campaign years;[22] in urban areas, in contrast, the annual rate was approximately 1.5 percent between 1951 and 1955.[23] Land reform, land, and administrative bumbling led to many requests for divorce as well as a high approval rate, as seen earlier on Chongming Island, as well as to marriages whose politics were the opposite of what state ideologues originally hoped for. What I leave *unanswered* in this chapter is whether such change can be attributed to suburban areas' close relationship to cities, or to "peasant" political culture, resources, geography, and experience. Chapter 4, which deals with the implementation of the Marriage Law in a rural area far removed from cities, settles this question.

"REFORMING LAND, REFORMING FAMILIES": THE IMPACT OF LAND REFORM

In the previous chapter, I suggested that having a tangible resource such as land allowed some working-class urban women to bolster their bargaining position vis-à-vis their spouses and the state. Having land, I pointed out, made a critical difference in the capacity of working-class and elite urbanites (particularly women) to sue for divorce. In addition, the case of Shen Ayuan presented above clearly demonstrates the role land played in divorce cases among women who lived at least part-time in suburban areas. At least in this respect, the suburban and urban working-class populations seem similar.

But even though these two populations received land from the state, the *manner* in which land was distributed was responsible for two divergent experiences with state power. Working-class urbanites who received land in the early 1950s were *passive recipients* of the fruits of the land reform movement. Many suburbanites, in contrast, experienced the policies responsible for giving them land *firsthand*. This divergent experience with the state and the conception of legitimacy it shaped were important factors in explaining what appears to be a rash of divorces in the Beijing and Shanghai suburbs. (See figure 2 in chapter 6 for a graph depicting the peaking of divorce cases in Shandong Province in 1953.)

Land Reform in the Suburbs

Conducted between 1949 and 1952, land reform almost invariably involved some violence, even if there were policies directing cadres to refrain from excessive force. Land reform work teams and cadres from county and district governments were sent to townships to mobilize peasants in struggle sessions and "people's courts" in which landlords and local bullies (*eba*) were often summarily executed. William Hinton's account of land reform in Long Bow Village in North China remains the classic account of peasants' "experience of the state." In one struggle session, described to Hinton by the chairman of the local peasant association,

> when the final struggle began Ching-ho [a landlord] was faced not only with those hundred accusations but with many, many more. Old women who had never spoken in public before stood up to accuse him. Even Li Mao's wife— a woman so pitiable she hardly dared look anyone in the face—shook her fist before his nose and cried out, "Once I went to glean wheat on your land. But you cursed me and drove me away. Why did you curse and beat me? And why did you seize the wheat I had gleaned?" Altogether over 180 opinions were raised. Ching-ho had no answer to any of them. He stood there with his head bowed.[24]

Edward Friedman, Paul Pickowicz, and Mark Selden, writing about the experience of Wugong Village in central Hebei (also in North China), also describe the violent, often unpredictable, nature of the land reform campaigns. Because Wugong lacked many individuals who could be clearly labeled as class enemies—a requisite for political struggle—CCP leaders chose a man whose "crime" was being the son of someone who was said to have bullied villagers, gambled, abducted widows, raped, and slept with prostitutes. Held accountable for the crimes of his father, this man, named Li Dalin,

> was dragged before the crowd. Li Rui . . . was carried up on the stage to denounce Li Dalin. People were silent as the woman poured out her grief. When she finished, the crowd engulfed the hapless Dalin and beat him for the sins of his father . . . Bound and dragged through the lanes, Dalin was smashed, twisted, and bullied, crippling his back. He was forced to confess to his alleged crimes, then jailed in the headquarters of the Poor People's Association.[25]

In another case, in a village several miles from Wugong, one man was active in anti-Japanese youth activity and later became secretary of the village party branch. But during land reform, as the village was split according to class categories, this man's political enemies accused him of oppressing poor peasants. Labeled a "counterrevolutionary rich peasant" despite his background, he was struggled and then shot.[26]

In these cases, land reform was manipulated to serve personal, and sometimes lineage-oriented, goals. Yet even with these miscarriages of justice, Hinton's account (less so in Friedman et al.) also shows that the idea of *fanshen,* "turning over"—the Chinese equivalent of our notion of "emancipation"—became part of the peasant vocabulary, as those who owned no land or rented out land received land confiscated from the pre-1949 village elites. Moreover, ordinary peasants witnessed the raw power of the Communist Party when other villagers were beaten or executed.[27] On the negative side, we can imagine that villagers also learned about the unreliability of village-level officials in handling political matters. Torn between satisfying local supporters and their political superiors, local leaders sometimes ended up satisfying neither.

The above two descriptions of the land reform process were based on either eyewitness accounts (Hinton) or subsequent interviews with participants (Friedman et al.) in North China villages. Other evidence from South China gazetteers also testifies to the dramatic changes in rural life after land reform. In Baoshan County near Shanghai, for instance, the first stage of land reform lasted between August and October 1950 with the training of cadres, the organization of peasant associations and militias, and the investigation of land holdings. According to the gazetteer, up until this point landlords were neither investigated nor subjected to land confiscation, and "used the opportunity to take revenge upon peasants." Peasants, the gazetteer notes, responded by taking their complaints directly to the county government and court, which received over 130 complaints involving the killing of farm animals, the breaking of farm equipment, and other acts intended to intimidate peasants and keep them from participating in CCP organizations. After October, land reform began in earnest, as eighteen townships in the county used struggle sessions and people's courts to prosecute landlords and other "counterrevolutionaries." Several were executed. By the end, much land, farm equipment, and livestock, as well as many homes belonging to the pre-1949 elite, had been forcibly confiscated and distributed to peasants.[28]

Gazetteers reveal not only the violence of land reform, but its equalizing nature as well. In Qingpu, prior to land reform those later classified as poor and middle peasants represented 88 percent of the local population, but owned only 27 percent of the land; landlords, who made up 4.5 percent of the population, owned approximately 50 percent.[29] Baoshan, which was closer to Shanghai, was more industrialized than Qingpu and therefore had less land and higher population concentration. In the remaining agricultural areas, however, landlords still owned land in proportions far higher (11.5 percent) than their percentage of the population (almost 2 percent). Their land holdings were larger as well, 9.6 *mu* per landlord family compared with 2.3 *mu* per average peasant family. Since many landlords left their land to live in Shanghai or other towns, their land was rented out to other peasants to till. After land reform, the land-ratio balance was changed in favor of peasants. Confiscated land was distributed to approximately fifty thousand poor and hired peasants; every household received 3.7 *mu*. Since land was distributed on an individual rather than family basis, this amounted to an average of 0.86 *mu* per person—not a lot, to be sure, but enough to scratch out a living. Those who had no land, or had even less than poor peasants, received approximately 1.5 *mu* on average. Homes confiscated by the state were distributed primarily to poor and hired peasants.[30]

The Impact of Land Reform on the Marriage Law: The State

"Solving All Problems at Once"   In the Shanghai and Beijing suburbs, campaigns to implement the Marriage Law either temporally coincided with or came directly after land reform. As the campaigns began, village and township cadres—many of them very new to their tasks—found themselves being called to district and county headquarters for training sessions to teach them how to implement the new law. Conflicts between time demands of competing political and agricultural tasks, together with the distances between village, township, district, and county, ensured that cadres would be impatient and unprepared for Marriage Law training sessions. According

to some reports, village and township cadres responsible for propaganda "studied" for only two days before "going to the masses" to tell them about the law; others trained for one day; and some never studied the law at all prior to implementing it. According to one of the more generous assessments of these meetings, "cadres have not studied and do not completely understand the directions and guidelines from the higher authorities."[31] In Tong County near Beijing, the Marriage Law coincided with efforts to organize village militias and mass organizations, and as a result, available village cadres were dispersed among several different tasks and could not concentrate on any one activity.[32] Unable to organize their calendar (which was based on the agricultural cycle of planting and harvest) to accommodate a tight political time schedule, village officials asked urban work team members, who had watches, for assistance in arranging their new schedule.[33]

Cadres who rushed from land reform meetings to Marriage Law study sessions and then returned to organize peasants found it extremely difficult to convey the law's most important articles. Two sorts of problems stand out in the reports. The first had to do with the origin of the revolutionaries who implemented state policies in the Yangzi Delta. In the Shanghai region as in other parts of the county, land reform was implemented by state cadres who hailed from older revolutionary base areas in the North, especially Shandong. Having just arrived in the delta, these cadres, most with only a primary school education, were expected to immediately enforce complex policies among a population that could not even understand their dialect.[34] In Chengqiao Township, Xinjing District, for instance, village cadres became so frustrated with a Marriage Law meeting that one-third left before the meeting was over, with the entire audience on their heels. While filing out, one complained, "We listened, but we couldn't understand a word!"[35] In Fengtai County, an area north of Beijing, peasants did not even wait until the end of the meeting. Prior to going to the meeting they borrowed a clock from a local school, and waited in anticipation as the minutes ticked away. When the scheduled end of the meeting finally arrived, the watch bearer stood up and announced, "Time's up! We have to go!" at which point they all left.[36] The second problem was that cadres, who had little time to study, were often unprepared for the questions hurled at them by suburban audiences. Much like the urban working classes, suburbanites were quite willing to humiliate unprepared officials in public forums. In one Marriage Law propaganda meeting in Xinjing District, a speaker said, "It's glorious for widows to remarry," to which one man responded, "If widows remarrying is glorious, from here on in it's best for women to have *several* husbands who die; that way they'll have even more glory!" In Chengqiao, when a cadre tried to clarify the benefits of marriage freedom by arguing that if two people married through a matchmaker, one would discover only upon marriage that the other had favus (a disease of the scalp causing baldness), some men in the audience shouted, "Now bald men won't be able to marry!"[37] Officials rarely answered these retorts, and stood there in embarrassed silence.[38]

Female officials seem to have faced even greater difficulties. Because women were still expected to take care of the household and children even though they had new political responsibilities, they were forced to bring their children to political meetings. In one case in Dachang District near Shanghai, half of the participants in a political meeting were children. As the meeting dragged on, the children became restless and began to cry. With all the noise, the audience was not even able to hear the report. People then complained, "The meeting hall has turned into a nursery!"[39]

Emerging from these chaotic training sessions was a campaign mode noted for a brand of radicalism born not out of ideology but out of a mundane frustration with busy schedules. According to official guidelines, cadres were instructed to "combine Marriage Law and production tasks," but few ever received instructions about how to do this in practice. For some cadres, this quandary was resolved in an ad hoc way: many decided just to get the Marriage Law campaign over as quickly as possible to allow themselves time for other tasks. In Qingpu, for instance, cadres in a training session said they wanted to use the Marriage Law campaign to "solve all marriage disputes at once," a method not unlike the one used by officials in Jin Xiangsheng's suicide.[40]

Radicalism and Fear   Lacking clear guidelines regarding whom to select as "targets" for the movement, cadres in Marriage Law training sessions frequently tried to avenge people who either were politically suspicious or had offended long-standing village sexual codes condemning excessive promiscuity. Older men and women were the most obvious targets: the Marriage Law targeted the "feudal" marriage system, and the older generation were the most obvious representatives of "feudalism," even though the Marriage Law and the central guidelines did not specifically make old people into the campaign's official targets. During Marriage Law study sessions in Zhennan Township, for instance, village and township cadres initially argued that "the only way to solve any problems is to line everyone up to see who are our friends and who is the enemy" (*jia jia zhandui*), that otherwise "it's only propaganda and won't accomplish anything." During the movement they looked forward to organizing "people's courts" to prosecute old women in the village.[41] Here, state officials transposed the language of land reform onto the Marriage Law: during the land reform campaign, cadres in one *xiang* reasoned, "we reformed land; in the Marriage Law campaign we should reform grandparents."[42] In a township in Shanghai's suburban Xinjing District, a female cadre proposed: "During this movement we should struggle against those stubborn old feudals. We can solve all the problems in this one movement."[43] And in a village in Fengtai County, village cadres proclaimed: "In this movement grandfathers have turned into landlords!"[44] Sometimes the criterion for struggle was even broader. In Shanghai's suburban Yangsi District the criterion for struggle expanded beyond "old feudals" and "those who committed mistakes" to include "everyone who has marriage problems."[45]

Targets selected for political struggle also reflected desires for personal revenge and, in true charivari style, the wish to maintain a modicum of control over residents' sexual practices (particularly adultery).[46] In Wusong District near Shanghai, a township cadre said, "We have to struggle against adulterers (*luangao guanxi de ren*) during the Marriage Law campaign; otherwise they won't change," and that "not handling adulterers will create chaos in social relations."[47] In Yangsi District near Shanghai, and in Songjiang County's Caojing District, cadres were particularly incensed that some residents, caring little about "bad" class status, had sex with family members of "counterrevolutionaries"; in Caojing alone, some seventeen people were said to have had sex with "family members of counterrevolutionaries and PLA soldiers' wives." In Yangsi, some cadres hoped that the Marriage Law campaign would "take care of them."[48] In Dachang District, a cadre said, "In our village there's a grandfather who's having sex with his daughter-in-law. In this movement we won't let him escape. We should struggle against them; the two should be locked up for one to two months. That'll teach them."[49]

When reports regarding struggle sessions, the unauthorized convening of people's courts, and the prosecution of adulterers were received by district and county party committees, orders were sent down to remind cadres that the Marriage Law campaign was not the same as previous campaigns conducted against "enemies of the people." Assuming that local officials had enough free time on their hands to patiently mediate, county officials instructed village and township cadres to use "persuasion" and "education," rather than violence, to resolve marriage disputes, all while adhering to the basic spirit of the Marriage Law—"protecting the rights of women." Policy now emphasized tight control (*kongzhi yan*) over the movement in order to prevent people from panicking.[50] In meetings in townships, the township party secretary would tell gathered officials, "When you go back, don't make irresponsible remarks (*luan shuo*), and be disciplined."[51] In January 1952 in Tong County, Li Zifan, the county party secretary, instructed lower-level party officials in no uncertain terms to accept divorce cases even without a letter of introduction from district, township, or village officials. Moreover, he instructed them to accept oral testimony as sufficient evidence "because the people's cultural level has not yet been sufficiently raised" and they thus could, not write. "Written testimony," he wrote, "is an unnecessary limitation, and should be immediately canceled."[52] With the issuing of these orders, cadres breathed a sigh a relief. Their personal behavior inside the family was often far from exemplary, and many were just as afraid of being investigated during the campaign as others; they, too, had witnessed the raw power of the party during previous campaigns. As one cadre in Yangsi District remarked, "If I hadn't studied this report I would have committed a big mistake (*fan da de cuowu*) when handling marriage problems."[53] Fearing punishment if they were to handle a case incorrectly, cadres in suburban areas often adopted a hands-off approach toward problems they encountered for fear of deviating from policy and being accused of being responsible for someone's death. At this point, district- and county-level officials complained that control over the movement was "too tight: cadres do not dare explain the policy and also do not dare handle any questions."[54]

For suburban plaintiffs, the road to court began with the fear that such directives instilled in local officials. Because the Marriage Law was enforced in the context of many political executions, cadres were understandably afraid of being held responsible if they handled a dispute incorrectly, a distinct possibility given their illiteracy and lack of training and experience in handling family disputes. To make sure that the fate that befell landlords and some erring cadres did not befall them as well, officials who had previously obstructed divorce cases by refusing to send them up to higher levels now perfunctorily dispatched women to districts and courts. In these settings, as we saw in the case of Shen Ayuan and as we will see again later in this chapter, divorce plaintiffs could receive a more sympathetic hearing.[55]

Legitimacy and Identity   Despite the violence of land reform and other early 1950s campaigns, it would be wrong to interpret land reform only as an event that inspired fear of prosecution. For many, land reform was a crucible wherein a new political identity was forged; many residents became "cadres" because of their activism during the movement. Furthermore, during the movement, officials received something even more tangible than political power: land. These two rewards—power and land— gave some party organizations more legitimacy than they had had in urban areas, even among the working class that the revolution was supposed to benefit the most. It was, in part, this new, and very much appreciated, identity as "the state" that helps explain why officials in Shen Ayuan's case and on Chongming Island often granted divorces, and why the Women's Federation complained that divorces in the suburbs were "easy." In Xinjing District near Shanghai, for instance, work team members complained that cadres "do not even know the law's basic spirit or content, but only that the law is the 'state's law' (*guojia dafa*) and that if it is a regulation promulgated by the Communist Party it must be beneficial to the masses . . . [Others say,] 'I'm a government cadre, how can I not support the government's laws?'"

These cadres, the report concluded, "praise and support the law, but [when asked] can't even say why they support it, and what exactly about it they support."[56]

"Blindly supporting the law" resulted in decisions that clearly went against the interests of many poor peasant men, as seen in the lack of sympathy evidenced by Policeman Wu and Marriage Law instructor Wang in their dealings with Jin Xiangsheng just prior to his suicide. In Jiangsu Province, Shanghai Women's Federation officials complained of cases of male township officials *overcompensating* women in divorce cases. In one case, officials ordered a poor male defendant to pay his ex-wife three years' worth of alimony in order to provide for her parents. Township officials believed that this decision was necessary to "protect women's rights."[57] In Jiangwan, officials in Marriage Law training were told that "women really suffered in the old society." When mediating divorce cases they refused to listen to men's objections. "By doing this," work team members reported, "they think they are correctly implementing the Marriage Law."[58] In a village in Kunshan County (northwest of Shanghai), officials told a man who was reluctant to divorce that he should agree to it because "the regulation of the new Marriage Law is to take appropriate measures to care for the woman" (*shidang zhaogu nüfang*).[59]

Not surprisingly, in both North and South China a substantial number of court cases dealt with "postdivorce property settlements" involving complaints of inequitable property settlements.[60] Women often found that the price of divorce was the loss of property, and state officials who rather casually granted divorce seemed to have a more difficult time implementing the clause in the Marriage Law guaranteeing equitable property settlements after divorce. The charge in the feminist literature on the Marriage Law is that the state dragged its feet in implementing the law, but this seems to be more true of *postdivorce* property arrangements than of divorce itself. Moreover, it was not always the case that higher-level state officials were always reluctant to enforce postdivorce property settlements. What sometimes happened was that the lack of administrative personnel in courts made it difficult to overcome determined, organized village resistance, best intentions notwithstanding. Take for instance an extreme case of resistance. In one village some twenty older women, together with some young men, pelted a divorcée with stones when she came with some state officials to take her property back to her natal home (a tactic we will see recurring in the next chapter). Faced with such organized opposition and clearly outnumbered, the officials and the woman, bleeding, beat a hasty retreat without the property. The divorce, however, remained in force, leading the village men to complain: "The people's government is great; it's just that it's too easy to divorce. She's divorcing only because she wants to marry a worker. If she does and others follow, we won't be able to find anyone to marry."[61]

Suburban Society: Transposing Land Reform onto the Marriage Law

How did family elders react to these political developments? Such a question is crucial, since if ever there were barriers between an individual woman and courts, these barriers were likely to be erected within the family and in local state institutions such as peasant associations and village governments. Kay Johnson, in *Women, the Family, and Peasant Revolution in China,* argues that these dual barriers were formidable, and frequently insurmountable, and cases such as the twenty women pelting a divorcée would seem to support this argument. The cases of Jin Xiangsheng and Shen Ayuan, however, together with evidence of the state's transposition of land reform onto marriage reform, show that resistance might not always be uniform or strong enough to prevent a determined woman from suing for divorce. Some state officials and institutions resisted granting women divorce, but others could be sympathetic, even though they were male. The case involving Shen Ayuan is particularly problematic for the thesis that patriarchal local officials were necessarily determined to resist divorce, since Shen's husband, who was a village chief, acceded to divorce on more than one occasion. Below I flesh out how land and marriage reform together interacted to loosen family relations, provide the state with popular legitimacy, and inspire new, unexpected marriage criteria.

Panic   When the Marriage Law campaigns reached their high tide (in winter 1951 and spring 1953), elderly suburbanites had much to fear. As noted above, cadres who had only a vague impression of the law organized "speak bitterness" sessions, land reform–style struggle sessions, mass meetings, and "people's courts." In "speak bitterness" sessions, suburban residents were encouraged to speak of their travails in the old society; in people's courts, violators of the Marriage Law were summarily sentenced. In Tong County, for instance, the state executed an old woman for having driven her daughter-in-law to suicide. After witnessing this, some young women, using the same language used by Jin's Xiangsheng's children, exclaimed, "We've been liberated! In the past we were abused by in-laws and grandparents; now we should get back at them!"[62] Events such as these sowed panic among older men and women. In one community, seven older women witnessed CCP organizers mobilizing young women and heard them air their family grievances. Together, the seven formed a pact according to which, "if one has to confess they will all go onstage together; if one is sent to detention, they'll all go to prison together."[63] In Zhennan Town, in an "old people's meeting," work team members found participants "very worried" and "stunned." One old man warned, "These days are the eye of the hurricane!"; and Old Lady Zhang went to the work team and asked, "Does everyone with an arranged marriage have to divorce?"[64]

Suicide statistics from Shanghai's suburbs from 1951 to 1953 lend some support to these anecdotal data.[65] Suburban women accounted for almost 70 percent of suicide (attempt) cases (n=128). In this, Chinese suicide in the early 1950s is consistent with historical patterns of suicide, but at variance with international patterns. In the United States (1970s), England (Victorian and Edwardian periods), and Singapore(1968–1971), men committed suicide more often than women, sometimes by a four to one ratio.[66] More consistent with international patterns, however, seems to be the correlation of age with suicide by sex. Among female suicide attempts in China, the average age was twenty-five, but among men the average age was almost ten years older—thirty-four. According to the statistics for suburban Shanghai, while there were only four female suicides over forty years old (4.7 percent), men over forty (Jin Xiangsheng included) accounted for 22 percent of the male cases.[67] Given the tensions generated by successive political campaigns, most of which targeted pre-1949 power holders who were often older men, it would not be unreasonable to suggest that some of these suicide cases resulted from cadre abuses and changes in state-family relations. That Jin was at pains to claim property rights over his family ("the wife is mine") to state officials who, in their effort to enforce the Marriage Law, made Jin a spectacle of weakness in managing his family reveals shifting power relations between the expanding state and the traditional family. An interpretation focusing on the impact of regime transition is also supported by a study by Frederic Wakeman Jr. of the Manchu conquest and reconstruction of power between 1644 and 1661. As in the early 1950s, the transition between the Ming and Qing dynasties witnessed a "wave of suicides," many by men closely associated with the outgoing regime.[68]

For some older men, suicides may not have resulted only from fear of "turning into landlords." As I mentioned earlier, the Shanghai suburbs were often commercially developed, boasting numerous shops and small enterprises. Those who were able to accumulate wealth could afford, and believed that they deserved, more than one wife.[69] These people were also targeted by state officials, who wanted to force the husband to divorce the younger wife or struggle against them.[70] Before one such struggle session, a manager of a store in Dongchang District contemplated his new predicament:

> In this movement I'm sure to suffer more than during the Five Antis. In that campaign all I did was confess and pay a fine. In this movement they want me to divorce a wife. That's really difficult. The older wife takes care of the household, so divorcing her isn't right (*bu xing*). As for the younger one, she works in a silk factory and makes eight hundred thousand yuan a month. Divorcing her is even worse (*geng bu xing*). What should I do now?[71]

Fearing political trouble, struggle sessions, and imprisonment, elderly Chinese in the suburbs frequently, but reluctantly, adopted a hands-off approach to their children's marital affairs at the same time that young men and women asserted their new rights to "freedom." Similar to complaints lodged against local officials, scores of reports indicated that parents felt that they "dare not" intervene with their children's affairs. In Tong County, one parent confessed: "Not caring [about their marriage] is wrong. If we make an introduction, we first have to obtain their consent before the match is finally arranged."[72] And an old woman complained, "Now it's 'marriage freedom,' [so] if my son marries a 'broken shoe' [a woman who has had sex before marriage, or is known to be promiscuous], there's nothing I can do about it. What's the point of caring whether she gives him face and is pretty? Now the government is promoting this idea [marriage freedom], so I have no choice [but to accept it]."[73] The Tong County Marriage Law Committee confirmed this account by noting that "some old people now no longer dare try to control their children's marital affairs. As a result, some youth marry while still underage, and mistakenly emphasize this as their right of 'marriage freedom.'"[74]

Community, Legitimacy, and Language   As these cases hint, there was more to the CCP's image than a prosecuting, executing organization. Although some suburbanites were reluctant to "bring up old scores" in highly political forums for fear of getting family and friends into political trouble,[75] many young and old women alike took advantage of "speak bitterness" meetings to tell of their travails prior to the Communists' arrival. Despite differences in age and status, many women nonetheless shared common experiences: poverty, early death of parents, becoming an adopted daughter-in-law, widowhood, and abuse. One old woman, for instance, looked at a picture of a man beating a young woman and cried out, "That's me! That's me!" Another woman was forced to abort several children and almost died of internal bleeding. At the "speak bitterness" session she said, "I was reincarnated too early [i.e., before the Communists' arrival]; that's why I suffered too much."[76]

What might be called the "linguistic residues" of land reform, as well as what seems to be a general confusion concerning the meaning of "revolution" and "distribution," also help explain elderly support, as well as some politically influenced marriage criteria. In cities, as the previous chapter showed, the operative metaphor elite businessmen used to understand the demands of the new Marriage Law was "confiscate" (*qingsuan*), which reflected their experiences during the Five Antis movement. In the suburbs, in contrast, people did not speak in terms of confiscation, but rather in terms of *distribution* (*fen*): in land reform, the CCP distributed (*fen*) land and rice to the poor peasants; now, with the Marriage Law, the party would distribute women to them, or else "assign" (*fenpei*) them women, much like the party assigned plots of land to poorer peasants during land reform. One older woman remarked, "You young people have nothing to worry about. The government will give you wives."[77] In Wusong and Yangzi Districts, old people said, "After the Marriage Law we won't have to worry about our children's marriage any longer."[78] But how would such distribution take place, and who should be allocated to whom? Here again, analogies from land reform shaped marriage considerations in ways unintended by the regime. For some peasants, for example, land reform's language of equalization (*ping*) was more important than its language of class. During a Marriage Law question-and-answer session in Pinghe County, Fujian Province, a peasant asked, "How should we get married?" The cadre replied, "The good will marry the good and the bad will marry the bad";[79] and in Zhennan Township near Shanghai, local cadres said, "The Marriage Law will even things up (*la ping le*): the good will marry the good, the bad the bad, cripples will marry cripples, and the blind will marry the blind."[80]

For poor suburban men, the transposition of land reform's language of "distribution" to the Marriage Law also seems to have partially alleviated worries over finding a spouse. In a town in Yangsi District, for instance, a middle-aged man suggested that "those who can't afford wives should be assigned one during the Marriage Law campaign";[81] a "bare stick" (bachelor) resident of Dachang Town proposed that "in this movement we should have the wives of executed counterrevolutionaries assigned to the bare sticks"; and in Pengpu *xiang* someone suggested, "We should have all women under twenty-five who aren't married registered and assigned."[82] In Zhenru District, a man said, "The Marriage Law is just like land reform: the poor people will get wives."[83]

Confusion over the name of the law itself sometimes combined with the transposition of land reform discourse to shape marriage considerations in unintended ways. The official name of the law was the "Marriage Law" (*hunyin fa*), the word "marriage"—in both Chinese and English—serving as an attributive noun. During the campaign, however, bumbling cadres misinterpreted the noun *hunyin* (marriage) as the verb for "to get married" (*jiehun*), and subsequently called the law a "get-married law" (*jiehun fa*).[84] Convinced that the CCP was actually legislating marriage, some acted accordingly. In Tong County, for instance, cadres called the law a "get-married law" and convened a mass meeting to force villagers to marry. As a result, several old widows panicked, afraid local officials would soon "assign" them some man.[85] Farther away, in suburban Minhou County in Fujian,[86] a township party secretary confessed to having written down all the names of a village's bachelors and widows; upon meeting one in the street, he would take out his list and tell him or her to "pick someone out."[87] In another area, when villagers saw Marriage Law work team members entering their village they would holler, "The wife-allocation work team has arrived!" and village women asked questions like, "When we are assigned, is it okay if I not be assigned to a hunchback?"[88]

By casting the party and state as "matchmaker," some peasants transposed the state's role concerning land to its role in governing the family. In the above example, the woman who asked not to be "assigned" to a hunchback did *not* question the *legitimacy* of allocation, but only *to whom* she would be assigned. What this suggests, it seems to me, is the remarkable acceptance of the new state's allocating role from land reform. Land reform gave a great deal of legitimacy to the Communists, and this legitimacy carried over to other policies. But what facilitated this sort of transposition, I suggest, was the relative lack of a "private sphere" in rural China. Absent rigid notions of privacy, it may not have been that difficult for peasants to accept, at a conceptual level, a state role in reshaping family relations in the village. Some evidence for this can be found in older women's reaction to the Marriage Law. When "speaking bitterness," for example, some older women praised Chairman Mao for land reform, as well as for being concerned about ordinary people's family matters. As one said, "Chairman Mao is great. He cares about everything, even our family relationships" (*yangyang shi dou guanxin, lian women de jiating guanxi*).[89]

SUBURBAN LEGAL CULTURE: EVERYDAY VIOLENCE, SUICIDE, STRIKES, SOCIAL PROTEST, AND "RUNNING TO THE DISTRICT"

In the report on Jin Xiangsheng's suicide, investigators stressed the economic and political changes that conspired to produce his depression and subsequent suicide. Inspired by the Marriage Law, officials pointed out, women "dared" to stand up to patriarchal authority. By focusing attention on the role of the party, however, officials perhaps underestimated the extent to which women asserted independence, resisted men, and exercised power in the family and community in daily life *prior to* and outside of the political framework of the Marriage Law. A determined pursuit of survival and rights through violence, suicide threats, hunger strikes, and community-based collective action, I suggest below, was an integral part of suburban women's legal culture, shaping their willingness to use state institutions, in addition to the form in which they presented their demands to the state.

Everyday Violence

Violence was an important method women used to exercise control in the family. Contrary to feminist scholarship on women in the PRC that has tended to emphasize women (and especially rural women) as victims of patriarchy, male violence, and state oppression or neglect, some suburban

Chinese women were agents of their own fate in the family who proved will-ing and able to beat men, albeit certainly not as often as men beat women.[90] Encountering everyday domestic violence, urban party officials disparag-ingly commented that, in the suburbs, people have a "poor peasant men-tality: everyone fights and yells" (*dada mama jiajia you*).[91] In Zhennan Town-ship, for instance, a man named Ren Guilin jumped into a well because his wife beat him up. The attempt at suicide failed, but when his wife clobbered him again, Ren stabbed himself with a knife.[92] The case of Yang Xiuzhen, a twenty-three-year-old peasant woman from Hetong Village (Caojing Town-ship) who worked in a Shanghai tobacco factory, is also a good case in point. Yang was married to a steel-factory worker, Wu Jinshan, in a "free-love" (i.e., not arranged) marriage. After the marriage, the two argued inces-santly, mainly because Yang demanded ten thousand yuan per month from her husband's salary. Wu refused, claiming that Yang spent her entire salary on herself, and contributed nothing to the family's household expenses. As a compromise, he agreed to give her a lump sum of twenty to thirty thou-sand yuan. Dissatisfied with the amount, Yang sank her teeth into his arm. According to the report, Wu "cried half the night." After this incident their relationship deteriorated, as Yang continued to beat her husband and re-fused to allow him to use his salary to buy urban amenities for himself, such as a watch. On the afternoon of March 29, 1953, Wu happened to meet Yang on the way home from work. She was on her way to her mother's home, and refused to return home with him. Upset, he walked behind her. At her natal home, Wu and Yang's mother made an unsuccessful attempt to persuade her daughter to return home. Angry at her husband's interven-tion, Yang whacked him on the ear and kicked him. The next day the humil-iated Wu attempted to commit suicide. When Yang heard the news, she ex-pressed no remorse, and brashly told the Women's Federation officials who were sent to investigate: "He means nothing to me; I don't give a damn."[93]

I do not think that this case was exceptional. Other cases show that women adopted very aggressive strategies toward other family members, particu-larly in poorer families where one member could not pull their weight. Pov-erty forced women to stand up, sometimes violently, in their own interests.[94] Suing for divorce, alimony, or subsidies for children, which likewise involved a willingness to stand up for oneself in opposition to others, was an exten-sion of this toughness. In Jiangwan, for instance, a man named Wu Jinfu had pneumonia for over a year. According to a work team report, Wu's wife despised him because he could not afford medicine or rice, and the family was on the verge of starvation. To get rid of him, his wife snuck up behind his bed and tried to strangle him with a belt. Wu thrashed around, alerting other family members. Fortunately for him, his mother was in the vicinity and heard his struggle. She burst into the room just in time to prevent his murder.[95]

Toughness within the family was also reflected in the way women interacted with state officials against whom they had personal grievances. In a case reminiscent of Jin Xiangsheng's wife going to the township to complain about her husband, a woman named Sun Xiuying filed criminal charges against a policeman with whom she had an affair. Sun went to court because she felt that the punishment that was meted out to the policeman, administrative discipline, was too light. Women such as Sun, the report complained, were excessively prone to "seek out punishment" against those who offended them (*zhengban sixiang*).[96]

Such contrariness and willingness to use state power to challenge those against whom women had personal grievances (husbands included) sometimes resulted in male suicide, as seen in the case of Yang Xiuzhen and her husband, Wu. As mentioned earlier, in 128 cases of reported suicide attempts in the Shanghai suburbs, men tried to take their lives in slightly over 30 percent. Thirty percent of homicide victims were also male. Men hanged themselves, took poison, or tried to drown themselves most frequently in response to domestic arguments (which represented 65 percent of male cases), in addition to experiencing physical abuse at the hands of their wives, and wives' extramarital affairs—conflicts that most probably resulted in a loss of face in the community. Others committed suicide because of economic difficulties, an inability to marry, or their wives reporting them to the police.[97]

Suicide and Divorce

Since the early part of the nineteenth century, some eighty years prior to the publication of Émile Durkheim's well-known study, *Le Suicide* (1897), suicide was used to prove that human behavior, even in its most solitary acts, is governed by certain laws and can be attributed to specific causes. From the 1830s onward, European investigators tried to establish links between suicide and a wide array of sociological factors, such as occupational and marital status, level of education, sex, industrialization, mental illness, and the like. Durkheim's contribution was not a new discovery of the causes of suicide, but rather, as Anthony Giddens has written, his argument that the suicide rate of a community or collective is distinct from the particular factors leading a particular individual to commit suicide, and this, in turn, makes the study of suicide more of a sociological enterprise than a psychiatric one.[98] In the field of Chinese history, owing to the absence of reliable quantitative data and a native Chinese sociological tradition, there have been no studies of the propensity of certain people to commit suicide. Nevertheless, accounts of suicide from official dynastic histories, novels, and works intended to encourage virtuous behavior suggest that Chinese suicide was often driven by dynamics quite different than in the West. Prior to the late nineteenth and twentieth centuries, China had few industries or large cities to speak of, two important causes of suicide in Durkheim's view. Rather, as Margery Wolf points out, suicide was often used as a way to protest injustice: should a person commit suicide as a result of maltreatment or abuse, in the afterlife their ghost might avenge the perpetrators.[99] In traditional Chinese society, defeated generals, princes, poets, and frustrated lovers all showed a willingness to take their own lives, often to express political, moral, or emotional protest.[100] Literature also shows, however, that suicide threats often were *not* carried out. The novel *Dream of the Red Chamber,* for instance, includes scenes where young women threatened suicide to affront opponents during arguments. In a society that offered women few means of public participation, threatening or even attempting suicide was a way to get family members to notice and try to resolve personal grievances.[101]

During the early 1950s, suicide, in addition to everyday violence, was frequently employed by women as a strategy to divorce or at least to maintain a modicum of leverage in the family. As during traditional times, many suicides were in fact threats that were never actually carried out. The Shanghai Women's Federation suicide report cited above reveals that, of 128 suicide attempt cases, only 23.4 percent (30 cases) actually resulted in death.[102] Studies of suicide elsewhere have shown a far higher "success" rate.[103]

Suicide methods in the suburbs reflected local topography, much like suicide in the San Francisco Bay area, where people prefer to hurl themselves off the Golden Gate Bridge, perhaps for one last look at the beautiful city.[104] As an area crisscrossed by shallow streams and railroad tracks, the suburban environment provided many public settings where aggrieved women could press their cases. In Shenbei *xiang,* for instance, the wife of a man surnamed Xu wanted to file for divorce, claiming irreconcilable differences. Court officials refused to hear the case, so she tried to commit suicide. After she was rescued, the court heard the case, but did not mediate it to her liking. In full view of state officials, she sat on nearby railroad tracks, waiting for the next train to run her over. She was then taken off the tracks by the township chief, who also accompanied her to court. The court eventually agreed to rehear her case.[105]

In the intense political atmosphere that characterized the early 1950s, the threat of suicide played into cadres' fear of state investigation. They worried that should a woman die as a result of suicide in their political jurisdiction, they would be held responsible and purged from the party, losing their job and newfound political identity in the process. Women's recourse to suicide thus provoked angry reactions from male cadres, who quickly learned that women were often using suicide as means to a different end. In a meeting in Xinjing District near Shanghai, a cadre complained that

> women are always pretending to die (*zhuang si*). They try to commit suicide over the most trivial problems. They're so stupid (*shisan dian*)! If we tell them, 'Go ahead, kill yourself,' then they don't dare. They jump into the river where the river is most shallow, and stand there screaming and crying that they're going to die. Next time it happens we'll dive in the water with them and dunk their heads in. That way we'll be able to see if they really want to die.[106]

In Kunshan County, officials dealt with similar circumstances. In Luqiao Township, the township chief confessed to his mishandling of a divorce case during Marriage Law study sessions prior to the implementation of the campaign. A woman named Chen had come to the township government to petition for divorce, on the (illegitimate) grounds that her husband "had a bad leg." The township chief and other local officials humiliated her by placing a large dunce hat on her head. Then

> we told her that if she wanted a divorce she had to meet five conditions, otherwise we wouldn't let her. In fact, we ourselves had no idea what the conditions for divorce were. Chen left, but returned a day later. She told us that if we didn't allow her to divorce she'd run off to the river by the *xiang* [township] government and throw herself in the water. We said, "Go ahead."[107]

Such confessions concerning the way local officials handled suicides resulted in criticism by work teams sent to enforce the Marriage Law. Reports indicated that local cadres, after being thus chastised, "guaranteed" that upon their return to the township they would no longer be afraid of hassle (*mafan*), and that they would propagandize the Marriage Law and handle marriage problems "quickly." This "guarantee" also proved problematic, however. Officials afraid of shouldering responsibility for a death and unclear about how to handle marriage conflicts were sometimes *too* willing to dispense with problematic cases. Herein lies an important part of the explanation for why the officials handling Shen Ayuan's divorce case were willing to bend over backward to accommodate her requests for divorce. Reports of cases such as Shen's were passed on to work teams, and led to complaints that, because "there wasn't enough study time, some cadres are now convinced that the old marriages are all bad and that *everyone* should be divorced."[108]

Strikes, Collective Action, and Divorce

In addition to violence and suicide attempts, suburban women used hunger strikes and work stoppages to resist men's power in the family and to counter the objections of officials unsympathetic to their divorce claims.[109] Whether used to attract the attention of the state or family to their plight or to gain sympathy for their cause, these methods allowed women to assert their interests against sometimes overwhelming odds. Take the case of a woman named Mao Linsheng, a worker in a Shanghai steel mill in the suburban Yangsi District. Mao's husband refused to give her some cash. To force him to relent, Mao then went on strike by refusing to cook, wash clothes, or take care of the children. Her husband then forked over the money.[110]

In other cases, strikes might be used in conjunction with suicide threats in divorce cases. In Worker-Peasant (*Gongnong*) Township in Jiangwan District, a woman named Zhao Di sought to divorce her husband. According to the report, Zhao was "very determined" to divorce. To make her point crystal clear, she threatened to commit suicide and went on a hunger strike for four days. Officials were forced to deal with her case, and persuaded her not to commit suicide. According to the village officials, Zhao was a "bad" (*bu hao*) woman, and was threatening suicide only because she was ridiculed.[111]

In addition to protesting for divorce, peasant women in the suburbs would also use hunger strikes to protest the breakdown of an arranged marriage, especially if one's prospective partner was an elite urbanite. Contrary to Western critiques of arranged marriages (whether in China, India, or the like) as oppressive, it seems that they were welcomed by some, especially if one's future spouse had high status. The case of a woman named Zhao Yutao, twenty-three, is a good example. Zhao's parents had arranged for her to marry a man with a university education whose parents owned a store in Shanghai. Zhao herself had only a primary school education. After the two were engaged, Zhao took her dowry and moved into her prospective husband's home, where she lived for the next three years. In 1952, he said that he wanted to call off the engagement. Zhao refused, claiming that they had a good relationship and that she loved him. She then began to cry, saying she "had no future," and that she had already given away her dowry to his family. She went on a hunger strike for four days and threatened to commit suicide in their home.[112]

Not all instances of protest were of women fighting injustice in isolation, however. In other cases, women banded together to protest what they considered a miscarriage of justice and the seeming contradiction between the political rhetoric of "liberation" and the resistance they encountered by some state officials. Collective action was used in the divorce process as well. In suburban communities, women often knew one another, went through similar rituals prior to marriage, and, prior to 1949, sometimes belonged to the same extrastate societies, such as the Yiguandao.[113] The trust that developed between people facilitated gender-based community action. Below, in the suicide case of Zhou Azhen, women circumvented state institutions to organize a protest against the state's miscarriage of justice by combining traditional symbols with their newfound political vocabulary.

Zhou was a twenty-one-year-old woman from Taizhou County, Jiangsu Province. Her parents died when she was seven. When she turned nine, she left Taizhou to move into the home of her future husband, Zhu Longbao. Zhu lived with his parents and siblings, working the land part-time and managing a fried dough-stick stand. According to the Women's Federation investigation report, Zhou's mother-in-law was extremely cruel to her, rarely letting her out of the house. Zhu and Zhou were married in 1949. Their marriage was fine at first, but before long Zhu began having affairs and the relationship deteriorated. Zhu and his mother then accused Zhou of stealing rice and giving it away, and beat her harshly. Zhou eventually found an ally in her father-in-law, but her mother-in-law accused him of having sex with her. This accusation was powerful enough to sever their relationship.

One day, Zhou returned home from a shopping trip. Upon her return, her family accused her of stealing their money for her shopping. Her husband, a cadre, accused her of being a "counterrevolutionary" for taking money to purchase a ring. Zhu then tried to organize a peasant association meeting where he would force her to confess and then divorce her. On August 11, 1953, mediators were sent to settle the conflict. None of these mediators were state officials, but rather people who had face in the community—a bean-thread store owner, two grandmothers, and the wife of a fruit seller. The mediators encouraged her to give the ring to her husband. Zhou agreed, but her husband threatened suicide: "I don't want it. In two days I'll teach her a lesson by changing the color of my face" (from red to blue, evidently). Not long after this, Zhou, rather than her husband, committed suicide.

Zhou's mother-in-law, upon discovering the corpse, tried to hide the body. Fearing she would be held responsible for the death, she claimed Zhou died of an illness. Other members of the community, however, suspected foul play, particularly a female leader of a small group, Chen Xiuying. Everyone in the village, after all, knew about the frequent arguments between Zhou and her husband and mother-in-law. When they got hold of the corpse, they inspected the body and discovered scars left from the rope around her neck.

Acting on their own initiative, the women reported the case to the local public security bureau and government. Zhu and his mother were arrested, but were released after brief questioning. Local women were furious. They said, "You say women have *fanshen*'ed and been liberated! If that's the case, how can we keep quiet about her death?" In response, the women organized three women's meetings, where they complained about the way in which the case was handled. They accused the government of covering up Zhu Longbao's actions. But this was not all. Soon the women began their own protest, whose form was very much in the tradition of Chinese political theater, complete with costumes, scripts, and symbols designed for maxi-

mum impact on the intended audience—in this case, potentially sympathetic officials and other women.[114] They ordered a funeral casket and invited a monk to read scriptures, then demanded that Zhu Longbao drape
himself with mourning apparel on his way to the grave site. In the meantime, they organized over one hundred other women, giving each one white
flowers to wear as they carried the coffin. As the women paraded down the
street they chanted slogans using *their* new political vocabulary: "All women
unite, down with feudalism!"; "Destroy feudalism!"; "Long live Chairman
Mao!" Confronted with this pressure, government officials relented: Zhu
and his mother were rearrested and an investigation ordered. In its assessment of the situation, the Women's Federation commented that "the form
of the parade was a deviation, but in cases where women are struggling for
independence, such deviations are unavoidable."[115]

Collective action organized to protest injustice was not the only occasion
when women found common ground. In other cases, young women in the
suburbs collectively petitioned for divorce, sometimes even threatening
collective suicide in the process. In a meeting of county, district, and township officials in a suburb of Fuzhou, Fujian Province, for example, a district
chief reported: "Ten women came for a divorce [evidently without their hus-
bands], and all ten were granted divorces. We were afraid that if one died
we would be held responsible."[116] Elsewhere, one township cadre said, "One
day four women came to the office and said, 'We want a divorce. All of us or
none of us.' What could I do? I granted them all a divorce."[117]

In many ways, these collective petitions were the polar opposite reaction
to the Marriage Law on the part of older women, who organized pacts to
protect themselves against the state and pelted a divorcée. Yet, at the same
time, these two types of collective action stemmed from the same organizational basis: in the suburbs, people still lived in relatively tight-knit communities. These cases suggest not only that divorce may not always be the
sort of individualistic enterprise it is conceived of as in the West, but also
that community "strength," or what have been called "primordial ties," may
not always be inimical to state goals. In fact, a case can be made that the very
processes that are said to facilitate divorce in urban areas in the West actually hindered such change in China. Even in cases where some state officials
dragged their feet in enforcing the law (as was clearly the case above), scores
of documents from the early 1950s show no instances of urban women
(core elites or peripheral working class) going *together* to the (urban) district
government or court and demanding a divorce. Elite women would probably consider this form of protest as hopelessly backward (i.e., rural). Moreover, the primary attachment of elite urban women was to their *family*
rather than the community at large. In this sense they were more isolated,
and thus less empowered, than women living among many other women. As
we will see in the next chapter, which examines an area where communities

were said to have been even more cohesive than in the suburbs, community life shaped reactions to the Marriage Law in similar, yet also very distinct, ways. Cases presented here suggest the hypothesis that opportunities to build trust within communities would also facilitate the sort of social change envisioned by the new Marriage Law.

"Running to the District": The Thin and Scattered State

When women such as Shen Ayuan and groups of women petitioned for divorce, it was often not in their own communities but in relatively remote courts and district governments. According to the sociolegal literature, the greater the geographic distances from communities to courts, the more difficult it is to enforce central state law, making customary law more salient. If this is the case, however, why and how were state institutions such as the district government, reaching which might require a few hours' walk in the Jiangnan region, the centerpiece of divorce petitioners' legal strategy? Why weren't village mediators, who lived only minutes away, used as the primary "address" for seeking legal restitution?

According to the Marriage Law, divorce cases were supposed to be mediated prior to granting a divorce. Prior to 1949, as China historians, anthropologists, and legal scholars have pointed out, disputes between villagers were often mediated by those with the most face in the village; face, in turn, was positively associated with social status and wealth.[118] Mediators only recently recruited into the ranks of the Communist Party because of their activism in land reform and other political movements, in contrast, had a modicum of political status, but often lacked face and experience conducting mediation. When implementing the Marriage Law, the lack of face or experience was a source of irritation to courts and petitioners alike. County-level organizations frequently complained that local cadres were "afraid of hassle" (*pa mafan*), "see abuse but don't criticize for fear of giving offense to anyone or getting someone in trouble," "have no confidence," "see abuse and run away," and "encounter a concrete problem and can't get a single word out of their mouths."[119] As one mediator recalled, "If we take the wife's position into consideration, the mother isn't happy, but if we consider the mother's, the wife is dissatisfied."[120] Anxious to rid themselves of quarreling couples, mediators often told disputants to go to the township or district government, the Women's Federation, or the court. As the director of the peasant association in Lunan Township, Kunshan County, confessed, "I hated the hassle (*xian mafan*), so I just wouldn't do it. I'd try to get the women cadres to mediate."[121]

When mediators nonetheless attempted to mediate divorce cases they were frequently unable to decide an issue to the satisfaction of all parties. When people petitioned for divorce, they often presented demands in unequivocal terms, such as "I want a divorce." Mediators were hard-pressed to find a satisfactory outcome to such a demand and thus incurred the wrath of disgruntled villagers. In Sanguan Village in Qingpu, for instance, a mediator who botched a reconciliation session was cursed by one of the disputants: "You people who have now become mediators. Damn you! May your generation be cut off with you! You're breaking up couples!"[122]

What stood in the way of successful mediation was frequently the knowledge generated by community life. In some cases, entire communities became involved in mediating divorce cases; in these villages, after all, everyone knew who argued and fought. When legal work teams set up mobile court units in townships (to make it easier to file suits), women from nearby villages headed over to hear and argue about other people's marriage problems, and were encouraged by local officials to serve as jurors in divorce cases.[123] Such participation, however, quickly got out of hand when *too many* women stood around arguing and trying to mediate; in some cases there were as many as fifty women milling around the township "introducing" and debating other people's cases. Suburban women would sometimes spend an entire day at the township before returning to the villages in the evening.[124] A Qingpu report noted that the women "think its perfectly reasonable (*heli*) for many officials to mediate their case in front of them while they are arguing about their problems."[125]

When going to court and other state institutions, suburban petitioners (most of whom were women) benefited from relatively long distances and their continued attachment to their natal homes, which were often some distance away. Whereas in cities density made it difficult for people seeking divorce to find refuge from abusive families, in the suburbs the more open spaces and proximity to the city were a resource used both to escape unsatisfactory relationships and to pursue new ones. In Xinjing District near Shanghai, a model worker surnamed Yang had a daughter-in-law who "objected" to his family. She then left his home. Sometime later, she ended up at her mother's home. Helpless to do anything by himself because his daughter-in-law was too far away, Yang then tried to enlist the government to help him convince her to return home.[126] In another case, in Kongcang Township, Kunshan County, the chairman of the peasant association reported that an adopted daughter-in-law broke off her engagement and married someone else. That relationship did not work out, and she wanted to divorce. Village officials and the chairman beat her up, but in the end she ran off to Shanghai. She returned a year later, in June 1951, and divorced at the district government. The same report also noted that women frequently "go to the district and look for the district chief," thinking him to be the only one who would solve their problem. If he could not be found, they would return. "Because they have a marriage problem," the report noted, "women run off (*pao*) to the district and township governments. At a minimum, they have to go twice, and at most, ten times; only then will their problem be solved."[127] In another Qingpu case illustrating the role of the district, a woman in Xinan Township "ran off to the township because she wanted a divorce." The township chief and Woman's Federation officer told her, "You were married with a red lantern and riding a bridal sedan. How can you so casually get a divorce? If you divorce, others will follow. If you want to divorce you have to give a reason, not just say, 'I want a divorce.'" The woman didn't say anything, and went away crying all the way to the district government.[128]

As this report indicates, suburban women might be shunted from one state institution to another before being granted a divorce. In this respect, there appears to be little difference between the behavior of officials in urban and suburban areas; many were clearly not enthusiastic about implementing the law (this, however, did *not* necessarily mean that change did not take place, as women found ways around recalcitrant officials). In other respects, however, the way in which state power was organized and *geographically structured* in suburban areas was different than in urban locales, particularly in relatively organized work units and large state-owned factories. In Shen Ayuan's case, if we recall, she went to an urban court, an urban district, and a suburban court and district. Each of these institutions had the power to grant her a divorce. For Shen, state power (to grant divorce) was *concentrated* in each of these institutions while at the same time *geographically scattered* among many of them. Suburban disputants might go to, and obtain decisions from, township governments (*xiang*), rural district governments (*qu*), county governments and court (*xian zhengfu, xian fayuan*), or even *urban* district governments. During the Marriage Law campaign itself they also could have pressed claims in local circuit courts. Having many authoritative institutions to go to increased the probability of finding one willing to accede to one's demands should a previous attempt fail. Yet, at the same time, this very feature made it very difficult for officials responsible for handling a case in different areas to coordinate action and make a well-thought-out decision. In cities, however, power and the state's "political geography" worked to frustrate petitioners. As noted in the previous chapter, state institutions were "thick" in the sense that local officials could force petitioners to go through many hoops just to get to court. At the same time, and probably most frustrating of all, only two institutions—courts and district governments—could grant divorces. Unlike suburban locales, where officials had a clear mandate and administrative jurisdiction to decide cases, in cities officials could get away with pushing them to a different level or institution just by claiming that they were not "responsible." In the end, this made the divorce process more complicated than in suburban areas.

At district governments and courts, state officials found themselves confounded by women's frankness about family and marriage problems, or what I called in the last chapter an open sexual culture. In contrast to elite urban women, who were often silent about marriage problems due to concerns with face, privacy, property, or fear of the state, suburban women, according to court officials, were *too* frank and open when dealing with family problems. Officials at the court and district levels complained that residents seeking divorce would constantly "quarrel with each other and with cadres and women's representatives, sometimes from morning until the offices closed at 5 P.M." Not bound to a factory schedule like urban workers, or to a tight political schedule like cadres, these women had the time to wait around until their cases were heard. In exasperation, court officials called upon local cadres to encourage divorce petitioners to have "civilized divorces" (*wenming lihun*): "They shouldn't get into such heated arguments at government offices."[129]

Not all cases ended in divorce, however. Many reports complained that suburban couples did not treat marriage and divorce with the seriousness appropriate to these supposedly "milestone," once- (or never-) in-a-lifetime events. Such criticism, I believe, reflected different meanings attached to marriage and divorce. For writers of these reports, who were educated, marriage was to be entered into after much consideration and deliberation. Hence, it is not surprising that they emphasized the "rashness" of suburban divorce suits. According to some reports, suburban couples would argue, run off to the township to demand a divorce, but then reconcile several minutes later, laugh, joke around, and return home.[130] Likewise, a work team report from Zhennan found that "there are not a few instances of people lightly/rashly petitioning for divorce" (*qingyi tichu lihun*).[131] Shen Ayuan's marriages and divorces were somewhat similar to this, at least in the informality of remarriage after divorce. We need not take this "lightly" appellation at face value, but I do think we need to be open to the possibility that for more rural residents, marriage and divorce meant something very different than for elite urbanites.

As it turned out, however, instructions to encourage "civilized divorces" and to give divorce more "consideration" were difficult to implement. Long distances between villages and districts, in addition to suburban residents' frankness about family problems, hindered proper investigation of cases. Petitioners who arrived at the district government or court after a train ride or long walk were tired and impatient, and wanted to have their case heard as quickly as possible. In Beijing's mining districts, for instance, a Bureau of Civil Affairs report criticized their cadres for "rashly" handling marriage and divorce registration. Apparently, cadres felt rushed because couples who arrived at the bureau after their train ride were "very irritable" and pressured the cadres into handling their cases quickly. As a result, the report complained, "cadres could not conduct a thorough investigation, and chaos resulted."[132] In Shanghai's suburban Xinjing District, cadres from the court, the Women's Federation, and the Bureau of Civil Affairs criticized their own "crude and careless" (*cuzhi daye*) methods for handling problems, and the fact that they were "substituting feeling for policy."[133] In Zhenru District near Shanghai similar complaints were directed at the court: "A couple quarrels, and then [she] goes to court to make an accusation. Cadres rigidly handle the case by forcing them to separate."[134] The situation became even more difficult to manage when women—like Shen Ayuan on several occasions—would arrive *without* their husbands. Instead of demanding that they return all the way to the village (which might be far away), officials would simply grant them divorces on the spot.[135]

Cadres in townships, districts, and courts who wanted to quickly dispose of cases found that settlements were fairly easy to achieve because suburban petitioners, after land reform, had a relatively easily divisible resource in land. In addition, because the Chinese revolution brought in cadres either from the outside (usually North China) or from villages different from those of petitioners, many officials suffered few consequences for how those cases were settled; they could distribute land with little thought as to how their decisions would affect individual plaintiffs' lives.[136] The four divorce cases in Chuijing Village in Qingpu, for example, were said to have been "straightforwardly and quickly resolved." In another village in the same township, one woman wanted to divorce her husband because he suffered from schistosomiasis. During township mediation she offered him four *mu* of land in return for his agreement to a divorce. He was satisfied with this settlement, and did not ask for anything else. Within ten minutes, the case was resolved and the two returned home.[137] County court mediation cases confirm the important role land played in facilitating divorce settlements acceptable by both parties.[138]

XICHENG, YANXIANG ("LOVE THE CITY, HATE THE VILLAGE"): MARRIAGE AND DIVORCE IN THE SUBURBS[139]

According to the new state ideology, marriages should be based on "love" (*lian'ai*) and consideration of political attributes, not on the quest for social status or material possessions. Couples married on the former basis, it was thought, would rarely argue, and would be faithful to one another and concerned about the welfare of children and the elderly. To the disappointment of party and state investigators of marriage relations in the Shanghai suburbs, few relationships met this ideal. In Yangsi District near Shanghai, urban-based work teams blamed the district's "complicated and chaotic marriage relationships" on "proximity to the capitalist city." Marriage Law work teams found men living with several women, several women in common-law relationships with one man, and cases of rape, incest, adultery, and "commercial" marriages.[140] Usually, investigators found, marriages were arranged by matchmakers or the parents, sometimes just after children were born. Formal marriages might occur as early as when the couple reached the age of fourteen, and by twenty-four most were married. To get married in the suburbs, men often had to go heavily into debt, sometimes selling off their land.[141] If parents could not afford it, their son would remain a bachelor, and there were not a few cases of this. In Zhennan Township between 1949 and 1953, according to reports, none of the village youths managed to marry.

Distrust of other villages and proximity to the city contributed to these difficulties. In Zhennan, it was customary for the prospective couple to come from the same village, limiting the possibilities for marriage.[142] Exacerbating this situation was the relatively high level of economic development in the area. Industry in the region attracted peasants from the poorer areas of the country who were seeking either refuge or economic opportunities. In the Beijing mining district, for instance, women came from distant provinces via personal introductions to work part-time in the mines and to marry workers who had difficulty in finding local wives. Miners were often required to pay for the woman's travel and food expenses, as well as for the introducer. When CCP officials interviewed the miners as to why they had to spend money and take out loans in order to get married, some explained, "We're coal-black boys (*mei heizi*), so it's difficult to find a wife." According to party reports, this situation resulted in many unhappy marriages, frequent affairs, and arguments.[143]

For suburban residents, whether native to the area or from other provinces, proximity to the big city left an indelible impression on how status and more money could improve one's lot in life. Thus, even though women who came to suburban areas from poorer areas were attracted by the area's relative wealth, the big city showed them that even more was possible. For those born in suburban villages and towns, the city likewise offered marketing opportunities, entertainment, and the possibility of finding a spouse with a better income than a peasant would provide.

Evidence shows that mobility between rural and urban areas, and the ambition it fostered, placed suburban men in an extremely precarious position in the marriage market. In the Beijing mining district, a Marriage Law work team found many "careless" and "rash" marriages and divorces among miners, and attributed the problem to the fact that miners were hastily married and that women "take advantage of marriage in order to obtain material goods." Most all miners, the report found,

> have to give the women many things before the women will even agree to talk to them. Miners who don't have much money go out to buy gifts locally even if they can't afford it, often on credit. But even in those cases women insist on going to Beijing to buy everything. Workers then have no choice but to bor-

row more money and go to Beijing. [In one case, a worker] promised to buy everything only after the marriage. After the marriage, however, his salary was lowered and he couldn't afford to buy the things he promised. His wife then petitioned for divorce. As for migrant women, after they arrive they want to go strolling and window-shopping in Beijing with their prospective husbands. There they spend a lot of money. Workers then marry them because they've spent so much money already. As a result of these rash marriages, many couples end up fighting and arguing all the time. There are few democratic and harmonious families among them.[144]

Another report—on Mentougou, an area to the west of Beijing—noted:

Because workers are anxious to solve their individual marriage problems, some meet a woman once, play cards, and they ask [her] to marry them. The government doesn't question the basis for the marriage (*hunyin jichu*) and grants it. Soon after the marriage, the woman takes off, leaving him with nothing.[145]

Men in the suburbs, as these reports make clear, lived under the shadow of divorce. Women were not unaware of this, and used their position to extort more material possessions. A Women's Federation report from suburban Tong County found that some women "got married only to trick the man into giving her material things. Then, as an excuse, they say that their 'relationship isn't good' and threaten to divorce. The only way the men can prevent the divorce is to accede to [their wives'] demands." These women, the report noted, "want to find a spouse who lives in the city."[146] On occasion, men could prevent this only by selling off all their family's land and possessions.[147]

Women's choice of gifts they demanded from prospective husbands reflected their desire to assume city ways. In contrast to bankers in Shanghai, who grew increasingly frustrated with routines governed by clocks and watches, and who became enamored with a rural life free from time measurements,[148] suburban women considered clocks and watches symbols of the urban modernity they lacked. Thus, even though suburbanites had little functional use for clocks and watches (except for holding cadres to their political schedule by shouting "Time's up!"), they often demanded them from their prospective husbands, in addition to other modern accouterments such as leather shoes, large and small overcoats, and gold jewelry.[149] For many women, I would tentatively suggest at this early stage of the study, having a husband who could give them a modern and urban watch was far more important than having a husband who could give them good political status.

Cities were envisioned not only as "modern," but also as places where women could enjoy a better life than in the countryside. Unlike urbanites in China and elsewhere who, out of ignorance and naïveté, sometimes imagined rural life as idyllic, women who lived in the suburbs and more remote countryside knew firsthand how difficult, and often boring, rural life could be. Cities were viewed as places where free time could be spent enjoying the exciting things cities had to offer, and where they could settle down at home and *not* work. A common complaint of county-level Women's Federations was that women in the suburbs did not want to marry peasants, only workers who lived in cities. According to these reports, peasant women detested rural poverty, "were afraid of hardship," and wanted only to "have fun." In Tong County, women wanted to marry workers in electric power plants or transport workers because with them, "after they marry they could go to the city." One Communist Youth League member—from whom we might have expected slightly more attention to the criteria for political virtue, said, "Once I've put down the straw basket, I never want to pick it up again."[150] In Shanghai, party officials also complained that women in the suburbs were interested only in money and status, and because of this were refusing to marry peasant men. One woman explained: " I want someone stronger than me, who has family money and who can make a lot of money. This way I won't have to work and can enjoy myself more."[151]

With only so many urban men of means to go around, however, it was inevitable that many women would still end up with peasants. These marriages, however, were seen as a last resort, a situation that might be "repaired" should the marriage bring the woman too much aggravation or if a better opportunity arose. In the Beijing suburbs, for instance, women sometimes refused to work after marriage, and threatened divorce if their husbands were too insistent. The young women interviewed by Women's Federation officials in the suburbs seemed to take divorce rather in stride, not as something that would shatter their or their family's reputation. According to one report, young women held the view that "if the relationship isn't good, they'll just separate" (*fufu bu hao, jiu san*).[152] Poor peasant men were quite aware of their predicament. In Tong county, some men, in what appears to be a phallic reference, complained, "If you want to marry, you have to be a worker. If you're a peasant, you'll be holding your own leg in bed your whole life."[153]

Although most divorce cases were initiated by women, suburban men were also interested in upward mobility through marriage. During the early 1950s, such mobility did not, however, come from marrying someone with good *political* status but from the more traditional measures of face and social class, such as wealth and beauty. One Communist Youth League member in Tong County said, "I'm looking for someone from a better family than my own, someone who can afford a dowry and is beautiful."[154] "Men," according to one report from Tangyan *xiang* near Shanghai, "want a beautiful wife, but if after the arrangements are made they see that their wife is not beautiful, they abuse them."[155] Because beautiful women were a relatively scarce "commodity," those who were particularly attractive had their choice of men. Male peasants whose position in the marriage market was weaker knew this and were indignant. "It's easy for beautiful women to find a husband," one griped, "but men who are blind or bald always have problems."[156]

These motivations for divorce, however, do not explain why divorces would be granted by the state. Thus far I have attributed court and district officials' willingness to grant divorce to political factors, such as the terror of land reform, weak investigative power, clear political jurisdictions, and impatience with angry and loud plaintiffs. There were, in addition, more sociological factors at work. Having come to suburban districts from other provinces, district-level cadres and court officials were often in the *same predicament* as suburbanites seeking divorce. Having participated in military struggle for many years and far away from home, many were in the process of divorce themselves. According to marriage registration forms in Qingpu County, for instance, many new marriages in the early 1950s were those of cadres from Shandong or Jiangsu to local women.[157] Few of these cases indicated a prior marriage, but, given the young age at which peasant males were married in Shandong, it is likely that either they misreported their former marital status or their superiors did not care. Township cadres also frequently divorced. In a meeting of such cadres in Xugan District in Qingpu, 87 out of 193 participants had already divorced by "going to the district."[158] Like the newly arrived rural cadres in Beijing discussed in chapter 2, cadres in the suburbs were tempted not only by local suburban women, but also by the nearby *urban* women they considered more cultured and beautiful than their peasant wives. Some local cadres resented these developments. Some argued that veteran cadres should not divorce because their peasant wives had "sacrificed their lives and youth" waiting for them to return home. Others explained that the rural northern cadres just could not help themselves, since they were "giddy and dazed" (*xuan guang tian*) after seeing Shanghai women "who have culture and are beautiful."[159]

Despite such objections, these cadres sought divorces in large numbers, attracted by the same images of the bright lights of the big city that made not a few suburban women ditch or divorce their peasant husbands. Having divorced themselves, district cadres in the suburbs often did not hesitate to grant divorces to plaintiffs, such as Shen Ayuan, who made it as far as the district government.

CONCLUSION

This chapter has argued that the impact of land reform on divorce and marriage in the countryside was manifold and profound. Land reform shaped cadres' and ordinary peasants' political experience with the state in crucial ways—most importantly, by the political and social transposition of that experience to marriage reform. After witnessing the power of the party, many officials—but particularly those higher up in the administrative hierarchy, who had less of a stake in village life—opted to grant divorce and overcompensate women in property settlements rather than risk punishment for violating a policy many did not understand in the first place. At the same time that land reform bolstered the legitimacy of the Communist Party center, it also contributed to the *delegitimization* of village cadres, who sometimes used land reform for personal vengeance. These officials, because they were already known to villagers before the revolution as just ordinary peasants, did not enjoy the same degree of legitimacy as their higher-level counterparts, many of whom came from the outside (especially Shandong and northern Jiangsu) to "make revolution" in suburban communities. This multilayered structure of legitimacy (low in villages, higher the further one goes up the administrative hierarchy) encouraged women seeking divorce to avoid village- and township-level political institutions and concentrate their efforts on those further up the hierarchy, where their petitions were often looked upon more favorably. Conceptually, this chapter raises the possibility that legitimacy is better seen in nonaggregated, institutional terms. Even in the 1950s it was not the case that "the" state—conceived as a unitary entity—had legitimacy; "the center" or Mao often did, as did courts and county governments, but legitimacy did not smoothly flow all the way down to officials who did the state's grunt work in villages. In addition to shaping a multilayered structure of legitimacy, the land reform process also contributed to women's empowerment. This chapter has shown that through its mass mobilization and "speak bitterness" sessions, land reform helped give many young women both the courage and the language to place and justify their private claims in the public/state arena. Land reform was also crucial in terms of the material resources it gave suburban residents. The land that suburbanites received during land reform was used to negotiate divorce settlements, much as it was among some working-class urbanites. Moreover, and ultimately ironically, land reform discourse of "distribution," "allocation," and "equalization" (*ping*) shaped suburbanites' understanding of the Marriage Law, resulting in unanticipated marriage criteria.

In addition to terrorizing state officials, land reform also induced fear among the older men and women in the suburbs. After witnessing the execution of landlords and other class enemies—many of whom were their age cohorts—elderly women in the suburbs feared the results of their intervening in marriage and divorce freedom. The evidence presented in this chapter challenges Kay Johnson's thesis that rural divorces were stopped through the resistance of older rural women and recalcitrant, "traditionalist" local officials. Although they may have shared common interests (such as preventing young women from leaving the village), this did not necessarily translate into action. Moreover, as we have seen, many women who encountered resistance at the village level (and here I agree with Johnson that the main obstacle to divorce was at this level) did *not* raise the white flag in surrender, but instead moved on to higher-level state institutions. The village was often the first, but usually not the last, station on the road to divorce.

In addition to examining the impact of land reform, this chapter also suggested that space and time might be seen as "resources" in securing divorce. In chapter 2, I argued that the modern infrastructure that enabled easy access to courts in urban areas also allowed the state the time to conduct thorough, and time-consuming, investigations. In the meantime, the lack of available housing, particularly in the urban core, made it difficult for women to escape abusive or unhappy relationships. For urbanites, space and time were important obstacles to divorce. In this chapter, I suggested that the more open suburban spaces and scattered but authoritative state institutions allowed women such as Shen Ayuan to sue for divorce with relative ease. If urban areas were "thick" political spaces, the spatial organization of political institutions in the suburbs might be described as far "thinner," allowing suburbanites, who were also less bound to urban, "modern" time discipline, to move rather freely from state institution to state institution. Long distances led to pressure to adjudicate quickly.

In the last chapter, I also suggested that a possible explanation of working-class divorces in Shanghai and Beijing was a particularly feisty legal culture, in combination with a willingness to be open about family and marriage problems and ambition to become more "urban." I posited several possible sources for such behavior: litigiousness might have resulted from incompetent local institutions, urban working-class culture, or the rural background of many working-class urbanites; becoming "urban" was of course the result of the quest for a better life in the city. The evidence in this chapter cannot conclusively trace the origins of all these behaviors. Shen Ayuan, after all, had access to urban institutions and had experienced city life, in addition to having the resources of living in a semi-industrialized rural area. Did she behave as she did because she was relatively "urban," or because she was still "rural"? The next chapter, which examines a remote rural locale where peasants had little access to "modernity" and were embedded in communities more typical of a "traditional" setting (unlike a place such as Worker-Peasant Village), answers the question posed in the second chapter more decisively.

CHAPTER FOUR

Family Reform in the Southwest Frontier, 1950–1953

WHY THE SOUTHWEST?

To assess more conclusively the hypotheses introduced in chapter 1, it is crucial that we examine the implementation of the Marriage Law in China's frontier. Here we have an area where few of the variables suggested in the secondary literature as conducive to state-led social change were present (in the early 1950s): the overwhelming majority of peasants living in frontier areas did *not* work in industry, lived in relatively isolated communities in mountainous areas, and had to travel days to get to court. Moreover, throughout Chinese history the southwestern provinces' geographical remoteness from the center of state power in Nanjing or Beijing led to an independent streak that made central administrative and legal directives difficult to enforce and easy to ignore.[1] On the surface, Yunnan's topography, level of economic development, and political history would all seem to pose obstacles to the implementation of state-led social change in the Communist period. But, if findings in the previous chapters about state administrative incapacity or "bumbling" and about the empowering role of community, land, time, and space as "resources" people could use to sue for divorce are plausible explanations, then Yunnan is an area where these factors might be said to have existed to an even greater degree than in the suburban areas of Shanghai and Beijing. Looking at the Southwest from my perspective, Yunnan becomes a *prime* candidate for change, rather than a least likely case as initially hypothesized. Only in one dimension does Yunnan seem least likely: land, which was important to both peripheral urbanites and suburbanites in their negotiations with their families and the state, was a rare commodity in the mountainous regions of the Southwest; in Chuxiong, for instance, mountains cover 90 percent of the prefecture's territory.[2] If awarding land to peasants in the Yangzi Delta facilitated divorce, in many areas of Yunnan this resource was largely unavailable.

The Yunnan case does more than just compare "pure" peasants with their suburban, urban working-class, and elite counterparts responding to liberalized divorce law. In addition to testing variables such as industrialization, state presence, urbanization, education, and technological infrastructure, examining the southwestern frontier adds important ethnic and cultural variation. In Yunnan we can observe not only how "peasants" as a socioeconomic *class* responded to the law, but also how peasants who in terms of ethnicity, culture, and history differed from the Han majority (who implemented the law) dealt with it. In this culture and history, we will see, there were few reasons to anticipate the law receiving a hearty welcome. The Communists, much like their missionary predecessors in the area and elsewhere, enforced the law (and other social changes, such as land reform) as part of a "civilizing project" designed to allow minorities in the area to attain the high level of Han culture developed elsewhere in the country.[3] Throughout southwestern history, many leaders of minority groups such as the Miao, Yi, and Muslim (Hui) deployed violence and other forms of resistance to deflect these efforts.[4] The sources and long history of these conflicts led me to the original hypothesis that the law would encounter a great deal of resistance, particularly on the part of community leaders whose power and status could be threatened by the imposition of central state law. Given that ordinary peasants are often dependent on such leaders, it seemed to me that they, too, would eschew confrontation with local authorities. Moreover, given the fact that those representatives of central state authority were Han Chinese, I did not expect women or men seeking divorce to go to a Han-dominated court instead of their "own," more familiar and perhaps trusted, local leader. From many social science perspectives, this would not make too much sense.

That said, this chapter will demonstrate that in Yunnan both Han women and women from various ethnic minorities very frequently petitioned state institutions to resolve their family disputes; the number of divorce suits reaching Yunnan courts and governments was not any lower than in the suburbs. To explain how this happened, I suggest that we need to examine Yunnan's political, economic, and cultural features in light of the factors identified in the previous chapters as (at least in the Chinese case) conducive to pursuing new rights in government institutions.

A WALK ON CHINA'S WILD SIDE

Moving westward to Yunnan from the Han-dominated North China plain and the Yangzi Delta, plains, industries, and midsize cities gradually give way to hills, small villages, raging rivers, and, eventually, high mountains dotted

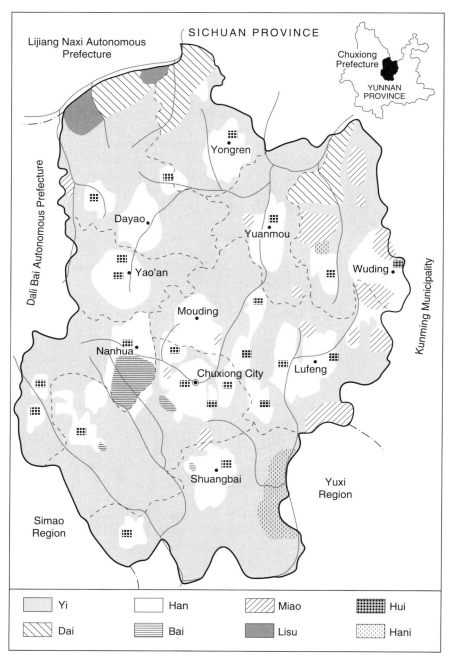

Map 4. Distribution of Minority Groups in Chuxiong. Adapted from *Chuxiong yizu zizhi zhou zhi,* vol. 1 (Beijing: Renmin Chubanshe, 1993). Dots indicate county seats.

with over four hundred different ethnic minority groups (see map 4). Yun-nan's location and social composition shaped a political and social history quite different from that of the cities and suburban areas discussed thus far. If cities were loci of political control, in Yunnan political control was highly decentralized; local strongmen wielded more power than remote central state authorities. When cities and their suburbs experienced eco-nomic growth, much of the Southwest, girded as it was by mountains and unnavigable rivers, remained locked in a preindustrial economy. In Yunnan social tension also exhibited a strong ethnic character. Although ethnicity was a source of conflict elsewhere in China, in Yunnan and the Southwest the range of potential ethnic-based conflicts increased exponentially due to the sheer size and variety of groups living in an area endowed with few resources.

Politics

If the implementation of state policy is at least partially dependent on the administrative capabilities and legitimacy of its central agents—a proposi-tion few political scientists would disagree with—there were few reasons to anticipate successful implementation of the 1950 Marriage Law in areas where the central state had never successfully established legitimate politi-cal control. Unlike political patterns in Beijing, which were strongly shaped by its historical position as the national capital, and Shanghai, whose politics reflected Western influence and industry, in Yunnan and other provinces of the Southwest (Guizhou and Sichuan) political traditions were structured by geographical distance from the center of political power, topographical terrain, and proximity to Burma, Tibet, Laos, and Vietnam. Separatism, ethnic conflict, and militarization led by local strongmen were endemic to the area. This is an area that seems to fit Joel Migdal's description of those places where resistance to state policies is most likely, particularly among "unassimilating minorities or vulnerable peasants . . . clinging for security to tried and true folkways."[5] Implementing a new family law in such an area immediately after the conclusion of a civil war is also reminiscent of the at-tempt by the U.S. government to enforce the Morrill Act of 1862 in frontier Utah territory. Much like the Chinese Marriage Law that made bigamy a crime and promoted the ideal of the monogamous, nuclear family, so too did the Morrill Act; the monogamous family, it was argued at the time, was a "cornerstone of American civilization." In the American case, however, federal authorities targeted a very specific religious group, the polygamous Mormons living in tight-knit communities in the territory that later became the state of Utah. According to Stephen Cresswell's account, even during this period of expansion of central state authority (much like post-1949 China), federal marshals dispatched to Utah territory found it extremely difficult to enforce the law because they were in "an alien land," far from their friends and families and "wholly ostracized from the close-knit Mormon majority." Twenty years later, in 1882, there were only two convictions.[6]

Throughout Chinese history, southwestern provinces' geographical remoteness from the center of power in Beijing or Nanjing led to an independent streak that made central administrative and legal directives difficult to enforce. From the Han dynasty to the Qing, many areas of Yunnan, Sichuan, and Guizhou were administered either by enfeoffing local tribal chieftains as either civilian administrators (*tu guan*) or military chieftains (*tu si*), or through military colonization; one scholar has estimated that roughly one-third of Yunnan province, over three-quarters of Sichuan, and at least one-half of Guizhou were "under native chieftainship control" in the sixteenth and seventeenth centuries.[7] Both of these systems of administration proved difficult to enforce over the long term: *tu si*, whose rule was hereditary rather than meritocratic as in the Chinese civil service, were concentrated in mountainous regions and often took advantage of their geographical remoteness and autonomy from the central state to build quasi-independent fiefdoms that often served as a rallying point against the state;[8] military colonization, for its part, contributed to tension between central state authorities and local leaders by forcing out native groups to mountainous regions, leaving to Han garrison leaders and troops the more fertile valley basins. During the Qing, tension between Han military administrators and *tu si* resulted in armed conflict.[9]

During the late Qing, social and political cleavages barely disguised and pasted over by the *tu si* system quickly unraveled. The Southwest, like other areas of China in this period of dynastic decline, was racked with local rebellions, leaving many areas virtually ungovernable.[10] As in many areas of China during the late Imperial period, local elites relied primarily on military forces to maintain a modicum of control over an increasingly restive, armed population.[11] In the Republican period, bandits, often led by ethnic minorities, proliferated, finding refuge and bases in the mountains from which they would plunder both Han and other ethnic communities.[12]

By the end of the Second World War and the outbreak of the Chinese Civil War (1945–1949), political control in much of the Southwest had almost completely devolved into the hands of local Han and ethnic minority elites. Although Chiang Kai-shek managed to establish some authority in the urban basins of Chongqing and Kunming after he retreated to Sichuan during the war, he was still forced to compete with secret societies such as the Gelaohui (Elder Brother's Society) and local warlords.[13] As the Communists advanced toward the Tibetan border and occupied southwestern cities, many GMD forces capitulated. Those who did not retreated to villages and hills, from where they harassed PLA troops and engaged in banditlike activities toward the local populace.[14]

Chiang's retreat into the Southwest during the war also had implications for the Communists. Rural areas in Yunnan, Sichuan, and Guizhou were the very last bastions of resistance to the Communists. In contrast to North and Central China, where the Communists had established wartime base areas during the 1930s and 1940s, in the Southwest the CCP was slow to establish party organizations or any significant military or administrative presence. Virtually all CCP officials were outsiders, hailing predominantly from the older revolutionary base areas in Northwest China.[15] As a result, local units of the CCP and PLA enjoyed limited legitimacy. A firsthand account of the PLA's entrance to Chengdu in Sichuan captures the general mood:

> Few farmers . . . did any cheering; fewer still had even a vague idea who the Communists were or what they were fighting for. Up to that time, knowledge of the Communists had derived largely from tales and rumors about the Red sweep through the rim of the Chengtu Plain during the Long March in 1935. These tales had been universally unfavorable.[16]

Confronted by hostile groups ranging from former GMD officers and troops, some of whom linked up with landlord militia in rural areas, to secret-society and bandit leaders (who might double as community leaders among the ethnic groups), the Communists had little reason to anticipate a warm welcome. Moreover, the CCP in the Southwest established its headquarters in cities such as Chengdu in Sichuan and Kunming in Yunnan, and from there began conquering the countryside—a reversal of the way power had been established in other parts of the country. As a result, their political and military infrastructure in rural areas was especially weak.[17]

Economy, Infrastructure, and Community

To the extent that divorce patterns are shaped by the level of economic development, there was little reason to expect much change in Yunnan after the promulgation of the Marriage Law. The Southwest's political and social geography worked against full integration into the Chinese economy. High mountain ranges, unnavigable rivers, and abundant forests that have drawn admiration from many urban Chinese also hindered the Southwest's economic development and, prior to 1949, gave rise to an extremely inequitable distribution of land and wealth.

Economic development in the Southwest was extremely uneven, reflecting the large disparities between plateau and mountain settlements. In the late Qing and early Republican periods, small-scale tobacco, mining, and cotton industries were established in the Han-dominated fertile basins, and even in some mountainous areas where transportation made marketing convenient; but for the most part mountainous areas remained mired in a preindustrial economy.[18] The mountainous topography of Yunnan, together with high population growth, created a large surplus of farm labor.

In one village studied by anthropologists, 90 percent of the villagers did not have enough land to allow them to make a living on it.[19]

The temporal discontinuity of agricultural labor exacerbated rural unemployment. Demands for labor expanded and contracted in accordance with the agricultural season: demand rose during the planting season, but as the crop matured, the need for labor decreased. Excess labor, inequitable land distribution, poverty, and free time encouraged the poor to engage in nonfarming activities such as handicrafts, duck raising, weaving, and the raising of pigs, mules, oxen, and sheep.[20] Products of these efforts were usually sold in local markets, very often by the women of the family or village.[21]

To escape poverty and the plundering of bandits and community feuds (both to be discussed below), peasants in the area also took to the road, looking for employment opportunities in other villages or cities. Migration frequently assumed one of two forms: individual peasants might leave the village looking for work, or entire families and communities might depart together. There were also cases of the village rich moving to cities to seek a better life.[22] Mobility, either individual or community-based, was thus very much a part of ordinary life in much of the Southwest.

Yunnan's agricultural economy and topography encouraged other sorts of nonfarming activities as well. In contrast to the fertile Yangzi Delta, in Yunnan and the Southwest, excluding the few basins and valleys, only 10 percent of the land was arable.[23] Poverty and scarcity of land gave many incentives to grow high-yielding cash crops, such as opium, which during the late nineteenth and early twentieth centuries was often a staple of southwestern regional and interregional trade.[24]

Rivalry over scarce and inequitably distributed resources shaped the nature of interaction with state authorities. Much as in poor areas of North China, conflicts over resources pitted one community against another, fostering a fairly rigid hierarchy of power among them and encouraging a militarized political culture that was inimical to the implementation of central state policies. Since many communities were based on ethnic ties, community conflict assumed ethnic forms. For instance, the Dai in Xishuangbanna were said to dominate the Hani; Hui were frequently in conflict with Han and the Bai, and among the Yi in Yao'an County in the northern part of Chuxiong Prefecture the "Black Yi" branch dominated both local Han and members of the "White Yi" branch.[25] Such conflicts also shaped interaction with Han political and legal institutions. Groups not able to muster military power to defend themselves often sought protection and redress in government courts, or at the county seat.[26] Local chieftains also relied on state courts when they were not able to come to terms with leaders of rival communities. One nineteenth-century commentator noted that "the lairds (*tu si*) . . . are constantly at law with one another in the Chinese courts . . . an opportunity for the magistrates to enrich themselves."[27]

In addition to conflicts over material resources such as land, water, and grazing rights, competition could surface over another scarce "resource": women. In northeastern Yunnan, leaders of the dominant Nisu took Miao and Han women as concubines, leaving few women available to the poor men of the subservient groups.[28] In northern Chuxiong, the Black Yi raided Han and other communities to steal women to serve as slaves and concubines,[29] and in southwestern Yunnan, members of elite Dai families would take in multiple wives from the lower-status Dai groups.[30] Marriage was frequently a political affair: community leaders forged alliances with leaders of other groups through the marriage of their offspring. Because marriage involved intricate arrangements between lineages, marriage disputes sometimes erupted into full-scale feuds. Among the Liangshan Yi, for example, there was a saying: "If something happens to a person, the whole clan (*jiazhi*) has to take responsibility."[31] Here, as in other poorer areas of China, state family laws (such as the GMD's 1931 civil code) had no impact whatsoever.

Culture: Marriage, Sex, and Family Customs in the Southwest

Relations between Han Chinese and ethnic minorities in the Southwest were characterized by domination, conflict, pacification, and co-optation. In many cultures, as Stevan Harrell points out, such relations are often expressed in sexual terms, and Han depictions of southwestern cultures were no exception.[32] In the Ming, Qing, and Communist eras, ethnic minorities were artistically portrayed as sensual, erotic, and promiscuous. According to Harrell, Norma Diamond, and Dru Gladney, defining ethnic minorities in this way was the state's way of asserting the cultural superiority of the more civilized Han, providing a justification for its "civilizing project."[33]

Depictions of minorities as "promiscuous" may reflect more than a state's effort to show a modern face to the outside world, however. To date, I have found no "smoking gun" demonstrating that state officials in Beijing, either in Imperial or in modern times, calculated just how to eroticize minorities in order to justify civilizing or modernizing them. Instead, I suggest that depictions of minority promiscuity are in part a reflection of the *class* prudishness about sexuality that I discussed in the chapter dealing with Chinese cities. Ethnic bias no doubt plays a role; however, it is equally significant that one finds very similar descriptions of "chaotic" sexuality in reports on Han peasants and workers as well. The common denominator seems to be the literacy (and thus class) of the authors and their condescending attitude toward peasants generally, instead of only ethnic bias toward minorities specifically. This does not suggest that there were no differences between Han and minority sexual practices—the Yi and the Dai and Bai are not ethnic Chinese—but that such differences are not nearly as stark as depicted in much of the Western and Chinese literature. No less an astute observer of rural life than Mao Zedong noticed considerable sexual freedom among poor Han peasants in Hunan (in his "Investigation into the Peasant Movement in Hunan") and Jiangxi (in his *Report from Xunwu*) Provinces, and also contrasted this sexuality to that of the more conservative upper classes.

According to most accounts of "minority culture" in the Southwest, minorities' "promiscuity" was reflected in their courting and marriage customs, many of which had a strong community orientation. In courting rituals among the Yi and Dai, for instance, youth often paired off during community public and religious festivals, where they were free from parental restraints. Among the Dai, youth met prospective partners during the Splash Water Festival (*po shui jie*) or New Year's festivals, or while bathing together in local streams. Among the Yi, village youth would gather together in the mountains for drinking sessions (*chi shan jiu*), for dancing, and for the Spring Festival and bonfire festivals (*huo ba jie*). In the mountains, they would sing songs, pick flowers, and, unseen by others in the forest, engage in sex. Unmarried women among both Yi and Dai, some noted, "are allowed the most absolute freedom, and have many lovers."[34]

Among the Yi in Yunnan, marriage customs varied in different areas. In some areas of Chuxiong, customs were similar to those of the Han. The marriage engagement would be facilitated by either a male or female matchmaker, usually a person with high social or political status in the community. This person would also be responsible for mediating marriage conflicts.[35] In other areas, however, Han culture was said to have had less influence. In Yongsheng County, for instance, Yi youth had frequent premarital sex; companionate marriages, as well as intermarriage between blood relatives, also occurred. Some women never formally "married," even as they had children and lived with a man.[36]

Community was also reflected in forms of collective action within certain marriage customs. A tradition common to many groups in the Southwest (Hani, Miao, Yi, Dai, Lisu) was to "steal a spouse," or *qiang hun*. Among the Liangshan Yi, bridegrooms would gather friends together to "raid" the home of their future wife, and then whisk her away on horseback.[37] Among Yi groups in the eastern and northern sections of Chuxiong Prefecture, when the bridegroom's family entered the village of his prospective spouse, the bride's female friends would together greet them by throwing water in their faces. Old men and women would sing drinking songs, while the bride, her mother, and other female relatives and friends sang marriage lamentations (*ku jia ge*). At this point the groom's party was required to "steal" his wife from among her female friends and hand her over to the groom's brothers, who would then carry her on their backs out the door, plop her down on a horse, and spirit her away.[38] Among the Bulang, roles were reversed: the bride and *her* friends might organize a raiding party and "plunder" the home of the groom, "whisking" him away on the back of a (plodding) mule to his future wife's home.[39]

Women's mobility was evident in marriage life as well. Among the Yi, women would rarely remain at their husbands' homes for an extended period, and as result, marriage during the first several years tended to be unstable. Four days after marriage the new groom returned from his bride's family's house, by himself, to his family home, while his bride continued to live with her own family. During festivals or the agricultural busy season she would spend some time with her husband to assist with the harvest, but after the work was over would return to her natal home. This intermittent cohabitation might last several years, usually until pregnancy. Only then would the wife move permanently into her husband's home.[40]

There were cases when it quickly became obvious that the new couple was incompatible. In this event, community leaders might mediate to prevent the break-up of the marriage. If these efforts were unsuccessful, separation procedures were very simple. Rather than going to a district magistrate, women and men from the Yi, Hani, Dai, and Bulang groups seeking separation would arrange to meet with the village head, who would handle issues of custody and property division.[41] Some communities had public "separation ceremonies." Separation among the Bulang, for instance, involved a ceremony in which the plaintiff was required to slaughter a pig, whose meat was distributed to children of every household in the village. The village children would then inform the villagers by yelling at the top of their lungs, "So-and-so are now separated!" In Yongren County in Chuxiong, a county with Yi, Han, and other minority groups, the process was also quite simple: the woman would return to her natal home. To formalize the separation, however, she would be required to compensate his wedding expenditures.[42]

Several features in southwestern marriage customs are crucial in explaining variation in the extent and form of resistance to the implementation of the Marriage Law, as well as the law's success in helping women leave relationships with which they were no longer satisfied. First, it seems that in the Southwest the division between "public" and "private" was highly blurred, probably more so than in Han-dominated suburban areas. Unlike educated couples in Shanghai, who sometimes sought to spare themselves the publicity of a court hearing by placing brief notices in newspapers, among many groups in Yunnan leaving a marriage was a *public* affair. While most of the scholarship on the Southwest deals with minorities and their customs, there is some evidence suggesting that the "open" sexual culture I discussed in the previous two chapters existed in Han communities as well. One 1930s study of southwestern village life, for example, found that Han peasant men and women who knew each other well displayed a fair amount of bawdiness and sexually oriented "horseplay."[43] As I pointed out earlier, I believe that the differences between Han and minorities in the extent of "openness" or frankness in marriage and family affairs are of degree, not kind. This issue, however, cannot be resolved in this chapter, however, since it deals only with the Southwest. Chapter 6, which presents more evidence about state-family relations in rural areas (minority and Han included) further strengthens my case.

Second, community—especially in the more mountainous areas—appears to have been more cohesive than in the suburbs, with its mixture of migrants from all corners of the Chinese map, as well as relatively advanced industrial development and infrastructure. Unlike North and South China, where, prior to 1949, village leaders often abandoned their communities to become absentee landlords in cities, in remote areas of Yunnan, like other peripheral and frontier areas, local elites were still mediating family disputes, protecting their communities, and leading raids and the like. Community was also reflected in nonelite practices. Rituals such as lamentation songs and raids on bridegrooms' homes brought women together; others, such as communal bathing, brought the two sexes together.[44]

Third, the community cohesion that fostered collective action led peasants on the periphery to be highly mobile, reinforcing preexisting tendencies to move when economic times were difficult, or to market handicrafts or produce in distant locales. To find a wife or husband, young people and their parents often looked outside of their own villages, perhaps because of the attention given to lineage hierarchy and status in marriage selection, or to the prohibition of intralineage branch marriages common in some groups.[45] Couples that gained experience with mobility and travel as they looked for spouses could call upon this experience to help them leave these relationships as well. As seen among the Yi, the path a woman took between her husband's home and her natal home was often well trodden.

PRELUDE TO THE MARRIAGE LAW:
THE STATE ON THE FRONTIERS, 1950–1951

Pacification and Intervention

According to Greenwich Mean Time, three hours separate Beijing from Yunnan and the rest of the Southwest China. But if time can also be measured politically, in 1949 the Southwest was separated from many areas of China by at least several years. Unlike North or Central China, where the

CCP had established an organizational presence during the Sino-Japanese War in the 1930s and 1940s, in the Southwest there were very few political foundations for the implementation of new social reform policies. These time differences notwithstanding, in 1949 the CCP followed in the footsteps of other revolutionary regimes by introducing a single time zone—based on "Beijing time"—and an almost unified political schedule.[46]

From one perspective, the introduction of a single time unit was emblematic of the new regime's quest for national unity, a quest that was also manifested in (at least officially) conciliatory policies toward intellectuals, the bourgeoisie, non-Han customs, and frontier elites.[47] From a different perspective, however, the introduction of a single time zone was also a symbol of the new regime's arrogance and impatience with the "political time" of different areas of the county. From 1949 on, the regime decided, all provinces, regardless of their history and different cultures, would march more or less in unison to the ticktock of Beijing's clock and political schedule. In the Southwest, this meant that officials who had only recently arrived in the area from the northwestern provinces were placed on roughly the same political schedule as cadres in the North and East. Political campaigns that were temporally separated elsewhere in the country were thus "telescoped" into a few short years in the Southwest; in many areas, these campaigns temporally overlapped.

This telescoping of a unified political schedule into an area several time zones away from Beijing turned out to be extremely problematic. In the Southwest, the CCP was forced to deal with a dearth of trained personnel, long-standing animosities among ethnic groups, widespread banditry, and armed communities determined to resist the CCP, while at the same time frantically trying to keep up with the various policies and instructions sent down from the distant center.[48]

In this hostile environment, the task of pacification and social reform fell largely to military and political officers who had begun their careers with the CCP in its pre-1949 base areas in the Northwest.[49] Schooled in military struggles against the Japanese and Nationalists and harsh intraparty struggles, battle-hardened PLA soldiers overwhelmed these hastily organized "armies." Rank-and-file members of these armies who were not killed in PLA counterattacks were usually released on their guarantee to longer participate in such activities; leaders of the movements who did not manage to flee abroad (to Thailand or Burma), however, were usually executed.[50]

During military pacification campaigns, it was often difficult for PLA soldiers and CCP officials to distinguish between leaders and rank-and-file soldiers of resistance movements and between Han and ethnic minorities, who often looked alike, lived together, and spoke similar dialects. Cadres whose primary experience was in the Northwest were accustomed to associating all "feudal" remnants—as these groups were termed—with "landlords" who should be either "struggled" or executed. Despite official policy, which called for conciliation with local elites and respect for minority customs, many cadres were reportedly unable or unwilling to distinguish between former GMD officials, Han, and minorities, or between Han and ethnic minority landlords.[51] In one district in Chuxiong, for instance, the local government convened a meeting of Yi leaders, and then shot in cold blood all twenty-eight of them.[52]

CCP and PLA counterattacks and political campaigns targeted not only local elite military power but the sources of their economic strength as well. As noted earlier, local elites in Yunnan (and Sichuan) enriched themselves and their communities through the opium trade. However, both the GMD and CCP viewed opium trade as a symbol of China's humiliation before the West, and consequently enacted laws banning the purchase and sale of opium. In Yunnan the opium problem was particularly vexing, given that ethnic minorities, who were now (at least in theory) a "protected" group, were heavily involved in its trade and consumption. Navigating these treacherous waters, state officials in Yunnan usually sided with those victimized by the wielding of opium's economic clout, and took a very firm stance against the use of arms to resolve intraethnic disputes. In one case in northern Yao'an County, for instance, the district government freed several White Yi serfs who had escaped from their Black Yi masters and sought refuge at the district, confiscated the Black Yis' opium, and warned them to no longer use force to resolve their community conflicts.[53] Weaker groups thus learned that district governments could be used to solve all sorts of community and resource-based grievances. Other evidence shows that during 1950–1951, district governments resolved disputes over water supplies, public land, and forests among a variety of ethnic groups. Each of these cases came to light after the weaker community petitioned the district for redress, and each was amicably settled by the district only after the conflict was on the verge of erupting into a full-scale feud.[54] Whether owing to their coercive power or their ability to serve as relatively objective outsiders to interethnic conflict, district governments came to be seen by local residents as legitimate and powerful organizations.

Such legitimacy, however, did not necessarily rub off on all Han officials in the area, best intentions notwithstanding. Drawing upon their experience in base areas in northwestern and eastern China during the Sino-Japanese War, the CCP and PLA also sought to become involved in improving agricultural production and assisting minority groups with basic health-care issues. Urban youth and demobilized PLA soldiers went into villages to assist with the harvest, reclaim land, and administer vaccination and other public-health programs.[55] Despite these efforts, community leaders remained suspicious toward these new intruders and, according to one PRC account, were "very worried" as to what policies the state might adopt toward them in the future.[56] Moreover, Han cadres working among minorities in their villages were not unaffected by what the sources referred to as "Han chauvinism": the Han belief that peripheral and minority cultures were "backward" in comparison to the Han Chinese. This resulted in frequent misunderstandings and conflicts.[57] In Guizhou, ethnic conflict between Han and Hui was reportedly particularly acute. In one case, Han cadres in a Hui village, irked that Muslims did not eat pork, tried to "enlighten" them by stuffing the meat down their throats at knifepoint, or by throwing chunks of pig meat down village wells, contaminating the water supply.[58]

Land Reform

Ethnic tensions in the area appear to have structured a multitiered conception of the state's legitimacy. Officials who had the most contact with minority groups in villages, simply by virtue of the amount of time they spent with the villagers, had many opportunities to reveal prejudices and insensitivity to customs, and otherwise foul up. As a result, they were not afforded the same degree of legitimacy as higher-level organizations (mostly in districts and counties), which were more anonymous but often successful in resolving flammable disputes. This dual structure of legitimacy intensified with land reform, which began in late 1951. According to official land-reform policy, local officials were required to study differences in land-holding patterns in different areas of the province (such as mountains and valley basins), as well as to consider the ethnic composition of each area. Land reform should commence only after investigation, and if there were a sufficient number of poor peasant "backbone" cadres. Implementing land reform, moreover, should not increase the hostility between ethnic groups or strike a crippling blow against elites; cadres should "emphasize each group's common interests."[59] Unfamiliar with the history of ethnic tensions in the area, policy-makers seem to have been unaware that minority groups had few common interests to begin with. Land reform intensified these disputes by throwing very tangible rewards and punishments up for peasants to grab. The results of land reform were threefold. First, community conflict over the distribution of land further enhanced the role of courts and district governments as authoritative mediators. Second, contrary to official intentions, land reform reduced the power of local elites through its use of organized terror. Third, land reform radicalized many village women, and thus changed family and gender dynamics in the period just prior to, or in some cases temporally coinciding with, the Marriage Law.

The account of the rent-reduction and land reform movement in Chuxiong's gazetteer gives few hints as to how land reform was implemented in practice, stating only the bare-bones facts: 1,046,907 *mu* of "feudal land" were confiscated and distributed to 957, 367 landless peasants. Farm animals, equipment, homes, and grain belonging to landlords were also confiscated. Local ruffians (*eba*), bandit leaders, and landlords were attacked and struggled. In the end, the gazetteer claims, land reform achieved a "basic change" in rural land relations.[60]

Fortunately, recently published intraparty documents from the early 1950s and archival sources allow us to fill in the picture. Land reform in Yunnan, these sources demonstrate, was greatly complicated by the area's political history, class structure, ethnic composition, and gender relations. To mobilize peasants to participate in struggle sessions against landlords, cadres first had to assure peasants that the area was militarily secure, and that later on landlords would not be able to take revenge. In Yunnan, this was a difficult task. Even by 1953, Nationalist soldiers and other predatory groups were still hiding in mountain lairs. For many, standing up and making a bold accusation against one's former landlord was simply too risky. Landlords and other pre-1949 power holders took advantage of peasants' wariness during the rent-reduction campaign by spreading rumors that the Nationalists would soon return to Yunnan, and that when they did, peasants who had made accusations would be executed. As a result, many peasants were reluctant to air their grievances publicly.[61]

Previous patterns of ethnic conflict also affected land reform. In one village, for instance, Han and Yi lived together in the same community, but had a very brittle relationship. Between the 1920s and the 1950s, Yi controlled most of the village land, renting it out to Han at very high interest rates. Tensions continued well into the early 1950s. When the Communists established health clinics in the village, Han and Yi would sit separately, and when two Yi assumed posts at the county seat, a dispossessed Han landlord organized three thousand peasants to struggle against the Yi. To retaliate, the Yi organized an attack against several Han. Conflicts prevalent earlier in the century over land use and water rights continued to divide the two communities.[62]

These complications in village land and ethnic relations were difficult to fit into the simplistic formulas and classifications of land reform. In the above village, the Yi had the most land, but were not well represented in county and district government. Were they the exploitative "landlord class" or historical victims of "Han chauvinism"? If the former was the case, they should be struggled against, but if local cadres were to implement Beijing's conciliatory policies toward minority customs and traditions, Yi, as an oppressed minority, should not be subjected to struggle. Official policy tried to steer a middle course: poor peasants of all ethnicities could unite to struggle against Han landlords, but minority peasants should take the lead in struggling against landlords of their own ethnicity.[63] Northwestern cadres, however, continued to rely on their previous political experiences, and persisted in advocating struggle.[64] When peasants did not mobilize on their own accord, frustrated and impatient cadres used force.

Redistributing land, however, did not eliminate the sources of ethnic tensions as originally hoped. Instead, in many cases the violent struggle over land widened preexisting cleavages in villages by terrorizing local elites, older people, and the better off, much as it did in the suburbs of Shanghai and Beijing. When a minority group (the Miao) installed a rich peasant as chairman of their village's peasant association, for instance, northwestern cadres threatened a violent purge. The chair, terrified, committed suicide. Other Miao then panicked, fleeing the village.[65] In a Yi community, a forty-year-old Yi woman was murdered by hanging,[66] and elsewhere there were complaints of northwestern cadres beating minority village headmen, secretly organizing unauthorized poor peasant associations to encourage peasants to withhold rent payments, and itching to struggle *tu si,* calling them by the same term used in Han areas—"village bullies." Some headmen, fearing struggle, abrogated their traditional responsibilities in the village completely. At minimum, many showed passive resistance. Some headmen told peasants, "If you have a problem, go to your government, not me!"[67]

Land reform did not resolve long-standing conflicts over land, either. Cadre radicalism raised villagers' expectations of the possible, particularly among the poorest peasants. All over the province there were reports of poor landless peasants making "new demands" and "taking initiative," with a concomitant rise in the number of land disputes handled in district governments and courts—peasants' long-standing address for petitioning the state.[68] But these demands were difficult to fulfill—particularly in the minority-dominated mountains, where there was little arable land. One Yi complained to senior Han officials, "In Luquan County the minorities are mostly in the high mountains. There are only a few landlords and not a lot of land. During land reform, the fruits of struggle were also few." A Miao said, "In our county the Miao are in the high mountains, and have suffered bitterness for several thousand years. Now, with land reform, we want to switch places with the landlords in the valley basin."[69] Officials who rejected these proposals as too radical could still not escape peasants' new demands. With land reform, the more intractable intraethnic disputes over land became, the greater became the government's role in resolving them.

Patterns of gender relations were also shaped by land reform, albeit not in ways the state anticipated. When peasants heard that land would be distributed on the basis of the number of persons per household, some quickly took in adopted daughters-in-law, thinking that in this way they could increase their land allotment.[70] Mobilizing women for struggle was not easy.

Initially, women were very reluctant to participate in land reform, fearing retribution from both landlords and their families. Some women, fearing that their husbands were going to political meetings only to have affairs, hindered their participation by accusing them of wandering eyes, or forcing bawling infants into their arms to take along to meetings.[71] Women with children were reluctant to participate because they were afraid of exposure to the light of shooting stars: many believed that a child who was exposed to such light would be cursed and soon die.[72] Others did not understand land reform policy, fearing that land rights would be turned over to the head of the household, not to them individually.[73]

But as cadres persisted and "speak bitterness" sessions began, officials soon found women to be quite radical, speaking openly and bitterly about their past experiences, exposing past offenses, and raiding landlords' homes for hidden stashes of cash (women, given their knowledge of domestic household space, were said to be especially good at this).[74] Yet, contrary to the party's expectation that young women would criticize landlords for their "class oppression," startled cadres found women spontaneously criticizing their husbands and in-laws. Old women in Yunnan who "spoke bitterness" about how they were treated by landlords soon found themselves facing their daughters-in-law, who, encouraged by the "speak bitterness" example, began to "speak bitterness" about their oppression. One report commented, "As soon as middle-aged women accuse the landlord of crimes, young women, as well as some young men, begin accusing their parents and grandparents. We encounter this problem very frequently." These women, the report complained, "do not see class oppression, only their in-laws and husbands."[75] Such accusations, coming as they did in the immediate wake of land reform, led some men to panic. Rumors only increased men's worries. In Wuding County, for instance, rumors spread that the International Women's Day holiday (March 8) would be used to "kill, arrest, and monitor men." Fearing persecution, men wandered around villages sobbing, and refused to participate in meetings.[76]

Accusations against in-laws and husbands often went hand in hand with demands for divorce. Reports show that the number of divorce cases received by state institutions in Chuxiong doubled and sometimes tripled after land reform.[77] Nevertheless, women seeking divorce (women were the overwhelming majority of plaintiffs) rarely received help from local Women's Federation representatives. Like their male counterparts, these officials were extremely harried with work they considered more important, such as production, and saw "women's work" as a burden. Women who were just recently promoted from among the poor peasantry also lacked the confidence to deal with women's land-related problems. When women came to them with land- and family-related problems, they would say, "Leave me alone. Go to court."[78]

THE MARRIAGE LAW

The establishment of a national political clock shaped not only the implementation of land reform and other early political campaigns, but the implementation of the Marriage Law as well. In Yunnan and the rest of the Southwest, land and marriage reform often occurred simultaneously. Provincial court directives instructed prefectures and counties that the Marriage Law campaign "must be combined" with land reform, land reform investigation, democratic reform, production, legal reform, and clearing the court docket.[79] The merger of these campaigns meant that cadres in the Southwest, like their counterparts elsewhere in China, framed the Marriage Law in the political methods and discourses of land reform. This framing was evident in the way in which they worded the law. Fresh from their land reform experience, cadres mistakenly called the "marriage law" (*hunyin fa*) campaign a "marriage *reform*" (*hunyin gaige*) campaign, even in official reports.[80] This linguistic overlap pointed to targets for the campaign: just as landlords were said to have perpetuated the inequitable "feudal" land system, so too should landlords be held accountable for the evil "feudal" marriage system.[81] Also associated with this wording was a conception of time based on the land reform analogy: if land relations could be speedily reformed through land reform, cadres reasoned, why not marriage relations and family structure as well? One instructor was thus forced to tell cadres, "Implementing the Marriage Law can't be done in one or two days. It's not like land reform and land reform investigation (*tugai fucha*), which have a deadline. Marriage reform is slow (*manmande*)."[82] Such framing relegated to the background other directives, such as those prohibiting implementation of the Marriage Law in minority or mixed Han-minority areas and advocating the use of nonviolent methods to implement the law.[83]

To understand how it happened that peasants went to court and district governments to divorce (despite the long distances between village and court) and why state officials frequently granted these requests, I will begin by examining the training of county, court, Women's Federation, district, and township government officials. As these officials were those who had the authority to deal with family disputes or to grant divorce (with the exception of Women's Federation officials), it is important to examine how they interpreted the law and the various objections they raised. I then treat the implementation of the law in villages and townships, discussing how villagers and local officials initially reacted to the law. After this, I examine the role of mediation and community in villages in order to explain why plaintiffs avoided local mediation and why women frequently went in groups to divorce. In a series of five cases detailing battles over the right to divorce, I will flesh out some of the arguments made earlier with regard to the role of community, mobility, and legal and sexual cultures. Finally, I conclude by looking at what happened within district governments and the court walls after people arrived with their divorce claims.

"I've Had Sex with a Counterrevolutionary! How Can I Implement the Law?"

In 1950, China had recently emerged from years of wartime mobilization. As in all wars, many family relationships were shattered. Soldiers (usually male) were separated from their families and fiancées for long periods, while the latter were forced to take up the extra burden at home. The results of wartime separation were clearly apparent in Beijing, where high-ranking cadres sought to divorce rural wives, and elsewhere in the county, where there were reports of increased illegitimacy and extramarital affairs. But in Yunnan and the Southwest, long separations were particularly problematic. Unlike soldiers stationed in less militarily sensitive areas who might be demobilized and sent home, soldiers in Yunnan were stationed in a border region adjacent to areas where Nationalist troops had recently retreated and where banditry was still rampant. To secure these areas, many soldiers and CCP officials remained on as an occupying army, without their wives or families.

Though for many state officials and soldiers the end of the war brought loneliness and new anxieties, it also brought relief and new opportunities. After years of military struggle, they could finally relax a bit and take advantage of the absence of a routine military grind and rigid discipline. Pent-up desires for pleasure could be released.

During the early months of CCP control over Yunnan, sexual inclinations found outlets in brothels, in offices, and in the fields. Very often, the objects of soldiers and cadres' desires were not those considered "politically correct." A Women's Federation investigation report on cadre discipline, for instance, found that cadres at provincial, county, district, and township governments, as well as Public Security Bureau officers, frequently engaged in illicit sex with prostitutes, family members of "counterrevolutionaries," "female criminals," and wives of bandit leaders. In a case in Gujin County, the county chief himself committed adultery with the wife of a bandit during the pacification campaign. After becoming pregnant, this former bandit wife rented a bridal carriage and scoured the countryside for the county chief in order to hold him accountable for his actions. In another county, the party secretary of the public security bureau lived with a prostitute until he was chased out and then captured by some militiamen led by the brothel's madam.[84] Han court officials in Lufeng County were also discovered to be having sexual relations with "counterrevolutionaries" or marrying women who had just been released from labor reform; there were also many reported incidents of rape and abuse of women among demobilized solders at district, county, and township levels.[85]

Because the party relied on the very same people who were committing these political mistakes to enforce the law, it was assured that cadres' own sexual improprieties would shape their reaction to the law's enforcement. In Marriage Law training sessions, cadres were forced to confess to these sexual transgressions, without knowing how the party would handle their testimony. As a result, many cadres panicked at the prospect that the methods the party used for bandits and counterrevolutionaries would apply to them as well. The Provincial Marriage Law Committee was aware of this problem when it wrote: "The struggle against external enemies was not over before the Marriage Law began. As a result, external struggles have turned into (*zhuanru*) internal struggles."[86] Some cadres were so fearful that they spent entire days vomiting, and nights unable to sleep; others' eyes swelled;[87] a township chief was worried that he would be punished for wanting to divorce his wife only "because she was pockmarked and ugly"; another heard about "marriage reform" and was worried that he would be forced to divorce his new wife, who was his cousin. When he went to the Marriage Law meetings, his wife stayed at home, "quaking." The lack of political awareness in marriage selection was also a cause for concern. One township chief confessed to having lied when divorcing his wife. He had claimed that she could not bear children, when in fact he already had two, both of whom had died. One month after his divorce, he married the widow of a landlord. During study, the report found, the township official "did not say a word."[88]

Court cadres in particular had many causes for worry. In Chuxiong Prefecture, court officials were either left over from the Nationalist regime or newly appointed CCP cadres. Since Nationalist judges were among the political elite, they were able to afford more than one wife. With the new monogamy clause of the Marriage Law, some were afraid they would be punished for their marital situation. One court official in Guangtong County said:

> Before liberation I had two wives, but after liberation I didn't dare say anything about it. I was very afraid of punishment. I couldn't do any work. During the day, all I would do was sleep. At night, I would lie on my bed, crying, scared that during the Marriage Law movement I would be the target of struggle, and that I would be struggled against like people during the Three Antis. I asked myself, "Should I say anything or keep quiet?"[89]

A Lufeng County Court cadre, Li Xuezheng, was also terrified. Li confessed: "I had illicit sex with a sister of a counterrevolutionary. During the legal reform movement I came clean and wasn't punished. Now, with marriage reform, I'm afraid I'll be purged and punished."[90]

Court cadres, however, were generally better off than local officials. While the former interacted with peasants mainly in the court setting in a fairly structured environment, village officials had to do the grunt work of propagandizing a law they were convinced would be unpopular, lead to suicides, or produce even more promiscuity than was already present in villages. Few had confidence in their capabilities of handling disputes likely to arise from implementing state policy. Many cadres had come from the ranks of poor peasants, and thus had no experience in handling other peasants' private issues; in pre-1949 Yunnan, family mediation had been conducted by village elites, many of whom were now purged or too terrified of entanglement with the CCP to exercise leadership. In addition, since marriage disputes were often entangled in ethnic and community politics, local officials also might become subject to harsh reprisals should they mishandle a dispute or favor one party over another. Village cadres thus voiced opposition to each article of the law: a "love marriage" (*ziyou lian'ai*) was "screwing around" (*luan gao guanxi*); granting legal protection to bastard children would result in "chaotic sexual relations" and increased illegitimacy; widows' remarrying was "shameful"; divorce would make it difficult for poor men to remarry; marriage freedom would "make it difficult for hunchbacks and cripples to marry."[91] Divorce, however, was clearly the most contentious issue, as it threatened existent property arrangements, custody, and continuity of the patrilineal line. Cadres feared that if one woman in the village divorced, others would surely follow her example, resulting in entire villages losing "their" women. Since peasants in the area were poor, they would not be able to afford another wife, and the cadres, who would be responsible for this, would incur the villagers' wrath.[92] Divorce requests, cadres argued, would surely result in violence, death, and "chaos." Death, however, was not an option. County- and district-level cadres instructed their village counterparts that "during the movement no one should die." After this warning, some village cadres panicked and refused to implement the law at all for fearing of making a mistake and inadvertently causing a death.[93]

Hearing these fears, Marriage Law trainers tried to reassure cadres that the Marriage Law was not land reform, and that cadres would not be struggled. Reports claimed that after receiving these reassurances, cadres, in their relief, "became active supporters of the law" and that cadres "easily accept the party's policy."[94] Others, however, were still worried. Even after study they said they "did not dare" propagandize the Marriage Law. The law, they said, "was a matter for the courts and the Women's Federation," probably because they dealt with "law" and "marriage," respectively.[95]

Women's Federation officials in counties, townships, and villages, however, did not necessarily share this assessment. Like their male counterparts, female officials were similarly conflicted about implementing the Marriage Law.[96] Since many Women's Federation officials had yet to go through party rectification or receive formal training, many were clueless about how to actually go about doing "women's work" in the state sphere. The Lufeng County Women's Federation cited village officials as saying, "I can't handle these affairs; I only know how to care for the home." Women cadres in Wuding County were said to have been "completely confused about women's work, even though they are all women." They wondered, "Will families be forced to sleep on the same bed after the Marriage Law is enforced?" Others complained that they would be less "valuable" because the Marriage Law prohibited the exchange of gifts for marriage. Arranged marriages, they said, "are better." Federation officials criticized other women who sought divorce ("Everyone spent a lot of money to marry you . . . if you divorce, the man will really suffer"), and would not offer them assistance, claiming, "We're too busy."[97]

Drawing the Battle Lines: The Marriage Law in the Villages

"Death to the Abusers!"   Cadres who left townships and villages to study the Marriage Law during land reform returned to implement the law as "speak bitterness" and struggle sessions continued. As a result, both the methods and the discourse of campaigns to suppress counterrevolutionaries and of land reform shaped the implementation of the Marriage Law. Using the methods of land reform, cadres organized Marriage Law study sessions: men and women were divided up into young and old and encouraged to "speak bitterness" about their travails in the old society.

Young women—the main target of mobilization of the Marriage Law—were not always easy to mobilize. In some cases husbands' families locked them inside their rooms, fearful they would file for divorce after a meeting.[98] Women who did go to meetings were often accused of having the ulterior motive of having extramarital sex and meeting new male friends.[99] Some women objected to the monogamy requirement: If they could not bear children, why couldn't they bring in someone who could and thus continue the family line?[100] Rumors about the purpose of the campaign complicated matters further. Bumbling cadres who had barely studied the law could do little to dispel rumors that, according to the new Marriage Law, people who were "not married by eighteen or twenty-one" would be taxed or fined, or that women who were twenty-five and still childless would be "kicked in the ass by the government."[101]

Deadlines forced cadres to adopt radical methods to overcome these obstacles. In Xikang Province—a border region between Sichuan, Yunnan, and Tibet—a district party secretary told work team members, "Now we're starting a movement to abolish illegal marriages, especially adopted daughters-in-law (*tongyangxi*). We're going to set a deadline by which all illegal marriages will end. The current situation can't continue any longer." As a result of this order, a work team member in a village ordered a cadre to gather seven *tongyangxi* couples and the one bigamy case and send them to the township. At the township, he told them to separate "all at once, because that will save us a lot of hassle (*mafan*)." The party secretary reportedly witnessed these events, but did nothing to stop the forced separations. Other *tongyangxi* who heard the news were so scared they ran away.[102]

Lacking the time to conduct proper investigations, cadres frequently selected targets they believed to be most representative of the "feudal" family order, regardless of whether they had committed any offense.[103] When propagandizing the law in villages, cadres used a simple formulation—"Men are bad, women are good; old people are wrong, daughters-in-law are right"—and told others that "whoever harms women has violated the law." Women were reported to be particularly radical, using the land reform vocabulary of "avenging old debts" (*suan xizhang*). Some women argued that "because in the past men oppressed women for thousands of years, now that women have *fanshen*'ed (been emancipated), we should oppress *them* for several thousand years." Others said, "Men and old ladies who abused women should all be executed."[104]

Young women's thirst for revenge was sometimes fulfilled. When targets for the campaign were located, they joined landlords together onstage as defendants in public trials and were sentenced to hard labor for two to eight years.[105] Witnesses to these events often panicked, fearful that they too would be selected as targets of struggle. Men—including local village cadres, one report noted—became terribly frightened when they saw village women congregating in separate rooms to "speak bitterness."[106]

Most reports on villagers' reaction to the Marriage Law emphasized some combination of bemusement, fear, apathy, and confusion. The law's regulations were complex, and so were the reactions to it. One report found that peasants "laughed and joked around" about marriage problems during propaganda sessions.[107] In Bai Family Village in Chuxiong, one man said, "Ai! She pissed me off once and I smacked her. I made a mistake; now I guess I'll go to labor reform."[108] In Yao'an County, work teams reported that "very many daughters-in-law spoke about their past bitterness, and are requesting that the government educate their mothers-in-law and husbands."[109] As in the Shanghai and Beijing suburbs, this willingness to draw in the state resulted in panic among the older generation, as they feared that methods employed in previous campaigns would carry over to the Marriage Law and that they, as representatives of the "feudal" order, would suffer.

Older women were not uniformly opposed to state intervention in the family, however. Stereotypes of the evil mother-in-law notwithstanding, some had not beaten their daughters-in-law, and thus were less fearful of retribution. Others were sympathetic to the plight of their younger counterparts, or welcomed the new state's intrusion into the family sphere. One sixty-year-old woman said, "Today's policy is really good. When I was younger, my marriage was arranged and I had a bitter life because of this. Now I'm over sixty, but if I were younger I would now have a better life." Middle-aged women complained that they were "reincarnated too early" and that now, with the Marriage Law, women would be "protected" by the state.[110] In Guangtong County, Dianwei Township, one woman welcomed the reassertion of the public/state domain *within* the "private" sphere—a response we also observed in the previous chapter. "Chairman Mao," she said, "cares about everything. He's aware of all our bitterness. He's taken care of (*zhaogu*) land, food, and now he wants to solve our domestic quarrels as well."[111]

Organized Rape and Illegal Prosecutions   Village men, however, were notably less sympathetic to the plight of younger women, and resisted efforts to implement the law—a reaction noted and emphasized by the earlier literature on the Marriage Law. Resistance to the law occurred at several levels of social organization. In the family, male family members tried to prevent young women from attending Marriage Law meetings, fearing that should they go, they would immediately seek to divorce. Others murdered their wives after they returned from court with divorce papers in hand.[112] Some, however, supported the law, arguing that in the past landlords had several wives but poorer peasants could not afford even one. With the ban on commercial marriages, poorer peasants would finally be able to afford a wife.[113]

More frequent than family-level resistance, however, were instances of peasants organizing violent opposition within newly created Communist organizations such as peasant associations and the community militia, and receiving the tacit or active blessing of village- and township-level officials. These low-level state organizations, which tended to be staffed by macho young men, were intended to replace the pre-1949, and now largely decimated, power structure in rural areas.[114] For peasants in the Southwest frontier, such violence had been commonplace prior to the Communists, but the organization and armaments the CCP provided to young male peasants who served in the peasant associations and militias made such resistance particularly lethal to divorce petitioners. In Chuxiong there were reports of village cadres locking up women divorce petitioners (for up to three weeks) and raping them while in prison, punishing women who requested divorce by assigning them to construction work, stringing up the first woman in the village who requested divorce at peasant association offices for other women to see, preventing "love marriages," struggling adulterers, chopping off body parts, and threatening widows seeking to remarry. In one case, peasant officials prevented a couple seeking a free-choice marriage by forcing them to write a "guarantee" that "they wouldn't marry during their entire lifetimes."[115]

Militiamen were said to be particularly fanatical in their efforts to prevent implementation of the Marriage Law. The same militias the state used to pursue bandits now turned against policies they found disagreeable.[116] During the Marriage Law campaign, however, militiamen often appeared to be more concerned about promiscuity and adultery than about their "class enemies." Reports complained that militiamen "kept watch over adulterers more vigilantly than over landlords" and took potshots at couples having sex in the fields. In response, the policy guidelines issued by the Yunnan provincial government instructed militiamen and cadres to cease "monitoring adultery and sex," forcing confessions, humiliating people and tying them up, hanging, beating, and organizing struggle sessions," and attributed to these actions the rash of suicide attempts by both men and women. The rise in suicide cases resulting from these abuses of power at the lowest level of the political structure was coupled, however, with a concomitant *increase* in the number of abuse cases received by higher-level institutions such as courts. Faced with village and township officials who were willing to take extreme measures to prevent them from leaving their villages, young women chose courts and counties in Yunnan as the preferred institutions to seek protection and get justice, much as they were for women seeking divorce in the suburban areas discussed in the last chapter.[117]

While many of these forms of resistance reflected older ways of exercising male authority, and certainly confirm accounts in the secondary literature, there was still something different and new about them, reflecting recent political and economic developments. The organization of mutual aid teams, the inclusion of women in village and township governments and meetings, early-1950s dance parties, and literacy classes increased opportunities for courtship and sexual encounters. After meeting someone who met their fancy at these venues, many men and women acted on their sexual impulses. A Women's Federation report found that many domestic abuse cases were caused by "adultery, women dancing [with men other than their husbands], going to classes, and early marriage."[118] Male resistance, as cruel and brutal as it was, can therefore also be interpreted as a *defensive* reaction to new developments in political, economic, and gender relations.

Pro-Divorce Resources: Language and Marriage Practices

Ironically, it was CCP discourse on marriage "freedom" and "liberation" that gave women the political cover to engage in the sexual activities party ideologues condemned. Extramarital affairs among peasants were nothing new, but with their new political language women were handed a powerful weapon to justify their love, desire, and pursuit of upward mobility through marriage.[119] A Women's Federation report from Fuyuan County found that many [peasants] misunderstand the Marriage Law. They blindly emphasize that the Marriage Law "liberated" them. This is the case for some women in particular, who have become very unconventional and dissolute (*fangdang*) in their sexual relations. They have several partners at once, and often switch among them, choosing whichever man appeals to them on that particular day. They also flirt with many men (*luan tan lian'ai*).[120]

Other reports, rather prudishly, complained that peasants, as well as party members (it is not made clear whether married or unmarried, or Han or ethnic minority) "do not treat marriage seriously, and rashly (*caoshuai*) marry," "treat love like a game," "marry after knowing each other for only a day," and "use the idea of marriage freedom to justify eating, drinking, and then requesting a divorce because of an argument."[121] Such behavior stands in sharp contrast to that of Han (and presumably better-educated) court officials, who were said to be "unable to bear the sight of men and women working together, talking, holding hands, taking walks and dancing, and flirting." Especially troublesome for these officials was some women's practice of changing partners if they found someone with more money to buy food and clothes. "Women," they complained, "eat up one man's resources and then move on to another." Struggle sessions organized by peasant associations, they argued, were necessary to curtail peasants' excessive sexuality; otherwise, "these people will be shameless, behaving just like animals."[122]

The overlap between new political developments and marriage customs also contributed to the rise in marriage conflicts and divorce cases among some ethnic minority groups. Prior to 1949, as I mentioned earlier, young men and women from the Yi would often gather to drink and dance around a bonfire in the hills surrounding their village, a custom known as *chi shan jiu*. When the CCP established political control during intense political campaigns, *chi shan jiu* was temporarily suspended. But as the intensity of campaigns subsided, young men and women resumed their mountain forays. During peasant association meetings, one report complained, men would whistle to the women, the women would give a shout in reply, and in a flash the group would run off into the mountains. During *chi shan jiu*, couples had sex. Some, after their moment of passion, became dissatisfied with their original spouses and soon afterward pressed for divorce.[123]

The language of emancipation and freedom during the early 1950s was also influential among ethnic minorities, despite the policy that instructed local officials to desist from implementing the Marriage Law in minority areas.[124] Owing to the lack of communication infrastructure in Yunnan, word of mouth and rumor frequently substituted for formal political communication. According to the investigation report cited above, minorities began to raise demands for divorce because they "were influenced by the implementation of the Marriage Law in the alluvial plain area," and because they became dissatisfied with their marriages after land reform. Even though many areas did not hear formally about the law, minority women, like their Han counterparts, were still influenced by its language. Young minority women, this report found,

> understand "freedom" as allowing them to behave rashly in sexual relations. If they are criticized by the court or by other peasants, they feel that their "freedom" is being infringed upon. Others who genuinely seek freedom might encounter the resistance of their family or the peasant association. If they do, they are incensed that their freedom is being limited and resist. Some even commit suicide or abuse and kill their own children to get revenge.[125]

Investigators of minority marriage disputes in even more remote border regions encountered a similar phenomenon. Among the Lisu in the border Nujiang region, CCP investigators found that "very many" young women began to petition for divorce. If their spouse refused, "the women threatened to commit suicide."[126]

Space

In the secondary literature on law enforcement, large geographical distances between plaintiffs and state institutions are said to hinder the implementation of state law. Here I take a different view: space could hinder the implementation of the law, but at the same time it also served as a *resource* and *refuge* for women seeking to leave their marriages or engagements. Women's mobility was nothing new, however. In the Southwest (and in other areas, as other research has shown)[127] women might return to their natal homes after a row with their husband, participate in groom raids, or sell produce in local markets. This mobility continued during the Marriage Law period. But, in a break with past practices, instead of returning to their native place to annul the marriage, they (both Han and minorities) might also run off to a government institution to formally divorce.

According to many reports from the early 1950s, women's mobility, in combination with the perception that they had "marriage freedom," sometimes resulted in a sort of "marriage-divorce roundabout": women would marry or be married off, argue with their husbands, and then either run off to the district government or find refuge at their parents' home. This way of taking advantage of the Marriage Law did not necessarily contradict the letter of the Marriage Law, since it encouraged women to use divorce to have more satisfactory relationships. A marriage-divorce roundabout did, however, fly in face of the spirit of the law and the CCP's marriage policy more generally. The *ultimate* goal of divorce was not to move on to short-lived affairs, but to remarry and have a happier, more "democratic," "modern," productive, and *stable* marriage. But as the CCP soon discovered, the scope of peasants' willingness to take advantage of new opportunities was quite broad and went well beyond the law's original intentions. In Yongren County, for instance, a woman named Yan Guiying married Tang Xinghan (it is not clear whether Han or Yi) after the couple had known each other for one day. On the second day of the marriage, Yan "ran to the district government to return her marriage certificate." In another township in Yongren, a woman named He Lanzhi was married five times before she turned eighteen. On one occasion, she married one Xu Jiazhu for one evening, but on the following morning "ran back to her natal home." The study narrowly concluded that the many marriage disputes were caused by women's "misunderstanding of marriage freedom" and "careless marriages," ignoring the possibility that several of these marriages may not have been voluntary choices on the part of the women in the first place.[128] If these marriages were indeed coerced, then the Marriage Law was working as it should have, and the reports probably reflect class bias on the part of the investigators.

The practice of returning to natal homes (the sources, reflecting the class bias of the authors, always refer to this as "running back" to natal homes rather than just "walking"; running seems more chaotic) upset both husbands and mothers-in-law, who together employed local militia to prevent this mobility. One Yang Lanying, eighteen, from Shangzhuang Village in Wuding County, for example, came from a poor peasant family. Her father died when she was five, and at six her mother sold her to another village. Because she was abused by her husband and in-laws she "frequently ran back to her mother's home." To prevent Yang's recurrent departures, her mother-in-law approached a blind fortune-teller for help. The fortune-teller told her, "Your daughter-in-law's returning to her mother's home represents the growth of wild hair. The way to control it is to burn some wild growing hair. If you do, she won't run away again." When Yang's mother-in-law returned to the village she grabbed Yang and pushed her into the chicken coop. She then scattered some hair around and chanted, "Burn wild hair, burn wild hair, burn wild hair and she won't run away." Despite these incantations, Yang continued to run away, until one day, as she was about to leave after an argument with her husband, her husband called in the local militia and had Yang hauled to the peasant association. A local cadre agreed to mobilize the peasants for struggle. They organized a parade that passed through four villages. As they walked, they demanded that Yang shout out "For the sake of others, don't be unfilial."[129]

Community, Mediation, and Collective Action

Any explanation of legal processes in rural China has to deal with the role of community. If communities are said to be "strong" in remote rural areas of China, how did it come about that people (usually women) seeking divorce frequently *avoided* local community institutions such as mediation committees? Why did many cases end up at court or district-level government institutions instead? According to sociolegal theory, we would not expect close neighbors who live for long periods together to seek out state institutions to resolve interpersonal disputes, particularly when mediation institutions are easily accessible. I have already hinted at several plausible explanations earlier in this chapter, such as the competition for scarce resources, the "decapitation" of pre-1949 village heads, land reform, and state officials' fear of purge. There were, however, other reasons for popular reliance on courts, as we will see below.

In the previous chapter, I examined cases in which women in the Shanghai suburbs, angered by a miscarriage of justice, organized a protest aimed at forcing the hand of the state. In rural areas of Yunnan there were similar forms of gender-based collective action. In a village in Yongren County, for example, a dispute arose between a brother, his sister (one Miss Zhang), and their uncle over her decision to marry a hired laborer in the village, Niu Lianyu. Zhang was thirty, and perhaps better off financially than Niu, so she gave him some cloth as a gift before the marriage. When Miss Zhang's uncle, Gao Yuqing, found out about this exchange, he berated her older brother, Zhang Jili, telling him that the family had lost face by giving a gift. To prevent the marriage, Zhang Jili locked his sister in a room. Left there for ten days without food, she starved to death. The brother then tried to cover his tracks by throwing his sister's body into a well in the mountains. In villages, however, secrets are difficult to keep, and it was not long before a village women's committee member, Wang Luofang, discovered what had transpired. She organized the village women into a search party and found the body. Furious, Wang mobilized other women to struggle the victim's brother and uncle. They also forced them to buy a coffin for her, so she could have a proper burial.[130]

Avenging injustice was not the only form of women's collective activity. Women would also gather to discuss family disputes and divorce. In a community where most aspects of life (including sexuality) were public, there was less of the shame that characterized discourse about divorce among elite urban women, who were often steadfast in their desire to uphold the traditional elite and modern "bourgeois" division between public and private spheres. CCP work teams from courts and other agencies thus found women to be willing and active participants in mediating family disputes. Women, they discovered, "like collective mediation" and "welcome outsiders," even when sessions turned into heated shouting matches.[131]

Young male cadres recognized the imminent danger of women's collective discussions of marital difficulties when they adopted drastic measures to prevent the *first* woman in the village from going to court or, if it was already too late to stop the initiator, from even discussing the divorce with other village women. For village men, who were often relatives and long-time neighbors, mobilization was relatively easy, and they used collective action to deter others, often successfully, from seeking divorce. But despite these efforts, it was almost impossible (short of locking up or killing all village women) to prevent such public discussion; even though village women came from different villages (in the usual patrilocal marriage), many found solace and strength in their common predicament. Take for instance the case of Zhang Chaoxiu. Zhang had an arranged marriage to a man named Zhu Rongsheng. In 1951, Zhang demanded a divorce. Encountering obstacles at the township, she reportedly "cried all the way from the township to the county court." The court granted the divorce and she returned to the village. The other village women, the report noted, "had been concerned about her marriage problems, so when they heard that the government had granted her a divorce, over twenty women went over to see her."[132]

While one can only guess at what was discussed in these informal gatherings, it would not be unreasonable to suspect that Zhang's divorce encouraged other women to follow suit. After her divorce, it was easier for others to follow her example, as they could simply point to Zhang's case as precedent. One report noted that in villages "women want to divorce, but cannot decide who will taken the lead," but would go when they "see others" who went to court.[133] Such an interpretation receives support from the historical literature. Nancy Cott, in her analysis of divorce during the U.S. Revolutionary War period, suggests that "communication about the granting of divorces may also have had a cumulative effect: the more divorces were allowed, the more likely it became for a discontented spouse to consider the possibility. *Especially in small towns,* news of divorces being obtained must have encouraged more men and women to petition."[134]

Women's reliance on courts to settle family disputes (which party officials claimed "wasted time" and reduced agricultural output) prompted moves to strengthen village-level mediation. These efforts, however, had only limited success. Sources show that women seeking divorce often viewed mediators with utter contempt and distrust. Most mediators, we should bear in mind, had been ordinary poor peasants (and thus had little face) until the revolution. Moreover, mediators might also be related to their husband's family, and thus could not be trusted to be impartial. One report found that in divorce disputes, "Women are not willing to go to village or township officials for mediation, and are not willing to accept village mediation at all." When women avoided local mediation by going to court, village and township mediators saw this as a personal affront to their authority. When one woman ran to court for a divorce, mediators berated her: "You look down on us, huh! You have some nerve!"[135]

Of course, not all mediators were so disrespected. There were some, although reports indicate that they were clearly in the minority, who had enough "cultural capital" to serve as sought-out mediators. But records show that even these people had a difficult time separating themselves from local politics and community. Because of the politicization of villages during anti-bandit, anti-counterrevolutionary, and land reform campaigns, mediators were frequently terrified of "violating policies" they did not understand. The price of committing a violation might be high: many cadres were reported to be deathly afraid of being held responsible for a suicide or murder that might result from a mishandled mediation case—a distinct possibility considering rural women's tendency to threaten suicide or hurl themselves into the village well. According to one report, mediators feared "committing an error and being criticized," and "being held responsible if someone dies." [136]

Embeddedness in community further limited mediators' effectiveness, for one of two reasons. First, because mediators knew almost everyone in their village, and had to continue living with them after mediation was concluded, they were hard-pressed to find common ground in family disputes. Should they criticize someone for abuse, the offender might later be singled out for struggle. The mediator would then be faced with the awkward possibility of confronting him and his family after the end of the campaign. According to court investigators, mediators were also afraid of "making an enemy out of someone" (*pa dezui ren*). Two mediators vividly described their dilemma in handling family disputes. In Shadi Township in Yuanmou County, a mediator said, "Mediating is like whipping a mule: you whip the mule and it farts, stinking you up; you try to mediate and everyone will be angry with you." Another mediator complained, "When you mediate a marriage dispute both sides threaten you, and each other, with murder or suicide. How can we possibly find a solution?" Mediators in minority villages had similar gripes. Local cadres in a Bulang village complained that divorce cases gave them "a headache." Unable to conciliate the parties, mediators—both Han and minority—adopted the pragmatic strategy of sending cases to courts, leading courts to complain that mediators were sending cases their way "as soon as there is a conflict in the village." [137]

Second, embeddedness in community led to small-time corruption in villages, as mediators tried to use their positions to gain material benefits or to curry favor with one of the parties to the dispute. In Zhennan County, mediators reportedly required villagers to pay a "mediation fee." Others were accused of using "personal connections" to manipulate mediation, yelling and cursing at plaintiffs, or trying to force reconciliations by having couples write "guarantees" and "pacts" not to divorce. [138] But whether mediators avoided handling cases or mediated on the condition that participants pay a fee, the result was often the same: women who prior to 1949 presented their problem to a local elite now did not trust the young and inexperienced CCP cadres (men and women) who replaced them and instead went to court. "Women," the courts complained, "go rushing off to court, traveling for days, just because of a trivial dispute."[139]

BATTLEFIELDS

Four cases described below illustrate the social and political tensions generated by the succession of political campaigns preceding and during the Marriage Law. In some cases, women's actions were shaped by their alliance with their family and their community. Attachment to natal homes, the first case demonstrates, gave some women refuge from abusive husbands and their adopted communities, as well as support for their divorce claims. The second case looks at the role community played in the struggles over divorce. When women were held captive by husbands, in-laws, and lineage groups, their natal communities came in force to help them. The other cases deal with the intersection of village family politics, district governments, and courts. Finally, and perhaps most importantly, these cases demonstrate peasant women's "legal culture": their boldness, resourcefulness, grit, and determination when confronted with obstructionist family members or officials, as well as their ability to use political vocabulary for their own ends.

1. Family Support in Divorce: The Case of Wang Huizhen

Divorce in the Southwest, as this and the following case show, was not simply a matter of an *individual* petitioning the state for a divorce, as divorce is generally conceived of in the West. In Yunnan, Guizhou, and Sichuan, families and entire communities might also initiate the divorce process. Cases such as these have been largely ignored by scholars, who have tended to portray communities and families as exclusively obstructionist. In the case of Wang Huizhen we can see precisely the opposite: her stepfather, Wang Guangming, and her mother actively supported her divorce claim after the promulgation of the Marriage Law. The entire family paid a heavy price for this support, as Wang Guangming's intervention led to the surfacing of latent family tensions between the couple's communities.

Wang, a poor peasant woman, was from Three Mountain Village in Weng'an County in Guizhou Province. Like Yunnan, Guizhou was very poor, mountainous, and historically resistant to central administrative control. When she was nineteen years old, Wang married a man named Zhou Changguo, a peasant from Pingyue County, Gulong Township. They were married in

1950; their union had been arranged by their parents from the time she was seven. After the promulgation of the Marriage Law, Wang sought a divorce by going to a small-group leader in her village. He was unsympathetic, and convinced her to reconcile.

Some time later, Wang's stepfather, Wang Guangming, was attending a class in a nearby district. There he participated in a Marriage Law study session, and as a result "understood something about the Marriage Law." Returning home, he decided to support his stepdaughter with her divorce claim, and went to Gulong Township to try to resolve the dispute. He spoke with a female member of the peasant association, Wang Guixian (who was also chairwoman of the township's Women's Representative Committee). Wang Guixian, perhaps relying on village customary law, told him that the conditions for divorce were: physical impairments, epilepsy (?) (*die*), bad eyesight, if the husband was old and weak, or if he "likes to eat but is lazy" (*haochi lanzuo*); otherwise, she said, divorce was impossible. Since her husband did not fall into any of these categories, Wang Huizhen's case was refused.

Wang Guangming's intervention in his stepdaughter's divorce opened a Pandora's box of personal and community resentments. Apparently, at some time in the past he had offended a member of the Zhou lineage named Zhou Changfu. Zhou decided to use the divorce request to his own advantage. He told other villagers, "Wang Huizhen's divorce request is all her stepfather's doing." Villagers then turned their anger against Wang and her stepfather. That evening, Wang Guangming and Wang Huizhen left the village to stay at her aunt's home. On the way, however, they were suddenly accosted by the chief of the village militia, who was accompanied by several others. With Zhou's support, the Wangs were tied up and hauled off to the township government, where they were accused of having illicit sex. The township chief and his deputy, without looking into the situation further, tried to force Wang Guangming to admit to "adultery," and sent them packing off to the district government. They also wrote a letter to Three Mountain Village requesting "materials" on them in order to prepare for a struggle session.

District officials did not believe their township counterparts' concocted story, and notified the township government about their decision not to pursue the matter. Returning to Gulong Village, Wang Guangming thought his ordeal was over, but when his wife shouted some obscenities at members of the Zhou lineage and township officials, Zhou Changfu, together with other members of his lineage, hauled the Wangs back to the township government under the trumped-up charge of "stealing Zhou's property." On the way to the township government, Wang Huizhen and her mother were beaten. Wang Guangming—Huizhen's stepfather—accompanied by several Zhous, went back in the direction of Three Mountain Village. On the way, the Zhous again tried to force Wang Guangming to confess to adultery, but he still refused. Frustrated, the Zhous eventually used a ruse to trick him into signing the confession. They procured new documents at the township and told him that the documents stated that the Wangs had *not* committed adultery. The Wangs, who were both illiterate, believed the Zhous and affixed their fingerprints.

Several days later, Gulong Township convened a struggle session. With eighty peasants present, Wang Huizhen "confessed" to adultery, and was sent to the district government for punishment. The district, seeing only the manufactured documents, believed the accusation. They sent her step-father to the district government of Three Mountain Village for "handling," while Wang Huizhen was handed over to Gulong Township's chief for "mediation."

At Gulong Township, the township chief organized a struggle session in-volving some twenty women, and with the support of Gulong Township's Women's Representative Committee chairwomen, demanded that Wang Huizhen bow her head toward a picture of Chairman Mao and the as-sembled masses and promise to "never divorce Zhou Changguo," "obey my husband," "not be unruly" (*bu tiaopi*), and "not spread rumors." Should she violate these promises, she would be "handled by the masses."

After the struggle session, Wang Huizhen was sent to a district govern-ment in Weng'an County, and only there were the facts of the case clarified (Wang Guangming had already been there for several days). The case was sent to the county government, which dispatched court and Women's Federation officials to the scene to investigate. The court reportedly gave "appropriate punishment" to the offenders, and Wang was granted her divorce.[140]

2. Community Involvement in Divorce among the Yi: The Case of Li Bangguo and Pu Lanfan

In addition to natal families, entire communities might support a woman's divorce claim. In the divorce case of Pu Lanfan and Li Bangguo, both of whom were Yi, communities mobilized to lend support to each party in the dispute. In part, community mobilization reflected the area's militaristic culture and past patterns of feuding over family disputes, but there was also much that was new. Unlike the GMD, which could do little to prevent such disputes from spilling over to armed community conflict, the CCP was de-termined to stamp out extrastate violence of this sort. Placing itself in the middle of such conflicts, the state added its weight to the claims of one side, and by doing so changed the outcome of the dispute. Much like the role the state played in settling land disputes prior to 1949 and in the aftermath of land reform, district governments and courts became, by default, *the* place where people could seek redress of personal/community grievances.

Li Bangguo, twenty-four, was a member of the elite Black Yi community, and hailed from Xuefang Township in Yongren County, Chuxiong. In 1949 he married Pu Lanfan, a distant cousin from nearby Yuanmou County. Before the marriage, the county report noted, the couple had an amiable relationship, but after the marriage Li beat her, and spent much of his money on opium. When Pu complained to her family about the abuse, some of her family members tried to take her back home, but the rescue party was stopped by Li family members.

In 1951, Pu managed to escape, taking her jewelry with her. When she returned, Li strung her up and beat her senseless. In retaliation, Pu refused to cook for him. Furious, Li beat her again. After this incident, Pu and her family were determined to break off their relationship with the Lis. On a pilgrimage to a local temple, twenty-three members of Pu's family formed a reconnaissance team, planning either to trick Li in order to get Pu back or, if that was not successful, to steal her away. Li, however, got wind of the plan and hid his wife.

Pu's family did not give up: they placed a watch on Li's home, hoping to figure out a way to get Pu back. While on watch, they were accosted by Chen Zhaofa, a Yi who served as a small-group leader. Chen demanded to see documentation proving they were allowed to stay in the area. When the Pus refused, Chen brought the matter before the township government. Pu Lanfan's sister, who served as the representative of the group, complained to the officials that Li abused her sister and beat "one of our own" (*da wo de ren*). "Today," she said, "we are going to beat him and take her back home." Township government officials sided with Li, first issuing a warning to the Pus not to exact communal revenge upon Li Bangguo, and then ordering the township militia to tie up some of the Pus and arrest them. Li Bangguo then took his wife from her hiding place and led her toward the village. On the way, however, Pu broke from his hold and ran away. Li—his eyesight failing—failed to catch up with her and returned home empty-handed.

The township chief in charge of the case, Wang Jiu'an, was at a loss for how to proceed. The Pus, after all, could not remain locked up indefinitely, and Li Bangguo, anxious to regain his wife, was pressing them to arrest the Pu family representative as well. This issue soon became moot, since several of the Pu family who escaped, much like bandits who had operated in the area not long before, raided the township offices and released their comrades. Emboldened by their success, the Pus raided Li Bangguo's livestock, driving all the animals away. They then sent a search party to look for Li, planning to tie him up and beat him. Li, in turn, mobilized several of his family members to attack the Pus.

As tensions escalated, a district-level official was dispatched to the scene. The district official brought six members of the Pu family to the district government compound to eat, sleep, and clarify the situation. The district also invited leading members of the Li family for a collective mediation session. In mediation, the Pus harshly criticized the township officials, and complained that the Lis abused and beat Pu Lanfang and prevented her from returning to her natal home, treating her "like a slave" (i.e., like the subordinate White Yi). Now, they said, "we are determined to break off relations, but we request that the government settle the issue in accordance with the new Marriage Law: property should be distributed equally; otherwise, we'll raid the livestock of the entire village." The Lis, in contrast, were equally determined *not* to break off relations and evoked traditional as well as new political justifications. Pu Lanfan, they argued, "will always be a member of the Li family, even when she turns into a ghost." Moreover, the government should follow its own policy of "respecting the customs and traditions of minorities" when handling such disputes. According to local custom, the Lis said, Pu Lanfan would have to be shamed in some way. This meant that a dog, a cat, and a chicken would be hung at a crossroads for everyone to see. This way everyone would know that Pu Lanfan was at fault. They also demanded that Pu return the silver she had taken back to her natal home. If their customs were not followed, they threatened, "we'll do whatever we have to do."

District officials attempted to mediate the case informally by conducting lengthy discussions with the Lis and Pus. After a day of discussions, Li agreed to the divorce, but refused to allow the property to be distributed. This settlement did not satisfy the Pus, who were rumored to be mustering their forces for a raid on the Lis' village. District officials then created a "formal consultation meeting" to move beyond the impasse. The role of the meeting, they said, was to "avoid violence." A compromise was struck: the couple would be divorced, Li would retain his original property (not acquired during the marriage), and Pu would be allowed to keep some of the silver ornaments she received after they were married. Li was forced to make a "simple self-confession" and give Pu one sheep for the cessation of all animosity between the groups. After both groups promised the district to keep the peace, they sat down for a feast, paid for by the district. The Lis apologized to the district for creating such a hassle.[141]

3. Courts and Villages: The Case of Chen Faying

Families, communities, and district governments were not the only sources of redress for personal/community grievances of Han, Yi, Lisu, Dai, and

Hui peasant women. They also traveled large distances to courts when they had difficulty separating from their husband's community and encountered the resistance of local officials.[142] By going to court, women continued previous legal traditions of invoking state power to solve personal and family issues. The ethnic composition of the court—officials were all Han—was not nearly as important as the court's ability to curtail the power of abusive husbands, families, and local officials. As these cases show, interaction between women and courts threatened the power of local officials in villages and townships, and the latter put up stiff resistance. In this power struggle, courts had the upper hand, as they had much better access to the machinery of the CCP and the government. Village and township authorities thus found themselves pitted against women, their natal families, and the machinery of the upper echelons of the power structure in rural areas. Methodologically, this case demonstrates the importance of disaggregating the state and looking at how individuals and communities deal with different types of state organizations. It also shows the importance of not assuming a smooth line of policy implementation from top to bottom or of assuming uniformity of interests and modus operandi among the (mostly male) officials staffing the myriad of organizations that, collectively, we call the state.

The divorce case of Chen Faying and Tao Yingxian (of Mai Diao Village, Luquan County) began when Chen fell in love with another man, Yang Chunfu, and wanted to marry him. Chen's father refused the match, and quickly married her off to a man from another village, Tao Yingxian. After the marriage, Chen moved into her new husband's home but, because she was dissatisfied with the match, "frequently returned to her natal home." Several months later, Chen went (by herself) to the Luquan County Court to petition for divorce. The court tried to mediate the case three times, but when she refused to conciliate, the court granted her a divorce.

Her husband refused to comply with the verdict, and brought the matter to the attention of the township government. The township chief, Li Qicai, agreed with Tao's refusal, and said, "Chen Faying was only recently married and now wants to divorce just like that (*san xin san yi de*); if things continue this way, who will dare get married when their wives can sue for divorce like that? If Chen divorces, I'm afraid all the village women will divorce." To prevent this scenario, Li issued a bulletin to gather all the women in the township, the militia, and Communist Youth League. On August 8, 1953, Chen was tied up and brought to the township government for a struggle session. Wielding her court verdict, Chen showed the crowd that she was now divorced, but the verdict was snatched from her hands by someone in the crowd and handed to Li. Li announced to the militia and the gathered peasants that they would follow the "old laws," not the new Marriage Law. Under the slogan "Injure the skin, not the bones," the gathered officials and peasants beat and spat on her. Grabbing her by the hair, they pulled her head back, pointed her face upward toward the sun, and forced her to "guarantee" that she would not divorce and would return to Tao's home, that in the next ten days she would not encourage anyone else in the township to divorce, and that after returning home she would "not hang herself or jump in the river to commit suicide." Under this pressure Chen agreed to the conditions, and was released.

Even though Chen escaped, Chen's mother was still furious at the local officials who led the struggle session. She ran off to the Luquan County Court to accuse the township cadres of not implementing the court's verdict. This complaint led to the arrest of the township chief, who received a one-year prison term. Chen's mother, even though she brought the suit, was criticized for arranging her daughter's marriage in the first place. The head of the township militia was also seriously reprimanded. The court brought the case to the attention of a districtwide peasant association meeting, where the cadres responsible for mishandling the case were roundly criticized.[143]

4. The Thin and Scattered State: The Case of Luo Caixian

The most important role the court served was as an institution of last resort for women whose divorce suits were stifled by village- and township-level cadres. But another important role courts played was fulfilled by their very presence as an institution required to listen to peasants' complaints. Peasants in Yunnan, like their counterparts in the Shanghai and Beijing suburbs, had a panoply of state institutions that could offer them redress. Divorce cases might be brought to peasant associations, township governments, district governments, county governments, and county courts. As the case of Luo Caixian demonstrates, if one institution proved recalcitrant, peasants could go to another one; the lack of communication between geographically scattered state institutions (in contrast to the ease of making telephone calls between the work unit and court in dense urban areas) made it very difficult for state officials to coordinate their actions and corroborate testimonies. As a result, women had the opportunity to receive multiple hearings. The more institutions there were, the higher the probability that one of them would finally grant a divorce request.

Luo Caixian, of Yikang Township, Da Village, was married to Song Jiafu in 1941. Their marriage had been arranged by their parents. The couple did not get along well, and after two years of marriage Luo returned to her natal home. By 1951 the couple had been separated for eight years, but not yet formally divorced. In June 1951 Song went to the township government to request one, but officials refused to hear her case. In early July she went to the district government, but the district official who heard her case told her to "go back to the village." This happened twice. On the third trip to the district Luo again encountered obstructionist tactics. Angered, Luo yelled at the district official, "Twice already you've told me to go back! I'm going to kill myself right here and now!" The official replied, "You want to kill yourself, go ahead. Do it here. I don't care. You shouldn't be so tough. If you want a divorce you only have to pay one hundred thousand yuan." Taking advantage of this opening, Luo bargained for a better deal, reducing the amount to thirty thousand, payable within three months. She returned home and tried, unsuccessfully, to scrape up the money. In October, Luo did not go to the district again, but instead to court. The court heard her complaints without having access to any of her materials. Relying solely upon her oral testimony, they decided to send a notice to the district instructing them to hand over the case. Luo divorced by December.[144]

DENOUEMENT: AT THE COURT AND DISTRICT GOVERNMENT

In courts and district governments, peasant women were granted divorces at an astonishingly high rate. At the same time that local officials and militiamen were busy finding ways to deter women from seeking divorce (often by intimidating the first woman who tried), some county courts granted divorces in 100 percent of the cases they heard. Moreover, the demand for divorce that we have witnessed in the cases above seems to have translated into a quite a few successful outcomes (as far as the plaintiff was concerned). One 1951 report from Chuxiong calculated that a divorce occurred in 5 percent of all households in one year. In Mianyang District, An County, in northeast Sichuan, we can cobble together the scattered numbers in the reports and calculate that some 4.5 percent of households experienced divorce. And in a Lisu township, documents show that as many as 14 percent of households experienced either a wife or an adopted daughter-in-law "returning to her natal home" or "petitioning for divorce" only during 1952. In one minority township, some eighty couples were said to be "considering and preparing for divorce." Sources also demonstrate that district governments also handled many cases. Reports indicated an increase from 517 divorce cases in 1950 to 6,600 cases in 1953, a twelvefold rise that is impressive even with some population rise.[145] Such an outcome would not have been anticipated by the feminist literature on the Marriage Law, which does not treat the state in a disaggregated fashion, assuming instead a uniformity of patriarchal interests and values throughout the state apparatus, but particularly in rural areas. Nor would it be anticipated in much of the modernization and law and social literature. In these areas, there was little urbanization or industrialization to speak of, and courts were far away from plaintiffs and staffed by chauvinistic, frequently inexperienced Han men. Courts and district government cadres often did not have time to study the Marriage Law, or to deliberate each case. For women in courts, however, these features of courts and district governments often worked to their advantage. What the evidence shows is that "the state" did not, and often *could not,* speak with one (male) voice on the issue of divorce; different institutions handled divorce requests in different ways, and the dynamics of divorce requests at the level of village and township could differ dramatically from such interactions in courts, and in district and county governments.

Court and district government officials in the early 1950s were subject to intense political pressure. Campaigns such as the anti-bandit, legal reform, anti-counterrevolutionary, and Three Antis instilled in these officials an illness-inducing fear of the same party state for whom they, somewhat ironically, served as executioners. For many, fear was the result of the realization that private family behavior would be made public and used as a political litmus test. When officials heard that the "basic spirit" of the Marriage Law was to "protect the legal rights of women," and that one of those rights included the right to divorce, many court and district officials adopted the risk-averse strategy of granting it to them, fearing that if they refused and women committed suicide in protest they would be held politically accountable and purged.

When women arrived in court, few were willing to leave without their case being heard. After traveling for days, these women were tired, angry, and impatient. One report, for instance, noted that Dai women would "not leave" the district government until their case was heard.[146] Officials, on the other hand, were scrambling to catch up to the national political schedule, and barely had time to study the Marriage Law, let alone conduct proper divorce hearings.[147] In Yunnan, the plethora of different minority groups complicated matters further: cadres were expected to "respect" local customs and traditions they did not have the time or inclination to learn about.[148] Granting a divorce simply to move on to more important things was the result.

The *manner* in which plaintiffs came to court did not make the state's work any easier. Women in Yunnan, like some of their counterparts in the Shanghai and Beijing suburbs and Fujian, frequently came to the court in groups either to petition for divorce or simply to "watch the fun" (*kan renao*)—a practice that was an extension of other community activities: gossip, the "stealing the groom" marriage custom, "marriage lamentations," religious organizations, festivals, secret societies, and, after 1949, women's meetings and organizations.[149]

In the confrontation between court and district officials and peasant women, it is also possible that two types of "sexual culture" collided. Some educated Han court officials who were chauvinistic, who were too "embarrassed" to even come into contact with women, and who studied the Marriage Law in the bathroom or under the bedcovers came into contact with peasants (some Han and some minority) for whom discussion of marriage and sex was, in relative terms, more casual, or who thought that witnessing a couple argue and come to blows was fun to watch.[150] Those plaintiffs who came with their spouses might spend hours arguing with each other until court and district officials would get so irritated with the racket that they would grant divorces simply to get rid of them. This modus operandi led peasant men and even the Women's Federation to complain that courts were rendering hasty verdicts (*luan pan*) that were frequently (but not always) in women's favor. It was often the case that women, both Han and minority, left courts with divorces but had to forfeit claims to property, perhaps as a quid pro quo for the divorce.[151]

But officials also may have been inclined to allow divorces even if they actually took the time to deal with the particulars of each and every case that came their way. This was because women and court officials, despite their obvious differences, shared something of a common vocabulary—that of "feudalism," "eating bitterness," "liberation," and "emancipation." Women came to courts or districts to circumvent village or township mediation, which many rightly felt was biased against them, and invoked their rights to use the Marriage Law to "be liberated" or "resist feudalism." Some court and district officials, chauvinistic as they were, were familiar with this vocabulary and could be sympathetic to women's predicament. According to one report, officials had a "one-sided viewpoint" (*pianmian guannian*), seeing minority women—but not men—as victims of their "feudal" and "backward" marriage system.[152] In Guangtong County, another court report noted, male district cadres, upon hearing the official policy about nonimplementation of the law in minority areas, "were not happy. They wanted to know why this was the case, as they too [minorities] had been subject to the feudal marriage system, and their women had eaten bitterness."[153] After training, district officials returned to their jobs and insisted that minorities "understood the Marriage Law," and should now be able to use it instead of their own customs. Cadres, the report noted, "ignore the special features of minority marriages and minority methods of handling cases. When they handle the cases, most use the Marriage Law, and grant divorces if the woman claims the marriage was arranged."[154]

The language of the CCP's civilizing project in Yunnan was thus Janus-faced. Innocent minority elites were executed because they represented the "feudal" system that needed to be abolished, but at the same time the language of "feudal oppression" worked to free women from relationships in which they did not desire to remain.

CONCLUSION

The situation in Yunnan in the early 1950s was very different from that in the two areas examined in the previous chapters. Here, unlike in the city or the suburbs, few of the causes predicting people's willingness and ability to use, and success at using, new state laws to divorce were present. In the mountainous areas of Chuxiong, mechanized transport was rare; land, which facilitated divorce in the suburbs of Beijing and Shanghai, was a scarce resource; state administrative capacity was historically weak; communities, often the bane of expanding states, were relatively cohesive. If the enforcement of law is said to depend in part on the "capacity" of the state, and on a willingness and ability to access courts on the strength of community ties, there was little reason to anticipate a twelvefold rise in divorce petitions and one out of twenty households experiencing either divorce or a breakup of engagement.

To explain this outcome, this chapter has built on insights from the previous two. In the chapters on Beijing and Shanghai and their suburbs, I attributed the tendency of "peripheral urbanites" and suburbanites to go directly to courts and district governments, as well as to argue in front of local officials about their family conflicts, to the following: (1) a relatively positive "experience of the state," which resulted in *less fear* of the state; (2) the multilayered structure of state legitimacy; (3) the resources they were able to marshal to support their claims; (4) a bold "legal culture"; and (5) a relatively open "sexual culture." By moving from the city to the countryside, I have tried to trace the origins of these urban and suburban patterns. Divorce among the urban working class, I propose, was largely a result of their *rural* upbringing, rather than of their having benefited from urban modernity. Of course, the fact that the Yunnan countryside is different from areas of North or South China complicates this argument, but we will see in chapter 6 enough evidence from more "typical" rural areas to further reinforce it.

In terms of political experience, there is no doubt that divorce and marriage patterns in suburban and rural areas were linked to previous patterns of political interaction. In Yunnan, unlike the suburbs, the "wild west" character of state-society relations prior to 1949 required particularly harsh pacification by the CCP and PLA in 1950–1951. While scores of local elites, bandits, and other opponents of the regime were killed, these very actions contributed to the legitimacy of the central state in the eyes of those who were the most oppressed; this was seen most clearly in the case of Li Banguo and Pu Lanfan. At the same time, however, errors committed in these campaigns often delegitimized village and township officials, who frequently used political campaigns to avenge personal enemies. Courts and district government officials—because they were several steps removed from the village—had "room" to step in as more objective and reliable mediators and adjudicators and in this sense were more legitimate than their lower-level counterparts. Thus, even though there was little direct *legal* penetration into villages, the Marriage Law campaign itself created an atmosphere of fear and provided new institutions, a rough legal framework, and opportunities for women to seek redress. While it would not be incorrect to argue that "the" state had an important role in rural social change, it would be more accurate to emphasize that many of these changes were unintended, and that only *certain* state institutions played a positive role. Even when courts and districts—the main addresses for filing cases—followed the letter of the law by granting divorces to women who "deserved" one owing to an arranged or coerced marriage, this was often done *without* undertaking serious investigation or mediation as stipulated in the law. Had such intervention taken place, it is very likely that the delays involved would have resulted in many divorce suits being withdrawn due to family pressure, or else denied because of conflicting evidence or absence of documentation. For women seeking divorce (especially for reasons not covered by the law), the state's administrative weakness clearly was an advantage.

In locating the sources of post-1949 patterns of family dynamics we also have to look at the role of land reform and previous patterns of disputes over scarce resources. Historically, conflicts engendered by scarce resources often led villagers into the arms of central or provincial authorities. As competition for resources intensified during land reform, the state—particularly districts and courts—became a crucial arbiter of community conflicts, if only to prevent these conflicts from erupting into armed confrontation. This institutional role carried over to the Marriage Law. In a more general sense, the land reform process in rural areas was important because it further displayed the power of the Communist Party and scared members of the older generation and pre-1949 political elites, while at the same time convincing young women that the CCP could counter the power of their adopted families, communities, and recalcitrant local officials.

In his landmark study of the civil rights movement in the United States, Doug McAdam wrote that "a conducive . . . environment only affords the aggrieved population the opportunity for successful insurgent action. It is the resources of the minority community that enable insurgent groups to exploit these opportunities."[155] In China, both Han and minorities used many resources to take advantage of new opportunities created by the law, some of which were provided by the state, others of which were indigenous. Land reform and the Marriage Law, for instance, provided peasants in Yunnan with an empowering language. Words like *fanshen* (emancipation) and *jiefang* (liberation), and new rights such as "marriage freedom," allowed people, as the legal scholar Michael McCann notes, to "imagine and act in light of rights that have not yet been formally recognized or enforced by officials."[156] Of course, there was no way the state could have anticipated that people—mostly women, according to the sources—would also use this new vocabulary and rights to pursue relationships that were also considered quite unorthodox.

But political language was not the only resource peasant women employed to seek divorce or break an engagement. They also benefited from community, particularly in the way it facilitated collective action, provided refuge, and shaped a relatively "open" sexual culture. In the suburbs, as we have seen, women organized protests and petitioned for divorce *in groups* to overcome the many obstacles in their way. The Yunnan case further demonstrates the importance of community support in the divorce process. "Running" to natal homes, parents stepping in to prevent abuse, and other community members interfering in relationships to protect "one of our own" were all essential to counter the violent opposition by militias, township and village cadres, and groups of older women. In some cases, despite these countermeasures, such opposition undoubtedly deterred many women from seeking divorce, but in other cases it proved self-defeating, as it pushed those determined to divorce to petition for redress in courts and district governments—institutions that were more independent of, and cared less about, village and township politics and interests. For courts and districts, the law was more important than a village leader's demand that "their" women not leave the community. All of these officials constituted "the state," but a disaggregated perspective on it shows that common gender or self-identification as a "cadre" did not guarantee a shared platform for action. Community also facilitated divorce because there was much less concern about "privacy" and bourgeois or Confucian "propriety" in villages. Because there was little separation between "private" and "public," complaints that in elite Shanghai or Beijing neighborhoods would often remain "private" were publicly discussed and loudly voiced in rural China. And problems heard were problems that could be solved. I did not encounter any scenarios in Yunnan similar to the case in Beijing involving an abused female intellectual who took a silent bike ride rather than complain to her family, friends, or the state.

Peasants had other resources many urbanites lacked—space and, I suggest, more time as well. Unlike workers, who might be disciplined should they show up late for work, ordinary peasants generally had more time on their hands. Having extra time (particularly during the slack season) often resulted in boredom and the quest for a more exciting life in the city, but it also had its benefits. Spending several days in transit to court and another two haranguing court or district officials was common among peasants in Yunnan, but rarer among those urbanites tied to work units, the factory clock, and production shifts. Another highly critical factor in southwestern divorces was people's relationship to *space*. In the suburbs, if we recall, residents might commute to and from cities for work or leisure. In the Southwest, however, rural mobility, particularly among ethnic minority women, seemed to be even more extensive, taking them many miles away from their villages, whether this be in order to sell produce and handicrafts in markets, return to their natal homes after marriage, participate in "bridal and groom raids," or migrate to other rural areas or urban locales in search of a better life. This mobility served them well during the Marriage Law, when many women took up their bedrolls and ran back to their natal homes, from township to district, and from district government to court in pursuit of their new rights.

Women's mobility was a particularly strong card in the divorce process because it was complemented by the *state's* position in space, or what I have called its "political geography." Unlike "thick" urban units that could coordinate action by telephone, conduct house-to-house searches, and rummage through personal papers, rural units in Yunnan could rely only on peasants' oral testimony. Separated from each other by large distances, many government institutions simply did not have the means to verify conflicting accounts. Moreover there were, numerically speaking, more rural state institutions responsible for family matters than comparable urban institutions, each of which was authorized to grant divorce. The more institutions there were, the better the chances that one of them would accede. For women seeking divorce for reasons not necessarily covered under the Marriage Law (such as illness, baldness, bad eyesight, crippled legs, and the like), the state's "scattered" nature across space, in combination with the political power concentrated in each institution, was an advantage. These features, when coupled with the relatively high legitimacy enjoyed by institutions associated with the center, allowed women to take advantage of the Marriage Law, even if male officials were personally unsympathetic to their cause and the end result was not what was expected.

While few of these features might have been anticipated by the secondary social science literature on family change, my findings will certainly sound familiar to China scholars who have read the recent and pathbreaking work in social movements and legal history. These studies all show that Chinese peasants had an extremely litigious, confrontational, and feisty legal culture, that women often availed themselves of the state legal system precisely because of the inequities and power imbalances in village mediation, and that courts were very prone to rendering all-or-nothing verdicts remarkably similar to the 100 percent divorce approval rate in some areas of Yunnan and the 96 percent rate near Shanghai.[157] This legal culture was very much present in Yunnan, where scarcity of resources compelled people—Han and minority—to adopt a panoply of strategies, legal included, to expand or protect their resources.

As much as I have in this chapter attempted to resolve issues and questions left over from the previous chapters by looking at an area more typically "rural," I have clearly complicated matters by choosing the Southwest as a rural case. Generalizations based on findings from this chapter might easily be contested on the grounds that minority customs such as *chi shan jiu,* returning to natal homes after marriage, and stealing brides and grooms, as well as minorities' supposedly less "prudish" attitudes toward sex, were not at all "typical" of Chinese rural communities, and that divorce in *Han* rural areas might have an entirely different dynamic. At this point in the study, I will offer only a partial defense, as chapter 6 will deal with rural divorce in both Han and ethnic minority communities from 1954 to 1966. First, even in Yunnan it would be wrong to sharply distinguish Han customs from minority ones, because there were many areas where Han and minorities lived in the same villages and absorbed each other's customs. To be sure, there were "pure" minority areas, but in Chuxiong Prefecture, the location of most of the villages in the chapter, many villages were of the mixed sort. Second, I think we should be very skeptical of accounts that dichotomize "Han" and "minority" marriage practices and customs. While some, such as nude bathing, might have characterized only the Dai, others were common to both groups, such as returning to natal homes after short periods. It might have been the case that Han peasants were somewhat more conservative than minorities, having been more influenced by traditional Confucian ethics, but, given the evidence we have seen, it would be difficult to conclude that this supposed "conservatism" might prevent them from airing personal grievances in a court of law. Generally, however, I am unconvinced that Han peasants are very prudish about sexuality; their "sexual culture" could be as "open" as that of some minority groups in Yunnan. As one Chinese physician who specializes in sex has remarked,

> Chinese peasants may have very conservative values, but when it comes to sexual knowledge and techniques, they are better than the factory workers, and the workers are better than the intellectuals. Why? Because life in the countryside is very dull. The peasants don't have a lot of other things to talk about. So you have these yellow jokes and sex songs, very brash, very colorful—some of them quite ingenious.[158]

Such a view regarding educated Chinese is also echoed by youth who were sent to the countryside after the Cultural Revolution. One such youth, Yang Rae, recounts that she knew virtually nothing about sex until she began to work on a pig farm in a village in the Northeast, a job that required her to make sure that the sows and boars copulated and the sows were impregnated. Pigs copulating marked the beginning of her own sexual awakening, at age seventeen. She writes:

> This job was a big eye-opener for me! By watching the pigs, suddenly I understood everything about men and women. The topic of sex was taboo in China in the years when I grew up. No adult was willing to talk about it with a minor . . . In spite of my pride, in spite of my reason and the so-called good upbringing, I felt a crazy urge to mate just like the pigs, right there and then, with whatever man.[159]

Following up on these observations and what we have seen in villages thus far, I would argue that the starkest contrast is not between Han and minority peasants, but between peasants and educated urbanites. Yang's observations that "no adult" was willing to talk with a minor about sex and that "sex was taboo" were true mainly for people of her own class background (upper-class businessmen during the Republican period, educated CCP officials in the 1940s and 1950s), but certainly not for everyone in China.

Some comparative evidence lends support to this argument concerning class differences. For instance, Laura Engelstein cites late nineteenth-century Russian academics who noted then that peasants "saw nothing mysterious in sex; everything was natural, out in the open, and therefore also completely social." Another educated observer, himself of peasant origin, noted that "sexual relations [were] simpler and more natural" in the village than in the city.[160] Christine Worobec, writing about family life in the post-emancipation period in Russia, also notes that during village festivals such as the *khorovody* (which was somewhat similar to the Splash Water Festival in Yunnan), peasants' songs "touched on the purely sexual aspect of love and first sexual encounters by juxtaposing images of girls sowing and growing flax with boys trampling it down." Other village rituals, such as "bundling" (similar to "stealing a wife" in Yunnan) and the "deflowering" of the bride (who was not always a virgin), were also public occasions.[161]

Research on French, Turkish, and Japanese rural communities has also found a rather frank attitude toward sex. Martine Segalen reports that one observer of a rural French wedding in the nineteenth century remarked, "It is enough to have been at a county wedding to understand the natural, one could also say the innocent, way in which the crudest jokes were made and received." When women gathered in groups, Segalen notes, they spent much time "criticizing, denouncing, insulting, slandering, relating family histories." The sense of community fostered by such interaction was not unnoticed by men: "Nothing was more feared" among French peasant men than "a group of women gathered together at the wash house or bake-house."[162] Even in Turkey, where the power of rural women in their families was limited both by exogamous marriages and by their subordinate position in Islam, women sued their husbands using the provisions of a secular family law enacted by Atatürk in 1926. With a feistiness we have seen in rural China, in rural Turkey women (as of the 1950s) were quite bold in bringing suit against their husbands, sometimes bringing witnesses to court to testify that their husbands were often drunk or visited prostitutes. Such willingness to disclose affairs is not that surprising given that many community festivals (such as weddings, circumcisions, and mourning rituals) were sexually segregated. This, according to June Starr, allowed women to exchange "news of marriages, births, deaths, crops, and schools, in fact everything imaginable, including who was divorcing," without male interference.

When men interfered, however, women counterattacked. As Starr noticed on one occasion: "When a drunken male once stumbled into a women's group at a wedding, a mature woman picked up a board and hit him over the head to drive him away."[163]

In Japan as well, peasants' family relationships were quite fluid and there was a good deal of frankness in dealing with such matters, at least prior to mass rural education. Anthropologists working in the Japanese village of Suye in the mid-1930s found peasant women to be "frank to the point of boldness, inquisitive, unrestrained and outspoken . . . eager to pass on gossip, and interested in instructing their young visitor in everything from the techniques of raising silkworms to the most intimate details of conjugal life." As Robert Smith writes,

> To a degree that no literature I know of would lead us to expect, Suye women divorced their husbands. Or, more precisely, they terminated marriages of their own accord, and very often for reasons having nothing to do with the classic male concerns of household continuity and the rest . . . over and over again we encounter women who had been married several times and who themselves were the instigators of the dissolution of the marriages and the rematches. The record was held by one older woman, universally described as an impossibly difficult person, whose current husband was her tenth. She had either abandoned or thrown out all the others.[164]

Such attitudes toward divorce and sexuality *declined* with the advent of education, when "respectability" became more closely associated with drawing a thicker curtain around the private sphere. Village women in the 1970s, he surmised, "would doubtless be mortified to hear of some of the behavior of their great-grandmothers and grandmothers."[165]

In addition to sharing a rather thin divide between private and public affairs, Turkish, Russian, Indian, African, and Chinese peasants relied on similar strategies to leave abusive or unsatisfactory relationships, some legal and others based upon community resources. In Turkey, for instance, women filed for divorce in district courts, where they found judges to be more sympathetic than local officials—a pattern we have also seen in China.[166] Russian peasant women, like their Turkish and Chinese counterparts, other studies have found, rarely went to village courts, where judges were often related to men in their communities, but instead sought assistance from the more distant, and thus more objective, justices of the peace. There, they would berate their husbands—"I'll get my rights! You'll answer for the blow, and that's the last you'll see of me!"—or else return to their natal homes, which were seen as places of refuge and warmth.[167] Legal scholars of India have also pointed to a "flood" of litigation that reached British colonial courts precisely because these courts were "foreign" and knew or cared little about village politics and stratification.[168] In colonial

Africa, Crawford Young notes in a similar vein, foreign "district officers found little difficulty in attracting as many disputes as they wanted to solve; those who believed themselves unlikely to prevail through African juridical institutions . . . viewed the district officer as an alternative opportunity for litigative action."[169] The fact that the district officer was British or French was not as important as the leverage he gave the litigant in dealing with village disputes. Minority women in Yunnan viewed Han district officials, I would suggest, in a similar light.

If French, Japanese, Indian, Turkish, African, and Russian peasants shared roughly similar legal orientations and attitudes toward privacy and sexuality as in China, then why was rural divorce almost nonexistent in the former cases? In the case of Japan (approximately 1.7 divorces per 100 households in 1883; far fewer in 1935) and many African countries, an important reason was the absence of a revolution that shattered traditional political structure and of a law liberalizing divorce requirements. But what about France, Russia, and Turkey—countries that, like China, experienced revolutionary changes in politics and society? Why did they experience so little rural divorce? Here we must consider two crucial factors. First, in China, there was no religious notion that divorce was an offense against God, nor was there an institution similar to the Catholic Church or the Russian Orthodox Church, which limited access to divorce in France and Russia respectively. After their respective revolutions, however, both of these countries severely curtailed the power of the church over family matters, but still divorce was rare in the countryside. Why? Here we have to recall what is perhaps *the* distinguishing feature of the Chinese revolution: only in China was the revolution *peasant based,* moving from rural to urban areas. In the early years of the Russian and French Revolutions, the revolutions began and became strongly institutionalized in urban areas, and only after the consolidation of power in cities did they move on to rural areas. Likewise in Turkey's "revolution from above": Atatürk's civil code of 1926 was implemented in urban areas well before the law reached more rural locales in the early 1950s. Undoubtedly it was the urban base of these revolutions that contributed to the relative absence of law-led change in the rural family. China, with its rural-based revolution—which gave greater priority to rural social change, empowered peasants vis-à-vis the state, and staffed thousands of government offices with rural-educated officials—exhibited a very different dynamic than these other countries.

CHAPTER FIVE

The Politics and Culture of Divorce and Marriage in Urban China, 1954–1966

The prevailing view of the 1950s and early 1960s in the secondary literature emphasizes the weakening of the state's legal commitment to the "emancipation" of women alongside its growing power over private life, heightened levels of state regimentation and penetration of social and private life, and rising social stratification along political class lines. For many urbanites during these years, China scholars have suggested, political class became "caste," "friendship" was transformed into "comradeship," schools and factories became divided along "activist" and "nonactivist" lines, political indoctrination was widespread, and divorce was often politically motivated.[1] Chinese, and others who have written about or studied Communist regimes, have echoed these views. Liu Binyan, a well-known intellectual, for instance, writes: "In the days of Mao Zedong, politics permeated *every aspect of life in China,* and was considered more important than happiness, love, and even life itself";[2] Yang Rae, a daughter of two highly educated officials, claims that "in the fifties *people in China* still believed Chairman Mao's teachings: 'All cadres, regardless of their ranks, are servants of the people'";[3] and Lie Jie, a Shanghai writer and critic of Mao, writes that "by 1966 *the Chinese* could only think in Mao Zedong Thought; they had undergone a complete stupefaction of their own thought processes. Hundreds of millions of people were turned into clones of Mao himself."[4] Jianying Zha, author of *China Pop,* similarly describes the 1950s and 1960s as a period when "sex practically vanished from sight in Chinese culture" because the CCP "promulgated a stiffly antibody, antiflesh, antisexuality attitude" and "systematically eradicated all palpable signs of bodily interest and institutions of carnal pleasure."[5]

In this chapter I take a different look at this period. Intraparty reports, memos, and investigations—many of them handwritten and never intended for public consumption or propagandistic purposes—show that many urbanites, particularly the working classes, ignored or avoided the state's attempt to regiment and organize private life by aggressively seeking divorce and marriage without reference to the state's understanding of political good and evil. Often, this happened as the *unintended* result of unrelated state policies, such as crash industrialization, mass arrests of men, and the Great Leap Forward. Urban elites, by contrast, frequently succumbed to state efforts to enforce "socialist" sexual morality, whether out of fear or because of the overlap between their own and the sexual values promoted by state propagandists. Where this chapter largely concurs with previous studies is in its depiction of the increasing difficulty in obtaining a divorce. After 1953, the actual number of divorces granted decreased dramatically, with the exception of a small bulge in 1962–1963. In Tianjin, for instance, the number of divorces in 1964 was only one-sixth of what it had been in 1953,[6] and in Shanghai, one 1955 report noted, a lane with fifteen hundred households had experienced thirty-two divorces between 1950 and 1955: fourteen between 1950 and 1953 (.09 percent), and eighteen between 1953 and 1955 (1 percent).[7] What I add in this chapter is not so much an argument regarding the *outcome* of the divorce process as a "thick description" of its process, the various institutions that the state comprised, the way in which different sorts of people interacted with these institutions, and the impact of politics on marriage, friendship, and sexual relations from 1954 to 1966. It asks, To what extent does new evidence corroborate what China scholars and Chinese intellectuals have told us about this period?

Taking the years 1954–1966 as a single unit is not at all common in studies of Chinese politics and society, which have tended to use various political campaigns as landmark dates. While useful for teaching purposes, the campaign-driven timeline is less helpful in understanding the relationship between politics, marriage, love, and divorce in urban and (in the next chapter) rural China. What unified the 1950–1953 period was the party's proactive stance toward family change; the party, in its campaigns, "went to the people" to enforce the Marriage Law. Between 1954 and 1966, however, there were no large-scale campaigns to enforce the Marriage Law. From the perspective of the main "independent variable"—the law—there was no substantial difference between, say, 1955 and 1965, even though there were significant differences in the national political climate. According to this line of reasoning, it is possible to see the integrity of the years 1954–1966. But the reasons for this periodization go beyond change in the modus operandi of the state after 1953. Taking 1954–1966 as a single unit underscores a conceptual point made in this chapter: the time has come (and the material *is* available) for us to shift attention away from the impact of dramatic, but ultimately fleeting, political campaigns on society toward people's more mundane, more "everyday" interactions with state institutions at multiple levels. This is possible even in a period seen as highly politi-cized, such as the 1950s and 1960s. Shifting the focus from campaigns to what I would call the politics of everyday life requires, I suggest, a time line quite different from the one determined by Beijing.

What forces shaped family relationships during this period? To what extent was politics a consideration in marriage, divorce, and interpersonal rela-tionships more generally? Previous chapters have suggested that, in the 1950–1953 period, politics was rarely a consideration in marriage among many urbanites, with the exception of intellectuals. This finding may not be very surprising, however, considering that the state had been established for only a few years. A project as ambitious as changing the way in which people think about such matters certainly requires more time than three years, one could easily argue in response to the previous chapters. But during the late 1950s and early 1960s, there were more reasons to expect heightened politicization of the family. It would make sense, given what we know about China in the 1950s and 1960s, to expect that social life would follow lock-step with political life, that as society generally became more politicized, so too would decisions regarding marriage and divorce. It would also make sense given what has been written about the secret polices of East Germany and other regimes that employed tens of thousands of informants in every nook and cranny of society.[8] That citizens under powerful regimes might abide by the state's classificatory program in making choices about marriage and interpersonal relationships would also not surprise social scientists in-terested in decision making or in the formation of personal identity. From a rational choice perspective, people generally tend to avoid unnecessary risks and choose the option that offers more opportunity for material gain and/or social status. Since the regime condemned former landlords, capi-talists, gangsters, and their progeny, friendship and marriage with such per-sons entailed certain risks, particularly during political campaigns, when "class enemies" were dragged out and struggled. Association with a "coun-terrevolutionary" might put a permanent stain on one's political dossier, which, in turn, might be used to deny access to opportunities for upward mobility. In this sense, it would be "rational" to avoid such dangerous rela-tionships.[9] Social psychologists interested in identity formation might predict a similar outcome. The literature on social deviation and group in-teraction emphasizes the extent to which negative labels powerfully, and usually detrimentally, influence personal and group identity; people la-beled as "social misfits" will often come to see themselves as misfits, tend to associate with others so categorized, and have hostile feelings toward those with better prospects.[10] If negative markers of group identity (such as bad class status) can produce higher levels of hostility, it would not be unreasonable to expect that a highly coercive state intent on dividing the population into good and bad groups and preventing relations between the two would enjoy considerable success.[11]

But what if we found a wider gap between what we might have expected given a certain literature and new findings from different sources? How might we account for this? The first, most "dramatic" explanation would be to argue that the new sources require that we revamp our understanding of the period to account for the new findings. The second, "deconstructionist" position would argue that these new sources say a great deal more about their authors than about any alternative "reality" out there; that what is being described in the sources is nothing but a "text" reflecting the interests and power of the authors themselves, describing little that is actually factual. For instance, Liu Binyan's portrayal of 1950s China or Václav Havel's description of Czechoslovakia in the same period might say more about them and their particular social class than about the reality of everyday living for millions of others; alternatively, the new archival sources say more about what concerned "the state" than what actually "happened" in society. Of course, how one falls on this question depends on the inclinations of each reader, but I will say up front that I more inclined to the first alternative than the second: these new sources, even with their limitations, demand that we rethink what has become conventional wisdom on this period. Yet, at the same time, we should not ignore the question of authorship. So much of what we know about China during this period has been shaped by intellectuals' experiences; they are the ones who are more inclined to write their memoirs. Now, with the opening of archives, we have a chance to hear others, all much less literate, "speak." These voices, as we will see, portray a China that is much more human, lively, bawdy, and chaotic than what we have come to expect.

This chapter is divided into two sections. The first deals with the extent to which motivations for marriage and divorce were shaped by political considerations, and the second with how marriage and family disputes were handled by state institutions. Common to both sections are many of the issues I have highlighted in previous chapters: class differences in how personal disputes were handled, the meaning of marriage and divorce, the "thickness" of the state, conciliatory and confrontational methods of dealing with state officials, and the role of time and space in shaping political behavior.

MOVING UP AND OUT: URBANITY, ECONOMICS, AND CLASS IN MARRIAGE AND DIVORCE

In a 1984 article on Chinese views of social classification, Philip Kuhn pointed out four major social distinctions in traditional Chinese thought:

divisions based on occupational status (peasant, merchant, etc.), rulers and ruled (officials and the people), free and unfree, and rich and poor. According to Kuhn, there was little to prevent people from moving between categories: an imperial decree could erase the stigma of slavery; the classification of "peasant" included both rich landowners and ordinary peasants; and there was considerable mobility between poverty and wealth. The only distinction seen as more or less "natural" to the social order was between rulers and the ruled.[12] Marriage patterns were shaped by the norms and expectations of belonging to one of these classes. During the Song, as Patricia Ebrey notes, gentry families hoped to bolster their class position by marrying their sons and daughters to other prominent families. To accomplish this, mothers tried to cultivate values and behavior to ensure success in their marital prospects: "Women in this class," she argues, "should differ from lower-class women in much the same way upper-class men should differ from peasants: by exhibiting restraint, composure, and knowledge of books."[13] In the mid-Qing, the scholar-literati class, partly in an effort to maintain their class status among much upward and downward social mobility, identified their wives and daughters as "women who carried forward the status of their families and the honor of their class in the face of threats from all sides . . . they [mid-Qing literati] were discovering ways to valorize the status of brides and wives in their class and to emphasize the differences that separated marriageable women from concubines and women of lower rank." Naturally, daughters were groomed, through learning ritual, education, and reading "guides" to family living, to marry into homes belonging to their social class.[14]

The Communist takeover and the subsequent reclassification of Chinese society according to Marxist and political criteria attempted to invert many traditional notions of social and political classification. Rather than assign high political status to the educated and wealthy, Mao awarded many administrative posts to those with neither education nor wealth. After "Thought Reform" campaigns in universities, and particularly after the Anti-Hu Feng campaign of 1955, educated people were instructed to learn from the poor, "good class," peasants.[15] Furthermore, after land reform in rural areas in the early 1950s and the expropriation of private property in urban centers in 1956, wealth was dramatically redistributed, and a new system of political classification was designed to ostracize people belonging to the "black" classes. At the same time, the state valorized those favored by Marxist class analysis and who contributed most heavily to the success of the Communist revolution, the so-called red classes (cadres, soldiers, workers, poor and middle peasants, families of revolutionary martyrs). Yet, despite this reversal of what was considered good status, evidence shows that good political status (which meant low social status in the traditional hierarchy) did not always translate into good marriage prospects.

Nowhere was the discrepancy between high political status and low cultural status more glaring than among CCP officials (male and female) in China's cities. During the Marriage Law campaigns in the city, as I pointed out in chapter 2, new urban officials took advantage of the law to divorce their peasant wives and marry more "cosmopolitan" urban women. This situation continued during the mid-1950s as well; peasants, despite their high political status, were clearly on the low end of marriage preferences. In 1954, the Women's Federation in Beijing complained that cadres sought to divorce their peasant wives because the wives "lacked culture" and were "backward," and because the men "did not want to be seen with them in public." According to statistics from the first six months of 1954, one-third of all divorce cases at the Beijing Municipal Court were those of cadres seeking to divorce their peasant spouses.[16] At Beijing's People's University, where many students had originally been village- and township-level cadres, students were reported to have been particularly enthusiastic about replacing their peasant wives with urban ones. "After they enter the city," one report noted, "they hate (*xian*) that their wives are peasant cadres without culture, and petition for divorce."[17] In early 1957, a Women's Federation discussion of love and marriage problems among youth implored cadres to "help" their peasant wives progress, rather than divorce them because they were "backward."[18]

Among ordinary workers in both Shanghai and Beijing, preoccupation with urban status at the expense of political ideology was pervasive as well. Many of these workers hailed from suburban and rural areas, coming to the city to seek refuge from rural poverty. In the process, many left behind husbands and wives in the countryside. After living in the city for some time, these former peasants sought to quickly upgrade their urban status by divorcing their spouses and taking up with new lovers. Some took desperate measures to rid themselves of unwanted spouses. In 1955 in Shanghai, for instance, a factory worker named Wang Shenchang had an affair with a coworker and wanted to divorce his wife, who lived in a nearby suburb and worked transporting goods on the Huangpu River. Fearing for her children's prospects, she refused to divorce. Knowing that the courts would likely block a divorce on account of his adultery, Wang instead tried to kill his wife by capsizing her boat as she was sailing on the river. When this plot failed, he decided to murder his children, whom he considered the main obstacle to divorce. Under the pretense of a family trip, he took the children to the nearby city of Wuxi. There he pushed his eleven-year-old daughter into Lake Tai, where she drowned. His other child ran away, and Zhang was arrested.[19]

Some jilted spouses of these urban aspirants put up furious resistance to divorce. In their effort to prevent divorce, working-class women in Shanghai sometimes forgot any concern they may have had concerning "face" and engaged in public (outside factory gates) arguments and fistfights with the husbands' lovers.[20] Other women directly petitioned unions and government offices, raising what report compilers considered a "ruckus."[21]

Rural male transplants into the urban setting were not alone in seeking to acquire urban status by discarding rural women. Rural women, too, were eager to divorce peasant men, whether for better jobs, pay, or identity as an urbanite. Even rural men with good political status could not prevent women's mobility to urban areas in search of what they hoped would be a better life. In mid-1950s Hunan, the records of one National Women's Federation meeting reveal, entire villages were depleted of young women (seventeen to twenty-four years old), who packed their meager belongings and moved to the city. This provoked local peasants to pen a collective letter to Chairman Mao complaining there were no young women left to marry.[22] A divorce case from 1957–1958 illustrates how this might occur. In 1958, the Shanghai Women's Federation received a letter from nearby Nanhui County, Zhoupu Commune, regarding a woman surnamed Shen, who had been "happily" married since 1952 to a production team party secretary surnamed Cai. In 1956 Shen moved to Shanghai to work in a cotton mill. Six months later Shen and Cai's relationship deteriorated, and in 1957 she petitioned for divorce in Nantong County. When they denied her petition, Shen, undeterred, appealed to the Songjiang Intermediate Court. The Songjiang court followed suit and instructed Cai and Shen to reconcile. According to the letter, Shen was "unwilling to make any efforts to improve the marriage." Commune members felt that Shen's divorce claim did not stem from irreconcilable differences, but rather resulted because she "looked down on peasant cadres" after she moved to Shanghai. Her factory, for its part, supported her divorce because she was a good worker and "lively." This did not satisfy commune officials, who complained that the factory was "covering up" for her.[23]

Such preference for urban life continued during the early 1960s as well, when there was a large movement of urban workers and students to rural areas during the "xiafang" (Send Down to the Village) campaign.[24] One 1963 report from Shanghai noted a rise in divorce claims filed by men and women whose spouse had been sent down to the countryside. These workers, the report complained, "do not sufficiently appreciate the importance of agricultural labor" and use "material things and money as the only basis of marriage." Clearly they were also upset about the way in which workers viewed marriage and divorce in a larger sense. Expecting that marriage was a lifelong commitment and divorce something that one should seek out only as a last resort after many attempts at reconciliation, report compilers were upset when workers told them, "Firewood and rice make a husband and wife; no firewood or rice, the two separate" (in Chinese the couplet rhymes: *you chai, you mi, shi fuqi; wu chai, wu mi, liang fen li*). When male workers went back to their parents' homes during the movement, their wives then designated them as "having no future" and requested a divorce. When they returned to the city on furlough, loud arguments between them were rapidly followed by petitions for divorce. Such cases, the report noted, represented the majority of new divorce claims filed in suburban courts, and probably account for the small bulge in the number of divorce cases in Tianjin during 1962–1963.[25] The case of Chen Yanzhang, a worker and CCP member from Shanghai who returned to Duxing Commune in Shanghai County, illustrates this early-1960s trend in urban divorces. At the factory, Chen's monthly earnings had been more than eighty yuan, a very respectable salary at the time. His wife, surnamed Xia, moved in with him "because his salary was high." When Chen returned to the countryside, however, his salary was transferred to the commune each month. Xia was upset by this turn of events. When Chen returned to Shanghai to visit, Xia locked him out and refused to give him a water vat and commode, forcing him to go elsewhere to take care of his needs. After this incident, she petitioned for divorce.[26] Urban men displayed similar feelings toward wives who returned to the countryside. Jin Cuilan, a female CCP member from Shanghai who was sent to the countryside, found that after her transfer, her husband "looked down upon her" and refused to allow her to live with him in Shanghai. In the autumn of 1963 she became ill and went to live with her grown daughter. In her despair, she tried to commit suicide.[27]

Preference for cities, and the concomitant difficulty that rural men had in finding wives, led to trafficking in urban women to rural areas—an activity that was in clear violation of the state's household registration (*hukou*) system. Here we can begin to trace a reversal of the causal link I initially posited between state family policy and family behavior (see chapter 1). Whereas earlier chapters have generally focused on the state's role in shaping family change, now we can see how people's *own efforts* to change their family situation, in disregard of the state, shaped political outcomes. Trafficking in women was a product of a long-standing preference to live in urban areas, but since it was now in violation of other state policies, the security apparatus and other agencies could not but try to identify and punish the perpetrators. In late 1963, for instance, the Shanghai Women's Federation reported a disturbing rise in the trafficking of women from Shanghai working-class districts to two particular counties in rural Zhejiang Province. According to their investigation, most of the women transferred to Zhejiang were between seventeen and twenty-one years of age, and already on the periphery of urban society: Most did not have household registration in the city, frequently moved between city and countryside, lacked stable employment, or were failing at school; only some of these women had "bad class" backgrounds. In other cases, the women's fathers were in labor reform, and matchmakers played upon the mothers' political fears that their daughters would have difficulty in finding a husband. Other women were told that their future rural husbands were either "workers," rural cadres, or relatively well-off peasants, such as accountants.

To ensure that urban women would remain in the countryside and not return to the city, organizers of this marriage market (often comprising an older female and seven or eight associates) used black-market connections to procure products rural men would be able to use to satisfy the material demands of their new spouses. In the meantime, the Zhejiang men hoarded products—such as grain, oil, paper, and selected fruits and vegetables—that were strictly rationed in urban areas after the Great Leap Forward. After their arrival in Zhejiang, groups of these urban women were met by local officials and gifts were exchanged between villagers and the women. Most "recipients" of these gifts were ordinary peasants, but there were also some accountants, production team leaders, and cadres. All of these men's wives, the report mentioned, had already moved to Shanghai.[28]

The relatively easy transfer of people and commodities between urban and rural areas in the early 1960s was encouraged by certain state policies, in addition to ordinary people's preference to live in urban areas. After the disaster of the Great Leap Forward, many previous restrictions on free markets were lifted to increase agricultural output. By 1963 there were signs that the economy was recovering as a result of these policies (attributed to Liu Shaoqi and Deng Xiaoping and others). Opening markets came at a certain price, however, in terms of both social stability and the party's effort to inculcate "class struggle" after 1963. In Kunming, for instance, a 1963 provincial Women's Federation investigation on the political situation in a working-class area reported a notable increase in criminal activity, such as theft, prostitution, and "profiteering." Given the renewed emphasis on "class struggle" in 1963, party ideologues and propagandists blamed these problems on the resurgence of "capitalism," and sought to remedy the situation through an ideological campaign of stressing "class struggle" and "socialist education." Local officials, in contrast, were less likely to blame only "capitalism" or propose ideological solutions. Some said that "overseas Chinese brought the problems over," while others attributed the difficulties to lower enrollment in schools after the Great Leap; too many students, they argued, were loafing around with nothing to occupy their time. Not all "profiteers" were vilified, however. In fact, to the consternation of higher-level officials, there were more lane and alley women representatives who were "envious" of the "profiteers" for their ability to make easy money than those who thought they should be subject to struggle. Efforts to instill class consciousness also failed because local representatives bluntly blamed the Communist Party for the lack of social stability. One woman said, "Profiteers have emerged because of the free market; if there were no free market, profiteers wouldn't have anywhere to sell." Others were nostalgic for the

Great Leap Forward. During the Leap, one representative remarked, "everyone had work. In the evening you could sleep with the door open and nothing would get stolen. These days, though, things will get stolen even if you lock the door. Things were better during the Great Leap."[29]

Throughout the 1950s and 1960s, marriage patterns were shaped not only by urban and rural status or the mobility that was encouraged by party policies. Among workers and other lower-class urbanites, marriage choice and divorce patterns were also based upon occupational status and skill level, more so than on class considerations. In scouring archival reports, I have seen little evidence that the intraworker cleavages between activists and nonactivists emphasized by Andrew Walder was very important in the urban workforce marriage market.[30] Instead, rank-and-file workers sought to marry better-paid factory staff and skilled cadres; staff members, in turn, wanted to marry technicians (*jishuyuan*), even if they were under a political cloud.[31] The same attitudes that led women's representatives above to admire profiteers for their gumption also made it difficult to inculcate the sort of class consciousness that made poverty a political virtue. In 1954, for instance, a Women's Federation investigation team was disappointed to find that women in a Shanghai cotton mill were interested in marrying cadres only because of their high skill level, rather than because of their political qualifications and "attitude toward work."[32]

Because skilled workers earned more than ordinary ones, assessing a worker's skill level was sometimes the first step in evaluating that person's marriage potential.[33] One worker in the Shanghai mill was reported to have been unsuccessful in finding a husband. When the workshop director asked why she refused to go to the factory's machine maintenance unit to find someone, she replied, "Workers who clean machines have no status. They aren't skilled, so they have no money." The quest to marry high-skilled workers who earned more placed those with low skill and therefore less money in a precarious position in the marriage market, leaving many young men in some of the mills unable to find spouses. Low-skilled cadres had similar difficulties in Shanghai and Beijing. In a cotton mill, a female worker was to be introduced to a factory security official, but she refused to meet him because "he had a low salary and no skill."[34]

In urban China in the 1950s, higher skill level was not the only avenue to a better income and a more comfortable life. In the eyes of women workers, members of the pre-1949 bourgeoisie were also seen as better marriage partners than workers, even though many of them were subjected to political attacks. Like women's preference to live in cities, their desire to marry a member of the former "exploiting classes" irked the more class-conscious investigators. In 1955, for example, a female worker in Beijing's Yi Li Food Company reluctantly married a cadre in the Public Security Bureau. In complete disregard for the state's political hierarchy, this worker, with the sort of frankness we have come to expect from her class, told the interviewers that she regretted not marrying a capitalist. Had she married a man of means, she thought, she would have been able to "ride in the car and hire servants."[35] Another Beijing report complained that among female workers, relationships were established primarily "on the basis of material possessions, money, and status." "Women," the Women's Federation found, "see this as the best way to raise their own status."[36] Shanghai workers had similar hopes. A trade union report commented that women workers sought to become wives of shop proprietors (*laoban*), skilled workers, or workers in heavy industry.[37] If they were able to marry such men, they would then be able to leave the "bitterness" of factory work, stay at home, enjoy life, and buy clothes and makeup to put on their children.[38]

The quest for an easier life after marriage shaped postrevolutionary patterns of courtship as well. State officials, who likely expected working women to live up to ideological expectations of proletarian, socialist austerity, emphasized in their reports that women ignored pleas for frugality and demanded that their future spouses demonstrate their financial solvency through such gifts as clothes, watches, and cash. Some women, officials complained, "refused even to talk" to male workers unless they were first given these gifts. Should men fail in fulfilling their demands, women would then break off relations; some of the men, fearing they would never marry, committed suicide.[39] Some were reported to have married simply to justify the amount of money they had spent, or perhaps "invested," during courtship. For example, a Beijing couple realized during courtship that their "personalities were not compatible" (which the state considered a legitimate reason for separation), but the man married her anyway "because he already bought her some gifts, and was afraid all his money would be wasted if they separated."[40]

A more common method of dealing with these demands, however, seems to have been fabricating and inflating one's salary and position. Some investigations found that when men wrote, or had someone else write, love letters to potential spouses, they included brief statements on the bottom of the letters indicating their salary. Often women discovered only *after* marriage that the salaries were inflated, a fact that clearly reveals the limitation of marriage registration bureaus' and work units' investigative power into people's private affairs in some peripheral working-class areas. In what may be a cautionary warning to other women, the Women's Federation emphasized how dangerous it might be to be overly concerned with material possessions. Such women, the Federation wrote, might easily become victims of "seduction" by false promises of watches and new clothes.[41]

Whether such stories were reported to warn other women or as representations of urban reality is difficult to know for certain. Although there are elements of warning in these reports, it is hard to see who the "audience" of these reports might be, since reports were often handwritten, internally circulated, and not intended for public consumption. Most of the people reading these reports were other state officials, *not* ordinary urban women (many of whom were illiterate). In this way, these stories are quite different from those published in the mass-circulation press, which served a more didactic purpose. Cautionary or not, it does seem clear that a good deal of behavior went against what was officially considered "appropriate" from a political or social class perspective; investigators' eyes would not have turned to such events otherwise. Thus, in addition to seduction through promises of watches and the like, the Women's Federation also reported that working-class women had been seduced by shady, but relatively well-off, underworld figures, gangsters, and even "counterrevolutionaries." One Shanghai woman, surnamed Zhang, for instance, was said to be "honest" but one day "suddenly left home and took up with a worker." She lived with him in the factory dorms for two days, then returned home and told her parents she wanted to marry him. A day later, she changed her mind, went out again, and hooked up with a "small-time hood." The two then had sex and strutted around the city together. "He has some money," the report noted, "so she's satisfied." Before long the two were arrested for criminal activities.[42]

Like some of their working-class counterparts, female cadres in cities were also interested in using marriage and divorce to advance themselves, rather than seeing it as something one did for "love," romance, and the like. For these women, however, status in the political hierarchy seemed to be more important than their prospective spouse's level of "urbanity." According to some reports, female officials in Beijing bureaucracies sought out only men with a "zhang" (chief, head) character attached to their title, and refused to marry any male with any rank lower than section chief (*ke zhang*). These officials, the Women's Federation complained, were far too "status-conscious" (*diwei guannian*). Low-level male officials thus frequently found themselves without spouses, and complained that arranged marriages were better than free ones, since under the former system, men with low status and incomes were able to get married. Rank-and-file PLA soldiers in cities, even with their good political status, found themselves in a similar predicament.[43]

Much to the consternation of the Women's Federation, which hoped to promote stable, nuclear families, relationships formed on the basis of misrepresentation of income and status, desire for economic security, or upward mobility through marriage often did not last long. Evidence that such relationships did not last long are scattered throughout the sources, but do not show up in the aggregated statistics on urban divorce trends during this period. In Beijing in 1954, for instance, a woman met a staff member of the Youth Cultural Department, who told her that his salary was 170 yuan a month. Within two weeks, the couple married; none of the relevant state agencies discovered the lie. Several weeks after the wedding, the woman discovered that her husband's salary was in fact far lower than he had originally indicated and immediately petitioned for divorce. Friends encouraged her to stay with her husband and work as a nursemaid to compensate for the unexpected drop in income, but she adamantly retorted, "Why get married if I'm still going to work as a nursemaid?"[44] In Shanghai some marriages ended in less than a week, something that should not surprise us all that much now given the evidence and aphorisms about how people understood "marriage" in rural and working-class communities. A female factory worker named Hu Xiuying, for instance, met an "accountant" at a hospital where she was recuperating from an illness. To woo her, the accountant bought her a coat and a watch. Because Hu "wanted to marry a staff member," the two were married after three months of courtship; once again, the deception was not detected by either of their work units. This marriage, however, lasted less than three days. After moving in with her new husband, she discovered that her "accountant" was actually a janitor at the hospital, and had borrowed the jacket and watch. Infuriated, Hu divorced him.[45] In Beijing's Qiangen *hutong*, another report griped, a couple met "only once" prior to moving in together. He married her because he thought she was rich, as she had been the wife of a ("bad class") landlord; for her part, she thought that because he owned a store, he was good at business. Only after the marriage did he learn that she had lost all her property during land reform. His wife was alarmed that he owned not a store, but rather a small room cluttered with odds and ends. Within forty days the couple had divorced.[46]

It is doubtful that women such as Hu Xiuying abandoned their quest for upward mobility through marriage even after being tricked by janitors posing as accountants. Much like working-class marriages, multiple divorces also piqued literate investigators. In Beijing, a report grumbled: "Women don't like it that their husbands are policemen or workers because they have no future. They meet someone with better circumstances and then demand divorce." Some women (all the instances cited were workers, sellers of odds and ends, and peddlers) had been married and divorced seven or eight times, motivated, according to their critics, by a desire to find someone with better circumstances than their previous husband. Marriage and divorce, the federation complained, had become matters of "routine" (*xichangle*) for workers, and not entered into with the seriousness required of such important events in one's life. Ironically given its institutional role, the Women's Federation was moderately sympathetic to the predicament of poor men. The report noted that some men, but especially those who were unemployed or employed only part-time, were forced by circumstance to accede to these demands for divorce, as they realized they did not have the income to support their wives.[47] As one 1959 Women's Federation report acerbically concluded:

> There are some women workers who look down on manual labor and refuse to marry workers, or hate that their husbands are policemen and pedicab drivers and want to divorce them. Some want to marry only a wealthy man, after which they will be able to stop working and lead a parasitic life, even to the point of leading the lifestyle of the exploiting classes . . . Because women want property and money for marriage, many men have had to make special efforts in order to attract a woman. Because of this, there have been cases of corruption, crime, suicide, and murder.[48]

The quest to marry the relatively few men with high status or income was said to have resulted in intense competition among women, and in a concomitant determination so strong as to violate the Marriage Law's prohibition against polygamous relationships. In one Shanghai cotton mill, married and single women workers allegedly ignored whether the object of their affection was married or not, if he had children, or if they were violating the law, "so long as his economic situation was relatively good."[49] The competition among women was sometimes so fierce that brawls broke out between women vying for the man's attention and pocket. Victors of this competition would then be seen with their "conquest," and sometimes his other wife, strolling around the factory and city. A worker in the machine room, surnamed Lu, for instance, was known to be living with two women. The federation, rather than heaping blame on the man for his violation of the Marriage Law, instead complained that when salary day arrives, both women "hold onto him and do not let him go to work; the two women go to the factory gate and wait for him to emerge. Later on, the three stay out late eating and drinking, and are late for work the next day. Sometimes they don't show up at all."[50]

Despite the politicization associated with the Anti-Rightist campaign and Great Leap Forward, many women remained steadfast in their quest for upward mobility through marriage. Rarely, however, was political class per se (i.e., "I will marry you because I like your political class") important in shaping new relationships. Cadre status was important more because it ensured a higher income than because it was a highly respected social position. A hand-scrawled 1959 report by the union of a Shanghai food factory found that, in courtship and marriage, "most workers do not ask about political status, only how much the other person makes and their social standing." Those who met such men, the report indicated, were willing to suffer the political consequences. A woman worker in Shanghai, for instance, surnamed Zhao, was criticized in a report for "making friends" with a technical specialist in the factory. Soon afterward, she found out that her technician had been designated a rightist during the Anti-Rightist campaign of

1957–1958 and was about to be sent to labor reform in the countryside. Despite his political status, Zhao still wanted to marry him because he had a good salary and social status.[51] Other reports from 1959 confirm the union's findings. In late-1950s Shanghai, the Women's Federation complained, workers remained basically uninterested in political class considerations in marriage. Instead, they sought to marry anyone of the "three *yuans*": zhi*yuan* (staff), yi bai *yuan* (anyone with a salary over one hundred yuan), or dang*yuan* (party members). Party members were the target of workers' marriage aspirations, the federation found, not because of their ideological commitment to the regime, but because their salaries were higher than those of ordinary workers.[52]

POLITICS, DESIRE, MARRIAGE, AND DIVORCE

What can possibly be "political" about beauty, passion, and sexual desire? In most of the secondary literature, and in the section above, marriage selection has been portrayed more or less as the result of very self-interested, pragmatic calculations in which women and men sought to use marriage to advance themselves materially and in social status. This approach fits well within rational-choice approaches to decision making, as well as Darwinian-inspired accounts of mate selection.[53] The emphasis on "choice," however, may obscure more about the way in which relationships are often formed than it illuminates. In everyday life, people marry not only after calculating their "objective" interests, but also after feeling sexual desire at first sight, enjoying nights of passion, becoming obsessed with beauty, and of course, falling in love; this is the stuff of romance novels, not rational-choice theory. Unfortunately, the literature on marriage and family in China pays scant attention to this, emphasizing instead the powerful role of ritual, community surveillance, and the highly "restrained," unemotional nature of courtship, especially among peasants. "One of the most important constraints [on marriage] is the attitude that relationships between men and women ought to be regulated by the strictest sort of puritanical decency," write the anthropologists Sulamith Heins Potter and Jack Potter. Emotions, they add, "are not thought of as significant in social relationships."[54] Historians, as Dorothy Ko notes, have also by and large neglected the role of emotions, dismissing them as "either unknowable or too physical and trivial to be of historical value."[55]

Historically, states have been quite concerned with some of the results of spur-of-the-moment sexual encounters. Out-of-wedlock births, abortions, and divorce have long been at the vortex of social and political debate and social reform movements. In the United States, advocates of "responsible sex," abstinence, and "strengthening" the nuclear family to reduce the divorce rate have gained clout in recent years as out-of-wedlock births and divorce rates have risen.[56] In China, marriage and family reformers also proposed such measures: in addition to weighing a prospective partner's political standing, future couples, reformers said, should also consider whether their personalities are compatible, preferably after an extended period of courtship. In 1962 *China Youth* magazine, for instance, cautioned, "Before a man and a woman get married, they should thoroughly understand each other. One must make a careful analysis and judgement of the political stand, ideological quality, attitude towards labor, habit of living, disposition and likes and dislikes."[57] Desire and passion might then be doused by cold "reason" and the possibility of unfavorable political consequences. The question addressed here is, Did politics and reason overcome passion, or did passion contribute to the unraveling of the regime's hopes for modern marriages based upon extended courtship and love between "good classes"?

Much as they were during the 1950–1953 period, during the mid- and late 1950s officials from Women's Federations, courts, and Bureaus of Civil Affairs in Shanghai and Beijing were struck by the extent to which passion inflamed social life among urbanites, particularly the working classes, as well as the publicness and frank sexuality of such displays. Such descriptions show up in actual divorce cases, where they might be expected to be found given the fact that divorce is often (but not necessarily) the end of a longer period of marital strife, as well as in the more routine bureaucratic reports on everyday marriage issues in the working class.[58] Such reports frequently referred to the "chaos" of sexual relations (such as adultery, sex with multiple partners, or perhaps even passion more generally) especially in "small firms where party organizations were weak."[59] While reference to "chaos" may reflect literate investigators' bias against those less educated and orderly than themselves, the pervasiveness of out-of-wedlock births does give some indication that passions were not contained by marriage or politics, and that, literate bias notwithstanding, there were objective grounds for concern. In a Beijing factory, for instance, one investigation revealed that in a one-month period there were fifteen out-of-wedlock pregnancies among three hundred female workers, and another complained that underage married women had sex some six or seven times, sued for divorce, and then killed their infants because they could not afford to raise them.[60] Similarly, in Shanghai 50 percent of all cases of nonregistered marriages were entered into by single mothers who were pregnant prior to marriage.[61] The high incidence of multiple sexual partners figured prominently in investigation reports. In a Shanghai factory, one woman "had at least eight lovers"; another woman "had affairs with three men, all married: everyday one goes and another comes to take his place."[62] In a quilt factory in Beijing, one woman had nine boyfriends, but during the New Year festivities she was seen with yet another man. Several days after the party, she moved into his room.[63] Some couples did not keep these affairs secret. In a display of the relatively "open" sexual culture I discussed in previous chapters, one report noted that, on occasion, women workers would go out dancing with their boyfriends, after which they would go home to have sex. After their night of passion, the report noted, "the man would casually walk over to her and give her a hug," which would soon lead to a passionate display of kissing in public.[64]

Statist language sometimes offered workers a justification for their open displays of affection—yet another unintended consequence of the Marriage Law. In some cases, workers had sex in full daylight, and in front of other people. But if they were discovered and admonished by an official, they were reported to be "unafraid," and retorted that they were merely following the party's call for "open social interaction among men and women."[65] In Beijing, for instance, one report from 1954 noted, women workers held the view that the Marriage Law's notion of "love marriage" (*ziyou lian'ai*) meant that you can "have sex with whomever you please."[66] As state officials discovered to their dismay, "political language," once learned, could be a powerful weapon to justify very *apolitical* and unorthodox behavior. In other cases, more "traditional" methods of remonstration were used. A sixteen-year-old girl in Beijing's working-class Xuanwu District, for instance, reportedly had sex with various young men on several occasions. When her party branch tried to interfere, she "fasted for several days, cried, and raised a racket" (*you ku you nao*).[67]

Some homosexual party members in factories were similarly steadfast in their determination to pursue sexual relationships regardless of their political propriety. Lesbian women had sex, and occasionally did so quite openly, despite the official condemnation of this behavior as a product of "bourgeois" decadence. Ordinary workers, by contrast, seemed to have treated such relationships with much less disdain. Take as an example the case of a woman surnamed Bao, deputy director of the party's Women Workers Committee (and a member of the factory committee as well) at a Shanghai rubber factory. Bao took advantage of her access to surplus rubber to fashion a dildo, which she used in her relationship with a woman surnamed Lin, also a party member. Bao and Lin slept together, the report noted, "just like a husband and wife." Bao, however, was unhappy with the fact that Lin was married, and tried to convince Lin to divorce her husband by yelling at and insulting him in front of other workers. This dispute was well known both to fellow workers and to cadres in their neighborhood. In the factory, when workers saw Bao, they would yell out, "Hey, Bao! Is the dildo as good as the real thing?!" Coworkers were not, however, pleased with her attempt to induce Lin to divorce her husband, since they considered him a decent fellow; they were also dissatisfied that Lin was a party member but was nonetheless "taking the lead in divorcing." Lin, however, was unrepentant, and accused the union members who were interfering with her relationship of having affairs themselves.[68]

Male party officials were also tempted by the flesh, and in the process disregarded consideration of political class and state sexual ideology. In a Shanghai drug factory, for instance, the party secretary and chair of the union, Pan Juyang, had an affair with Xu Suzhen, the mistress of a capitalist. Despite being "educated" by the party on several occasions, Pan said that he would rather be dismissed from his union job than break up with Xu. Pan brought Xu to his home, where the two lived together with Pan's wife. Loud fights between Pan, Xu, and his wife were said to keep the neighbors awake for hours.[69]

Living and working conditions in factories contributed to the flourishing of relationships born in moments of passion. In factories in Shanghai and Beijing there were many workers who had arrived by themselves, and without the threat of immediate spousal sanctions, temptations of the flesh were easily acted upon. In addition, dense living conditions in shack areas and factory dorms made intimate encounters common. "Most illicit sex," one report noted, "occurs in small factories or in shack areas," and many divorce cases were reported to have been the result of men and women pursuing extramarital affairs; politics, reports found, figured only marginally.[70] In Shanghai's working-class Putuo District, for instance, Yang Delin, a pedicab driver from Anhui, lived with another pedicab driver, Yang Baoqin, and his wife, in a very small room. Delin was also married, but his wife remained in the village. One day, when Baoqin was out of the room, Delin and Baoqin's wife were sleeping close together when both succumbed to temptation and had sex. When Baoqin found them in bed, he was so furious that he "ran off to court." In a small factory in Shanghai, similar conditions resulted in "chaotic" sexual relations and "very many" women becoming pregnant.[71]

In addition to dense living conditions, the sexually segregated nature of urban factories contributed to what the some officials deemed "chaotic" sexual relations. In Kunming in Yunnan Province, some "unmarried workers in industrial districts" were said to be extremely anxious (*sixiang hunluan*) about their marriage prospects owing to the fact that there were very few members of the opposite sex in the factory. In one concrete factory, for instance, there were over two hundred unmarried men, but only four female workers. As a result, several workers requested to be transferred a cotton mill, where, among the very many women there, they would be in very high demand. In a mining district, similar anxieties among male workers led to relationships with women with unsavory political backgrounds, as well as cases of theft. To satisfy the women's material demands, as well as to fend off competition from fellow workers, workers stole money and property. Only in this way could they afford to marry.[72]

In addition to demographics of the work force, political campaigns in factories, ironically, also undermined the state's ideological goals regarding marriage and love. Campaigns were intended to strengthen party and state presence in local institutions, as well as to inculcate a certain threshold of fear among the population. The problem was that during campaigns against "counterrevolutionaries," secret societies, and the like, many male workers (but fewer women) were sentenced to reform through labor camps, leaving behind wives and lovers who continued to work alongside members of the opposite sex. In the absence of the husband's watchful eye, "very many" wives of convicted counterrevolutionaries and "elements under state supervision" had affairs with other workers, who seemed to care little about their lover's husband's bad political label. When party officials reprimanded them for committing adultery, workers shot back, "Adultery is no big deal. At most I'll be lectured at by the union or courts." In court, workers promised to change their behavior but, upon their return to the factory, often continued to engage in their sexual dalliances as frequently as before.[73]

In other cases, rather than political persecution leading to adultery, adultery was said to have resulted in political persecution. In a Shanghai cotton mill, for instance, investigators criticized a fifty-four-year-old female worker surnamed Xu for having an affair with a married man. This affair resulted in frequent arguments with her husband. According to the report, Xu went to court to accuse her husband of abuse and sue for divorce in order to get rid of him. The union and the court believed Xu's testimony and granted the divorce, in addition to sentencing her husband to a year of labor reform. After Xu's husband was hauled away, she continued to have sex with her lover, and tried to force him to divorce his wife.[74]

Not all were as bold as Xu, however. In some cases, women who were caught having affairs while their husbands were serving time felt so ashamed they committed suicide. One Huang Gendi, an unemployed worker, was said to have been engaged in several simultaneous affairs while her husband was serving time in labor camp for shady business dealings. Huang had an affair with a repairman at another factory. Their tryst was abruptly interrupted, however, when they were caught in the act by her adopted son, who informed the local police station. After "education" by the union and the local police, the two were afraid of being seen together, and in a lover's pact, they swallowed poison and died soon after.[75]

In other cases, infuriated husbands murdered their wives after they discovered them having affairs while they were serving time in prison. In Shanghai, for example, one Li Shiyou, the husband of a female cotton mill worker, was sentenced to two years in labor reform for "spreading rumors and causing destruction." During his sentence, Li's wife had multiple affairs and lived with a number of other men. Even after Li was released, his wife continued her affairs; on occasion, she stayed away for stretches of seven or eight days, accumulating substantial debt in the process. One night, after her husband caught her talking with another worker, he stabbed her. Li survived the attack, and her husband was sent off to labor camp again.[76]

Violence resulting from conflicts over adultery was also the cause of another man's sentence to labor reform in 1955. This case, much like Li Shiyou's and Huang Gendi's above, is interesting not only for its outcome, but also for its vivid description of workers' aggressive and bold legal culture. While this culture facilitated their willingness to expose family problems in state institutions, it also made them frequent visitors to courts and police stations as either plaintiffs or defendants. The plaintiff in this case was a woman surnamed Chen, a Shanghai housewife who was married to a transport worker surnamed Cao. Chen and Cao were married in 1948, and had three children. In 1952 Cao had an affair, and became "cold" toward his family, leaving home for days at a time. Whenever he returned from his lover's place, Cao pressured Chen for a divorce, but Chen refused. She told Women's Federation officials: "I'm a mother of three kids. How can I agree to divorce? He comes home at ten P.M. and leaves at five in the morning. I'm pregnant now, but he doesn't recognize the baby as his own. He humiliates me by saying I'm having an affair."

After the baby was born, the divorce case came before the court. Cao denied he had a lover, but neighbors refuted his account. As a result of this investigation, the court denied his petition. Cao then appealed to the Shanghai Municipal Court. During the hearing, Cao told Chen that her refusal was "unreasonable," because "the regulation of the Marriage Law is that if one party is determined to divorce, a divorce should be granted" (this was the version of the Jiangxi Marriage Law, not the one promulgated in 1950). Cao was confident his appeal would be successful because "the government lacks people with skill, so even if I break the law, I won't be sent to prison." But even if the appeal failed, Cao was still willing to commit bigamy for the sake of living with his new lover. "Violating the Marriage Law," he argued, "isn't the same as being a counterrevolutionary. I'll get six months at the most." After investigation, the appeals court also denied his appeal.

When Cao received word of the verdict, he realized he would never be able to divorce. Furious, he slapped Chen, and headed toward the kitchen for a knife. Chen took the children to a neighbor's home. Cao saw her escape, dashed upstairs, and proceeded to destroy all of her furniture. In the meantime, Chen, together with some neighbors, sought refuge at the neighborhood government offices and the local police station, which led to Cao's arrest. In court, Cao refused to "accept" the court's education (i.e., he did not express remorse) and was thus sentenced to five years of labor reform.[77]

In court cases from the 1960s, passion, or suspicion of having affairs, also figures prominently, even with the intense politicization that characterized the period from 1963 to 1966. A 1965 case from Shanghai's Changning District Court, for instance, involved a fifty-four-year old female servant named Shen Amei, who accused her worker husband of having sex with his neighbor in 1963; and in a 1965 case, a female temporary worker from Subei surnamed Tian accused her temporary worker husband (surnamed Hu) of being unable to maintain a steady job and of going to Hangzhou with his lover. The couple had been married for twenty-four years, and Hu had already served a one-year prison sentence for theft in 1953.[78]

To be sure, affairs were not only a working-class phenomenon; businessmen, doctors, and intellectuals also had extramarital liaisons.[79] In 1965, for instance, a deputy workshop director (with a capitalist family background) accused his teacher wife (their marriage was arranged in 1950) of having an affair with a fellow teacher, having sex at home, going to movies with him, eating good food, and selling her jewelry to pay for her and her lover's expenses. She countered by claiming that he had not "drawn the line" between his capitalist parents and himself.[80] Among students, however, there is little evidence of such promiscuity until the breakdown of social order during the Cultural Revolution in 1966. Informal conversations with intellectuals who were students in the 1950s and 1960s, as well as recently published memoirs of sent-down youth (which reveal how shocked urban youth were at peasants' sexual practices), show that the sexual conservatism I pointed to in chapter 3 continued into the early 1960s. As one teacher told me, "Sex among students was very rare. Should a couple be found out, they would be met with serious sanctions, gossip, and ridicule."[81] For Liang Heng, another student, it was virtually inconceivable that young people would have sex before marriage. Moreover, he assumes that in Chinese society generally, parents were the arbiters of their children's marital affairs. "Most young couples in our society," he writes,

> would never have dreamed of staying together in opposition to their parents' wishes. The Confucian tradition of obedience and filiality had been instilled over thousands of years, and even after marriage it was unclear whether your main loyalty was to your spouse or your parents.[82]

Not much seems to have changed with the advent of revolutionary marriages in the PRC. Even after Mao himself called for population growth in the early 1950s, Chinese youth remained shockingly ignorant and naively ideological about sexuality. As with most ideologies, such a view regarding sex could have originated only with intellectuals themselves and, given what we have seen about their views in the 1920s and 1930s, is not all that surprising. According to Rae Yang,

> Sex was bourgeois. No doubt about it! In my mind, it was something very dirty and ugly . . . Revolutionaries had nothing to do with it. When revolutionaries fell in love, they loved with their hearts. They didn't even touch hands. Of course, at the time it never occurred to me to ask: if our revolutionary parents

had nothing to do with sex, where did we come from? In fact, I was too ignorant about human reproduction even to raise such a question.[83]

Given these notions of "proper" marital conduct and ideologically inspired ideas about sex, Liang and Yang no doubt would have been shocked if they had witnessed what was happening in working-class districts in their respective cities (Changsha and Beijing), let alone in society in general. Such ignorance would prove lethal during the Cultural Revolution, when these sexually puritanical, Confucian-minded youth—ironically, in the name of the bawdy working class—were called upon to purify Chinese culture and "re-revolutionize" Chinese society. The conflict between these class differences in sexual morality and behavior will be discussed in chapter 7.

THE PURSUIT OF LEISURE AND FUN

In *The German Ideology,* Marx portrays the citizen in communist society as no longer subject to the division between mental and manual labor that prevails in capitalist countries. Communism, he prophesied, would "make it possible . . . to do one thing today and another thing tomorrow, to hunt in the morning, fish in the afternoon, rear cattle in the evening, criticize [culture] after dinner, just as I have in mind, without ever becoming hunter, fisherman, or critic."[84] At the heart of this vision was an interesting understanding of time. As Stephen Hanson points out, on the one hand, even in Communism people would continue to be subject to some time discipline—this in order to produce the necessary goods for society; "labor" still exists and requires some organization. On the other hand, the destruction of capitalist society would unplug a tremendous reservoir of time that knew few boundaries and would allow people to develop their creative capacities. According to Hanson's analysis of Marx's views on time, "socialism must abolish abstract, rational time itself." Lenin also tried to combine two very different notions of time. His novel conception of the "revolutionary" combined extremely rationalist or "bourgeois" elements: he was to be a modern "professional" at his task. Yet, at the same time he would devote every moment to the revolutionary cause and not measure his commitment by hours, days, and weeks. At the end of this revolutionary struggle, the party would eventually be able to transcend "bourgeois time." Likewise for the proletariat: in the postrevolutionary state, workers should not be subjected to the same sort of time restraints as they had been under the capitalist system. However, people would still have to work, and this required a rational, capitalist organization time. "The post-revolutionary state," Hanson' s analysis of Lenin sums up, "must be both proletarian and bourgeois, based simultaneously on a faith that time constraints will be overcome and on a recognition of the need for societywide enforcement of time discipline." Lenin's insistence that the revolutionaries who will lead the proletariat to socialism be full-time professionals who care little about other aspects of social life led to the exclusion of those people who were more time bound and had less time to spare.[85] This, in essence, lies at the basis of Oscar Wilde's simple, yet penetrating, critique of socialism: socialism, according to Wilde, would take too many evenings.[86] The political theorist Michael Walzer, echoing Wilde's critique, acerbically commented, "Socialism means the rule of the men with the most evenings to spare."[87]

Even if Marx and other revolutionaries often overestimated people's willingness and ability to pursue many different activities in a day, they were nevertheless aware of the importance of a decent amount leisure time to the development of human potential. Less sympathetic to untrammeled leisure, however, have been modern states and industry, which have fingered too much undisciplined leisure time as the cause of crime, licentiousness, and low productivity. Maximum productivity and social stability are maintained not by allowing people to do whatever they please in their off-hours, but by channeling their free time into organized, disciplined activities, such as clubs, sports groups, and the like.[88] At least officially, Maoist views of leisure time in the Chinese socialist state were similar to those in the capitalist countries that Mao railed against in public speeches and documents. According to Shaoguang Wang, the Maoist interpretation of Marx was that "leisure is merely the time given to workers for their recuperation . . . meaningful only if people use the time to rest, to reduce stress, or to enhance their physical and mental ability so that they can work more productively later."[89] Maoist opposition to leisure for leisure's sake was also based on a class analysis of Chinese society. Leisure was suspect because of its association with wealth, decadent urban living, and the disparagement of manual labor. It was in cities that most "bourgeois" vices (such as gambling, opium, bars, dancing, and prostitution) were concentrated, and it was the Western-oriented "leisure class" that took advantage of these opportunities. By emphasizing labor, productivity, and the utilitarian value of leisure, the state would transform not only the productive forces of the country, but its values as well.[90]

The natural outgrowth of this view toward leisure was the regimentation, organization, and politicization of time and space, much as society generally was said to have been organized and regimented in work units, villages, and the like. In the 1950s and 1960s, Wang argues, "students and workers were often *organized* to go to the movies, sporting events, dances, and the like together regardless of their personal preferences." In the early 1960s, free time became increasingly politicized, as the official media tried to convince people that all forms of entertainment had hidden messages that would subvert communist ideology.[91]

In its attempt to regiment and politicize leisure time, the state eventually encountered the same sort of obstacles that frustrated entrepreneurs and industrialists in the early stages of industrialization.[92] In the West and in China, many workers in emerging industries were peasants or farmers, whose idea of leisure was not shaped by an industrial conception of time or work-discipline, nor by Communist collectivist ideology or Leninist conceptions of party organization. In villages, leisure was not regimented: when not engaged in agricultural labor, peasants might go to hear local opera at the township or county seat, sit around and smoke and gossip, or play cards and gamble.[93]

The pursuit of entertainment and leisure, even in highly politicized environments, was the third shoal against which state efforts to politicize relationships crashed. My evidence shows that dancing, gambling, and the appetite for good food and drink made it very difficult for the state to politicize intimate relationships among a wide swath of the urban population, particularly among the urban working class. In addition, suspicions of extramarital affairs and the squandering of precious resources during all-night gambling and drinking sessions led to a substantial number of divorce cases.

In the 1950s, the dance floor was where the regime's production quotas and ideological goals regarding marriage often floundered. Dance parties—usually of the Western ballroom style—were hardly as regimented and organized as the regime hoped. In late 1954, a party report on the marriage situation in a Shanghai factory complained that there were "very many illicit affairs" among workers. Because workers liked to go dancing, they would take off early from work and wander about the city frequenting various places of entertainment until the wee hours, often with the assistance of street-savvy pedicab drivers. The next morning, many found it difficult to muster the strength to show up for work on time.[94] In Shanghai's Number One Cotton Mill, some party officials likewise griped that workers were "irresponsible toward love" because they "wanted to have a good time," "irresponsibly chose boyfriends at random" (*luan jiao pengyou*), "and left work to go to dances." One woman in the factory reportedly "specialized in making friends," taking off from work to go dancing, sometimes as often as six times a week. Other workers in the factory followed her example.[95]

The structure of the industrial labor force encouraged these visits to dance halls. Factories producing goods such as textiles employed many women but very few men, whereas the opposite situation prevailed in shipyards and steel factories, the vanguard industry according to the Soviet development model. For young women and men who had yet to marry, finding a spouse in such sexually segregated firms was a very difficult and frustrating enterprise. For these bachelors and bachelorettes, the dance floor was not only a place to escape the drudgery of factory labor but also a place where they might find a future spouse, as men and women from different factories congregated on the floor. In an agricultural machinery plant in Beijing, for instance, some women workers reportedly went to dance at the Beijing Cultural Palace "because they were not able to find a spouse" in the factory.[96] The dance floor, reports noted, soon became a quasi "pick-up" bar: couples met during a dance, and then went home to have sex.[97] In a 1957 speech to workers, a Women's Federation official complained about "flash marriages: couples go to eat, a movie, a dance, and in their passion get married . . . some take longer, but when they court the only thing they talk about is food, drink, and entertainment, not each others' thought (*sixiang renshi*)."[98]

Women, of course, were not alone in their desire to have a good time. As Mao's personal physician's memoirs make clear, high-ranking CCP cadres in Beijing (most of whom were male) also enjoyed late-night dance parties as late as 1958, and Mao is on record as supporting dancing as a legitimate leisure activity. "If you don't dance," he said, "you are culturally impoverished, and I have nothing in common with you."[99] Lower-ranking officials, however, were no less interested in promenading around the dance floor. This required not only a certain knowledge of the dance steps, but also, in order to make a decent showing, a woman who would be looked upon with envy by other dancers. On the dance floor, young cadres thus sought out beautiful (but not necessarily politically correct) women able to give them "face" in front of their peers. In 1957, a soldier and CCP member on Hainan Island wanted to divorce his peasant wife. He lamented, "How good it would be to find someone I could take for a stroll, or take dancing, out to dinner, and to the opera after work." The compilers of the soldier's case attributed this to his interest in "face," and to his having succumbed to "bourgeois and capitalist thinking."[100]

Passion inflamed by dancing could get couples in serious trouble with the authorities, especially if it led to a bigamous relationship. A good example is the court case of Yang Liying, a twenty-five-year-old woman from Wuxi, and her husband, surnamed Bao, twenty-six, from Chuansha County in the Shanghai suburbs. Bao met Yang at a dance hall in 1951. After dancing they became close friends, frequently going out to the theater and touring around the city. In December 1953, the court found, the two had sex. After this, Yang discovered that Bao was already married to a peasant woman. Nonetheless, because Yang became pregnant the couple decided to marry anyway, and had a public feast of good food and wine in December 1954. "After her consciousness was raised," the court claimed, she "became dissatisfied with this relationship" and sued for divorce. The court, finding Bao guilty of bigamy, sentenced him to a year in prison and annulled the marriage. Yang did not receive a very sympathetic hearing, either. "The plaintiff," the court wrote in its verdict, "had sex with him even after she knew he was married, and went through with a marriage ceremony anyway."[101]

In addition to the dance floor, the gambling table was another forum in which the pursuit of leisure time and state ideology of the family and marriage clashed. Gambling has always been a favored leisure activity in China, among both upper and lower classes. But concomitant with gambling's popularity has been its ability to attract the ire of the state and social reformers. The Imperial government, missionaries, the GMD, and later the CCP all condemned gambling as leading to, or associated with, crime, waste, and laziness. In the early 1920s, Sidney Gamble complained in his *Social Survey* that "it is one of the most unfortunate features of the entire Chinese recreational system that so much of their play involves gambling, often for huge stakes."[102] During the New Life Movement of the Republican period, gambling was similarly condemned, and the Communists, as seen earlier in this chapter, sometimes arrested people for the practice, even though Mao himself loved to play mah-jongg.[103]

Despite the state's condemnation of gambling and attempt to organize more wholesome and regimented leisure activities, many urbanites continued to throw the dice and shuffle the mah-jongg tiles. As with dancing, movies, and late-night pedicab rides, gambling was also said to have important repercussions in marriage and family relationships, leading to attempted suicides, divorce, and the sort of "rash" marriages that undermined state hopes for politicized relationships. In working-class districts in Shanghai, it was not uncommon for public confrontations to result from one spouse having lost precious resources during a gambling session. In 1955, in Shanghai's Xingxing Lane in Changshu District, for example, the wife of a peddler surnamed Wang "frequently gambled, and did not look after the household," resulting in loud arguments between the couple. Investigators reported that Wang was "thinking of committing suicide." Men also gambled, with similar results. A ticket seller on a tramcar was reported to "love gambling," spending hours away from home squandering away his family's meager savings. His wife was so upset that she too contemplated suicide.[104] According to Beijing's Dongcheng District's *Chronology of Major Events* (1957), gambling was particularly common among pedicab drivers, and "flourished" before and after Spring Festival. Losses at the gambling table, the *Chronology* noted, resulted in theft, arrests, and exasperated and desperate wives hanging themselves.[105]

Given that gambling always results in winners and losers, it is not very surprising to find that losses from gambling resulted in intrafamily conflicts. But in addition to being a game of risk and potential profit, gambling was also a social activity that brought people together. Prior to 1949, gambling and other recreational activities were usually segregated by sex, but after the Revolution, men and women came into increasingly frequent contact both in literacy classes and at work. State-sponsored recreational activities mirrored these developments. Despite the regime's attempt to sanction only certain recreational activities as appropriate for the intermingling of the sexes, the desegregation of the sexes could not but spill over into non-state-sanctioned recreational activities, such as gambling. One 1957 report, for instance, complained about "rash and careless" marriages and divorces among workers, who, after playing one game of poker, eating at a restaurant, and seeing a movie, "fell in love" and did not give due attention to politics. After marriage, such relationships frequently ended in divorce: "They get into a fight, and the relationship is soon over."[106]

Those who sat down to play cards met new people, but in the meantime they left their spouses at home brewing, worried both that their money was being squandered and that their husband or wife was having an affair. Violence and divorce suits often resulted from these tensions. A report from Shanghai's working-class Yulin District noted that domestic violence sometimes resulted from conflicts over gambling losses: if the wife refused to provide money to sate her husband's penchant for cards, he would beat her until she submitted.[107] In Beijing, gambling, and suspicion regarding extramarital affairs, were also said to be particularly prevalent in working-class neighborhoods; in 1953–1954, 50 percent of divorce cases in a working-class district were said to have been caused by "mutual suspicions" between spouses who feared that their spouses had someone on the side.[108]

Women beaten for trying to prevent their husbands from gambling away their money were not without recourse, however. Unable to change their husbands' ways, they invoked the authority of an institution that perhaps could, the courts. The high number of divorce cases resulting from "mutual suspicion" was one result of this. Take as an example the case of Tang Lai'a, a thirty-one-year-old Zhejiang woman of peasant background living in Shanghai's Changshu District. From the age of twelve, Tang lived as an adopted daughter-in-law with the man who was now her husband, Bing Yongquan. Tang and Bing married when Tang turned nineteen. By 1955, they had three children. According to the Changshu District Court's investigation, Bing "frequently gambled" and, as a result, "has not taken any responsibility toward his family's livelihood." To force him to stop gambling and take responsibility for her and the children, Tang went to court and threatened to divorce him. The court agreed that the couple should separate, but denied her request for alimony because Tang had already returned to the countryside. Moreover, the court argued, Bing was too poor to be able to afford alimony payments anyway.[109]

In Shanghai's working-class districts, charges of gambling, excessive eating, and drinking continued unabated on the eve of the Cultural Revolution. When we look beyond the official press (which has been the primary source of many previous studies of the period), we can see that ordinary life, for many working-class urbanites, continued pretty much as it always had, even with the growing calls of class struggle and the emerging cult of Mao among educated youth. What was particularly hypocritical from the state's perspective is that these calls for class warfare, which would be led and waged by the proletariat, were advanced at the very same time that internal party reports almost invariably depict workers as politically and sexually unruly, lacking in political consciousness, and generally unworthy of their assigned historical role. By 1966, writers of these reports must have silently wondered how the Great Proletarian Cultural Revolution could possibly be led by such "chaotic" people. A case from Shanghai demonstrates how ordinary concerns, tastes, and indulgences were more important in working-class divorce than politics at approximately the same time that this class was being exulted and charged with leading a new revolution. In 1965 Ji Meizhen, a twenty-five-year-old worker from Yanchang (Subei), sued her worker husband, Xu Zixian, for divorce. In her suit, Ji maintained that Xu "liked to eat but is lazy" (*haochi lanzuo*), "lies," "gets into debt," and "is concerned only with the pursuit of leisure." Moreover, Xu forced her to live with him against her will, and beat her even when she was pregnant. Xu did not deny his abuse or gambling, but justified his behavior by arguing that the "real reason" she demanded a divorce was owing to his debt and poverty. The reason he slapped her around, he argued, was that Ji herself had a bad temper. Court inquiries found that Xu in fact led a rather lavish lifestyle, spending a good deal of his time eating, and spending whatever he had in his pockets at the moment (the court referred to this as *luan chi, luan yong*). The case was eventually dismissed after Yu promised the court he would change his ways.[110] Nowhere in this claim, filed and handled on the eve of the Cultural Revolution, were there references to politics or class. This absence of political consciousness would soon have important implications for how workers dealt with those who were condemned (primarily by intellectuals and students) as political enemies during the Cultural Revolution, as we will see in chapter 7.

THE STATE

How did state institutions deal with marriage and family disputes during the 1950s and early to mid-1960s? Memoirs, the secondary literature on divorce, and interviews suggest that divorce was difficult to obtain. Li Zhisui, one of Mao's personal physicians, writes that, in 1958, divorce was "a difficult thing to arrange," a view echoed by Emily Honig and Gail Hershatter, who argue that after the campaigns to implement the Marriage Law, divorce (prior to the Cultural Revolution) was rare owing to the state's preference for mediation over adjudication. The main exceptions, they suggest, were instances of politically motivated divorce. An interview with a music teacher at the Shanghai Music Conservatory confirms these arguments. "In the late 1950s we wouldn't think of divorcing," he told me, "because it would be interpreted by the government as 'not being united' (*bu tuanjie*) when the government called for unity."[111]

Outside the lofty heights of Mao's inner court and the tranquillity of the courtyards of the Shanghai Conservatory, the reasons for divorce, and the state's way of handling divorce claims, were far more complex. First of all, there were many cases of divorces suits, but few of these seemed to be caused by conflicts over political ideology or bad class status. In a random sample of twenty divorce cases from 1955 in Shanghai's working-class Changning District, only three suits were filed because one spouse (the man, in all cases) was in prison; the rest were based on claims of adultery, drinking, unemployment, abuse, gambling, and the like. Second, courts still adjudicated marriage disputes, granting divorce in 65 percent of the cases heard, in comparison with 25 percent that were denied or reconciled through mediation. (Another 10 percent were dismissed). In cases from 1965, divorce outcomes (relative to the number sought) were indeed less common than in 1955, but courts still granted divorces. In a sample of cases in 1965 of the same size, 40 percent were granted divorces, 35 percent were mediated and reconciled, and 25 percent were dismissed. If we interpret "dismissed" as indicative of the difficulty petitioners had in pressing their claims, then the proportion of "nondivorce" outcomes was higher than the positive responses. From 1955 to 1965 there was only a slight increase in the number of petitions based on political claims (from three to four).[112]

How can we explain the discrepancy between the secondary literature, various memoirs, and the new evidence from China's working-class districts? In chapter 2, I discussed the different ways in which "core" urban elites and "peripheral" working-class people interacted with state institutions and the extent to which they were able to discuss matters of the heart and family in public forums. One plausible explanation for this discrepancy is simply that much of what we know about politics and the family in urban areas is based either on elite witnesses, whose own sexual and legal cultures are reflected in their analysis of the period, or on articles in the official press, whose writers also came from a certain class. Another possible explanation might build upon the *geographical* conceptualization of the state presented earlier. Where the state was "thick"—where there were many layers of institutions between the plaintiff and the court, such as in well-organized work units like state-run factories, banks, universities, and research institutes—filing claims was indeed difficult, but for the very many people who lacked stable work units and whose ties to the city were less dense, there were fewer bureaucratic hurdles to overcome. Which of these explanations helps account for divorce patterns among different sectors of the urban population after 1953? To what extent did different legal and sexual cultures and/or degrees of state "density" result in different experiences with state institutions in family matters, experiences that, in turn, explain the discrepancy between elite and archival sources? Our sample of cases from Changning provides some clues: in 1955, 90 percent of divorce cases (in the sample of twenty cases) were filed by people occupying marginal status in the urban hierarchy: nursemaids, pedicab drivers, vegetable and tofu peddlers, and unemployed and temporary workers. Where native place is indicated in the summary, *all* plaintiffs hailed either from northern Jiangsu (Subei) or from Anhui Province (even though Subei and Anhui natives constituted 60 percent of the Changning population),[113] areas known for their contentious legal culture. In the two "elite" cases in the sample, one was a no-contest suit that involved a physician whose spouse had already left for Hong Kong (meaning that there was no need for face-to-face confrontation in court) and the other a teacher who divorced her "counterrevolutionary" husband (who was sentenced to ten years in labor reform) because her work unit leaders and friends pressured her to "draw a line" between her and her husband.[114]

According to official policy in the 1950s and 1960s, "ordinary" disputes among urban residents were supposed to be mediated within residents' work or residential units prior to their adjudication in court. Factory workers were therefore expected to present their problem to their workshop director or union official (if the plaintiff was female, she might also present her case to the factory's Women's Worker Committee). In administrative work units such as schools, hospitals, and banks, personal problems were expected to filter up through the administrative hierarchy prior to a court hearing. In addition to work units, both blue- and white-collar residents might also have to deal with local neighborhood residence and mediation committees, who served as intermediaries between residents and the higher administrative authorities, as well as with local constables preserving public peace. According to official policy, residence committees were supposed to: (1) help arrange residents' public and welfare work, (2) relay residents' opinions to the local government, and (3) ensure that residents obey laws and regulations.[115]

In both neighborhoods and factories, problems that vexed these organizations during the first three years of the People's Republic continued well into the late 1950s and early 1960s. Inexperience with hands-on mediation work, the lack of time and local knowledge, and the interpenetration of personal prejudices with mediation work decreased their effectiveness and legitimacy at the same time they were being called upon to play a more active role in solving people's interpersonal disputes.

By establishing local institutions such as unions and residence and mediation committees, which gave representation almost exclusively to the regime's favored classes, the CCP virtually guaranteed that these institutions would enjoy little legitimacy in the eyes of the local population. Although the favored classes were the majority of the population, people still believed that high cultural status (viewed in traditional Confucian terms), adherence to norms of decency, civility, and good work habits were more important than good politics. This clash between the criteria for high political and cultural status can be seen in material detailing the 1954–1955 local elections for positions such as directors of mediation committees, women's representative committees, and residence committees. Problems began when the party did not allow all residents to become candidates or even participate, and were further complicated when many residents were befuddled about these committees' function. One resident in Beijing, for instance, confused the term *jumin weiyuanhui*—"residents' committee"—with the phonetically similar, but functionally quite different, *junmin weiyuanhui*—"soldiers' committee." After being nominated by local residents, candidates for these committees were required to submit to a battery of political litmus tests before being formally placed on the ballot. This process involved disclosure of past political and social activities, family history, and views toward the Communist Party. Such vetting disqualified a substantial number of candidates: in one election, some 12 percent of potential candidates were considered politically unacceptable due to past participation in GMD organizations, secret societies, "political problems," or bad class or family background (such as being relatives of landlords, or being counterrevolutionaries). Sometimes, however, the vetting process worked in reverse, when residents disqualified candidates suggested by district work team members. One work team, for example, went door-to-door to persuade residents to elect a local fruit seller, but residents, who knew this particular individual for a long time, refused. When pressed for a reason, they said, "That guy drinks so much he can't even recognize east from west or north from south! Why elect someone like that?"[116] If officials persisted and engineered the election of someone residents opposed, the latter showed their displeasure by quickly electing people they knew the regime despised, such as former GMD officials.[117]

In general, political litmus tests usually resulted in committees whose composition was heavily skewed toward working-class residents with more or less clean political histories, but with little experience or "face" in the community. In three districts in Beijing, for example, 80 percent of elected committee members were either "factory workers," "worker family members," or "independent workers," and in Shanghai's Yulin District, among thirty-seven cadres in Lane 623, all but a few were workers' family members and "ordinary workers." In the lane's Women's Committee, "almost all" committee members were promoted from among residents who had become activists during 1952–1954. According to a 1955 investigation, these women's political status was "relatively pure," and their work style "enthusiastic."[118]

Political purity and an enthusiastic work style, important as they were to the regime, appeared to do little to reassure residents that their officials would be capable of successfully mediating marriage and family disputes. Most internally circulated neighborhood reports from the 1954–1956 period complained that, because local officials lacked "culture," "experience," and "confidence," they often failed to explain policies, or help residents deal with everyday difficulties or disputes. Frustrated by their own inability to persuade residents to obey certain regulations, local officials frequently fell back on ordering them around. These difficulties prompted charges that local officials lacked a "democratic work style," were "impatient," "acted blindly," "poked around in things they shouldn't [such as illicit sex] and don't care about things they should [mediation]," and "do not trust the masses' opinions."[119] Residents resented the fact that these officials had been chosen only because of their ideological purity, rather than on a meritocratic basis. If given the opportunity, they tried to reverse the regime's status hierarchy by electing residents whose political status might be shaky, but who were able to work well with people. "Residents err," one report complained, "by looking only at activists' work ability, without considering their political class." In Beijing's Baochao *hutong*, residents thus chose eight deputy group leaders, none of whom met the political qualifications to serve, and in another district, residents wanted to elect a man surnamed Wang, a former capitalist, but cadres told them they had to "elect a worker."[120]

Despite their lack of legitimacy among urban residents, a good number of local officials nevertheless became infatuated with the small amount of power placed in their hands. During mediation sessions, evidence shows, manipulation of the proceedings for personal or political ends was not uncommon and severely hindered the operation of the committees. In both Shanghai and Beijing, officials on mediation and residence committees were frequently unwilling to discuss a resident's problem with other committee members, preferring instead to solve the problem independently, and thereby receive all the credit should a solution be found. In Shanghai's Xingxing Lane, one Women's Committee member was reported to be "active, but wanted to do everything by herself." Work team investigators complained that she "sees all achievements as her own, seeks status, doesn't listen to anyone, and is impetuous (*jizao*) when dealing with people and their problems." Other cadres were terrified of incurring her wrath, and rhetorically asked: "Who's not afraid of her?" Similar accusations were made against a second mediation committee member, and others were accused of "seeking status," "pettiness," and "jealousy."[121]

These problems were not as dangerous to local residents as cadres' propensity to use the state apparatus to enforce unwanted settlements or settle personal scores. Reports on how residence committees worked pointed out that many of them ignored their roles as mediators and conveyors of residents' opinions and instead focused almost exclusively on their public security function.[122] In Beijing, a report on mediation committees' work instructed mediation committee members not to "punish or arrest" parties to a dispute, and reminded them that "mediation was different from adjudication: you can't force people into mediation." The same report also warned mediators not to take "revenge" against local residents during mediation. "Mediation," the report stressed, "should not be used as an opportunity to get back at someone for personal grievances."[123]

To deal with mediators and residence committee members who used their official roles to bestow favors and punishment, urban residents adopted one of two strategies. Some, one report noted, tried to curry favor with mediators by giving them gifts, which mediators accepted as tribute.[124] Others, however, became increasingly wary of local officials and reluctant to divulge personal problems. A report on lane and alley mediation in Shanghai in 1955, for example, noted a decline from previous years in the number of cases presented to residence and mediation committees.[125]

But there were other reasons for avoiding local institutions. After 1954, lane and alley mediation committees were reluctant to send problems they considered "ordinary disputes" to courts, believing them to be too "insignificant" to merit courts' attention. In Zhaofeng Road in Shanghai's Xuhui District, for instance, the mediation committee handled 371 disputes between October 1954 and October 1955, but of these, only seven (1.8 percent) were forwarded to court. In Xingxing Lane in Changshu District, work team (comprised of court, civil affairs, police, and Women's Federation officials) reports complained that local cadres "overemphasize reconciliation" in divorce cases.[126] Residents may thus have avoided mediation committees because of their inability or unwillingness to offer decisive resolution to their disputes.

District-level investigators of lane and alley cadres, in contrast, did not cite such calculations as an explanation of local officials' behavior. Instead, investigators argued that local officials' conservative stance toward divorce cases was rooted in their wrongheaded "thinking" (*sixiang*) toward marriage and the family. When female cadres who were reluctant to divorce or sue their husbands for abuse explained their hesitation by arguing that "men will be men," or that, should they divorce, they would be unable to collect alimony, they were criticized by work team members as having a "mistaken viewpoint." Male officials who refused to send marriage disputes to court because they were convinced that women were petitioning for divorce only because of their own illicit affairs, or their husbands' poverty or unemployment, were similarly criticized for "chauvinism" or for not understanding the Marriage Law.[127]

According to Andrew Walder in his *Communist Neotraditionalism,* one of the major cleavages in Maoist society was between "activists"—those who played a certain role in implementing state policies—and nonactivists. "The party," he argues, "reaches out to the citizenry through constantly cultivated patronage relationships, in which active support and loyalty are exchanged for mobility opportunities, material advantages, and social status." As a result, in the Communist factory, "the distinction between activists and non-activists . . . is easily the most politically salient social-structural cleavage." Such activists, as his research and research by Stanley Rosen, Hong Yung Lee, and others have shown, tended to be those who had "good" political class, while nonactivists came from the "black" classes.[128] A "bottom-up" or "anthropological" look at how the state worked on a day-to-day level, however, reveals that the cost of "activism" could outweigh its benefits, and caused not a few activists to rue the day they agreed to undertake the state's grunt work. When handling marriage disputes, for example, many activists found that they were too busy running around the neighborhood or participating in endless meetings to mediate or accompany residents to court. Not a few harried activists came to realize that such political participation did not always lead to new opportunities or more resources, as these tended to be monopolized by cadres who were on state payroll and had far better connection to higher authorities. Unlike local activists, cadres on state payroll (or *tuochan ganbu*, "cadres who have left production") did not have to balance their everyday jobs with neighborhood political activities, and the glaring disparity in privileges led to a good deal of resentment toward them. In these circumstances, activists' family members refused to support their parents' political involvement, loyalty to the regime notwithstanding. In 1956, for instance, the daughter of a neighborhood activist in Beijing wrote a letter to the district government complaining that her mother "was so busy with neighborhood work she has no time to look after the household. She has no time to cook, and there is no one else in the house to help her." Some local officials looked in desperation for an escape from their relentless schedule of meetings: "Life," one surmised, "can't be as good as death."[129]

Payrolled cadres were frequently unsympathetic to the plight of their more harried counterparts. When neighborhood officials were unable to participate in police precinct meetings because of their schedule, they criticized them as "backward" (*luohuo*). Neighborhood activists were also resentful that, unlike payrolled officials, they received no time off on Sunday and were not allocated state housing or provided with child-care facilities. When they complained about this, they were again criticized by higher-level officials as "backward." In retort, neighborhood officials asked, "Can this really be Marxism-Leninism?"; "Is this 'serving the people'?"; "Is this the 'mass viewpoint'?"; "How can there be the same demands for activists as full-time cadres?"[130]

Conflicts between neighborhood officials and payrolled cadres some-times came to a head in marriage and family disputes. Busy with meetings, some neighborhood officials found themselves mediating and cooking at the same time, children scurrying around their feet.[131] Court officials also had food on their minds, but seemed to be completely unaware of the time constraints experienced by lower-level cadres when mediating cases. In Shanghai's Yangpu District, for instance, neighborhood cadres who accom-panied a couple to court were in the midst of presenting their evidence when, at noon, the lunch bell rang. Judges promptly ended the discussion and dismissed the parties. When neighborhood officials complained, court officials cut them off: "I want to eat! I don't need to see any more evidence or listen to any more testimony!"[132]

Not surprisingly, hungry court officials rarely displayed wisdom in their disposition of marriage dispute cases, frustrating neighborhood cadres and plaintiffs alike. When courts either dismissed cases perfunctorily or handed down verdicts on the basis of the situation of their stomachs, they placed the already harried neighborhood cadres in the awkward position of imple-menting their decisions, almost guaranteeing that decisions regarding al-imony and property would not be successfully carried out. Neighborhood officials and residents in Shanghai's Hongkou and Yangpu Districts fre-quently complained that court officials' work was "slapdash"(*cuzhi daye*), particularly concerning property and custody issues.[133] Bureau of Civil Af-fairs officials were no better. In 1955 in Shanghai's Xuhui District, an in-vestigation into problems with marriage and divorce registration bureaus found that "in not a few districts, those who come to divorce for the first time are not even issued a formal application. Many cadres say that 'this is a very good method.' They figure that if the couple does not return for a formal application, they will have saved themselves a lot of hassle (*mafan*)." As a result of this, there were not a few couples that were living in biga-mous relationships, at least according to law.[134] In other cases, municipal reports criticized district-level registration bureaus for approving "rash" marriages: "some people do not take marriage seriously, but the registra-tion bureau lets them register anyway; a short time afterward they petition for divorce."[135]

For working-class urbanites who sought to sever their ties to rural ar-eas through marriage and divorce, marriage bureaus' mishandling of cases might have harsh consequences. Even as registration bureaus, in their de-sire to avoid *mafan*, turned a blind eye to the possibility that some couple seeking to marry may not have formally divorced, courts might still consider them guilty of bigamy, which was considered a criminal offense. Take as an example a divorce case in Shanghai's working-class Lao'zha District. A man from Henan surnamed Jia married in 1953, even though his wife was still living in Henan. Registration officials did not investigate properly and approved the marriage. When Jia's wife heard about his marriage, she made the trip from Henan to Shanghai to "negotiate" (*jiaoshe*) the divorce terms. Jia was eventually accused of bigamy, and his case came before the district court. The Shanghai Bureau of Civil Affairs complained that Jia's case caused his wife to "waste a lot of money on travel expenses, and also harmed production." The "masses," too, reportedly complained: "How can women's rights be secured if the government issues marriage certificates without investigation?" Although the ultimate responsibility for the mistake was the defendant's, the bureau found, "the case might have been prevented had the registration officials conducted a proper investigation."[136]

Slapdash methods of handling cases were not the only problem residents encountered when dealing with the state. Residents and investigation teams complained just as often about bureaucratic obstruction and delays as they did about irresponsible behavior. Courts, registration bureaus, and district governments frequently passed responsibility for divorce and property issues to each other, each hoping to save itself *mafan*. In a divorce case involving one Ding Guiyou and his wife, Li Suzhen, for instance, neighborhood cadres complained:

> We accompanied them to court, but the court comrade told us: "The couple agrees to the divorce, so they should go the district government." When we arrived at the district, though, officials said that they don't have the authority to deal with the matter, since there are still some unresolved issues. They told us: "You need to go back to court."[137]

Local residents sometimes sympathized with the plight of their neighborhood officials. In one divorce case in Shanghai's Changshu District, plaintiff Zhou Hubao expressed his frustration with the slow pace of the proceedings: "I want these proceedings to be over with. If anything happens [i.e., a suicide], I'll be held responsible. If we don't divorce this time, the residence committee members will surely drop dead from exhaustion. Each time they mediate takes up half a day. At this rate, they won't get anything done."[138]

Of course, it is not uncommon for bureaucracies to "pass the buck," as anyone who has dealt with bureaucracy knows very well. But what distinguished urban China in this respect was not so much the official reluctance to take responsibility for decisions, but rather the sheer *number* of institutions that, together, enveloped the lives of urban residents. It was this dense and sometimes dangerous web of institutions, coupled with complex property, custody, and housing issues, that slowed the pace of proceedings and contributed to the virtual freezing of urban family structure in the 1950s and 1960s. The intrafamily tensions resulting from these stifled divorces, in combination with the information gathered on urban residents by these political institutions, would soon have important implications for patterns of violence in the Cultural Revolution.

A court case in Shanghai's Changshu District involving two food-stand peddlers is a good, and I think quite typical, example of how several layers of local institutions might become involved in marriage disputes. The couple, Wang Jinrong and his wife, Dong Jindi, were often embroiled in loud arguments and fights. As a result of their fighting, the couple were frequent visitors at the local police station, residence committee, and court. According to the court's preliminary investigation, the root of the problem was that Wang was "very chauvinistic." When Dong wanted to work, Wang suspected that her real motive was to "have a good time" with a boyfriend. But later in the proceedings, a court investigator and local policeman confirmed Wang's suspicions: Dong was indeed having an affair. Urging them to reconcile, the court sent them back home, but when the fighting continued, the residence committee, located next door to the couple, tried to mediate, as did local household registration officials. All of these officials urged them to reconcile. When mediation failed, residence committee officials told Wang and Dong to "ask the higher authorities for a solution."[139]

"Higher authorities," however, were unlikely to ride in and save the day for frustrated residents. From the mid-1950s until the mid-1960s, district governments and the Women's Federation gradually lost their role as advocates for residents seeking assistance with family difficulties, most probably owing to their giving higher priority to ideology and propaganda than to solving people's practical problems. From 1954 to 1955, the Shanghai Women's Federation noted a 30 percent decline in the number of letters of complaint regarding family problems from the previous year, and from 1955 to 1956, a 64 percent drop-off. In all of 1959, the federation and other second-tier municipal institutions received only fourteen letters concerning marriage problems.[140] The Women's Federation interpreted the near absence of visits and letters from women in distress as a sign that, with the utopia of the Great Leap Forward, social tensions had completely dissipated.[141] A similar situation was noted at district governments. In 1956 in Beijing's Dongdan District, the district's complaint office received many complaints regarding unemployment and the "bad service attitude" among shopkeepers in the ritzy Wangfujing area, but none regarding marriage problems. Eight-five percent of those seeking assistance with jobs, the district found, "were those who lost their jobs [during the nationalization of industries] and [are] already registered to work, but have not received any notification regarding their prospects." Those who bothered to write letters, however, were usually disappointed with the results. District letter handlers considered letters a hassle (*mafan*), and the Bureau of Civil Affairs "rarely did anything with the letters it received."[142]

TOWARD 1966: STATE AND SOCIETY
ON THE EVE OF THE CULTURAL REVOLUTION

The sources we have seen thus far, ranging from party investigations to letters of complaint, are revealing not only because they give us an inside look at how the state worked in everyday life between political campaigns and remind us that the state, even in China, is a composite creature, made of different institutions often at odds with each other.[143] Analysis of the types of problems depicted in these sources and the way in which problems came to the attention of the government also tells us a good deal about society, especially the *class-based* differences in how urbanites dealt with the web of urban institutions surrounding them. A quantitative breakdown of the types of letters written to the Women's Federation in 1954 in two Shanghai districts with roughly similar populations—elite Xincheng in the core, and working-class Zhabei in the periphery—is suggestive. In the letters from Xincheng, 16 percent (n=602) involved either "accusations" or requests for assistance to go to court, in contrast to 40 percent of the 150 Zhabei letters. That there were fewer letters overall from Zhabei than Xincheng is not surprising given that the former district was home to many of Shanghai's poor, many of whom were illiterate migrants.[144]

Qualitative evidence from the mid- and late 1950s fleshes out the legal culture behind these admittedly inconclusive numbers. Working-class men and women habitually used courts and local governments to solve marriage and family disputes, even though these institutions became increasingly reluctant to intervene in the family. Often, reports about marriage and divorce in working-class districts were laced with complaints about the seemingly "casual" attitude with which workers dealt with family disputes. Much as the educated officials working in the state apparatus viewed marriage as the culmination of extensive courting and serious deliberation, so too did these officials view divorce as moral and legitimate so long as it too was undertaken with due consideration. For state officials writing about the subject, multiple divorce, like adultery and having many lovers, was yet another sign of the "chaos" and immorality of the working class. In Beijing, for instance, Bureau of Civil Affairs officials complained: "Some couples do not want to conciliate and do not give their relationship much consideration. Instead, they get into an argument and run to the district government demanding a divorce."[145] In one case in the capital, a woman surnamed Jin was married for eight years, but one day "ran to court" to sue for divorce because her brother-in-law from the countryside addressed her too informally—and, to her mind, disrespectfully—as "sister-in-law" (*saozi*).[146] Courts might also be used to regain face lost over a relatively trivial matter. Another Beijinger, surnamed Song, returned home from work one day and knocked on the door to be let in. His wife was in the bathroom at the time, and so rushed to the door half naked. Embarrassed that she looked like a wreck, he slapped her, and then went to the district government to petition for divorce.[147]

In other cities, party officials also complained about working-class urbanites' frequent visits to courts, in addition to the casualness (or, what *they* considered to be excessive casualness) of divorce. In a cotton mill in Shanghai, party officials groused that people were "too casual in seeking divorce: they argue, and then run off to petition for divorce. Picking up and leaving, they think, will do away with the problem."[148] In marriage problems among workers, investigators in another Shanghai factory (in late 1954) found that

> divorce is a relatively common phenomenon. Prior to the Marriage Law, couples frequently argued. They argued and that was that. They didn't petition for divorce on account of an argument. Now if a husband and wife quarrel, they demand divorce and can't be reconciled. They say, "Relationships are just like shattered glass: when shattered, the glass can't be put together again."[149]

A Bureau of Civil Affairs investigation from Kunming produced similar findings. During the first six months of 1954, Kunming Municipal Court handled 514 divorces cases; of these, 106 cases were classified as "rash." All examples cited involved workers. For instance, Wang Yunhua and Zhou Binyuan were divorced in February 1954, and in early April of that same year Wang married someone named Li. By April 17 Wang and Li had filed for divorce. In another case, a worker married on December 5 and filed for divorce on December 7, while others were reported to have sex "without knowing each other very well," marry soon after, and then divorce a month or two later.[150]

Such behavior continued well into the late 1950s and early 1960s, even as the official stance toward divorce hardened and disgruntled couples were told to "conciliate" in increasingly large numbers. Even so, there is little evidence to suggest that the change in state policy made a significant difference in terms of workers' propensity to seek out state institutions to demand divorce or to request other forms of assistance in dealing with abusive family members. It is likely, I believe, that the statistical evidence suggesting a rapid decline in the number of divorces granted by the state overlooks many *informal* separations that took place during these years. In 1959 in Shanghai's working-class Zhabei District, the Women's Federation recorded a case involving a worker at an oil-drill equipment factory, Xu Runsheng, who married a man named Xu Juanxian. The couple had met in a lane and alley study session in 1956, had sex, and then married; their daughter was born within the year. The couple frequently argued, however, and in 1957

Runsheng "ran back to her mother's home" and refused to return. From there she filed for divorce. Her husband was reportedly willing to conciliate, but Runsheng did not trust him, and refused a compromise.[151]

As in the early 1950s, throughout the later half of the decade working-class urbanites continued to draw the state into their family affairs. Even as the state used police, courts, unions, and party committees to mount harsh campaigns against intellectuals and other "class enemies" (resulting in many being shipped to labor camps), some workers still viewed the court, police station, and other state institutions as the address where they could exact revenge against those who treated them unfairly in courtship and marriage. State power thus worked in both directions. The state, to be sure, employed coercive power to repress many in Chinese society; at the same time, some were quite willing to use the state's coercive power against other members of society. For example, a woman named Dai Tianfeng, a servant from a poor family in Subei, requested that the Women's Federation help her "punish" a village cadre who reneged on his promise to marry her. The Women's Federation, however, was unsympathetic, and criticized Dai for having sex with this cadre "without proper consideration." This experience, the Women's Federation, hoped, "should teach her a lesson."[152]

Even though working-class urbanites used state institutions for a variety of goals, obtaining a divorce was made much more difficult by the consolidation of the "work unit" (*danwei*) as the primary institution governing the lives (salary, benefits, housing, food rations) of many urbanites during the 1950s and early 1960s. This, in combination with the state's preference for mediation over adjudication, resulted in fewer divorce outcomes than during the early 1950s, even if it did not necessarily stifle demand for divorce. As the following two cases show, the state, at least in urban areas, was often "thick" enough to frustrate plaintiffs seeking to extract themselves from relationships with which they were dissatisfied.

The case of Zhu Yunshen, a worker in the women's clothing department at the Bai'le Department Store, shows how work units' access to urbanites' private lives and their ability to contact courts with all the necessary documentation could stifle a divorce claim. After moving to Shanghai from a village in the late 1940s, Zhu met a man and moved in with him soon afterward. Her husband then introduced Zhu to a friend who worked at the department store, who arranged for her job. In the early 1950s, Zhu became involved in union work. Because union meetings often ran late, she either stayed at the dormitories for the night or returned home late in the evening. This situation continued for several years. In 1958, however, Zhu's husband became convinced his wife was having an affair. Suspecting that her late-night meetings were being used for extracurricular activities, he demanded that she cease her involvement with the union. After a particularly bad argument in late 1958, Zhu left home to live with the relatives of a coworker, a man surnamed Dong, who was a demobilized soldier. Incensed that Zhu had left him, her husband went to court to accuse Dong of "breaking up his family." Taking advantage of the opportunity, Zhu petitioned for divorce during the court hearing. The court investigated, and found that, in fact, Zhu and Dong's relationship had already "moved beyond that of comrades." The court thus denied the suit, and criticized all parties to the case. Zhu, however, was unwilling to relent. She refused to return home, and petitioned for divorce at the Shanghai Intermediate Court. The court contacted the department store's personnel department for their opinion on the case. The personnel department told the court that, since 1957, Zhu's "work style" was bad and that she "enjoyed going to local opera performances" with Dong. In addition, the court found that she was having an affair, and even "liked to put on makeup." As a result, Zhu's petition for divorce was denied.[153]

In factories, native-place ties might add another layer to already dense political institutions. As the political atmosphere intensified between 1962 and 1966, working-class urbanites found it increasingly difficult to obtain a divorce and even remarry as unions and party organizations began to pry more deeply into their private lives, often under the pretense of "correcting" their political thinking. The high number of dismissed cases in the sample from 1965 is probably a reflection of this. Take as an example the 1965 case of a thirty-two-year old woman worker named Xia Wenxiu. In 1965, Xia wrote a letter of complaint to the Women's Federation detailing a confrontation with her factory union. In 1955, Xia, an orphan, married a man who had been introduced by the aunt and uncle who raised her. The couple's relationship was never good; after their marriage, Xia discovered that her husband, a man surnamed Liu, was a "hoodlumlike" character who loved to gamble and had been having sex since he was sixteen years old. After their marriage, Xia wrote, her husband continued his affairs and his gambling, causing frequent arguments between them. In 1960, she was transferred from a Shanghai cotton mill to a machine plant in the Shanghai suburb of Minhang. The factory was impressed with her, and recommended her for university study. Xia was elated at the prospect of studying.

Liu, however, was upset that his wife had moved away, and repeatedly exhorted her to request transfer back to Shanghai. When she refused, he went to Minhang to confront her directly. Unable to concentrate on her studies because of her husband's harassment, she requested transfer back to Shanghai in 1961. Her transfer was approved, and she began work at a glass factory.

Despite her return to Shanghai, Liu continued with his old ways, frequently leaving the house for late-night gambling sessions. When Xia objected, he pummeled her. In June 1964, she petitioned for divorce at Hong-kou District Court. After a six-month investigation, the divorce was finally approved.

In August 1964, Xia met a man who worked in the security department of the Number Seventeen Cotton Mill, Jin Shunwei. Jin was sympathetic to her plight, and Xia was anxious to marry, as she feared that her age (thirty-two) and having a daughter would make it difficult for her to find another husband. In November 1964 she approached her section chief and branch party secretary to inform them about her relationship with Jin, and to inquire if she could continue to have a relationship with him. Xia's unit approved, as did Jin's after a three-month investigation. In January 1965, Xia went to the factory's union for its seal of approval. The factory union was unwilling to expedite the matter, and gave Xia numerous excuses for the delay. In the meantime, the union demanded that she submit a detailed political history so that the union could conduct a more thorough investigation. Xia was also asked to undergo political criticism (*sixiang piping*). Incensed, she asked, "What crime did I commit? To marry I have to go through political criticism?"

Because she was anxious to marry, however, Xia reluctantly agreed to submit to political criticism. This was to no avail, however. The union chairman demanded further investigation, and delayed approval for another two months. When Xia went to the union office, the chair avoided her by rushing off to meetings, or claiming he had no time. Fed up with Xia's persistent pleas for assistance, he finally told her that the approval was denied because her aunt disapproved of the marriage, as did the Number Seventeen Cotton Mill. When she expressed disbelief, the chair divulged the real reason: her ex-husband did not want her to marry. The union chair, as it turned out, hailed from the same native place as her ex-husband, had entered the factory at the same time, and the two were good friends.

Furious that her rights had been so flagrantly violated, Xia went to the Municipal Women's Federation office, where she discussed the matter for several hours. The Women's Federation, however, was unsympathetic. It argued that marriage between a bachelor and a woman with children should not be "hastily" concluded. Xia and Jin, they suggested, should spend more time getting to know each other prior to marriage. Moreover, the couple should both "rely on their organizations" (*yikao zuzhi*) to resolve their difficulties.[154]

To what extent was political class important in these divorce cases? The cases above give little sense that political class was ever the decisive issue leading working-class men and women to divorce, even though officials may have used class as an excuse to block divorces. Working-class urbanites did divorce husbands and wives sent to labor reform, but often this was many years after the sentencing. In other cases, political accusations were used as a *complement* to other claims, such as affairs, gambling, unemployment, and the like. Rarely was political class per se a reason to divorce. In the sample cases I have from 1965, a female worker sought to divorce her husband seven years after he was sentenced to labor reform during the Anti-Rightist campaign (the claim was denied).[155] In a dispute between Deng Chengfu and his wife, Dong Mingzhen, Dong accused her husband of "not drawing the line" between him and his capitalist parents only *after* Deng accused her of extramarital affairs and spending money on her lover, and in another Shanghai case, He Dinglin, a worker from Subei, sought to divorce his wife, Shen Baoxin, because he found out in 1963 (during the Socialist Education campaign) that, prior to their marriage, Shen had been a concubine to a landlord who was now in labor reform. In court, Shen took full responsibility for not informing He of her political history, and hoped that he would reconsider his claim. The court sided with her, and persuaded him not to divorce. According to the report, He "reluctantly" accepted the verdict.[156]

Elite urban women and men differed from their working-class counterparts in several respects. First, evidence shows that throughout the 1950s and early 1960s such women were very reluctant to expose family problems in state forums, seek punitive measures against their husbands, or divorce. For these women, the shift in state policy toward mediation made little difference, since they were reluctant to bring the state into their family affairs for their own reasons. Such women, after having "married well" (presumably after a good deal of thought and family consultation), were reluctant to separate, fearing that as divorcées they would not be able to find someone else of high status. Because marriage itself meant something different to elite women than it did to working-class women (who said, "If there's no food, we separate"), so too did divorce—differences reflected in their respective willingness to use state institutions. But even if there was a strong tendency to cause a rupture in their relationship, few trusted the state to deal with their problems in a fair and impartial manner—something that is understandable given their already shaky class status and local committees' impulse to "punish" and courts' "slapdash" or "bureaucratic" methods. Moreover, lacking the sort of mobility between city and countryside that was a prominent feature of working-class life, few would be able to muster the spatial resources to leave their families, even if they finally decided to ask for assistance; urban housing (especially in "core" areas) was scarce and often controlled by work units. Second, among elites, relationships seem to have been more politicized than among the working class. Bad class labels, in addition to restricting access to state institutions, were a stigma and sufficient cause for divorce. As a result, on the eve of the Cultural Revolution, an event that would place tremendous strains on the family, relatively high-status women and men found themselves "frozen" in relationships, unwilling or unable to seek outside assistance.

Four cases, drawn from letters received by the Women's Federation in the mid-1950s to the mid-1960s, illustrate the difficult predicament of urban elite women, whether owing to cultural, structural, or political reasons. The first example of elite women's conciliatory stance toward abusive husbands is a 1955 letter to the Women's Federation written by a woman surnamed Ma, who was married to a physician, a man surnamed Liu. According to Ma's complaint, Liu was extremely abusive toward her, demanding that she "wait upon him" after he returned from work. Even though Liu admitted that she had financial independence, and was busy with her own job as a teacher, she nonetheless gave him her entire salary, and did nothing to protest his mistreatment. "This is my heavy psychological burden," she wrote. When she finally discussed the matter with the Women's Federation, she stopped short of accusing him of wrongdoing. She also did not want the federation to tell him that she had even visited. If he knew, she feared, "he would be angry with me." Ma also requested that the Women's Federation not inform hospital or lane and alley cadres about their problem because, she said, "my husband is a man who likes face." Instead, Ma hoped that the federation could somehow persuade him to change his behavior toward her.[157]

In 1959, another woman married to a man at the top of the urban marriage market showed similar reluctance to make a formal accusation, or to seek divorce. Li Dexu, who was married to an engineer at the Shanghai Railway Bureau's telegraph factory, wrote the Women's Federation that her husband, like Ma's in the case above, did not allow her to eat until he returned from work. If she ate before he did, she complained, her husband would beat her. Even though she recognized that they could no longer live together as a couple, Li was not willing to petition for divorce. Her main fear was that she would not receive alimony or custody of the children. Even though she lived in the same apartment complex as the factory director and party secretary, Li was unwilling to press her claims to them directly. The Women's Federation tried to mediate the case, but was unsuccessful. Li's unwillingness to divorce led the Women's Federation to criticize her as "weak."[158]

The case of a thirty-year-old Shanghai woman illustrates how the intensification of calls for "class struggle" several years prior to the Cultural Revolution placed women and men of capitalist and intellectual backgrounds in an increasingly vulnerable position vis-à-vis their family and the state. Zeng Caifeng, a daughter of a capitalist, hailed from Nanjing, but now worked in a Shanghai dye factory. In 1962 she was introduced by the factory's union chairman to a worker named Wang Kunxiang. Wang, who was apparently uninterested in her suspect family background, began to court her. Within a short time, Zeng and Wang were sleeping together, using a birth-control device obtained by Wang. The device failed, however, and Zeng became pregnant. Zeng then proposed that they marry, but Wang turned her down, claiming he did not have the cash to pay for a wedding. "I was shocked," Zeng wrote. "This sort of thing is very shameful for us women. How could I now face my parents?"

Unable to turn to her parents for assistance, Zeng discussed the matter with the woman who introduced them in the first place. The matchmaker told Wang Kunxiang that he should take responsibility for his actions and marry Zeng. Wang again refused, arguing that Zeng had had sex with another man and that he was not responsible for the pregnancy. Wang softened his position only when the matchmaker threatened him with a lawsuit, which would likely have resulted in a detailed investigation into his private life, and possible criminal charges.

In October 1962, Zeng and Wang married, but Zeng paid for the wedding. Not long afterward, Wang had several extramarital affairs. Unafraid of Zeng's retribution, Wang hung several photographs of his lovers on the apartment wall, and proposed to Zeng that they invite one of his girlfriends to live with them as his mistress. When she refused, he became even more abusive toward her, occasionally beating her so badly she ended up in the hospital. Zeng also wrote that Wang made excessive sexual demands on her, forcing her to have sex right after a tubal ligation. Nonetheless, Zeng hesitated to reveal her family's "dirty laundry": "Our sex life was private," she wrote, "so how could I tell another person (*qi ke wai yang*)?" Only because her life was threatened did she decide to write the federation.

Several months after her operation, Wang petitioned for divorce, but Zeng contested the suit. In her letter, she appealed to Mao's promise for a better life for women after the revolution: "Owing to the leadership of Chairman Mao and the Communist Party," she wrote, "women's lives are now protected . . . I don't have the words to express how kind the party has been toward me." According to her letter, her situation was going from bad to worse because Wang "does not distinguish between public and private (*bu fen gong si*)" and told other workers at the factory about his exploits. He also threatened to kill her. Rather than go directly to court as many working-class women did, Zeng requested that the Women's Federation contact the Xuhui District Court to force Wang to compensate her for the wedding expenses. In the meantime, she returned to Nanjing.

The Women's Federation investigated and found that Wang was indeed having several affairs. In April 1966, two months before the onset of the Cultural Revolution, Zeng returned to the Shanghai Women's Federation to inquire about the investigation. The federation told her that there was little it could do because it had already contacted their respective work units; if the work unit did nothing, the federation was powerless. If Zeng was unhappy with her organization, the federation advised, she should go to court. Unwilling to do this, Zeng remained married to Wang as the Cultural Revolution began.[159]

Another case in Shanghai involved Lu Guiqiu and her husband, Zhang Qingyun. The Women's Federation summary of the dispute was relatively straightforward: Lu and Zhang both had "capitalist" class labels; after their marriage both had multiple affairs but were "unwilling to divorce." Sexual matters in Zhang's family were also quite irregular as far as the federation was concerned: there were reports that Zhang's mother was promiscuous, and that Zhang and his sister had had sex, but such issues were "kept silent." Because Zhang abused her, Lu moved in temporarily with another family in a crowded apartment. Unhappy with the arrangement, this family also mistreated her, largely at the instigation of Zhang. Zhang admitted to the abuse, as well as to taking away all of her clothes.

Underneath this broad sketch, however, is a more detailed depiction of social and political relations among relatively high-status urbanites, involving abuse, divorce, black-market activity, and suspicions of extramarital affairs. According to Lu's letter, Zhang was an assistant lecturer at Tongji University. Lu and Zhang were distantly related: Lu's mother was Zhang's uncle's second wife. The two met after Zhang's mother met Lu during a family gathering. Impressed with Lu's honesty, Zhang's mother told Lu that her son had a good temperament, and that they would be a good match. Lu agreed, and in 1961, when Lu graduated from middle school, they were married.

Five months into their marriage, Zhang purchased two train tickets to Jiashan County in Zhejiang Province. His plan was to go to Jiashan to buy meat at low cost, which he would then resell at a large profit back in Shanghai. His success in this venture led to more black-market transactions. In the fall of 1962, Zhang again asked Lu to accompany him to Zhejiang, this time in order to buy black-market cigarettes. He ordered Lu to roll tobacco, while he made the sales. Unfamiliar with tobacco rolling, however, Lu was very slow, and as a result sales were down. Returning home with only a marginal profit, Zhang berated her, but Lu remained silent: "All I could do was get angry; I didn't dare speak out."

In early 1963, their relationship deteriorated further. Zhang forced Lu out of their common room to live in the basement of their building, allowing her upstairs only in his absence. On occasion, he slapped her. No longer able to tolerate her situation, Lu returned to her family's home, but there, unlike many rural women who were sheltered by their natal families, she found no refuge. Her parents immediately forced her back to Zhang's, because, Lu wrote, they were "concerned about face." Zhang, who seems to have been somewhat of an exception among intellectuals, had no such concern, however, and petitioned for divorce at Yangpu District Court. The court, however, denied his suit as groundless.

In early 1964 Lu began to work as a teacher at a primary school, and by mid-1964 she had been invited to teach at "Broadcast University" (*Guangbo Daxue*). Zhang was not happy about the prospect of Lu's absence from home, and threatened her with a beating should she go. Lu did not put up much of fight and subsequently turned down the offer. In early 1965, Zhang became suspicious that Lu was having an affair with another teacher. On one occasion, as Lu was leading her class back from a day of labor in the countryside, Zhang confronted her on the road, announcing to her students, "Lu is a capitalist and is having affairs with Teacher Wu." As a result of his mockery, Lu left the school in June 1965. Later that year the couple separated residences, but fights continued. When cadres asked him to stop beating her, he replied, "This is an issue among the people (*renmin neibu de shi*); beating women is not a crime."

In her letter to the Women's Federation, Lu asked that the federation help her complete the divorce process. Without its assistance, she pleaded, she had no way to resolve the matter. Her husband, she complained, was a "monster" (*mo gui*) who would kill her if she did not leave him immediately. The federation, as in the other cases, was unable to offer much help. It sent a letter to Tongji University requesting that it speak with Zhang. The university, as well as the local police station and lane and alley cadres, insisted that there was nothing they could do, since the matter "had already been handled in court." Because the court mediated rather than adjudicated the case, none of these institutions could deal authoritatively with the matter. By March 1966, three months prior to the Cultural Revolution, Lu's case was still not resolved; she remained married, without a job or salary.[160]

Lu and Zhang's case is interesting not only for its depiction of lack of recourse available to women in instances of serious family disputes, but also for the absence of reference to political class: at no point did Lu argue that she wanted to "draw the line" between herself and her capitalist husband, calling him a "monster" instead. This may not be very surprising, given that drawing attention to her husband's class would also focus attention on her own politically suspicious background. Was this case, then, typical in its lack of politicization?

Other evidence shows that politics may have been more important than is suggested in this one case. In his memoir of his youth in China, Liang Heng recalls that his father, an intellectual, immediately divorced his mother (who had been unjustly accused as a "rightist") because he was worried about his children's fate as the sons and daughters of a rightist, and because "his commitment to the Party won out" over his "traditional Confucian sense of family obligation." "The Party," his father believed, "could never make a mistake or hand down a wrong verdict." This conviction shaped their personal relationships. When his wife returned from working in the countryside, Liang's father was upset. According to Liang, "he poured out a stream of words, political words—on the meaning of the Anti-Rightist movement, on her obligation to recognize her faults and reform herself. It was as if he had turned into a propaganda machine." When his wife argued back, he shouted, "Rightist element! Have some thought for your influence on the children."[161] Other memoirs written by intellectuals of the 1950s show that Liang Heng's father was not exceptional is this regard,[162] and appear to confirm Liu Binyan's claim that "in the days of Mao Zedong, politics permeated every aspect of life in China, and was considered more important than happiness, love, and even life itself."[163] This perspective on politics, love, and happiness, however, seems more true of Liu's class than of other sectors of the population. Among workers, the party was not nearly as charismatic, reified, powerful, and infallible as it was seen to be among many intellectuals.

CONCLUSION

Contrary to expectations of China scholarship and the more theoretical literature on decision making and identity formation, this chapter has argued that in considerations of marriage and divorce, political notions of class did not figure very prominently for many urbanites, and that this was especially true among the working classes. Even given the limitations of archival sources, the evidence presented here should prompt a reevaluation of the primacy given to political class during 1950s and 1960s China. My sources show that factory workers, tailors, peddlers, seamstresses, and clerks often entered into friendship, marriage, and sexual relations driven by status and economic concerns, urban or rural residence, sexual desire, and the pursuit of fun and leisure more so than by politics or political class. This does not mean that politics and political class were *entirely* unimportant, but only that, compared with what we might have expected given the extent of our knowledge of the period (from Westerners and Chinese), they were, in relative terms, not that important. Looking at divorce, my evidence suggests that decisions as to whether to file suit continued to be shaped by factors suggested in the previous chapters: the meaning of "marriage" and "divorce" and understandings of "private" and "public," legal culture, resources, and political experiences with the state. Among members of the working class, official state policy regarding divorce changed little in their propensity to *file* suits, but apparently made a difference in the outcomes of cases, as work units, unions, courts, and other state officials stifled them in increasing numbers (but not completely) even before they got to court. Among workers, demand for divorce remained high, even if the actual numbers of

cases with a divorce outcome declined dramatically after 1953. Among intellectuals and other core urbanites, on the other hand, it is not clear that
state policy made that much of a difference, since many were reluctant to
demand divorce anyway, and so were probably affected less by the mid-
1950s emphasis on mediation over adjudication—a shift that was a clear
reflection and manifestation of their own long-standing understanding of
the "seriousness" of marriage and divorce, and their Confucian-like disdain
for courts and open conflict.

Even as we acknowledge the power of the state to stifle family change (albeit not always the demand for it), we see that the relationship between the
state and family was not completely one-sided. This chapter also has shown
that, at the same time that state policy made it more difficult to divorce, the
way in which people went about trying to change their family situation—
their agency—ultimately shaped the nature of the state and the legitimacy
of its officials. That a person seeking divorce might cast aspersions on the
legitimacy of the mediator based on the latter's behavior in the family is as
important as the fact of mediators preventing the divorce. At least in this respect, the question I posed at the beginning of this study—To what extent
can states change family relations?—has been partially reversed; how family relations shape the nature and legitimacy of the state seems now to be
just as important a question. Answering this sort of question requires a different sort of methodology than those employed in studies of politics during this period. Rather than study the 1950s and 1960s as a period characterized mostly by intermittent political campaigns, I would argue that we
need to focus on what happens to ordinary people in everyday life *between*
these campaigns. Now that there is access to urban archives, we can begin
to reconstruct the politics of this crucial period in a different light. This
chapter has attempted to begin this process.

CHAPTER SIX

The Family in Flux:
Family and Personal Relationships
in Rural Areas, 1954–1966

The 1950s and 1960s witnessed some of the most dramatic changes ever in the Chinese countryside. During this period, whether in the suburbs of Beijing and Shanghai or in the frontier areas of Yunnan, the agricultural economy shifted from one based on household plots and small-scale mutual aid teams to one based on large-scale cooperatives in the mid-1950s, and the commune in 1958–1959. After 1958, the state introduced the household registration system (*hukou*) on a large scale, severely limiting peasant migration to urban areas. In the early 1960s, rural China suffered from one of the most devastating famines in human history after the failure of the Great Leap Forward. The mid-1960s ushered in intense political mobilization, targeting corrupt cadres in the "Four Cleanups" campaign and peasants' "feudal" and "superstitious" practices and "class struggle" during the Socialist Education campaign. Many of these events were the result of Maoists' impatience with the pace of economic and cultural change in the countryside after the revolution, disillusion with the city- and industrial-centered Soviet model of development, and conviction that political will alone can overcome objective limitations of the natural environment.[1]

According to the secondary sources on this period, these political and economic changes had mostly deleterious effects on the Chinese family, particularly on the rights, status, and freedom of women. The prevailing wisdom is that after 1953 there was very little rural family instability (divorce) because the state, preoccupied with class struggle and production, did not actively push for marriage reform. Absent such efforts, rural patriarchy succeeded in maintaining family stability, even as young people gained more say than before in choosing a partner.[2] Because divorce has been viewed both by left-leaning states and scholars as an instrument for "progressive," "liberating," and "modern" social change, the post-1953 curtailment of divorce rights has concomitantly been seen as a conservative, reactionary backlash against the earlier implementation of new rights. For instance, Edward Friedman, Paul Pickowicz, and Mark Selden's account of a North China county over the course of thirty years, and Sulamith Heins Potter and Jack Potter's study of a South China village, vividly portray changes in the social and political scene without any mention of divorce after 1953. What accounts for this neglect of women's rights during this period, both sets of authors suggest, are peasant patriarchal values, the lack of enforcement of state law when power shifted into the hands of local officials, and, related to the former, the "maintenance of male property rights." As Friedman, Pickowicz, and Selden write: "The court in Zoucun closed in 1953. For the next thirty years, Raoyang residents seeking legal recourse in personal disputes involving divorce, inheritance, and injury could in theory go to the county seat for help, but in practice they turned to village party officials. There was no law."[3] Potter and Potter make virtually the same argument for South China: "In the new society as in the old society, women fell between two stools, structurally speaking. They literally had nowhere to go after a divorce . . . In spite of the fact that the right [to divorce] existed in theory, the social structure made it a practical impossibility."[4]

At the same time that the state "postponed the revolution" in rural families by emphasizing the importance of family stability, scholars have also suggested that the state was often successful in revolutionizing the way in which peasants went about forming these stable families. The intensified political atmosphere that accompanied collectivization, the Great Leap Forward, the Four Cleanups, and the Socialist Education campaigns is said to have made it close to impossible for "bad class" peasants, stigmatized by their class label, to find spouses, friends, or assistance in time of need. Friedman, Pickowicz, and Selden write that "the paralyzing and poisonous consequences of imposing permanent categories of class struggle would frame *in frozen status* and color in blood the politics of Raoyang and all of China."[5] William Parish and Martin Whyte, too, found that people of poor peasant background tended to marry those with a similar class background, and that landlords and rich peasants likewise married within their status group, if they were able to marry at all.[6] During rural collectivization, Elisabeth Croll argues, class origins were a consideration in mate choice, with the status of "poor" and "lower-middle" peasant ranking fairly high up the ladder.[7] By the end of the Cultural Revolution, Potter and Potter argue, former landlords became "mostly broken people" and "the new embodiers of despised status in the village" owing to the politically inspired destruction of their social world.[8]

Politics also limited people's freedom to marry someone outside of a very limited geographic horizon. After 1958 the state vigorously enforced the household registration system, making it difficult for peasants to leave their villages in search of urban or suburban spouses. According to Friedman, Pickowicz, and Selden the *hukou* system "bound rural people to the village of their birth, now reorganized as their collective, or in the case of married women, to their husbands' collective village. By 1956 all villagers were tied to land they no longer owned and could not leave and to jobs assigned by party-appointed village leaders."[9] Vivienne Shue similarly maintains that opportunities for residential and occupational mobility were "close to zero for Chinese rural dwellers after the Great Leap Forward [as] the welfare of every individual must increasingly have come to be regarded as permanently tied to the welfare of that person's village or commune."[10] Should peasants seek to move outside of their village, they were required to obtain permission from their village officials and from the "receiving" village— permission that, according to William Lavely, was "usually impossible to obtain."[11] The household registration contributed to what eventually became a "cellular" rural political geography, particularly after the Cultural Revolution: with movement between villages made more difficult, peasants were able to easily identify "insiders and outsiders," and communities became increasingly insular.[12]

This association between post-1953 changes in the economy, politics, and mobility and the subsequent absence of change in the rural family level also seems very plausible in light of our findings on rural areas in previous chapters. Earlier I identified several features of rural political, economic, and social life conducive to peasants' ability to take advantage of the Marriage Law. In the early 1950s, peasants (of whom the great majority were women) extricated themselves from family relationships by relying on courts and district governments (which countered the power of village or township officials), by using the land they received in land reform in bargaining sessions, and by "running" to districts, courts, cities, or back to their parents' homes. In addition, land reform gave the CCP (especially those organizations associated with the center) much legitimacy, which carried over to support for the Marriage Law as well. During the late 1950s and the 1960s, however, the institutions and resources that served peasants well during the early 1950s were no longer easily accessible or available: mediation was given preference over adjudication, power was decentralized, district governments were often eliminated, the private land peasants used to bargain for divorce was all but abolished by 1957, and rural mobility was restricted by the *hukou* system.[13] After land reform, peasants had few emancipatory political experiences to speak of. Instead, they were burdened with campaigns targeting "superstition" in the mid-1950s and "feudal" culture more generally during the Socialist Education campaign in 1963–1964. From the perspective developed earlier in this study, there were few reasons

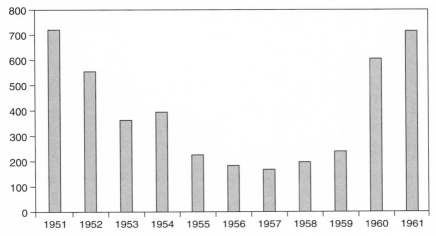

Figure 1. Registered Divorces in Songjiang County, 1951–1961.
Source: Songjiang County Archives, 8-1-32, p. 32.

to anticipate the continuation of the changes that took place in rural families between 1954 and 1966.

For all of these reasons, the findings of this chapter are particularly surprising. In contrast to urban areas during these years, where divorce became increasingly difficult to obtain, in many rural areas (ranging from the Shanghai suburbs to Yunnan) there were as many divorces in the early 1960s as during the height of the Marriage Law campaign in 1953. Moreover, only in rare instances did courts deny petitions for divorce. A random sample of forty court cases from 1955 and 1965 in Qingpu County, which I believe to be representative of general trends, reveals a 98 percent divorce approval rate throughout this period, despite the change in official policy toward adjudication.[14] Peasants continued, for reasons we will see below, to make extensive and creative use of courts and other central government institutions to get what they wanted, and were quite inventive at continuing with sexual practices unsanctioned by state ideologues. This happened sometimes despite and sometimes because of the state's attempt to gain control over marriage, divorce, sexual behavior, and rural mobility. Figures 1 and 2, which include the number of registered divorces (i.e., not including divorces in courts) in Songjiang County (outside of Shanghai) and the number of divorces in Shandong Province (in North China), respectively, present evidence unexpected either by my earlier findings or by the secondary literature. As I pointed out earlier, in the best works on this period by Western sociologists, historians, and political scientists, there is almost no

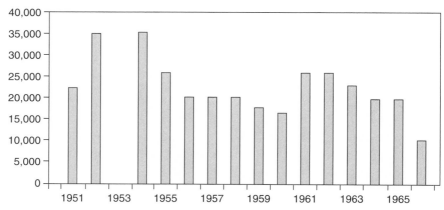

Figure 2. Divorces in Shandong Province, 1951–1966. Source: *Zhongguo renkou— Shandong fence* (Beijing: Zhongguo Tongji Jingji Chubanshe, 1990). The above represents the number of divorces in the province without differentiating between urban and rural areas. Shandong, however, is a predominately rural province, so it stands to reason that very many of these divorces are occurring in rural areas. Data for 1953 are missing.

mention of divorce after 1953, although Chinese legal journals of the time repeatedly called attention to the phenomenon.

County gazetteers also show a significant increase of divorce cases in the early 1960s. In Nanhui County in the Shanghai suburbs, divorces peaked in 1962 (410 cases) and registered only a slight decline in 1963 (334 cases). In 1964, the last year records were kept on divorce in the county, 201 peasant couples registered to divorce. This 1964 figure was twice the number of cases received in 1954.[15] The decline after 1962 was not universal, however. In Taicang County in eastern Jiangsu, for instance, there were as many divorces in 1965 as in 1962 and 1963 (159 cases).[16] There was a similar trend even in mountainous areas of Yunnan, where there were many ethnic minorities. In Lufeng County, Chuxiong, for instance, the county court received 1,174 divorce petitions in 1953 and 1,126 in 1962. The total number of divorce cases shot up from between one thousand and fifteen hundred per year between 1958 and 1960 to over fifty-eight hundred in 1961 *alone*.[17] Minorities in the province, the court found, divorced at the same rate as Han.[18]

New archival evidence challenges not only the conventional wisdom concerning the stability of the rural Chinese family in the 1950s and 1960s but also the idea in the secondary literature that marriage prospects and causes for divorce were largely shaped by political considerations. In contrast to studies that have emphasized the role of good class status in marriage choice, new evidence shows that favorable marriage prospects were often *inversely* related to good class status. Moreover, political differences did not seem to lead to many divorces.

Because these findings were unanticipated, they offer an excellent opportunity to assess the validity and causal "weight" of competing explanations. Previously I focused attention on the role of political movements (land reform, the suppression of counterrevolutionaries), the multi-layered structure of state legitimacy, the availability of resources (such as land, space, and language), the role of community, and legal and sexual dimensions of rural culture without addressing the extent to which these factors could explain changes *after* 1953. The findings above present a puzzle: peasants continued to seek divorces and obtain them despite significant changes in every one of the causal variables that I suggested facilitated divorce. Moreover, divorce continued, albeit in lower numbers, in the mid-1950s, despite the state's retreat from enforcing the Marriage Law through campaigns and the persistence of peasant patriarchy—factors emphasized in the secondary literature. This raises three questions: (1) Are my explanations for divorce between 1950 and 1953 essentially "time-bound" to that period? (2) What explains the decline between 1953 and 1959? and (3) Do the new findings suggest that we need to reevaluate well-established characterizations of rural life during this period in the secondary literature?

This chapter, like the previous one, departs from the conventional method of chronology and organization. As in urban areas, scholars have usually used the national political schedule to explain the rural scene after 1953. Hence the 1950s and 1960s have been organized around events such as the formation of mutual aid teams in the early 1950s, larger cooperatives in the mid-1950s, communes in 1958–1959, the more liberal economic policies of 1961–1963, and finally the radicalization of national policy toward the countryside after 1963—a period that served as the prelude to the Cultural Revolution. In contrast, this chapter takes the years 1954–1966 as a single unit and examines dimensions of politics, resources, community, and culture and their relationship to divorce and marriage with only partial adherence to the policy-driven time line. Section 1, which most closely follows the usual demarcation of important dates, deals with the impact of two political junctures in the 1954–1966 period: "decentralization" between 1954 and 1958, and the political and economic liberalization of 1961–1963. Section 2 examines the role of peasants' material and other resources on divorce, and the impact of changing land tenure relations on the power relations in the family. In Section 3, I focus on the role of culture and community in shaping family dynamics.

1. COMPETING POLITICAL FORCES IN THE COUNTRYSIDE: LOCAL LEADERS AND COURTS IN FAMILY RELATIONS

Bumbling Registration Bureaus and Township Mediation Committees

According to findings of previous chapters, decentralization of power from district governments and courts to township and village officials after 1954 should have resulted in a dramatic decline in the number of divorce cases, or even in the absence of divorce altogether. Peasant women seeking divorce, we have seen, tended to go to courts, counties, and districts, as these organizations were all seen as more legitimate than their local counterparts and more closely affiliated with the center. Part of the decentralization process involved the transfer of authority to register marriages and divorces to townships, rather than to more remote district officials.[19] Prior to granting divorce, registration officials were expected to mediate and investigate to determine if the relationship might be salvaged. They might deny a divorce claim for several reasons. First, having been promoted from among the ranks of village leaders and activists, township officials usually had closer connections to villages than court and district officials, who were on government payroll and had fewer connections to or stake in villages.[20] Second, it is precisely those officials, according to Friedman, Pickowicz, and Selden, that are said to have been embedded in a "local culture fraught with violence and patriarchy."[21] As such, they had both the incentive and cultural inclination to side with husbands whose wives petitioned for divorce. But if this was the case, then how did decentralization not entirely eliminate divorce?

Explanations that emphasize rural officials' patriarchal values or position vis-à-vis the peasant in rural political structure fail to account for post-1953 divorces because they downplay other crucial features of rural administration—most importantly, rural officials' lack of experience, competence, patience, and investigative capacity; peasants seeking to marry or divorce could encounter official bumbling and indifference as often as they might patriarchal values, if not more so. In fact, it may have been these "patriarchal" values that actually allowed divorce to continue. Because men frequently designated marriage as "women's matter," they sometimes took a *passive* stance toward women requesting divorce (women remained the primary petitioners). Indifference resulting from such attribution, in combination with general administrative incapacity, probably explains why reports on divorce and marriage registration work in the 1950s and 1960s often refer to local officials' "careless" and "slapdash" methods of handling divorce cases. The Yunnan Provincial Civil Affairs Bureau, for instance, found that divorce and marriage registration officials understood their work as involving only "issuing documentation" rather than conducting mediation,[22] and a 1955 report from Yongren County, Chuxiong, accused township officials of "lacking patience" when registering marriages and divorces. On occasion, this resulted in "coerced divorces": a couple would go to the township registration office, but preliminary questioning would reveal that only one spouse sought the divorce. Thinking that conducting mediation in such cases was too "bothersome" (*mafan*), the registration official would order them to divorce.[23]

In addition to registration bureau officials, some township government officials considered peasants' marriage difficulties too *mafan* and difficult an undertaking. In 1955, in a mixed Han-minority district of Yunnan, a Miao deputy township official (surnamed Zhang) tried to mediate a dispute between a quarreling older couple. Zhang simplistically asked them, "Was the marriage coerced? If it was, let's talk about divorce." This hasty solution did not sit well with the woman, who replied, "Our marriage was coerced, but I'm old now. If you divorce me, I won't be able to find someone else!"[24] Officials in predominantly Han areas shared their frontier counterparts' reluctance to deal with peasants' marriage disputes. A 1964 Women's Federation report on the marriage situation in Songjiang County complained that brigade (i.e., village-level) cadres were "afraid of encountering problems" when handling marriage disputes. This assessment is probably only partially accurate, however. The brigade leader they cited complained not only of "difficulty" in handling cases, but also of administrative incapacity. Unlike factory union cadres, who could call upon an employee's personal dossier, brigade leaders had little time or administrative reach to investigate the personal life of peasants seeking divorce. As one brigade leader said, "The countryside is like an open-air factory (*lutian gongchang*): they're both hard to manage."[25]

Female officials in local governments were often as indifferent and/or incompetent as their male counterparts. Sensitive to community reaction should their intervention fail to produce a satisfactory outcome, many Women's Federation officials avoided dealing with marriage and other problems associated with what they pejoratively termed "women's work" (*funü gongzuo*). At a conference of local Women's Federation representatives in Chuxiong's Guangtong County, village and township federation officials said that they hesitated to mediate because they "feared that villagers with whom they have a minor conflict will falsely accuse and slander them." Such passivity led village women to ask, "Does the Women's Federation exist anymore?"[26]

Actually, local federation representatives themselves were often unable to answer this question. Most of their training classes took place in jam-packed meetings at the district or county seat, where speakers could rarely be heard above the noise. In Lufeng County, for instance, local representatives who were bored by the proceedings sewed, made shoes, chatted, joked around, or left the meeting hall to wander around the county seat. Compilers of the final report complained that "women came to the meeting only in order to satisfy their desire to have fun in the city" and that, after the meeting, "they can't remember what the policy is."[27]

Although some of these complaints might be attributed to cadres' lack of experience in office at the time of these reports (1954–1955), there is little evidence suggesting that the situation had improved much by the 1960s. In Yao'an County, Chuxiong, a 1965 report on the work methods of local Women's Federation cadres classified only 13 out of 103 officials as having "good" work methods. How such officials were "elected" to their posts virtually guaranteed that village women would not have forceful advocates in local governments. Because so many women refused to serve as village and township representatives because of the extra burden and "trouble" (*mafan*) involved in mediating disputes and in implementing birth control, "late marriage," and other unpopular policies,[28] many women became representatives solely on the basis of their not having any children. This resulted in pre-1949 matchmakers assuming the post of local women's representative, as well as others "who had no idea how to do women's work and solve women's problems."[29]

By decentralizing authority to lower levels of rural political administration, the CCP gave power not only to those with the least administrative competency, but also to officials who enjoyed little legitimacy among the peasants. Because local officials were ordinary poor peasants prior to their elevation to cadre status, other peasants were often well aware of their weaknesses and failures to live up to official moral standards. As in the 1950–1953 period, knowledge of officials' sex lives complicated their roles as mediators and enforcers of state family policy. This gave added importance to higher, geographically more remote, levels of rural political administration such as courts and districts, which could not be easily delegitimized or stigmatized by such knowledge. Investigation reports on the behavior of local officials in the mid-1950s and the 1960s complained that Women's Federation officials were "always having illicit sex" (*yi guan luan gao guanxi*) and then giving birth to illegitimate children. In a district in Yao'an County, peasants brazenly yelled "wild pisser!" (*luan niao*) at their local federation representative because of her multiple affairs, and asked, "How can she be a women's representative?" Other peasants reportedly "lacked respect" for representatives who had illegitimate children; state officials, after all, were expected both by the state and by ordinary citizens to be a bit more respectable in their private behavior than commoners. District officials blamed these difficulties on decentralization, which resulted in districts "relaxing their control" over local officials.[30]

Such problems were not geographically confined to frontier areas, where the state was traditionally weak, or even temporally to the mid-1950s. In 1964, a work team report on the marriage situation in Jinshan and Qingpu

Counties in the Shanghai suburbs found that among three women's representatives and deputy directors in a brigade, two were having illicit affairs: "The current Women's Federation director and the party branch secretary had a child together, and the deputy director and the number 8 production team leader also had illicit sex. Peasants want them both removed."[31] Such local officials were unlikely to be seen as credible mediators of marriage problems, thereby enhancing the role of central state officials.

Center-Local Relations

"Relaxing control" over local level officials resulted not only in lax supervision, registration procedures, and promotion methods. Sometimes, the lack of supervision over local officials made it easier for peasants to divorce, particularly when registration officials felt that dealing with marriage problems was far too *mafan*. The other face of decentralization was that it gave more leeway for local officials to enforce village moral codes, even if these codes contradicted the Marriage Law and were strongly resisted by peasant women who sought to use the law to extricate themselves from coerced relationships. Below I examine two types of conflicts between legal and community officials involving the Marriage Law. These cases demonstrate how decentralization, by rendering community officials unaccountable for their public and private behavior, forced peasants seeking free marriage, divorce, or justice out of villages to the more legitimate courts, counties, and legal officials. In some cases, the state's security and legal apparatus continued to serve as a check on the arbitrary power of local officials, much as it did between 1950 and 1953. In other cases, however, courts *shared* with local officials a common understanding of the Marriage Law and adultery. This partially explains why people were able to divorce throughout the 1950s, even though the balance of power shifted from central state to community leaders. The first case involves a conflict with strong moral overtones over the right to a noncoerced marriage in a suburb of Huainan City, in Anhui Province; the second examines the interaction between central state and local officials over the Marriage Law's clause 19, which vowed to "protect" the marriages of People's Liberation Army soldiers, and how this affected the legitimacy of rural administration. The latter case is particularly important from a methodological perspective, since scholars have suggested that in the pre-state period the CCP made it increasingly difficult for women to divorce due to fears of harming military morale. We might expect similar concerns in the 1950s and 1960s, a period encompassing several international crises threatening state security. Such a conclusion would not really surprise anyone who studies the state. All states are concerned with national security and thus with the morale of their armed forces. Why would a state move to advance women's rights if their enforcement would clearly come at the expense of its uniformed soldiers? Hence the importance of examining PLA marriages in the context of the Marriage Law: What would finding widespread *violation* of the Marriage Law's clause protecting PLA marriages tell us about the nature of the Chinese state and the constituencies that benefited and suffered from the Marriage Law? How might we explain a large gap between the intentions of clause 19 and actual outcomes? As we will see, the case of PLA marriages demonstrates the need to disaggregate the state into its composite elements, and to avoid simplistically assuming that state officials will necessarily act in a certain way because of their gender or their identity as the state. It further suggests that we prioritize in our research the gray area between what is proclaimed and legislated in Beijing—the proverbial cue ball—and what actually happens as policies move their way down the administrative hierarchy and are deflected both by entrenched interests and administrative bumbling—the subsequent shots taken after the cue ball strikes the others.

The Suicide of Tao Chengying   Tao Chengying, who turned twenty years old in 1963, had been abandoned as an infant and adopted by Tao Longshi, a member of her lineage in the township of her birth. Longshi raised Chengying to adulthood, hoping she would marry her son when she came of age. In 1962, Longshi formally requested that Tao Chengying marry her son.

To Longshi's surprise, Chengying refused the match. To back herself up, she sought out the assistance of the political-legal section (*zhengfa bu*) of the commune (or what used to be called "township") to break their engagement. The political-legal officer told Chengying to return to her production team for documentation. Chengying, however, refused to return to her adoptive village because she was aware that the party secretary there, Cheng Jiakang, opposed her breaking off the engagement. Instead of returning to the village, she went to a more hospitable locale—her natal home—to secure the necessary documents. There she received a more sympathetic treatment, and was able to secure the documents. With them in hand she again went to the commune to request separation. The registration official saw her papers, but was suspicious about her motives. He asked that she return to the village for permission from Cheng Jiakang, the party secretary. Chengying again refused to talk to Cheng, and pleaded with the commune Women's Federation and political-legal officers to talk with him. Only after this intervention did Cheng agree to issue the documentation requested by the civil affairs officer.

But even after breaking off the engagement, Cheng Jiakang nevertheless tried to induce Tao to marry her former fiancé. Each request was met with refusal. Frustrated at her obstinacy, Cheng threatened to cut off her grain rations, but this also failed to sway her.

Tao's adoptive mother, Longshi, was equally upset at Chengying's refusal to marry her son, as she considered her raising the abandoned baby the quid pro quo for the marriage arrangement. Afraid that Chengying would marry someone else, Longshi went to the district Women's Federation to ask that federation officials discuss the matter with Chengying's biological mother, who was still in good relations with her daughter. Longshi and the official hoped that Chengying's mother could convince her daughter to repay the debt incurred to Longshi for raising her. Prior to their visit, they met with the commune party secretary, Cheng Jiakang, in order to "borrow" twenty yuan as a marriage fee. These machinations failed to move Chengying, however. She argued that "getting married is easy, but later on, divorce will be more difficult."

After this refusal, party secretary Cheng Jiakang went to see a district Women's Federation official, Chen Chuanying. Chen was upset at Tao Chengying's refusal to marry, and proposed that the commune not issue her a certificate allowing her to change her household registration. That night, Chen visited Chengying and told her that "she had an obligation to marry since she was taken in destitute as a small child." Cheng Jiakang added to the pressure, demanding to know if she would marry within a few days. That evening, Chen of the Women's Federation accompanied Chengying to the political-legal officer to complete the registration procedure. The officer remembered her earlier demand to break off the engagement, and asked if she agreed to the marriage. Tao said that she did not. Exasperated, the federation official said, "You'd better think again. If you refuse, everyone will be upset." This plea failed to move Tao, and she returned home. That night, however, she committed suicide by hanging herself. An investigation followed, resulting in the dismissal of Chen Chuanying, the Women's Federation official, and Cheng Jiakang, the party secretary, from their posts.[32]

Tao Chengying's case, abbreviated as it is, illustrates important features of rural social and political life that, in other cases, contributed to rural divorce, but at the same time made it more difficult to attain. First is Tao Chengying's determination. Even though she was separated from her natal home and subject to repeated pressure to marry, she refused an arranged marriage on several occasions. Her eventual suicide appears to have followed the "script" described in earlier chapters—that of women committing suicide as a final form of revenge against abusive parents or in-laws. The second feature worthy of notice is that Chengying returned to her *natal home* to secure documentation to prove she could break her engagement. Knowing that the commune party secretary would disapprove of her breaking off the engagement, she went "home," where she might receive a more sympathetic hearing. Officials too recognized the strength of the mother-daughter bond when they appealed to Chengying's mother for assistance. Finally, Chengying's first response to Longshi's attempt to coerce her into marrying her son was an appeal to the commune's *legal* officer, rather than to village leaders or commune officials. It was this same officer who in the end frustrated the combined efforts of the party secretary and Women's Federation officials. Chengying's reliance on legal officers was likely a direct result of the obstacles she encountered when powerful members of her adoptive community united around a common understanding of obligation and duty, as well as a shared interest—in this case, preventing village women from marrying outside of the community. It was such shared understandings and interests that, in combination with decentralization, contributed to the decline in divorce cases after 1954. At the same time, however, the "strength" of local communities often forced women to courts, ensuring that at least some cases would be heard. In several of the cases involving PLA marriages described below, courts were also used to circumvent or avenge abuses of authority by local political officials, albeit for different reasons.

Civil-Military (Sexual) Relations   The devolution of authority to brigade and commune party officials during the mid-1950s and the 1960s did not result only in violations of the Marriage Law's promise of free marriages. The absence of effective supervision over local party leaders also gave them free reign to indulge their sexual desires with little fear of punishment. Villagers, especially the poorest ones, who often could not afford a wife, could only seethe in anger as they witnessed officials enjoying access to village women. In their account of collectivization in the 1950s, Friedman, Pickowicz, and Selden also note that local officials took advantage of decentralization to have their way with village women, resulting in a "plague of rape."[33] Evidence from Yunnan, Jiangsu, and Jiangnan only partially supports this observation, however. There were instances of rape, but it appears that, in many cases, multiple sexual liaisons between local officials and village women were consensual and self-interested. These sexual encounters help explain how divorce continued in the countryside despite decentralization; according to many reports, PLA divorces were common throughout this period.[34]

Nowhere was the conflict between central state legislation and local power more apparent than in cases defined legally as "destroying soldiers' marriages." Article 19 of the Marriage Law made special provisions and guidelines for handling separation and divorce cases filed by fiancées and wives of People's Liberation Army soldiers, the overwhelming majority of whom were peasants. Since recruitment and morale of troops depends on their perception of a stable home front, the state had an obvious interest in reassuring soldiers that their wives could not file for divorce solely on the grounds of long separation.[35] In addition to the Marriage Law, the criminal code mandated punishment for "ruining a soldier's marriage" by "seducing" and having illicit sex with his wife.[36] Decentralization, in combination with active recruitment of peasants for military service during periods of heightened international tensions (the Korean War in 1950–1951, the Quemoy and Matsu crises in 1958, the U.S. military buildup in Vietnam in the early 1960s), it turned out, made these articles extremely difficult to enforce.

Worldwide, it is not uncommon for war, with its attendant period of protracted mobilization, to produce tensions that might result in the annulment of engagements or divorce. When husbands are away at war, women continue to live among other men—a situation rife with opportunity for second thoughts about one's engagement, marriage, and vows of fidelity. For instance, the divorce wave in early-1950s China might have been the result of the breakup of relationships owing to the Sino-Japanese War, in addition to state-led changes such as the Marriage Law. During World War II in the United States, extramarital affairs and divorces were common among soldiers' families. Karen Anderson writes that, during the war, "social and sexual contacts outside marriage as men and women worked together to a greater extent than they ever had before . . . contributed to marital discord during the war years."[37] Since many wartime marriages were hastily arranged just prior to soldiers' departure, the divorce rate among serviceman following the war was twice as high as that among the non-military population.[38] Among PLA soldiers in China, few had relationships based on "bourgeois" ideals of romantic love and extended periods of courtship; a 1957 court report in Yunnan found that in divorce cases involving PLA soldiers, 100 percent of those soldiers' marriages had been arranged.[39] In addition, the long separation of PLA soldiers from their families placed the latter in difficult financial straits. Unlike women who entered U.S. industry and saw a substantial rise in their income, the departure of able-bodied young men from villages was not always alleviated by measures that made their families less dependent on the mobilized soldier.[40] Instead, decentralization made PLA families highly dependent on community officials, who had access to and control over scarce resources such as good job assignments, welfare allowances, and food.

Reports from the 1950s and 1960s attest to the tensions and temptations of PLA families in their communities. During 1955, the Lufeng County court (in Yunnan) handled twelve cases of violations of the Marriage Law's Article 19. Of these cases, eight were reported to have been perpetrated by pre-1949 village elites and "local hoodlums," and the other four by "basic-level cadres, especially village cadres and militia heads who used their position as an excuse to conduct night-time investigations to have sex with soldier's wives."[41] A report on military marriages in Jiangxi Province found that in one prefecture (*zhuanqu*) there were over 1,100 cases of "ruining military marriages," including 330 that resulted in pregnancy. Among the perpetrators were 23 county and district cadres and 149 township and village cadres; others were ordinary peasants and militiamen.[42]

Despite their violation of Article 19 of the Marriage Law, PLA wives and their cadre lovers were frequently remorseless when confronted by central state investigators and other peasants. Emboldened by their relationship with officialdom, many women pressed to divorce their soldier-husbands, which were then granted by bumbling administrators. Some were quite bold when explaining their motives. One woman argued, "My husband's out making revolution. Because of this I'm at home and am so busy I have no spare time. How come this isn't considered working for the revolution? How come the party only looks after him? In a couple of years the spring of my youth will pass."[43] To justify their violation of Article 19, some women invoked the Marriage Law's Article 1, which granted them the right to "marriage freedom." In Chuxiong, for instance, a PLA wife surnamed Wang wrote a petition to the county court demanding "marriage freedom" because "her parents arranged the marriage." This marriage was not formally registered; the couple married the traditional way, by having a feast. The court sent the case to the district government, which "rashly" granted her a divorce without even bothering to contact Wang's mobilized husband, as was required by law. Not considering the circumstances of the case, the district relied on a formalistic reading of the law: "Having a feast doesn't mean you're married; to marry, you have to go through formal procedures. The marriage was thus invalid in the first place."[44]

If appealing to the language of the Marriage Law was unsuccessful, women might also try to cast doubt on the credibility of their detractors in order to avoid criticism of their affairs. In Tang'yin County in Hunan, for instance, a PLA wife surnamed Hu was reportedly "seduced" by the township chief, Zhang Chengmei. When Hu was reprimanded, she disclosed that Zhang was also having illicit sex with the chair of the Women's Federation.[45]

To be sure, not all soldiers' wives wanted to divorce their husbands. Some tried to preempt the possibility of a long separation by convincing their husbands to avoid military service or threatening divorce should they dare leave.[46] When fiancés and husbands joined the army, however, their wives found themselves separated from their natal homes and surrounded by their husband's family. In this situation, the wife was often at the mercy of family heads and soldiers' brothers. In Chuxiong, reports circulated that divorce cases among soldiers' wives were sometimes caused by pressure from a PLA soldier's father who wanted the wife to marry another family member, or sometimes because the woman was raped by the soldier's brothers and they wanted to marry her. In other cases, ex-servicemen in the village pressured the PLA wives to divorce and marry them instead. In some instances, this pressure was effective and women divorced.[47]

Soldiers discovered their wives' affairs and rapes in one of two ways. In some cases, cadres having affairs with PLA wives tried to instigate their lover's divorce by writing letters to the soldiers informing them of their wives' adultery.[48] In other instances, soldiers who returned home on furlough discovered their spouses in bed with cadres, or heard community gossip about them. Such discoveries prompted immediate countermeasures: furious soldiers stormed off to courts and district governments for revenge, without knowing that it was the courts and districts that had granted their wives divorce in the first place. The road to court, however, was full of obstacles. In Shimen County, Hunan, a soldier returned home on furlough only to discover that his wife had been "seduced" by the township chief. The distraught soldier ran to court to file an accusation, but was waylaid by "leading district cadres, who, with the local militia, pummeled him, and locked him away."[49]

Even when soldiers reached court and filed charges, the results were usually disappointing. Officials in townships, districts, and courts denigrated the political import of sex. According to one report, some cadres "openly say, 'It's no big deal when a soldier's wife gets pregnant and has a kid,' or consider illicit affairs an ordinary social problem."[50] In Hubei Province, a soldier returned home and discovered that his wife was having an affair with a village cadre. He then went to the district government to file an accusation. Unmoved, district cadres told him, "This is a social problem left over from the old society. We don't have the authority to deal with it." The soldier then telephoned the county court. The local court, ignoring the statute dealing with these matters, also saw no ground for legal action: "Your wife is having an affair because you've been away for so long. All we can do is tell the district government to educate him. We can't prosecute a peasant because of something like this."[51]

Unable to get revenge at district governments or courts, some soldiers simply filed for divorce when they discovered their wives' affairs. Some wrote letters home ridiculing and insulting their spouses—an action that prompted their wives to seek divorce.[52] Others wrote letters to the National People's Congress or traveled all the way to Beijing in the hope that central state authorities, as more powerful and apparently more legitimate institutions, would intervene in their favor.[53] A more serious consequence, however, was the substantial number of suicides among soldiers resulting from their spouses' affairs with cadres and ordinary villagers. In 1956, the Bureau of Civil Affairs reported that, in Chuxiong, there were 693 suicide cases among demobilized soldiers, with the largest number of cases resulting from wives' adultery or rape (47 percent). In other cases, soldiers who received letters informing them of unpunished rape and affairs went AWOL to return home to "reclaim" their wives.[54] Sex and divorce among cadres and local women also affected recruitment campaigns and army morale. In the mid-1950s, court investigations found that many young peasant men were discouraged from joining the military after witnessing divorces, affairs, and rapes of wives of PLA soldiers who had already been recruited.[55]

Problems of illicit affairs, divorce, and rape of PLA wives continued well into the 1960s. During and after the Great Leap Forward, many supervisory controls over local officials were decimated. At the same time, heightened tension between China and the Soviet Union after the Sino-Soviet split, and later between China and the United States, required substantial recruitment of peasants to the PLA. As during the 1950s, mobilization efforts were hampered by the hearty sexual appetite of local CCP officials. In Jinshan County near Shanghai, a 1964 investigation revealed that between January and October 1963, fifteen out of twenty-four defendants in PLA marriage cases were cadres; of these, over one-half were CCP members in production teams and brigades or members of the Communist Youth League who "used their position to attract PLA wives."[56] In a commune in the Shanghai suburbs, 267 village youth were recruited into the PLA during 1963. Of the 131 soldiers who were engaged or married at the time they were recruited, 18 had problems resulting from their wives' having affairs with other villagers and cadres, and six women were already divorced as a result. In Songjiang County, the Women's Federation found that "the great majority" of perpetrators in PLA marriage cases were cadres. "When soldiers hear that their wives are sleeping around," the federation found, "they request leave to return home in order to settle accounts. Others are completely depressed, while some want to leave the military altogether." During a recruitment drive in 1964, village youth refused to undergo physicals, believing that this would allow them to avoid military service. Recruiters' efforts to assuage their fears by having wives and fiancées give them a "guarantee" of chastity failed because the men "did not trust women to keep their promises."[57]

During the anti-corruption drives of the Four Cleanups and Socialist Education campaigns in the early 1960s (and later during the Cultural Revolution, as we will see in the next chapter), these relationships were used as ammunition for political critique. Investigations of cadre corruption during the movements revealed that, during soldiers' absence, party members used their access to the commune bank, police, and granary in order to secure good food, gifts, and travel documents for lovers to see local opera performances. PLA wives themselves, the Federation complained, "do not value their own honor. All they want to do is to eat and drink well and have fun."[58] In Chuxiong, Yunnan, cadres were criticized for using their position to give PLA wives more work points (and thus more money), more grain, gifts, and, with their power over job assignments, plum jobs in the brigade. Since many of these officials were already married, a substantial number of them were involved in de facto bigamous relationships—not unlike some of the village elites they had so violently replaced in 1951.[59]

Work teams administering these campaigns also criticized PLA wives for their indifference to the bad class status of their paramours and benefactors. One former landlord in Chuxiong, surnamed Yang, was reported to have used "cash, rice rations, and clothes" to seduce the wife of a PLA soldier, surnamed Wen. Using a horse-drawn carriage, Yang took Wen to the city to "eat, drink, and have a good time."[60] In Songjiang county as well, "good class" PLA dependents were involved in sexual liaisons with sons of "bad class" landlords.[61] When criticized for such affairs, women invoked the language of the Marriage Law. A provincial report from 1965 instructed local officials not to accept "claims of marriage freedom as an excuse to ruin a revolutionary soldier's marriage."[62]

The power decentralization vested in local officials virtually assured that few would receive harsh punishment for violating PLA marriages. Among sixty-five cases (involving seventy people) handled by local courts in Chuxiong, thirty-seven were given mere reprimands, and seven "administrative discipline" (shorthand for a brief criticism session within a unit). Only five perpetrators were sentenced to labor reform, while twenty were temporarily suspended from their posts. According to the Chuxiong intermediate court's report, "courts think these cases are complicated and hard to handle, and so are not serious about looking into the real situation." Light sentences, the court found, were given largely because "local court officials see that the defendants are party members." As a result of this attitude, divorce petitions, whether by the cadre or by his PLA wife-lover, were sometimes granted on demand, Article 19 notwithstanding.

But even when courts took such cases seriously, local officials knew they were virtually immune from punishment. In 1962, for instance, Wu Jiacheng, a cadre in Dayao County, Chuxiong, acquired a reputation among peasants as an unabashed philanderer. Peasants called him "a cadre who screws around like a donkey" because he committed adultery over five times, and on several occasions, with PLA wives. When court officials investigated, Wu brashly called them "dogs" who had come to "bark" at him. Wu confidently informed court officials: "No matter how much I fuck around, there's nothing you can do. I'm promoted every year no matter what I do. I've already been promoted from the commune to the district." But even if courts were not intimidated by such blustering, their sentences were difficult to enforce. Some cadres, they found, "continue to cohabit with PLA wives (*pin zhu*) even after they've received a suspended sentence."[63]

Forces of the Center

Even with the abuses of power so vividly captured in these documents, it was not always the case that decentralization completely undermined the role of central state agencies when dealing with family relations in rural areas. Although China's top leadership called for decentralization in increasingly strident tones toward the end of the 1950s, peasants still sought out the state agencies they associated with the more legitimate center—namely, courts and county governments. Throughout the 1950s and 1960s, peasants continued to use their well-worn legal strategy of directly petitioning these institutions; courts, for their part, continued to grant peasants divorce, despite the official policy advocating mediation and conciliation rather than adjudication and separation. In 1956, for example, the Lufeng County court in Chuxiong granted divorces in sixty-four out of eighty-six cases they heard (74 percent).[64] How can this be explained? Why did peasants go to court, and why were courts willing to grant divorce?

Court behavior and peasants' continued reliance on legal institutions during the 1950s and 1960s was undoubtedly shaped by the impact of decentralization. Officials who took advantage of their power to rape village women, arrest protesting husbands with local militia, and boast about their immunity from supervisory controls were the sort of people who were either uninterested in mediating peasants' family disputes or unable to do so. In the countryside, decentralization thus made central state institutions all the more necessary to get justice. Peasants' legal culture, which frequently focused on appeals to power holders in the county seat, suicide threats, and mobility from village to court or natal homes, could not be repressed, even by the abuses of power at the village and township levels. One 1957 report published in a legal journal found that peasants "*immediately come to court* demanding divorce as soon as they have an argument," bypassing local institutions in the process.[65] In Anhui, a judge's memoirs also testifies to this litigious culture. In 1958, a worker in a cotton mill on the outskirts of Wuhu City threatened the judge: "I definitely want a divorce. If I can't get one, I'll kill myself!" When this tack proved unsuccessful, she began "crying in court," dropped her two kids, and then "ran back to her natal home."[66]

If abuses of power at the local level and a contentious legal culture help explain appeals to court, why would courts be sympathetic to their claims? One possible explanation is that by granting peasants divorce, courts were able to regain some of the power they had lost to local officials after processes of decentralization began. During the early years of the PRC, as previous chapters have shown, conflicts over the scope of the Marriage Law's divorce clause resulted in tension between courts, districts, and village and township leaders. The willingness of courts and districts to grant peasants' divorces irritated local officials, who worried that all of "their" village women would divorce en masse. When power shifted to local leaders during the mid-1950s and courts found themselves increasingly impotent in the rural political structure, their control over the divorce process enabled them to restore a modicum of the authority they had lost. Separated from the village by long distances, they also had little stake in the outcome of cases.

Other explanations of court behavior can be found at the level of language. According to one report, judges decided cases on the basis of two legal languages: that of the Marriage Law, and that of communism. Because marriages cases were often difficult to decide, and because courts had a difficult time verifying the veracity of plaintiffs' testimony, some judges relied exclusively on what they understood to be the "basic spirit of the law"—in particular, the law's promise of "marriage freedom." For instance, a 1956 report on rural family and marriage disputes found that court officials "have a one-sided view of marriage freedom and, as a result, rashly grant divorce . . . if the woman wants the divorce. They don't inquire about the concrete circumstances of the case, don't do any further investigations, and then rashly (*qingshuai*) grant divorce."[67] Court officials also decided cases by relying on the rhetoric of recent economic policies. Investigation reports by the Chuxiong intermediate court, as well as reports on court work in legal journals, charged courts with "absolute egalitarianism" (*juedui pingjun zhuyi*) because they divided property equally between husband and wife, regardless of how much each party brought into the relationship. In other cases, however, the spirit of the Marriage Law's advocacy of "protecting women" proved more powerful than egalitarian notions of property settlements—a situation similar to one we have already described in the early 1950s. When lower courts granted women the lion's share of property and land (prior to full collectivization), the intermediate court complained that such decisions were unenforceable at the village level.[68] In fact, in none of these reports were investigators impressed with the lack of access to courts, or with courts' refusal to grant divorces. The most serious charge concerning the latter possibility was that, on occasion, courts had a "poor peasant outlook": they allowed divorce, but did not grant women property, fearing, correctly, that should a man lose both his wife and property, he would be left without the two most critical things in his life.[69]

In Yunnan, the intermediate court criticized lower court officials not only for ignoring differences in income and land holdings in divorce settlements, but also for disregarding differences among different ethnic groups. Even by the late 1950s, court officials were still largely ignorant about minority marriage and divorce customs, preferring instead to handle cases on the basis of the Marriage Law and the "experience and principles" of legal work in Han Chinese areas. In Chuxiong, for instance, a Yi couple married in 1953 when the woman (Zhang Kaixin) was only fourteen. Because her in-laws mistreated her, she soon returned to her natal home. By 1956, when Kaixin petitioned for divorce, she had lived in her husband's home for only three months. The court, on the basis of Article 4 of the Marriage Law (setting the legal age for marriage at eighteen years for women and twenty for men), declared the marriage null and void. Kaixin's husband, upon hearing this, demanded that his ex-wife return the gifts he had sent her prior to their marriage, as was required by Yi custom. The court, however considered this exchange a "voluntary transfer of gifts" that need not be returned. As a result, Kaixin divorced and retained the gifts she received during courtship and marriage, leaving the husband's family bereft of resources to allow their son to marry again.[70]

Court officials in Yunnan were also hampered by language barriers. Lacking the time or inclination to study minority languages, court officials continued to grant divorces simply because they could not deal with determined peasant women speaking in foreign tongues. In Luquan County, Yunnan, only eighteen out of eighty divorce cases at the court during 1956 were properly translated, for instance. Such barriers, however, did not prevent ethnic minority peasants from seeking divorce in Han courts. One Yi woman, Li Guangrong, went to the county court three times, and to a different court four times, but "because no one understood her," the case remained unresolved. On one of these trips she managed to find a judge willing to grant her a divorce. The Luquan report noted similar difficulties in divorce cases among the Miao.[71]

As Li Guangrong discovered, determination in and of itself proved a potent method of securing a favorable outcome in divorce cases. Lacking time and modern technology to investigate each and every divorce claim in remote villages (in Yunnan, mountains made such investigations even more difficult and time consuming), courts relied primarily upon plaintiffs' testimony. It was as if courts reasoned that if a woman was "undetermined" she must be lying, but if she was "determined" she must be telling the truth. But probably more important than this was courts' inability to properly investigate the veracity of peasants' claims. Unlike courts in urban areas, which used material provided by work units to decide cases, in rural areas peasants' domestic life was on the very far periphery of courts' administrative vision. Without such information, courts were often at the mercy of resolute peasants. A 1957 Luquan County court report on how courts handled "rash divorces" among peasants (the causes of which will be discussed later) criticized court officials for "not knowing what to do when they get a case in which both or one party to the dispute are determined to divorce." Instead of investigating, the report found, judges "rely only on the plaintiff's attitude. If [the plaintiff is] determined, they grant a divorce . . . they don't do any investigation before deciding if a case should be dismissed." The lack of a strong rural investigative apparatus gave peasants wide berth to fabricate testimony. As one report found:

In courts, plaintiffs often exaggerate or lie about certain reasons for divorce. They say that their free marriages were actually arranged by a matchmaker;

that their spouse is sleeping around when they're not; that because they're in different production teams they are never together when they are always together; that they're abused when they are treated well; or that they have no feelings toward one another (*ganqing*) only because they had one or two arguments or fights.[72]

Peasants' frank sexual culture continued to make courts' work difficult. Rural courts rarely encountered the concerns and behavior we discussed in the previous chapter regarding urban intellectuals. In court reports, peasants seeking divorce rarely failed to speak frankly and openly about their domestic situation because of concern with "face" or privacy. A Chuxiong intermediate court report, for instance, complained that peasants "argue when entering court" and hurl explicit, sexually oriented accusations at one another. To make court proceedings more "civilized," the intermediate court instructed county courts to individualize hearings for plaintiffs if they persisted in discussing their sex lives or spouses' illicit affairs.[73]

Granting divorce on the basis of misleading testimony did little to improve the already brittle relationship between courts and local officials. As we have seen in previous chapters, village and township officials on the one hand and court officials on the other were often at odds over divorce, with the latter far more inclined to grant divorces than local officials. This tension, which continued well into the 1950s and 1960s, reminds us of the need to look at *multiple levels* of the state apparatus, and not assume a uniformity of interests on the part of male officials because of their gender, or a smooth line of policy implementation. The divorce case of Tuo Shuzhen and her husband, Wu Chunming, is a good example of how different officials handled demand for divorce. According to the intermediate court's investigation, the county court "did not investigate the quality of their marriage, their postmarriage situation, or even their reasons for divorce. Instead, the judge decided on his own accord that a divorce was warranted." As a consequence of this decision, Tuo was granted a divorce and a substantial property settlement. Wu Chunming complained that the judge's decision was "too subjective," and township officials felt that because the marriage had not been arranged there were no grounds for divorce. The ease with which Tuo was divorced led other peasants to wonder, "If Tuo and Wu can divorce just like that, who knows how many will divorce in the future?" Subsequent events proved that the court was, in fact, too careless in its decision. After Tuo and Wu were divorced, they returned to the village and continued to live together. By July 1957, they had another child.[74] Peasants' remarks, spoken in 1957, still proved quite prescient: after 1957 the number of divorce cases did increase—in some years dramatically so, as we will see in the next section.

2. RESOURCES

In previous chapters, I suggested that owning land, either directly or in absentia, facilitated divorce in the countryside. Land was used to negotiate the terms of divorce with one's family or the state, and gave peasants confidence that they could maintain a livelihood after divorce. By 1957, however, most individual or household plots were collectivized in some form, leaving peasants without the land they had gained during land reform. Looking at the divorce trend, the decline in the number of divorce cases from 1953 to 1958 correlates with changes in the land tenure system. During 1961–1963, the failure of the Great Leap Forward led to Mao's retreat from the front line of politics. Liu Shaoqi and Deng Xiaoping, with Mao's grudging approval, restored private plots and relaxed previous restrictions on how much and what peasants could grow on their plots. At the same time, the party, through the PLA, preached the ethical virtues of communism.[75] This period of economic liberalization and political indoctrination largely overlaps with the dramatic rise in the number of divorce cases seen in figure 1, particularly between 1960 and 1963, and the still substantial number of cases received between 1964 and 1965.

These data raise several interesting issues and questions. First, even though the number of divorce cases decreased from its peak in 1953, peasants continued to divorce throughout the 1950s, despite collectivization. Related to this, the correlation between the expansion of private plots and the increase in number of divorce cases suggests that peasants' willingness, ability, and success in getting a divorce were related to a land tenure system that allowed the maintenance of private plots. If this was the case, what were the causal mechanisms underlying this relationship? In the early 1950s, for instance, peasants not only received land, but did so in a *revolutionary process* that terrified both local officials and members of the older generation. In chapters 4 and 5, I argued that the land reform process provided the link between land and the willingness to seek divorce. Similar questions might be raised for the 1960s: Exactly how did the expansion of private plots and markets after the Great Leap lead more peasants to seek divorce? Was the rise in divorce after 1959 a direct reaction to the liberalization policy, or perhaps the consequence of changes set in motion earlier—during the Great Leap in 1958–1959, for instance? This section assesses these issues.

Collectivization

How did collectivization contribute to divorce during the mid-1950s? The main impact of collectivization, I suggest, was its contribution to the further erosion of parental authority in the family. Without the power to grant inheritance (as land became collectively owned), older Chinese peasants lost much of their authority over their children. This happened at the same time that women continued to assert their right to divorce either by threatening to divorce or by actually going to court. The combination of the decline of parental authority and peasant women's willingness to boldly exercise new rights (even though there was no longer a special campaign to enforce those rights) resulted in the persistence of divorce throughout the 1950s.

An investigation of the marriage situation in Wuxiang County, Xinyi Township, in Shanxi Province in North China reveals the extent to which collectivization, in combination with divorce, strengthened the hand of women in their families. Unlike the Jiangnan region and the southwestern frontier, Wuxiang was classified by the Communists as an "old liberated area" (*lao jiefang qu*) because it had been "liberated" in 1946. The Marriage Law was implemented in the region in 1947, and mutual aid teams organized in 1948. In this sense, it was not very different from the area studied by Friedman, Pickowicz, and Selden in *Chinese Village, Socialist State:* Raoyang County in Hebei. As a result of these changes, the report found, almost as many women as men participated in agricultural labor (252 men to 237 women), brides rode on trucks instead of bridal sedans to marriage ceremonies, domestic violence was reportedly less frequent, and "free marriages" were more common. Still, old attitudes persisted, particularly with regard to the sexual division of labor in the family: women wanted to rely on men to provide the bulk of the household income, and men continued to believe that women worked best at home.[76] In this respect, Wuxiang appears to have been similar to Raoyang.

The most dramatic changes were not in views toward the sexual division of labor, but rather in how divorce and women's participation in labor changed power dynamics in the family, even in this supposed bastion of patriarchy in North China. In Wuxiang, evidence shows that peasant women boldly used the Marriage Law to raise their status in the family—a goal sanctioned by the state—as well as to acquire material possessions—a consequence that was not quite intended. Sometimes even the threat of divorce was enough to cower husbands into submission. According to the report, "men are afraid their wives will divorce them, so they give in to their every whim. Men buy them whatever they want. If their wives do not feel like working, they don't dare say anything." In one mutual aid team, investigators found, five out of nine households experienced instances in which "the wife refused to work, but the husband did not dare say anything to her."[77] Clearly men were very aware of the danger this threat posed. Should their wives divorce, they would have a very difficult time marrying again, especially since there were generally fewer young women than men in many poor areas.[78]

In some cases, women's awareness of their right to divorce led them to demand radical changes in the traditional domestic division of labor. Usually, men worked in the fields while their wives remained at home caring for the children and cooking for the family. After the work day was over, men came home and expected that a meal would be ready. Some women, however, found this arrangement unsatisfactory and pressed for change. Village women, the report complained, "loaf around at home and don't cook," but instead "demand that their husbands cook and serve them" even after they return tired from work. Complaints were ineffective: when husbands "tried to reason with them," the women reportedly "threatened to divorce" (*yao nao lihun*). Some threats *were* carried out: marital relations among some youth in the township were described as "unstable" (*quefa gonggu*), and "rash divorces," usually initiated by women, were said to be "relatively common." In the township's Hebei Village, 25 percent of all married couples under the age of twenty-five were either divorced or in the process of divorce within a sixteen-month period—a rate that is extremely high by any standard; in the township, 6 out of 329 households experienced divorce between April 1953 and May 1954 (1.8 percent), almost double the urban rate for the same period (see chapter 5).[79] Except for one case involving a legless war veteran, all these couples had "free marriages." This surprised the investigators, who believed that "among freely married couples there should be only a few instances of divorce." Not surprisingly, women's willingness to divorce and a general sense of family instability (said to be "bourgeois") caused no small sense of panic among village men. According to the report, men's "three fears" were of "not being able to find a wife because women set their sights too high" (*yanguang tai gao*); "finding a wife but not being able to afford her" (marrying was said to cost half of the average household's annual income); and "after finally being able to afford her, losing her in a divorce." Men, the report concluded, "are especially afraid" of the third possibility.[80]

Relations between young couples and their parents were also affected by CCP policies. As a result of attacks on the "feudal" land relations and family structure during land reform and the Marriage Law, 19 out of 329 households had older family members "distributed out of" (*fen chu lai*) their homes into new dwellings, allowing young couples to form the nuclear families CCP marriage reformers (who were invariably intellectuals) had long advocated as the "modern" antidote to thousands of years of "feudal" oppression caused by multigenerational families living under one roof. Having been forced out of their "traditional" homes into more "modern" ones, many older people became concerned that sons and daughters would now neglect them. "Old folks," the report noted, "complain that [young] women's status is too high; they say, 'Young women's status has been pushed up and we've been pushed out!'"[81]

In July 1955, Mao called for a rapid speed-up in the pace of agricultural collectivization in his speech "On the Question of Cooperativization in

Agriculture." Impatient with the pace of rural socialist transformation and worried about a "rightist" resurgence, Mao insisted that more villages form cooperatives of agricultural producers, even though there was widespread reluctance to form larger units.[82] Hard-working peasants were reluctant to join co-ops with lazy and/or weaker peasants, fearing the latter would not contribute their fair share. Adding to these worries was the regime's insistence that collective units be as "politically pure" as possible. Not a few cadres and ordinary peasants preferred to work with rich peasants and landlords rather than poorer ones, believing that the latter were poor because they were either weak, lazy, or scoundrels, even if they were the politically privileged class.[83] Gender issues also got in the way: the government encouraged women to participate in labor, but was slow to organize child care facilities. In some instances, couples divorced because one spouse wanted to join the co-op but the other refused, or because one spouse did not work hard once in.[84] Men did not make the conflict between household chores and agricultural labor any easier for women. If the state wanted women to have "equality" with men, they reasoned, why shouldn't they haul the same loads and work the same number of hours? [85]

Family relations during these years were further strained by other policies associated with the collectivization drive. The mid-1950s witnessed massive public work projects to repair roads, dikes, and canals. To complete these projects, peasant men were mobilized on a massive scale, leaving their families behind. According to a 1956 report by the Jiangsu Province Women's Federation,

> when male peasants leave to repair dikes, women are left by themselves to look after six to seven *mu* of land. As a result, work is very intense. They have no time to look after the household, no time to wash clothes, prepare food, and so forth. In response, in Kunshan County some peasants have taken the initiative to organize cooperative dining rooms and laundries.[86]

Because men were either unavailable or unwilling to assist with household chores, the extra burden of caring for children fell upon women and older peasants who could not work outside of the home. Forced to take care of the household and agricultural work without their husbands' assistance, peasant women during these years had little time for anything except work—a process Philip Huang has called the "familization of rural production."[87] Women's extensive participation in production both in and outside of the home undoubtedly took a toll on their ability to sue for divorce. Without any time for cooking or tending the land, it is doubtful that many would have the time to go to remote government agencies and begin the often time-consuming process of obtaining a divorce.

By increasing the burden on individual households, collectivization also increased intergenerational conflicts, particularly between daughters-in-law and their husbands' parents. To deal with the extra labor, elderly women and men were pressed into service to care for children while their daughters-in-law were out in the fields. For those enfeebled by old age, and who expected that after their hard lives as wives and mothers they would finally be able to rest some in their last years, this extra burden was deemed "too heavy to carry." According to one report, the elderly had "three fears": of "being bothered" (*pa mafan*), of children getting sick, and of fighting with each other.[88] Either living separately from their children, or saddled with extra responsibilities at home, many were left dependent on the good-will of their children to provide for them.

State efforts to provide the elderly with minimal welfare provisions sometimes (and unexpectedly) made their situation even worse. Some sons, daughters, and daughters-in-law believed that with collectivization, the state, rather than the family, would provide for all of their parents' needs. This reasoning further frayed filial bonds and rationalized neglect. In other cases, however, neglect was far more calculated. A report on civil disputes in Hebei, for instance, found that collectivization reduced the number of land disputes, but increased the number of cases involving children neglecting their parents. Children either believed that the state welfare program obviated the need for their care, or calculated that there would be few costs in neglecting parents because "they can't inherit the land anyway."[89]

By the late 1950s, postcollectivization neglect of elders had become common enough to warrant special state investigations into the situation. Such investigations revealed that, in most cases, older folks suffered at the hand of their own families. Reports found that daughters-in-law used divorce, control over the household, mobility, access to natal homes, and political language to abandon in-laws, abuse them, or drive them to suicide. In 1958, the investigation *yuan* (*jiancha yuan*) in Yunnan reported an alarming rise in the number of criminal cases involving the abuse, poisoning, murder, and abandonment of parents "since the high tide of collectivization." Involving both CCP cadres and ordinary peasants, the bureau's initial probe concluded that

> most abuse cases are the result of children hating that their parents are old and cannot work. Usually the son and daughter-in-law collaborate. In other cases, the daughter-in-law initiates the beating and the son joins in, fearing that if he goes against her, she will petition for divorce. For instance, the wife of one Xiao Yuxian hates that her mother-in-law is poor and dependent on her work. Because of this, Yuxian's wife refuses to feed her. She threatens her husband and mother-in-law by saying that she will return to her natal home and divorce in order to get what she wants . . . [In another example], the wife of Xiao Zuxian doesn't allow her husband to talk with his mother. If he does, she refuses to feed him.[90]

State intervention appeared to do little to alleviate the plight of aging parents. Daughters-in-law could wield political language like a cudgel, intimidating officials, husbands, and in-laws alike. For instance, a woman surnamed Hu despised her mother-in-law and refused to feed her. At the dinner table, Hu's mother-in-law pleaded for some food. Hu refused and told her, "Even if this food was shit, I still wouldn't give it to you!" Close to starvation, Hu's mother-in-law brought the matter to the attention of the township government (another tack we have seen previously), whose officials tried to mediate the cases several times, but without success. During one mediation meeting, Hu repeatedly confounded officials by yelling and accusing them of "supporting the old and oppressing the young." Nor were in-laws spared the wrath of this language. A woman surnamed Yang berated her mother-in-law: "You're just like a landlord! All you do is eat and exploit people! Why don't you work!?" Other women called the collective's welfare program (the "Five Guarantees") "exploitation" because it contradicted the socialist principles of "to each according to his work," and "you eat what you can work."[91]

In addition to political language, mobility was a crucial resource that gave young women leverage over elderly parents and in-laws. Hobbled by old age, or perhaps by bound feet, there was little parents could physically do to prevent daughters, daughters-in-law, and sometimes sons from running away from the village. In the Beijing suburbs, for instance, a 1954 report noted several cases of family conflicts caused by "young men and women ignoring parents who threaten to cut them off and then leaving the village to go get married."[92] But running away was instigated not only by desire to elope. In Luquan County, Yunnan, a woman surnamed Li (nineteen years old) married one surnamed Bai (twenty-three). They met in March 1956 and married fifteen days later. Two weeks after the marriage, Li argued with her mother-in-law and then "ran back to her natal home and petitioned for divorce." Other women "ran off" because they were unaccustomed to the difficult physical effort demanded in agricultural work; having been raised to sew, cook, and the like, they found more physical labor intolerable. In Yunnan, a report criticized a woman surnamed Li for divorcing despite a happy marriage. Li, the report complained, "frequently ran away" (*jingchang zai wai pao*) because she "hated to work," thereby angering the village.[93]

Elderly Chinese peasants were terribly upset over this turn in their fate. Some tried to bring their children to township government legal departments, hoping the state would intervene on their behalf. Township officials, busy with organizing communes and production schedules, rarely assisted. Others took solace in the company of other women. In one township, several abused old women got together and "told each other that they shouldn't be happy if they have a son, or unhappy if they don't. If they don't have chil-

dren and are old, they can still go to the commune and get the Five Guarantees." Other elderly people found relief only in death. Shocked at how
"their world had changed," some committed suicide, believing that the next
world would surely be better than the present one.[94]

The state's explanation of children's unfilial behavior toward their parents was remarkable in its admission of past and present political error. During the Marriage Law campaigns, party officials confessed, "we attacked the
'feudalism of old people' abuse, and so on, without any mention of the
need to 'respect and support the elderly.' As a result, bourgeois selfishness
took root." The state also attributed abuse to postcollectivization property
arrangements and men's fear of losing a wife in a divorce, which led sons to
collaborate with their wives against their parents. Neighbors and relatives,
even as they witnessed the elderly starving to death and committing suicide,
did not intervene because they "have gotten used to the young no longer
caring for the old."[95]

Further contributing to rural family instability was a new conception of
state-society relations, one inspired directly by collectivization. By seizing
peasants' land and assuming responsibility for marketing and distribution, the state unwittingly gave some peasants the impression that it would
also be responsible for any misfortune that might happen to one of their
family members. This notion of state-family relations made severing family
and marital relationships a simple matter, as it gave women and men free
reign to pursue self-interest without concern for the consequences of their
actions. The Jiangsu Province Women's Federation reported that, "especially since collectivization, there had been many instances of parents abandoning their children, and of CCP officials abandoning their wives. When a
child is born, the report noted, "they place it on the steps of government
offices in the hope that the government will raise it. After giving up the
child, the woman leaves and tries to get a job as a nursemaid."[96] Viewing
the cooperative as guarantor of the needy also extended to children born
out of wedlock, even in cases when the fathers were officially categorized as
counterrevolutionaries. In the Nanjing countryside, the Jiangsu Women's
Federation reported:

> Not a few fifteen-to-sixteen-year-olds become pregnant out of wedlock.
> There are also family members of counterrevolutionaries whose husbands
> are in labor reform who are now pregnant. There are even cases of incest. In
> all these cases, the women give birth and insist that the government help them
> take care of the children. If the government doesn't agree, they curse, yell,
> and scream at the cadres.[97]

Separating from undesirable wives was also less complicated now that
land was collectivized. In Chuansha County near Shanghai and in Chuxiong, male cadres who "looked down upon their peasant wives" because

they were "crude" (*tuqi*) or illiterate frequently petitioned for divorce, or else deliberately provoked conflicts to force their spouses to initiate proceedings. After divorce, they ignored their responsibility toward their families, believing that the collective would now take care of them.[98]

In addition to facilitating divorce by providing a new conception of the state's role in the family, collectivization further contributed to it by reducing the number of property conflicts associated with divorce cases. A 1957 court report from Yunnan found that among peasants "there are very few disputes over postmarital property"; disputes arose in only two out of the fifty-five divorce cases the court handled. The court attributed this to the fact that, between 1953 and 1957, women had been participating in production, been paid according to their work, and therefore become no longer dependent on their husbands or families. Property settlements remained problematic only in relationships involving a sick spouse, or in households in which many family members were unable to work. How the state distributed work points also facilitated settlements. By 1956, peasants in Yunnan had each been distributed a booklet to record their work points. Peasants received food and other resources based on the number of points recorded in this booklet. "After divorce," the court noted, "women can take their booklet wherever they go." If they did not have enough points to get by, the court would "take care of" their points.[99]

What complicated divorce settlements was not universal male opposition to divorce, as has been suggested by feminist scholars of the family under the CCP, who tend to portray men generally as patriarchs and women as victims. Collectivization, after all, eased the burden on some men by providing their wives with alimony payments and the like. Moreover, men might be just as frustrated and angry with their wives (for gambling and adultery in particular) as wives were with their husbands.[100] More problematic from the state's administrative perspective was women's mobility between their natal and husbands' homes (even after the implementation of the household registration system).[101] In Chuxiong, for instance, the county court handled a case involving a woman surnamed Shao who "returned to her natal home" after one month of marriage. During the courtship and month of marriage, Shao on several occasions "ran back and forth" between her husband's home and her own. The court persuaded her not to divorce, but Shao demanded that the court solve her "grain allocation problem." The court found that in cases such as Shao's, a common problem arose when work points and grain were distributed in two different locations (work points were distributed at husbands' homes). Should women divorce and their families not receive an extra grain ration, families might have difficulty feeding them. To resolve this problem, the court ordered that when women returned to their natal homes after divorce, their families should receive an extra grain allotment.[102]

Postdivorce land settlements also reflected rural marriage practices. In 1957, just prior to the Great Leap Forward, peasants were still allowed to maintain some land as a household plot. When peasants from the same village divorced, this land could theoretically become a source of conflict between the households. But court reports surprisingly give no indication of serious disputes over such land. When women demanded land in court, the court agreed to allocate it on the basis of the number of people in the woman's household and how many family members were able to work. That there were few disputes over such land is perhaps explained by the support divorcing women received from their natal homes, which may have welcomed their return to augment the family labor force. When women married outside of their village and then divorced, however, "their" portion of their husband's plot was considered abandoned.[103]

In comparative perspective, the relative ease with which divorce cases were settled after collectivization is not all that surprising. In other collectivized economies, divorce is also quite common, and facilitated by the lack of concern over alimony payments, property, and land settlements. In the Israeli kibbutz, for instance, divorce does not affect one's status, occupation, income, or future prospects because the kibbutz assumes responsibility for both partners' livelihood. There are, of course, disincentives to divorce. In such a small community, encounters with estranged spouses are unavoidable. Nonetheless, the divorce rate on the kibbutz as of 1982–1983 was only slightly lower than in major metropolitan areas, but still higher than the national average.[104]

The Family and the Great Leap Forward

Although sharing features of common property and land, the Israeli kibbutz differed from the collective in China in important ways, most significantly in organization and the amount of resources available to individual members and families. On the kibbutz, members join voluntarily, and can now enjoy a level of prosperity equivalent to that in some Western European countries. In China, by contrast, during the high tide of collectivization peasants were often coerced into communes, and remained destitute after they entered.[105] As China hurtled toward the Great Leap Forward in 1958, peasants were mobilized to join massive public work projects, often working around the clock to the point of complete exhaustion. Peasants were ordered to build backyard furnaces and smelt their cooking utensils in sufficient quantity to enable China to catch up to England's steel production within sixteen years. When men were away, women, who were generally less experienced than men in fieldwork, were forced to take up the slack in the fields. As a result, many villages failed to bring in the fall harvest.[106]

By 1959 and 1960, the results of the Great Leap's utopianism were slowly becoming apparent. Many areas of China, but particularly in the arid North, suffered famine on a massive scale. In Anhui, peasants excavated corpses for food and scraped bark from trees. Ignoring household registration restrictions, peasants abandoned communes in search of food in more hospitable locales; in Hebei Province, there were reports that migrants fled to the Northeast, and there established new communities. Rural political administration in the province, already in chaos after the massive amalgamation of cooperatives into full-scale communes, could do little to prevent massive migration, food riots, and raids of granaries.[107] In contrast, state policies assured that whatever food supplies were available would be shipped to urban areas, where inhabitants rarely suffered from starvation throughout the Leap years.

The post-Leap famine, like famines elsewhere, strained family relations to a breaking point.[108] Competition for scare resources often pitted young against old, and spouses against each other. Liu Shaoqi privately admitted that, during the Leap, "people starved and families were torn apart."[109] It was these family tensions, and the migratory survival strategies they produced, that contributed heavily to the rash of divorces in 1961–1962.[110] Evidence suggests that women usually initiated the proceedings. Compilers of the Kunshan County gazetteer attributed divorce to the fact that some women, as in earlier periods, "blindly ran away" (*mangmu wailiu*) because of economic hardship.[111] In Lufeng County in Yunnan as well women were the majority of plaintiffs, but men also initiated many proceedings.[112] Family elders, who had already lost a great deal of influence during collectivization, were often abandoned and left to die of starvation. Weak and hungry, few were in a position to prevent women and men from leaving. At the same time that very few couples divorced in cities, the rural family—particularly in those areas most affected by the famine—was an institution very much in flux.

Contributing heavily to these divorces was the organizational and social chaos resulting from the Great Leap, which removed some obstacles on the road to divorce. Commune officials who implemented the radical policies and were then left scrambling to pick up the pieces could do little to prevent divorce; nor was this their highest priority. It is also possible that officials might actually *encourage* villagers to leave in order to have fewer mouths to feed.[113] Commune mediation committees were also in disarray, as hungry officials tended to their families' needs. As state layers that had built up between peasants and courts during 1954–1958 peeled away, there were fewer administrative structures between villages and the courts.

Even as the extent of the disaster of the Great Leap Forward became clear, the top CCP leadership was slow to respond with emergency measures. Mao was reluctant to admit that his economic policies were misguided, and there were few brave enough to risk his wrath by explicitly criticizing him. In 1959–1960, factional struggles and purges in the leadership made it difficult to devise, let alone implement, a coherent new economic policy.[114] Only in 1961, after a series of investigations into the economic situation of the countryside and Mao's grudging withdrawal from the front line of politics, were a series of economic measures approved to ameliorate the famine and raise peasant production and living standards. Known as the Sixty Articles, the new policies reduced the amount of cereals peasants were required to deliver to granaries and increased welfare expenditures to rural areas. In mid-1961, peasant households were allowed to restore cultivation of private plots; other small-scale peasant enterprises, such as weaving, and raising pigs, chickens, ducks, and the like, were also sanctioned. Products from these household enterprises could then be sold in reopened rural markets. Throughout the early 1960s, however, these policies only partially improved peasant income; many areas of China remained dirt-poor, even if they were better off than during the Great Leap.[115]

Politically, change also came slowly. Although some cadres at the commune and brigade levels were purged, lower levels of rural administration remained intact, leaving cadres in control of scarce resources and the allocation of goods on the basis of the recently restored work-point system (in which production team members would be paid according to their work, instead of in accordance with the communist principle of "to each according to his need"). Between 1961 and 1962, if the experience of a South China village is representative of other parts of the county, less emphasis was placed on good political class as a criterion for recruitment into state service.[116] This shifted dramatically only after 1962, when Mao began his campaign to regain power by emphasizing class struggle.

How did the aftermath of the Leap and the economic policies of the Sixty Articles shape family relations? Did the renewed emphasis on class influence family dynamics? Evidence shows that economic policies that rewarded work, opened markets, and gave material incentives to families to increase production frequently, but unintentionally, undermined both the Marriage Law and campaigns to increase peasants' class consciousness. According to party and government reports after the Great Leap, the years 1961–1966 witnessed a widespread revival of "feudalistic" marriage practices, such as arranged and coerced marriages, bride-prices, exchanging gifts, wedding feasts, and underage marriages.[117] At the same time that these "feudal" marriage practices spread, however, the number of divorce cases (a "modern" sort of family change) was as high in 1963 as it had been in 1953 in areas as ecologically and economically different as the Yangzi Delta and Yunnan. How can we explain these seemingly paradoxical outcomes? Why would certain cultural practices persist in the face of politicization and economic upheaval?

The post-Leap economic policy allowing the expansion and revival of household plots, rural markets, and the work-point system gave peasants incentives—all unintended—to circumvent the Marriage Law and avoid relationships based on statist notions of "good" and "bad" political classes. According to many reports, cadres at the production team and brigade levels often took the lead in violating the law. Since the Sixty Articles policy gave incentives to households to increase sideline production, cadres with access to scarce resources augmented their household labor force by purchasing wives and adopting or purchasing *tongyangxi*. In Beiyin Commune (township), Chuxiong, for instance, a production team leader and CCP member surnamed Wang cited purely economic reasons to justify his adoption of a thirteen-year-old girl for his young son:

> Since the promulgation of the Sixty Articles, everything is calculated on the basis of work points. If I bring in a young girl, even though she won't add to the labor force in the short term, I can still increase my income by having her raise pigs and ducks and do household work. When she's at home, more adults can work in the fields. This way we can collect more work points.[118]

In addition to the desire to increase work points, cadres also adopted daughters-in-law because many mistakenly believed that, after the Great Leap, the CCP was completely abandoning communes in favor of a land tenure system based on household plots. In Biji Commune, another production team leader gambled that the party would liberalize land policy even further and adopted a young girl:

> In 1961, the party abandoned the policy of collective dining halls. In 1962, the party restored some land and farm animals to households. In 1963, it's possible that all land will be returned to households. I have a son, so the earlier I bring in a young daughter-in-law, the better. That way there will be more people in the household. When land is distributed back to the household [on the basis on the number of people per household], we can then get an extra piece of land.[119]

Witnessing party officials bringing in *tongyangxi,* peasants who were able to afford the expense followed suit. In Yunnan's Sanjie District, sixty households were reported to have brought *tongyangxi* into their families. Of these, five were families of commune cadres, ten were production team leaders, and thirteen were party members; the rest were "ordinary" peasants. With political leaders violating the law, few ordinary folks feared retribution. When outside work teams criticized peasants for this practice during the Socialist Education campaign, some peasants simply responded, "The cadres lead and the masses follow."[120]

Behind cadres' confidence that they would not be prosecuted for violating the Marriage Law was an acute awareness of their own power in the community. With their connections to higher levels of government, local officials were perfectly placed to secure scarce resources (such as food) for themselves, family, and friends. This enhanced power was not lost upon parents and relatives of young village women. Success in selling a daughter into a cadre family would virtually guarantee the family's survival in the post-famine years. The more money one could get for a daughter, the better off parents would be, even if the daughter eventually divorced. Many parents were thus anxious to arrange marriages for their young daughters, and demanded a high price for their "hand," a price only some could afford to pay. Bride-prices were very expensive considering the general poverty of the time, probably reflecting, at least in part, the scarcity of women in the area and their mobility.[121] Because women were willing to divorce, sometimes after only a few days, a high bride-price might give them added incentive to stay in place. The average price in Yunnan (as per 1963), party reports indicated, was between four hundred and five hundred yuan, but beautiful or middle-school-educated peasant girls were said to fetch an astronomical twelve hundred yuan. In the Liangshan area of Yuanmou County, Yunnan, even mentally ill women could cost ninety yuan.[122] This happened at the time when the monthly salary for an *urban* worker was approximately one hundred yuan.

But it would be simplistic to argue that parents were the only ones demanding a high price for daughters. Young women were not mere pawns or putty in their parents' hands; they had both agency and ambition, and demanded a great deal for themselves. In the post-Leap period as in previous years, prior to consenting to a proposed marriage young peasant women presented suitors with a shopping list of demands. Reports from the 1960s criticized women for making excessively long ones, which included large apartments, cash, watches, alarm clocks, wool blankets, clothes, leather shoes and purses, a formal photograph, and a meal with candy and pork, in addition to a night on the town to see opera performances. In relatively well-off Songjiang County, men had to sew three or four pairs of woolen pants and build an extra room for their new bride as a condition for marriage; without the extra room, women refused even to consider the match. Similar demands were made in poorer areas farther away from cities. In Wujiang County in Jiangsu Province, women reportedly demanded eight "zi's": a gold earring (huan zi), a gold ring (jin zi); a silk quilt cover (chou bei mian zi), a multicolored quilt (hun tan zi), a ride in a bridal sedan (zuo qiao zi), a pig being killed (sha zhu zi), and a two-room apartment (liang jian fang zi), in addition to some cash (qian zi). According to the report, "women will agree to marry only after receiving all of this." As during the early 1950s, young women refused to marry (good class) peasants unless there was absolutely no other alternative; in Yunnan, "good class" soldiers were also undesirable because "they might die in war." And, in a clear shift from the past, some women were reluctant to marry "good class" urban workers because they feared (rightly, it turned out) that state policies forcing workers back to the countryside would reduce them to the lowly status of peasant.[123]

In demanding a high price for their agreement to marry, some women seemed to have been very aware of their clout in the marriage market. Taking advantage of their right to divorce, women gravitated toward those men with more means, such as cadres and other wealthier peasants. Such cadres were the only ones who, usually through corruption, could gather the resources to satisfy their demands. Evidence shows that women could press their advantage to the hilt. As reports from the Shanghai suburbs remarked, "It's easy for young women to find a partner. Because of this, they have very high demands: a big apartment, furniture, gifts, strong workers, and good looks." A marriage's failure did not seem to be cause for much concern. With many available men, women could easily remarry, even if they had already lost their virginity. As one woman explained, "Even if I divorce I'll always be able to find a husband. All I have to do is not make so many demands."[124]

The multiple marriages of a peasant woman named Chen Qiaolin is a case in point. Prior to her marriage, Qiaolin was said to have "flirted and talked about marriage with three different men" until finally agreeing to marry a worker at the railroad bureau. Married in August 1961, Qiaolin soon spent the six hundred yuan the railroad worker gave her as a gift for marriage. After her marriage, she reportedly "flirted" with three other men: Chen Zhongyuan, a state purchasing agent; and two truck drivers, Liu Zhong and Wang Shaochang. Qiaolin decided that purchasing agent Chen could offer her the best of two worlds—access to food supplies and extensive travel opportunities within the county. Qiaolin then had sex with Chen, and sued to divorce her railroad worker husband. After the railway worker heard of these developments, he chased after her, but when he caught up with her Qiaolin quickly spun around and socked him in the nose, breaking it. Furious, the now broken-nosed railway worker complained to the court, "If you have money you can stay married; if you don't, you can forget about your wife." In the hearings, he agreed to divorce, but demanded that Qiaolin compensate him for his wedding expenditures. The court agreed to the divorce, and instructed Qiaolin to write a self-confession and return 250 yuan and some clothes.[125]

Qiaolin's case was not an isolated incident.[126] Investigations of female party officials in the Four Cleanups and Socialist Education campaigns often complained that cadres, who were supposed to serve as examples to the rest of the population, also used divorce as a method of advancing themselves materially. In Yuanmou County, Yunnan, the county party committee complained that "some female cadres, because they want money, material possessions, and to have a good time, have cheated men by accepting gifts from three men at a time and promising to marry each of them." The director of the Women's Federation in the county was criticized for using 250 yuan of pilfered money to divorce her husband, supposedly because he had tuberculosis, and remarrying soon afterward.[127] Similar events occurred in wealthier rural areas. In Jinshan and Qingpu Counties, women reportedly "returned to their natal homes after they spent all their husband's money, and the husband and his family were no longer able to afford them."[128]

Male cadres, who had the best access to scarce resources, were quick to take advantage of post-Leap economic difficulties to improve their family situation and enhance their personal status. Whereas female cadres tended to use marriage and divorce to increase their material resources, male officials—rather than being sexually puritanical, as suggested by Judith Stacey—had many affairs and multiple marriages, most likely in order to increase their "face" among other cadres. In 1963 in a commune in Chuxiong, four out of six party members at the commune level had more than one wife, and adultery and "chaotic sexual relations" were said to be "common." In District 3 of the commune, the deputy party secretary "used his position and ability to allocate jobs" in order to commit adultery with eight women, and another cadre at a key gastronomic post—Ji Guofu of the food storage facility—pilfered two thousand yuan of goods, including three thousand *jin* of pork, to "have illicit sex with over twenty women, including several PLA wives." In Lufeng County, married women were reported to have "eaten, lived together, and had sex with people who had access to food storage facilities, and justified these affairs by citing 'marriage freedom.'"[129] In other cases, cadres abducted other peasants' wives, had ménages à trois, and exchanged wives among themselves. As among the urban working class—many of whom hailed from rural areas—few of these relationships were kept secret. In Jiujue Commune, for instance, the production team leader "openly committed bigamy" with a beautiful nineteen-year-old, inviting enough guests to their illegal wedding to fill fifteen tables. Peasants who witnessed these officials complained, "These days it's impossible to control the cadres."[130]

Cadres were not the only ones able to use the new economic policies to attract *tongyangxi*, lovers, and wives. In Yunnan, some peasants—ignoring household registration restrictions—picked up their meager belongings and moved to wherever they could collect more work points in return for their labor in what seems to be an early-1960s prelude to the "floating population" in the post-Mao period. With their notebook of work points, all they needed to do was record the number of points they had earned (with an official seal) and then proceed to a public granary to collect their rations. Along the way some collected wives, many of whom were eager to find a hard-working and enterprising man. One He Zhengmin, a peasant from He Family Village, for instance, was reported to have three wives, all living in different villages. Other peasants from the village pointed out that Zhengmin "was hardly ever at home working . . . He lives a couple of days in one place, fools around, and goes somewhere else for several days." Other peasants committed "bigamy" by taking advantage of bumbling civil affairs bureaus. Anxious to increase their welfare allotment, peasants registered to marry several times, each time at a different locale. Having secured these "marriages," they would then file for benefits at different agencies. From 1958 to 1963, reports indicated a threefold increase in the number of rural bigamy cases. Many of these cases were attributed to the registration bureaus' practice of "casually issuing documentation" and not investigating peasants' family situations.[131]

In their pursuit of economic security and upward mobility, neither young women nor their parents seemed to pay much attention to the political class of men supplying these goods. In Jinshan County near Shanghai, a woman surnamed Lu was reported to have "forgotten her class standing" because she married a handsome son of a "counterrevolutionary," who provided her with a large apartment.[132] In Yunnan's Lufeng County, Fanguang Commune, a woman surnamed Yin (a "middle" peasant) was orphaned and was raised by her paternal grandmother. The grandmother introduced her to a landlord family from a nearby village to become their adopted daughter-in-law, believing that this would give her granddaughter a better life. The young woman's grandmother was not afraid to tell a Four Cleanups investigation team in late 1965 that "landlord families live well, work hard, and have nice homes."[133]

CCP cadres, who may have had more incentive to marry a "good class" poor peasant than "bad class" landlords and rich peasants, also placed economic over political concerns. Landlord families, even though they had much of their property and land holdings confiscated and had been reduced to the lowest political status, still seemed to have retained their reputation as those most capable of making money. (It would be interesting to see if, in the 1980s and 1990s, those classified earlier as landlords have emerged more prosperous than those categorized as "poor" or "middle" peasants). In 1961 in "New Village" Commune in Yunnan, a female CCP cadre surnamed Wu agreed to marry a landlord's son. When the party branch tried to persuade her to break the engagement, Wu defiantly said, "I'm definitely getting married, even if it means no longer being a CCP member." After the marriage, Wu and her husband reportedly engaged in selling state food supplies at double their price in a nearby county. Wu expressed no remorse for her marriage: "Even though his class status is bad, he's still an honest guy."[134] Another female CCP member threatened to commit suicide in front of her mother if the latter did *not* allow her to marry into a landlord's home. Some male cadres also ignored class. In Tianxin Commune a production team leader and CCP member "married the daughter of a counterrevolutionary and decided to give up his position as team leader after that," and in other areas, cadres in the state security apparatus also sought to marry into landlord homes.[135] That such marriages were not uncommon nor limited to Yunnan is confirmed by interviews with rural officials. The vice–country magistrate of Jiangpu County in Jiangsu, Li Xianqing, when asked about interclass marriages among cadres in the 1950s and 1960s, told me that "cadres married landlord daughters even though they knew this might affect their promotions." He admitted that landlord sons might have some difficulties (but most managed), but that landlord daughters, particularly if they were beautiful, had very few difficulties in getting married; poor peasants, he added, really did not care if their spouse was from a landlord background.[136]

Notions of cultural refinement and gender difference reinforced these economic considerations. Poor peasants may have had good political class, but rich peasants and "landlords" were still perceived to be more "culturally cultivated," even on the eve of the Cultural Revolution. Some cadres considered landlord and rich peasant families to be "better workers, kinder, *and more polite*" than poorer peasants. Women were particularly confused by the state's renewed concern with political class. For some, their role in the household and family negated class consciousness. Only men, who had more important roles in the public sphere, could concern themselves with such matters. As one female cadre in Yunnan remarked:

> Only men can concern themselves with class struggle; women can only care for babies and look after the household. For women there is no such thing as class struggle . . . These last few years the only thing we think about is production to improve our livelihood. Class struggle is way back in the recesses of our mind."[137]

In the more affluent county of Songjiang in the Yangzi Delta, sons and daughters of rich peasants and landlords also managed to marry, despite their "bad class" background.[138] "Peasants," complained one 1964 report, "don't discuss class status when choosing a wife." This may not be that surprising given that some matchmakers themselves were "wives of counterrevolutionaries," who may have lacked political status, but evidently retained enough connections and face to make them important community assets. In a village in Songjiang County, a "counterrevolutionary" matchmaker had already matched twenty-six couples in 1962–1964, including "cadres, and poor and lower-middle peasants."[139]

What often militated against the adoption of a political class-based system of social classification were villagers' everyday experiences and the post-Leap economic program. State efforts to pit one political class in the countryside against another flew in the face of the one common experience villagers shared: agricultural labor. In one production team in Chuxiong, three cadre households married sons and daughters of landlords and rich peasants, and five households were already engaged to "black class" families. When prefectural officials in Yunnan criticized county and district Women's Federation cadres for these choices, women retorted, "Now that we all work, we aren't divided into classes anymore" (*bu fen jieji le*); others said, "Land reform has been over for over ten years now; there aren't any classes anymore" and "The revolution has succeeded, so there's no need to continue making revolution."[140] Not only did everyone "work" in the fields, but all peasants—including landlords' progeny—earned their living on the basis of work points. During the Socialist Education campaign in 1964, the director of the Women's Federation in a commune in Yunnan confessed:

> In the past I didn't distinguish between friends and the enemy (*di wo bu fen*). I thought that landlords and rich peasants rely on work points to eat just like us, that there are no classes anymore, and that they're honest and haven't destroyed anything.[141]

The absence of a class-based social hierarchy, in combination with peasant women's desire to improve their livelihood during the relatively liberal economic atmosphere of the early 1960s, placed poor peasant men in a difficult position in the rural marriage market. Women who gravitated toward cadres or toward relatively well-off peasants left few young women available for the poorest of the poor. Reports from Jiangnan, Subei, and the Southwest found that poor and lower-middle peasants fretted about how they would be able to marry without constructing an extra room for the new daughter-in-law, or buying expensive gifts obtainable only in cities or through black-market connections. In some cases, poor families were able to meet prospective spouses' (or their families') material demands only by pawning household items or borrowing money at high interest rates from relatives and other village members, including families of the "bad classes."[142]

Families unable to muster such resources had no choice but to rely on their own efforts. In Songjiang, there were reports that poor fathers did not allow their sons to be drafted into the military in order to help build an extra room for a new daughter-in-law: if the son were to leave home to join the PLA, the productive capacity of the household would be drastically reduced. Lacking the income earned from his work, the family would not be able to add the room, and the son would forever remain a bachelor.[143] Desperate peasants might also resort to illegal means to raise funds. In Yunnan, a Women's Federation report noted other unintended consequences of the Marriage Law: "very many" single poor and lower-middle peasants robbed, gambled, sold drugs, and engaged in black-market trade in order to raise funds to marry or purchase *tongyangxi*. On occasion, these efforts paid off. In Dali County, Xiangyang Commune, a peasant named He Shicai won 340 yuan during three successive nights of gambling and then used 280 yuan of his profits to purchase a ten-year-old girl for his nine-year-old son.[144] Peasants who lacked Shicai's luck at the gambling table remained in difficult straits, however, and were said to express strong support for the CCP's Marriage Law.[145] Even though the law made it easier to divorce, the law also banned the "commercial marriages" that placed poor men at a clear disadvantage; only with state intervention in the form of a strengthened Marriage Law, some argued, could such men afford wives.[146]

Peasants who despaired because they were unable to purchase wives might have taken heart at the fact that cadres and peasants who managed to purchase *tongyangxi* often found themselves without their new wife soon after the completion of the transaction. Short of locking *tongyangxi* or brides in rooms or killing them, there was little husbands' families could do to prevent new daughters-in-law from running away, usually back to their natal homes. In Chuxiong's Sanjie District, for example, nine out of twenty-five women who were married in 1962 (most were between sixteen and seventeen years old and had arranged marriages) "had [by early 1963] already returned to their natal homes and broken off relations," and five were reportedly about to follow suit.[147] Although most of these cases seem to have ended with the woman running back to her natal home, it is also likely that some ended up in court, where a more formal resolution to a marriage could be had. Thus, in addition to the family tensions resulting from the Great Leap, it is highly probably that some of the cases ending up in court, and the early 1961–1963 statistics, resulted from women running away from commercial marriages.

Families who spent years saving to satisfy women's material demands did not take such escapes lightly. In some cases, family elders invoked the power of brigade (village) and commune (township) officials to prevent women from running away after deals were signed. These officials sometimes shared elders' interests in sustaining population growth in their communities, which could be accomplished only by making sure that village women who married into the village could not easily leave. According to one report, "cadres, including the Women's Federation, collaborate with family heads to make sure that the woman lives with the man." In Baoshan County near Shanghai, two family heads, local cadres, and peasants forced a woman who repeatedly "ran away" from her marriage to return to the village and have sex with her husband, presumably because they thought that forcing the daughter to lose her virginity would lower her chances of finding another husband. Her mother agreed with these measures because the family "had already received numerous gifts" for her daughter. Anxious that she would lose her daughter-in-law, the mother-in-law sought out the help of local officials. As a result of their discussions, the production team's deputy party secretary, production team leader, and Women's Federation cadre then "tried to tell her to follow the old customs" by ripping her clothes and humiliating her. This intervention failed, and the woman remained at home.[148]

Even though it appears that many male cadres ignored the issue of political class status when selecting wives or *tongyangxi* for their young sons, they were nonetheless willing to use the *language of class status* as a weapon to deter young daughters-in-law from seeking divorce. In this sense, language was a very flexible resource, available to many villagers depending on their individual or family circumstances; class might be completely ignored during marriage, but later tactically invoked during the divorce process. Take for instance the case of Li Kaichang, a party branch secretary in Chuxiong. In 1960 Li brought (or bought) into his household a seventeen-year-old girl to marry his ten-year-old son. This girl, who was also surnamed Li, came from a village in the same commune. Their wedding was a huge affair: over ninety guests were invited, and there was plenty of food and beverages; hosts and guests kowtowed to the ancestors. After the marriage, the young bride was reported to be extremely unhappy with the match, not surprising given the age difference between the couple. After "frequent arguments" with her adopted family, she threatened to divorce on several occasions. Party branch secretary Li then accosted her and said, "You're a member of the upper-middle peasant exploiting class (*shangzhong nong boxue jieji*), so no one cares what you have to say. If you divorce, you have to return all the jewelry, clothes, and other things my family bought you when you were married." Undeterred, the young woman "ran to the commune" to request assistance. Sometime later in 1963, a commune official—who apparently cared less about her class background—went to their village to see how he might help, but Li Kaichang did not allow his daughter-in-law out of the house. After the official left, his family beat her. The young daughter-in-law was at this point said to have "become insane" because of her terrible predicament. In December 1964 she deteriorated further, and was seen "aimlessly wandering around" (*dao chu luan pao*) the countryside. Luckily for her, her mother found out about her situation and brought her home. Soon after this, she recovered from her "insanity."[149] Whether this "insanity" was truly the result of her predicament, as the report noted, or perhaps feigned in order to draw attention to her case, we will never know for certain, but given the tenacity and resourcefulness we have already seen among many village women, the latter possibility does not seem so farfetched.

Cultural Revolution Overture: Sexual Tensions during Political Campaigns

Ad hoc alliances between disgruntled villagers and outside officials against village political administration were bolstered during the Four Cleanups and Socialist Education campaigns. In contrast to ordinary times, when peasants ventured to the district or county seat to file accusations against family members, neighbors, and officials, during the Four Cleanups, state authorities streamed into villages to collect material on abusive practices of local officials. Such material was certainly abundant: during the years of economic liberalization, cadres took advantage of their positions to secure good jobs and work-point bonuses for lovers and second wives, or to seize good land to attract *tongyangxi*. Villagers who lacked such resources probably seethed in silence, waiting for an opportunity to strike back. Cadres seemed to have been aware of this tension: reports indicated that the entrance of work teams into villages produced general panic among local officials and their families. According to reports on the Four Cleanups and Socialist Education campaigns in Yunnan, local officials were reportedly terrified of struggle sessions, labor reform, and administrative discipline because they had consorted with the enemy classes, "borrowed" public funds, and appropriated good land for themselves. Many feared that villagers would either seek revenge for past injustices or, goaded by outside officials, make false accusations. Other officials feared prosecution of illicit sexual relations. For instance, the jilted lover of an accountant in the granary of Qianliang Commune went to the work team to accuse her former lover of sleeping around. Prior to heading off to the village cadre meeting, the accountant took with him three pairs of pants, shoes, and socks so that he would be prepared should he be sent to labor reform after the struggle session.[150]

During the high tide of the campaigns, as struggle sessions intensified and accusations were hurled at officials, cadres' family members and wives were often fearless in trying to protect their husbands and sons from angry villagers and work team officials. Having secured access to power through marriage or family blood ties, cadres' families had a large stake in preventing their own from being sentenced to prison or labor reform. During the campaign, these women were subjected to serious criticism for their "bourgeois" values. Wives of commune-level officials were criticized for refusing to allow their husbands out of the house to attend cadre meetings because they feared a struggle session and a possible purge. In this event, they would have to forfeit their husbands' economic perks. According to one critical report, such women "rely only on their husband's income, don't work, don't care about the collective economy, don't participate in social activities, and have separated themselves from the masses."[151] Wives of brigade (village)-level officials, although enjoying far fewer perks than their commune-level counterparts, were also worried about their husbands, and resisted the state's efforts to prosecute them. According to a report on the Socialist Education campaign in Jianshui County in Yunnan,

Cadres' family members go to struggle session to find out who has made accusations against their husbands. After the meeting, they run around the village crying and screaming, searching for poor and lower-middle peasant
women representatives to yell at. Because of this, the representatives are very
worried. They say, "We're not afraid of the cadres; we're afraid of their wives
cursing and screaming at us."[152]

Cadres' mothers also closed ranks around their sons. When the mother
of a production team's accountant heard that her son was going to a cadre
meeting, she "feared he was going to be struggled." She then

went to the meeting and began hollering and screaming, not allowing anyone to say anything negative about her son. She ran to wherever they held
meetings in order to raise a racket and prevent disclosures of her son's behavior. She then berated whoever accused her son of something. Only after we
calmed her down did she stop arguing, screaming, and cursing people.[153]

Often, threats by family members were effective in silencing peasants
who wanted to make accusations. After the work team left, some wondered,
who would prevent cadres and their families from taking revenge? Who
could guarantee that accountants, at the instigation of their wives, would
not shave off work points when calculating their income? Past experience,
according to some peasants, showed that campaigns come and go, but cadres still retain their power: "If we stomp on a snake's head but it doesn't die,
we still can get bitten," they complained.[154]

That families of cadres closed ranks during the Four Cleanups and Socialist Education campaigns would later shape the way the Cultural Revolution—which began one year after the Four Cleanups campaign in some
areas—would develop. Cadres who escaped criticism for abuses of power
during the Four Cleanups would soon face a more terrifying ordeal in the
Cultural Revolution. During the Cultural Revolution, Mao, with the help of
sexually puritanical urban-educated youth, would give poor peasants the
opportunity to criticize local cadres' abuses of power.[155]

3. CULTURE AND COMMUNITY

A search of the secondary literature on China for a hypothesis suggesting
cultural causes for divorce in the 1950s and 1960s would leave the researcher empty-handed. Although "women were brought into the work
force and the schools, and women's rights to property ownership and divorce were written into law," Friedman, Pickowicz, and Selden argue, "no
practical challenge was mounted to the values, practices, and institutions of
male supremacy."[156] During the mid-1950s, they point out, village fathers
continued to insist that their daughters stay at home, even though some

opportunities for high school education were opening up; women were "forced into early marriages"; domestic violence was condoned by party officials, and even by the Women's Federation.[157] Rural culture, according to the authors, remained deeply patriarchal, and the state remained uncommitted to the enforcement of the Marriage Law.

The secondary literature on rural culture during the mid-1950s and the 1960s is not alone in its stress on the relative absence of family change. In terms of the cultural hypotheses developed earlier in this study as well, there were also many reasons to anticipate a steep downward decline in divorce cases after 1953. The political radicalization of the countryside during collectivization, the antisuperstition campaigns of 1955, and the Socialist Education campaign in the early 1960s might have led to rural cultural change or to peasants hiding cultural practices deemed "feudal" by the state. If elite cultural values filtered down to the countryside during these years, peasants would treat marriage and divorce in a more "civilized" manner: they would see marriage as a milestone in one's life and divorce as something undertaken only as a very last resort after many attempts at reconciliation, rather than seeing marriage as a pragmatic arrangement entered into or dissolved according to changing circumstances (an attitude exemplified by the peasant woman who said, "I marry to eat; if I don't eat, I divorce"). Studies of the family in rural Japan have pointed to this exact phenomenon.[158]

Much like Western critics of Chinese culture who emphasize "patriarchy" and the lack of "sexual equality" (often without acknowledging the cultural bias involved in seeing "equality" as a "progressive" social value and its absence as equivalent to "oppression"), Chinese critics also point to the stubborn persistence of peasants' "feudal" marriage practices throughout this period. In 1957, for instance, state officials complained that deep-rooted "feudalism" resulted in arranged and underage marriages four years after the 1953 Marriage Law campaign ended, yet the same report officials also attributed *divorce* in this period to this very same "feudal" culture; peasants, they complained, still do not treat marriage with appropriate seriousness. In this memorandum the Interior Ministry in Beijing instructed local officials to put an end to peasants' "feudal" practices, such as "arranged marriages" and "marrying and divorcing over three times."[159] By 1963 the causes had changed somewhat, but the practice remained the same: part of the early-1960s surge in divorce cases was attributed to bourgeois-influenced "rash" marriages among peasants, which in same cases accounted for over 25 percent of divorce cases in courts.[160] In Fujian Province, county-level officials spoke not in terms of "feudal" or "bourgeois" culture, but simply of "bad customs" that were responsible for a young girl marrying and divorcing thirteen times in the mid-1960s. The eradication of such customs, whether deemed "feudal" or "bourgeois," was a major goal of the Socialist Education campaign.[161]

To what extent do peasant attitudes and practices concerning marriage and divorce, whether classified as "patriarchal," "feudal," or "bourgeois," help explain the continuation of divorce after 1953, during the period when the state mounted vigorous attacks on rural culture? Did divorce reflect the state's political agenda, as it did among intellectuals who divorced spouses because the regime labeled them rightists and counterrevolutionaries, or were there other, perhaps more prosaic, causes at work?

Contrary to the arguments of Western scholars, who have emphasized the extent to which peasants do not form relationships based on desire, love, or other such emotions,[162] or have proposed that peasants' courtship practices are highly restrained and monitored by the community, evidence shows that love and sexual desire led to the formation and break up of relationships, a good deal of which were in opposition to state ideology. Peasants, as we have seen in the last section, were certainly interested in marrying "up" the political and cultural ladder, but they (in both Han and minority areas, suburbs and frontier) were also subject to the same passions and emotions that scholars have usually located only in urban areas. Such passions, and the short-term relationships they brought about, were a major irritant to more literate critics investigating marriage practices in the countryside. In the Beijing suburbs, for instance, a 1954 party report on the marriage situation there made it a point to complain that a certain woman surnamed Wang "has slept with four or five men, and the village party secretary has already slept with her twice." In other rural areas, the report continued, "some women publicly live together with three or four men." The result, according to the report, was "chaos" in marital relations and many out-of-wedlock children.[163] Even in the more rural province of Shanxi, marriage and divorce were deemed "rash" because peasant youth took the Marriage Law's promise of freely chosen marriages seriously and married and divorced more than once.[164] In northern Jiangsu, the Provincial Women's Federation complained that "many couples get married because they have already had sex and she is pregnant," only to divorce several days later.[165] Moving south to Yunnan, a Bureau of Civil Affairs investigation found that "in rural areas, illicit sex (*luangao guanxi*), adultery *(tongjian)*, and seducing minors (*youjian*) is very common. Sexual relations are particularly chaotic (*hunluan*) among youth."[166]

By repeatedly emphasizing the "chaotic" nature of sex, marriage, and divorce in the countryside, investigators failed to pay attention to more "structural" causes for the flourishing of sex before or outside of marriage. In fact, a case could be made that state collectivization policy unintentionally produced the very conditions that undermined its hope for more orderly, "civil," and politicized relationships. Many have already written about the economic consequences of collectivization, but only few have noticed its *sexual* dimension: all across China and under state auspices, millions of young men and now-mobilized women gathered in the fields in close proximity, forming ad hoc communities where there were opportunities for chat and banter, and later for love and sex. The anthropologist Yunxiang Yan notes that "the emphasis on collectivism and the mobilization of female laborers in collective farming encouraged young women to make personal choices in mate selection . . . As a result, a new type of courtship and marriage emerged, one characterized by romantic love and conjugal affection."[167] This new emphasis on "conjugal affection" most probably led to not a few impromptu (i.e., "chaotic") relationships among peasants and to subsequent divorces.[168]

Even though complaints about "chaotic" relations spanned the Chinese map, it would be inaccurate to conclude that certain ethnic customs made no difference in marriage and divorce patterns. Collectivization was a national policy, but in some areas youth found opportunities for sex in the fields and mountains before the latter half of the 1950s. In Yunnan's Chuxiong Prefecture, where there are many of the Yi ethnic minority, courtship, sex, and adultery during community drinking sessions in the mountains (*chi shan jiu*) led some couples to hastily marry, and others to go to court to file for divorce. In a breakdown of eighty divorce cases from 1956 in Luquan county, thirteen were caused by adultery during *chi shan jiu,* and thirteen by "rash marriages." One Yi, for instance, a man surnamed Chen, met his wife, (surnamed) Yang, during *chi shan jiu,* had sex, and married her soon afterward. Arguments over "household matters" finally led Yang to file for divorce. *Chi shan jiu* was not only Yi youth's most popular venue for premarital romps, but also for postmarital adultery. Some Yi were notorious home wreckers during drinking sessions. A Yi man surnamed Zhang, for instance, was said to have "destroyed marriages" by his persistent forays into the mountains. "Even after accusations led to his arrest and reform," the court complained, "Zhang and his friends continued to go with other women to the mountains, sometimes as many as four men and three women at a time." Some Yi became alcoholics after one-too-many drinking sessions, and sold their bed quilts to make money to purchase wine. When spouses discovered the theft, they petitioned for divorce.[169]

"Rash" marriage and divorce in Yunnan during the 1950s did not necessarily depend on *chi shan jiu,* however. Peasants in Yunnan—Yi and Han Chinese—entered and left marriages as quickly as some of their North Chinese counterparts, but much more rapidly than urban elite women. Few seemed to hold the latter's view (which was represented in state propaganda as well) that the "life milestone" quality of marriage justified multiple efforts to "get along" or reconcile after a particularly bad argument. Nor did young peasant women seem particularly worried about their prospects for remarriage should they divorce their first husband. In one township in Yongren County, a woman surnamed Xu married a man surnamed Sun in 1955 but "returned to her natal home after three days" because she did not like digging ditches. Another couple "did not know each other well" prior to marriage. They were married one morning in 1955, and the new bride "ran back to the district" to return her marriage certificate the very next day. Such women did not remain single very long, as there were many men anxious to find wives in an environment in which there were fewer women than men. For instance, a woman named He Lanfang, who was only eighteen years old in 1955, had already been married and divorced five times. Her last marriage endured only one evening before "she ran back to her natal home."[170]

When they were criticized for what some state officials considered an excessively cavalier attitude toward relationships, some peasants justified their relationships by citing the Marriage Law itself. The language of the law, once it entered popular circulation, turned out to be a powerful weapon to parry the state's criticism because it could be countered only by citation of the laws' various subclauses and articles, something that most local officials were not capable of doing. A Yi woman named Na La Yong, for instance, argued that the Marriage Law's clause of marriage freedom "allowed her to get together with five men at a time and have sex without a formal marriage."[171] In another minority county, a special court report on "rash marriages" complained that youth "have a one-sided view of the meaning of marriage freedom: they think that 'marriage freedom' means there are no limitations at all" (*haowu yuezhi de hunyin ziyou*) and that "parents should have no say whatsoever as to whom we should marry."[172]

Yi women, such as Na La Yong above, did not always petition for divorce by themselves. Yi (and other ethnic minority women) often traveled in small groups to market centers to sell fruits, vegetables, and other goods. While in town, many stopped off in court just to witness whatever disputes were being heard at the time (*kan renao*); others, however, took advantage of the opportunity to divorce. Township officials who happened to see Yi women in court were concerned: "They're not coming to listen to cases or policy. They all want to divorce!" This concern led to a small controversy between court and township officials over the issue of "whether or not Yi women love suing for divorce" (*ai nao lihun*). Whereas township officials attributed Yi divorces to Yi women's litigiousness, courts argued that Yi women divorced because their "consciousness had been raised." The court did admit, however, that "the more we intervene, the more divorces there are."[173]

The mid-1950s expansion of mutual aid teams into cooperatives and the concomitant politicization of the countryside during 1956–1957 apparently had little effect on peasant marriage and sexual practices, or on the language they used to justify their relationships. In 1956, the Jiangsu Women's Federation complained that in Chuansha and Pei Counties, women "flirt with three men at a time," tricked men into giving them engagements gifts and then "refuse to talk to them again," married only for money without any regard for the age or political class of their spouse, and "divorce after using up all their husbands' money," sometimes only a few days after marriage.[174] A 1958 article by a law student on the causes of divorce in the countryside (area unclear) pointed out a bit condescendingly that in "some backward rural areas," peasants have a "one-sided view of the meaning of love marriage. They think that 'falling in love at first sight' (*yi jian zhongqing*) is the same thing as 'free love' and then immediately want to get married. One or two months later they'll demand a divorce. In the hearing they will tell the judge: 'I didn't know that he was ten years older than me' or 'I didn't know that s/he was married and already had children.' The student also found that some peasants frequently visited court compounds. A woman surnamed Huang, he wrote, was only nineteen, but had divorced and married four times between 1950 and 1958, the last divorce being on account of an illness that caused her husband to become bald. The way Huang dealt with her relationships irritated the student. A nineteen-year-old could not even see if her husband had hair on his head or not!" he complained.[175] Rural parents—their authority weakened by campaigns and changes in the economy—appear to have played little role in these affairs. As one mother commented, "No one now dares to intervene in other people's freedom to divorce; it's just that it will be embarrassing if our children divorce *many times*."[176]

Despite the intensified political atmosphere of the early to mid-1960s, there is little evidence suggesting that Mao's call for class struggle led to political considerations in marriage and divorce. The evidence shows only a moderate drop in the number of divorces after 1963, probably owing to political radicalization, but not a significant change in the meaning people gave to marriage and divorce. The persistence of these attitudes bothered peasants' more educated state critics, who hoped that peasants would treat relationships more seriously (i.e., like them) and consider class when selecting a spouse (also like them). Thus, in 1964, Women's Federation officials in suburban Jinshan and Qingpu Counties emphasized the extent to which "marriage" in the countryside was considered an arrangement subject to constant review, reevaluation, and, if necessary, termination should things not work out. Deemed "casual" by literate officials in reports, what lay behind this appellation, I believe, were two incompatible conceptualizations of marriage and, as a result, different ways of dealing with the state in divorce matters. "Some youth," the federation complained, "are quite casual in handling their relationships. If they get along, they stay together; if not, they just separate. Some divorce on account of a trivial argument."[177] Such attitudes cannot be explained by the proximity of these counties to the "liberating" influence of the more "cosmopolitan," or "decadent" Shanghai, as modernization and Marxist theorists might argue. In remote rural areas of Yunnan, similar attitudes also irked party ideologues during the 1960s. In Chuxiong's Lufeng and Yuanmou Counties, court and party reports from 1963 lamented that "not a few youth misunderstand the notion of marriage freedom, do not treat relationships seriously, and rashly marry and divorce."[178]

Divorce registration forms provide yet additional evidence that divorce was rarely motivated by political differences. As they appear in such forms, the causes for divorce stemmed from frequent arguments, illness, bigamy, theft, incompatible personalities, domestic violence, and "rash" marriages, but rarely because of political differences. In a random sample of twenty divorcing couples in Qingpu County in 1957, politics was not listed as a motive in any case. In a list of twenty-two couples from 1959, registrars wrote down reasons ranging from "she isn't willing to live at his home" (three cases) to "he's ill" to "she's insane," but never political differences.[179] In 1964, in a sample of forty-five cases, politics was not mentioned once either, as can be seen in the partial list of causes of divorce given in table 3.[180] In some instances, peasants (or officials) listed plaintiffs' occupations as "class status," so that "fisherman" appears in the box for class. Also of interest are the cases (in italic type) where marriages were de facto terminated, usually by the woman returning home, well before the divorce was officially registered.

In addition to attitudes toward sex, marriage, and divorce, certain customs in rural communities contributed to nonpoliticized relationships and divorce. Much like the urban working classes discussed in previous chapters, peasants also gave their desire for enjoyment and leisure priority over more serious political considerations. In the countryside, wedding ceremonies had traditionally been a time for good food and celebration. The CCP, however, condemned lavish wedding ceremonies as wasteful and "feudal," particularly during the 1963–1964 Socialist Education campaign. Despite this official condemnation, traditional weddings continued well into 1966. Matchmakers sometimes helped find partners, and peasants used different types of sedans to carry brides to husbands' villages, consulted these "feudal" fortune-tellers, and exchanged gifts prior to marriage—practices that undermined the party's ideological goals for political relationships. For instance, in the Jiangnan region peasants sometimes used small boats to carry brides to their husbands' homes, even if their respective villages were less than one hundred yards away. In 1966, the female leader of the Lu family production team, Lou Juanbao, married a man who lived just on the other side of the railroad tracks. Rather than walking, Lou demanded to use a boat, even though drought had almost dried up the stream separat-

TABLE 3   Some Causes for Divorce in Qingpu County

Year of Marriage	Cause for Divorce
1956	Arranged marriage; don't get along; argue a lot.
1956	He breaks household items, doesn't work hard, is lazy.
1948	She is a bit too cheap; he's violent. No *ganqing* (don't get along).
1960	Fight over sex; no *ganqing*.
1960	Rashly married; argue and fight.
1960	Personality clash; frequently argue. *Already separated for a year.*
1960	Arranged marriage; no *ganqing*. *Already separated for a long time.*
1960	Introduced by someone else and then rashly married; don't get along.
1960	Were forced to marry.
1960	He is sick; they argue and fight.
1960	Introduced by someone else and then rashly married; argue.
1946	She is having an affair.
1960	He cheated her into a rash marriage; beats her.
1950	He is lazy but likes to eat (*hao chi lan zuo*); beats her; sold her household items. *Already separated three years.*
1956	"Everyday disputes" (*shenghuo jiufen*). *Already separated for a year.*
1956	Small disputes and arguments led to a change in the relationship.
1960	Arranged marriage; no *ganqing*. She has "committed" (*fan*) an affair.
1960	She is having an affair and steals; doesn't take care of the household; wants to eat without working.
1955	Don't get along because of trivial arguments. *Already separated for a year.*
1958	Arranged marriage. After marriage, she had an affair. Now argue.
1955	He has bad temper; beats her.
1959	"Everyday arguments"
1961	Rash marriage; argue over everyday problems.
1958	Everyday disputes (*shenghuo jiufen*).
1958	Everyday disputes.
1961	After marriage, she still goes out to have affairs (*zai wai luan zhao duixiang*); lies and cheats to get stuff.
1961	Introduced by someone else and rashly married; argue and fight.

ing the villages. Determined to carry out her plan, Lou invited all able-bodied youth in the villages—regardless of class—to push her and the boat through the muddied water to the other village.[181]

In addition to the custom of using sedans to carry the bride, peasants used fortune-tellers to make sure the bride and groom would enjoy health and good fortune during their marriage. In early 1965, party reports complained that over 20 percent of villagers who married used fortune-tellers and divination of some sort.[182] Fortune-tellers were also consulted during the course of a marriage, when events did not turn out as planned. In Yun-nan, some divorce cases were instigated by fortune-tellers who predicted that terrible misfortune would beset couples who did *not* immediately di-vorce. In Chuxiong, a woman surnamed Li went with her husband to a fortune-teller for advice. The fortune-teller replied, "You must divorce now; you'll die if you don't." In another case, a fortune-teller told a disputing couple, "You'll go blind in one eye if you don't divorce."[183]

The exchange of gifts and the holding of feasts were also staples of the traditional marriage ceremony in Chinese communities. As with other prac-tices, this custom continued despite the official crackdown. Evidence shows that politics was rarely a consideration when drawing up the expense ledger and compiling the guest list to weddings. To afford such feasts, the groom and his parents often went into debt, or borrowed money from relatives and friends, even if lenders were officially branded as "bad class" landlords and rich peasants; a nice wedding with tasty food would give a family face, and this outweighed the relevance of the creditors' bad political class. In the actual ceremony, cadres, poor peasants, and former landlords alike participated; taking part in someone else's celebration, but not inviting that person to one's own, was considered bad form. In Gusong Commune, for instance, a man surnamed Zhuang, a production-team accountant, had been praised during the Socialist Education campaign as a cadre who "took the lead in changing his customs and habits" because he, unlike many others, did not want to host a lavish wedding feast for his two sons. After the meeting, however, Zhuang's seventy-four-year-old mother admonished him: "We've eaten at other people's weddings; how can we not invite people to our own festivity?" One month later, Zhuang spent two hundred yuan for a large feast, bought a variety of gifts, and invited all the villagers.[184]

In other cases, cadres helped arrange festivities for other peasants, in-cluding those of the "bad classes." Because they had access to scare re-sources, cadres were well placed to secure loans or provide foodstuffs for the wedding feast. At the same time that radical urban intellectuals were incit-ing class culture war, in Yunnan there were reports that a CCP official "got so drunk" at a wedding he left his pistol next to a member of the "enemy class." Others were so helpful in making wedding preparations that they earned the position of "master of ceremonies" at rich peasants' weddings. In other instances, cadres as high as district committee members and gra-nary officials "asked landlords to take the seat of honor" at their relatives' wedding, and even "kowtowed in their direction."[185]

CONCLUSION

The above discussion of rural divorce places us in a good position to answer some of the questions put forth at the beginning of this chapter. More than anything else, this chapter challenges several important characterizations of Chinese rural life in much of the secondary literature concerning this period. During the mid-1950s and the 1960s, divorce was not "almost nonexistent," nor did peasants always remain "tied to the land" or limited by the household registration system to increasingly insular villages. Throughout the 1950s and 1960s, rural space remained a resource and refuge from coerced marriages, famine, and abuse. Peasants' mobility, whether in the form of women "running back to natal homes," "blindly running away," "wandering around the countryside" engaging in black-market trade, or pursuing more work points or urban jobs and spouses, continued well into the 1960s, and certainly contributed to divorce and marriage patterns. Politically, rural divorce and "politically incorrect" relationships after 1953 were often the *unintended* result of state political and economic policies (such as decentralization and the Sixty Articles); the lingering residue of land and marriage reform discourse of "freedom" and "exploitation"; and women's ability to assert their agency even without political campaigns such as the Marriage Law, or even active support of organizations such as the Women's Federation. Often enough, peasants' contentious legal culture was enough to compensate for the state's retreat from active intervention in the family. This does not suggest that the state's retreat did not have certain costs, however. Between 1953 and 1959 the number of divorces declined, most likely because of intense political mobilization and the power that decentralization gave obstructionist local officials, and the elimination of the district-level governments in the mid-1950s. Nonetheless, there is substantial evidence to support the argument that political mobilization did not put a stop to peasants' (rural officials included) behaving in ways some officials considered quite unorthodox.

In addition to politics, state economic policies reverberated strongly within the family, affecting both its structure (seen through marriage and divorce) and power relations. Collectivization in the mid-1950s created more opportunities for young men and women to meet by mobilizing women in massive numbers to work in the fields. Flirting and bantering sometimes led to sex (another unintended consequence), shotgun marriages, and then demands for divorce. In the late 1950s and early 1960s we might distinguish between two types of divorce claims, both of which were the unintentional result of state policies. The first type was likely motivated by purely economic or survival reasons, such as women "blindly running away" during the famine resulting from the Great Leap Forward. This group of women were probably more numerous in the late 1950s and early 1960s than after 1963. The second type were, I believe, promoted by the return of material incentives and the general loosening of controls after 1963 until the Cultural Revolution. With increased commercialization and the return of some private plots, some women were able to focus on the best bargain they could get on the rural marriage market, even if this meant trading in old husbands for new ones. Underlying both of these motives, however, was the weakening of familial authority, which, unlike multiple divorces, was an *intended* outcome of state policy. Collectivization, as we have seen, weakened the authority of the family elders in ways similar to land reform, allowing women (and some men) the "social space" in which to leave their adopted homes out of dire necessity or else find men who they thought could provide them with better lives.

In many respects, this chapter confirms many of the arguments I made concerning different types of Chinese rural areas and about peasants in other locales. Evidence in chapter 4 showed that, worldwide, peasants frequently seek out *higher-level* political institutions to get justice, and are often willing to draw the state into their domestic affairs and to be frank when discussing such affairs in state forums. As I have pointed out in earlier chapters, studies of state-society relations would do well to disaggregate the state and look at how different sorts of people interact with different types of state organizations. But these commonalties in peasant "legal" or political culture should not lead us to forget about important differences in politics in revolutionary states. In France and in Russia, poor peasants did not gain nearly as much political power as in China; in the former cases, the urban base of the revolutions meant that fewer peasants actively participated in implementing key policies.[186] In China, however, millions of people who grew up in peasant communities gained power owing to the rural nature of the revolution. This proved to be a crucial factor in Chinese peasants' ability and willingness to use supravillage state institutions to change their family situation, even if they did not always get what they wanted. Peasants in China were generally less fearful of the state than educated urbanites owing to the state's *class* composition and the legitimacy that geographical distance afforded higher-level political institutions. Not embedded in village political or social structure and cognizant of their position as central state officials, districts, counties, and courts granted divorces even if they held the women who came to them in contempt. For their part, ordinary villagers did not know about the personal lives of such officials, and so they were generally seen as more objective, and thus more legitimate, than local officials, whose personal, political, and sexual affairs were common knowledge. State legitimacy, like the state apparatus, I suggest, is best viewed in disaggregated terms: in rural China, legitimacy was concentrated at the top of the political hierarchy but became diluted the farther down the ladder one went.

Such a view of the state and legitimacy calls into question the analytical usefulness of the term most favored by feminist critics of the PRC's Marriage Law—namely, "patriarchy." While "patriarchy" can be a useful concept to explain the behavior of many village and township officials (but certainly not all; as we have seen, village officials, in their confusion, might send disputing cases to court, or implement the Marriage Law using radical methods based on their experience from previous campaigns), it is far less helpful in accounting for the behavior of higher-level state officials, who often granted divorces with a casualness that must have surprised petitioners themselves. Even if such officials held what Westerners would consider to be sexist views and believed in male primacy in society, these attitudes did not automatically translate into decisions. In fact, based on evidence in this chapter we might even make a case for a certain *overlap* in attitudes regarding marriage and divorce among the largely female divorce petitioners and the mostly male district and court officials. That is, sociologically speaking, "the state" and "society" were not that different in rural China.[187] To the extent that state officials came from rural backgrounds, it is likely that marriage was *not* perceived by them as a once-in-a-lifetime event to be preserved at high costs, and for this reason such officials were not necessarily judgmental about women who married and divorced on multiple occasions. As we have seen in the case of military marriages, court officials did not see adultery by the wife as a major political or even cultural offense. As one court official explained to a soldier who was ditched by his wife: "Your wife is having an affair because you've been away for so long."

Given this overlap in "sexual culture" among peasants and officials in rural China, one can only speculate whether peasants would have been able to sue for divorce had judges and political officials been urban intellectuals. Judging from what we have seen in this and earlier chapters, this stratum, much like Confucian moralists in the Imperial and Republican periods, was more interested in family *stability* than change. Those favoring a more puritanical sexual code, "careful" divorces and marriages, and "proper" family relations would eventually have their opportunity to enforce their vision, however: in the Cultural Revolution, as we will see in the next chapter, the "sexual culture" of the Communist Party itself would soon face a conservative backlash.

CHAPTER SEVEN

The Conservative Backlash: Politics, Sex, and the Family in the Cultural Revolution, 1966–1968

Several years ago the thirtieth anniversary of the Great Proletarian Cultural Revolution (GPCR) came and went virtually unnoticed in the Chinese press. State propaganda departments may have felt that commemoration of the Cultural Revolution—condemned since the reform period as the "Ten Years of Chaos" (1966–1976)—would prompt uncomfortable analogies to the present-day political problem of corruption, which was a major grievance in the pre-GPCR period. Despite this official silence, however, memories of the Cultural Revolution, and its violence in particular, run deep in the post-Mao Chinese polity.[1] Images of Red Guards ransacking homes and offices and parading various "class enemies" in the streets are indelibly etched in the minds of top leaders, many of whom were targets of political attack. Such memories of "chaos" probably shaped the party leadership's extreme reaction to the 1989 protests, and have likely tempered the pace of economic reforms in the 1990s, particularly in the industrial sector. The silence of the thirtieth anniversary, understandable considering these memories, was nevertheless slightly disingenuous. Even as the GPCR has been officially condemned, the regime has used its memory to shore up its political legitimacy. By identifying Maoist tactics (such as class struggle) with China's "feudal" peasant culture and then disavowing them, the state can now proclaim itself as the truly "modern" alternative to Mao. Such attacks on "peasant" culture dovetail with those of intellectuals, many of whom blame "peasant consciousness" for the excesses of Maoist China and for the everyday tyrannies of life in urban China.[2]

In contrast to the cursory treatment of the GPCR in the official press, Western students of China have devoted enormous resources to locating the origins of this political and social watershed. Over the past thirty years, a scholarly consensus has emerged explaining the forces that produced much of the conflict during the GPCR. Looking at the state, the GPCR has been viewed as an extension of Mao's Trotsky-inspired vision of "permanent revolution," long-standing CCP mobilization tactics (such as campaigns), and a culmination of an intra-elite struggle pitting advocates of two mutually incompatible visions of China's development strategy. Sociologically, what drove many people to participate in the GPCR were mainly pent-up personal hatreds and socioeconomic and political grievances, some stemming as far back as the 1930s. In factories, temporary laborers attacked full-time employees, who were the main beneficiaries of the socialist system; in urban schools, "bad class" rebels attacked the privileges and status of "good class" students, in addition to conducting struggle sessions against teachers and party officials; in villages, peasants who had been slighted by fellow villagers or officials found in Mao's argument that "to rebel is justified" ample excuse to take revenge.[3] In addition to the origins of the GPCR, scholars have also agreed about *where* it had its greatest impact. Even though the GPCR was intended to rid China of "feudal" culture, which was presumably more entrenched in rural than in urban areas, the aims of the Cultural Revolution were embraced most fervently in cities, and among intellectuals in particular. Peasants, for the most part, were mystified by the GPCR, and were often angered by its interruption of their efforts to recover from the Great Leap Forward.[4]

In this chapter, I propose new hypotheses concerning some of the sources and forms of political critique, and responses to it, during the GPCR. I want to argue that in addition to the well-documented elite and socioeconomic cleavages between the winners and losers under socialism, other important dimensions of conflict were the result of different conceptualizations of "proper" marital and sexual behavior and changes in family relations after the Communist Revolution. Class-based, mutually incompatible differences in "sexual culture" were sometimes as important in shaping the content of criticism and even the form of collective action during the GPCR as the social and political cleavages caused by differences in status, opportunity, and income. In this sense, my approach to the Cultural Revolution shares some ground with that of Richard Madsen in his *Morality and Power in a Chinese Village;* Madsen also sees moral and ethical issues as central to the understanding of political dynamics and conflicts in rural China. But whereas Madsen focuses on a very wide range of moral dilemmas shaping politics in one rural village mainly in the mid-to late 1960s, I look at a smaller "slice" of moral understandings—those concerning "proper" sexual, marital, and divorce behavior—among different social strata, in several areas of the country, and with a look back to how politics in the 1950s shaped morally driven sorts of conflict during the Cultural Revolution.[5] In addition to conflicts generated by these different conceptualizations, I also suggest that other phenomena, such as the propensity of intellectuals to commit suicide after mass struggle sessions, might also be explained by what happened in families prior to 1966.

This chapter is different than previous ones in two important ways. First, unlike earlier chapters, which were based almost entirely on archival sources, this one relies mostly on more conventional ones, such as auto-biographies, newspapers, and magazines from the period. Second, rather than testing various hypotheses of the secondary literature and proposing new arguments to explain unanticipated outcomes, this chapter is more of the hypothesis-generating sort. That is, I do not claim here to have discovered *the* roots or *the* origins of the Cultural Revolution, but instead suggest plausible, though not always provable, ideas linking family and sexual dynamics in the pre-GPCR period to types of criticism and forms of conflict during the GPCR. To my knowledge, no account of the Cultural Revolution has looked at the Cultural Revolution in quite this way, and this I hope makes up for the lack of novelty in source material. By cutting off one or two slices of "what happened" during the Cultural Revolution, linking these to past events, and suggesting hypotheses to explain them, I hope to provoke further inquiry in two directions. First, what were the cultural sources of conflict during the "Cultural" Revolution? Second, how did families respond to the unprecedented political tensions during this period?

A SKETCH OF WHAT HAPPENED

Accounts of the Great Proletarian Cultural Revolution that trace its origins to intraparty elite conflicts are of little help in explaining how it happened that the opening salvo of its violent stage was a *nonpolitical* slogan featuring elements of the very culture the GPCR intended to destroy. On June 1, 1966, an editorial on the front page of *People's Daily* called for a cultural revolution that would "sweep away ox ghosts and snake demons" (*niugui sheshen*) that had infiltrated the Communist Party and were now posing a mortal threat to the dictatorship of the working class, the Communist Party, and the People's Republic of China. Chen Boda, the radical intellectual credited with the headline, asserted that "proletarian" values and culture were in danger of being usurped and replaced by "bourgeois," capitalist culture on the one hand, and undermined by the persistence of feudal culture on the other. While the economic base of the People's Republic had been effectively changed through land reform and the socialization of industry, the cultural "superstructure" remained much as it had been prior to the revolution. The "proletarian cultural revolution," the article asserted

is aimed not only at demolishing all the old ideology and culture and all the old customs and habits, which, fostered by the exploiting classes, have poisoned the minds of the people for thousands of years, but also at creating and fostering among the masses an entirely new ideology and culture and entirely new customs and habits—those of the proletariat. This great task of transforming customs and habits is without any precedent in human history.[6]

To stage such a revolution, Maoists issued a clarion call to youth, entrusting them with the task of re-revolutionizing Chinese society. Such a revolution would ensure that the achievements of the revolution would not be lost in stifling bureaucracies and that culture would reflect the revolutionary values of the working class. Only youth—who were seen as untainted by China's feudal past—could carry forward this holy grail of the Chinese revolution. As a 1967 article in *People's Daily* proclaimed: "The Red Guards are precious new born things . . . a new born force brimming with vigorous spirit and capable of fighting bravely . . . to wash away all the sludge and filthy water left over from the old society."[7]

Initially, participation in the movement to "sweep away ox ghosts and snake demons" was restricted to sons and daughters of the "good classes." The choice of targets was also limited. As in other campaigns, those initially selected for political struggle belonged to the "bad classes," often teachers with problematic political histories. Under orders to confiscate and destroy artifacts of the "old" culture (such as Confucian classics and traditional art) or the trappings of "bourgeois" materialism (jewelry, makeup, or leather shoes), young "Red Guards," often wearing workers' clothing to look more "proletariat," pillaged homes, interrogated families, and dragged people to struggle sessions.[8]

The second stage of the Cultural Revolution, beginning in late 1966, was characterized by a broadening of the criteria both for participation and for targets of attack. "Bad class" urban youth, who initially had been excluded from the GPCR, demanded that they too be allowed to show their fealty to Chairman Mao. On the "target" side, Mao called upon the student masses to attack the "headquarters"—that is, the Communist Party itself. According to Mao and his radical allies, the party itself was rife with "capitalist" and "bourgeois" tendencies, and its members had removed themselves from the concerns of the ordinary citizens. At Mao's behest, formerly disenfranchised students attacked party members, accusing them of having become "capitalist roaders." In many cases, party offices were raided and secret personnel documents stolen, later to be published in student newspapers. This second stage of the Cultural Revolution led to the near decimation of Communist Party organizations throughout the country. By mid-1968, Mao had grown tired of the chaos caused by incessant attacks on the party and the factional infighting among different student organizations and called in the PLA to disband armed youth groups and take over the day-to-day administration of schools, factories, and rural governments. With this military intervention the most radical stage of the GPCR was over. From 1969 to 1978, Chinese politics was dominated by the military.[9]

THE SEXUALIZATION OF POLITICAL CRITIQUE

What social and political forces might lead participants of mass movements to raise issues concerning sexuality? A comparative perspective suggests some clues: sexuality appears to play an important role in movements with strong religious or ultranationalistic overtones. The Cultural Revolution, with its cult of Mao as the "Supreme Leader," Red Guards wielding the "Little Red Book" like the Bible, and xenophobia, seems to generally fit in this category.[10] In early modern France, for example, Natalie Davis has noted that youth played an important role in purifying the community from its vices because they were seen as the "conscience of the community in maters of domestic accord." As such, they were given license "to do violence in the religious rite."[11] In the French Revolution, crowds sometimes shouted "Austrian whore" at women they considered impure, and considered as "counterrevolutionary" women who used the freedoms promised by the revolution to use "impure" language—that is, curses and other profanities."[12] In Russia, as I noted in chapter 2, young intellectual revolutionaries of the late nineteenth century developed a cult of celibacy, according to which abstinence from sex would somehow "purify" the nation from vice and help reconstitute society on a new moral basis. In such movements, youth can easily cast themselves as "cleansers" of the national community largely because of their own naïveté, black-and-white worldview, and innocence with respect to the complications of love and passion. Having little experience in matters of the heart, they contrast their own purity to the sordid transgressions of the adult world.

But the concern with sexuality has not been limited to ordinary participants of mass movements. Leaders and propaganda artists in nationalist and revolutionary movements have also used sexualized symbols to mobilize citizens. As Eric Hobsbawm noted in his study of socialist iconography, a recurring image in socialist art was the naked and muscular torso of an attractive male worker.[13] Such images have also been put to use for more evil purposes than socialist artists' idealization of the working-class body. In Germany, Hitler and Goebbels and others (such as the writer Ernst Jünger) promoted images of Aryan youths' virility and sexual purity, associating this imagery with a strong, "virile" body politic. Images of robust, healthy, and clean "Aryan" youth were juxtaposed to those of Communists, Jews, Gypsies, and others whose bodies were dirty, sick, contagious, and weak. These stark, contrasting images of the body were often successful in dehumanizing those the regime considered as the national enemy.[14] Chinese artists in state and army propaganda departments before and during the Cultural Revolution likewise depicted handsome male workers with tremendously muscular arms and bulging torsos marching in unison under a sun that is Mao himself. Such virile and militaristic images were contrasted to various enemies of state, who were depicted as thin, weak, and often resembling rodents that could be crushed underfoot; in young Red Guards' donning working-class clothing we can see their effort to transpose some imagined working-class strength onto their own, often underdeveloped, bodies.[15] Not surprisingly, some youth worked out with weighs to build up their musculature;[16] others, after seeing in person Lin Biao, Mao's designated successor, worried that he would not be able to lead the Chinese revolution and world revolution because he was "very short and resembling an invalid" or "skinny, little and stooped . . . who sounded like a cock crowing."[17]

In China, however, in contrast to France, Russia, and Germany, there were other reasons why youth might have been chosen to carry out the new revolution, and why sexuality might play a role in political critique. According to party propaganda, sexual behavior was directly related to *class* status. An attack on the culture of "capitalists" or the "bourgeoisie" might also, simply by way of association, imply condemnation of the *sexual practices* of those classes. For instance, since adultery was said to be a symptom of the "decadent" bourgeois lifestyle (even among peasants in remote villages!), a political assault on the latter might be interpreted as justification for criticism of the former. Only through such a sexual purge—led by the "new born force" of sexually untainted youth—might a cultural revolution successfully promote the supposedly more ascetic values of the proletariat.

In the GPCR's mass rallies, parades, and struggle sessions, urban Chinese youth embarked on a political and sexual crusade similar to those of youthful rioters in France and the Hitler youth in Germany, but still different in their Marxist assumptions about the connection between class and sexual conduct. As in France and Germany, highly polarized images for good and evil, sexually pure and impure, led urban youth (primarily students) to look toward sexual behavior, and how people conducted their private lives more generally, as criteria for participation in, or exclusion from, the new, revolutionary community. The overlap of sex and politics was initially evident in the banner headline in *People's Daily* calling for the "sweeping away" of class enemies, now called "ox ghosts and snake demons," but later even more so as the violence against class enemies intensified.[18] Images conjured up by the "ox ghosts and snake demons" slogan may not always have been explicitly sexual, but the slogan tapped into the rich pantheon of the gods, demons, and ghosts in Buddhist folklore, a rich cultural repository of sexualized images. In the traditional pantheon of spirits and gods in Chinese folklore (ox ghosts and snake spirits among them), women's bodies and sexuality were often associated with such malevolent and powerful spirits. The womb, for example, was seen to contain a malignant spirit in the shape of the dreaded water monkey, and the "fox spirit" was extremely beautiful and preyed on young, sexually innocent men.[19] Together with the class-based attacks on the sexual decadence of "bourgeois" culture, the Buddhist-inspired sexuality conjured up by the "ox ghosts" and "snake demon" slogan provided youth with ample justification for making sexual behavior a criterion for participation in or exclusion from the new revolutionary community.[20]

Looking at how the Cultural Revolution began, we can find even more proximate causes to these historical ones. What gave sexual critique added relevance at the very beginning of the Cultural Revolution was the all-too-common vagueness and ambiguity of central guidelines concerning exactly who could be legitimately attacked as a political enemy. Top leaders themselves sent conflicting messages about just how much violence would be tolerated for the sake of revolutionizing Chinese society. For instance, in August 1966 Lin Biao was quoted as saying that "chaos is a necessary part of the Cultural Revolution,"[21] but in the "Sixteen Points" dealing with how to conduct the GPCR, the Cultural Revolution leadership called for "struggle by reason, not force."[22] While Mao's wife, Jiang Qing, often pressed for more violence, Premier Zhou Enlai told Red Guard units that "Chairman Mao is not in favor of dealing a person a fatal blow" at the very time that he was responsible for a special unit responsible for the torture of senior party members. Another leader who would later be sentenced as part of the radical Gang of Four, Chen Boda, also claimed that the Cultural Revolution leadership "did not permit the smashing of dog's head xxx or putting people in a jet plane [position]."[23] Complicating matters even further was that the "Sweep Away Ox Ghosts" headline did not identify who, exactly, these "ox ghosts" were, or how such "sweeping" would have to be done.[24] Lacking guidelines or time to figure out what the movement was about, students followed the script from previous political campaigns by attacking people against whom the party had already justified struggle: the five "black" classes (former landlords, rich peasants, counterrevolutionaries, "bad elements," and rightists). Later, when the movement shifted to attacks on the "headquarters," high-level party members themselves were subject to withering criticism. Yet, while the selection of targets was often determined by decisions from the center and notions of good and bad political class, the content of the accusations youth hurled against these political "enemies" were often sexual in nature.

Where can such criticisms or charges best be discerned? Scholars of the "New Cultural History" have suggested the close examination of the symbols, language, and rituals used in collective movements as a middle road between "national character" studies, which argue for a direct causal relationship between culture and politics, and Marxists' tendency to deny or overlook the role culture plays in shaping political action.[25] As in the path-breaking works on the French Revolution and Chinese student movements that have used analysis of ritual and language to better understand politics, looking at Cultural Revolution political rituals such as parades and rallies also provide us with clues as to where a different interpretation might begin.[26]

As the first example, let us examine the configuration of sex and politics in students' interrogation of a teacher named Guo Pei in a middle school on the North China plain.[27] For many students, Guo's identity and behavior represented a threat to the political, as well as sexual, purity of the new, revolutionary community Mao called upon them to forge. First, they accused her of being a daughter of one of "Chiang Kai-shek's most notorious strongmen, Yan Xishan." This, according to a student poster, made her an "Alien Class Element," and a "counterrevolutionary who wormed her way into the heart of the party." Next to this "political" charge, however, was a second, and seemingly unrelated, accusation originating in the language of *People's Daily*'s "ox ghost and snake demon" headline: "Guo Pei," they claimed, "is a venomous snake who disguised herself as a beautiful woman . . . We must break the venomous snake's spine!" Guo, the poster continued, was also guilty of using her womanly wiles to "corrupt her husband," a man who, unlike the politically suspicious Guo, came from a working-class background.

Accusations against Guo soon escalated. Red Guards stormed her office and ordered her to "confess" her crimes. When she refused, one of her interrogators, on a lark, made another sexual accusation. Students told Guo that Ding Yi, the school's Communist Party secretary, had already confessed to an affair with her. Coincidentally, this happened to be true, and further questioning forced Guo to admit that she had been the party secretary's mistress for more than a year. Students were shocked: "How incredible! Every day, Teacher Guo taught us to observe socialist morality, but she herself is a worn shoe!" (i.e., a woman who had sex). Interrogators soon delved into the details, asking Guo what she and Ding Yi talked about in bed, and when they had sex. When Guo told them that, on one occasion, she went to Ding Yi's house in the snow, a student commented, "This wild pheasant is not afraid of cold when in heat." Interrogation of Ding Yi himself led to further intimate disclosures. Not only was the party secretary sleeping with Guo Pei, but with another woman as well, Tang Hong, the general secretary of the Communist Youth League. Students quickly drew another big character poster, proclaiming that Ding Yi was a "Cavalier Riding Two Horses" because he "had rolled in bed with both women at once." With the interrogations near completion, students embarked on a search of Guo Pei and Ding

Yi's property. This turned up "big piles of grain coupons, wads of money, cigarettes, good wine," and a Panda brand radio, all of which were then exhibited as evidence of the couple's "decadent" lifestyle. "Where," one student wondered, "had the party secretary gotten so many? Did he have so much meat and fruit to eat that he could not use up his grain rations?" The search and confession led to a plan: the next day, Guo Pei, Ding Yi, and Tang Hong would be paraded down the street as adulterers.

In a discussion of twentieth-century American parades, Mary Ryan, a social historian, has noted that "parades acted out a social vocabulary."[28] In the Chinese context as well, parades are interesting to study for what they can tell us about the concerns and interests of the participants: What sort of banners are unfurled? How are people dressed? What music is played? In our case, Guo Pei's parade began on a dusty road, the sun beating down. Ding Yi led the procession wearing a five-meter-high dunce cap (a political costume) decorated with paper cutouts of "skeletons, monsters, turtles, and ox heads" (the tortoise was used to indicate a man who was cuckolded). Around his neck was a drum. Guo Pei walked next to Ding Yi wearing a *qipao,* a traditional tight-fitting dress. Red satin shoes hung around her neck, and she held a gong and stick in her hands. Tang Hong, the second adulteress, wore a long black gown and leather shoes around her neck. She carried a pair of cymbals in her hands. Students of the middle school followed the threesome. Because the parade took place on market day, the sides of the roads were lined with peasants who had come to sell their produce. Gao Yuan recounts the parade route: as Ding Yi beat his drum, Guo Pei sounded her gong and Tang Hong her cymbal.

> The crowds gawked as we escorted the three new demons through the streets. On orders from the rebel leaders, the three had to chant in turn as they walked: "I am Ding Yi, ox demon and snake spirit." "I am Guo Pei, and I am a worn shoe." "I am Tang Hong, and I am a worn shoe too" . . . Our three demons were drenched in sweat. Guo Pei's tight dress clung to her so that her underwear could be seen. Ding Yi's paper dunce cap was soggy and coming apart. Rivulets of perspiration ran down his red, puffy face.[29]

This was not an isolated incident occurring in a remote area of the North China plain. Events similar to this one took place even in more "cosmopolitan" urban settings. In Beijing, student Red Guards discovered during a house search that two of their teachers were having an affair. Both were under political attack at the time, and their respective spouses had already been expelled from the city to labor reform. Comforting each other, the two fell in love and had sex. Red Guards stripped off their clothing and paraded them through the city with a placard around their necks similar to the one worn by Ding Yi. Rather than labeling the teachers as counterrevolutionaries, the placards simply stated that the two were an adulterer and adulteress.[30] In Shanghai, students also accused a teacher (who was also a CCP member) of having an affair with a former student who had relatives in the United States. This made him suspicious on sexual, political (relations with the enemy), and cultural grounds (as he was influenced by bourgeois culture). "Look!" the big-character poster exclaimed, "A Communist Party Member is Sleeping with a Bourgeois Wench!—A Real Class Struggle."[31] In Changsha, the capital of Hunan Province, students criticized teachers for their "bourgeois" tendencies such as wearing "high heels," having a "co-quettish voice," and wearing "perfume in the summertime."[32]

In some cases, willingness to divorce defined what were considered "proper" sexual morals. For students, divorce was not seen as an exercise in rights guaranteed by the CCP's Marriage Law signed by their Supreme Leader Chairman Mao, as was often the case among peasants, but instead as a manifestation of promiscuity and unethical behavior unbefitting a true communist. Nie Yuanzi, a philosophy teacher at Beijing University who took the lead in attacking school authorities, was thus vociferously attacked on both political and sexual grounds. When her political enemies were not attacking her by using various quotations from Chairman Mao or references to the Qing dynasty's empress dowager (Nie was called "Old Buddha"), they condemned her for "loose" morals. According to her detractors, Nie was promiscuous (a "broken shoe") because she had recently divorced and re-married a high official, a man who was a confederate of Head of State Liu Shaoqi.[33]

"Bad class" teachers and administrators in schools were not the only ones who suffered from students' criticism of sexual and marriage practices under the guise of making revolution. Material possessions such as bathtubs, high heels, nice clothes, perfumes, and jewelry could be used to show how "bourgeois" cadres betrayed Mao's revolutionary line and lived bourgeois-inspired, sexually decadent lives. In the second stage of the Cultural Revolution, when Mao ordered youth to "Bombard the Headquarters," politburo members, provincial leaders, generals, and their wives also came under sexualized attack, blending traditional cultural images and class language. When Gao Yuan and his Red Guard comrades traveled to spread the word of the GPCR, they encountered a poster at Wuhan University that accused the provincial party secretary of "having illicit relations with a famous acrobat whose body was so flexible that she could coil up like a snake."[34] In the city of Amoy in Fujian Province, students from a middle school broke into the house of the provincial party secretary, a "veteran CCP member with thirty years' experience." There, students discovered expensive goods such as beef juice, rooms for two female servants, foreign liquor, and cigarettes. In his defense, the party secretary justified these items as "gifts." Moving from the living room to the bedroom, students grew even more excited: "Come up and see how corrupt Yeh Fei and [his wife] Wang Yu-keng are!" they yelled. Ken Ling (a pseudonym) describes how students reacted:

> We all dashed upstairs to Yeh and Wang's bedroom. It reeked with fragrance, and in the wardrobe there were expensive cloth, high-heeled shoes and a big stack of French perfumes. Whoever would have thought this old lady close to fifty was still so coquettish? What made us really wonder was the size of the tub in the bathroom, larger than anyone had ever seen.

The tub, foreign goods, and other material that students found rifling through the couple's personal papers would eventually be used as "evidence" against them in a parade similar to that in Gao Yuan's school.[35]

Sexual and political critique also intertwined in one of the most celebrated Red Guard "victories" during the Cultural Revolution—the arrest and interrogation of Mao's former second-in-command Liu Shaoqi and his most recent wife, Wang Guangmei, by students of Qinghua University (Ken Ling claimed that Wang was Liu's sixth wife).[36] Despite their high level of political sophistication, Qinghua students were as fascinated by Wang Guangmei's body and sexuality as they were interested in her politics. Wang's young interrogators were particularly curious about the dress she had worn during a state visit to Indonesia in 1963, the body-clinging *qipao,* and the pearl necklace and earrings she had donned. Students were also aghast that Wang had the audacity to slow-dance with Sukarno in the presence of other scantily clad "palace girls" (who were merely folk dancers). As Ken Ling reports:

> Kuai [a Red Guard leader at Qinghua] showed us the most valuable materials, including family photographs of Liu and Wang's families, the "ugly photograph" of Wang and Sukarno laughing together in the company of half-nude palace girls and a complete series of photographs of Wang from infancy to the time she became an evil vixen-spirit infatuating men.[37]

By dancing and "flirting" with Sukarno while wearing the *qipao,* her interrogators charged, Wang had "put the whole Chinese nation to shame."[38]

Their investigation finished, Qinghua students, with the support of top GPCR leaders such as Jiang Qing (who had a personal vendetta against Wang),[39] hauled her to be struggled before the masses. Looking at Wang's bedraggled appearance after her interrogation sessions, Ken Ling had a hard time "imagin[ing] that this was the same flirting and lustful Communist Party cadre member in Indonesia."[40] Onstage, Wang was first accused of various political offenses: suppressing the nascent Red Guard movement at the university, supporting programs offering peasants incentives in the early 1960s, and protecting landlords and rich peasants during the Socialist Education campaign. Then the students shifted to other matters. After one accuser told the crowd that, on foreign visits, Wang "had made frequent changes of clothing and had her hair done twice a day," the assembled student masses shouted: "Let her show off her ugly look. Make her put on the *chi-pao* she wore in Indonesia!"

Student leaders onstage obliged. Bringing Wang backstage, they forced her to wear the *qipao* and high heels, but instead of the pearls she had worn in Indonesia, they draped her neck with a mock necklace made of table tennis balls. To assure the audience a good look, she was repeatedly forced to climb on top of a table in her scandalous regalia. As Wang struggled each time to get down, students took photographs of this "historic" scene. Six minutes later, Wang was led offstage and the struggle session was declared over.[41] With this, the Red Guards believed that Wang's capitalist-inspired lifestyle had been trounced by a "proletarian" moral code.

The critique of Wang for sexual behavior inappropriate for a communist was used as political leverage against her husband, Liu Shaoqi, who was then under severe political attack.[42] For students, Wang Guangmei was suspicious not only for displaying her body and slow-dancing, but also owing to her family background. Wang's father had been a high-level government official in Beijing in the 1920s and was thus labeled a "bureaucrat-bourgeois" by the Red Guards. This background apparently explained her unproletarian sexual behavior, as well as her ability to attract and seduce a high-ranking official such as Liu Shaoqi. Liu, in his attraction to someone with such a background, confirmed that he had taken the "capitalist road." According to a Red Guard newspaper in Canton,

> Liu Shao-ch'i chose to establish ties with this wicked family by marriage. It can be seen that he has long ago ceased to be a communist cadre and a true communist. He is a simon-pure favorite of the bureaucrat-bourgeoisie, the protector of the bourgeoisie, and the No. 1 revisionist chieftain of China.[43]

In fact, by marrying someone from a well-off and well-educated family with less than reputable class background, Liu was quite *typical* among high-ranking officials in Beijing. As seen in chapter 2, so-called red and black marriages between high-ranking cadres and "black"-class women were common throughout the 1950s. But in the "proletarian" Cultural Revolution, these marriages came back to haunt political careers.

Wang Guangmei, and Liu Shaoqi by association, were not alone in being attacked on moral/ethical grounds relating to sexuality and marriage. Although it is common in Chinese political discourse to attack powerful women such as Wang for sexual indiscretions, in the GPCR high-ranking men were also investigated and attacked on such grounds. In an article attributed to the "Anti-Revisionist Revolutionary Rebel Detachment of the Yangfengchiatou Physical Culture School," Peng Zhen (the mayor of Bei-

jing), Deng Xiaoping, and Liu Shaoqi were attacked for establishing an exclusive club for high-ranking cadres and enjoying themselves at workers'
and peasants' expense. In this club, students complained,

> Orders for any kind of food could be taken. Balls were held two nights a week,
> and on important festive days, food and drinks were supplied free of charge.
> Their dance partners were invited from cultural work troupes and various
> leading hospitals, and they were as a rule beautiful girls . . . They danced, and
> played *mahjong* and bridge up until midnight, and Western films were also
> constantly shown up to midnight, and sometimes until dawn. Not only tea and
> cigarettes, but also bath and pedicures were served free. They were also sup-
> plied with perfume, soap and towels . . . There were also special rooms, pri-
> vate rooms etc., and it is not possible to enumerate all of them.[44]

Accusations against Tao Zhu, a politburo member, Zeng Sheng, the
Mayor of Canton, and Marshall He Long of the People's Liberation Army
also centered on their sexually "corrupt" lifestyle. Tao (who, like Liu
Shaoqi, had also married a "black class" daughter) was condemned for not
objecting to Wang Guangmei's wearing a "semitransparent dress," which required her to bare her legs when she hitched it up to walk. Tao, students
charged, was "submissive as a Pekinese dog to that enchantress Wang
Kuang-mei." They also criticized Tao because in 1957 he supposedly demanded that female cadres "put on skirts." Even further demonstrating his
departure from the socialist road, Tao was said to have "energetically publicize[d] and extol[led] the bourgeois way of life of the West:

> He constantly attended balls and invited those tiptop actresses with good
> figures from the Fighters' Song and Dance ensemble and other troupes to
> dance with him. These partners were required to wear lipstick, high-heeled
> shoes, and clinging garments. All of this showed how corrupt and decadent
> T'ao Chu's soul was.[45]

Accusations against Mayor Zeng Sheng and Marshall He Long went even
further. A veteran revolutionary, Zeng was condemned as "utterly corrupted" because of his sex life, extensive wardrobe, purchase of foreign
goods such as radios and refrigerators, and penchant for Hollywood films
and mah-jongg. "He led a befuddled life," Red Guards charged. "His face
was really that of a foreign slave."

> He would lust after a woman as soon as he saw one . . . In recent years, he had
> raped four women, including a young girl, a married woman and the wife of
> an army man. This human-faced beast violated women by threatening them
> with force and tempting them with money. Reveling in lust the whole day, how
> could this mayor and overlord spare time to handle the affairs of state?[46]

He Long, a dashing PLA marshal, was accused of even greater sexual im-
propriety. On these grounds, He Long was a relatively easy target, having

been married and divorced nine times. Divorce, however, was not his only "misdemeanor." According to the Red Guard account, He Long had the gall to publicly brag about his sexual conquests: "Should I invite all my past concubines to dinner," he proudfully [*sic*] said, "they could make a table!" His other "crimes" included "carry[ing] away any young and beautiful girl he saw in the street" during his days as a bandit (before joining the PLA), lusting after Cantonese women (because they had "curved eyebrows and high cheekbones"), hiring a mistress of a GMD officer to teach him dancing during his tenure in Yunnan in the early 1950s, dancing and then sleeping with Cultural Work Troupe members during the antibandit campaigns in the Southwest, consorting with prostitutes, and always discussing women. "After Liberation," they charged, "he was addicted to dancing" and "playing cards," never taking along Chairman Mao's collected works on any of his numerous trips.[47]

Although these accusation may seen frivolous, it is important to keep in mind that they contributed to fatal consequences: neither Liu Shaoqi, Tao Zhu, or He Long survived the Cultural Revolution.

SEXUAL POLITICS IN RURAL AREAS

Although the GPCR, especially in its early stages, was largely an urban political movement centered in schools and factories, the countryside was also affected. As in other political movements, urban-based work teams were dispatched to rural areas to mobilize the peasants to join them in their revolution. In Beijing, for example, the police provided Red Guards with information pertaining to which peasants in a nearby suburb belonged to the "black" classes. The following day, Red Guards went to the county and ordered the listed residents to produce old land titles. These would then be used as "proof" that they were secretly hoping for the return of the Nationalist government in Taiwan. When villagers could not produce the papers, Red Guards beat them mercilessly, killing many. In one month alone (September 1966), 325 of these "class enemies" (including old peasant women and infants) were murdered by urban Red Guard units.[48]

In some areas of South China as well, sent-down urban-educated youth, not villagers, responded most enthusiastically to calls for the persecution of class enemies. Since 1964, urban youth in villages generally came from two different social backgrounds: "street youth" recruited from unemployment lines who had minimal education (many of whom were probably peasants seeking urban jobs), and high school–educated youth. The former tended to look upon their tenure in the countryside in pragmatic, and sometimes opportunistic, terms. According to testimony from educated youth, the working-class urbanites frequently argued with peasants over the allocation of work points, ran away from work whenever possible, and stole chickens.

Sexual relations in this group seemed quite casual to the educated contingent. They "even bedded down together," one remarked.[49]

In contrast, the high school youth combined idealism with strong ideological and political commitments. Many believed that by working in the countryside they were contributing to the national cause. At the same time, they were also politically ambitious; many hoped to advance to leadership positions in the village. From the moment of their arrival in the village, these students tried to prove how "revolutionary" they were by adopting the sort of asceticism noted earlier among educated Russian revolutionaries in the 1870s and among Chinese intellectuals in the 1930s and 1940s. Given the opportunity to eat rice with tasty soy sauce, many refused on the grounds that self-induced hardship would make them as "spiritually steeled" as peasants were prior to the Communist Revolution. Others collected wild vegetables for their kitchen, the same vegetables that peasants used only to feed their livestock. Peasants who observed this asceticism advised the youth to eat better, but to no avail. At the same time that ambitious youth were struggling to enter the few prized spots in the village's Communist Youth League by trying to "outpeasant" the peasants, peasants themselves were generally uninterested in politics. After the just-completed Socialist Education campaign, peasants and village cadres were busy rebuilding the village infrastructure and improving agricultural output.[50]

The Cultural Revolution came to "Chen Village" (a pseudonym, located in South China) by way of frustrated urban-educated youth. Denied leadership positions in the village because of their "bad class" status, these youth organized a unit called the Maoism Red Guards and tried to stir up the political winds. As one recalled, "We discussed among ourselves why the Cultural Revolution was erupting in the cities and not in the countryside . . . The atmosphere in the Commune seat was so dull at that point." The Maoism Red Guards' first action was to write a poster accusing lower-level cadres of "only taking care of production and not paying any attention to the Cultural Revolution." This attack, they felt, was justified by Mao's call to purge the party ranks of so-called capitalist roaders. Calls for the village to enter the fray of GPCR politics, however, usually fell on deaf ears: party leaders' attention was focused elsewhere, and ordinary villagers were disturbed by what they had already heard about urban Red Guards' violence. Bolstered by orders from above that members of Red Guard units were required to have impeccable class background, village leaders were quickly able to squash this nascent organization and replace it with one devoted to protecting the privileges of the village's political elite.[51]

Soon this new Red Guard unit began to wreak havoc in the village. To prove how "red" they could be, Red Guards ordered girls to cut their hair short, smashed villagers' ancestor tablets, and burned "feudal" books and inscriptions for good luck. "Bad class" villagers were subjected to intense struggle sessions to force them—often to no avail—to confess to a plotted counterrevolution. For show, a good-class village leader was also attacked for being a "capitalist roader" because his older sister sent him small gifts from her home in Hong Kong.

The reign of "good class" Red Guards ended in late 1966, when national directives ordered the withdrawal of the work teams that supported these organizations. The recently suppressed "bad class" Red Guard unit then sprang into action, first trying to seize power from the local government and then attacking local cadres for petty corruption. Still, they found many peasants indifferent: "We'll just worry about taking care of our private plots," one said. Faced with solid opposition from the village leadership, many returned to Canton. Cadres also withdrew from politics; after being accused of corruption during the Four Cleanups and again in the Cultural Revolution, few saw any benefit in shouldering the responsibility and hassle of being a cadre. By early 1967, many villages were left without a functioning governing apparatus. According to testimony from the educated youth, the breakdown in political order also led to a collapse of the village's sexual order. Political disorder was said to have resulted in a "peeping tom prowling the village" and "worse yet . . . stories circulated of adulterous sex in the hills." "Many villagers," youth recalled, "agreed that private property, personal security, and public morality were all endangered."[52]

We cannot for certain know whether this "breakdown" in public morality was something altogether new to the GPCR, or more the perception of puritanical educated youth. Evidence from previous chapters shows that "adulterous sex in the hills" was not unknown in many areas of rural China prior to the breakdown of political authority during the Cultural Revolution. Then, as in the GPCR, educated urbanites who wrote about the social and sexual situation in the countryside emphasized peasants' "chaotic" sexual relations. That adulterous sex was not only a product of the GPCR is supported by the way sex and politics intermingled during the Cultural Revolution. As during the Marriage Law campaigns, when village cadres and ordinary peasants used the movement to prosecute women and men against whom they had sexual, personal, or family grudges, the GPCR too allowed cadres and villagers to bolster their political authority by pursuing sexual or political enemies. The aborted prosecution of adulterers in Chen Village (a man nicknamed "Shorty"; his lover, Lilou; and his scorned wife, Maiyan) is a case in point.[53]

"Shorty," according to accounts of what transpired in the village during the GPCR, was a good candidate for political struggle. Known as a "woman chaser," he was well placed to prevent another village cadre from occupying a key post on an important political body—the village's public security committee. To prevent him from blocking his political ambitions, the village leader found an ally in Shorty's wife, Maiyan, who at the time was furious that her husband was having sex with Lilou, known as "the most infamous woman in the village." Maiyan "loudly let it be known throughout the village that she was out for revenge against both her husband and his rumored paramour." As we have seen in previous chapters, it was not uncommon for peasant women to go public with problems that in more cosmopolitan settings were considered private, and to draw in the state to punish other family members when such opportunities arose.

Further questioning revealed that Shorty was not the first or last of Lilou's lovers in the village. Frustrated in her attempts to divorce her "dull-witted, irritable, and half-blind man," Lilou sought satisfaction elsewhere; each of her children, gossip had it, "resembled a different man in the village." Even with these sexual indiscretions (which were apparently known to all), in 1958 Lilou was still admitted to the party on the basis of her support for CCP programs and work ability. In 1964, however, the Four Cleanups work team—one-third of whom were educated urban youth— were outraged by her "flouting of Communist moral standards" and expelled her from the party.

The Cultural Revolution provided the perfect opportunity for Maiyan and the ambitious village cadre to make an example of Shorty and Lilou. To justify struggle against them, the village cadre asserted that the reputation of the entire village was at stake because of their affair, and that something had to be done to "revolutionize" the village. This appeal probably sat well with the urban-educated and politically ambitious radical who controlled the village's public address system, a girl in her late teens who did little to oppose this blatant misuse of the Cultural Revolution to pursue such personalistic ends. She used the public address system to assemble all the villagers, and the struggle session against Shorty was ready to begin.

The cadre's well-designed political plans were soon waylaid by peasants' frankness about sexuality and urban youths' prudishness. Shorty climbed onstage, but instead of offering a brief confession, he began to shout about his wife's sexual problems: "Every time I wanted to do things with her, she said she was bleeding," he complained to the assembled audience. His wife, Maiyan, countered with accusations of her own: "You're talking a lot of bunk! When you go to bed, you just go to sleep," after which she began to disparage "his potency in intimate detail, with withering asides about Lilou." Lilou, not one to be slighted, then jumped to her feet, resulting in her and Maiyan "trading ribald sexual insults."

As the three peasants were shouting sexual obscenities at each other, the urban youth in the audience, who were expected to join the session by shouting various accusations, sat still in embarrassed silence. "We had never heard anything like this before, and we were blushing . . . We were over 20 years old and we didn't know what they were talking about!" Village men, however, were content to sit back and enjoy the show, as they were "sympathetic" to Shorty and had no intention of "meddling in his affairs." With the struggle session on the verge of chaos, the village cadre, who had planned to use the meeting to discredit Shorty, stepped in. Rather than accuse Shorty of political shortcomings, however, he disparaged his masculinity: "If a cow doesn't drink," he said in reference to Maiyan's refusal to have sex, "you push its head into the water." In other words, none of this would have happened had Shorty simply forced himself upon his wife. This intervention only worsened the situation. The trio's verbal arguments turned into a fistfight between Shorty and his wife. Maiyan emerged victorious and "chased him [Shorty] off into the night."

In the end, the struggle session, despite its chaotic nature, accomplished some of its original objectives. Maiyan's goal of avenging her husband was accomplished in the speedy approval of her divorce suit. Shorty, for his part, was not dismissed from his post, but was no longer invited to meetings of the public security committee. His vacant position was taken by his now ex-wife, Maiyan.

The connection between class, sex, and politics in rural areas has also been the subject of modern fiction about the Cultural Revolution. In Bai Hua's *Remote Country of Women*, for instance, the Cultural Revolution in an ethnic minority village in Yunnan is also described as a political movement with strong sexual overtones. Much of the conflict in the story centers on different conceptions of appropriate sexual behavior among youthful and puritanical Red Guards on the one hand, and Naxi villagers on the other. Red Guards decamped in some villages in Lijiang, a frontier area near the Burmese border. A matriarchal society, the Naxi were deemed by two urban intellectuals running the GPCR from Beijing (Zhang Chunqiao and Yao Wenyuan) to be one of "the most primitive" groups in China because "primitive" societies were matriarchal and nonmonogamous. The Red Guards' mission was to make the Naxi more "modern" by criticizing their family structure and sexual behavior; if necessary, they would also prosecute adulterers. As in Chen Village, peasants' earthy frankness about sex placed a few bumps in this road to modernity. After the Naxi described their origins, female Red Guards "blushed," and the men made noises and gestures indicating discomfort. After recovering, Red Guards appealed to the Naxi peasants:

> We're not asking you to climb a mountain of swords or wade a flaming sea, but you must be trailblazers. Just think—everything is being done for your sake. We want you to live a decent, monogamous, legitimate life. What kind of life are you leading now? Only cavemen living ten thousand years ago had lives like yours, so chaotic that a child knows his mother but not his father. This is the residue of group marriage. You are party members. Aren't you ashamed of yourselves? This is far from the morality of a party member. We cannot put up with this anymore.[54]

In this story, as in Chen Village, Naxi peasants had little tolerance for Red Guard speeches. One village cadre retorted, "During the Great Leap Forward they said the same thing. But later . . . the women and men who married ended up separating and returning to their mothers."[55] The Red Guard leader assured the cadre that, despite her objections, "we will not give up until we have carried the revolution through to the end!" and threatened her that should she refuse, she would be dismissed from the party. This also failed to have its intended effect. In a display of the bold legal culture similar to that of "real life" peasants discussed in earlier chapters, the cadre in the story said, "So be it . . . I don't see why the members of the central committee should give a damn about what's inside a man's trousers or under a woman's skirt! . . . Why are you forcing us to accept marriage?"[56] This response further infuriated the young revolutionaries: "Your head is on backward! Only monogamy fits current moral standards."[57] They then warned the assembled peasants that having sex without a marriage certificate would be deemed a crime punishable by labor reform. When peasants left the meeting, the Red Guard leader, in a modern incarnation of nineteenth-century Russian revolutionary youth, yelled after them, "Let's see who is tougher! Let's see how long you can bear celibacy!"[58]

The Cultural Revolution not only gave opportunities for rural cadres and disgruntled peasants to avenge political enemies, or for enthusiastic Han youth to force monogamy on minorities with different family and sexual practices. In other cases, rather than peasants and cadres closing ranks against outsiders, peasants used the movement to criticize and attack local officials. By 1966 there was no lack of reasons to resent village officialdom: campaigns against corruption in the early 1960s yielded only partial and temporary successes; as we saw in chapter 6, cadres used their access to scarce resources to secure brides and lovers (who would agree to marry only a man with such resources) at a time when poorer peasants could not afford to marry.[59] In late 1966, for example, army veterans, who had long suffered cadres' abuse of power, were among those who organized and pressured the local party committee (in suburban Shanghai) to improve their economic position.[60]

During the GPCR, charges of economic corruption blended with those that reflected poorer peasants' difficult marriage predicament; unlike students, peasants did not seem to make the connection between cadres' having led a "capitalist" lifestyle and their "inappropriate" sexual behavior. In Chen Jo-hsi's short story "The Execution of Mayor Yin" (Yin was actually a *rural* county chief, not an urban "mayor"), for example, Magistrate Yin was accused of being "rotten and corrupt, and . . . behav[ing] immorally with women."[61] In Long Bow Village in Shanxi Province, peasants criticized party officials for using their power "to engage in a wide variety of illicit sexual liaisons."[62] In his memoir, *Son of the Revolution,* Liang Heng recalls the frank discussions he and his father had with poor peasants in Hunan who were confused about the goals of the Cultural Revolution. "Old Liang," they complained, "we don't understand. Why is raising chickens and ducks rotten Capitalism? How can we buy oil and salt if we don't sell eggs?" One thirty-five-year-old bachelor complained, "I have almost two hundred yuan now. But if I can't raise more than one pig a year, I'll be sixty before I can look for a wife. Do they want me to dream about women for the rest of my life?"[63]

Party officials who tried to enforce the radical leftist policies of the time sometimes encountered peasants' frank and feisty legal culture. When a peasant named Guo Laoda was told to hide his ducks from a party official, he swore, "His mother's . . . Can a Party Secretary eat me up? If my ducks like the fields, let them stay there." Urged again to remove his ducks, Guo retorted, "Six ducks have a nibble on public land. Well, who knows how much public food that farter has eaten, dropping in everywhere at mealtimes. We poor peasants don't know how to write, but we keep our accounts with our bellies!" Even at a public meeting, Guo refused to back down. After being criticized by the party secretary for raising capitalist ducks, Guo, in his anger over the sexual and economic perks of party officials, shouted back, "What makes you think your cock is any bigger than anyone else's?"[64]

Liang Heng, as the son of an intellectual who not once openly questioned party policy, was unaccustomed to such blatant displays of defiance by mere peasants. For him, *education* was a prerequisite for intelligent and effective critique: "I never dreamed that this uneducated peasant could render a Party Secretary speechless, but he did," he comments in surprise. In the end, however, Guo's defiance was not sufficient to defy the power of the work team. Soon after this incident, the work team blew up Guo's pigsty, killing the "capitalist" hogs he planned to sell to market.[65]

In other cases, village cadres, rather than work teams, responded to peasant violence in kind. In doing so, they found trustworthy allies in village or township militias, organizations with which they had established close ties in the pre–Cultural Revolution years.[66] As we observed in previous chapters, an important facet of the cadre-militia alliance was their mutual interest in gaining sexual access to women: cadres used militia to abduct widows of executed landlords, PLA wives, and other women, while militia leaders were often given a free hand to conduct nighttime searches to have sex. During the Cultural Revolution, this alliance came under attack by powerless male peasants and radical students.

Despite party and militia retribution, peasant attacks on the party were not completely futile. The protracted nature of the Cultural Revolution allowed many peasant grievances to surface, and when Mao ordered party and PLA units not to restrain Red Guard activity, some peasant complaints were given their due attention. As usual, local cadres used their access to material resources to satisfy these demands. This time, however, resources that had been given to lovers, second wives, and family members were diverted to other recipients. In suburban Shanghai, for instance, reports indicated that local power holders "distributed over ten thousand yuan [forty-two hundred dollars] to various groups of local dissidents to buy off their opposition." As one report noted:

> In the name of "showing concern for the masses," they illegally distribute a large portion of the general [grain] reserves and public welfare funds . . . They even contract loans from the state under various pretexts and make forced withdrawals from banks and credit cooperatives.[67]

In other cases, local leaders urged peasants to go to cities to demand various economic and welfare benefits. Later on during the Cultural Revolution, more meaningful reforms were introduced. During 1968, public health, consumer credit, technical support, fertilizers, and farm tools were all made more available than they had been in previous years.[68] From the poorer peasants' perspective, then, the Cultural Revolution, and its violence in particular, was not a total loss. Rebellion against pre–Cultural Revolution party perks forced local officials to agree to ameliorative measures and be more responsive to peasants' needs. Now, in the 1990s, after the Cultural Revolution and Maoist-style political campaigns have been repudiated, one wonders what force might instill the fear necessary to convince many local cadres to cease engaging in corruption and become more responsive to their constituency. Mao and many peasants understood that violent campaigns were just about the only way to check the power of local officials, if only temporarily.

FROM SEXUAL CRITIQUE TO SEXUAL VIOLENCE

To date, there have been very few scholarly accounts of the violence that permeated everyday life during the Cultural Revolution. Lynn White III, who has written the only book-length work specifically devoted to this topic, argues that violence was the result of CCP administrative policies, such as class labeling, assigning bosses and monitors, and organizing campaigns. Such policies, White suggests, created animosity between groups and pent-up frustration toward the state: "They were mad," he writes. "Pastels would not do; so they chose red . . . relaxed muscles could not let out enough of their anger, after their lives had been exploited so egregiously for years; thus they shouted loud slogans and clenched their fists, instead."[69] Anne Thurston, in contrast, focuses more on psychology than specific policies. In traditional Chinese culture and in the modern period, she argues, people accepted violence as "necessary or even inevitable." Chinese under Mao's rule, she adds, lost all capacity for moral reasoning: "So much did many people love Chairman Mao, so greatly did they admire the Communist Party, so timorous were they before authority . . . [that] the[ir] capacity for independent human judgement was grotesquely, pathetically maimed."[70] Richard Madsen, in an article examining the downward spiral of violence in Long Bow Village during the Cultural Revolution (as chronicled by William Hinton in *Shenfan*), emphasizes peasants' "felt duty to take revenge." Peasants, he suggests, saw revenge as having "moral meaning as the fulfillment of obligations to carry out retribution against those who had harmed the members of one's community."[71] Given what we have seen in previous chapters, it is clear that White's and Thurston's accounts of violence require some revision. With the exception of intellectuals, few heeded the regime's black and red line in matters of marriage, friendship, and sex. The frequent blurring of class categories challenges one of White's main causal arguments—that "violence" was the cumulative result of state labeling policies. Thurston's argument that "most" Chinese "admired" the party would surely have been dismissed by Mao himself, who understood very well that many officials were taking advantage of their positions for less than honorable goals and otherwise not "serving the people." Certainly evidence of peasants calling cadres "wild pisser" or "donkey," or remonstrating in Beijing (chapter 6), does not quite support the contention that all or even most Chinese admired the party. Just as peasants disaggregated the state in terms of legitimacy and knowing which sort of organization was more likely to look favorably upon their demands, so too did they disaggregate the party: some may have worshipped Mao at the very same time that they despised their local party organization and adopted a more respectful stance toward the county. In contrast, the available literature on intellectuals reveals their tendency to reify and anthropomorphize the party, treating it as an all-knowing, all-powerful, godlike organization devoid of human form and the possibility of failure. The "blind obedience" Thurston writes about rings far more true of the intellectuals she sympathizes with than of any representative sample of ordinary Chinese. Madsen's approach to violence seems far more promising, as revenge, at both the elite and local levels, was so central to politics of the Cultural Revolution. His argument that revenge had *moral* meaning for individual participants, however, seems more questionable given that his article is based on one secondary source, which leads him to infer more morality than probably existed at the time. People sought revenge because they had certain grievances, whether based on interests or ethical concerns, but how the desire for revenge translated into "violence" is not very clear.

Part of the problem in previous accounts of violence during the Cultural Revolution is that "violence" is too large a category of analysis; "violence" as it occurs in everyday life assumes different *forms* and involves systems of legitimization. Assault and rape, for example, commonly figure in crime statistics as separate subcategories, and in the popular mind are associated with different causes. Criminals themselves will likely explain assault and rape in very different terms. A first step to toward explaining "violence" during the GPCR, therefore, is to disaggregate the concept into smaller, more manageable units.

Below, I briefly examine one specific form of violence, as part of what might become a larger effort to explain violence more generally. The questions I am particularly interested in are the following: If the GPCR was primarily a political movement, why would violence take sexual forms? In what way might sexual violence be a product of the puritan sexual ethics among youth discussed above?

One possible answer linking the political goals of the Cultural Revolution to sexual violence was the sort of youthful concerns for sexual purity and class-based notions of proper sexual morality I discussed earlier. Take for instance a Red Guard struggle session against a teacher at Beijing University. During the Cultural Revolution, students organized a violent struggle session against a teacher for "allowing" a fellow student to have sex with a forty-year-old widow. The department, students charged, permitted the student to read "yellow novels" (pornography). This, in turn, "corrupted" his "socialist morality."[72]

Ad hoc struggle sessions designed to condemn sexual transgression were only one forum within which violence occurred. Many societies organize institutions of violence that reflect their cultural norms. In Nazi Germany, for instance, the mass, methodical execution of perceived "enemies" in the concentration camps was at once a manifestation of Germany's long history of virulent anti-Semitism and the German concern, if not obsession, with efficiency and order. Red Guards, like the Nazis, also had their institutions of violence, and they were as much a reflection of their culture as the German camps were of theirs. In the GPCR, the imagery and associations of "Ox Ghosts" (*niu gui*) in the *People's Daily* headline took institutional form in hastily organized "Ox Sheds"; *niu peng* or *niu lan*). In many cases, these *niu peng* were located in basements of buildings. Spatially separated from society, Red Guards could perpetrate violence without much fear of public criticism or intervention.

Within the *niu peng*, the forms violence took were sometimes a direct result of (usually male) Red Guards' obsession with sexual and class purity, concern with women's erotic power (especially in the imagery of the "snake demon"), and a desire to prove themselves as "real men" by humiliating class enemies in sexual ways. At the same time, the puritanical sexual code among students in the years prior to the GPCR led to a bizarre voyeurism about sex, a curiosity that could be satisfied by forcing others to engage in sex in public view. In Amoy, Fujian Province, for example, a chemistry teacher who had once mentioned in class that the "mutual attraction of

positive and negative electrons is like the union of man a woman" was ordered to remove his pants and have sex with his wife.[73]

Not all instances of violence were inspired by chemical principles. In the
hastily erected *niu peng*, male Red Guards tortured and raped women who
belonged to "enemy" classes or factions. On occasion, violence was justified by reference to the "Snake Demon" headline in *People's Daily*. In North
China, for instance, Red Guards tortured a female student in the *niu peng*.
When other students felt that the torture was out of proportion to her
"crime," the student torturer replied, "We can't show mercy for this venomous snake."[74] In the same school's *niu peng*, a female student was violently raped. A doctor who examined her bruised body found her genitalia
stuffed with dirty socks and twigs.[75] Can it be only coincidental that violence
against this student would target sexual organs? The womb, as I pointed out
earlier, was said to contain an evil spirit (in the form of the fearsome water
monkey) dangerous to men. By stuffing her genitalia with socks and twigs,
male students may have been acting on their fear of women's sexual power,
a power associated with the sexualized images in the Buddhist pantheon of
demons and ghosts. Rape was thus a way of reasserting male power against
an imagined, folk-religion-inspired threat to young men.

Sometimes, forms of torture reflected a more literal than sexual understanding of the "Ox Ghost and "Snake Demon" couplet. Red Guards would
use coal or black paint to darken the face of people in the "black" classes
and then force them to crawl around on shards of glass and sharp rocks, and
eat grass, like real oxen.[76]

Sexual violence in the *niu peng* also spread to the streets. During the factional fighting between Red Guard units in 1968, captured male "soldiers"
would occasionally have their sexual organs cut off.[77] In other cases, male
sexual organs were the target of punches and blows.[78] In Tibet, the reli-
giouslike fervor stirred up among youth combined with sexual puritanism
to produce some of the most horrifying atrocities. Red Guards castrated
Tibetan monks and gouged out their eyes, and forced nuns and monks to
have sex in front of them.[79]

It was rare for urban youth witnessing these events to actively step in to
stop the violence. Doing so might result in accusations of aiding and abet-
ting the enemy classes seeking to overthrow Chinese socialism. But when
minimal efforts to tone down the violence were made, the criticism also
reflected concerns with sexual purity. In Fujian, a Red Guard leader who
"never let a good-looking girl get away from him" was scolded by a fellow
comrade-in-arms. Rather than criticizing him for multiple rapes, the friend
asked, "How can you ejaculate revolutionary sperm into a counterrevolutionary womb?"[80] In a school in North China, a woman who was called a
"counterrevolutionary whore" was sexually molested by a Red Guard leader
and killed by him soon afterward.[81]

Sexuality, however, was not used only as a justification for attack; it could also be a resource that victims might deploy in the context of a violent struggle. Given the ignorance and sexual puritanism among many Red Guard youth, overt displays of sexuality could also be used as a way of *defending* oneself and exhibiting defiance against Red Guard attacks. In Rae Yang's memoir, *Spider Eaters,* for instance, she and some of her Red Guard comrades-in-arms captured a man who then "confessed" to being a Nationalist spy and admitting to hating Red Guards. As the Red Guard group began to beat him, this man found a simple way both to scare off his attackers and to show that he was not cowed by them. Yang writes:

> The next thing he did was a real shock to all of us. In a shower of fists, kicks, curses, and thrashes he suddenly straightened up and pulled his white cotton shorts down. He had no underwear on. So there was his thing, his penis. Large and black. It stuck out from a clump of black hair. To me it seemed erect, nodding its head at all of us. I couldn't help staring at it. I was dumbfounded. I was embarrassed. I was furious. My hands were cold and my cheeks were on fire. For a few seconds none of us moved. We were petrified. Then the dike burst . . . All the female Red Guards ran out of the classroom.

In the end, however, this sexualized display of defiance was to no avail. After running away, the embarrassed "iron women" called in the boys, who then proceeded to beat the man to death with bamboo sticks. They hated him, Yang writes, "because he was a scum of their sex. By exposing himself, he had exposed all of them. They were stripped. They were shamed."[82]

"SEXUAL" CLEAVAGES: INTERPRETING
PURITANISM AND SEXUAL CONFLICTS

Jung Chang, in her memoir, *Wild Swans,* argues that the Cultural Revolution "produced a large number of militant puritans, mostly young women." In her view, state policies, more so than society or culture, better explain how sexuality became a contentious issue during this period.[83] In contrast, my study suggests not only that sexual puritanism among educated urban youth—male and female—preceded the GPCR, but also that there were important differences in the way different social classes dealt with the issues of sexuality and class throughout the conflict. The issues that preoccupied Red Guards did not necessarily interest others.

When Red Guards attacked political enemies and ordinary Chinese for their lack of revolutionary consciousness in dress, choice of sexual partners, and the conduct of their private lives, they unwittingly stepped into the historical shoes of many of those they attacked. From the May 4th Movement in 1919 to the 1940s, Chinese intellectuals criticized fellow citizens who, in their pursuit of the good life and pleasure (such as playing cards, dancing, and sex), did not see any necessary connection between private morality and political virtue. According to many intellectuals, building a strong state and moral society required a citizenry committed to their own ethical reformation, and this meant leading an austere private life, refraining from pleasure for pleasure's sake, and channeling one's physical energies toward the nation. These qualities were largely thought of as "proletarian" or "peasant" values. Given what we have seen about workers and peasants' material aspirations, however, one wonders if was possible for students to have been more gullible and naïve: at the same time that they tried to demonstrate their revolutionary zeal by wearing workers' clothing and eating food fit for animals, workers and peasants sought to acquire nice clothes, put on perfume, wear leather shoes and makeup, and own property and jewelry—a far cry from the austerity attributed to their social class by state intellectuals.

When many intellectuals were given important positions in the state apparatus after 1949 (particularly in education and propaganda bureaus, which required a high level of literacy), criticism of Chinese with a more lax notion of private morality mounted; acerbic comments in intraparty reports concerning "rash," "careless," and "chaotic" sexual relations among workers and peasants were only one manifestation of this statist-cum-intellectual puritan ethic. Party officials who actually investigated the family and marriage situations of workers and peasants knew very well that there was a wide gap between what workers and peasants desired to acquire and how they wanted to live on the one hand, and what was expected of them in Communist propaganda on the other. Young students, however, were much less knowledgeable about workers and peasants' private lives and ambitions and, as a result, were easily taken in by the notion that by demanding that women chop off their hair, remove makeup and jewelry, and so forth, they were actually helping to forge a more "proletarian" society. This was one of the many ironies of the GPCR: in their attack on "bourgeois" and "capitalist" culture in the name of a "proletarian" cultural revolution, students condemned the aspirations and cultural practices of the proletariat itself. Moreover, by beating teachers and other intellectuals, students were in effect attacking those who were probably the *most* committed to fulfilling the revolutionary quest for a more pure and austere (i.e., "proletarian") private life.

Students' attacks on teachers were not the only manifestation of misguided and naïve ideas about "proletarian" culture. When youth went to villages or ransacked homes and CCP offices to uproot "capitalism" and "revisionism" within the party, many, for the first time in their short lives, came face to face with a rural-based sexual culture, one in which the meaning of marriage, divorce, and probably sex was quite different than their own.[84] Discovering evidence of party officials (many of whom, presumably, had spent a good deal of time in rural areas or were themselves of peasant extraction) having their way with several women, divorcing several times, having sex with assorted "black class" individuals, hiring GMD dance teachers, consorting with secretaries and cultural troupe members, and exchanging material benefits for sexual favors probably came as quite a shock. As seen in the prosecution of Ding Yi and Guo Pei and the charges leveled at Marshall He Long, Tao Zhu, and Zeng Sheng, "discovery" of these sexual practices might even overshadow political critique. While students' brandishing of sexuality as political critique was misguided in the case of many state-serving intellectuals, in the case of CCP officials accusations *were* often factual. As we have seen in previous chapters, many peasant CCP members *did* have sex with landlords' daughters, wives of executed landlords and bandits, rich peasants, and the like; in the Southwest, the subject of chapter 4, PLA officers and county officials (Marshall He Long probably included) had sex with bandit wives and prostitutes; in other areas, many officials used their power to give special treatment to lovers, hence all the "gifts" found in party officials' spacious homes; in chapter 6, we witnessed CCP officials committing adultery and rape of PLA soldiers, acts similar to the one in the accusation leveled at Mayor Zeng Sheng during the Cultural Revolution; some party members actually had more than one wife—a practice that was most clearly associated with the exploitative behavior of capitalists and landlords prior to 1949. In other words, if one of the goals of the GPCR was to attack "capitalist roaders" within the party, and "capitalism" was understood to produce promiscuity, bigamy and the like, then student attacks on the party on sexual grounds were not unjustified. Of course, that students launched these attacks in the name of Chairman Mao, of all people, is yet another irony of the GPCR. Recent memoirs suggest that Mao was quite fond of good liquor, mah-jongg, dancing, and beautiful women. Like Shorty, Lilou, and Maiyan of Chen Village, Mao and his peasant guards discussed these affairs quite openly. Mao's physician, in contrast, was as befuddled by these frank conversations as the educated youth in Chen Village who blushed and were embarrassed by peasants' willingness to go public with "private" problems.[85]

Attacks on party officials on sexual grounds may not have been limited to students, however. A hypothesis suggested by this chapter is that male peasants who were unable to scrape money together to marry criticized and attacked party officials in part owing to the way in which power was used to gain access to women. Women, for their own self-interested reasons, often refused to marry unless prospective husbands could offer material possessions or property. Easier access to divorce after the 1950 Marriage Law and the lack of attention to poor peasants' good political class made the long-term marital prospects of poor males even more precarious. The GPCR exacerbated tensions further by forcing local officials to espouse policies that made it even more difficult for a poor peasant to marry.

DEALING WITH CONFLICT: FAMILY DYNAMICS, LEGAL CULTURE, AND SUICIDE DURING THE CULTURAL REVOLUTION

Early accounts of violence during the Cultural Revolution tended to emphasize its impact in urban rather than rural areas. According to a quantitative analysis of fatalities and injuries caused by violence during the early years of the GPCR, the number of deaths showed a positive correlation with proximity to an urban area.[86] However, more recent scholarship—much of it based on research in the PRC—has added an important corrective to these earlier accounts by describing, in grisly detail, incidents of violence in rural areas, including cannibalism.[87]

Absent reliable quantitative measures of violence, the question of where the GPCR had its greatest impact or death toll will remain an open one. Less controversial, it seems to me, have been arguments concerning how different social classes related to politics, both during the early to mid-1960s and during the Cultural Revolution. Prior to the Cultural Revolution, harsh-toned debates concerning "proletarian" and "capitalist" culture were largely confined to radical urban intellectuals, and the ideology of class warfare was imbibed most fully by students; in the GPCR itself, students and intellectuals were the most "zealous disciples" of Mao.[88] It was not coincidental that students were used to foment class war in the countryside.

At the same time that students and intellectuals were instrumental in fomenting the ideology of class warfare that preceded the Cultural Revolution, some accounts of the GPCR published in the post-Mao era tend to emphasize Chinese intellectuals as innocent victims of Chairman Mao and his marauding Red Guards. According to these accounts, some written by former Red Guards and others by sympathetic Westerners, intellectuals sometimes reacted to violence directed at them by committing suicide, a final gesture of defiance against the miscarriage of justice very much in the Confucian intellectual tradition.[89] Although there is no quantitative evidence of suicide in rural areas, the extant literature does not give the impression that peasants or workers responded to political attacks by taking their own lives. If the cases of Guo Laoda (the Hunanese peasant who was criticized by the party secretary for raising capitalist ducks but who turned the tables on him in a public meeting), "Shorty" and Lilou of Chen Village, and the Naxi peasants are at all representative of what happened elsewhere in the countryside, peasants generally seemed to have been less cowered by political threats than were urban intellectuals, and certainly much less enamored of the party to act out the role of sacrificed martyr. Below I take up the question of why it may have been the case that social classes responded in different ways to political attacks during the Cultural Revolution. If further research confirms Richard Baum's quantitative analysis suggesting a higher death toll in urban areas than rural, an explanation of why suicide occurred among intellectuals (who resided mostly in urban areas) will help explain this outcome.

Although the causes of suicide are extremely complex, previous chapters suggest that different reactions to the GPCR are partially explainable by looking at what happened within the family in the years prior to the Cultural Revolution and how different classes dealt with the state, or what I have earlier called "legal culture." I hypothesize that the pre-1966 politicization and "freezing" of family in urban areas (particularly among intellectuals and those from capitalist background) and the relative fluidity of family structure and relations in rural areas, in addition to peasants' feisty way of dealing with the state, contributed to urban intellectual radicalism and suicide on the one hand, and the reportedly fewer incidents of suicide in response to struggle in rural areas on the other. In urban areas, we have seen that the number of people granted divorces decreased dramatically from 1954 to 1966 at the same time that urban life became increasingly politicized. Among intellectuals in particular, fear of the state, the density of work units, and bureaucratic institutions, in combination with concerns about face and propriety, resulted in many relationships that, by 1966, were fraught with tensions that had no outlet. In contrast, throughout this period, peasant wives continued to demand divorce by "running to court," separate more informally by leaving the homes of their husbands, and, most importantly, publicly complain about family members or obstructionist officials. To be sure, this does not suggest that peasants were necessarily "happier" in their relationships. Instead, it suggests that because peasants were willing to use state institutions, confront officials, discuss their problems in a frank manner, and use rural space and social structure to escape from abusive or unhappy relationships, there were, in relative terms, fewer politically based intrafamily tensions than among intellectual families in the years just preceding the Cultural Revolution.

I am convinced that these different family dynamics had profound implications for how different groups responded to the violence in the GPCR. For many urban intellectuals, by 1966 the family was no longer a secure refuge from national politics: politicized, class-conscious children might attack parents, and ideologically literate spouses might "draw a line" and ostracize their partner should they be attacked. When the private sphere of family and home was attacked with unprecedented thoroughness during the Cultural Revolution, when behavior in the family was forcibly exposed and made public, and when sons and daughters tried to become "revolutionary" by "drawing a line" between themselves and their parents, intellectuals under assault felt they had no place to which to turn. One result of this was suicide.[90] Lines were not drawn only *within* the family, however. In the politicized environment of urban China in the mid-1960s, entire families labeled as "capitalist," "counterrevolutionary," and the like often found themselves ostracized. Thus, in addition to individuals committing suicide owing to intrafamily tensions, there were also cases of entire families committing suicide because of fear and isolation.[91]

Ostracism of people labeled as class enemies was not common to all Chinese, however. Although there is not enough evidence to demonstrate this point conclusively, fragmentary evidence suggests that it was more likely for intellectuals to ostracize other intellectuals than for workers and peasants to ostracize people labeled as "class enemies." Given the relative absence of politicization of these classes during the pre-GPCR years, perhaps this is not very surprising. As Anne Thurston writes about one intellectual's experience in a factory:

> Huang Chaoqun was once taken to a factory where the workers were supposed to participate in a struggle session against him. But the workers refused to attend. The struggle session, for lack of participation, was canceled. One winter, the Red Guards took [him] to a rural commune where the poor peasants were supposed to organize a struggle session against him and where Huang Chaoqun was supposed to receive reeducation from the rural poor. Seeing [Huang] shivering visibly . . . one of the poor peasants removed his own greatcoat and gave it to [him]. Another brought him tea.[92]

For intellectuals under political attack, feelings of hopelessness may not have resulted only from ostracism or the absence of refuge within the family. Refuge was also limited by the urban environment itself; in the dense, politicized city, there were few places where one could escape the storm. At the same time, the city environment made it easier to attack political enemies. Distances between Red Guard units and police stations and residence committees (where much important information was kept) were short, and authorities in urban work units kept dossiers recording political history, past political activities, and personal foibles. This made it difficult for people to escape when a crisis arose. Those who would suffer the most were those with the weakest ties to rural areas, the most "cosmopolitan" of the urban population. As a daughter of a "capitalist" family attacked during the Cultural Revolution lamented, "Oh, how we longed to find a refuge, but where?"[93] Perhaps another reason why the GPCR may have had a more limited impact in rural areas was that space *could* be used as a resource to escape from politics, much as it was utilized to flee abusive families in the 1950s and 1960s. This study suggests not only that there was less tension in rural than urban families, but also that peasants had an easier time running away from politics. In Bai Hua's novel about Yunnan, for instance, a GPCR work team trying to instigate revolution among the Naxi minority had difficulty in organizing peasants because children scampered away and jumped into a lake.[94]

This analysis does not suggest that the ultimate responsibility for suicide during the GPCR was intellectuals' pre-1966 family predicament, legal culture, or the absence of escape routes from political attack. It was Mao Zedong, not urban intellectuals, who initiated class conflict in order to eliminate political rivals. Nonetheless, intellectuals' behavior as perpetrators and victims during the GPCR demands explanation without reference to the edicts of Chairman Mao. Why did Mao's call for struggle against class enemies find fertile ground among intellectuals, and why were their enemies attacked on sexual or family-related matters?

This chapter has suggested that some of the reasons can be discerned by looking at the language of critique and the form of political struggle. That "political" critique and struggle often had strong sexual overtones suggests that the call for the prosecution of class enemies was given extra potency because it meshed well with intellectuals' *own* sexual understanding of marriage, divorce, and "appropriate" sexual relations, in addition to their willingness to sacrifice mundane pleasures to attain statist goals. When their commitment to the state was betrayed and their families ostracized them, the hollowness of their political and private lives and their disappointment in the party drove them to suicide. It is doubtful that workers and peasants, who, as we have seen in previous chapters, were less beholden to a puritanical vision of sex and leisure, felt the same sense of betrayal by Mao during the Cultural Revolution. These groups, who continued to dance, gamble, and whore throughout the 1950s and 1960s, did not raise the issue of sexuality as a form of ideological critique, but did not hesitate to point to party officials' (and others) sexual peccadilloes (of which there were many, as we have seen) if this helped advanced or defend their cause; such improprieties, however, did not seem to motivate attacks or shape the form of violence.[95]

THE BIG PICTURE: THE GPCR IN COMPARATIVE PERSPECTIVE

Sexual forms of critique and violence during the GPCR suggest something larger than contrasting class views concerning appropriate revolutionary and sexual behavior. In comparative perspective, sexual puritanism as a criterion for "worthiness" in a community and sexual violence appear to be the common stock-in-trade in social conflicts in which religion, race, and ethnic identity are primary forms of identification. In the Salem witch trials in the United States, violations of appropriate sexual conduct led communities to burn sexual transgressors at the stake; in the racial laws of Nazi Germany, it was a crime for "pure" Aryans to have sex with "inferior" Jews; in the U.S. South, sex between blacks and whites occurred but was condemned by both communities, and blacks might have been lynched for sexually "defiling" a white woman. More recently, issues of sexual purity and ethnic identity have figured prominently in the violent conflicts in Rwanda and Bosnia. In both these places, rape and mutilation were, not coincidentally, common in battles for territory with "pure" religious, ethnic, or tribal characteristics.

From one perspective, it seems very odd that conflict in China, a country that is quite homogeneous in race and ethnicity (over 95 percent of the population is Han Chinese), and that since 1949 is officially atheist, would bear any sort of resemblance to social strife in more ethnically and religiously diverse societies. Looking at how "class" was interpreted in the pre-GPCR years and how the cult of Mao resulted in his being viewed as a god-like figure gives some indication of why there might be some similarities. Among students in particular, the infusion of notions of "purity of blood" into Marxist class analysis merged with a quasi-religious notion of sexually pure communities to produce ethnic and religious forms of identification and association; friends and enemies could be identified and targeted by questioning class background *and* sexual behavior. And, as in these other cases of community boundaries drawn along ethnic and religious lines that resulted in widespread sexual atrocities, so too was the GPCR, with its tightly drawn divisions between good and bad, pure and impure revolutionary and counterrevolutionary communities, characterized by sexual critique and violence.

To date, social conflict in the Cultural Revolution has usually been ascribed to concrete socioeconomic grievances. While this explanation accounts for the motives for participation in Red Guard units and the choice of which unit to join, it is less helpful in explaining some of the GPCR's rhetoric, forms, and meaning of violence. Interpreting social conflict during the GPCR as conflict between class-based quasi-ethnic and religious *communities* helps account for the sex-laden forms of critique and violence. Many of the issues that surfaced in these forms of critique, however, cannot be understood without reference to the Marriage Law, which, to an unprecedented degree, inserted the state into marital relations and sexual practices, and foisted people's decisions about marriage, divorce, and sex into the public arena.

CHAPTER EIGHT

Conclusion

Given my training in political science, it is not surprising that the question I posed at the beginning of this study focused on the role of the state and its laws in shaping family relations. Such an orientation made sense both in terms of my training and in terms of the methodological inclination of many scholars of comparative politics; the movement to "bring the state back in" to studies of revolution and economic and political development had already produced several pathbreaking works, all of which shaped the ideas and hypotheses of this study.[1] Studies of social change by non-political scientists concurred that changing "traditional" social structure requires a "strong," "capable," or "modernizing" state. Scholars of women in the People's Republic of China, for instance, looked toward the revolutionary Communist state as *the* agent capable of "liberating" women from the multiple oppression of family, community, and tradition. The tone of disappointment in these works is in part reflective of the high expectations the authors had of the state in the first place.

So then what was the role of state in changing family relations in China? Despite the state-centered orientation of the initial question, what I have come to appreciate in this research is how the most "traditional" of women could, and often did, change their situation *without* the state's helping hand, frequently despite criticism for their "unorthodox" behavior and violent resistance on the part of state officials and community members. Rural and working-class women, and some men, annulled engagements, left marriages, and petitioned for divorce even though the "party line" toward divorce hardened. Moreover, they did so for reasons that the state (or, to be more precise, educated Chinese in the state apparatus) considered "rash," "careless," or unwarranted. Even as many Chinese women continued to hold what many Western feminists would consider "traditional" views toward the sexual division of labor in the family, they still went to courts and other state agencies to complain about husbands and in-laws or to sue for divorce. I thus have found little incompatibility between an understanding of sexual *inequality* as the natural order of things and a willingness to take an active role in changing one's family situation. In short, achieving "gender equality," a principal concern of Western feminists and often the criterion by which they judge women's "progress" in the Third World, was clearly not a precondition for taking advantage of the Marriage Law or changing power dynamics in the family. In some cases, we can even make the argument that "modern" state-led social change can actually be *facilitated* by "traditional" *inequality* between the sexes, as a fairly rigid division between the sexes can make it easier for women to forge identities and communities based on common experiences and grievances. The trust established between women, in turn, can pave the way for collective action oriented toward solving shared problems or attaining common goals. We have seen such cases in China, as well as in the comparative literature on Japan, Turkey, Russia, India, and France discussed in chapter 4. Attention to ordinary people's *agency*—whether on the individual or group level—was an important modification of the original state-centered hypothesis.[2]

But in the case of the Marriage Law, which challenged local norms and customs on multiple levels (making it easier to divorce, setting the legal age of marriage, approving only certain kinds of marriages, etc.), it is also clear that individual agency was not always enough to counter stiff resistance on the part of officials and others; the state still had an important role to play in shaping family dynamics. At the risk of some simplification, it might be helpful to think of its impact in terms of *fear, legitimacy,* and *opportunity*. Political campaigns such as Land Reform and the Marriage Law, whether intentionally or unintentionally, often had the result of terrifying citizens and state officials alike. As we have seen in chapters 3 and 4, such fear on the part of officials often resulted in "rash" handling of divorce claims, which, in turn, contributed directly to the high divorce approval rates in rural areas. Fear was also important in preventing alliances between members of the older generation and obstructionist local officials, as both of these parties were afraid of violating what they believed to be party policy. Such fear was clearly responsible for the cases in which women were overcompensated in property settlements and the many "rash verdicts" rendered in the early 1950s. A key dynamic in the Marriage Law was not only "the state" acting upon society, but also "the party" generating fear among its own membership and officials. This latter perspective on the state has largely been ignored in the previous scholarship on the Marriage Law, since it was simply assumed that Mao and the party central and other, much lower, officials were of a "like mind," and implemented the Marriage Law and other policies through the cultural lens of "patriarchy."

Fear—whether among citizens or party officials—was not the only reaction to CCP policies, however. In rural areas, land reform, in addition to generating terror, also, and somewhat ironically, contributed mightily to the legitimacy of the Communist Party, particularly at levels that had a more direct association with the party central and Mao; if the Marriage Law was promulgated by "Chairman Mao" or "the Communist Party," who were responsible for land reform, it must be good for poor peasants. We usually do not think of these feelings toward the state as mutually compatible—how could citizens fear and trust the state at the same time?—but in our case we have seen that the CCP, through violent campaigns against pre-1949 elites, managed to instill terror while generating legitimacy among poorer peasants. The fact that the CCP had legitimacy in rural areas virtually ensured that the law would have a great deal of impact. This legitimacy, I have argued, was largely the result of the fact that the CCP state was generated by a revolution that moved from the countryside to the city (despite having originated in the city). Because of this, many urbanites, particularly during the early years of the PRC, did not hold such a positive view of the Communist Party and had a different "experience of the state" than did peasants in the early 1950s. Evidence in chapters 2 and 5 shows that there was much confusion, skepticism, and fear about new Communist policies and institutions, and that few felt personally "liberated" (*jiefang*) or "emancipated" (*fanshen*) by the Communists, even as some welcomed the imposition of social order and the expulsion of foreigners.[3] That the PLA and CCP comprised primarily "backward" peasants from North China certainly did not make it easy for the new state to establish legitimacy in urban areas. As a result, many urbanites, intellectuals, and the pre-1949 bourgeoisie in particular, avoided as much as possible dealing with state institutions.

Finally, it would be difficult to argue that the law in itself "caused" social change. As we have seen, the Marriage Law rarely affected villages unmediated by other factors, and when the law was enforced, the results were quite often completely unintended (such as women ditching their husbands because they were "too poor," using the language of "marriage freedom" to justify having sex with landlord progeny, interpreting the Marriage Law by calling for the "distribution" of wives, illicit sexual liaisons between military wives and local officials, etc.). We might illustrate the way in which policy was implemented in the Marriage Law, and in other cases of legal and political reform as well, using the metaphor of billiards. In billiards, players aim the cue ball in the general direction of the assembled, numbered balls. The cue ball strikes the other ones and the formerly orderly balls scatter in numerous directions, some of them falling into the intended side and corner pockets, while others scatter randomly on the board. For the player, the end result was partially successful, even if the balls that ended up in the pockets were not the ones originally intended. Still, given the difficulty of planning something as complex as shooting many balls into small pockets, the number of unintended consequences is not that surprising. After the first shot, the situation facing the player is far more complex than before the rack was broken, since many of the balls are in randomly scattered places. For the rest of the game, the player plays "catch-up" to the situation created by the very first ball. I believe that this metaphor goes far in describing policy implementation in China generally, as well as in the specific case of the Marriage Law. Studies of Chinese politics using rational choice, patron-client, principal-agent, or leadership approaches are, I believe, too elegant or structured to capture policy implementation in a country where many officials have a hard time even reading, let alone comprehending, the often vague and unrealistic guidelines set forth in central directives, are minimally educated, often lack face, and are buffeted by social forces that have taken initiative into their own hands; we need concepts, metaphors, and models to account for the "mess" of Chinese politics, as well as for its patterns. This study of policy implementation thus suggests that we be very attentive to both intended and *unintended* consequences, to the balls that fall in the pockets correctly as well as mistakenly; state influence, we have seen in each of the chapters, rarely flows from careful, intentional implementation of policies, and can be obstructed (or facilitated) not only by entrenched interests but also by incompetence and bumbling. This is pretty much what happened with the Marriage Law. Even when the central directives were clear, officials, many of whom could not even read them and had little time to work with them, interpreted them in different ways, ensuring that their implementation would be distorted in many ways. Such distortions, and the conflicts that ensued because of them, should caution us to avoid speaking of the "party" and "state" as unitary, monolithic entities and instead adopt a disaggregated, sociological perspective on the state. Here I have attempted to put a much more human face on the Maoist party-state, to view the state as "officials *in action*" and to, as Joseph Esherick has suggested, analyze "the internal composition of the party-state and the complex relations among its different levels." The party-state, he reminds us, is indeed a "structure" comprising many sorts of institutions, but inside these structures are people whose actions cannot simply be reduced to their small role in the party machine.[4] The historian R. Keith Schoppa has expressed this analytical perspective very eloquently in his study of the revolutionary Shen Dingyi:

> To understand the revolution, we must give substantial attention to the daily human experience and social processes from which ideas developed and ac-

tions were taken, to flesh-and-blood human beings whose commitments and motives could stem from a wide variety of motives.[5]

Looking at the state in a disaggregated way and at the (highly fallible) people inside its institutions allows us to appreciate just how politics and administration during the Maoist years (and, I believe, today as well) were characterized by outright bumbling, mismanagement, and improvisation.

Because the law's impact on society was often indirect, mediated, and unintentional, it is useful to conceptualize its role in terms of new *opportunities* that allowed people to extract themselves from families. Prior to the Marriage Law, divorce, by almost all accounts, was very rare (*informal* separations, however, were probably much more common), in part because there were very few state institutions designated to handle marriage disputes; the Republican civil code had virtually no impact on rural society. This changed dramatically after the promulgation of the 1950 Marriage Law, which, for the first time on a nationwide scale, inserted many layers of the state into family relations. Courts, townships, districts, counties, and prefectural governments were all required to deal with peasants' divorce suits; if one proved recalcitrant, there were others to go to. In urban areas, by contrast, there were simply fewer institutions authorized to grant divorce, only courts and district governments. Just a numerical comparison of the opportunity structure provided by the state in urban and rural areas suggests a greater probability of success in the latter.

But there was clearly more than numbers at work. Feminist scholars have rightly pointed to the gendered nature of the state—the fact that the overwhelming majority of officials are male has to be relevant to any account of state-led change—but they have exaggerated the extent to which this sociological or physiological fact *necessarily* worked against women's interests. In China, as we have seen, many in the state apparatus were poor peasants prior to becoming "officials," and therefore unaccustomed to dealing with marriage disputes, since these and other such family issues were often considered women's matters or handled by elites. For many male officials, granting women a divorce was often a way of avoiding *mafan,* or "hassle." But what made this strategy particularly attractive was the feisty and confrontational manner in which divorce claims were presented. For impatient and harried officials, granting a divorce, sometimes on the spot, was simply easier than dealing with angry women, whom they disparaged anyway, banging at their doors threatening to commit suicide.

In addition to this feisty way of interacting with the state, what made a peasant woman's chances of a favorable outcome even more likely was *space.* Many peasant women—whether in North China or in the Southwest—were quite mobile, moving from natal to adoptive homes for visits, migration, selling produce in markets (in suburbs, goods would also be sold in cities), or engaging in community rituals such as "stealing the bride" in the Southwest. Such mobility, which is probably more characteristic of peasant life than the more usual depiction of peasants being confined to their villages or stuck on their land, served them very well when seeking divorce, as state institutions were invariably located some distance away from their villages. The "political geography" of the state in rural areas and the extent of their authority in dealing with marriage cases was also crucial in shaping the outcomes of cases. As shown in the chapters of this study dealing with rural areas, township, district, and county governments, courts, and registration bureaus were all authorized to grant divorce and yet, owing to the wide expanses in the countryside, had great difficulty in coordinating their decisions. For peasants, then, both the number of political and legal institutions and the state's "scattered" political geography gave them many opportunities to sue for divorce and made divorces relatively easy to obtain. In urban areas, by contrast, the law also led to a proliferation of state institutions dealing with the family, but more opportunities did not translate into great demand for divorce or a quick approval process. This was largely because many state institutions in cities were not authorized to grant divorces (such as work units, unions, mediation committees, and residence committees) but *were* able to coordinate their handling of a divorce case. The more low-level institutions became involved in a case, the more difficult it became for the petitioner to even reach a court or district government (the only two institutions authorized to grant divorce) and secure a positive judgment. As we have seen in chapter 5, urban divorce petitioners might have to get approval from their party committee or union director well before even going to court, and courts could telephone work units' personnel departments or residence committees to investigate someone's personal behavior. In many cases petitioners would just be sent home—something that was easy to do given the density of urban areas. Peasants, in contrast, packed a few belongings and went directly to court, often bypassing local officials. Having traveled far, they refused to leave until their case was heard. Whereas for peasants the state's "scattered" political geography often made it easier to divorce, for urbanites, particularly those in the urban "core," the state's "dense" or "thick" political geography led to the opposite outcome.

In addition to appreciating the role of agency and unintended consequences in state-led social change, the evidence has also forced me to rethink a commonsensical understanding of the causal direction of change. When I embarked on this research, it did not occur to me that family politics and dynamics might have as much influence on the state as state policy on the family. Yet in this study we have seen that adultery, conflicts over marriage and divorce, and different ideas about sexuality shaped how state officials were perceived by the general population. This was reflected in the disdain villagers and workers frequently showed for their immediate superiors, many of whom were involved in all sorts of rather unconventional and politically suspect sexual practices (such as swapping wives, abducting wives of executed landlords and bandits, and having sex with wives of PLA soldiers), as well as in the form of critique against officialdom during the Cultural Revolution, discussed in chapter 7. There was a circular causal chain: the Marriage Law created new opportunities to divorce and at the same time (intentionally) forced local officials to deal with issues of marriage and divorce and (unintentionally) sex. When male officials took advantage of divorce to marry women they considered more attractive (even if they were very "politically incorrect"), when they committed adultery with PLA wives, when they bungled mediation, and when they tried to use their power to stifle divorce suits, whatever legitimacy they might have had in the eyes of many villagers was undermined. When this happened, peasant women went to those institutions they saw as more representative of the central state (such as districts, courts, and counties), which had more legitimacy in their eyes. Geographically remote from villages, few peasants were aware that judges and district officers (and, of course, Mao) had often engaged in the same sort of misconduct as local officials. State legitimacy, this study suggests, should therefore be looked at in *disaggregated* terms; it was not something that "the state" could win or lose, have or squander. Different institutions were afforded different degrees of legitimacy by different classes, at different times and in different regions of the country. Speaking of "the party" as having legitimacy in the early years only to lose it after the Anti-Rightist campaign (as Liu Binyan suggests),[6] or even speaking of states more generally as "having" legitimacy or not, misses important *variations* in the way people view the state. Some intellectuals may not see the political center as very legitimate (particularly after the Tiananmen uprising of 1989), but their view is not shared by many rural Chinese. As Kevin O'Brien and Li Lianjiang, who have studied the way in which peasants lodge complaints in China, point out, a popular maxim in the countryside is: "The Centre is our benefactor (*enren*), the province is our relative, the county is a good person, the township is an evil person, and the village is our enemy."[7] It seems to me much more useful to think of legitimacy in China, at least as far as peasants are concerned, as being concentrated at the top but growing more diluted the farther down the administrative hierarchy.

The notion that legitimacy is differentially distributed in the state helps explain not only patterns of social change inside China, but also developments in comparative Communism. By far one of the most interesting events in world politics since the end of World War II was the sudden collapse of Leninist states in the former Soviet Union and Eastern Europe. In contrast to these dramatic changes, China, Vietnam, and North Korea remained Leninist stick-in-the-muds, stubbornly refusing to revamp their political systems. Why was this the case? One explanation might focus on the *nationalist* element in these Asian Communist regimes: unlike the former Communist states in Eastern Europe, where Communism was imposed from without, in China, Vietnam, and North Korea the Communist parties came to power after long and difficult struggles against foreign aggression, and this gave their leaders the credentials or legitimacy to rule after victory was achieved.[8] Another explanation might focus on the role of peasants in supporting authoritarian regimes. According to Chinese intellectuals and some Western theorists, peasants' parochialism, inclination to blindly obey authority, ignorance, and superstition lead them to support authoritarian regimes. Daniel Chirot, for instance, attributes the fall of the regime in East Germany to the fact that, unlike China, it had "no reserve of ignorant, barely literate peasant boys [in the army] to bring into the breach."[9] My evidence and arguments modify all of these views. First, patterns of peasant appeals for justice in which institutions above the township level are often the preferred address suggest that the "legitimacy" that supposedly supports the regime *as a whole* might instead be limited to *certain* critical institutions. It appears to be the case that at its lowest levels the regime is not very legitimate, mainly owing to corruption, but this has not led to the crumbling of the regime because of higher concentrations of legitimacy in institutions associated with the center. Thus we can have peasants who consider Communist party officials in their village their "enemy" and township officials "evil" but who will travel all the way to Beijing or write a letter to the National People's Congress; if this were not the case, the CCP probably would have gone the way of its Soviet and East European counterparts. Second, this study has demonstrated that peasants, far from being obedient to authority, were often willing to act in a bold and feisty manner vis-à-vis state officials. This was also reflected in their relationship to the military: draft dodging was often the response to local officials' abusing their power with soldier's wives and fiancées. The "ignorant" peasants Chirot blames for carrying out the crackdown on Tiananmen protesters, therefore, should not be seen as mere cogs in the party security apparatus.

Moving away from the comparative analysis of Leninist regimes to the larger issues involved in the study of law and social change, I have argued in this study that, at least in the Chinese case, there are many reasons to question any necessary causal connection between "modernization" and social change. In the areas I examined, peasants in villages (whether in the Shanghai suburbs or in Yunnan) and former peasants in cities (peripheral urbanites), rather than intellectuals, were the most aggressive and capable, and the most successful in using state institutions to change their family situation; this, I believe, is reflected in many reports from urban and rural areas and in the partial statistics indicating more divorce cases in working-class districts than in elite ones, in countryside than in city, and the upward swing in rural divorce cases in the early 1960s as opposed to the downward shift in urban areas after 1953. Modernization does explain some of the change in Shanghai, Beijing, and their suburbs—many divorced rural spouses came to be seen as more "modern"—but in rural Yunnan, where few if any of the independent variables posited in modernization theory were present, we have proof that something else besides modernity was at work. Peasants were able to take advantage of the new opportunities and institutions created by the Marriage Law for many of the reasons modernization theorists would have predicted the absence of rural social change. In addition to the scattered and thin political geography in rural areas, peasants benefited from the state's *inability* to use modern technology such as telephones, or roads that offered easy transportation. Peasants were also able to use their ties to land to negotiate for divorce. Peasant marriage practices and community—features of "traditional" rural life that are said to hinder change—likewise made it easier for peasants to take advantage of the law. Peasant women (whether living in the countryside or in cities), as we have seen, tended to view marriage, separation, and divorce in practical, no-nonsense terms; as some said, "I marry to eat; If I don't eat, I leave," and "Firewood and rice make a husband and wife, no firewood or rice, the two separate" (*you chai, you mi, shi fuqi; wu chai, wu mi, liang fen li*). Usually, they married to guarantee for themselves, and perhaps their families, a better life. When things did not work out as hoped, they often did not hesitate to break up and return to their natal homes, where soon enough they would be courted again; with more men than women in the rural population, they could afford to switch among men without worrying that they would remain spinsters; as one said, "It's easy to marry again. All I have to do is not make so many demands." Poor men may not have liked this, but given their fragile position in the marriage market and the state's granting of legal protection to women, there was not very much they could about it. As a result, separation and divorce were not nearly as traumatic or face-losing events as they were for urban elite women, who realized that their chances of finding another elite male to marry them were quite slim.

But it would be wrong to call attention only to hard-headed calculations in rural marriage and divorce. Peasants, like most people, sometimes acted on impulse, having sex based on sexual desire and falling in love "at first sight," frequently without considering the political or social consequences of their actions. It is high time we make room for love, passion, and romance in the study of peasant behavior. Why should urban sophisticates have a monopoly on such fundamental emotions of human nature? For their part, state officials were not unaware of the power of emotions when they castigated citizens for their "unruly" or "careless" sexual encounters and then attempted to channel passion into other venues. In the case of peasants and workers, these efforts were largely unsuccessful; few took the state's prerogatives concerning marriage or divorce very seriously. Looking at who was doing the castigating provides some clues as to why: "state" values concerning marriage and divorce were by and large a reflection of intellectuals' own concerns, which went back well before the promulgation of the Marriage Law. Educated Chinese in the ministries and departments dealing with culture, propaganda, and education, as well as students in work teams, were those calling most loudly for "civilized" divorces and "good class" marriages—not county or district officials, or even Mao or Liu Shaoqi, both of whom, incidentally, married "bad class" women. For these educated officials, neither pleasure nor marriage existed only for the sake of individual satisfaction, but to appease or please one's family and the state. The restrained, conservative, and puritanical sexual code of the PRC, a code ascribed by Judith Stacey to *peasant* patriarchal sexual culture, might be better thought of as a reflection of intellectuals' own puritanism and prudery.[10] The rhetoric and forms of violence during the Cultural Revolution were, I believe, a reflection of this.

In addition to taking a new look at peasants' and intellectuals' "sexual culture" and the role sexuality played in the Cultural Revolution, this study has also taken a new look at the role of community in state-led social change. In examining this issue, modernization theorists and their critics alike have tended to focus on the ways in which "traditional" community structurally *inhibits* the enforcement of new, modern state legislation; in much of the third world, "strong societies" have blocked even the most well-thought-out social reform programs.[11] In contrast, I have argued in this study that community could also *facilitate* the implementation of state laws, often in unintended ways. As we have seen, some women found that community ties made seeking divorce very costly, since men organized collective action against them. This capacity, coupled with men's willingness to use violence, undoubtedly deterred even more women from seeking divorce. However, this sort of collective action was not without its problems, since one of its unintended consequences was to push women who wanted to divorce *out* of villages and into the arms of higher-level state institutions, where they could receive a more sympathetic hearing. We also have seen cases where trust and common experiences among women led them to divorce in *groups* or to organize collective protests against the state. In rural areas, natal families and communities often served as refuge for women who were unhappy or suffering at the hands of their adoptive families and villages. For many urban women, however, these community resources were not available. True, urban women did not have to deal with being dragged by their hair to pray to Chairman Mao or locked up in local governments, but they had a more difficult time leaving unhappy relationships because they were more isolated and more dependent on families and work units.

This perspective on the role of community in facilitating divorce also challenges studies that have emphasized peasant parents' utilitarian calculations vis-à-vis their daughters. According to conventional wisdom, daughters, because they marry out of the family and community into another village, are given less attention than sons while growing up and, after marriage, gradually lose their connection to their natal families. In their adoptive families, they occupy the bottom of the family hierarchy. Susan Mann argues: "Weak ritual ties with her natal family and the unacceptability of a return to her natal home forced the bride into near-complete dependency on her husband's family"; Deborah Davis writes: "Because rural women usually live outside their natal villages, ties between the rural elderly and their daughters are fragile, and they atrophy steadily with each year that the daughter lives away from the parents' home";[12] and according to Margery Wolf, in traditional China "Daughters were goods on which one lost money. They could contribute little or nothing to their natal families in the way of enhancing their status, increasing their wealth, or providing for their care in their old age." A strong connection to natal families, Wolf contends, exists almost exclusively in *urban,* not rural, families.[13] That peasants prefer sons to daughters is undeniable, as is the fact that parents sometimes sell girls to the highest bidder. These preferences, however, should not blind us to the fact that, even as parents prepared to marry their daughters out of the family, they and their communities could also feel a strong sense of caring, love, and duty to look after them after their marriage. For many young women, returning to their natal home *was* a viable solution to an unhappy marriage, and their parents and kinsmen did not always force them out; surely many of the women who "ran back to their natal homes" knew that they would be taken back, or that their families might fight on their behalf.

Such a view is supported by both historical and contemporary evidence. In late nineteenth-century North China, Ida Pruitt tells us in *A Daughter of Han,* male relatives of an abused female family member might take up arms to avenge the death of a sister. In other cases, women returned to their natal homes for extended periods when their in-laws or husbands were abusive, and were clearly aware that their parents and natal communities could be a place of refuge.[14] Such relationships also perform an important function in the lives of Chinese rural women in the contemporary period. According to Ellen Judd's research on women's relationships with their natal families in three North China villages (in Shandong Province), neither marriage out of the natal family nor having children in her husband's village necessarily broke the strong emotive and instrumental ties between parents and their married-out daughter. In the early years of marriage, Judd notes, "there is a rhythm of coming and going between the families . . . a constant movement back and forth" (which the women simply referred to as their "custom" or "tradition" [*xiguan* or *chuantong*]; after having children such visits declined owing to the increase in responsibility and identification as "mother" rather than only as "daughter," but they did not disappear altogether. In some villages, repeated visits to the natal home could continue for several years after the birth of the first child, which typically occurred after one year of marriage).[15] Although Judd does not mention divorce (even though the theme of divorce has been shown to figure "not infrequently" in North China peasant operas),[16] such visits, particularly in the early years of marriage, surely facilitated it, as divorce, in China and many other societies, is most common during the first five to six years of marriage as well, even if there are children involved.[17] During the years when divorce is most likely to occur, therefore, rural women were aware that their natal families and communities were places of refuge, caring, and protection, even if they knew that they would not be able (nor would they necessarily want) to remain there indefinitely. They knew that the act of marriage, even with its well-established rituals and extensive preparations, did not sever the bonds nurtured during eighteen to twenty-one years of growing up in a family. To cite Judd again: "The pattern of women's ties with their natal families is often *protective* and *nurturative,* especially in the early months of their transition to adult status elsewhere."[18]

In addition to looking at the way family and community structure contributed to patterns of interaction between the state and families, we have also called attention to the way *community life* facilitated peasants' ability (and women's in particular) to take advantage of the Marriage Law. The Marriage Law, I noted in chapter 1, required people to discuss, in a public forum, problems with their marriage, their family, and even their sex lives. For people who did not make a sharp distinction between "public" and "private" (whether out of Confucian or bourgeois sensibilities), this requirement presented few difficulties; hence the constant complaints that peasants were not having "civilized" divorces or were yelling and screaming when they came into court or using sexually explicit epithets when cursing one another (see chapter 6). Living in rural communities where there were few private spaces led to a culture in which matters of the heart could be gossiped about (which often embarrassed the more prudish urban-educated youth or educated court officials) and, most importantly for our purposes, *frankly presented* to state authorities. This "open" sexual culture was also present among workers, many of whom hailed from rural locales. Getting a problem solved first required getting it out in the open, and neither peasants nor workers had much difficulty with this. In contrast, among educated people in the more "cosmopolitan" cities, concern with privacy, status, or face, in combination with fear of the state, militated against the exposition of private affairs. This was perhaps best expressed in the last chapter, by the educated woman who complained that her working-class husband "did not separate public from private" (*bu fen gong si*).

That peasants rather than urban educated elites were the most aggressive, capable, and in the end successful in taking advantage of the new Marriage Law has important implications for how we view the Communist revolution in China in comparative perspective. This study suggests that comparativists, in their effort to develop theories of revolution and the formation of regime type, have been too willing to overlook what was unique in the history of the Chinese revolution, at least until the victory of the North Vietnamese and the Vietcong in Vietnam and the Khmer Rouge takeover in Cambodia in the 1970s. Among the social revolutions of the modern era (e.g., France and Russia), only in China were cities conquered by peasants, only in China did peasants staff many state institutions, only in China was the regime ideologically hostile to large cities and urban elites. In suggesting the hypothesis that the state would have a greater impact on the family in urban than in rural areas (a hypothesis that was suggested by the history of other revolutions) I, too, overlooked the *incomparability* of these revolutions when they are analytically sliced along an urban-rural dimension. The social dynamics generated by the implementation of the Marriage Law thus forces us to rethink the nature of revolutionary change. Why was it that in China, but not in Russia or France, peasants were the most active in seeking to change their family situation? An important part of my answer has been that only in China were peasants so radicalized by politics to demand such change. I have argued that such demands cannot be explained without reference to the *peasant* nature of the Chinese state and revolution. Classifying China as a revolutionary state without noting and emphasizing its *sociocultural* features—in this case, the rural background of the officials who staffed its ranks—is to gloss over what was most important about it.

But even as this study makes a case for Chinese exceptionalism, I have also tried to find concepts that allow comparisons between cases. In writing up my findings, this undoubtedly was one of the most difficult challenges. The concepts of "legal culture," "political geography," "sexual culture," "community," and an expanded view of "resources" to include universal properties such as space, time, and language represent my best effort to capture what seemed to be common to peasants in several areas of China, as well as what distinguished peasants from urbanites, and different types of urbanites from each other. This is not a theory of state-society relations or law-induced social change. I, like Max Weber, believe that the essence of social inquiry should be the development of clear concepts, rather than general causal explanations valid across many different historical contexts. The challenge is to create or develop concepts that allow enough space to fit contextualized, local facts and that also permit a reasonable degree of "stretching" to other contexts. For instance, the same feisty "legal culture" that led many Chinese peasants and working-class urbanites (who came from villages) to county courts led to a similar strategy among Russian peasants after the legal reforms in the 1870s.

To return to our initial question of the extent to which states can shape family and intimate relations, this study of one country has shown the answer to be highly contingent. Much seems to depend on the nature of the state itself: its history, structure, and legitimacy in particular regional settings and among certain social strata, the culture and attitudes of its officials, its organization in geographical space. At the same time, state-led change also hinges upon people's willingness and capacity to change themselves. While the state provided opportunities for people to leave relationships, it was ultimately people's own decisions, taken individually or collectively, that made the law a source of power in relationships and families.

How should we judge the "success" of the Marriage Law and other CCP policies toward the family? The answer will probably depend upon how individual readers view the benefits and costs of divorce or arranged marriages, so I imagine that little consensus will emerge (this, I think, is a good thing, given the near uniformity of feminist voices condemning the Communists for their "failed" Marriage Law). Liberals might view the fact of family instability resulting from people's pursuit of rights as a positive thing, while conservatives will likely emphasize the costs of divorce borne by society and children. But more than this predictable division, what makes any judgment of success or failure more difficult is that the Marriage Law meant different things, and had different sorts of implications, for a variety of people in China; the results of Marriage Law clearly were a mixed bag. For elite women the law—both in its articles and in its "spirit"—did not seem to have a great effect, but for many rural women the law offered a way out of unsatisfactory or abusive relationships; for male officials in Beijing and in other cities, it offered opportunities to divorce "uncultured" rural women and marry "colorful" and educated urban ones. While rural women and high officials were those best able to take advantage of the law, it is equally apparent that poor men were greatly disadvantaged by it. After witnessing women climbing social ladders through multiple marriages and divorces, many poor, bald, or otherwise unattractive men yearned for the days when their marriages were arranged by parents; at least in this way they could marry and have children. Framers of the Marriage Law (who all belonged to the highest stratum of Chinese society), however, condemned arranged marriages as "arbitrary," and in doing so refused to acknowledge that they served a social function. The same goes for other elements of prerevolutionary family arrangements condemned by the Marriage Law: concubinage could give poor women an opportunity to move up the social ladder through a relationship with a wealthy man; becoming a concubine to a wealthy urban male was certainly preferable to marriage to a poor peasant.

The traditional system compromised individual happiness for a modicum of family stability and upward mobility, and had some benefits and costs for women and men alike. When the Marriage Law "liberalized" the marriage market, women pursued a greater degree of upward mobility than had been possible under the old system, and this, in turn, placed poorer men in a more precarious position. On this score, the consequences of the Marriage Law revealed not only its framers' failure to account for the functionality of traditional marriage arrangements (seeing them all as agents of oppression of the young by the old and women by men) but also their extreme naïveté: the law was based on expectations that new relationships would be formed on the basis of love, equality, and mutual respect, but in the real world people also desire power, money, and sex—all "commodities" that are *unequally* distributed in society and therefore subject to competition. In this competition, poorer, unattractive male peasants—despite their high political status—clearly came out on the short end. By telling poor, bald, and unattractive men's part of the story, I have offered a more balanced account of state-family relations in the PRC, previous accounts of which focused their attention on women's predicament at the expense of men's. The fact that most all research on women in the PRC has been conducted by women and not men has not been, in my opinion, unproblematic. Peasants' comments to William Parish and Martin Whyte and to William Hinton sum up poor men's experience with the Marriage Law. In Parish and Whyte's account a peasant laments:

> At liberation, when they propagandized the marriage reform, there was a 180 degree change in the situation, and for males to find a marriage object became a hard problem. Those who had a daughter to marry off saw their daughters become "money trees"—they could get as much as 200 *yuan* in bride price, and the average was even over 100 *yuan* . . . As I reflect now on the past I think it is quite remarkable how much things have changed. I don't know whether to laugh or cry.[19]

Similarly, a male peasant in North China complained, "You have raised women too high. No one dares cross a woman anymore. If you do they ask for a divorce."[20] Such voices have not become part of the conventional wisdom regarding the impact of the Marriage Law, however.

Of course, the ultimate irony is that the Communist Revolution was based on poor peasants' support, and many of its goals were carried out in their name. It was they, not rural women, whose status in society was damaged by the party during the many years that the Marriage Law shaped family relations.

Observations on State-Family Relations in the Reform Period

Although this study has focused on the interaction between state law and the Chinese family in the 1950s and 1960s, its findings also allow us to assess, albeit briefly, the question of change and continuity in state-family relations in the post-Mao period. Both scholarly and journalistic accounts of the reform period have emphasized the many *transitions* between politics and society under Mao and those that began under the leadership of Deng Xiaoping. Whereas the 1950s and 1960s were dominated by "politics," in the reform period economics has "taken command"; Marxism has been replaced by a combination of consumerism and nationalism; socialist aestheticism has been shunted aside by new demands for bourgeois accouterments such as beauty products, plastic surgery, good clothes, makeup, cars, and other material indicators of high social status; "illicit" sexual liaisons are now flourishing in the more liberal political atmosphere. Political liberalization, economic modernization, and the influx of books and movies from the West are also said to have resulted in a more "fluid" family situation, with soaring divorce rates in cities and among intellectuals in particular. According to a report of the Beijing Bureau of Civil Affairs, one out of every four marriages in the city ends in divorce, "with the highest rates found among the highly educated and those working in arts and communication fields." Seth Faison of the *New York Times* reported that "many Beijing residents say [that] one of the most profound changes in their society is the surge in divorce . . . and a remarkable increase in adulterous affairs." Marriage in the pre-reform period, said a Beijing woman who runs a women's hot line, "was very stable, but the quality was very low . . . most Chinese women traditionally had sex only for the purposes of bearing children."[1] Divorce rates in the countryside, while on the rise, are said to be significantly lower than in the city. According to one Shanghai lawyer I interviewed, this was because "life in the countryside is much calmer and less stressful than in the big city, where the fast pace of life and the pressures lead more people to divorce."[2] If these numbers and observations are all true, I would have to agree that the 1980s and 1990s—a period that has witnessed both economic liberalization and the loosening of many political controls, including a new Marriage Law (1980) that made divorce a bit easier to obtain[3]—does in fact represent a major transition from the period examined in this study; as we have seen, by the Cultural Revolution, very few urbanites were successful in taking advantage of the Marriage Law to change their family status, and intellectuals were among those least willing to do so, and least capable of doing so, for reasons of fear (often justified) and concern with losing face.

Evidence from the 1950s and 1960s and interviews with those involved in handling marriage and divorce issues in the 1990s, however, suggest that there might be more continuity than transition in state-family relations between the Maoist and post-Mao periods, and that the notion of transition may apply only to a particular segment of the population during the Cultural Revolution years. As we have seen, in the 1950s and early to mid-1960s there were workers who bought makeup, married for looks, money, or on a whim, and whose behavior was a far cry from the socialist aestheticism common to, and desired by, many intellectuals and which was manifested most blatantly during the Cultural Revolution years.[4] Nor can it be argued that adultery and divorce suddenly "reappeared" with the economic reforms, since officials in the Maoist period repeatedly complained about peasants and workers' "chaotic" sexual relations and excessive eagerness to take advantage of the Marriage Law. Nor was it the case that Chinese had sex "only for the purpose of bearing children"; if this was the case, officials would hardly have been as perturbed as they were about sexual practices and attitudes in working-class and rural communities. Looking at the way in which ordinary people interacted with the state in the Maoist period is one indication that the notion of a sharp transition between the zeitgeist of politics and society under Mao and Deng is probably a reflection of intellectuals' experience with the state, not everyone's. Finally, it seems, intellectuals are taking advantage of a law that peasants and workers were skilled at taking advantage of forty years before. With greater contact with the distant West, it seems that intellectuals' "sexual culture" is growing more similar to that of peasants living only twenty miles away.

But it is not only evidence of what happened to the Chinese family in the 1950s and early to mid-1960s that suggests greater continuity than change in Chinese family relations, even among intellectuals. Formal interviews and more casual conversations with lawyers, intellectuals, mediators, and court and Bureau of Civil Affairs officials also point to a great deal of continuity with past practices, even among those intellectuals who are said to be taking advantage of the 1980 Marriage Law most enthusiastically. Divorce lawyers and Women's Federation officials I interviewed in Shanghai and Nanjing in 1994 told me that workers were more likely than intellectuals to take advantage of the new Marriage Law to divorce, all things being equal. The latter, informants said, were frequently reluctant to divorce because of a combination of long-standing housing problems, concern with face and with keeping family problems "private," fear of their *danwei's* response, and concern that their children would face discrimination and name-calling— many of the same problems that limited their access to divorce in the 1950s and 1960s.[5] In Shanghai's elite Jing'an District, for instance, a Women's Federation official I interviewed said, "People here don't really know when intellectuals have a problem until after a divorce because they keep things inside and don't want to talk about it," and a divorce lawyer told me of an intellectual couple who did not get along, but did not petition for divorce because there was no way they could find alternative housing. Instead, they simply hung a curtain in the middle of their small apartment and continued living together.[6] Intellectuals in other cities seemed to face similar difficulties. According to Ms. P., a lawyer in Nanjing who previously served as a judge in the Jiangsu Provincial Court for many years, intellectuals were still very concerned about face (but workers and peasants less so) and feared that their children would be ridiculed in school should they divorce. In her experience, intellectuals were generally very reluctant to discuss their family problems with friends and coworkers and hesitated for a long time before submitting their request to the proper authorities.[7] A certain amount of elitism also accounts for such silence. A legal scholar I knew well laughed out loud when I asked him if he would consult with a member of his lane and alley mediation committee if he had a tiff with his wife. If they were going to have an argument, he told me, they would go outside to a place where no one would hear them. Should their row become public knowledge, they would both lose face. What's more, why would he, as an intellectual, go ask for help from the "old ladies" that serve on resident committees? What do they know that he doesn't?[8] As a result, divorce cases among intellectuals are frequently devoid of interpersonal confrontation and involve only minimal contact with the state—a continuation of pre-reform patterns of interaction. In the late 1970s and early 1980s, for instance, many former Red Guards who had been sent out to the countryside during the Cultural Revolution and married peasant women for their favorable class status abandoned them, returned to the city, and then sued for divorce. Other cases involved intellectuals who were accepted into foreign universities but had to leave China without their spouse. Once abroad, they met someone else and then filed for divorce from their new locale.

Workers, on the other hand, were said to be quite willing, and often *too* willing, to "draw the state into" their affairs, much as they had done in the

1950s and 1960s. In early 1994, for example, I interviewed judges in Yangpu District Court, located in Shanghai's largest working-class district. I had spent the fall and winter of 1993 poring over archival materials from that district and so was interested in whether the "variable" of people's willingness to go public with domestic tiffs was still an important part of workers' legal culture. During the interview I asked the assembled judges whether Yangpu's residents were reluctant to go to court or to go public with their families' "dirty laundry." Trying to suppress a grin, one of the judges told me about a case she had recently handled involving a female factory worker. This worker had come to court to file for divorce on account of her husband's gambling problem; all her income, she complained, went to support his gambling, leaving the family without money for food and other necessities. The court, in response to her filing the case, began a brief investigation and soon found that the woman was telling the truth: neighbors, nearby shopkeepers, and other family members confirmed that the worker's husband gambled and because of this they were at each other's throats. The court then sent three officers to talk to the gambler face-to-face, warning him that if he continued with this activity he could be sent to detention and probably lose his wife in the process as well. Faced with the prospect of losing his job and wife, he promised to stop. Soon after this, his wife reappeared in court to withdraw her complaint, getting a partial refund of the court's handling fee. According to the judge, this had been her legal strategy all along. She had never really wanted to divorce, only to get him to stop gambling. By drawing the state into her family she made her "private" problem public, and was thus able to get it solved. Such a solution would not have occurred to Chinese intellectuals owing to their fear of losing face and unwillingness to draw the state apparatus into their affairs.

Chinese studies of workers' marriages in the late 1970s and early 1980s also highlight the same sort of cultural divide in attitudes toward marriage and divorce that we have seen in the Maoist period. As part of the effort to revive social sciences after the Cultural Revolution, many sociology students at China's major universities were sent out to conduct interviews and surveys of family life in various areas of their cities' often poorer districts. These surveys are interesting not only for their findings regarding marriage in the late 1970s and early 1980s, but also as "texts" that allow us to read into the concerns of students and their academic supervisors. Reading these reports immediately conjures up a palpable sense of déjà vu: much like the 1950s and 1960s, students noted many instances of their fellow urbanites—nearly all of whom happened to be factory workers—"rashly" divorcing, and attributed this to a tendency to "view sexual life as trifling matters" and to adopt "Western" theories of "sexual freedom"; others were said to be lacking the "correct relationship between economics and marriage, often lacking lofty revolutionary ideals and the spirit of arduous struggle, unrealistically demanding to satisfy the enjoyment of material life . . . choosing a person because of his or her wealth." Here is one case demonstrating the pernicious effects of the "Western trend of thought of sexual freedom" on marriages. Though these conclusions were drawn from an investigation in Beijing's Dongcheng District in the late 1970s, such behavior drew similar ire in the 1950s and 1960s as well:

> There is a telephone operator who married a driver, after which there did not [*sic*] develop any contradictions. The woman liked to dance, to mix with people, but the man did not like to talk or do things. Later, it was discovered that the woman many times [*sic*] had relationships with others. She said, "I like a world free [to be free?]; after divorcing, I won't get married. I play with whomever I like."[9]

In addition to complaints about excessive sexual freedom resulting from increased contact with the West, other complaints also sound eerily familiar: people did not understand their legal obligations; couples got married only because of pregnancy and later divorced (supposedly because of "bourgeois thinking"); there was a high frequency of extramarital affairs, hasty marriages, and fights over "trivial matters," such as a woman petitioning for divorce because of an argument resulting from her "being dissatisfied with a crack in an old set of mahogany furniture."[10] A similar willingness to trade in spouses for other ones, but attributed to different causes, was conveyed to me by a lawyer I interviewed in Shanghai, Ms. N. According to her, "More so than among intellectuals, women workers' expectations have risen together with economic progress. If their situation improves, they think that they should have someone better, preferably someone with outside connections like Hong Kong or Taiwan. If they manage to find someone else, they'll petition for divorce."[11]

It is obvious, however, that in the reform period many workers are not doing well, high expectations notwithstanding. During the 1980s most of the economic reforms took place in the countryside, but by the mid-1990s millions of workers were being laid off from firms failing to compete in the marketplace. Many of these workers are given only a pittance in severance pay, but a hefty dose of propaganda focusing on the possibilities of entrepreneurial success. Structural changes in the economy, unemployment, and other insecurities have led to a rising number of work stoppages, strikes, and violent protests. They have also taken their toll on family relations. In divorce cases from Shanghai's working-class Changning District Court, arguments and domestic abuse resulting from "economic difficulties" figure prominently (in addition to adultery or suspicion of affairs, gambling, rash marriages, bad tempers, conflicts related to sex, imprisonment, and conflicts with in-laws).[12] Judges, mediators, and legal officials who have written about conflicts among workers in the 1990s have also pointed out how forced retirements, firings, and industrial restructuring generate tremendous tensions in families, particularly when husbands can no longer fulfill the role of the family's breadwinner. In this event, husbands become frustrated and feel useless and wives complain that they have no money. Divorce claims often follow.[13]

When such couples arrive at court or other state institutions to sue for divorce, officials are confronted with a population often willing to go to far-reaching lengths to secure their goal. Much like the periods discussed in this study, state officials dealing with working-class divorces in the 1990s are often perturbed by their "messiness." Dire threats of suicide, threats to abandon children, and violence make it difficult to patiently mediate cases, and this has prompted efforts to change working-class "legal culture" into one a bit more amenable to state control. The following quote is from an article entitled "Education in Civilized Divorce," published in the *Beijing Review* in 1996; however, it could just as easily have been written by a law student or a senior Women's Federation official in the 1950s or 1960s:

> A special school for divorcing couples in Nanjing, Jiangsu Province, has helped check the rising number of divorce [*sic*] in the city's Gulou district . . . Some couples initiated divorce for common conflicts inherent in everyday life. Some even went to court with scissors, hammers, pesticide or written wills threatening to commit suicide if the decision was against their will. Some couples both refused to be the guardian of their child, or fought for guardianship to demand the lion's share of property or punish their ex-spouse by hiding the child and denying access to the child. Crimes caused by marriage disputes thus increased. It has become urgent to educate divorcing couples to properly handle their disputes . . . A marriage and family school for divorcing couples . . . would help them reunite, if possible, or educate those with no hope of reunion to have civilized divorces and to properly plan the upbringing and education of their child.[14]

Although the article did not mention the background of these petitioners, it is more than likely that many of them were workers, or *former* peasants who transplanted to the city the same rural feistiness we have seen so often in previous chapters, during a time when the country is often said to have marched to a completely different tune than today.

How have political and economic changes in the post-Mao period affected divorce in the Chinese countryside? To date, statistics and interviews seem to suggest that divorce has largely been an urban phenomenon, concentrated among cultural elites in particular, and not very pronounced in the countryside. According to the *China Daily* (April 22, 1994), in 1993 the divorce rate in Beijing reached 19 percent; in 1995 it reached 25 percent. But divorces in the countryside barely register in the official statistics.[15] Chinese sociologists, however, are skeptical about the reliability of such figures, given that those responsible for data collection in courts and in bureaus of civil affairs lack appropriate training and do not consider such work particularly important. In the *Encyclopedic Yearbook of China* of 1981, for example, there are divorce statistics for the years 1978 and 1979 and for some of 1980 (based on information supplied by provincial civil affairs offices), but the figures are all aggregate, are often incomplete, and lack an urban-rural comparison. Regarding such differences, the encyclopedia notes only that in cities "bourgeois marital viewpoints" cause some 30 percent of divorces but divorce resulting from "the pernicious influences of feudal, arranged, mercenary marriages" is more common in rural areas.[16] Even smaller locales fail to make a systematic urban-rural comparison. In Shanghai, for instance, figures compiled by the Bureau of Civil Affairs do not differentiate between divorce in the city's semi-industrialized suburbs and the more rural areas of the municipality, even though the administrative jurisdiction of the city covers all of these areas. Although it is never stated, it is likely that the absence of such statistics is indicative of the difficulty in defining basic terms. Given the massive movement of peasants from villages to suburbs and cities in search of work, as well as the development of cities and township and village enterprises, defining the boundaries of concepts such as "city," "countryside," "peasant," and "urbanite" is as problematic as it was in the 1950s. Absent reliable statistical indicators (only recently the State Statistical Bureau uncovered over sixty thousand "irregularities" in data supplied by official agencies and businesses; undiscovered "irregularities" would drastically increase this number),[17] we should look to other sources to get a reasonably clear picture of what has been happening in rural families.[18]

My interviews with lawyers, registration officials, township chiefs, and Women's Federation officials in Qingpu and Jiangpu Counties in 1993 and 1994 (Jiangpu is in Jiangsu Province, near Nanjing) reveal the tenacity of many of the patterns we observed in the 1950s and 1960s. As in these earlier periods, larger structural changes in the economy have profoundly affected the rural family. At the same time, peasant initiative and boldness in taking advantage of new openings for the betterment of family and self have left the state fumbling to find solutions to keep the family more stable. In interviews with officials responsible for marriage and divorce issues in rural China I repeatedly heard that new economic opportunities and greater mobility between countryside, suburb, and city have made rural marriages very unstable, perhaps even more so than during the revolutionary political changes of the Maoist period. For instance, in Jiangpu County, Jiangsu, peasant men who had struck it rich by leaving their village and opening a restaurant or some other business often sought to divorce their peasant wives in order to marry women they considered more beautiful or who were younger than their previous spouses—the Chinese peasant equivalent of the "trophy wife" in American parlance. If state officials refused their request, the entrepreneurs would simply take their money and buy or build another apartment for their lovers and then move in with them, effectively abandoning their wives. In such cases, wives agreed to tolerate the situation provided that the husband continued to provide for them; if he did not, they would initiate the divorce and it would then be granted.[19] Housing problems, which often limit the options for family change among many *danwei*-bound intellectuals, were also said to be far less intractable in the countryside, where rural space continues to be a resource facilitating change, much as it was during most of the Maoist period. In Qingpu County in Shanghai Municipality, registration officials also emphasized the impact of the economic reforms on the family. In the county many divorce cases were initiated by men and women who had moved from poorer rural areas (especially northern Jiangsu and Anhui) to Qingpu and wanted to remain there and marry someone else—a pattern that we have seen in family dynamics in the Shanghai and Beijing suburbs in the 1950s as well. These ambitious peasants often formed the workforce of township and village enterprises popping up all over this prosperous area. There were also not a few cases in Qingpu of Taiwanese businessmen buying apartments for live-in mistresses while their "formal" wives remained back home.[20]

Divorce, however, is not always motivated by peasants' desire to climb up the social hierarchy. As in the 1950s, peasants divorced because they did not pay enough attention to the character of their spouse prior to marriage or because they were overly suspicious of their spouse having an extramarital affair, suspicions that often turned out to be well founded. According to the Qingpu Bureau of Civil Affairs, 47 percent of uncontested divorces in 1993 resulted from "rash marriages"; the next largest category (18 percent) resulted from "mutual suspicion of having an affair and illicit sexual relations."[21] In transcripts of divorce cases we can also see similarities with the 1950s and 1960s. As in the past, women were the primary initiators of divorce proceedings; in a sample of twenty cases from 1985, for instance, seventeen of the plaintiffs were female. The Qingpu women complained about their husbands' gambling, drinking, or abuse (which some men denied, or blamed on their wives' having affairs), insufficient income (to which men replied that their factories were inefficient, so it wasn't their fault), conflicts with in-laws, not knowing their husband well enough before marriage, sickness, impotence or unreasonable sexual demands, and "everyday arguments" over household chores and children. In other cases, women initiated divorce because they themselves had affairs and wanted to divorce their husbands to marry their lovers. In the three male cases, two resulted from adultery and the man's desire to marry his lover and one from the wife's having "gone insane." In some cases, men agreed that their wives go their separate way. In other cases, however, they resorted to violence. In one case in Qingpu, a man surnamed Sun was suspicious that his wife was having an affair. As it turned out, he was right; he soon discovered that when she went to court to petition for divorce. In response, he beat her and physically tried to prevent her from leaving the village. Despite these efforts, the court eventually convened. Before the session began, however, Sun took out a knife that he had brought with him, walked over to the township official attending the hearing, and unabashedly rammed it in the table at which he was sitting. Sun then threatened: "If the court grants her a divorce, I'll kill her." This tactic worked and she withdrew her case. Whether the couple is still together or Sun's wife found another way to leave him is not recorded in the case, but it would seem likely, given what we have seen from the past, that she returned to her natal home. Other Qingpu sources reveal instances of men dousing ex-wives with gasoline and setting them alight, or else shooting them and then committing suicide.[22]

These preliminary data suggest that there are few differences between the pre- and post-reform periods in terms of the causes and motivations for marriage or divorce. The main difference between the periods seems to be not of type but of *scale*: post-Mao China has offered peasants more opportunities for upward mobility than before, and since many peasants feel that their spouses should reflect their socioeconomic status, many have clamored to "change in" old spouses for new ones. Intellectuals almost universally describe this as peasants' succumbing to "bourgeois thinking" owing to greater contact with the West during the period of "reform and opening up," but this study has made it very clear that such things went on even at the height of Maoist China's socialist aestheticism in the 1950s and 1960s, at least among peasants (and workers). Of course, all this does not suggest that *all* those making money, moving to the city or suburbs, and the like are seeking divorce. Instead, my point here is that macro-level changes in the economy, especially greater opportunities for wealth and mobility, are affecting family relations in rural China in ways as destabilizing as the politically induced changes of the early 1950s and pre–Cultural Revolution 1960s. Many of these changes, however, are not likely to be reflected in the official divorce statistics.

What, then, does the "low" rural divorce rate really mean? Here again, we can see some similarities with the past. Much as state officials in the 1950s and 1960s often complained about peasant women's overzealousness in taking advantage of the Marriage Law's article advocating marriage and divorce "freedom" and the subsequent "chaos" in social relations, so too are their reform-era counterparts worried that the rural family will become too unstable. Officials I interviewed in Qingpu and Jiangpu Counties were all concerned that a high divorce rate was inimical to their townships' economic development. Since there were already so many changes in rural society, they argued, it was preferable that that basic institution—the family—

remain as stable as possible. Should they allow all those demanding divorces to actually obtain them, the countryside would become too chaotic (*luan*). As a result, village and township leaders and bureaucrats in civil affairs bureaus frequently demand that peasants undergo extensive local mediation, fill out lengthy forms, and submit to questioning before being granted a divorce—things that in the more chaotic 1950s and 1960s were often considered far too *mafan,* or bothersome. According to the Bureau of Civil Affairs representative of Baihe Township in Qingpu, many disputes are successfully resolved because "every village has someone monitoring civil disputes" and township officials are "able to persuade peasant women who come crying to them demanding divorce to reconsider their decision."

In the 1980s and 1990s, however, peasants seeking divorce have greater legal options than "crying" to local officials, options that might, ironically, also lower the official divorce rate. One important feature of the backlash against the lawlessness and violence of the Cultural Revolution has been greater interest in the "rule of law"; the 1980s and 1990s witnessed hundreds if not thousands of new laws dealing with everything from marriage to personnel administration to real estate to foreign investment. Concomitant with this new interest in law has been the growth of legal professionals (albeit rarely trained in professional law schools) in urban and rural areas. Now peasants in many areas have access to lawyers who can help them file the necessary paperwork and help them present their cases in court. While there still are cases of peasants "rushing to court" after a heated argument with a wife or neighbor, peasants' access to the official legal system is now frequently mediated by a new quasi-professional class, who, in the interest of professionalism and greater efficiency, try to make sure that their clients refrain from wild outbursts in court or explicit denigration of their spouse's sexual performance. As a result, the divorce process—at least according to officials and lawyers I spoke with—has become more structured than during the 1950s and 1960s, when peasants' access to court was rarely mediated by professional agents, and judges were often pressured by crowds of angry peasants banging on the court gates. Cases of *luan pan,* or "rushed judgments," are thus said to be on the decline. The state, to use the terminology developed in the previous chapters, appears to have "thickened" in the countryside during the reform period.

Other evidence, however, suggests that state efforts to channel conflict into mediation and conciliation might not always be the preferred solution from peasants' perspective, particularly women's, nor always successful. As in the past, peasant women who are frustrated by low-level intervention in their cases proceed directly to court, claiming that in villages and townships they are unlikely to get a fair hearing since members of the local mediation committee might be kinsmen or friends of their husbands. Peasants, according to BCA officials in Jiangpu and Qingpu, prefer courts because they are required to adjudicate within a specific time frame (a couple of months) and they allow oral testimony; peasants, the Jiangpu vice county magistrate said, cannot write very well, but can speak their mind. Moreover, when couples begin to fight over custody of the children and the possession of the TV, courts are seen as the institution best able to force the hand of the husband and family.[23]

To be sure, not all divorce cases are filed in order to actually secure a divorce. As in the 1950s, rural women are often successful in maintaining or gaining power in their families by invoking the power of courts, county governments, and the law, or by threatening to return to their natal homes. In Qingpu, women were said to use a panoply of tactics to gain greater leverage in their families: some threatened to expose husbands' gambling problems to their bosses, or their affairs to courts and to the local Women's Federation; in other cases, they threatened to divorce, boycott domestic chores, or return to their parents' place—acts that would force the husband and his family to take up the slack in cooking and cleaning. Since many Qingpu men do not really know how to cook or clean and are not interested in learning, they consent to writing "guarantees" of better behavior. In some cases, men even agree to a 50 percent division of labor in cooking and cleaning, fearing their wives' sanctions.[24] Here, it seems, the "traditional" division of labor in the family has given women more leverage than they would have had if their husbands had been "progressive" enough to learn how to cook and clean for themselves; monopolies, whether seen in terms of resources, skill, or knowledge, can be a source of power, even in the case of cooking rice, vegetables, and noodles.[25] Behind this exercise of power, however, is a simple fact of life confronting many young men in rural China: owing to female infanticide and sex selection prior to birth, there are fewer adult women than men (in 1989 there were 114 boys to 100 girls in rural areas; by 1997 the ratio stood at 118 to 100. The world average is 104 to 100). Demographers estimate that by the year 2010, some 23 percent of rural men will not be able to marry for lack of women.[26] Those girls who survive infancy and childhood are therefore a relatively scarce "commodity," and this can make their threats to divorce or leave their husbands highly effective.

Peasant women's willingness to invoke courts to maintain or gain leverage in their families is not the only reason why official accounts of a more orderly rural divorce process might be somewhat misleading. Other evidence suggests that the divorce process remains almost as messy as in the 1950s, albeit due to different causes. Whereas in the 1950s and 1960s political campaigns made rural governance extremely difficult, in the 1980s the main cause for disorder appears to be new opportunities in the market economy. The economic reforms in the countryside have turned not a few officials into entrepreneurs, whose main priority is to bring "pork"—investments, contracts, and supplies—home to their families and villages. The rush to make money in response to new economic opportunities—particularly in prosperous suburbs such as Qingpu—has made mediation at the village and township levels even less attractive than it was in the 1950s, when village officials saw virtually no benefit in mediating aside from the money they collected as mediation fees. Many village cadres, an internally circulated investigation report from Qingpu complained, neglect mediation because their efforts are unremunerated (only the chair of the mediation committee is given a small reimbursement for his efforts). Investigations also found that many village mediation "committees" are committees in name only, having only one member—all this owing to the dearth of incentives and the attraction of the market. As a result, many conflicts between villagers, whether due to contract, property, or adultery, end up being handled by courts, which, as in the past, find themselves overburdened with letters, telephone calls, and visits by irate peasants.[27]

In light of both this evidence and what we have already seen in the 1950s and 1960s I would hesitate to conflate low divorce rates in rural areas in the 1980s and 1990s (to the extent that this is the case) with either "stability" or a sharp "transition" between the Maoist and post-reform periods. What seems to me far more plausible in light of the past is that many rural families, particularly those experiencing separation due to the pull of new economic opportunities, continue to be in a state of flux, and that this is probably reflected in many *informal* separations—taking in more than one wife in the absence of a formal wedding and other such methods of evading the state's attempt to "stabilize" rural family relations—rather than the more-difficult-to-obtain "official" divorces. And these efforts are not insignificant. During 1997 and 1998 a newly revised Marriage Law was drafted to stifle these trends. Including two hundred new regulations, the revised law bans domestic violence and the practice of keeping mistresses. Regarding divorce, the main requirement will no longer be the "termination of affection" but "actual termination of marital relations for three years."[28] How this law will affect family relations is difficult to predict, but there is little new in it of practical value. As we have seen in chapter 6, rural courts in the 1950s and 1960s were already granting divorces on the grounds of long-term, de facto separations. What seems to be the case now as in the 1950s and 1960s is that the state, interested in stability, is once again lagging behind the social changes it has unleashed and is trying to deal—in its usual scattershot and bumbling manner—with the many unintended consequences of its policies. At the level of state goals and modus operandi, and the relationship between the state and different social classes, I am suggesting that there has been a great deal of continuity from pre-reform patterns, even in a period that has been deemed China's "Second Revolution."

These, however, are mere observations based on several months of interviews and a smattering of primary and secondary sources. A second volume, to be based on hundreds of court and mediation cases from urban and rural areas in the 1990s, will look into state-family relations in the reform period in much greater depth.

APPENDIX

Texts of the "Decree Regarding Marriage" and the 1950 Marriage Law

The following are two texts that convey both the spirit and content of Chinese Communist Party (CCP) marriage policy. The first, "Decree regarding Marriage," was written in 1931 while the CCP was based in rural Jiangxi Province after having been ousted from its urban bases. This decree was accompanied by a twenty-three-article law ("Marriage Regulations of the Chinese Soviet Republic of December 1, 1931"), which established both "freedom of marriage" and the "freedom of divorce . . . whenever both the man and the woman agree" or when "one party . . . is determined to claim a divorce, it shall have immediate effect." The second text is a reprint of the 1950 Marriage Law. Between these two dates, the Marriage Law was revised several times—in 1934, 1939, 1943 and 1944—with the general trend being a gradual curtailment of the right to divorce without undergoing any form of state intervention, as was the case according to the 1931 law. The translation of "Decree regarding Marriage" is drawn from Stuart R. Schram, *The Political Thought of Mao Tse-tung*, 337; the text of the 1950 Marriage Law is reprinted from Kay Anne Johnson, *Women, the Family and Peasant Revolution in China*, 235–39.

DECREE REGARDING MARRIAGE (1931)

Under feudal domination, marriage is a barbaric and inhumane institution. The oppression and suffering borne by woman is far greater than that of man. Only the victory of the workers' and peasants' revolution, followed by the first step toward the economic emancipation of men and women, brings with it a change in the marriage relationship and makes it free. In the soviet districts, marriages now are contracted on a free basis. Free choice must be the principle of every marriage. The whole feudal system of marriage, including the power of parents to arrange marriages for their children, to exercise compulsion, and all purchase and sale in marriage contracts shall henceforth be abolished.

Although women have obtained freedom from the feudal yoke, they are still laboring under tremendous physical handicaps (for example, the binding of the feet) and have not obtained complete economic independence. Therefore on questions concerning divorce, it becomes necessary to protect the interests of women and place the greater part of the obligations and responsibilities entailed by divorce upon men.

Children are the masters of the new society. Under the old system little attention was paid to children. Consequently, special regulations have been established concerning the protection of children.

These present regulations are hereby made public and shall enter into force as of 1 December 1931.

> (Signed)
> Mao Zedong
> Chairman of the Central Executive Committee

THE 1950 MARRIAGE LAW

General Principles

Article 1. The feudal marriage system based on arbitrary and compulsory arrangements and the supremacy of man over woman, and in disregard of the interests of children, is abolished.

The new democratic marriage system, which is based on the free choice of partners, on monogamy, on equal rights for both sexes, and the protection of the lawful interests of women and children, is put into effect.

Article 2. Bigamy, concubinage, child betrothal, interference in the remarriage of widows, and the exaction of money or gifts in connection with marriages, are prohibited.

The Marriage Contract

Article 3. Marriage is based upon the complete willingness of the two parties. Neither party shall use compulsion and no third party is allowed to interfere.

Article 4. A marriage can be contracted only after the man has reached twenty years of age and the woman eighteen years of age.

Article 5. No man or woman is allowed to marry in any of the following instances:

a. Where the man and woman are lineal relatives by blood or where the man and woman are brother and sister born of the same parents or where the man and woman are half brother and half sister. The question of prohibiting marriage between collateral relatives by blood (up to the fifth degree of relationship) is determined by custom.

b. Where one party, because of certain physical defects, is sexually impotent.

c. Where one party is suffering from venereal disease, mental disorder, leprosy, or any other disease which is regarded by medical science as rendering a person unfit for marriage.

Article 6. In order to contract a marriage, both the man and the woman should register in person with the people's government of the district or township in which they reside. If the proposed marriage is found to be in conformity with the provisions of the law, the local government should, without delay, issue marriage certificates. If the proposed marriage is not found to be in conformity with the provisions of this law, registration shall not be granted.

Rights and Duties of Husband and Wife

Article 7. Husband and wife are companions living together and enjoy equal status in the home.

Article 8. Husband and wife are duty bound to love, respect, assist, and look after each other, to live in harmony, to engage in productive work, to care for their children, and to strive jointly for the welfare of the family and for the building up of the new society.

Article 9. Both husband and wife have the right to free choice of occupation and free participation in work or other social activities.

Article 10. Husband and wife have equal rights in the possession and management of family property.

Article 11. Husband and wife have the right to use his or her own family name.

Article 12. Husband and wife have the right to inherit each other's property.

Relations between Parents and Children

Article 13. Parents have the duty to rear and to educate their children; the children have the duty to support and to assist their parents. Neither the parents nor the children shall maltreat or desert one another. The foregoing provision also applies to foster parents and foster children. Infanticide by drowning and similar criminal acts are strictly prohibited.

Article 14. Parents and children have the right to inherit each other's property.

Article 15. Children born out of wedlock enjoy the same rights as children born in lawful wedlock. No person is allowed to harm them or discriminate against them.

Where the paternity of a child born out of wedlock is legally established by the mother of the child or by other witnesses or material evidence, the identified father must bear the whole or part of the cost of maintenance and education of the child until the age of eighteen.

With the consent of the mother, the natural father may have custody of the child.

With regard to the maintenance of a child born out of wedlock, if its mother marries, the provisions of Article 22 apply.

Article 16. Neither husband nor wife may maltreat or discriminate against children born of a previous marriage by either party and in that party's custody.

Divorce

Article 17. Divorce is granted when husband and wife both desire it. In the event the husband or wife alone insists upon divorce, it may be granted only when mediation by the district people's government and the judicial organ has failed to bring about a reconciliation.

In cases where divorce is desired by both husband and wife, both parties should register with the district people's government in order to obtain divorce certificates. The district government, after establishing that divorce is desired by both parties and that appropriate measures have been taken for the care of children and property, should issue the divorce certificate without delay.

When one party insists on divorce, the district people's government may try to bring about a reconciliation of the parties. If such mediation fails, it should, without delay, refer the case to the county or municipal court for decision. The district government should not attempt to prevent or to obstruct either party from appealing to the county or municipal people's court. In dealing with a divorce case, the county or municipal people's court should, in the first instance, try to bring about a reconciliation between the parties. In case such mediation fails, the court should render a decision without delay.

After divorce, if both husband and wife desire the resumption of marriage relations, they should apply to the district people's government for a registration of marriage. The district people's government should accept such a registration and issue certificates of remarriage.

Article 18. The husband is not allowed to apply for divorce when his wife is pregnant, and may apply for divorce only one year after the birth of the child. In the case of a woman applying for divorce, this restriction does not apply.

Article 19. In the case of a member of the revolutionary army on active service who maintains correspondence with his or her family, that army member's consent must be obtained before his or her spouse can apply for divorce.

Divorce may be granted to the spouse of a member of the revolutionary army who does not correspond with his or her family for a period of two years subsequent to the date of the promulgation of this law. Divorce may also be granted to the spouse of a member of the revolutionary army who did not maintain correspondence with his or her family for over two years prior to the promulgation of this law and who fails to correspond with his or her family for a further period of one year subsequent to the promulgation of the present law.

Maintenance and Education of Children after Divorce

Article 20. The blood ties between parents and children are not ended by the divorce of the parents. No matter whether the father or the mother has custody of the children, they remain the children of both parties.

After divorce, both parents continue to have the duty to support and educate their children.

After divorce, the guiding principle is to allow the mother to have the custody of a breast-fed infant. After the weaning of the child, if a dispute arises between the two parties over the guardianship and an agreement cannot be reached, the people's court should render a decision in accordance with the interests of the child.

Article 21. If, after divorce, the mother is given custody of a child, the father is responsible for the whole or part of the necessary cost of the maintenance and education of the child. Both parties should reach an agreement regarding the amount and the duration of such maintenance and education. Lacking such an agreement, the people's court should render a decision.

Payment may be made in case, in kind, or by tilling land allocated to the child.

An agreement reached between parents or a decision rendered by the people's court in connection with the maintenance and education of a child does not obstruct the child from requesting either parent to increase the amount decided upon by agreement or by judicial decision.

Article 22. In the case where a divorced woman remarries and her husband is willing to pay the whole or part of the cost of maintaining and educating the child or children by her former husband, the father of the child or children is entitled to have the costs of maintenance and education reduced or to be exempted from bearing such costs in accordance with the circumstances.

Property and Maintenance after Divorce

Article 23. In case of divorce, the wife retains the property that belonged to her prior to her marriage. The disposal of other family property is subject to agreement between the two parties. In cases where agreement cannot be reached, the people's court should render a decision after taking into consideration the actual state of the family property, the interests of the wife and the child or children, and the principle of benefiting the development of production. In cases where the property allocated to the wife and her child or children is sufficient for the maintenance and education of the child or children, the husband may be exempted from bearing further maintenance and education costs.

Article 24. In case of divorce, debts incurred jointly by husband and wife during the period of their married life should be paid out from the property jointly acquired by them during this period. In cases where no such property has been acquired or in cases where such property is insufficient to pay off such debts, the husband is held responsible for paying them. Debts incurred separately by the husband or wife should be paid off by the party responsible.

Article 25. After divorce, if one party has not remarried and has maintenance difficulties, the other party should render assistance. Both parties should work out an agreement with regard to the method and duration of such assistance; in case an agreement cannot be reached, the people's court should render a decision.

By-Laws

Article 26. Persons violating this law will be punished in accordance with law. In cases where interference with the freedom of marriage has caused death or injury to one or both parties, persons guilty of such interference will bear responsibility for the crime before the law.

Article 27. This law comes into force from the date if its promulgation.

In regions inhabited by minority nationalities in compact communities, the people's government (or the military and administrative committee) of the greater administrative area or the provincial people's government may enact certain modifications or supplementary articles in conformity with the actual conditions prevailing among minority nationalities with regard to marriage. Such measures must be submitted to the government administration council for ratification before enforcement.

NOTES

PREFACE

1. J. H. Hexter, *On Historians,* 241–43.

2. James F. Clarity, "Irish Cabinet Backs Lifting Ban on Divorce," *New York Times,* 17 September 1995.

3. Dirk Johnson, "No-Fault Divorce Is under Attack," *New York Times,* 12 February 1996; "The War over Marriage and Divorce," *New Republic,* May 1996; Barbara Dafoe Whitehead, "Dan Quayle Was Right," *Atlantic Monthly,* April 1993.

4. Steven Weisman, "India's Agonies: One Divorce Deepens Hindu-Muslim Mistrust," *New York Times,* 27 May 1996.

5. "A New Law in Iran Helps Divorced Women," *New York Times,* 19 November 1994.

6. Howard W. French, "For Ivory Coast Women, New Battle for Equality," *New York Times,* 6 April 1996.

CHAPTER 1. INTRODUCTION

1. See Newt Gingrich, "Speech to the Washington Research Group," 11 November 1994.

2. George Lakoff, *Moral Politics: What Conservatives Know That Liberals Don't,* 19. Emphasis added.

3. On Plato see Susan Moller Okin, "Philosopher Queens and Private Wives: Plato on Women and the Family," in Jean Bethke Elshtain, ed., *The Family in Political Thought,* 44–49; on Aristotle see Jean Bethke Elshtain, "Aristotle, the Public-Private Split, and the Case of the Suffragists," ibid., 51–52; on Montesquieu see Mary Lyndon Shanley and Peter G. Stillman, "Political and Marital Despotism: Montesquieu's *Persian Letters,*" ibid., 66–67. Lynn Hunt's family metaphor of political revolution is

in *The Family Romance of the French Revolution*. On Wu Yu see Ono Kazuko, *Chinese Women in a Century of Revolution, 1850–1950*, 93–96.

4. Cited in W. Muller-Freienfels, "Soviet Family Law and Comparative Chinese Developments," in David Buxbaum, ed., *Chinese Family Law and Social Change in Historical and Comparative Perspective*, 331.

5. James Traer, *Marriage and the Family in Eighteenth-Century France*, 49, 121. On the "rehabilitation" of the family after the enactment of radical changes in family law in 1793 see Hunt, *Family Romance*, 151, 161–62.

6. In 1776 John Adams wrote: "[T]he new Government we are assuming...will require a Purification from our Vices, and an Augmentation of our Virtues or there will be no Blessings." In Revolutionary usage, the power of the words "vice" and "virtue" derived in part from their *sexual* connotations, and the Revolutionaries' critique of the British was based upon a perceived "looseness" in the British aristocracy's sexual standards. See Gordon Wood, *The Creation of the American Republic, 1776–1787*, 123–24.

7. Bernice Glazer Rosenthal, "Love on the Tractor: Women in the Russian Revolution and After," in Renate Bridenthal and Claudia Koonz, eds., *Becoming Visible: Women in European History*, 378; Muller-Freienfels, "Soviet Family Law," 324.

8. I emphasize here the notion of "active" intervention since it was the case that the Imperial Chinese legal codes included many statues regulating aspects of family life such as divorce, marriage, incest, adultery, and the like. By liberalizing the requirement for divorce, the Republican state attempted to realize a new vision of more equitable gender relations.

9. Franz Michael, "The Role of Law in Traditional, Nationalist, and Communist China," *China Quarterly*, no. 9:138–40.

10. On the skepticism and anomie among Chinese students in the 1930s see Wen-hsin Yeh, *The Alienated Academy: Culture and Politics in Republican China, 1919–1937*, 253–54. On divorce see Kathryn Bernhardt, "Women and the Law: Divorce in Republican China," in Kathryn Bernhardt and Philip C. C. Huang, eds., *Civil Law in Qing and Republican China*, 188–89; Philip C. C. Huang, *Civil Justice in China: Representation and Practice in the Qing*, 30.

11. These views are in Friedrich Engels, *The Origin of the Family, Private Property, and the State*. For a useful summary see H. Kent Geiger, *The Family in Soviet Russia*, 12–16.

12. For the case in Thailand see David Buxbaum, "Introduction," in David Buxbaum, ed., *Family Law and Customary Law in Asia: A Contemporary Legal Perspective*, xxxii; David Engel, *Code and Custom in a Thai Provincial Court*, 168. For Turkey, whose 1926 civil code (which was based on the Swiss model) also endorsed monogamy and rejected polygamy, see June Starr, "The Role of Turkish Secular Law in Changing the Lives of Rural Muslim Women, 1950–1970," *Law and Society Review* 23, no. 3:498.

13. M. J. Meijer, *Marriage Law and Policy in the Chinese People's Republic*, 281.

14. Delia Davin, *Woman-Work: Women and the Party in Revolutionary China*, 29–30. Mao, in describing his experience in implementing new marriage regulations in Xunwu County in the early 1930s, notes how young women were quick to use CCP courts and township governments to press for divorce. See his *Report from Xunwu*, 213–17.

15. Meijer, *Marriage Law,* 63.

16. Despite this, evidence shows that peasant women were not nearly as hidebound to tradition as many of these urban feminists believed. Even though peasant women in the North were said to be among the least "modern" in China (illiteracy rates among women were as high as 95 percent, and many still had bound feet), quite a few were reported as quite aggressive when seeking divorce and new marriages on the basis of the Marriage Law; wives of the rich, however, proved to be much more reluctant. See Davin, *Woman-Work,* 36, 48–49; Kay Ann Johnson, *Women, the Family, and Peasant Revolution in China,* 54–58. Joseph Esherick, "Deconstructing the Construction of the Party State: Guling County in the Shaan-Gan-Ning Border Region," *China Quarterly,* no. 140:1061–62.

17. Cited in Davin, *Woman-Work,* 48.

18. In contrast, Mao, in his rural investigations, found that peasants had quite a variety of marriage arrangements that did not easily fit into the dichotomy of "free" and "arranged." See "An Investigation into the Peasant Movement in Hunan," in Stuart Schram, *The Political Thought of Mao Tse-tung;* also see C. K. Yang, *The Chinese Family in the Communist Revolution,* 54. On intellectuals' marriages see Vera Schwarcz, *The Chinese Enlightenment: Intellectuals and the Legacy of the May Fourth Movement of 1919,* 107–17.

19. *Nanfang ribao,* 13 February 1952.

20. Susan Shirk, *Competitive Comrades: Career Incentives and Student Strategies in China,* 126; Richard Kraus, *Class Conflict in Chinese Socialism;* Ezra Vogel, "From Friendship to Comradeship: The Change in Personal Relations in Communist China," *China Quarterly,* no. 21:46–60; Lynn T. White III, *Policies of Chaos: The Organizational Roots of Violence in China's Cultural Revolution;* James L. Watson, "Introduction," in James L. Watson, ed., *Class and Social Stratification in Post-Revolution China,* 13; Elisabeth Croll, "Marriage Choice and Status Groups in Contemporary China," ibid., 181.

21. All of these provisions can be found in Meijer, *Marriage Law,* 300–302.

22. Johnson, *Women, the Family, and Peasant Revolution,* 147.

23. On violence against women perpetrated by macho male village officials and women's incapacity to get redress in state institutions see Edward Friedman, Paul G. Pickowicz, and Mark Selden, *Chinese Village, Socialist State;* on divorce being "almost nonexistent" in rural areas see Emily Honig and Gail Hershatter, *Personal Voices: Chinese Women in the 1980s,* 206; see also Johnson, *Women, the Family, and Peasant Revolution,* 215. The phrase "on the back burner" is in William L. Parish and Martin K. Whyte, *Village and Family in Contemporary China,* 159; "Individuals expect . . . " is on p. 192, emphasis added. See also Margery Wolf, *Revolution Postponed: Women in Contemporary China,* 260; the Marriage Law campaign, she argues, was "ill-fated" (25).

24. Wolf, *Revolution Postponed,* 260, 164.

25. Here I must admit my own preference for research whose main goal is the development of useful *concepts* to understand political change rather than nomothetic theory. I have found such theories [particularly those of rational choice] far too elegant to capture the richness and complexity of my primary material. Moreover, the advantage of concept-driven research is that it can appeal to scholars in other disciplines. The more political science relies on formal models, the less relevant and useful the discipline will become to other disciplines.

26. Here I draw upon Timothy Mitchell's reconceptualization of the "state" in "The Limits of the State: Beyond Statist Approaches and Their Critics," *American Political Science Review* 85, no. 1:89.

27. This approach has recently been advocated by the political scientist Joel Migdal. He writes, "We need to break down the undifferentiated concepts of the state—and also of society—to understand how different elements in each pull in different directions, leading to unanticipated patterns of domination and transformation . . . we must look at the multiple levels of the state through a new 'anthropology of the state.'" See Joel Migdal, "The State in Society: An Approach to Struggles for Domination," in Joel Migdal, Atul Kohli, and Vivienne Shue, eds., *State Power and Social Forces: Domination and Transformation in the Third World,* 8, 14–15.

28. Wolf, *Revolution Postponed,* 164, 261. Emphasis added.

29. See Joan Wallach Scott, "Gender: A Useful Category of Historical Analysis," in her *Gender and the Politics of History,* 30.

30. William P. Alford, *To Steal a Book Is an Elegant Offense,* 7.

31. James Hammick, *The Marriage Law of England,* 220–21.

32. National Center for Health Statistics, *Marriage and Divorce Registration in the United States,* 3.

33. The term "legible" has been used by James C. Scott to describe the process by which modern states "arrange the population in ways that simplified the classic state functions of taxation, conscription and prevention of rebellion." Unlike the premodern state, which was often "blind" about many aspects of its population, modern state officials sought to take "exceptionally complex, illegible and local social practices" and fit them into a "standard grid whereby it could be centrally recorded and monitored." See his *Seeing Like a State: How Certain Schemes to Improve the Human Condition Have Failed,* 2.

34. C. M. Ch'iao, Warren S. Thompson, and D. T. Chen, *An Experiment in the Registration of Vital Statistics in China,* 6.

35. Cited in Meijer, *Marriage Law,* 179.

36. See Patricia Buckley Ebrey, *The Inner Quarters: Marriage and the Lives of Women in the Sung Period,* 257–58, on the shame of divorce, especially among the upper class. For lower-class women, divorce appears to have been less problematic, however.

37. Catherine A. MacKinnon, *Towards a Feminist Theory of the State,* 163.

38. Catherine A. MacKinnon, "Reflections on Law in the Everyday Life of Women," in Austin Sarat and Thomas R. Kearns, eds., *Law in Everyday Life,* 109–10.

39. See "Toward a Phenomenology of Feminist Consciousness," *Social Theory and Practice* 3, no. 4:430.

40. See Jon Elster's brilliant critique of Marx's functionalism in *Making Sense of Marx.*

41. People interested in these subjects would do much better to consult the work of legal anthropologists, who, far more than law professors, study how ordinary people use the law in everyday life. Not surprisingly, their works quickly reveal the hollowness of many of MacKinnon's arguments. See especially Sally Engle Merry, *Getting Justice and Getting Even: Legal Consciousness among Working-Class Americans.*

42. Johnson, *Women, the Family, and Peasant Revolution,* 122, 222; Wolf, *Revolution Postponed;* Judith Stacey, *Patriarchy and Socialist Revolution in China,* 188.

43. In contrast, more historically oriented studies of women in the Ming and Qing (by Susan Mann and others) show women's ability to circumvent state regulations.

44. Edward Shorter, *The Making of the Modern Family*, 3, 5, 7, 47–48, 96, 214–15. Shorter, of course, was one in a long line of European and American scholars positing rural conservatism and urban progressiveness. From Marx to Toennies to Daniel Lerner, social theorists anticipated the hypothesis of a low correlation between "strong" communities and "modern" social change by focusing on the role of urbanization and industrialization (which are located in urban areas) in "loosening" traditional social ties in the gemeinschaft community and thereby freeing people to pursue their own options to become cosmopolitan "individuals" within the gesellschaft city.

45. See *China's Peasants: The Anthropology of a Revolution*, 263. Emphasis added.

46. As Johnson argues, "Chinese cities in the early 1950s clearly presented a more hospitable environment for marriage reformers . . . Urban Chinese women were less likely to live among and be controlled by social networks based on rooted male kin groups." See *Women, the Family, and Peasant Revolution*, 117.

47. For the "law and social change" perspective in the Chinese case see David Buxbaum, "Family Law and Social Change: A Theoretical Introduction," in David Buxbaum, ed., *Chinese Family Law and Social Change in Comparative Perspective*. For comparative views see P. H. Gulliver, *Disputes and Negotiations: A Cross-Cultural Perspective*.

48. John O. Haley writes: "In societies where illiteracy rates are high or little is communicated about the courts, the judicial model will be less successful. A lack of law trained persons and the absence of published reports of court decisions . . . are serious barriers to the effectiveness of the judiciary." See "The Myth of the Reluctant Litigant," *Journal of Japanese Studies* 4, no. 2:380.

49. William Felstiner, "Influences of Social Organization on Dispute Processing," *Law and Society Review* 9, no. 1:74, 79, 83; also see Haley, "Myth of the Reluctant Litigant," 378.

50. Engel, *Code and Custom*, 143–44.

51. Joel Migdal, *Strong Societies and Weak States: State-Society Relations and Capabilities in the Third World*, 269, 275. Also see Charles Tilly, "Does Modernization Breed Revolution," *Comparative Politics* 5, no. 3:425–47; Theda Skocpol, *States and Social Revolution: A Comparative Analysis of France, Russia, and China;* Chalmers Johnson, *MITI and the Japanese Miracle: The Emergence of Japanese Industrial Policy, 1925–1975;* Peter Evans, "The State as Problem and Solution: Predation, Embedded Autonomy, and Structural Change," in Stephen Haggard and Robert Kaufmann, eds., *The Politics of Economic Adjustment: International Constraints, Distributional Conflicts, and the State*.

52. Kenneth Lieberthal, *Revolution and Tradition in Tientsin, 1949–1952;* John Gardner, "The Wu-fan Campaign in Shanghai: A Study of the Consolidation of Urban Control," in A. Doak Barnett, ed., *Chinese Communist Politics in Action;* Ezra Vogel, *Canton under Communism: Programs and Politics in a Provincial Capital, 1949–1968*. The strongest argument to date in this respect has been in Franz Schurmann, *Ideology and Organization in Communist China*. For a recent exception to this view see Elizabeth J. Perry, "The Shanghai Strike Wave of 1957," *China Quarterly*, no. 137.

53. To date there are very few studies of the "suburbs" as distinct subregions within larger macroregions. Studies that have focused on either the North or South China regions include Philip C. C. Huang's *The Peasant Economy and Social Change in North China* and the same author's *The Peasant Family and Rural Development in the Yangzi Delta, 1350–1988.*

54. The "prefecture," or *zhou,* is the administrative unit below the province but above the county.

55. Yasheng Huang, "Information, Bureaucracy, and Economic Reforms in China and the Soviet Union," *World Politics* 47:113, 127–28.

CHAPTER 2. THE STATE AND THE FAMILY IN URBAN CHINA

1. "Demand for divorce" and "divorce rates" describe two different phenomena. The former deals with changes within society that lead people to want to change their family situation, while the latter is a measure—usually quantitative—of how many divorces there are among the population of married people in a given year. In many cases there might be a large discrepancy between the two: people may want to divorce but the state will not let them. In this chapter I deal with both the demand for divorce and some quantitative evidence suggesting higher rates of divorce among the least "urban" urbanites.

2. Roderick Philips, *Family Breakdown in Late Eighteenth Century France,* 94, 96; William Goode, *World Revolution and Family Patterns.*

3. This was not an uncontroversial policy. Fiennes Trotman, an opponent of the first British Marriage Act, argued that not needing to promise faithfulness on "religious grounds" would be "license to wholesale legal prostitution." See Fiennes Trotman, *An Address on the New Marriage Registration Acts,* 7–8.

4. On France see Philips, *Family Breakdown,* 93–94; for Russia, Bernice Madsen, "Social Services for Women: Problems and Priorities," in Dorothy Atkinson, Alexander Dallin, and Gail Lapidus, eds., *Women in Russia,* 311; and Beatrice Farnsworth, "Village Women Experience the Revolution," in Abbott Gleason, Peter Kenez, and Richard Stites, eds., *Bolshevik Culture,* 254 n. 121.

5. Karl Deutsch has argued that the "inner source of political power depends on existing facilities for social communication . . . Such facilities are, however, unevenly distributed. Towns, libraries, archives, telephone and railroad networks, school systems . . . all these show the characteristic cluster distribution, with relatively crowded central areas separated by regions of relatively lower density." The denser the means of communication, he suggests, the easier it will be for the state to exercise power. See his *Nationalism and Social Communication: An Inquiry into the Foundations of Nationality,* 49.

6. G. William Skinner, "Cities and the Hierarchy of Local Systems," in G. William Skinner, ed., *The City in Late Imperial China,* 276.

7. G. William Skinner, "Introduction: Urban Development in Imperial China," in G. William Skinner, ed., *The City in Late Imperial China,* 25.

8. Patricia Buckley Ebrey, *The Inner Quarters: Marriage and the Lives of Chinese Women in the Sung Period,* chap. 1, has an excellent discussion of these divisions of private/female and public/male.

9. In *Civil Justice in China* and in "Codified Law and Magisterial Adjudication in the Qing" (in Kathryn Bernhardt and Philip C. C. Huang, eds., *Civil Law in Qing and Republican China*), Philip C. C. Huang argues that informal and formal systems of justice were used by ordinary Chinese. Huang does not, however, argue that the state proactively attempted to change family relations.

10. Stephen MacKinnon, "Police Reform in Late Ch'ing China," *Ch'ing-shih wen-t'i* 3, no. 4:82–99; on the development of the police in Beijing see David Strand, *Rickshaw Beijing: City People and Politics in the 1920s,* chap. 4.

11. Prasenjit Duara, *Culture, Power, and the State: Rural North China, 1900–1942,* 3–4, 180–93. See Huang, *Civil Justice in China,* 58–59, for a characterization of successful village mediators.

12. Bernhardt, "Women and the Law."

13. The Ningbo native-place association in Shanghai (which was one of the wealthiest and best-established in the city) mediated only five marriage conflict cases in 1946–1947. Between 1900 and the mid-1940s the association mediated a total of sixty-five cases. See Shanghai Municipal Archives (hereafter SMA) no. 6-5-963. (Here and throughout, sources will be indicated only by the name of or abbreviation for the archive and the file number; full citations, which include author [usually institutional] and the precise title of the report, can be found in my doctoral dissertation, "Revolutionizing the Family: Law, Love, and Divorce in Urban and Rural China, 1950–1968" [Dept. of Political Science, University of California, Berkeley, 1996].) Also see Bryna Goodman, *Native Place, City, and Nation: Regional Networks and Identities in Shanghai, 1853–1937,* 249–50.

14. Johnson, *Women, the Family, and Peasant Revolution,* 115, 117. For a similar account see Yang, *Chinese Family,* chap. 4.

15. Johnson, *Women, the Family, and Peasant Revolution,* 117.

16. See Thomas J. Schlereth, *The Cosmopolitan Ideal in Enlightenment Thought: Its Form and Function in the Ideas of Franklin, Hume, and Voltaire, 1694–1790,* 5–6.

17. Paul M. Hohenberg and Lynn H. Lees, *The Making of Urban Europe, 1000–1950,* 275.

18. Ibid., 251.

19. For urban disdain of recent immigrants to New York see Irving Howe, *World of Our Fathers: The Journey of East European Jews to America and the Life They Found and Made,* 121. Interestingly, even elite critics of the city (including, but not limited to, Rousseau, Jefferson, Melville, Durkheim, Henry James, Friedrich Engels, and the U.S. sociologists Robert Park and Louis Wirth), who naively imagined a more bucolic and peaceful life in the countryside, rarely left the city to live full-time in the rural areas they romanticized. See Morton White and Lucia White, *The Intellectual versus the City, from Thomas Jefferson to Frank Lloyd Wright,* 1–2, 200, 233–39.

20. F. W. Mote, "The Transformation of Nanking," in G. W. Skinner, ed., *The City in Late Imperial China,* 114; Skinner, "Introduction," 269; Rhoads Murphy, "City and Countryside as Ideological Issues: India and China," *Comparative Studies in Society and History* 14, no. 3:253.

21. See Frederic Wakeman Jr. and Wen-hsin Yeh, "Introduction," in Frederic Wakeman Jr. and Wen-hsin Yeh, eds., *Shanghai Sojourners,* 13. William Rowe, by contrast, has emphasized the development of a distinct urban identity for the city of Hankou in his *Hankow: Commerce and Society in a Chinese City, 1796–1889.*

22. On the development of the Shanghai middle class see Wen-hsin Yeh, "Corporate Space, Communal Time: Everyday Life in Shanghai's Bank of China," *American Historical Review* 100, no. 1:97–122; and Wen-hsin Yeh, "Progressive Journalism and Shanghai's Petty Urbanites: Zou Taofen and the Shenghuo Enterprise, 1926–1945," in Frederic Wakeman Jr. and Wen-hsin Yeh, eds., *Shanghai Sojourners,* 186–238.

23. See Betty Peh-t'i Wei, *Old Shanghai,* 37–38. Urban elite women in Beijing were also interested in buying clothes that reflected their social status. Jermyn Chi-hung Lynn (Lin) wrote that "along with the Bannerman's gown and the sleeveless garment have come all sorts of hats and caps mostly imported from Paris. In fact the wardrobe of a Chinese flapper has become just as complete as those of her sisters in Europe and America. The bob-haired girl of Peking as elsewhere is always clamoring for new style coats and hats." See his *Social Life of the Chinese (in Peking),* 170.

24. Yeh, "Corporate Space, Communal Time," 109–10, 113.

25. Lynn, *Social Life,* 112, 119, 127.

26. On these divisions see Elizabeth Perry, *Shanghai on Strike: The Politics of Chinese Labor,* chap. 1; Emily Honig discusses prejudices toward those hailing from northern Jiangsu (known as Subei) in *Creating Chinese Ethnicity: Subei People in Shanghai, 1850–1980.* Also see Lu Hanchao, "The Workers and Neighborhoods of Modern Shanghai, 1911–1949" (Ph.D. diss., University of California, Los Angeles, 1991). Lu makes the important and useful distinction between full-time workers who lived in settled areas and the poorest of the poor who lived in shacks. Both groups were part of the "working class," yet occupied very different places in the city's social hierarchy.

27. Yeh, "Corporate Space, Communal Time," 117–18.

28. According to an investigation of a working-class neighborhood in Shanghai (populated primarily by migrants from Anhui and Subei), one-third of all married couples lived apart, because of one partner either residing in the countryside or working in a different area of the city. See Xuhui District Women's Federation, "Xuhui qu hunyin fa xuanchuan zhongdian gongzuo zongjie" (Summary report of key point Marriage Law propaganda work in Xuhui District), Xuhui District Archives (hereafter XHA), (1951), p. 32.

29. See Emily Honig, *Sisters and Strangers: Women in the Shanghai Cotton Mills, 1919–1949,* 185–86.

30. According to Lu ("Workers and Neighborhoods," 161), a shack could be built in two or three days by the resident; rent was also easy to manage.

31. Lu, "Workers and Neighborhoods," 31.

32. Perry, *Shanghai on Strike,* 186–87.

33. SMA C32-1-6, p. 7.

34. SMA C32-2-122, p. 37. These statistics, I emphasize, are not conclusive. It is, for instance, possible, but I think highly unlikely, that those demanding divorce in Changning were the few educated students who lived there. Unfortunately, the lack of access to courts themselves has prevented me from building a case on individual divorce petitioners.

35. According to statistics from three hundred cases in Shanghai Municipal Court from September 1949 to November 1950, divorce was usually three times more prevalent among unemployed women than among women workers (in the

category of females aged nineteen to twenty-five, the ratio was 48 to 15). See Zhongyang renmin zhengfu fazhi weiyuanhui (State legal committee), ed., *Hunyin wenti cankao ziliao huibian* (Collection of Marriage Law–related materials) (Shanghai: Xinhua, 1950), 98–99.

36. On the frequently exploitative relationship between the GMD and Shanghai capitalists see Parks Coble, *The Shanghai Capitalists and the Nationalist Government.*

37. See Perry, *Shanghai on Strike,* 99–100, 203–5, 155–57.

38. Mao Tse-tung, "Report to the Second Plenary Session of the Seventh Central Committee of the Communist Party of China" (March 1949), in *Selected Works,* 4:374. Also see Mao's comments in *Mao Tse-tung Unrehearsed,* ed. Stuart Schram, 288.

39. H. Arthur Steiner argues that Chinese peasants have a "puritanical distrust of the cities." See his "Chinese Communist Urban Policy," *American Political Science Review* 44:62.

40. The best works on CCP mobilization efforts in the countryside are Chen Yung-fa, *Making Revolution: The Communist Movement in Eastern and Central China, 1937–1945;* William Hinton, *Fanshen: A Documentary of Revolution in a Chinese Village;* and Odoric Wou, *Mobilizing the Masses: Building Revolution in Henan.*

41. For an excellent account of this process see Esherick, "Deconstructing the Construction," 1057–58.

42. The term "Great Tradition" has been used to contrast elite and official culture with that of the "Little Tradition" of ordinary people.

43. See Tiejun Cheng and Mark Selden, "The Origins and Consequences of China's *Hukou* System," *China Quarterly,* no. 139:646.

44. As the newly appointed deputy mayor of Shanghai, Pan Hannian, noted, "In the past hundred years the imperialists made [Shanghai] their formidable fortress for invading and enslaving China, and it was, moreover, the heart of the Guomindang reactionary clique which oppressed the Chinese people for more than twenty years." See Gardner, "*Wu-fan* Campaign," 481.

45. SMA C31-2-159, p. 61.

46. *Beijing shi Dongcheng qu dashiji* (Major events in Beijing's Dongcheng District), 2:3, 7; ibid., 1:13–14.

47. Ibid., 1:10–12.

48. Marc Galanter uses the term "radiating" to explain the impact of a court's decision on how people view law and the courts. See "The Radiating Effect of Courts," in Keith O. Boyum and Lynn Mather, eds., *Empirical Theories about Courts.*

49. Gardner, "*Wu-fan* Campaign," 496.

50. Beijing Municipal Archives (hereafter BMA) 84-3-21, p. 34.

51. BMA 84-3-15 (1951), p. 3.

52. BMA 84-3-21 (November 1952), pp. 12–14. For other cases see *Xinwen ribao,* 11 November 1951.

53. *Xinwen ribao,* 2 December 1951.

54. BMA 84-3-15, p. 4.

55. BMA 84-3-15 (1951), p. 38.

56. BMA 84-3-15, p. 24.

57. SMA C32-1-4 (1953), p. 8.

58. XHA 8-1-414 (1953), p. 8.

59. On the Yiguandao see David K. Jordan and Daniel Overmeyer, *The Flying Phoenix: Aspects of Chinese Sectarianism in Taiwan.*

60. SMA C31-2-222 (1953), pp. 61–63.

61. BMA 84-3-21 (1951), pp. 12–14; BMA 84-3-15 (1951), p. 4. According to estimates from Putuo District in Shanghai, 320,000 out of 370,000 residents heard some form of propaganda. See SMA C31-1-2 (May 1953), p. 81.

62. Li Rong, "Hunyin shi bu shi 'geren sishi'" (Are marriage problems personal and private matters?), *Xinwen ribao*, 23 November 1951. Another report found that before being educated, officials in Shanghai held that marriage problems were "private matters" (*sishi*), "family matters" (*jiawushi*), and thus were not concerned about them. This attitude, they claimed, was "very common." See SMA C32-1-2, pp. 82–83.

63. SMA C32-1-4 (1953), p. 27; SMA C32-2-5, p. 3. Here it is interesting to note that in drafting mediation rules, the central government itself did not make any distinction between rural and urban areas, an oversight that shows the extent to which the Communists were not very well prepared for urban political work. See Jerome A. Cohen, "Drafting People's Mediation Rules," in John Wilson Lewis, ed., *The City in Communist China*, 50.

64. *Guanche hunyinfa yundong qingkuang jianbao* (Bulletin on the implementation of the Marriage Law), 7 March 1953, p. 2, in SMA C32-2-5.

65. SMA C32-1-2 (1953), pp. 82–83.

66. Perry, *Shanghai on Strike*, esp. chap. 1; Honig, *Creating Chinese Ethnicity*, 44–53.

67. SMA C32-1-5, pp. 59, 61–63.

68. Hinton's *Fanshen* mentions incidents of cuckolding and the like, but little systematic research has been done on this topic in the China field; see p. 307 for one example. In any event, Hinton's account certainly substantiates (as does Mao Zedong's rural investigations in Hunan) my argument that extramarital sex was quite common in villages, even in "backward" North China. Peasant promiscuity seems to have gone hand in hand with community efforts to regulate sexuality. For the British case see G. R. Quaife, *Wanton Wenches and Wayward Wives: Peasants and Illicit Sex in Early Seventeenth Century England*, 200; for France see Natalie Zemon Davis, "The Reasons of Misrule," in her collection of essays *Society and Culture in Early Modern France*, 100; and Eugen Weber, *Peasants into Frenchmen: The Modernization of Rural France, 1870–1914*, 399–406. According to Weber, "The most frequent inspiration of *charivaris* was marriage outside the acceptable norms: a widow or a widower remarrying too soon after the spouse's death, an older man or woman wedding a partner judged too young, notorious partners in adultery marrying after the spouse's death . . . " (400).

69. SMA C32-2-3 (1953), pp. 1–2.

70. SMA C32-1-2, pp. 90–91.

71. *Guanche hunyinfa yundong qingkuang jianbao* (Bulletin on the implementation of the Marriage Law), 7 March 1953, p. 1, in SMA C32-2-5. In Beijing, municipal officials had similar complaints. See BMA 84-1-32 (December 1952), p. 17; Dongcheng District Archives (hereafter DCA) 6-1-7 (May 1953), p. 12–13.

72. SMA C32-2-3, (1953), p. 64.

73. BMA 101-331 (1951), p. 13.

74. For the French case see Traer, *Marriage and the Family,* 145–49.

75. Duara, *Culture, Power, and the State,* 182–83.

76. SMA C31-2-222, pp. 61–63.

77. BMA 84-3-22, p. 26.

78. BMA 84-3-22 (1951), p. 25.

79. Ibid., p. 28.

80. BMA 84-3-22 (1952), pp. 3–4. Reports such as this one invite skepticism about the ability of the state to implement the mediation laws it drafted in the early 1950s. The laws may have been carefully drafted and flexible but, given the quality of the personnel responsible for enforcing them, were not used by low-level cadres. On the drafting of mediation laws see Cohen, "Drafting People's Mediation Rules," 29–50.

81. SMA C31-2-222 (1953), p. 77.

82. BMA 84-3-21, pp. 45–46.

83. One breakdown of participants in a training session for women activists in the Beijing Federation of Trade Unions found that in twelve large factories, twenty-three out of the twenty-six activists either were illiterate or had only a primary school education. The overwhelming majority of new officials were between seventeen and twenty-five years old. See BMA 101-331 (September 1951), p. 16.

84. BMA 101-331 (August 1951), p. 24.

85. BMA 101-412 (1951), p. 28.

86. BMA 84-3-15 (November 1951), p. 72–73.

87. BMA 84-1-32, pp. 46–47.

88. BMA 101-412, p. 9.

89. SMA C32-1-5 (1953), p. 35; BMA 101-412, p. 28.

90. BMA 84-3-21 (November 1952), p. 16.

91. SMA C32-2-5 (May 1953), p. 11.

92. SMA C32-2-3, p. 15.

93. SMA C32-2-5, pp. 11–12.

94. XHA (1951), p. 38.

95. SMA C32-2-5, pp. 11–12.

96. Erving Goffman, *The Presentation of Self in Everyday Life,* chap. 5, discusses the arts of "impression management."

97. SMA C32-2-5, p. 12.

98. In *Law and Society,* Lawrence Friedman defines "legal culture" or "legal consciousness" as the "attitudes, values, and opinions held in society, with regard to law, the legal system, and its various parts" (76). Sally Engle Merry (*Getting Justice and Getting Even*) defines "legal consciousness" more broadly as "the way people understand and use law" (5). In China, since "law" is usually coterminous with the state and its policies, I use the term to refer to the way people deal with law, *policies,* and those who enforce them.

99. See Yue Daiyun, *Intellectuals in Chinese Fiction,* 110.

100. Liu Binyan, *A Higher Kind of Loyalty,* 61; for other examples see Perry Link, *Evening Chats in Beijing: Probing China's Predicament,* 140–42.

101. On these campaigns see Merle Goldman, *Literary Dissent in Modern China.* See also Link, *Evening Chats in Beijing,* 140, on intellectuals' wanting "ideological remolding."

102. SMA C32-2-3, p. 42. Her father, Liu Hongsheng, was a match entrepreneur.

103. BMA 84-1-32 (March 1953), p. 38.

104. DCA 11-7-17 (November 1951), p. 14. For similar cases see DCA 11-2-16, (December 1951), p. 2. The manager of a bookstore, in discussing his family situation, argued that "we can still get along" (*hai bu cuo he de lai*). His main fear was that the government would force him to divorce one of his wives.

105. BMA 84-1-32, p. 38.

106. SMA C32-2-5, p. 6.

107. Jing'an District Archives (hereafter JAA) 23-2-2, pp. 11–13.

108. SMA C32-2-3 (1953), pp. 5–6.

109. DCA 11-7-66 (1951), pp. 3–4. Other men tried to use the law to get rid of their older wives by "faking a divorce," then returning to live together with their younger ones.

110. SMA C32-2-3, p. 42.

111. Shao Jun, "Qing shuai tichu lihun shi bu shi dui de" (Is it correct to casually petition for divorce?), *Xinwen ribao*, 30 November 1951. In Shanghai's elite Xincheng District, there were nine cases of suicide caused by conflict between number one and number two wives. Of the nine suicide attempts, eight were women and one was a man. All of the women were number one wives. In one case, a number one wife committed suicide because her husband favored the number two wife, and criticized her when the two wives got into a dispute. The one male case resulted from his number two wife asking to leave him, and his discovering that his number one wife had had an affair with an employee with whom she had just had a child. See SMA C31-2-222, p. 11. On suicide in the secondary literature see Stacey, *Patriarchy and Socialist Revolution*, 178; Johnson, *Women, the Family, and Peasant Revolution*, 132.

112. SMA C32-2-3, p. 15

113. Luo Qingyu, "Zai tiaojie jiating jiufen zhong de yi dian jingyan" (Some experiences mediating family disputes), *Xinwen ribao*, 17 April 1951.

114. BMA 84-3-21, p. 48.

115. Cheng and Selden ("China's *Hukou* System," 648) argue that the "relocation processes were accomplished smoothly in the early years of the People's Republic." My overall impression from reading scores of Bureau of Civil Affairs documents in municipal, district, and county archives was that this process was more chaotic than smooth. One report stated that many refugees did not want to return to the countryside because peasants in the village, having already distributed much of the land they received during land reform among themselves, would give the person returning from the city a bad plot. When this occurred, they would return to the city and complain to the Bureau of Civil Affairs. After accepting aid from the BCA, they would then go out to a local restaurant for a feast!

116. SMA C32-2-3. p. 15.

117. DCA 6-1-57 (1951), pp. 6–7; SMA C31-222 (1953), pp. 1–2.

118. SMA C32-2-3, p. 15.

119. SMA E81-2-115 (1953), p. 18.

120. Xiong Nong, "Bu neng wujie hunyinfa: Chuan Naiwen he Wang Ye (Wang Shou) de gushi" (Do not misunderstand the Marriage Law: The story of Chuan Naiwen and Wang Ye (Wang Shou), *Xinwen ribao* (Shanghai), 6 October 1951. The

Women's Federation wrote a very detailed report on court abuses in Xincheng District. See JAA 32-2-19.

121. *Guanche hunyinfa yundong qingkuang jianbao* (Bulletin on the implementation of the Marriage Law), 4 March 1953, p. 1, in SMA C32-2-5. See ibid. for another case resulting in suicide.

122. Xu Anqi, a sociologist at the Shanghai Academy of Social Sciences who has worked in court archives, told me that the divorce case files are very thick. Each case includes testimony by petitioner and defendant, neighbors, and work unit.

123. SMA C32-1-2 (1953), pp. 89–90. See DCA 1-1-143, pp. 25–27, for a similar report in Beijing.

124. SMA C31-2-222 (1953), p. 80.

125. SMA C31-2-222, pp. 3–4.

126. SMA C32-1-6 (1953), p. 20.

127. On suicide as protest in Chinese society see Margery Wolf's essay "Women and Suicide in China," in Margery Wolf and Roxane Witke, eds., *Women in Chinese Society,* 112. The theme of suicide will be developed further in the next chapter.

128. SMA E81-2-115, p. 18.

129. "Xuhui qu diqu hunyin zhuangkuang" (The marriage situation in areas in Xuhui District), XHA (1953), pp. 9–10. Emphasis added.

130. DCA 6-1-57 (1951), pp. 10–11. It is unclear from the report whether she rode around in the daytime or evening. If she rode around during the daytime, her bruises would be exposed, thus defeating the purpose of not telling anyone about her problems.

131. BMA 84-3-15 (September 1951), p. 45.

132. SMA C1-2-611 (1953), pp. 37–38.

133. SMA C1-2-611, pp. 37–38; DCA 11-7-17 (1951), p. 16.

134. SMA C1-2-611, pp. 37–38; DCA 11-7-17, pp. 14–15. More contemporary recollections of this period also emphasize the extent of intellectuals' commitment to the state, and their willingness to sacrifice their individuality to the state. See Link, *Evening Chats in Beijing,* 142–43.

135. DCA 11-7-17, p. 7.

136. On Hu's marriage and his defense of the system see Patrick Hanan, introduction to his translation of *The Sea of Regret: Two Turn-of-the-Century Chinese Romantic Novels,* by Wu Jianren, 7–8.

137. Schwarcz, *Chinese Enlightenment,* 111.

138. See Yeh, *Alienated Academy,* for an analysis of the views of Chen Xuexin (255). Chen was an advocate of marriage freedom, but dared to annul his engagements only *after* the death of his father.

139. DCA 11-7-17, p. 7. Evidently, some parents threatened their children with suicide should they refuse to marry the person they selected for them.

140. Ibid.

141. DCA 11-7-17, p. 14.

142. See, for instance, Chow T'se-tsung, *The May Fourth Movement: Intellectual Revolution in Modern China;* Schwarcz, *Chinese Enlightenment.*

143. See Timothy Weston, "Beijing University and Chinese Political Culture, 1905–1923" (Ph.D. diss., Dept. of History, University of California, Berkeley, 1996).

144. Hanan, introduction to *The Sea of Regret,* 6–8.

145. Colleen She, "Toward Ideology: Views of the May Fourth Intelligentsia on Love, Marriage, and Divorce," *Issues and Studies* 27, no. 2 : 111, 105.

146. Yeh, "Progressive Journalism," 214.

147. Jerome A. Cohen, "Chinese Mediation on the Eve of Modernization," in David Buxbaum, ed., *Traditional and Modern Legal Institutions in Asia and Africa,* 59.

148. Frank K. Upham, *Law and Social Change in Postwar Japan,* 13.

149. See Lawrence Stone, *The Road to Divorce: England, 1530–1987,* 16, 21.

150. John D'Emilio and Estelle B. Freedman, *Intimate Matters: A History of Sexuality in America,* 142. They write: "Members of northern middle class considered themselves more civilized than blacks, immigrants and the poor, whom they stereotyped as sexually promiscuous."

151. Ibid., 183–84. Concern with privacy was not limited to the American middle and upper classes. As noted in Michelle Perrot, ed., *A History of Private Life: From the Fires of Revolution to the Great War,* the growth of privacy was associated with economic changes and increasing differentiation in class structure. With their wealth, the French bourgeoisie could afford to build more private spaces in the home (separate bedrooms for parents and children, for instance), as well as cultivate themselves in dress, manners, and grooming. A good deal of this behavior was also motivated by a desire to distinguish themselves from the working classes, who lived in squalid, crowded rooms and whose behavior, described as vulgar, rude, and burlesque, was consistently condemned as unbefitting civilized society.

152. Merry, *Getting Justice and Getting Even,* 64. For more evidence see M. P. Baumgarten, *The Moral Order of a Suburb,* 55.

153. Laura Engelstein, *The Keys to Happiness: Sex and the Modern in Fin-de-Siècle Russia,* 118.

154. Barbara Alpern Engels, *Mothers and Daughters: Women of the Intelligentsia in Nineteenth-Century Russia,* 53, 125, 150, 178; also see Sheila Fitzpatrick, "Sex and Revolution: An Examination of the Literary and Statistical Data on the Mores of Soviet Students in the 1920s," *Journal of Modern History* 50, no. 2 : 273.

155. DCA 11-7-66 (1951), pp. 3–4.

156. *Guanche hunyinfa yundong qingkuang jianbao* (Bulletin on the implementation of the Marriage Law), 3 February 1953, in SMA C32-2-5, p. 17.

157. SMA C32-1-5, p. 35.

158. SMA C32-1-4 (1953), p. 26.

159. SMA C32-2-3 (1953), pp. 5–6.

160. BMA 84-3-21 (1952), p. 8.

161. SMA C32-2-3, p. 64.

162. "Xuhui qu hunyin fa xuanchuan zhongdian gongzuo zongjie" (Summary report of key point Marriage Law propaganda work in Xuhui District), XHA (1951), p. 44.

163. DCA 11-7-66, p. 1.

164. SMA C32-2-3, p. 3–4, 5. The reference to "Buddhist monk" is actually to the Communist Party; some thought CCP officials were nonsexual.

165. DCA 11-2-16, p. 3; DCA 6-1-7 (1953), p. 17, for examples in Beijing. Sympathy was also a basis for support for the Marriage Law. As one female worker in Shanghai's Yong'an Textile Mill related: "When I was in the bridal sedan chair I had

no idea whether my future husband's house was facing north or south or whether he was tall or short." The report noted that many older women were tricked by matchmakers with promises of a tall husband and an apartment, only to find out later that their husband was poor and an invalid. "Thus they are in support of marriage freedom." "If Chairman Mao came ten years earlier," they said, "I would not have eaten so much bitterness." See SMA C32-1-5, p. 37.

166. DCA 11-7-66, pp. 3–4.

167. "Xuhui qu hunyin fa xuanchuan zhongdian gongzuo zongjie," XHA (1951), p. 48.

168. Ibid.; DCA 11-7-66, pp. 3–4; SMA C32-2-3 (1953), pp. 2–3, 5–6; SMA C32-1-5 (1953), pp. 5–6.

169. *Guanche hunyinfa yundong qingkuang baogao*, 3 February 1953, in SMA C32-2-5, p. 17.

170. BMA 84-1-32, p. 38.

171. Xuhui District Women's Federation, "Zhongdian hunyin qingkuang diaocha baogao" (Report on the marriage situation in a key point area), XHA (1951), p. 21.

172. SMA C32-1-4 (1953), p. 20.

173. DCA 1-1-141 (1953), p. 3.

174. DCA 11-2-16 (1951), p. 3.

175. BMA 84-3-21 (November 1952), p. 17. Another report noted that neighbors "tell the work team about each other's problems, whether they fight or not." See DCA 11-2-16, p. 3.

176. BMA 84-3-15 (1951), pp. 102–3. Actually, they were right: the Marriage Law gave "illegitimate" children the same rights as "legitimate" ones.

177. SMA C31-2-222, pp. 64, 72.

178. BMA 84-3-15, p. 43.

179. This was common in cases handled according to the "mass line" in legal work implemented by the CCP during and after the legal reform movement. According to the mass line, courts were required to solicit the masses' opinions about a legal case and make a decision taking these opinions into account. See Victor Li, "The Evolution and Development of the Chinese Legal System," in John M. H. Lindbeck, ed., *China: Management of a Revolutionary Society*, 228.

180. In Beijing, reports from 1953 estimated that 50 percent of court decisions were problematic because they did not rule on violence or property issues. Women's Federation officials attributed this to court officials' attitude of "qing guan nanduan jiawu shi" (even upright officials cannot adjudicate family affairs) and "min bu gao, guan bu jiu" (if the people don't accuse, officials don't investigate). See BMA 84-3-15, p. 35.

181. *Hai Dingxiu v. Wang Dequan*, in SMA C32-2-4, pp. 15–18. For another example of such willingness to draw in the state see DCA 11-2-16 (1951), p. 3. In this case a woman in a *hutong* said, "My husband used to beat me whenever he got drunk. If he hits me again, I'll come looking for you [i.e., the investigation group]."

182. Because Yu was not the legal wife she was not required to go to court for a separation. (Whether she knew this or not is impossible to know, however. In the event that Yu did know this, she still might have sought to go to court to settle outstanding property issues.)

183. *Huang Aliu v. Sun Zengyi,* in SMA A71-2-1860, pp. 106–8.

184. BMA 84-3-21, p. 8.

185. XHA 8-1-414, pp. 9–10.

186. In one case, a Beijing worker was criticized by the union chairman for breach of discipline. The worker retorted: "The capitalist doesn't care, but you do. You are the capitalist's running dog!" See DCA 1-1-141 (1951), p. 34.

187. DCA 11-7-17 (November 1951), p. 19.

188. BMA 101-331 (October 1951), p. 13.

189. Luo Shuru, "Hunyinfa de xuanchuan gongzuo shi geming gongzuo zhongyao yi huan" (Marriage Law propaganda work is important revolutionary work), *Xinwen ribao,* 30 November 1951.

190. DCA 11-7-72 (1951), p. 3.

191. DCA 11-7-225, p. 17.

192. For an example of this see BMA 101-331 (September 1951), p. 14.

193. Elizabeth J. Perry, *Rebels and Revolutionaries in North China, 1845–1945,* 79.

194. M. P. Baumgarten, *The Moral Order of a Suburb,* 55; Merry, *Getting Justice and Getting Even,* 65.

195. Enid Hill, *Mahkama! Studies in the Egyptian Legal System,* 83–85. She notes that the better off do not go to court to divorce . . . because "that is what the 'common people' do."

196. Ned Levine, "Social Change and Family Crises—The Nature of Turkish Divorce," in Ligdem Kagitcibasi, ed., *Sex Roles, Family, and Community in Turkey,* 330, 332.

197. G. N. Ramu, *Women, Work, and Marriage in Urban India,* 184; J. N. Choudhary, *Divorce in Indian Society,* 36,102, 165. For a different view emphasizing the conservatism of the urban lower classes see Rama Mehta, *Divorced Hindu Women.*

198. Johnson, *Women, the Family, and Peasant Revolution,* 117.

199. BMA 101-331, pp. 12, 14.

200. XHA 8-1-417. Close to 10 percent of the claims stemmed from unemployment-related conflicts.

201. Zou Yiren, *Jiu Shanghai renkou bianqian de yanjiu* (Research on demographic change in Old Shanghai), 108–9.

202. XHA 8-1-418, p. 84.

203. XHA 8-1-417, p. 19.

204. Lawrence Stone, *Broken Lives: Separation and Divorce in England, 1660–1857,* 13.

205. DCA 11-7-66, p. 5.

206. SMA C32-1-5 (1953), pp. 50, 58, 63. For similar problems in early nineteenth-century Russia see Diane Koenker, "Urban Families, Working Class Youth," in David Ransel, ed., *The Family in Imperial Russia: New Lines of Historical Research,* 285.

207. BMA 84-3-21, pp. 27–28.

208. DCA 11-7-72, p. 3.

209. "Dongxi qu hunyin gongzuo zongjie" (Marriage work in Dongxi District), DCA 11-7-211, n.p.

210. XHA 8-1-414, p. 10; "Xuhui qu hunyin fa xuanchuan zhongdian gongzuo zongjie," XHA (1951), p. 46.

211. SMA C1-2-611 (1951), p. 3. Older people also commented on the younger generation's rather loose sexual norms. One elderly woman said, "Marriage freedom means old people are not allowed to arrange and interfere in marriages. But young people today are not behaving properly—today falling in love with that one, tomorrow with another one. I can't bear the sight of it." See DCA 11-7-66, p. 5.

212. BMA 101-331, p. 14.

213. DCA 1-1-141, p. 34; BMA 101-412, pp. 20–21.

214. SMA C1-2-1154, p. 123. What happened to babies conceived in these circumstances is hard to know for certain. My suspicion is that not a few women aborted their fetuses, got rid of the infant in some way after birth, or sent the baby back home to the village.

215. SMA C31-2-222, p. 67. Evidence of the role of poverty in the high divorce rate is seen in the following admonishment to court officials: "Legal cadres should stop writing on the mediation record 'Because the woman does not like being poor, the man, abiding by the basic spirit of the marriage law, agrees to a divorce.'" See SMA C31-2-122, pp. 38–9.

216. Diane Koenker, "Men against Women on the Shop Floor in Early Soviet Russia: Gender and Class in the Socialist Workplace," *American Historical Review* 100, no. 5:1442, 1445, 1448.

217. SMA C31-2-159, p. 14.

218. SMA C32-1-5 (1953), p. 47.

219. SMA C1-2-1154, p. 123.

220. BMA 84-3-15, p. 45.

221. Xuhui District Women's Federation, "Zhongdian hunyin qingkuang diaocha baogao," XHA (1951), p. 23.

222. Koenker, "Men against Women," 1442.

223. SMA C1-2-1154, p. 123.

224. SMA C1-2-611, p. 3.

225. BMA 84-3-21, p. 29.

226. DCA 1-1-194, p. 11.

227. BMA 84-3-15, p. 46.

228. Ye Lin, "Bu yao huang lianpo de sixiang" (Don't have "old hag" thinking), *Xinwen ribao,* 18 December 1951.

229. BMA 84-3-21, p. 29.

230. Untitled report, in DCA 6-1-7, p. 37.

231. DCA 1-1-194, pp. 11–13.

232. BMA 84-3-21, p. 29.

233. DCA 1-1-194, p. 13.

234. Unfortunately, I was not able to gain access to court records for the post-1949 period, which would allow me to build a "profile" of *individual* divorce petitioners in urban China. Scholars who have looked at court records in the Republican period, however, have also noted the high proportion of lower-class urbanites in their samples (see Bernhardt, "Women and the Law"). Because of this problem, I am forced to rely upon the more general characteristics of the communities petitioners lived in, and from this deduce patterns of interaction with state institutions.

CHAPTER 3. BETWEEN "URBAN" AND "RURAL"

1. SMA A71-2-1860 (April 1953).

2. Qingpu County Archives (hereafter QPA) 48-2-56 (1953), p. 151. This case is particularly helpful because it emerges from correspondence between several levels of government agencies and was never published in summary form. These reports—unlike some municipal and county-level work team materials—were never revised to present the implementation of state policy in a positive light, or used for educational purposes when training local cadres.

3. Ibid., pp. 152–55.

4. Ibid., pp. 157–62.

5. Johnson, *Women, the Family, and Peasant Revolution,* 117.

6. As Lynn T. White III rightly points out, the "problem with an emphasis on urban boundaries is that it obscures as much as it illuminates about the complex webs of human activity that center on cities, but also spread out far from them." See his "Shanghai-Suburb Relations, 1949–1966," in Christopher Howe, ed., *Shanghai: Revolution and Development in an Asian Metropolis,* 241. For a more recent treatment of the problem in defining "urban" by using only state-imposed administrative boundaries see Harry Xiaoying Wu, "Rural to Urban Migration in the People's Republic of China," *China Quarterly,* no. 139:670–71.

7. For the case of France see Philips, *Family Breakdown,* 92–94. After the enactment of the French family law, the city of Toulouse had 374 divorces between 1792 and 1803, but the number of divorces "decreased the farther one went away from Toulouse." More rural districts had only two divorces during the same period. In Rouen the rate was one divorce for every 89 people, but in the surrounding counties, one for every 407.

8. *Chongming xian zhi,* 219; SMA C32-2-5, p. 5.

9. Skinner's analysis of China's macroregions appears in his "Regional Urbanization in Nineteenth Century China," in G. William Skinner, ed., *The City in Late Imperial China,* 211–52.

10. Quantitative indicators clearly reveal key differences between the two areas. Philip Huang counted only twenty major floods in the Yangzi Delta between 1401 and 1900, whereas the Yellow River burst its dikes almost annually. The Tong County gazetteer listed either floods or locusts in every year between 1916 and 1920. See *Tong xian zhi yao,* 1941, 3:15, Tong County Archives (hereafter TCA). Huang, *Peasant Family,* 40–43, 95–96. On the role of the North China environment in shaping patterns of social protest see Perry, *Rebels and Revolutionaries;* Joseph W. Esherick, *The Origins of the Boxer Uprising.*

11. Skinner, "Regional Urbanization," 211–49, 275–351.

12. *Tong xian zhi yao,* 1941, 3:4–8, TCA.

13. *Qingpu xian zhi,* 308–9, 338–39. Qingpu was not serviced by rail. The railway linking Zhejiang to Jiangsu (built during the first decade of the twentieth century) passed through Songjiang. See *Songjiang xian zhi,* 616.

14. *Tong xian zhi yao,* 1941, 6–7.

15. BMA 84-3-28, pp. 1–2.

16. *Qingpu xian zhi,* 236.

17. *Baoshan xian zhi,* 480; SMA A71-2-1859, pp. 49–51. In Zhennan *xiang* in

Jiangwan District, for instance, of 849 married males, 49 worked in factories and 97 in handicrafts; the rest were classified as peasants. Married women were not as frequently employed in industrial labor. Of 938 married women, only 10 worked in factories, and only 42 in handicrafts. See SMA C32-1-4, p. 72.

18. Zou Yiren, *Jiu Shanghai renkou bianqian*, 116–17. The majority of Jiangwan residents were from either Shanghai or Jiangsu, followed by Zhejiang and Guangdong. Xinjing District, on the other hand, boasted far more residents from Jiangsu than Shanghai.

19. Honig, *Sisters and Strangers*, 67–68.

20. *Qingpu xian zhi*, 553. For Jiading County see *Jiading xian zhi*, 714.

21. Rate calculated on a village household (*hukou*) basis. In Qingpu there was an average of 80.22 households per village (in a random sample of 100 villages) in 1950. In Songjiajiao, village reports indicated nine couples divorcing in 1953, and in a 1953 report from Xinjing Village (100 households), four couples. The exact number of households in Songjiajiao is not recorded, but if we use the average number of households in Qingpu as the baseline, the divorce rate is 11 percent. In Jinkuang District there were 6,563 households (one town and seven townships) with four hundred divorce cases at the district government (not including those handled at the township). This represents a 6 percent divorce rate. Population statistics are in QPA 48-1-6. On divorce in Songjiajiao see QPA 48-2-31, p. 117; on Xinjing Village see QPA 48-1-13, p. 100. On Jinkuang District see QPA 48-1-13. In Xiaohongmen Village in the Beijing suburbs eighteen couples were divorced (BMA 84-3-15, p. 72), which was approximately 9 percent of village households. According to population statistics and gazetteers we can calculate that there was an average of 190 households in the villages of the nearby North China county of Fengning. See *Fengning manzu zizhi xian zhi*, 90–101; *Hebei sheng di si ci renkou pucha shougong huizong ziliao*, 304–5. Interviews conducted with rural officials in 1994 in Jiangsu Province (Jiangpu County, near Nanjing) confirmed that "very many" divorces took place during this period. During my interview, the foreign affairs official who accompanied me was surprised to hear that peasants in the area divorced at all, let alone that many had.

22. Meijer, *Marriage Law*, 114. He estimates that there were 1.3 divorces per 1,000 people. Since I have calculated households as having on average of five people, the rate per household is 0.05 percent.

23. On the 1.5 percent rate in Shanghai see SMA C31-2-369, p. 38.

24. Hinton, *Fanshen*, 137.

25. Friedman, Pickowicz, and Selden, *Chinese Village, Socialist State*, 105–6.

26. Ibid., 107.

27. I use the term "raw power" in the sense that Foucault uses it in his opening chapter of *Discipline and Punish*. There he describes a criminal dragged through the streets with severed limbs and the like. This is later contrasted with the "disciplinary power" of the state within "modern" and purportedly liberal institutions.

28. *Baoshan xian zhi*, 153. In Qingpu County, land reform also took place during the last months of 1950. As in the north, violence was a staple of the campaign. Work teams organized 1,072 struggle sessions in the county, peasants hurled accusations at "class enemies," and 437,337 *mu* of land were confiscated. See *Qingpu xian zhi*, 200. In Jiading County there were 565 mass struggle sessions at township level and

above, involving 130,000 people. Close to 5,000 landlords "were forced onstage to be accused and exposed," and 705 were personally subject to struggle. See *Jiading xian zhi,* 615.

29. *Qingpu xian zhi,* 200.

30. *Baoshan xian zhi,* 153–54.

31. SMA A71-2-1859, p. 57; SMA A71-2-1859, p. 65; SMA A71-2-1859, p. 24.

32. TCA 1-2-31, p. 9.

33. TCA 1-2-31, p. 11. For a similar problem in the Shanghai area see SMA A71-2-1859, p. 42. See David S. Landes, *Revolution in Time: Clocks and the Making of the Modern World,* for an explanation of why clocks and watches were unimportant and unnecessary in most areas of China. According to Landes, "It was simply not important in China to know time with any precision—neither life nor work had ever been organized on the basis of hours and minutes" (44).

34. The county gazetteers show very clearly the prevalence of Shandongese cadres in Shanghai's county administration, with 1949 clearly demarcating the shift from local to outside cadres. See *Shanghai xian zhi,* 254–56. In this county, every party secretary from 1949 to 1957 hailed from rural Shandong. Among cadres in 1952, 388 out of 505 (76 percent) had primary school education. Unfortunately, many of the other county gazetteers do not include native place. See *Baoshan xian zhi,* 153, and *Jiading xian zhi,* 615, for the role of courts and the Bureau of Civil Affairs in the land reform and rural reconstruction periods.

35. SMA A71-2-1864, p. 4; SMA A71-2-1859, p. 198; SMA A71-2-1859, p. 214; SMA A71-2-1859, p. 196; SMA A71-2-1859, p. 216.

36. BMA 84-1-32, p. 43.

37. SMA A71-2-1864, pp. 4, 6.

38. SMA A71-2-1859, p. 213.

39. Ibid., p. 214.

40. QPA 11-2-1, p. 11; TCA 1-4-6, p. 22.

41. SMA A71-2-1859, p. 55.

42. Ibid., p. 84.

43. SMA A71-2-1858, p. 5.

44. BMA 84-1-32, p. 41.

45. SMA A71-2-1864, p. 75.

46. For studies of the charivari in Europe see Quaife, *Wanton Wenches,* 186–201; Charles Tilly, *The Contentious French,* 30–36.

47. SMA A71-2-1859, p. 109; SMA A71-2-1864, p. 70.

48. SMA A71-2-1864, p. 83; Songjiang County Archives (hereafter SJA) 8-2-2 (August 1952), p. 26.

49. SMA A71-2-1859, p. 55.

50. Ibid., p. 96.

51. SMA A71-2-1859, p. 109.

52. TCA 3-1-31 (Party Secretary file), n.p.

53. SMA A71-2-1864, p. 82.

54. SMA A71-2-1859, pp. 99, 96.

55. QPA 48-2-31, pp. 85, 120; SMA A71-2-1958, p. 30.

56. SMA A71-2-1863, p. 10.

57. SMA C31-2-60, p. 7.

58. SMA A71-2-1859, p. 68.

59. QPA 48-2-31, p. 93.

60. TCA 1-2-31, p. 7.

61. SMA A71-2-1858, p. 29.

62. TCA 7-1-4, pp. 108–9.

63. BMA 84-1-32, p. 41.

64. SMA A71-2-1855, pp. 38–39.

65. The data on suburban suicide in the early 1950s do not allow for fine-tuned studies of the link between socioeconomic characteristics and suicide. The reports filed by the Suburban Women's Federation Office to the Shanghai authorities include only information on whether or not the person died and the person's sex and address, and sometimes contain an abbreviated case history ("Committed suicide after a family quarrel"; "Is beaten by wife/husband"). I do not know whether this report includes all instances of suicide that occurred within the office's jurisdiction.

66. Olive Anderson, *Suicide in Victorian and Edwardian England,* 45; Howard Kushner, *Self-Destruction in the Promised Land: A Psychocultural Biology of American Suicide,* 95; Riaz Hassan, *A Way of Dying: Suicide in Singapore,* 174.

67. SMA A71-2-1861. For the British case on the falling suicide rates for older women and the rising rates for aging men, see Anderson, *Suicide,* 63.

68. See Frederic Wakeman Jr., *The Great Enterprise: The Manchu Reconstruction of Imperial Order in Seventeenth-Century China,* 568–69.

69. SMA A71-2-1864, p. 70. As one businessman said, "If you have more money you should have more wives."

70. SMA A71-2-1859, p. 96; SMA A71-2-1864, pp. 64, 102.

71. SMA A71-2-1859, p. 89.

72. TCA 1-2-31, p. 14.

73. Ibid.

74. Ibid., p. 10. For a similar example in Shanghai see SMA A71-2-1858, p. 28.

75. TCA 1-2-31, p. 4.

76. Ibid., p. 5.

77. Ibid., p. 6.

78. SMA A71-2-1864, p. 70; SMA A71-2-1858, p. 27.

79. SMA E81-2-117, p. 90.

80. SMA A71-2-1856, p. 69. In North China, where some villages had already begun organizing mutual aid teams, marriage choice was also affected by the language of new political institutions. In Daqiao Village, a female cadre said, "In the past I thought that once you get married you shouldn't separate. Now I understand that love is just like buying cloth in a mutual aid team: you inspect which one is good and then take whatever you please." See TCA 1-4-6, p. 21. Another possibility is that these marriage criteria were inspired by the language of equalization derived not from land reform but from the more "traditional" concept of *mendang huidui*—that marriage partners should have equal status.

81. SMA A71-2-1859, p. 143.

82. Ibid., p. 55.

83. Ibid., p. 10.

84. Ibid., p. 90; SMA A71-2-1863, p. 11.

85. TCA 1-2-31, p. 14.

86. Minhou was a suburb of Fuzhou City, the largest in the province.

87. SMA E81-2-117, p. 61.

88. Ibid., p. 96.

89. SMA A71-2-1855, p. 31; for another example see ibid.

90. See Christina Gilmartin, "Violence against Women in Contemporary China," in Stevan Harrell and Jonathan Lipman, eds., *Violence in China: Essays in Culture and Counterculture,* 203–25; Ann Anagnost, "Family Violence and Magical Violence: The Woman as Victim in China's One-Child Family Policy," *Women and Language* 11, no. 2:16.

91. SMA A71-2-1856, p. 4.

92. SMA A71-2-1855, p. 29.

93. SMA A71-2-1860, p. 90.

94. In her study of the impoverished Huaibei area, Elizabeth Perry suggests that a harsh environment might foster fatalism about the environment (as peasants could not control flooding, droughts, and the like) as well aggressiveness toward elements of the environment that they could control, such as interaction with their fellow villagers. See *Rebels and Revolutionaries,* 45–46.

95. SMA A71-2-1859, p. 85.

96. SMA A71-2-1854, p. 2.

97. As calculated from a report on suicides in SMA A71-2-1861.

98. For a useful review of this literature see Anthony Giddens, "The Suicide Problem in French Sociology," *British Journal of Sociology* 16:3–5.

99. Wolf, "Women and Suicide in China," 112.

100. See the letter written by the great Chinese historian Si-ma Qian to a friend explaining why he preferred castration to suicide after falling into the court's disfavor. In the letter he remarks: "Even the lowest slave and scullery maid can bear to commit suicide." See W. T. deBary et al., eds., *Sources of Chinese Tradition,* 232–34. On the promotion of ideals of female virtue and chastity through stories about women who were willing to take their own lives instead of submitting to humiliation (in the "Biographies of Virtuous Women" and elsewhere) see Mark Elvin, "Female Virtue and the State in China," *Past and Present,* no. 104:111–52.

101. In the more contemporary period, the issue of female suicide became the subject of much intellectual debate, particularly during the May 4th Movement of 1919. The suicide of a woman named Zhao Wujie as the final act of protest to an arranged marriage inspired Mao Zedong to write at least nine articles on the role of women and the evils of the traditional marriage system. See Roxane Witke, "Mao Tse-tung, Women, and Suicide in the May Fourth Era," *China Quarterly,* no. 31:128.

102. SMA A71-2-1861. In Zhennan Township there were eleven suicide attempts between 1951 and 1953 (eight women, three men), but of these, only one woman died; SMA C32-1-4, p. 76.

103. Anderson, *Suicide,* 145.

104. In London people also committed suicide by jumping off bridges and buildings. See Anderson, *Suicide,* 128–29.

105. SMA A71-2-1864, p. 24.

106. SMA A71-2-1863, p. 24.

107. QPA 48-2-31, p. 85.

108. Ibid.

109. For the use of a hunger strike during a Republican-period labor dispute at a silk-weaving factory see Perry, *Shanghai on Strike,* 196. The hunger strike was a favored protest method among Buddhists, and, as James Watson points out, was used by Chinese scholar-officials to protest injustice as early as the Zhou dynasty. Among students, the hunger strike gained prominence during protests of the 1980s, and in 1989 in particular. The above, by contrast, focuses on the hunger strike within the family unit, with little or no consciousness of the relevance of the strike to larger political issues. For the reference to hunger strikes in the Zhou dynasty see James Watson, "The Renegotiation of Chinese Cultural Identity in the Post-Mao Era," in Jeffrey N. Wasserstrom and Elizabeth J. Perry, eds., *Popular Protest and Political Culture in Modern China: Learning from 1989,* 81 n. 4.

110. SMA A71-2-1864, p. 83.

111. SMA A71-2-1859, p. 85.

112. Ibid.

113. For an excellent discussion of women's community in Han villages see Margery Wolf, *Women and the Family in Rural Taiwan,* 32–52.

114. For an excellent discussion of the concept of political theater in the Chinese context see Joseph W. Esherick and Jeffrey N. Wasserstrom, "Acting Out Democracy: Political Theater in Modern China," in Jeffrey N. Wasserstrom and Elizabeth J. Perry, eds., *Popular Protest and Political Culture in Modern China: Learning from 1989.*

115. SMA A71-2-1958, pp. 57–60.

116. SMA E81-2-117, p. 102.

117. Ibid., p. 57.

118. Duara, *Culture, Power, and the State,* chap. 6.

119. TCA 1-2-31, p. 5; TCA 7-1-3, p. 128; SMA A71-2-1859, p. 43; SMA C32-1-4, p. 76; SMA A71-2-1864, p. 6; QPA 11-2-1, p. 5.

120. SMA A71-2-1859, p. 83.

121. QPA 48-2-31, p. 85

122. QPA 11-2-1, p. 81.

123. SMA A71-2-1855, pp. 40, 45. This might be related to the peasant practice of *kan renao,* or "getting in on the excitement."

124. QPA 48-2-31, p. 120.

125. QPA 48-1-13, pp. 100, 102.

126. Ibid., p. 9.

127. QPA 48-2-31, p. 84; QPA 48-2-56, pp. 113, 115.

128. QPA 48-2-31, p. 84.

129. SMA A71-2-1859, p. 96.

130. SMA A71-2-1855, p. 38.

131. Ibid.

132. BMA 84-3-28, p. 8.

133. SMA A71-2-1863, p. 58. Elsewhere in the district, work team officials were investigating several cases of people who were granted divorces "even though they were not supposed to have been." See SMA A71-2-1964, p. 69.

134. TCA 23-1-9, p. 39.

135. SMA A71-2-1859, p. 16.

136. When a township official had a connection to a particular village where someone was divorcing, a divorce case might result in tension between townships and districts. The chief of Shizhuang Township in Kunshan, for instance, wrote a letter to the district government pointing out that "a poor peasant's family spent a lot of money to get a wife. Now you district cadres just allowed her to divorce." See QPA 48-2-31, p. 84.

137. QPA 48-1-13, pp. 101–2.

138. QPA 58-2-51.

139. TCA 7-1-5, p. 20.

140. SMA A71-2-1864, pp. 76, 101, 19–20; also see SMA A71-2-1864, p. 34.

141. SMA A71-2-1856, p. 2.

142. Ibid., p. 3.

143. BMA 84-3-28, pp. 6–7.

144. Ibid.

145. DCA 11-7-224 (1954), p. 4.

146. TCA 7-1-5, p. 20.

147. TCA 7-1-3, p. 8.

148. Yeh, "Corporate Space, Communal Time," 97–122.

149. TCA 7-1-3, p. 127.

150. TCA 7-1-4, p. 109; TCA 1-2-31, p. 15.

151. BMA 84-3-28, p. 4; SMA A71-2-1856, p. 68.

152. BMA 84-3-28, p. 4.

153. TCA 1-2-31, p. 15.

154. Ibid.

155. SMA A71-2-1858, p. 28.

156. SMA A71-2-1859, p. 145.

157. Unfortunately, I did not get precise numbers. I did, however, look at many files of marriage registration forms, and the first thing that impressed me, aside from peasants listing their class status as "fisherman," was the number of men from Subei (listed as Jiangsu) and Shandong who were married to Qingpu women but whose forms were completely blank except for the name and native place. At the time I was more curious about political status (which I did write down) than native place and its role in divorce.

158. QPA 48-1-13, p. 87.

159. SMA A71-2-1859, p. 149. Cadres in Zhenru and Wusong Districts also commented that they "don't agree with veteran cadres who after coming to Shanghai divorce their wives." See SMA A71-2-1859, p. 10; SMA A71-2-1864, p. 70.

CHAPTER 4. FAMILY REFORM IN THE
SOUTHWEST FRONTIER, 1950–1953

1. See Dorothy Solinger, *Regional Government and Political Integration in Southwest China, 1949–1954*, 1–3.

2. *Chuxiong yizu zizhi zhou zhi* (Chuxiong Prefecture gazetteer; hereafter cited as

Chuxiong zhou zhi), 1 : 9. The Yi are a minority group whose members make up close to 50 percent of the population of the prefecture. According to George B. Cressey, as of 1946 only 4 percent of Yunnan's land was arable; see *Land of the Five Hundred Million*, 228.

3. On this point see Stevan Harrell's introduction to his edited volume *Cultural Encounters on China's Ethnic Frontiers*, 22–36. As defined by Harrell, a civilizing project includes "the assumption of cultural superiority by the politically and economically powerful center and the use of that superiority, and the supposed benefits it can confer on the peripheral peoples, as an aspect of hegemonic rule" (36).

4. The history of minority-Han relations were characterized by more than resistance, however. As Stevan Harrell points out, Yi might also buy into the system by taking the official examinations and entering politics. (Stevan Harrell, personal correspondence with author.)

5. Migdal, *Strong Societies and Weak States*, 14, 33.

6. Stephen Cresswell, *Mormons and Cowboys, Moonshiners and Clansmen: Federal Law Enforcement in the South and Southwest, 1870–1893* (Tuscaloosa and London: University of Alabama Press, 1991), 95, 119, 124.

7. James Lee, "Food Supply and Population Growth in Southwest China, 1250–1850," *Journal of Asian Studies* 41, no. 4:715; also see Chi Jen Chang, "The Minority Groups of Yunnan and Chinese Political Expansion into Southwest China" (Ph.D. diss., University of Michigan, 1956), 27–28.

8. *Chuxiong zhou zhi*, 1 : 11; John Herman, "Empire in the Southwest: Early Qing Reforms to the Native Chieftain System," *Journal of Asian Studies* 56, no. 1 : 50–52. A. Doak Barnett, *China on the Eve of Communist Takeover*, 283, discusses the ethnic composition of different topographical areas. According to David Goodman, the *tu si* system was only "marginally successful," as it "strengthened local non-Han feelings of identity (and autonomy) to such an extent that friction between the Chinese and other ethnic groups, and amongst non-Han, often erupted into violence"; see *Centre and Province in the PRC: Sichuan and Guizhou, 1955–1965*, 35–36.

9. This is recorded in the Tengyue County gazetteer, and cited in Joseph Ford, *The Local Histories of Yunnan*, 10. As one *tu si* described his family's relationship with the Chinese: "The Chinese overpowered us, because we did not fight together, and they took from us the Hsiao-chin and Ta-chin valleys. This was the most fertile part of our country. The Chinese began to dig and carry off our gold, which grieved us very much. Many battles were fought, but not enough to drive the Chinese out." See "The Tribes of North-Western Se-chuan," *Geographical Journal* 32, no. 6:596. On Guizhou see Edward McCord, "Local Military Power and Elite Formation: The Liu Family of Xingyi County, Guizhou," in Joseph Esherick and Mary B. Rankin, eds., *Chinese Local Elites and Patterns of Dominance*, 165.

10. *Chuxiong zhou zhi*, 1:11, 145. Violence was not directed only against the Qing, however. On occasion, Hui might fight with Qing troops against other Hui.

11. Philip Kuhn, *Rebellion and Its Enemies in Late Imperial China: Militarization and Social Structure, 1769–1864*. On the militarization of frontier elites see Joseph W. Esherick and Mary Rankin, eds., *Chinese Local Elites and Patterns of Dominance*, 24. See Goodman, *Centre and Province*, 27, on Sichuan; Barnett, *China on the Eve*, 284, on the 1920s in Yunnan. On Long Yun and Yunnan's independent streak during the Re-

publican period see Lloyd Eastman, *Seeds of Destruction: Nationalist China in War and Revolution, 1937–1949,* chap. 1. For a firsthand account of popular militarization see J. McCarthey, "Across China from Chin-kiang to Bhamo, 1877," *Proceedings of the Royal Geographical Society* 1, no. 8:499.

12. The Yi near the Sichuan border were reported to have the most notorious reputation for wanton pillage and plunder. Yi would descend upon Han villages to rob them of their property and women, taking the latter as slaves. As a result, Han communities, and even single residences, were equipped with watchtowers and ammunition. See Alexander Hosie, *Three Years in Western China: A Narrative of Three Journeys in Ssu-ch'uan, Kuei-chow, and Yun-nan,* 66. For another account on Han-Yi tensions see Samuel R. Clarke, *Among the Tribes in South-West China,* 116.

13. On the reassertion of Guomindang control in southwestern cities during the war and after see Solinger, *Regional Government,* 61–63.

14. On the problem of refugee troops see Barnett, *China on the Eve,* 293; on warlord politics see Cornelius Osgood, *Village Life in Old China: A Community Study of Kao Yao, Yunnan,* 201.

15. *Chuxiong zhou zhi,* 2:23. In An County, Sichuan, top government and party leaders all hailed from Shaanxi until the early 1960s. See *An xian zhi,* 460, 506; G. William Skinner, "Aftermath of Communist Liberation in the Chengtu Plain," *Pacific Affairs* 24, no. 1:63.

16. Skinner, "Aftermath of Communist Liberation," 62.

17. On the timing of the PLA takeover and relative absence of CCP officials see Goodman, *Centre and Province,* 39; Solinger, *Regional Government,* 28. On the alliance between the GMD and landlord militia, and on the urban base of CCP power, see Jung Chang, *Wild Swans: Three Daughters of China,* 156.

18. *Chuxiong zhou zhi,* 1:152. The gazetteer's authors emphasize the large disparity between the Han-dominated basin areas and the minority-concentrated mountainous regions.

19. Fei Hsiao-tung and Chang Chih-i, *Earthbound China: A Study of Rural Economy in Yunnan,* 141, 219.

20. Ibid., 25.

21. Ibid., 166. On the presence of women in the marketplace hawking their goods see Gabrielle M. Vassal, *In and Round Yunnan Fou,* 60.

22. Fei Hsiao-tung and Chang Chih-i, *Earthbound China,* 268.

23. H. L. Richardson, "Soil and Man in Western China," *Journal of the West China Border Research Society* 12:123.

24. McCarthey, "Across China," 498. McCord, "Local Military Power," 165. Hosie, *Three Years in Western China,* 37. For early twentieth-century commentators see Fei Hsiao-tung and Chang Chih-i, *Earthbound China,* 46.

25. Yunnan wenshi ziliao weiyuanhui (Yunnan Province historical materials committee), *Yunnan minzu gongzuo huiyilu* (Memoirs of work among minorities in Yunnan), 2:170–71; on the relationship between the Dai and other minority groups in Xishuangbanna see Shih-chung Hsieh, "On the Dynamics of Tai/Dai-Lue Ethnicity: An Ethnohistorical Analysis," in Stevan Harrell, ed., *Cultural Encounters on China's Ethnic Frontiers,* 301–28.

26. Ford, *Local Histories of Yunnan,* 21.

27. Clarke, *Among the Tribes,* 122.

28. Ibid., 123.

29. Chuxiong Prefectural Archives (hereafter CXA) 11-1-14B-1, pp. 107–8.

30. Yunnan Provincial Archives (hereafter YNA) 89-1-82, p. 50.

31. Ba Mo Qu Bu, ed., *Yizu fengsu zhi* (Yi customs), 69–70. Ch'eng Te-kun and Ling Ch'ao-t'ao, "An Introduction to the Southwestern Peoples of China," *Journal of the West China Border Research Society* 16, ser. A:27.

32. Harrell, ed., *Cultural Encounters,* 10–13.

33. Norma Diamond, "Defining the Miao: Ming, Qing, and Contemporary Views," in Stevan Harrell, ed., *Cultural Encounters on China's Ethnic Frontiers,* 100–101; Dru Gladney, "Representing Nationality in China: Reconfiguring Majority/Minority Identities," *Journal of Asian Studies* 53, no. 1:92–123.

34. *Chuxiong zhou zhi,* 1:373; YNA 89-1-36, p. 75; Gao Fayuan, ed., *Zhongguo xinan shaoshuminzu daode yanjiu* (Research on morals among China's southwestern minority groups), 39; Fred W. Carey, "Journeys in the Chinese Shan States," *Geographical Journal* 15, no. 5:490, 494, 509; Ford, *Local Histories of Yunnan,* 7.

35. *Chuxiong zhou zhi,* 1:373.

36. Yunnan lishi yanjiusuo, *Yunnan shaoshuminzu,* 29–30.

37. Clarke, *Among the Tribes,* 130–31. According to the Chuxiong gazetteer (1992), this custom persisted into the 1950s, but even in the 1980s there were remnants of it.

38. *Chuxiong zhou zhi,* 1:373.

39. See Gao Fayuan, ed., *Zhongguo xinan minzu,* 40.

40. *Chuxiong zhou zhi,* 1:373–74.

41. I use "separation" here because "divorce" is a legal process involving formal procedures *in state institutions.* According to Gao Fayuan, prior to the establishment of the PRC minority groups did not go to government agencies to seek permission to divorce. As Stevan Harrell points out in a personal communication, Nuosu customary law had detailed and "formal" provisions regarding divorce, but "divorcing" couples did not have to go to court. Thus I prefer to use "separation" to describe this process.

42. Gao Fayuan, ed., *Zhongguo xinan minzu,* 46; Shi Di, *Shenhua yu fazhi: Xinnan minzu fawenhua yanjiu* (Mythology and legality: Research on legal cultures in Southwest China), 156.

43. Osgood, *Village Life in Old China,* 230.

44. Ibid., 255.

45. See ibid., 277, for the role of family status in spouse selection in Gao Yao, a Han peasant community in Yunnan. Also see Fei Hsiao-tung and Chang Chih-i, *Earthbound China,* 256. On intralineage prohibitions among the northern Chuxiong-Sichuan Yi see Ba Mo Qu Bu, ed., *Yizu fengsu zhi,* 126.

46. See Eviatar Zerubavel, *Hidden Rhythms: Schedules and Calendars in Social Life,* chap. 6. On the French revolution's concern with the reorganization of time see Mona Ozouf, *Festivals and the French Revolution,* 158–96, and Lynn Hunt, *Politics, Culture, and Class in the French Revolution,* 70–71. For the Soviet Union see Hanson, *Time and Revolution.*

47. Wang, *Yunnan minzu gongzuo,* 142.

48. For accounts of resistance to the CCP see *Chuxiong zhou zhi,* 2:106–8; Yunnan wenshi ziliao weiyuanhui, *Yunnan minzu gongzuo huiyilu,* 1:84–98; *Chuxiong zhou zhi,* 2:108.

49. *Chuxiong zhou zhi,* 2:23. District and county-level officials almost always hailed from the Northwest.

50. Ibid., 2:107–9. Solinger, *Regional Government,* 96, cites the figure of four hundred thousand "bandits" killed.

51. This problems was called "experiencism" (*jingyan zhuyi*). See Yunnan wenshi ziliao weiyuanhui, *Yunnan minzu gongzuo huiyilu,* 209; Wang, *Yunnan minzu gongzuo,* 45, 125, 133. According to Wang (68), minority and Han elites intermarried. If this was the case, demarcating class differences between Han and ethnic elites would be an impossible task.

52. CXA 11-1-14B-1, p. 134. Other reports from around the province found local elites in panic, afraid they too would be executed or criticized. See Wang, *Yunnan minzu gongzuo,* 16.

53. The details of the case can be found in CXA 11-1-14B-1, pp. 103–12.

54. Duan Zhengqun, "Women jiejuele Mansao, Maoqin, Manyanghan san zhai de shuili jiufen" (We resolved the water rights dispute among the Mansao, Maoqin, and Manyanghan), 271–73; "Zai Nanqiao shan qu tiaojie minzu jiufen" (Mediating ethnic disputes in the Nanqiao mountain district), 278–81, in Yunnan wenshi ziliao weiyuanhui, *Yunnan minzu gongzuo huiyilu.* It would not be unreasonable to presume there were conflicts not amicably resolved. The above compilation of essays was published by a political organization, and was thus more likely to report on cases of success than failure.

55. Solinger, *Regional Government,* 96; Liu Chunpei, "Kaizhan weisheng gongzuo pianduan" (Developing health work), in Yunnan wenshi ziliao weiyuanhui, *Yunnan minzu gongzuo huiyilu,* 260–62.

56. Wang Lianfang, *Yunnan minzu gongzuo,* 37.

57. Tai Kaiting, "Zunzhong fengsu xiguan juefei xiaoshi yi zhuang" (Respecting customs and habits is no trifling matter), in Yunnan wenshi ziliao weiyuanhui, *Yunnan minzu gongzuo huiyilu,* 174.

58. CXA 11-1-14B-1, pp. 126, 130. Similar events were reported in many areas of the country, including Tianjin, Beijing, Hubei, Hunan, and Guangzhou.

59. *Chuxiong xian zhi,* 2:117. Wang Lianfang writes of three "contradictions" in land reform in border areas: between the party and minorities and GMD remnants/ "special agents"; between different minority groups; and between upper- and lower-class people within minority groups. See Wang Lianfang, *Minzu wenti lunwenji* (A treatise on minority problems), 273–74.

60. *Chuxiong zhou zhi,* 2:115–19.

61. Wang Lianfang, *Yunnan minzu gongzuo,* 31; CXA 16-8-B1, p. 3.

62. Wang Lianfang, *Yunnan minzu gongzuo,* 10–11.

63. Ibid., 59.

64. Ibid., 54. As some cadres said, "We have valley basin experience. Implementing land reform in the mountainous districts won't be a problem."

65. Wang Lianfang, *Yunnan minzu gongzuo,* 89.

66. CXA 11-1-14B-1, p. 134.

67. Ibid., pp. 164, 121–22.
68. Wang Lianfang, *Yunnan minzu gongzuo,* 73, 141.
69. CXA 11-1-14B-1, p. 140.
70. YNA 89-1-15, p. 42.
71. CXA 16-8-B1, p. 2.
72. Ibid., p. 3.
73. CXA 4-1-A1, p. 27.
74. CXA 16-6-B1, pp. 32–33.
75. CXA 4-1-A1, p. 27.
76. CXA 4-2-A1 (1952), p. 80.
77. CXA 16-8-B1, p. 69; CXA 16-3-A1, p. 180.
78. CXA 16-6-B1, pp. 33, 35.
79. YNA 103-1-45, p. 150.
80. CXA 16-3-A1, pp. 18–20; CXA 16-15-B1, p. 137.
81. CXA 16-3-A1, p. 20.
82. CXA 16-15-B1, p. 138.
83. YNA 89-1-24, p. 28.
84. Ibid., p. 45.
85. CXA 16-15-B1, pp. 85, 89; CXA 16-8-B1, pp. 131–33.
86. YNA 89-1-36, p. 40.
87. CXA 16-3-A1, p. 51.
88. CXA 16-15-B1, pp. 135–36.
89. Ibid., p. 13.
90. Ibid., p. 84.
91. CXA 16-3-A1, p. 51; CXA 16-15-B1, p. 141
92. CXA 16-15-B1, p. 17; CXA 16-16-B1, p. 75.
93. CXA 16-15-B1, p. 135.
94. Ibid., p. 14; YNA 89-1-22, p. 26.
95. YNA 89-1-15, p. 40.
96. Most Women's Federation officials at the district and county levels were Han Chinese. With regard to village-level officials, the sources make it difficult to distinguish between Han and ethnic-minority women cadres.
97. CXA 16-8-B1, p. 2; CXA 4-2-A1, pp. 95–97; CXA 16-15-B1, p. 141–42.
98. CXA 16-14-A1, p. 2.
99. CXA 16-8-B1, p. 68.
100. Ibid., p. 69.
101. CXA 4-2-A1, p. 97; CXA 16-16-B1, p. 75.
102. CXA 16-10-B1, p. 39.
103. Cadres, one report noted, "are not clear on what behavior is 'feudal'; they associate feudal behavior with the landlord class." See CXA 16-3-A1, p. 20.
104. YNA 89-1-22, pp. 27–28; CXA 16-15-B1, p. 176.
105. YNA 89-1-15, p. 42.
106. CXA 16-3-A1, p. 18; CXA 16-15-B1, p. 89.
107. CXA 16-3-A1, p. 67.
108. Ibid., p. 184.
109. CXA 11-4-14B, p. 54.

110. CXA 16-3-A1, p. 18; CXA 16-2-B1, p. 61.

111. CXA 16-15-B1, p. 22.

112. YNA 89-1-55, p. 12.

113. CXA 11-4-14B-1, p. 53.

114. See Friedman, Pickowicz, and Selden, *Chinese Village, Socialist State,* 194–95, 251, for the violent culture in rural militia units.

115. For cases see YNA 89-1-24, p. 27; CXA 16-3-A1, p. 52; YNA 103-1-45, p. 149; CXA 16-5-B1, p. 11; CXA 16-14-A1, p. 3; CXA 16-3-A1, p. 181.

116. See YNA 89-1-24, p. 46.

117. In Chuxiong District, in 1953 women accounted for 57 percent of suicide and murder cases (n=119), men 23 percent, and children 20 percent. Close to 37 percent were attributed to "abuse and humiliation." Abuse cases rose from nineteen in January–February 1953 to forty in November–December of the same year. See CXA 16-3-A1, pp. 184, 186. For instances of these deviations from policy see CXA 16-5-B1, pp. 10–11; CXA 16-3-A1, p. 181; CXA 16-14-A1, pp. 3, 5; YNA 103-1-45, p. 149; YNA 89-1-24, p. 27.

118. CXA 16-14-A1, p. 3.

119. CXA 16-15-B1, p. 89. In their investigation of marriage in West Village Township in Luoci County, party officials found relations to be "very chaotic." See CXA 16-15-B1, p. 28.

120. YNA 87-1-82, p. 47.

121. CXA 16-3-A1, p. 188; CXA 11-36-14B-1, p. 84; CXA 4-2-A1 (1952), p. 166.

122. CXA 16-15-B1, p. 84. Marriage registration officials in Wuding County had similar problems. One Zeng Qiongxian's face reportedly "turned red" when he heard about people discussing their marriage problems, and was "too embarrassed to listen and too embarrassed to ask the couple any questions." See CXA 11-36-14B-1, p. 84. Of course, it takes two to tango: there were obviously men who were quite willing to have sex with these women. Reports indicated that demobilized solders were also in the practice of switching partners very frequently. See CXA 16-8-B1, p. 132; CXA 16-15-B1, p. 89.

123. CXA 11-4-14B1, p. 125.

124. The following is based on reports specifically indicating ethnicity, unlike the accounts above, which are vague in this regard.

125. CXA 11-4-14B-1, p. 126.

126. Ibid.

127. Huang, *Civil Justice in China,* 28.

128. YNA 89-1-82, p. 40.

129. CXA 4-2-A1, p. 44.

130. CXA 16-8-B1, p. 68.

131. CXA 4-4-A1, p. 29. Also see the Chuxiong court's 1953 report, "Tiaojie gongzuo baogao" (Report on mediation work), CXA 11-4-14B-1, p. 136.

132. YNA 89-1-15, p. 40.

133. CXA 16-14-A1, pp. 2–3.

134. Nancy F. Cott, "Divorce and the Changing Status of Women in Eighteenth-Century Massachusetts," *William and Mary Quarterly* 33, no. 4:593. Emphasis added.

135. CXA 11-11-14B-1, p. 46.

136. CXA 11-4-14B-1, p. 141; CXA 11-11-14B-1, p. 46.

137. CXA 11-4-14B-1, p. 141; see CXA 11-4-14B-1, p. 126, for the Bulang case.

138. CXA 11-11-14B-1, p. 46.

139. Ibid., pp. 104–5.

140. CXA 16-10-B1, pp. 32–33.

141. CXA 11-36-14B-1, pp. 80–82.

142. For a Yi and Hui case see CXA 16-2-B1, p. 32–35.

143. CXA 4-4-A1, pp. 39–40.

144. CXA 11-4-14B-1, p. 54.

145. Rates are calculated on a household basis. On the 100 percent divorce approval rate see CXA 4-4-A1, p. 38. For the number of couples divorcing in villages in Chuxiong see CXA 16-3-A1, p. 185. In Guangtong County, Dianwei Township, twenty couples out of 304 households divorced (6 percent) in one year; see CXA 16-15-B1, p. 21. On Mianyang District, see CXA 16-5-B1, p. 8. The report indicated ninety-seven couples divorcing in one township (Huaxi). According to the 1992 An County gazetteer (p. 125), there was an average of 2,167 households per township in 1944. In addition, fifty-two adopted daughters-in-law returned home. For the statistic on 14 percent of the Lisu minority in Gezhi Township returning home and demanding divorce see YNA 103-1-45, p. 149. On the increase of cases at the district see CXA 16-3-A1, p. 184. The Chuxiong gazetteer points to a population rise from 1,264,280 in 1952 to 1,430,911 in 1957 without noting the population for the years 1953 to 1956. See *Chuxiong zhou zhi*, 1:314.

146. YNA 89-1-82, p. 50.

147. Court officials themselves complained that a major problem was that "there are few cadres who have a lot to do" *(ren shao, shi duo)*. See CXA 16-2-B1, p. 62.

148. CXA 11-1-14B-1, p. 117. The Wuding County Bureau of Civil Affairs, an agency assigned to mediating Yi disputes, for instance, admitted this problem in a letter to the Provincial Ethnic Affairs Commission: "We have no experience with, nor any method of dealing with, intraethnic disputes."

149. Women's Federation officials confessed to "hating" *(taoyan)* seeing "many women seeking divorce at the gates of the court." See CXA 4-2-A1, p. 97; CXA 11-4-14B-1, p. 126.

150. YNA 89-1-24, pp. 44–46; CXA 16-15-B1, p. 12; CXA 16-15-B1, p. 84; CXA 16-15-B1, p. 17.

151. CXA 16-15-B1, p. 86; CXA 16-14-A1, p. 5.

152. YNA 89-1-15, p. 43.

153. CXA 16-15-B1, p. 19.

154. CXA 11-4-14B-1, p. 126.

155. Doug McAdam, *The Political Process and the Development of Black Insurgency, 1930–1970*, 43.

156. Cited in Michael W. McCann, *Rights at Work: Pay Equity Reform and the Politics of Legal Mobilization*, 7.

157. For Fujian in the high Qing see Melissa MacCauley, "Civil and Uncivil Disputes in Southeastern Coastal China, 1723–1820," in Kathryn Bernhardt and Philip

C. C. Huang, eds., *Civil Law in Qing and Republican China,* 84–109. On Anhui see Perry, *Rebels and Revolutionaries,* 79. John Watt's account of the role of the district magistrate in Qing China similarly points to that official's important legal role, as well as peasants' litigiousness. See *The District Magistrate in Late Imperial China,* 212. Nancy Park's article on popular conceptions of corruption in China argues against the new legal history's emphasis on peasant litigiousness by noting the high costs and risks involved, but nevertheless offers wonderful cases describing peasants going as far as the emperor in Beijing to file suits against a corrupt official. See "Corruption in Eighteenth Century China," *Journal of Asian Studies* 56, no. 4:986–89. For the most comprehensive revisionist account in Chinese legal history see Huang, *Civil Justice in China.*

158. Cited in Jianying Zha, *China Pop: How Soap Operas, Tabloids, and Bestsellers Are Transforming a Culture,* 152.

159. Rae Yang, *Spider Eaters: A Memoir,* 196–98.

160. Engelstein, *Keys to Happiness,* pp. 118–19.

161. Christine D. Worobec, *Peasant Russia: Family and Community in the Post-Emancipation Period,* 130, 138–39, 144. "Bundling," according to Worobec, involved (in some provinces) "nocturnal intimacy between courting couples."

162. Martine Segalen, *Love and Power in the Peasant Family: Rural France in the Nineteenth Century,* 129, 139.

163. Starr, "Turkish Secular Law," 499–500, 518–19.

164. Robert J. Smith, "Japanese Village Women: Suye-mura, 1934–1936," *Journal of Japanese Studies* 7, no. 2:264–65.

165. Ibid., 262–63, 282; also see Ronald Dore, *Shinohata: A Portrait of a Japanese Village,* 166. Some statistical evidence on divorce rates before and after World War II in Japan strengthens my argument concerning a possible causal connection between features of rural living and high rates of divorce litigation. In his longitudinal study of civil action suits filed in Japanese courts, John O. Haley found that "when the ratio of agricultural employment to the total population is included [in the regression], the results show a *positive* correlation [to the number of suits filed]. That is, *lower* rates of agricultural employment coincide with *decreases* (or smaller increases) in the number of new civil actions ... This result is ... inconsistent with the notion that litigation in Japan is an index to modernization, or at least industrialization." See Haley, "Myth of the Reluctant Litigant," 385.

166. Starr, "Turkish Secular Law," 500.

167. Engelstein, *Keys to Happiness,* 121, 124; Worobec, *Peasant Russia,* 120, 129, 190; Beatrice Farnsworth, "The Litigious Daughter-in-Law: Family Relations in Rural Russia in the Second Half of the Nineteenth Century," *Slavic Review* 45, no. 1:57. According to Peter Czap Jr.'s study of courts in rural Russia in the late nineteenth century, Russian peasants generally were "highly litigious," frequently making use of courts to settle interpersonal or land-related disputes. See Peter Czap Jr., "Peasant Class Courts and Peasant Customary Justice in Russia, 1861–1912," *Journal of Social History* 1, no. 2:161.

168. Marc Galanter, *Law and Society in Modern India,* 19–20.

169. See Crawford Young, *The African Colonial State in Comparative Perspective,* 115.

CHAPTER 5. THE POLITICS AND CULTURE OF DIVORCE
AND MARRIAGE IN URBAN CHINA, 1954–1966

1. Vogel, "From Friendship to Comradeship," 46–60; Merle Goldman, writing on the Hu Feng Campaign of 1955, claims that the campaign "went beyond the intellectual community *to indoctrinate the population as a whole* and went beyond urban centers to become nationwide in scope." See "The Party and the Intellectuals," in Roderick MacFarquhar and John K. Fairbank, eds., *The Cambridge History of China*, vol. 14, part 1, *The Emergence of Revolutionary China, 1949–1965*, 239. Shirk, *Competitive Comrades*, emphasizes growing class divisions in schools; and Andrew Walder, *Communist Neotraditionalism: Work and Authority in Chinese Industry*, stresses the role of having good political class in shaping authority relations in factories. Richard Kraus, in *Class Conflict*, argues that, by the Cultural Revolution, class turned to caste.

2. Liu Binyan, "Jiang Zemin's 'Stressing Politics,'" *China Focus* 4, no. 4:1; emphasis added. Also see memoirs by former Red Guards, many of whom were sons and daughters of intellectuals. See, for instance, Liang Heng and Judith Shapiro, *Son of the Revolution;* Zi-ping Luo, *A Generation Lost: China under the Cultural Revolution.* For East European examples see Václav Havel, "The Power of Powerless," in his collection of essays *Living in Truth*, 45, 49.

3. Yang, *Spider Eaters*, 51. Emphasis added.

4. Cited in Geremie R. Barme, "Private Practice, Public Performance: The Cultural Revelations of Dr. Li," *China Journal*, no. 35:123. Emphasis added.

5. Zha, *China Pop*, 139.

6. Xu Anqi, "Zhongguo lihun zhuangtai, tedian ji qushi" (The situation, special characteristics, and trends of divorce in China), *Xueshu jikan* 18, no. 2:157. Her statistics are from the city of Tianjin.

7. SMA C31-2-369, p. 38.

8. Tina Rosenberg, *The Haunted Land: Facing Europe's Ghosts after Communism*, 302–5; Václav Havel, *Living in Truth*, 45–55.

9. Ezra Vogel emphasizes the high risk involved in befriending a person with shaky political reliability. See "From Friendship to Comradeship," 46–50.

10. Howard Becker, *The Outsiders: Studies in the Sociology of Deviance.*

11. For an example in a small political setting see Dean Jaros, Herbert Hirsch, and Dennis Chong, "The Malevolent Leader: Political Socialization in an American Subculture," *American Political Science Review* 62:564–75.

12. Philip Kuhn, "Chinese Views of Social Classification," in James L. Watson, ed., *Class and Social Stratification in Post-Revolution China*, 20–28.

13. Ebrey, *Inner Quarters*, 130.

14. Susan Mann, "Grooming a Daughter for Marriage: Brides and Wives in the Mid-Ch'ing Period," in Rubie S. Watson and Patricia Buckley Ebrey, eds., *Marriage and Inequality in Chinese Society*, 206, 212, 221. As Mann points out, in China as in other societies, "marriage . . . was a contract that aimed above all at reproducing class structures."

15. Hu Feng was a disciple of Lu Xun, one of the most prominent authors and essayists in the 1920s and 1930s. Hu was criticized for trying to loosen party control over intellectuals. See Roderick MacFarquhar and John K. Fairbank, eds., *The Cam-*

bridge History of China, 14: 239–42. On the impact of thought reform on Chinese intellectuals see Robert Jay Lifton, *Thought Reform and the Psychology of Totalism: A Study of Brainwashing in China,* and Merle Goldman, *China's Intellectuals: Advice and Dissent.*

16. BMA 84-3-28 (October 1954), p. 34.

17. DCA 11-7-212 (1954), p. 29.

18. DCA 6-1-36 (March 1957), p. 10.

19. SMA C31-2-417 (1955), pp. 10–11.

20. Ibid., p. 11

21. SMA C31-2-371 (1955), p. 3.

22. "Quanguo fulian huiyi jilu" (Records of All-China Women's Federation meeting), Jiangsu Provincial Archives, 1956. My notes from this document were confiscated by archive officials; hence there is no file number.

23. SMA C31-2-636 (1959), p. 60.

24. On this campaign see Thomas P. Bernstein, *Up to the Mountains and Down to the Villages: The Transfer of Youth from Urban to Rural China.*

25. See Xu Anqi, "Zhongguo lihun zhuangtai."

26. "Bufen zhigong huixiang hou fasheng hunyin jiating jiufen he zisha shijian," (Incidents of suicide and marriage disputes occurring after workers return to the countryside), *Funü qingkuang fanying,* no. 7 (December 1963): 2, SMA. In Shanghai County court, fifty-four of the sixty divorce cases between January and June 1963 were filed by disgruntled spouses of sent-down workers.

27. Ibid.

28. "Linong funü zhong yi zuo jieshao ren wei huangzi cong zhong huoli weifan hunyinfa de qingkuang fanying" (Lane and alley women violate the Marriage Law by becoming intermediaries under false pretenses and reaping a profit), *Funü qingkuang fanying,* 15 November 1963, in SMA C31-2-906, pp. 131–33.

29. CXA 16-77-B1 (September 1963), p. 26.

30. For this distinction see Walder, *Communist Neotraditionalism.*

31. SMA C31-2-228 (December 1954), p. 47.

32. Ibid., p. 39.

33. Elizabeth Perry has identified skill as an important variable explaining the political affiliation of Shanghai workers. See *Shanghai on Strike,* 131–34.

34. SMA C31-2-228 (December 1954), p. 39.

35. BMA 84-3-30 (January 1955), p. 24.

36. DCA 11-7-105 (1955), p. 17.

37. SMA C1-2-1443 (February 1955), p. 14.

38. Ibid.; also see SMA C31-2-417 (December 1956), p. 45.

39. SMA C31-2-394 (May 1956), p. 8.

40. DCA 11-1-67 (April 1956), p. 93.

41. DCA 6-1-36 (1957), p. 9.

42. SMA C31-2-369 (August 1955), p. 11.

43. DCA 11-7-212, p. 29.

44. BMA 84-3-28 (October 1954), p. 33.

45. SMA C31-2-620 (August 1959), p. 33; also see DCA 6-1-36, p. 9.

46. DCA 11-7-212 (1954), p. 28.

47. DCA 11-7-102, p. 17. Family tensions among struggling temporary workers in Shanghai sometimes resulted in suicide. For some cases see SMA C31-2-417, p. 3.

Other evidence for women divorcing men who lost their jobs is in SMA C31-2-228 (December 1954), p. 41.

48. SMA C31-2-620 (1959), p. 77. In Beijing, a woman worker at a printing press wanted to marry someone with "high status and a lot of money." After being married for one year she was divorced, dissatisfied with her husband's income. The Women's Federation complained about her because she took off two days from work in order to make the proper arrangements. See BMA 84-3-28 (December 1954), p. 19.

49. SMA C31-2-228, p. 51.

50. Ibid., pp. 51, 46.

51. SMA C31-2-620 (August 1959), p. 92. Other women, the union found, tolerated philandering husbands and boyfriends, so long as they were able to provide them with money and good clothes, which they could flaunt in front of other workers.

52. SMA C31-2-620, p. 32.

53. On the latter see Richard Posner, *Sex and Reason*, chaps. 5–6; Robert Wright, *The Moral Animal: Evolutionary Psychology and Everyday Life*, 93–107.

54. Potter and Potter, *China's Peasants*, 199, 182–83. Also see Croll, *Politics of Marriage*, 49–50.

55. Dorothy Ko, "Thinking about Copulating: An Early-Qing Confucian Thinker's Problem with Emotion and Words," in Gail Hershatter et al., eds., *Remapping China: Fissures in Historical Terrain*, 60.

56. On the divorce *cum* family values controversy in the popular press see Elizabeth Gleick, "Should This Marriage Be Saved," *Time*, February 1995, 48; Michael Kinsley, "No, Quayle Was Wrong," *Time*, May 1994, 78; and "Happy Families," *New Republic*, 15 June 1992, 6. See also Francine Russo, "Can the Government Prevent Divorce?" *Atlantic Monthly*, October 1997, 28–42.

57. Cited in Croll, *Politics of Marriage*, 42.

58. On the other hand, as Lawrence Stone notes, the bias toward "pathology" in divorce cases has its positive side, since "it is only at times of crises, such as revolutions in society and marital breakdown in families, that the innermost workings of a social system and the values which support it are exposed to the historian's gaze. Moments of crisis and rupture reveal secrets which in normal times remain hidden since they are taken for granted." See *The Road to Divorce*, 28.

59. SMA C31-2-417 (1955), p. 9.

60. BMA 84-3-30 (1955), p. 24; DCA 11-7-212, p. 27.

61. SMA C31-2-394 (1956).

62. SMA C31-2-417 (December 1956), p. 42.

63. DCA 11-7-212 (1954), p. 27.

64. SMA 84-3-28 (1954), p. 20.

65. Ibid.

66. Ibid. There were other cases where relationships were established on an even more tenuous basis. According to the same report as the one on the quilt factory above, some Beijingers went to register their marriage "without even knowing each other's names." See DCA 11-7-212, p. 27.

67. SMA 84-3-28, p. 20.

68. SMA C31-2-417 (December 1956), pp. 43–44. Lesbian relationships were

also noted in Beijing in the early 1950s. One Marriage Law investigation report from that period noted that in one *hutong*, "women married other women." The writers attributed this relationship to "physiological problems" (*shengli quedian wenti*). See DCA, Party Committee File, 20 November 1951.

69. SMA C31-2-417 (1956), p. 12.

70. SMA C31-2-369 (1955), p. 38.

71. SMA C31-2-417, pp. 13–14.

72. YNA 89–1-55 (1954), pp. 8–9.

73. SMA C31-2-228 (December 1954), p. 46

74. Ibid., p. 40.

75. SMA C31-2-417 (1956), pp. 1–2.

76. Ibid., pp. 2–3. All the cases above are of women having affairs while their husbands were in labor reform. What of men whose wives were imprisoned? Unfortunately, the sources do not mention what happened to relationships in this event.

77. SMA C31-2-371 (1955), p. 4.

78. *Shen Amei v. Wang Huaqi* (file no. 35), *Tian Jiaoling v. Hu Huan* (file no. 73), *Pu Liaodi v. Chen Raifang* (file no. 183), Changning District Court, Shanghai, 1965. Summaries of these cases are in the author's personal library.

79. BMA 84-3-28 (October 1954), p. 35; SMA C31-2-371 (1955), p. 8.

80. *Deng Chengfu v. Dong Mingzhen* (file no. 120), Changning District Court, Shanghai, 1965.

81. Zhang Jishun, Zhan Kaidi, and Li Xun, conversations with author, Berkeley, Calif., 1994–1995.

82. Heng and Shapiro, *Son of the Revolution*, 262.

83. Yang, *Spider Eaters*, 136.

84. Karl Marx, "The German Ideology," in Robert Tucker, ed., *The Marx-Engels Reader*, 2d ed., 160.

85. Stephen E. Hanson, *Time and Revolution: Marxism and the Design of Soviet Institutions*, 46–53, 77–81, 90.

86. See "The Soul of Man under Socialism," in Hesketh Pearson, ed., *Essays by Oscar Wilde*, 233.

87. Michael Walzer, "A Day in the Life of a Socialist Citizen," in Nicolaus Mills, ed., *Legacy of Dissent: 40 Years of Writing from "Dissent" Magazine*, 105, 109.

88. On this point see Shaoguang Wang, "The Politics of Private Time: Changing Leisure Patterns in Urban China," in Deborah Davis, Richard Kraus, Barry Naughton, and Elizabeth J. Perry, eds., *Urban Spaces in Contemporary China: The Potential for Autonomy and Community in Post-Mao China*, 150.

89. Wang, "Politics of Private Time," 152.

90. On entertainment in Beijing in the early part of the twentieth century see Sidney Gamble, *Peking: A Social Survey*, 223–41. Similar to the Maoist critique, Gamble begins his chapter by noting: "Many writers in the past have pointed out the lack of wholesome recreation among the Chinese . . . Unofficial amusement frequently involved gambling."

91. Wang, "Politics of Private Time," 153–54. Emphasis added.

92. See E. P. Thompson, "Time, Work-Discipline, and Industrial Capitalism," *Past and Present* 38:56–97.

93. Fei and Chang, *Earthbound China,* 40–43. Elizabeth Perry notes that "gambling had long been a favorite pastime for Huai-pei peasants during the slack season"; see *Rebels and Revolutionaries,* 53.

94. SMA C31-2-228, p. 45.

95. SMA C1-2-1443, p. 17.

96. BMA 84-3-30 (January 1955), p. 24.

97. SMA C31-2-228, p. 46.

98. DCA 6-1-36, p. 10.

99. Li Zhisui, *The Private Life of Chairman Mao,* 173. Mao said this at the 1958 Zhengzhou Conference. See Roderick MacFarquhar, Timothy Cheek, and Eugene Wu, eds., *The Secret Speeches of Chairman Mao,* 471 n. 76.

100. SMA C31-2-521 (June 1957), p. 26.

101. *Yang Liying v. Bao Tianying,* XHA 8-2-300, p. 107.

102. Gamble, *Peking: A Social Survey,* 223, 230.

103. Li Zhisui, *Private Life of Chairman Mao,* 82–83. Li, Mao's physician and an intellectual, on the other hand, held quite a different view. He writes: "My family had always disapproved of gambling, and since middle school I had regarded mah-jongg and opium addiction as two cancers eating away at Chinese society. I had never learned to play."

104. SMA C31-2-369 (August 1955), pp. 13–14; for cases of divorce resulting from men and women gambling and feasting in Beijing see DCA 11-7-10 (1954), p. 14. Such cases were said to be particularly prevalent among workers.

105. *Dongdan, Dongxi qu dashiji* (Chronology of major events in Dongdan and Dongxi Districts), 3:20, DCA.

106. SMA C31-2-368 (1956), p. 9.

107. SMA C31-2-369 (March 1955), pp. 60–61. In working-class Hongkou District, an investigation report noted that there were still marriage problems resulting from bigamy, adultery, gambling, arranged marriages, and conflicts between mother-in-law and daughter-in-law; see SMA C31-2-369, p. 38.

108. DCA 11-7-225 (1954), p. 17.

109. *Tang Lai'a v. Bing Yongquan,* XHA 8-2-300, pp. 122–24.

110. *Ji Meizhen v. Xu Zixian* (file no. 194). Changning District Court, Shanghai, 1965.

111. Li Zhisui, *Private Life of Chairman Mao,* 149; Honig and Hershatter, *Personal Voices,* 206; Mr. Dai, interview by author, Shanghai, 16 February 1994.

112. Changing District Court, cases from 1955 and 1965. Summaries of these cases are in the author's personal library.

113. Zou Yiren, *Jiu Shanghai renkou bianqian,* 116–17. This figure does not include people listed as hailing from "Shanghai."

114. Changning District Court, cases from 1955.

115. DCA 11-7-211, p. 28; DCA 11-7-216 (1954), n.p.; DCA 11-7-213, n.p.

116. DCA 11-7-213, n.p. In another case, residents refused to elect candidates who had good class but were also involved in extramarital affairs. Standards for political officials were, it seems, higher than for the ordinary people.

117. Ibid.

118. Ibid.; SMA C32-1-369 (1955), p. 56.

119. SMA C312-369, pp. 27–28; SMA C31-2-369, p. 15; DCA 11-7-211, p. 26.

120. DCA 11-7-211 (December 1954), pp. 16, 18; DCA 11-1-45 (December 1954), p. 98.

121. SMA C31-2-369, p. 10.

122. DCA 11-7-211, p. 28. Also see Donald Clarke, "Dispute Resolution in China," *Journal of Chinese Law* 5, no. 2:273–74.

123. DCA 11-7-216, n.p.

124. Ibid.

125. SMA C31-2-417, p. 51; SMA C31-2-369, p. 15.

126. SMA C31-2-417, p. 51; SMA C31-2-369, p. 15.

127. SMA C31-2-369, p. 18.

128. Walder, *Communist Neotraditionalism,* 246–47, 166. Also see Hong Yung Lee, *The Politics of the Chinese Cultural Revolution: A Case Study;* Stanley Rosen, *Red Guard Factionalism and the Cultural Revolution in Guangzhou (Canton).*

129. DCA 11-1-45, pp. 105–6; DCA 11-1-67 (1956), pp. 11–12. For similar complaints see *Jumin weiyuanhui tongxun* (Residence committee newsletter), June 1956, in DCA 11-1-67, pp. 43–44.

130. *Chuli renmin laixin fanying huibao,* 11 April 1956, in DCA 11-1-67, pp. 19–20.

131. DCA 11-7-199 (December 1954), p. 5.

132. SMA C31-2-369 (March 1955), p. 62.

133. SMA C31-2-369, p. 32; SMA C31-2-369, p. 62.

134. XHA 8-2-300 (1955), pp. 1–2.

135. DCA 11-7-115 (1957), p. 3.

136. XHA 8-2-300, p. 2. The Bureau of Investigation in Taiwan also noted the prevalence of mishandled cases and inappropriate arrests in courts in the mid-1950s. See "Gongfei yi nian lai sifa gongzuo de qingkuang fenxi" (Analysis of legal work during the last year [1957] in Communist China), document no. 589.8026, pp. 2–3, Bureau of Investigation Archives, Taipei.

137. SMA C31-2-369, p. 62.

138. *Zhou Hubao v. Zhang Changyou,* XHA 39-27-24 (1955), p. 73.

139. *Wang Jinrong v. Dong Jindi,* XHA 39-27-24 (1955), pp. 54–57.

140. SMA C31-2-394, p. 5; SMA C31-2-417, p. 9; SMA C31-2-636 (1959), pp. 97–105. "Second-tier" refers to CCP organizations, district governments, and the Women's Federation. The total number of letters, 217, represents a 300 percent reduction in the number of letters received only by the Women's Federation in 1953.

141. SMA C31-2-620, p. 46.

142. DCA 11-1-67 (1956), pp. 24, 29–30.

143. I thank Gail Hershatter for suggesting the word "composite." Personal correspondence.

144. SMA C31-2-369, n.p. The population of Xincheng was 286, 919 (as of 1950) and that of Zhabei, 243, 206. See Zou, *Jiu Shanghai renkou bianqian,* 125.

145. DCA 11-7-100 (1955), p. 7.

146. DCA 11-7-100.

147. DCA 11-7-212, p. 27. For another case see SMA C31-2-417 (1955), p. 51.

148. SMA C31-2-228, p. 41. Also see BMA 84-3-30 (1955), p. 24.

149. SMA C31-2-228 (December 1954), p. 45.

150. YNA 89-1-55, p. 8. In 1957, the GMD's Bureau of Investigation also noted a "gradual increase in cases involving careless marriages and divorce" (*caoshuai jiehun, caoshuai lihun*). See document no. 589.8026, p. 5, Bureau of Investigation Archives, Taipei.

151. SMA C31-2-636 (1959), p. 20. For similar cases in Beijing in 1956–1957 see DCA 6-1-38, n.p. Nonarchival evidence includes a similar analysis of "rash" divorces in factories. See Gu Zhou, "Lun hunyinfa lingbu hou jiu nian lai chuli lihun anjian de yuanzi" (Principles for how divorce cases should be handled several years after the promulgation of the Marriage Law), *Zhengfa yanjiu* 5:43.

152. SMA C31-2-636 (1959), p. 20. Punishment was also on the mind of another Shanghai nursemaid, Shi Yunzhen. Shi, unlike Dai, received a more sympathetic treatment from the Women's Federation, although not from courts. Shi worked in the home of Gu Su, a worker at the Number Thirteen Cotton Mill. One night, Gu raped Shi, and she had a child. After receiving the letter of complaint, the Women's Federation went to the factory to speak with the party leaders. As a result, Gu lost his party membership. In their discussions with the Women's Federation, Gu agreed to give her 180 yuan for child expenses. Shi was dissatisfied with this arrangement, and went to court to accuse him of rape. The court, however, decided that their relationship involved adultery, not rape.

153. SMA C31-2-636 (1959), pp. 18–20.

154. Xia Wenxiu to the Shanghai Women's Federation, 11 March 1965, SMA C31-2-1064, pp. 1–4.

155. *Wang Songqing v. Tian Jun* (file no. 65/66), Changning District Court, Shanghai, 1965.

156. *He Dinglin v. Shen Baoxin* (file no. 430), Changning District Court, Shanghai, 1965.

157. SMA C31-2-371, p. 20.

158. SMA C31-2-636, pp. 20–21.

159. Correspondence between Zeng Caifeng and Shanghai Women's Federation, SMA C31-2-1110, pp. 20–22.

160. Correspondence between Lu Guiqiu and Shanghai Women's Federation, SMA C31-2-1110, pp. 20–23, 30–36.

161. Heng and Shapiro, *Son of the Revolution,* 9–10.

162. Link, *Evening Chats in Beijing,* 139–42; Yang, *Spider Eaters,* 263, 265–66. When Rae Yang, after spending some five years in the countryside, expressed disillusionment with the party, her mother told her, "Stop! . . . Your thoughts are very dangerous! How come you talk like a counterrevolutionary?" What is particularly striking about this is that these comments were made after her mother had suffered a great deal during the Cultural Revolution. According to Yang, "Mother belonged to a generation that came of age in the fifties. For many of them, the Nationalist Party was corrupt to the core and the Communist Party was the savior of China . . . Thanks to their privileged positions and limited scope, the harsh reality in China did not seem to strike them as hard . . . they not only obeyed authority, they identified themselves with it."

163. Liu Binyan, "Jiang Zemin's 'Stressing Politics,'" 1.

CHAPTER 6. THE FAMILY IN FLUX

1. Key speeches on these developments are "On the Ten Great Relationships," in Stuart Schram, ed., *Chairman Mao Talks to the People: Talks and Letters: 1956–1971,* 61–83; and "China Is Poor and Blank" and "The Question of Agricultural Cooperation," in Stuart Schram, ed., *The Political Thought of Mao Tse-tung,* 343–46, 351–52.

2. "Divorce," according to Honig and Hershatter, was "almost nonexistent in rural areas" after the end of the second Marriage Law campaign in 1953; see *Personal Voices,* 206. See also Johnson, *Women, the Family, and Peasant Revolution,* 157. Parish and Whyte point out that young peasants had more choice in marriage partners; see *Village and Family,* 174.

3. Friedman, Pickowicz, and Selden, *Chinese Village, Socialist State,* 153.

4. Friedman, Pickowicz, and Selden, *Chinese Village, Socialist State,* 153. Potter and Potter, *China's Peasants,* 263.

5. Friedman, Pickowicz, and Selden, *Chinese Village, Socialist State,* 107, 212. Emphasis added.

6. Parish and Whyte, *Village and Family,* 179.

7. Croll, *Politics of Marriage,* 89–92.

8. Potter and Potter, *China's Peasants,* 57, 55.

9. Friedman, Pickowicz, and Selden, *Chinese Village, Socialist State,* 192. According to Franz Schurmann, the household registration system, in combination with the establishment of rural militia and police, resulted in the countryside becoming "under control" by 1955; see *Ideology and Organization,* 443.

10. Vivienne Shue, *The Reach of the State: Sketches of the Chinese Body Politic,* 49. For a similar view of the impact of the household registration system on marriage patterns see Potter and Potter, *China's Peasants,* 305.

11. William Lavely, "Marriage and Mobility under Rural Collectivism," in Rubie S. Watson and Patricia Buckley Ebrey, eds., *Marriage and Inequality in Chinese Society,* 290.

12. For a discussion of the impact of state policies on the increasingly cellular nature of rural society see Shue, *Reach of the State,* 50–53.

13. On the shift to mediation see Mao Zedong, "On the Correct Handling of Contradictions among the People," in Stuart Schram, ed., *The Political Thought of Mao Tse-tung,* 304–12.

14. Cases are in author's personal collection. I am grateful to Xu Anqi of the Shanghai Academy of Social Sciences Sociology Institute for access to these cases.

15. *Nanhui xian zhi* (Nanhui County gazetteer), 219.

16. *Taicang xian zhi* (Taicang County gazetteer), 602.

17. *Chuxiong zhou zhi,* 2:255.

18. CXA 1675-B1 (1963), p. 89.

19. On this policy shift in registration see CXA 11-17-14B-1, p. 146; CXA 11-45-14B-1 (1955), p. 35.

20. After collectivization, when the township became the commune, state cadres there also came from outside, as part of an intracounty "law of avoidance." (Joseph Esherick, personal communication with author.)

21. *Chinese Village, Socialist State,* 188.

22. CXA 11-45-14B-1 (1955), p. 35.

23. CXA 16-12-B1 (August 1955), p. 62.

24. YNA 89-1-55, (1955), p. 35.

25. SJA 8-1-37 (November 1964), p. 139.

26. CXA 16-19-B1 (1954), pp. 138, 141.

27. CXA 16-33-B1 (1956), pp. 10–11.

28. Peasant women had many objections to both late marriage and birth control policies in the early 1960s. In Jiangning County, Jiangsu Province, women complained that "the government's stomach is full and now they have nothing better to do than meddle in trivial affairs" (*chile fan mei you shi zuo, duo guan xian shi*). See Jiangsu Provincial Archives (hereafter JPA) 332 (1963), p. 71.

29. CXA 16-82-B1 (1964), pp. 52, 54–55, 62.

30. CXA 16-33-B1 (1956), pp. 56, 59.

31. "Nongcun hunyin wenti de qingkuang" (Marriage problems in the countryside), *Funü qingkuang fanying*, 30 January 1964, in SMA C31-2-979, p. 88.

32. CXA 16-77-B1, pp. 2–3.

33. *Chinese Village, Socialist State*, 188. The authors argue that rape was covered up because "collectivization made awesome the already great power of party secretaries and militia chiefs. If one thought the party secretary unjust and complained to Raoyang [the county seat], the county party asked the local party to look into it. The accused would be judge and jury."

34. CXA 16-12-B1 (1955), p. 63; YNA 89-1-82, p. 41.

35. The clause required that "consent be obtained" from the soldier "before his or her spouse could apply for divorce."

36. See the Supreme Court decisions in such cases in 1957–1958 in Wang Huai'an et al., eds., *Zhonghua renmin gongheguo falü quanshu* (Compilation of laws of the People's Republic of China), 201.

37. Karen Anderson, *Wartime Women: Sex Roles, Family Relations, and the Status of Women during World War II*, 81.

38. Anderson, *Wartime Women*, 76; Susan M. Hartmann, *The Home Front and Beyond: American Women in the 1940s*, 165.

39. CXA 16-27-A1 (1957), p. 30.

40. In 1954 the Bureau of Civil Affairs in Chuxiong found that welfare work among military dependents was erratic, and in some cases military dependents were ignored altogether. See CXA 16-13-B1, p. 64.

41. CXA 16-12-B1 (1955), pp. 58–59.

42. CXA 11-77-14B-1, p. 22.

43. BMA 84-3-28 (1954), p. 46.

44. CXA 16-13-B1, p. 64.

45. CXA 11-77-14B-1, p. 22.

46. CXA 16-15-A1 (1955), p. 49.

47. CXA 16-13-B1, p. 60.

48. JPA 35 (Women's Federation Files) (December 1955), p. 31.

49. CXA 11-77-14B-1, p. 23.

50. Ibid.

51. Ibid.

52. JPA 35, p. 31; CXA 16-13-B1, p. 61

53. DCA 11-7-405 (1963), p. 2.

54. CXA 11-77-14B-1 (1956), p. 23.

55. CXA 11-87-14B-1, p. 272.

56. "Nongcun hunyin wenti de qingkuang" (The situation concerning marriage problems in the countryside), *Funü qingkuang fanying*, 30 January 1964, in SMA C31-2-979, p. 88.

57. "Nongcun zhong de hunyin wenti" (Marriage problems in the countryside), *Funü qingkuang fanying*, 25 November 1964, in SMA C31-2-984, p. 92. This report was compiled by the Jinshan County Women's Federation.

58. Ibid.

59. CXA 16-75-B1 (1963), p. 102.

60. Ibid.

61. "Nongcun zhong de hunyin wenti," *Funü qingkuang fanying*, 25 November 1964, in SMA C31-2-984, p. 92.

62. CXA 16-77-B1 (1966), p. 27

63. CXA 16-75-B1 (1963), pp. 104–5.

64. CXA 11-96-14B-1 (1957), p. 55.

65. Fei Yuke, "Luetan chuli nongcun diqu hunyin wenti de tihui" (How marriage problems in rural areas are handled), *Zhengfa xuexi* 5–6:57. Emphasis added.

66. Anhui Sheng Gaoji Renmin Fayuan (Anhui Province Supreme Court), ed., *Shenpan jishi* (A chronicle of judgments), 172. As a cotton mill worker on the outskirts of the city, this woman very likely hailed from a village.

67. Gu Zhou, "Lun hunyinfa," 44.

68. CXA 16-27-A1, p. 6; Li Yangxi and Tian Ye, "Hebei sheng nongcun minshi jiufen de diaocha" (An investigation of rural civil disputes in Hebei Province), *Zhengfa yanjiu* 4:33; Gu Zhou, "Lun hunyinfa," 44.

69. Gu Zhou, "Lun hunyinfa," 44.

70. CXA 16-27-A1 (1957), p. 6.

71. Ibid., pp. 5–6.

72. CXA 11-96-14B-1 (1957), p. 55. The extensive quote above is from page 56 of the same report.

73. CXA 16-27-A1 (1957), pp. 36–37.

74. CXA 11-96-14B-1, p. 56.

75. On the liberalization of economic policy after the Great Leap see Friedman, Pickowicz, and Selden, *Chinese Village, Socialist State*, 252–55; Baum, *Prelude to Revolution*, 2–3. According to the new policy, peasant households were given bonuses for anything produced over the state quota. Free markets were also allowed to reopen. In factories, the piece-rate system was reintroduced.

76. QPA 48-2-59 (1955), p. 78.

77. Ibid.

78. See, for instance, *Hebei sheng di si ci renkou pucha shougong huizong ziliao*, for the demographic imbalance between males and females in a North China province.

79. QPA 48-2-59, pp. 78–79.

80. Ibid., p. 81.

81. Ibid., pp. 80–81. In 1955, there were similar developments in Tong County in the Beijing suburbs. "In families," a Women's Federation work report remarked, "young women don't respect or take care of older people"; see TCA 7-1-8 (May 1956), p. 42.

82. Schurmann, *Ideology and Organization,* 442–44; Friedman, Pickowicz, and Selden, *Chinese Village, Socialist State,* 188–92.

83. CXA 16-14-A1 (October 1955), p. 263. On the political criteria for joining mutual aid teams see Vivienne Shue, *Peasant China in Transition: The Dynamics of Development toward Socialism, 1949–1956,* 158–59.

84. CXA 11-96-14B-1, p. 54; Li Yangxi and Tian Ye, "Hebei sheng," 34.

85. CXA 16-14-A1 (August 1955), p. 256; CXA 16-18-B1 (August 1954), p. 168.

86. JPA 35 (1956), p. 28.

87. Huang, *Peasant Family,* 52.

88. CXA 16-18-B1 (1954), p. 168.

89. Li Yangxi and Tian Ye, "Hebei sheng," 33. In her study of the elderly under Chinese Communism, Deborah Davis notes: "Rural residents . . . are strikingly unsentimental and oriented towards the present. Children define their obligations to elderly parents in terms of specific financial arrangements between the generations, frequently focusing on the conditions for the division and inheritance of family property"; see *Long Lives: Chinese Elderly and the Communist Revolution,* 54.

90. CXA 16-65-B1 (September 1958), p. 171. This report was compiled by the *jiancha yuan* of Qilu County.

91. Ibid., p. 172.

92. BMA 84-3-28, p. 40.

93. CXA 11-96-14B-1 (1957), pp. 54, 56. According to the report, twelve out of eighty divorce cases in 1956 were caused by fights between the husband's mother and her daughter-in-law: "The mother-in-law yells at her daughter-in-law over trivial matters, and the latter disobeys." For other mid-1950s cases of women returning to their natal home over arguments with their mothers-in-law see CXA 16-27-A1, p. 29. These cases note that women were "incessantly returning to their natal homes" after arguments, returning to their husbands after several days, arguing again, and once again "returning to their natal homes."

94. CXA 16-65-B1, p. 172.

95. Ibid.

96. JPA 35 (1956), pp. 28, 31.

97. Ibid., p. 30.

98. Ibid., pp. 28, 31. For Chuxiong see CXA 16-27-A1 (1957), p. 30.

99. CXA 16-27-A1 (1957), pp. 33–34.

100. In the sample of court cases from Qingpu, adultery was the main cause of divorce among male petitioners in both 1955 and 1965.

101. Prior to collectivization and the household registration system, peasant women worried that their "freedom" to move between their husbands' and their natal homes would be curtailed. They also worried that "women's rights" would no longer be protected. See CXA 16-48-A1 (December 1956), p. 142.

102. CXA 16-27-A1 (1957), p. 34.

103. Ibid., p. 35. Housing was considered a more serious problem in the city than in the countryside in Yunnan. In divorce, the court noted, "the couple usually requests separation of walls and different entranceways in order to prevent postdivorce conflicts." In one case, the couple agreed to split their room in half. If the woman married again, she agreed to return her half to him. See Ibid.

104. Mordecai Kaffman, Sheryl Shoham, Michal Palgi, and Menachem Rosner,

"Divorce in the Kibbutz: Past and Present," *Contemporary Family Therapy* 8, no. 4: 302–5.

105. For examples of such coercion see Friedman, Pickowicz, and Selden, *Chinese Village, Socialist State,* 216–22.

106. For general accounts of the origins of the Great Leap Forward see Kenneth Lieberthal, "The Great Leap Forward and the Split in the Yenan Leadership," in Roderick MacFarquhar and John K. Fairbank, eds., *The Cambridge History of China,* vol. 14; and Nicholas R. Lardy, "The Chinese Economy under Stress, 1958–1965," ibid.

107. This account is largely based on Friedman, Pickowicz, and Selden, *Chinese Village, Socialist State,* 230–45.

108. See Sheila Fitzpatrick, *Stalin's Peasants: Resistance and Survival in the Russian Village after Collectivization,* 218–21; Mikiso Hane, *Peasants, Rebels, and Outcastes: The Underside of Modern Japan,* 114–17.

109. Cited in *Chinese Village, Socialist State,* 240.

110. For historical evidence of migratory survival strategies in North China, see Perry, *Rebels and Revolutionaries,* 54–58.

111. *Kunshan xian zhi* (Kunshan County gazetteer), 546, 566. The difficult economic situation was also cited in the dramatic increase in cases in Jinshan County, near Shanghai. According to the gazetteer, there was an average of two hundred cases every year between 1954 and 1962, but in 1962 and 1963 there were over four hundred cases per year. See *Jinshan xian zhi* (Jinshan County gazetteer), 696.

112. CXA 16-B1-75 (March 1963), p. 89. Women were petitioners in 57 percent of cases.

113. I am grateful to Joseph Esherick for pointing this out.

114. Lardy, "Chinese Economy," 382. On the ouster of one of the most outspoken members of the politburo, Defense Minister Peng Dehuai, at the 1959 Lushan Conference see Union Research Institute, *The Case of P'eng Teh-huai,* 393–95.

115. Lardy, "Chinese Economy," 388–92. The "Sixty Articles" document was published in final form in September 1962. See Union Research Institute, *Documents of the Chinese Communist Party Central Committee, September 1956–April 1969,* 719–22.

116. Anita Chan, Richard Madsen, and Jonathan Unger, *Chen Village: The Recent History of a Peasant Community in Mao's China,* 26.

117. Most all reports in my collection from this period document, or at least make it a point to criticize, the revival of these practices. The series in Chuxiong labeled "16-75-B1" are particularly useful in this regard.

118. CXA 16-75-B1 (March 1963), p. 52.

119. Ibid., pp. 52–53.

120. In Chuxiong, in the twenty-to-twenty-nine-year-old category, women outnumbered men by roughly two thousand people. See *Chuxiong zhou zhi,* 1:319.

121. Yunnan Province Women's Federation, "Guanyu hunyin wenti de qingkuang fanying" (Marriage problems), *Funü qingkuang fanying,* August 1965, in CXA 16-85-B1, pp. 34–35; on Liangshan, see CXA 16-75-B1 (March 1963), p. 73.

122. "Guanyu hunyin wenti de qingkuang fanying" (Marriage problems), *Funü qingkuang fanying,* August 1965, CXA 16-85-B1, p. 36; CXA 16-77-B1 (1963), p. 57. On Songjiang see "Nongcun hunyin wenti de qingkuang," *Funü qingkuang fanying,*

30 January 1964, in SMA C31-2-979, p. 88. For Jiangsu see JPA 1898 (April 1965), p. 14.

123. SMA C31-2-1106 (March 1966), p. 58; "Nongcun hunyin wenti de qing-kuang," *Funü qingkuang fanying*, 30 January 1964, in SMA C31-2-979, p. 88.

124. CXA 16-75-B1 (March 1963), p. 92. Secondary sources recount similar incidents. In rural Sichuan, a sent-down urban youth recalled a case in which a woman from the county town had "allegedly slept with a lot of city youth as well as peasants, and every now and then in the fields someone would come up with a lewd story about her." See Chang, *Wild Swans*, 419–20.

125. For other cases in both the pre- and post-Leap periods see reports in CXA 11-96-14B-1, p. 53; JPA 35, pp. 29–30; BMA 84-3-28, p. 45; TCA 7-1-8, p. 42; SMA C31-2-469, pp. 69, 72; CXA 11-97-14B-1, p. 64.

126. CXA 16-55-B1 (March 1963), p. 65; CXA 16-75-B1 (March 1963), p. 74.

127. "Nongcun hunyin wenti de qingkuang," *Funü qingkuang fanying*, 30 January 1964, in SMA C31-2-979, p. 88.

128. CXA 16-82-B1 (1963), p. 16.

129. CXA 16-75-B1, pp. 52–53. See CXA 16-75-B1 (March 1963), p. 57, for the Jiujie Commune case. Reportage from the post-Mao period also hints that sex was a major preoccupation of county-level cadres in the early 1960s. In his collection of essays *People or Monsters*, Liu Binyan writes than in Bin County, Heilongjiang Province, "at the meetings of the Standing Committee of the County Party Committee, and at the study classes for Party members at Two Dragon Mountain, all the talk was about women." See Liu Binyan, *People or Monsters?*, 13. Similarly, William Hinton's account of the postrevolutionary years in Long Bow Village in Shanxi notes several occasions in which cadres had multiple affairs and married or had sexual relations with "bad class" women; see *Shenfan: The Continuing Revolution in a Chinese Village*, 43, 665–69.

130. CXA 16-75-B1 (March 1963), p. 73; CXA 16-77-B1 (October 1963), p. 43

131. SMA C31-2-979, p. 88.

132. CXA 16-92-B1 (January 1965), p. 27; for another account see CXA 16-92-B1 (August 1965), p. 26.

133. CXA 16-82-B1 (November 1964), p. 57.

134. CXA 16-75-B1 (March 1963), p. 87.

135. Li Xianqing, interview by author, Jiangpu County, 14 July 1994.

136. CXA 16-73-B1 (August 1963), p. 81.

137. SJA 8-1-37 (November 1964), p. 136.

138. "Nongcun zhong de hunyin wenti" (Marriage problems in the countryside), *Funü qingkuang fanying*, 25 November 1964, in SMA C31-2-984, p. 92.

139. CXA 16-73-B1, p. 81; CXA 16-82-B1 (November 1964), p. 56.

140. CXA 16-79-B1 (April 1964), p. 57. Generational differences also contributed to the absence of class considerations in marriage. According to a Provincial Women's Federation's report, "women see the world in terms of 'old,' 'middle-aged,' and 'young,' rather than class." See CXA 16-55-B1, pp. 65–66.

141. SMA C31-2-1106 (March 1966), p. 58; "Guanyu hunyin wenti de qing-kuang fanying," *Funü qingkuang fanying*, August 1965, in CXA 16-85-B1, p. 37; JPA 1898 (April 1965), p. 15. In Liuhe County, Ma'an Commune, local statistics showed

that there were twenty-two poor and lower-middle peasant households who "are engaged but cannot afford to marry."

142. SMA C31-2-1106 (March 1966), p. 58.

143. "Guanyu hunyin wenti de qingkuang fanying," *Funü qingkuang fanying*, August 1965, in CXA 16-85-B1, p. 37. For evidence of the drug trade see CXA 16-92-B1 (January 1966), p. 27. In some cases, over three thousand *jin* of state food supplies were stolen in order to buy a daughter-in-law.

144. CXA 16-77-B1 (March 1963), p. 58; SJA 8-1-37 (1964), p. 139.

145. In Chen Village in South China as well, poor men had great difficulty in finding wives after land reform and collectivization. Before the CCP, even poorer villagers had found wives because of the general prosperity of the village, but by 1964 "some twenty or thirty Chen men over the age of thirty were still bachelors, with few hopes of ever marrying." See Anita Chan, Richard Madsen, and Jonathan Unger, *Chen Village under Mao and Deng*, 188–89. The authors, however, explain this not by the resurgence of commercial marriages, but by the raising of the standard of living of nearby villages after land reform and collectivization.

146. CXA 16-75-B1 (April 1963), p. 53.

147. "Nongcun zhong de hunyin wenti," *Funü qingkuang fanying*, 25 November 1964, in SMA C31-2-984, p. 92.

148. CXA 16-84-B1 (March 1965), pp. 113–14.

149. CXA 16-79-B1 (April 1964), p. 55; CXA 16-92-B1 (1965), p. 37. One cadre complained, "When a movement comes, everyone says something, even if they have nothing of substance to say."

150. CXA 16-82-B1 (November 1964), pp. 54–55.

151. CXA 16-77-B1 (September 1963), p. 54.

152. Ibid., pp. 40–41.

153. CXA 16-92-B1 (August 1964); CXA 16-92-B1 (1964), p. 49.

154. In a South China village, Richard Madsen points out a similar dynamic: "The accusations flung around and the humiliations inflicted during the Four Cleanups campaign had undermined trust and generated bitterness. Many villagers had ample reason to hate one another and plenty of excuses for seeking revenge." See *Morality and Power in a Chinese Village*, 158.

155. *Chinese Village, Socialist State*, 122.

156. Ibid., 122, 179.

157. Smith, "Japanese Village Women," 282.

158. YNA 103-1-131, p. 110.

159. CXA 16-75-B1 (March 1963), p. 90; CXA 16-55-B1 (March 1963), p. 66.

160. This report is from the "Lianchiang Documents." These material were stolen by Taiwanese frogmen from the coastal province of Fujian. See Richard Baum and Frederick C. Teiwes, *Ssu-Ch'ing: The Socialist Education Movement of 1962–1966*, app. A, 53.

161. Potter and Potter, *China's Peasants*, 183. They write that "an emotion is never the legitimizing rationale for any socially significant action . . . social relationships persist legitimately without an emotional basis, either real or fictive." The anthropologist Ellen Judd, who has conducted research in villages in North China, similarly notes that in the formation of marriages "parents and children weigh numerous factors in a nonromantic manner to find a good match for the children."

See her *"Niangjia:* Chinese Women and their Natal Families," *Journal of Asian Studies* 48, no. 3:533 n. 3.

162. BMA 84-3-28 (October 1954), pp. 45–46.

163. QPA 48-2-59, p. 81.

164. JPA 35 (1956), pp. 29–30. Children who were the product of such relationships were sometimes killed or abandoned by their parents.

165. CXA 16-12-B (1954), p. 55.

166. Yunxiang Yan, *The Flow of Gifts: Reciprocity and Social Networks in a Chinese Village,* 40.

167. This did not go unnoticed by one astute Western observer. M. J. Meijer wrote that even in the late 1950s, "frivolous marriage and divorce were also reported among the farmers." See Meijer, *Marriage Law,* 139.

168. CXA 16-27-A1 (1957), p. 4.

169. CXA 16-12-B1 (1955), p. 62.

170. CXA 16-12-B1 (August 1955), p. 62.

171. CXA 11-96-14B-1 (1957), p. 55; YNA 89-1-55 (1955), p. 37. "Careless marriages," the Lufeng court reported, "were common." Among eighty-six cases, over 70 percent were marriages arranged not by parents, but by the youth in consultation with their parents. In Shuangbai County there were also reports of peasants divorcing four times. See CXA 11-97-14B-1 (1957), p. 64.

172. CXA 16-27-A1 (February 1957), p. 2. Marriage conflicts were said to be handled differently among the Miao and Dai. Miao couples separated from their parents' household after marriage, resulting in fewer intrafamily conflicts. Should a conflict flare, it was "handled within the group, not by going to court."

173. JPA 35 (1956), pp. 29–30.

174. In *Wild Swans,* Jung Chang recalls that "one unfailing topic of gossip" among the peasants was sex. See p. 419.

175. Fei Yuke, "Luetan chuli," 57.

176. YNA 89-1-55 (1955), p. 37. Emphasis added.

177. "Nongcun hunyin wenti de qingkuang," *Funü qingkuang fanying,* 30 January 1964, in SMA C31-2-979, p. 88. The number of divorces reflected this attitude. In one brigade during 1964, twelve couples had either arranged marriages or marriages in which youth consented to parents' choice. Of these twelve, six had bad relationships, and four had already divorced or were in the process thereof. Somewhat ironically, this brigade was called the "Harmony Brigade" (*Hemu dadui*).

178. CXA 16-75-B1 (March 1963), p. 73; ibid., p. 91

179. QPA 66-2-28; QPA 58-2-36.

180. QPA 77-2-9.

181. SMA C31-2-1106 (March 1966), p. 58.

182. JPA 1898 (April 1965), p. 14.

183. CXA 16-55-B1 (March 1963), p. 66.

184. SJA 8-1-37 (1964), p. 138. For other reports on the continuation of lavish ceremonies see SMA C31-2-1106 (March 1966), p. 58.

185. CXA 16-75-B1 (March 1963), p. 87; CXA 16-77-B1 (October 1963), pp. 36–37.

186. For the near absence of Russian peasant leadership in social change see Richard Pipes, *Russia under the Bolshevik Regime,* 374–75; Moshe Lewin, *Russian Peas-*

ants and Soviet Power: A Study of Collectivization, 21–23, 32, 88; Jan Meijer, "Town and Country in the Civil War," in Richard Pipes, ed., *Revolutionary Russia,* 264–65.

187. Here I admit to simplifying the situation for analytical purposes. There were, as studies by Steven Averill and Ralph Thaxton have shown, CCP officials who came from rural areas but also spent some time in the city before returning to the countryside. How the time spent in cities shaped their views on marriage and divorce is difficult to know, and unfortunately there is little accessible information on the personal background of district and court officials (such materials are in party organization files that are not open to foreign researchers). Even openly published county gazetteers do not provide this sort of information. As a result, I have not been able to link the cultural attitudes of a particular judge with the outcome of a specific divorce suit, and have relied instead on class generalizations.

CHAPTER 7. THE CONSERVATIVE BACKLASH

1. Lowell Dittmer, "Learning from Trauma: The Cultural Revolution in Post-Mao Politics," in William Joseph, Christine Wong, and David Zweig, eds., *New Perspectives on the Cultural Revolution,* 19–20.

2. On the tendency of intellectuals to blame peasants for Maoist excesses and China's "backwardness" see Ernest Young, "Imagining the Ancien Régime in the Deng Era," in Jeffrey N. Wasserstrom and Elizabeth J. Perry, eds., *Popular Protest and Political Culture in Modern China: Learning from 1989,* 20; Link, *Evening Chats in Beijing,* 135–39.

3. The literature on the Cultural Revolution is quite vast, so here I will cite only those works that best represent a particular argument. Mao-centered theses can be found in Stuart Schram's *The Political Thought of Mao Tse-tung.* Roderick MacFarquhar's *Origins of the Chinese Cultural Revolution,* vols. 1–3, and Lowell Dittmer's *Liu Shao-chi and the Chinese Cultural Revolution: The Politics of Mass Criticism* are excellent examples of the "elite conflict" school. Hong Yung Lee's, *The Politics of the Chinese Cultural Revolution: A Case Study* and Stanley Rosen's *Red Guard Factionalism and the Cultural Revolution in Guangzhou (Canton)* combine both of these approaches. Another important work in the sociological vein is Richard Kraus's *Class Conflict in Chinese Socialism,* which emphasizes the role of political class in the formation of antagonistic status groups. Cleavages between winners and losers under the socialist system are discussed in Perry, *Shanghai on Strike,* 253–258, "Shanghai's Strike Wave," and *Proletarian Power.*

4. Elizabeth Perry, "Casting a 'Democracy' Movement: The Role of Students, Workers, and Entrepreneurs," in Jeffrey Wasserstrom and Elizabeth Perry, eds., *Popular Protest and Political Culture in Modern China: Learning from 1989,* 148; Madsen, *Morality and Power,* 174.

5. Given that Madsen (and his collaborators in the writing of *Chen Village*) studied only one village, it is difficult to know just how generalizable the conclusions are nationwide. It is also problematic that the main source regarding peasants' moral universe is an urban-educated youth—Ao Meihua—who spent several years there and then left. In general terms, Madsen sees the Cultural Revolution in Chen Vil-

lage as the final tear in an "extremely fragile" moral fabric composed of Confucian tradition and "a version of Maoist orthodoxy." His discussion of actual conflict during the GPCR, however, focuses largely on the issue of personal revenge, albeit motivated in part by morally conceived imperatives. I discuss this issue later in the chapter.

6. Translated in *Foreign Broadcast Information Service,* 2 June 1966, 3.

7. P'an Tz'u-nien, "Long Live the Red Guards," *Renmin ribao,* 9 April 1967, translated in U.S. Consul General, Hong Kong, *Selections from Chinese Mainland Press* (hereafter *SCMP*), no. 3923:13.

8. See Anne Thurston, *Enemies of the People: The Ordeal of Intellectuals in China's Great Cultural Revolution,* 121–22. See the photo of Jung Chang in worker's garb in Chang, *Wild Swans,* 191–92. The way Red Guards from intellectual backgrounds tried to be more "working class" by wearing dirty clothing occurred in other movements associated with the intellectual upper-class left. Writing about the socialist movement in postwar England, George Orwell lamented: "It is a pity that those who idealize the working class so often think it necessary to praise every working class characteristic and therefore to pretend that dirtiness is somehow meritorious in itself." See *The Road to Wigan Pier,* 130.

9. Mao's instruction to broaden the Red Guard movement can be found in "Talk to Leaders of the Centre," in Stuart Schram, ed., *Chairman Mao Talks to the People: Talks and Letters, 1956–1971,* 253–55. Mao's big character poster calling on the masses to "Bombard the Headquarters" was posted in August 1966; see p. 345 in the above volume for references to the actual text.

10. One of Anne Thurston's interviewees commented, "We were young. We were fanatics. We believed that Chairman Mao was great, that he held the truth. I believed in everything Mao said." See Thurston, *Enemies of the People,* 96.

11. Davis, "Rites of Violence," 183–84.

12. Simon Schama, *Citizens: A Chronicle of the French Revolution,* 860. This was a reference to Marie Antoinette. For the "counterrevolutionary" charge see Hunt, *Politics, Culture, and Class,* 84.

13. Eric Hobsbawm, "Man and Woman in Socialist Iconography," *History Workshop,* no. 6:127–28.

14. George Mosse, *Nationalism and Sexuality,* chaps. 6 and 7. The theme of "purification" during the GPCR (albeit without reference to sexuality) has been argued very persuasively by Robert Jay Lifton in his *Revolutionary Immortality.*

15. For an example of such art in the PRC see the work of Yang Shengrong "Ouyang Hai" (1964) in Ellen Johnston Liang's, *The Winking Owl: Art in the People's Republic of China.* For other examples of Cultural Revolution art see Julia Andrews, *Painters and Politics in the People's Republic of China,* chap. 6. For Red Guard art see the tabloid newspaper *Wei dong,* 26 May 1967.

16. Ken Ling [pseud.], *The Revenge of Heaven: Journal of a Young Chinese,* 316.

17. Gordon Bennett and Ronald Monteperto, *Red Guard: The Political Biography of Dai Hsiao-ai,* 96; Ling, *Revenge of Heaven,* 173.

18. The irony of revolutionary youth using the symbols of traditional culture to destroy traditional culture has also been noted by Maurice Meisner. Meisner writes that "it may have been the case that the traditional forms and archaic rituals had a

greater impact on popular consciousness . . . than the new revolutionary values which Mao and Maoists hoped to impart." See Meisner's *Marxism, Maoism, and Utopianism: Eight Essays,* 169.

19. On the gendered nature of these images see Marilyn Young, "Chicken Little in China: Some Reflections on Women," in Arif Dirlik and Maurice Meisner, eds., *Marxism and the Chinese Experience: Issues in Contemporary Chinese Marxism,* 262; R. David Arkush, "Love and Marriage in North Chinese Peasant Opera," in Perry Link, Richard Madsen, and Paul Pickowicz, eds., *Unofficial China: Popular Culture and Thought in the People's Republic,* 81; Anagnost, "Family Violence and Magical Violence," 18. Such views of the female body, and the danger it posed to men and the social order, were also common in early modern Europe. According to Natalie Davis, "every physician knew in the sixteenth century [that] the female was composed of cold and wet humors . . . and coldness and wetness meant a changeable, deceptive, and tricky temperament. Her womb was like a hungry animal; when not amply fed by sexual intercourse or reproduction, it was likely to wander about her body, overpowering her speech and senses . . . her disorderliness led her into the evil arts of witchcraft, so ecclesiastical authorities claimed." Davis, *Society and Culture in Early Modern France,* 124–25.

20. This does not suggest that these symbols formed a *coherent* sexual message to youth. In fact, it is not important whether these symbols were coherent; people can be mobilized for a cause without realizing the inconsistency or incoherence of political messages. Images, according to John Dower, might be even more powerful when they are "quick, disjointed, and condensed." See Dower's *War without Mercy: Race and Power in the Pacific War,* 28. On the "multivalent" character of images in the French Revolution see Hunt, *Politics, Culture, and Class,* 104. E. P. Thompson, discussing the status of images as a causal variable in the study of history, writes: "Imagery is itself evidence of powerful subjective motivations, fully as 'real' as the objective, fully as effective . . . in their historical agency. It is the sign of how men felt and hoped, loved and hated, and of how they preserved certain values in the very texture of their language." See Thompson, *The Making of the English Working Class,* 49.

21. See Margie Sargeant, "The Cultural Revolution in Heilongkiang," in *The Cultural Revolution in the Provinces,* 45.

22. *Renmin ribao,* 5 September 1966.

23. *SCMP,* supp. 178:21; *SCMP,* no. 3905:10. On Zhou Enlai's role in the torture of senior party members see Michael Schoenhals, "The Central Case Examination Group, 1966–1979," *China Quarterly,* no. 145:87–111.

24. Thurston, *Enemies of the People,* 96. For similar uncertainly see Bennett and Monteperto, *Red Guard,* 36.

25. For a useful summary of this position see Elizabeth J. Perry, "Introduction," in Jeffrey Wasserstrom and Elizabeth Perry, eds., *Popular Protest and Political Culture in Modern China: Learning from 1989,* 4–6. In general terms, for new cultural historians, culture is best seen as an arena of contestation between social actors; culture, they argue, is *not* a cause, or an independent variable, but rather something in flux and subject to power and authority relations.

26. Hunt, *Politics, Culture, and Class,* Ozouf, *Festivals and the French Revolution,* and Jeffrey Wasserstrom, *Student Protest in 20th Century China: The View from Shanghai,* are good examples of this scholarship.

27. The following account is in Gao Yuan, *Born Red: A Chronicle of the Cultural Revolution*, 68–76.

28. Mary Ryan, "The American Parade," in Lynn Hunt, ed., *The New Cultural History*, 139.

29. Gao Yuan, *Born Red*, 76. This case, vivid as it is, is still somewhat problematic for the purposes of the argument about conflicting sexual cultures because I do not know Ding Yi's personal history. My case would be weakened if he was also an intellectual.

30. Thurston, *Enemies of the People*, 228–29. Although much of the physical violence was by males, young women contributed to the atmosphere of sexual puritanism that led to these attacks. Jung Chang comments that the Cultural Revolution "also produced a large number of militant puritans, mostly young women." See Chang, *Wild Swans*, 317.

31. Zi-ping Luo, *A Generation Lost*, 20.

32. Liang Heng and Judith Shapiro, *Son of the Revolution*, 47.

33. Yue Daiyun, with Carolyn Wakeman, *To the Storm: The Odyssey of a Revolutionary Chinese Woman*, 207.

34. Gao Yuan, *Born Red*, 146.

35. Ling, *Revenge of Heaven*, 135–38.

36. Liu's marriage to Wang was yet another example of the absence of political concerns in marriage among top cadres. Wang's family was quite well off. She was educated at Beijing's Furen University (which was founded by Catholics), studied physics, and was reported to be a social butterfly. See Ling, *Revenge of Heaven*, 221; Li Zhisui, *Private Life of Chairman Mao*, 661.

37. Ling, *Revenge of Heaven*, 207.

38. "The Three Trials of Wang Kuang-mei," in U.S. Consul General, Hong Kong, *Current Background* (hereafter *CB*), no. 848:5.

39. Li Zhisui, *Private Life of Chairman Mao*, 175. According to Li, their mutual animosity resulted from Jiang Qing's jealousy over Wang's sociability toward other top leaders, including her husband: "Wang Guangmei would greet Mao warmly whenever she saw him and sometimes swam with him out to the platform. Jiang Qing made little effort to hide her displeasure with Liu's wife and I sensed a certain jealousy towards her." For another account portraying Jiang Qing as the main protagonist behind the struggle session see Yen Chia-chi and Kao Kao, *The Ten Year History of the Chinese Cultural Revolution*, 155–56.

40. Ling, *Revenge of Heaven*, 214.

41. Ibid., 219–20; Thurston, *Enemies of the People*, 123.

42. For a comprehensive list of Liu's political crimes see Richard Baum, "The Cultural Revolution in the Countryside: Anatomy of a Limited Rebellion," in Thomas W. Robinson, ed., *The Cultural Revolution in China*, 370 n. 3.

43. "A Glimpse of the Wicked Family," in U.S. Consul General, Hong Kong, *Selections from Chinese Mainland Magazines* (hereafter *SCMM*), no. 574 (1967): 4. The article was translated from the Canton newspaper *Ba-er-wu zhan bao* (August 25 battle news).

44. "Uncovering the Inside Story of the So-Called High Ranking Cadres' Club at Yangfangchiatou: Misdeeds of Liu Shao-ch'i, Teng Hsiao-p'ing, and P'eng Chen," *SCMM*, no. 576 (1967): 4, 6.

45. "T'ao Chu's 6 Major Crimes against the Thought of Mao Tse-tung, the Party, and Socialism," *SCMM*, no. 578 (1967): 28, 31

46. Liu Xiangdong, "Look! What Is Hidden in the Dark Recesses of Tseng Sheng's Soul," *SCMP*, no. 4018 (1967): 5–7.

47. "Collection of Materials against Ho Long," *CB*, no. 859 (August 1968): 5, 25–26.

48. Zhen Zhaihua, *Red Flower of China*, 96.

49. Chan, Madsen, and Unger, *Chen Village under Mao and Deng*, 103–7. "Even bedded down together" is cited on p. 125.

50. Ibid., 105–8. Richard Baum also describes the frustrations of these youth; see "Cultural Revolution in the Countryside," 395–96.

51. For similar cases in other part of China see Baum, "Cultural Revolution in the Countryside," 377.

52. Chan, Madsen, and Unger, *Chen Village under Mao and Deng*, 138; Baum, "Cultural Revolution in the Countryside," 408. Whether these events were factual or only representations or metaphors for "chaos" (*luan*) is difficult to know for sure. More important from my perspective was that the educated youth were disturbed by such events, even if the "rumors" were unsubstantiated.

53. The following account is based on Chan, Madsen, and Unger, Chen Village *under Mao and Deng*, 138–40.

54. Bai Hua, *A Remote Country of Women*, 7–8.

55. Ibid., 8.

56. Ibid.

57. Ibid., 9.

58. Ibid., 10.

59. On the persistence of corruption after the Four Cleanups see Baum, "Cultural Revolution in the Countryside," 373.

60. Ibid., 402; for other incidents of peasant attacks on the party see pp. 378, 408, 421. Such attacks are recounted in many gazetteers. See for example, *Chuxiong zhou zhi*, 2:146–47.

61. Chen Jo-hsi, *The Execution of Mayor Yin and Other Stories from the Great Proletarian Cultural Revolution*, 16.

62. Cited in Richard Madsen, "The Politics of Revenge in Rural China during the Cultural Revolution," in Jonathan Lipman and Stevan Harrell, eds., *Violence in China*, 191.

63. Heng and Shapiro, *Son of the Revolution*, 182.

64. Ibid., 183–84. For other examples of peasant resentment concerning restrictions on cultivation of private plots see Baum, "Cultural Revolution in the Countryside," 396.

65. Heng and Shapiro, *Son of the Revolution*, 184, 185–86. Rae Yang seems to hold a similar view of the locus of political opposition in China. She writes, "Only a small group of people, often those who are privileged, can afford to raise questions, challenge and defy authority." See *Spider Eaters*, 254.

66. Baum, "Cultural Revolution in the Countryside," 392.

67. Cited in Baum, "Cultural Revolution in the Countryside," 412.

68. Ibid., 403, 452.

69. White, *Policies of Chaos*, 270.

70. Anne Thurston, "Urban Violence during the Cultural Revolution: Who Is to Blame?" in Jonathan Lipman and Stevan Harrell, eds., *Violence in China: Essays in Culture and Counterculture,* 150–51.

71. Madsen, "Politics of Revenge," 194–95.

72. Yue Daiyun, *To the Storm,* 161.

73. Ling, *Revenge of Heaven,* 18.

74. Gao Yuan, *Born Red,* 226.

75. Ibid., 289–90.

76. Luo, *A Generation Lost,* 30–31.

77. Heng and Shapiro, *Son of the Revolution,* 130.

78. Gao Yuan, *Born Red,* 213.

79. Thurston, *Enemies of the People,* 136. In Bai Hua's *Remote Country of Women,* he describes cases in Yunnan in which some women were castrated by Red Guards (4). Given that this is a work of fiction, this may or may not be true.

80. Ling, *Revenge of Heaven,* 262. Such terms were also used in Hunan. Liang Heng's sister was called a "little crossbreed" because of her mixed-class background. See Heng and Shapiro, *Son of the Revolution,* 73.

81. Gao Yuan, *Born Red,* 285, 289.

82. Yang, *Spider Eaters,* 137–38.

83. Chang, *Wild Swans,* 317.

84. Judith Stacey, in contrast, attributes the CCP's "stringent sexual code" in part to the party's effort to appeal to "traditional patriarchal peasant values," since peasant men were those who insisted that their wives and women remain pure. See *Patriarchy and Socialist Revolution,* 187–88.

85. Li Zhisui, *Private Life of Chairman Mao,* 294–95, 307, 444.

86. Baum, "Cultural Revolution in the Countryside," 453–68.

87. For incidents of cannibalism in Guangxi Province see Zheng Yi, *A Scarlet Memorial: Tales of Cannibalism in Modern China.*

88. See Perry, "Casting a 'Democracy' Movement," 148. She writes: "In fact . . . most of China's twentieth-century political follies have been centered in the cities, where intellectuals themselves have played a central role. Certainly this was true for the Cultural Revolution; not ignorant peasants but educated students proved the most zealous disciples of Chairman Mao."

89. For a discussion of intellectuals' tendency to see themselves as martyrs for a higher cause while denigrating others who participate for more bread-and-butter issues see Perry, "Casting a 'Democracy Movement," 152.

90. Incidents of individual intellectuals' suicides can be found in Thurston, *Enemies of the People,* 139–40; Gao Yuan, *Born Red,* 57–58; Luo, *A Generation Lost,* 31. B. Michael Frolic, *Mao's People: Sixteen Portraits of Life in Revolutionary China,* 78–79.

91. Feng Jicai, *Voices from the Whirlwind: An Oral History of the Chinese Cultural Revolution,* 38–45.

92. Thurston, *Enemies of the People,* 120.

93. Feng Jicai, Voices from the Whirlwind, 40.

94. Bai Hua, *Remote Country of Women,* 3.

95. See, for instance, Elizabeth Perry and Li Xun, *Proletarian Power: Shanghai in Cultural Revolution,* 61–62.

CHAPTER 8. CONCLUSION

1. Among these were Stephen Skowronek, *Building a New American State: The Expansion of National Administrative Capacities, 1877–1920;* Skocpol, *States and Social Revolution;* Dietrich Rueschemeyer and Peter Evans, "The State and Economic Transformation: Toward an Analysis of the Conditions Underlying Effective Intervention," in Peter Evans, Dietrich Rueschemeyer, and Theda Skocpol, eds., *Bringing the State Back In,* 44–77; Johnson, *MITI and the Japanese Miracle.*

2. Another example of rural women's power to act upon their collective interests is the antiliquor protests in India in the early 1990s. According to one report, "the protest began in a handful of villages where women in a government literacy program read a fictitious story about a young heroine who mobilized women in her village to close the local liquor shop where husbands passed evenings spending money on liquor rather than on food for their families. Many of the women recognized themselves in the story, and began discussing the domestic violence that came with their husbands' drunkenness . . . the village women began attacking the liquor shops, pouring the booze into the streets and shaving the heads of men found drunk there . . . groups of women seized drunken patrons [of liquor shops], wrapped their skirts around them and paraded them through villages on donkeys to humiliate them." See Molly Moore, "India's Anti-Liquor Women Start a Social Revolution," *International Herald Tribune,* 20 December 1993, 1.

3. For a more positive view of early CCP rule see Suzanne Pepper, *Civil War in China: The Political Struggle, 1945–1949.*

4. The term "officials in action" was originally used by John Commons in *The Legal Foundations of Capitalism* and later cited in Skowronek, *Building a New American State,* 24; emphasis added. See also Esherick, "Deconstructing the Construction," 1053; Esherick and Wasserstrom, "Acting Out Democracy," 54.

5. R. Keith Schoppa, *Blood Road: The Mystery of Shen Dingyi in Revolutionary China,* 7.

6. See Liu Binyan, *Higher Kind of Loyalty,* 28, 91. He writes that in the early years of the PRC, the CCP "commanded the faith and following of almost every stratum of the population . . . As a member of the Communist Party, I took for granted that such a relationship between the Party and the population would be permanent."

7. Kevin O'Brien and Lianjiang Li, "The Politics of Lodging Complaints in Rural China," *China Quarterly,* no. 143:761 n. 18.

8. See Chalmers Johnson, *Peasant Nationalism and Communist Power.*

9. Daniel Chirot, "What Happened in Eastern Europe in 1989," in Daniel Chirot, ed., *The Crises of Leninism and the Decline of the Left: The Revolutions of 1989,* 15; for Chinese intellectuals see the writings of the Chinese astrophysicist and "democracy" advocate Fang Lizhi in Richard C. Kraus, "The Lament of Astrophysicist Fang Lizhi," in Arif Dirlik and Maurice Meisner, eds., *Marxism and the Chinese Experience,* 294–315.

10. Stacey, *Patriarchy and Peasant Revolution,* 188.

11. Joel Migdal, in his *Strong Societies and Weak States,* rightly focuses on the difficulties state leaders encounter when trying to modernize, but does not pay enough attention to the wide variation in types of local leaders and different sorts of communities, some of which may want to "draw the state into" their communities

for their own goals. In his contributions to Joel Migdal, Atul Kohli, and Vivienne Shue, eds., *State Power and Social Forces: Domination and Transformation in the Third World,* he corrects this omission.

12. Susan Mann, "Widows in the Kinship, Class, and Community Structures of Qing Dynasty China," *Journal of Asian Studies* 46, no. 1:44; Davis-Friedmann, *Long Lives,* 49. Scholars of peasant society elsewhere have also underestimated emotive bonds between parents and children. Eugen Weber argues that what bound the French peasant family was basically "need and greed." See *Peasants into Frenchmen,* 176.

13. Wolf, *Revolution Postponed,* 1–2.

14. See Ida Pruitt, *A Daughter of Han: The Autobiography of a Chinese Working Woman,* 31–32, 40–42, 50. For similar cases in rural Taiwan see Emily Ahern, "The Power and Pollution of Chinese Women," in Margery Wolf and Roxane Witke, eds., *Women in Chinese Society,* 199–200.

15. Judd, *"Niangjia:* Chinese Women," 525–37.

16. Arkush, "Love and Marriage," 78.

17. This was conveyed to me in conversations with Chinese sociologists specializing in marriage relations and is confirmed in the marriage registration and court records I collected for various years in Qingpu County. In a sample of twenty-five cases from 1957, sixteen out of twenty-five couples divorced within five years; in a sample of forty cases from 1985 and 1989 (twenty from each year), twenty couples divorced within five years, and ten between the sixth and tenth year. These records also show that over 60 percent of divorce cases involved children (of both sexes). Children were probably some deterrent to divorce, but the records show enough cases involving custody arrangements to demonstrate that they would not prevent a determined woman from taking advantage of her individual rights to seek divorce.

18. Judd, *"Niangjia:* Chinese Women," 542. Emphasis added.

19. Parish and Whyte, *Village and Family,* 184.

20. Hinton, *Shenfan,* 96.

AFTERWORD

1. Cited in *China News Digest—Europe/Pacific,* 13 August 1995 (http://www. cnd. org); Seth Faison, "In China, Rapid Social Changes Bring a Surge in the Divorce Rate," *New York Times,* 22 August 1995, 1,6.

2. Ma Jianjun, interview by author, February 1994; Cailian Liao and Tim B. Heaton, "Divorce Trends and Differentials in China," *Journal of Comparative Family Studies* 23, no. 3:425–26. Basing their report on the "China In-Depth Fertility Study" of 1985, they conclude: "Women with higher education, especially those residing in urban areas, experience higher divorce rates."

3. According to the 1980 Marriage Law, "complete alienation of mutual affection" (*ganqing polie*) was the main criterion by which courts would evaluate the reasonableness of divorce. In dealing with such cases, however, courts were enjoined to "try to bring about a reconciliation between the parties" through mediation.

4. Chinese sexual prudery was brought to the attention of the American public through best-sellers such as Fox Butterfield's *China: Alive in Bitter Sea.* According to

Butterfield, official puritanism was the result of love and sex being "equated with being cheap and bourgeois, with promiscuity; they are unrevolutionary, not worthy of brave hearts that should be beating with thoughts of building a new socialist nation." He gives an example of a high school student who asked for advice from *China Youth News:* "Dear Comrade: I've already fallen in love with a girl student. But I don't have the courage to break off relations. What shall I do?" In response, a high school teacher wrote, "You have to make a decision. High school is a time of high aspiration. If you fall in love now, you will lose precious time . . . You should concentrate on training yourself to be useful to the motherland" (142–43). At issue here, I suggest, is not so much the issue of revolutionary or not, but the social *class* of the writer. This teacher's advice is hauntingly similar to advice handed out by intellectuals about love and divorce in the May 4th Movement, the 1920s, and the 1950s. I cannot imagine county or district officials relating "love" to the "motherland" in such a manner.

5. One such name was *tuo you bing*—a hot cake taken out of the oil. Throughout the 1980s and early 1990s there were very few changes in the structure and role of the *danwei.* Only in the mid-1990s has the *danwei* become less important to the everyday lives of intellectuals. On Shanghai housing problems see Yanjie Bian, John Logan, Hanlong Lu, Yunkang Pan, and Ying Guan, "Work Units and Housing Reform in Two Chinese Cities," in Xiaobu Lü and Elizabeth J. Perry, eds., *Danwei: The Changing Chinese Workplace in Historical and Comparative Perspective,* 223–50.

6. L.P., interview by author, 19 April 1994; N.B., interview by author, 14 April 1994; Jing'an Women's Federation, interview by author, 16 April 1994. According to a report in *China News Digest,* a survey of six thousand people in Shanghai conducted by the Shanghai Academy of Social Sciences showed that 41.2 percent had considered divorce but then backed away from the idea after they considered the economic costs and housing problems. See *China News Digest—Global,* 3 November 1997 (http://www.cnd.org).

7. P.A., interview by author, Nanjing, 12 July 1994.

8. Evidence shows that it is probably best to avoid these institutions. In a report on domestic violence, a lawyer tells of a case involving a woman whose husband beat her when she refused to have sex with him. The "old ladies" in the residence told her that it was basically the man's right to demand sex and that the fault lay with her. See Xiu Linfeng, "Jiating baoli cunzai de yuanyin qianxi" ("Rudimentary analysis of the causes of domestic violence"), typescript. According to another analysis, many of these elderly mediators are increasingly reluctant to bother with such disputes because they have been influenced by "market mentality": they are unwilling to serve unless they receive better monetary or other forms of compensation. Many of them receive little to no support from family members, who see no point in their roles. See Huang Deyuan, "Shishu shichang jingji dui renmin tiaojie gongzuo de yinxiang" (The influence the market economy on mediation work), typescript, 4–5. When Westerners interview mediators, in contrast, the conclusions are often the exact opposite. According to James Wall and Michael Blum, "Chinese mediators—as in preindustrial societies—are quite well known in the community and, as one would expect, they know the people quite well. As a result, they have *close relationships* with the disputants." See their "Community Mediation in the People's Republic of China," *Journal of Conflict Resolution* 35, no. 1 : 9. Emphasis added.

9. Fourth Year Sociology Students, Chinese People's University, "The Divorce Situation in Dongcheng District of Beijing after the Implementation of the New Marriage Law," *Chinese Sociology and Anthropology* 16, nos. 1–2. Other quotes are drawn from "Why Can They Not Remain Devoted Couples to the End of Their Lives? An Investigation of Conditions of Divorces in Hongkou District, Shanghai," ibid.

10. Xue Suzhen et al., "An Investigation of Some Marriage Cases in Urban Shanghai," *Chinese Sociology and Anthropology* 16, nos. 1–2:91.

11. Interview by author, 14 April 1994.

12. Summaries of forty Changing District Court cases, 1985. Author's personal library. Conflict over money accounted for 35 percent of divorces in this sample.

13. See Wu Biaoxin, "Qiye shenhua gaige zhong minjian jiufen de tedian yu qi duice" (The features of civil disputes during the deepening of industrial reform and suggestions for countermeasures), n.p., 4; Geng Zhong, Tian Zhangfeng, and Xu Ji-awei, "Dui qiye xiagang renyuan jiufen de fangfan he duice" (Anticipating and preventing conflicts among unemployed workers), typescript, 5.

14. Xu Yao, "Education in Civilized Divorce," *Beijing Review*, 23–29 December 1996, 24.

15. Reports on national divorce trends either focus exclusively on cities or mention in passing that rates in cities are "far higher" than in the countryside, but without citing any figures. See *China News Digest—Global*, 18 April 1997, 13 August 1995, 13 February 1998.

16. Renjiadake, "Lihun qingkuang tongji fenxi," *Chinese Sociology and Anthropology* 16, nos. 1–2:131–37. According to David Chu, "extreme caution" should be used in making any calculation from the encyclopedia's data on divorce.

17. "China Finds 'Irregularities' in Statistics," *International Herald Tribune*, 31 March 1998.

18. Unfortunately, much of the secondary literature on the rural reforms, including those specifically devoted to the position of women, has virtually ignored the issue of the revised Marriage Law and rural divorce. In one of the best studies of the Chinese family after 1978, Stevan Harrell and Deborah Davis's edited volume *Chinese Families in the Post-Mao Era*, divorce figures only in the context of responses to mental illness.

19. Known as "helper mates" (*bang jia*) rather than concubines, these rural women are willing to become the permanent mistresses of wealthy businessmen. In return for their services, the businessmen set the women up with an apartment, money for shopping, and the like. Some of my friends, in a parody of the CCP's tendency to give movements a number (such as the Three and Five Antis, the Four Cleans, etc.), have called this period of family relations in the PRC the era of *yifu, yiqi, yibangjia*: one husband, one wife, and one helper mate.

20. Baihe Township registration officials, interview by author, 28 April 1994.

21. Qingpu Marriage Registration Office, "1993nian shenqing lihun falü zixun tiaojie jiedai chuli qingkuang" (The situation regarding providing legal advice to divorce petitioners in 1993), n.p.

22. Hu Wenqi, "Lun maodun jihua de yuanyin yu fangzhi" (Causes for the intensification of conflicts and ways to prevent them), n.p., 3–4. Hu is an official in the Qingpu County Court.

23. Newspapers similarly complained that peasants are too eager to avail themselves of the court system to settle matters that courts or journalists considered "trivial" or occurring due only to personal grudges. See Gui Haiqing, "Mou da 'douqi guansi'" (Settling personal grudges in court), *Xinhua ribao,* 8 May 1994. For cases of women going directly to court or returning to their natal homes see Feng Ertai, ed., *Zenyang chuli lihun jiufen* (How to mediate divorce cases), 147–49

24. Interview by author, Qingpu.

25. Peasant women, however, were not entirely reliant on the state or mobile solutions to solve their domestic problems. Peasants, more so than urbanites, one study found, are likely to respond to domestic violence by returning a blow for a blow; analyzed by education level, the more educated the woman, the less likely she was to respond to abuse by hitting back. The general rule was: the more educated, the more "restrained" (*kezhi*) in handling marital conflicts. See Xu Anqi, "Jiating baoli de faduan" (The reasons for domestic violence), *Shehuixue,* no. 1 (1994): 27, 30–31. According to her survey, in the Shanghai suburbs 13.2 percent of women would hit their husbands back, compared with 9.5 percent in the city. By education, in the city, 16.7 percent of "illiterate/primary school" respondents said they would hit back, compared with 8.7 percent educated in high school or above; in the suburbs, the respective percentages were 15.5 and 3.1.

26. For statistics on the sex imbalance in China during the reform period see Susan Greenhalgh and Jiali Li, "Engendering Reproductive Policy and Practice in Peasant China: For a Feminist Demography of Reproduction," *Signs: Journal of Women in Culture and Society* 20, no. 3 (1995): 601. For the 1997 figure and the demographer's estimate see "Skewed Sex Ratio Raises Serious Concern in China," *China News Digest—Global,* 20 October 1997.

27. Hu Wenqi, "Lun maodun jihua de yuanyin yu fangzhi," typescript, 7–8.

28. Reports on the new regulations are in *China News Digest—Global,* 8 April 1997, 5 December 1997; Erik Eckholm, "Divorce Reform Plan Splits China," *New York Times,* 18 November 1998.

BIBLIOGRAPHY

CHINESE SOURCES

Archives

Beijing Municipal Archives (BMA)
Chuxiong Prefectural Archives (CXA)
Dongcheng District Archives (DCA)
Jiangsu Provincial Archives (JPA)
Jing'an District Archives (JAA)
Qingpu County Archives (QPA)
Shanghai Municipal Archives (SMA)
Songjiang County Archives (SJA)
Tong County Archives (TCA)
Xuhui District Archives (XHA)
Yunnan Provincial Archives (YNA)

Gazetteers

An xian zhi. 1991. Chengdu: Bashu Publishers.
Baoshan xian zhi. 1992. Shanghai: Shanghai Renmin Chubanshe.
Chongming xian zhi. 1989. Shanghai: Shanghai Renmin Chubanshe.
Chuxiong yizu zizhi zhou zhi. 1993. Vols. 1 and 2. Beijing: Renmin Chubanshe.
Fengning manzu zizhi xian zhi. 1994. Beijing: Zhogguo Heping Chubanshe.
Jiading xian zhi. 1992. Shanghai: Shanghai Renmin Chubanshe.
Jinshan xian zhi. 1990. Shanghai: Shanghai Renmin Chubanshe.
Kunshan xian zhi. 1990. Shanghai: Shanghai Renmin Chubanshe.
Nanhui xian zhi. 1992. Shanghai: Shanghai Renmin Chubanshe.
Putuo xian zhi. 1991. Hangzhou: Zhejiang Renmin Chubanshe.

Qingpu xian zhi. 1990. Shanghai: Shanghai Renmin Chubanshe.
Songjiang xian zhi. 1991. Shanghai: Shanghai Renmin Chubanshe.
Taicang xian zhi. 1991. Nanjing: Jiangsu Renmin Chubanshe.
Tong xian zhi yao. 1941. Tong County Archives.
Xinzhou xian zhi. 1992. Wuhan: Wuhan Chubanshe.
Zhongxian xian zhi. Wuhan: Hubei Renmin Chubanshe.

Chinese-Language Books, Newspapers, and Articles

Anhui Sheng Gaoji Renmin Fayuan (Anhui Province Supreme Court), ed. 1959. *Shenpan jishi* (A chronicle of judgments). Hefei: Anhui Renmin Chubanshe.
Ba Mo Qu Bu, ed. 1992. *Yizu fengsu zhi* (Yi customs). Beijing: Zhongyang Minzu Xueyuan Chubanshe.
Beijing shi Dongcheng qu dashiji (Major events in Beijing's Dongcheng District). 1952–May 1958. Vols. 1 and 2. Typescript.
Fei Yuke. 1958. "Luetan chuli nongcun diqu hunyin wenti de tihui" (A brief discussion of how marriage problems in rural areas are handled). *Zhengfa xuexi* 5–6:56–58.
Feng Ertai. 1993. *Zenyang chuli lihun jiufen* (How to mediate divorce cases). Shanghai: Renmin Chubanshe.
Gao Fayuan, ed. 1990. *Zhongguo xinan shaoshuminzu daode yanjiu* (Research on morals among China's southwestern minority groups). Kunming: Yunnan Minzu Chubanshe.
Hebei sheng di si ci renkou pucha shougong huizong ziliao (Materials from the fourth population census of Hebei Province). 1991. Beijing: Zhongguo Tongji Chubanshe.
Li Yangxi and Tian Ye. 1957. "Hebei sheng nongcun minshi jiufen de diaocha" (An investigation of rural civil disputes in Hebei Province). *Zhengfa yanjiu* 4 (March): 31–38.
Remin ribao (Beijing)
Shanghai Academy of Social Sciences. 1962. *Shanghai penghu qu de bianqian* (The transformation of Shanghai's shack areas). Shanghai: Shanghai Renmin Chubanshe.
Shi Di. 1992. *Shenhua yu fazhi: Xinnan minzu fawenhua yanjiu* (Mythology and legality: Research on legal cultures in Southwest China). Kunming: Yunnan Jiaoyu Chubanshe.
Wang Huai'an et al., eds. 1989. *Zhonghua renmin gongheguo falü quanshu* (Compilation of laws of the People's Republic of China). Changchun: Jilin Renmin Chubanshe.
Wang Lianfang. 1989. *Yunnan minzu gongzuo shijian yu lilun tansuo* (Explorations on the theory and practice of minority work in Yunnan). Kunming: Yunnan Minzu Chubanshe.
———. 1993. *Minzu wenti lunwenji* (A treatise on minority problems). Kunming: Yunnan Renmin Chubanshe.
Xinwen ribao (Shanghai)
Xu Anqi. 1994. "Zhongguo lihun zhuangtai, tedian ji qushi" (The situation, special characteristics, and trends of divorce in China). *Xueshu jikan* 18, no. 2:156–65.

————. 1994. "Jiating baoli de faduan" (The reasons for domestic violence). *Shehuixue* 23, no. 4:27–31.

Yunnan wenshi ziliao weiyuanhui (Yunnan Province historical materials committee). 1993. *Yunnan minzu gongzuo huiyilu* (Memoirs of work among minorities in Yunnan). 2 vols. Kunming: Yunnan Renmin Chubanshe.

Zhongguo renkou—Shandong fence (China's population—Shandong). 1990. Beijing: Zhongguo Tongji Jingji Chubanshe.

Zhongyang renmin zhengfu fazhi weiyuanhui (State legal committee), ed. 1950. *Hunyin wenti cankao ziliao huibian* (Collection of Marriage Law-related materials). Shanghai: Xinhua.

Zhou Gu. 1956. "Lun hunyinfa banbu hou jinian lai chuli lihun anjian de yuanzi" (Principles for how divorce cases should be handled several years after the promulgation of the Marriage Law). *Zhengfa yanjiu* 5 (October): 42–45.

Zou Yiren. 1980. *Jiu Shanghai renkou bianqian de yanjiu* (Research on demographic change in Old Shanghai). Shanghai: Renmin Chubanshe.

ENGLISH-LANGUAGE SOURCES

Ahern, Emily. 1975. "The Power and Pollution of Chinese Women." In Margery Wolf and Roxane Witke, eds., *Women in Chinese Society*. Stanford: Stanford University Press.

Alford, William P. 1995. *To Steal a Book Is an Elegant Offense*. Stanford: Stanford University Press.

Anagnost, Ann. 1988. "Family Violence and Magical Violence: The Woman as Victim in China's One-Child Family Policy." *Women and Language* 11, no. 2:16–22.

Anderson, Karen. 1981. *Wartime Women: Sex Roles, Family Relations, and the Status of Women during World War II*. Westport, Conn.: Greenwood Press.

Anderson, Olive. 1987. *Suicide in Victorian and Edwardian England*. Oxford: Clarendon Press.

Andrews, Julia. 1994. *Painters and Politics in the People's Republic of China*. Berkeley and Los Angeles: University of California Press.

Arkush, David. 1989. "Love and Marriage in North Chinese Peasant Opera." In Perry Link, Richard Madsen, and Paul Pickowicz, eds., *Unofficial China: Popular Culture and Thought in the People's Republic*. Boulder: Westview Press.

Bai, Hua. 1994. *A Remote Country of Women*. Honolulu: University of Hawai'i Press.

Barme, Geremie R. 1996. "Private Practice, Public Performance: The Cultural Revelations of Dr. Li." *China Journal*, no. 35:121–26.

Barnett, A. Doak. 1985. *China on the Eve of Communist Takeover*. Boulder: Westview Press.

Bartkey, Sandra. 1975. "Toward a Phenomenology of Feminist Consciousness." *Social Theory and Practice* 3, no. 4:425–39.

Baum, Richard. 1971. "The Cultural Revolution in the Countryside: Anatomy of a Limited Rebellion." In Thomas W. Robinson, ed., *The Cultural Revolution in China*. Berkeley and Los Angeles: University of California Press.

————. 1975. *Prelude to Revolution: Mao, the Party, and the Peasant Question, 1962–1966*. New York: Columbia University Press.

Baum, Richard, and Frederick C. Teiwes. 1968. *Ssu-Ch'ing: The Socialist Education Movement of 1962–1966*. Berkeley: Center for Chinese Studies Research Monographs.

Baumgarten, M. P. 1988. *The Moral Order of a Suburb*. Oxford: Oxford University Press.

Becker, Howard. 1973. *The Outsiders: Studies in the Sociology of Deviance*. New York: Free Press.

Bennett, Gordon, and Ronald Monteperto. 1980. *Red Guard: The Political Biography of Dai Hsiao-ai*. New York: Doubleday.

Bernhardt, Kathryn. 1994. "Women and the Law: Divorce in Republican China." In Kathryn Bernhardt and Philip C. C. Huang, eds., *Civil Law in Qing and Republican China*. Stanford: Stanford University Press.

Bernstein, Thomas P. 1977. *Up to the Mountains and Down to the Villages: The Transfer of Youth from Urban to Rural China*. New Haven: Yale University Press.

Bian, Yanjie, et al., 1997. "Work Units and Housing Reform in Two Chinese Cities." In Xiaobu Lü and Elizabeth J. Perry, eds., *Danwei: The Changing Chinese Workplace in Historical and Comparative Perspective*. Armonk, N.Y.: M. E. Sharpe.

Butterfield, Fox. 1982. *China: Alive in Bitter Sea*. New York: Bantam.

Buxbaum, David. 1969. "Introduction." In David Buxbaum, ed., *Family Law and Customary Law in Asia: A Contemporary Legal Perspective*. The Hague: Martinus Nijhoff.

———. 1978. "Family Law and Social Change: A Theoretical Introduction." In David Buxbaum, ed., *Chinese Family Law and Social Change in Comparative Perspective*. Seattle: University of Washington Press.

Carey, Fred W. 1900. "Journeys in the Chinese Shan States." *Geographical Journal* 15, no. 5 (May): 486–517.

Chan, Anita, Richard Madsen, and Jonathan Unger. 1984. *Chen Village: The Recent History of a Peasant Community in Mao's China*. Berkeley and Los Angeles: University of California Press.

———. 1992. *Chen Village under Mao and Deng*. Berkeley and Los Angeles: University of California Press.

Chang, Chi Jen. 1956. "The Minority Groups of Yunnan and Chinese Political Expansion into Southwest China." Ph.D. diss., University of Michigan.

Chang, Jung. 1991. *Wild Swans: Three Daughters of China*. New York: Simon and Schuster.

Chen, Jo-hsi. 1978. *The Execution of Mayor Yin and Other Stories from the Great Proletarian Cultural Revolution*. Bloomington: Indiana University Press.

Chen, Yung-fa. 1986. *Making Revolution: The Communist Movement in Eastern and Central China, 1937–1945*. Berkeley and Los Angeles: University of California Press.

Ch'eng, Te-kun, and Ling Ch'ao-t'ao. 1945. "An Introduction to the Southwestern Peoples of China." *Journal of the West China Border Research Society* 16, ser. A, 26–29.

Cheng, Tiejun, and Mark Selden. 1994. "The Origins and Social Consequences of China's *Hukou* System." *China Quarterly*, no. 139:644–68.

Ch'iao, C. M., Warren S. Thompson, and D. T. Chen. 1939. *An Experiment in the Registration of Vital Statistics in China*. Oxford, Ohio: Scripps Foundation.

Chirot, Daniel. 1991. "What Happened in Eastern Europe in 1989?" In Daniel

Chirot, ed., *The Crises of Leninism and the Decline of the Left: The Revolutions of 1989.* Seattle: University of Washington Press.

Choudhary, J. N. 1988. *Divorce in Indian Society.* Jaipur: Printwell Publishers.

Chow, T'se-tsung. 1960. *The May Fourth Movement: Intellectual Revolution in Modern China.* Cambridge: Harvard University Press.

Clarke, Donald. 1991. "Dispute Resolution in China." *Journal of Chinese Law* 5, no. 2:245–96.

Clarke, Samuel R. n.d. *Among the Tribes in South-West China.* London: Morgan and Scott.

Coble, Parks. 1980. *The Shanghai Capitalists and the Nationalist Government.* Cambridge: Harvard University Press.

Cohen, Jerome A. 1967. "Chinese Mediation on the Eve of Modernization." In David Buxbaum, ed., *Traditional and Modern Legal Institutions in Asia and Africa.* Leiden: E. J. Brill.

———. 1971. "Drafting People's Mediation Rules." In John Wilson Lewis, *The City in Communist China.* Stanford: Stanford University Press.

Cott, Nancy F. 1976. "Divorce and the Changing Status of Women in Eighteenth-Century Massachusetts." *William and Mary Quarterly* 33, no. 4:586–614.

Cressey, George B. 1955. *Land of the Five Hundred Million.* New York: McGraw Hill.

Cresswell, Stephen. *Mormons and Cowboys, Moonshiners and Clansmen: Federal Law Enforcement in the South and Southwest, 1870–1893.* Tuscaloosa and London: University of Alabama Press, 1991.

Croll, Elisabeth. 1981. *The Politics of Marriage in Contemporary China.* Cambridge: Cambridge University Press.

———. 1984. "Marriage Choice and Status Groups in Contemporary China." In James Watson, ed., *Class and Social Stratification in Post-Revolution China.* Cambridge: Cambridge University Press.

Czap, Peter, Jr., 1967. "Peasant Class Courts and Peasant Customary Justice in Russia, 1861–1912." *Journal of Social History* 1, no. 2:149–78.

Davin, Delia. 1979. *Woman-Work: Women and the Party in Revolutionary China.* Oxford: Oxford University Press.

Davis, Natalie Zemon. 1975. "The Reasons for Misrule." In *Society and Culture in Early Modern France.* Stanford: Stanford University Press.

Davis [-Friedmann], Deborah. 1983. *Long Lives: Chinese Elderly and the Communist Revolution.* Cambridge: Harvard University Press.

deBary, W. T., et al., eds. 1960. *Sources of Chinese Tradition.* New York: Columbia University Press.

D'Emilio, John, and Estelle B. Freedman. 1988. *Intimate Matters: A History of Sexuality in America.* New York: Harper and Row.

Deutsch, Karl. 1953. *Nationalism and Social Communication: An Inquiry into the Foundations of Nationality.* Cambridge: M.I.T. Press.

Diamant, Neil J. 1996. "Revolutionizing the Family: Law, Love, and Divorce in Urban and Rural China, 1950–1968." Ph.D. diss., Dept. of Political Science, University of California, Berkeley.

Diamond, Norma. 1995. "Defining the Miao: Ming, Qing, and Contemporary Views."

In Stevan Harrell, ed., *Cultural Encounters on China's Ethnic Frontiers*. Seattle: University of Washington Press.

Dittmer, Lowell. 1974. *Liu Shao-chi and the Chinese Cultural Revolution: The Politics of Mass Criticism*. Berkeley and Los Angeles: University of California Press.

———. 1991. "Learning from Trauma: The Cultural Revolution in Post-Mao Politics." In William Joseph, Christine Wong, and David Zweig, eds., *New Perspectives on the Cultural Revolution*. Cambridge: Council on East Asian Studies, Harvard University.

Dore, Ronald. 1978. *Shinohata: A Portrait of a Japanese Village*. New York: Random House.

Dower, John. 1986. *War without Mercy: Race and Power in the Pacific War*. New York: Pantheon.

Duara, Prasenjit. 1988. *Culture, Power, and the State: Rural North China, 1900–1942*. Stanford: Stanford University Press.

Eastman, Lloyd. 1984. *Seeds of Destruction: Nationalist China in War and Revolution, 1937–1949*. Stanford: Stanford University Press.

Ebrey, Patricia Buckley. 1993. *The Inner Quarters: Marriage and the Lives of Chinese Women in the Sung Period*. Berkeley and Los Angeles: University of California Press.

Elshtain, Jean Bethke. 1982. "Aristotle, the Public-Private Split, and the Case of the Suffragists." In Jean Elshtain, ed., *The Family in Political Thought*. Amherst: University of Massachusetts Press.

Elster, Jon. 1985. *Making Sense of Marx*. Cambridge: Cambridge University Press.

Elvin, Mark. 1984. "Female Virtue and the State in China." *Past and Present*, no. 104:111–52.

Engel, David. 1978. *Code and Custom in a Thai Provincial Court: The Interaction of Formal and Informal Systems of Justice*. Tucson: University of Arizona Press.

Engels, Barbara Alpern. 1983. *Mothers and Daughters: Women of the Intelligentsia in Nineteenth-Century Russia*. Cambridge: Cambridge University Press.

Engels, Friedrich. 1985. *The Origin of the Family, Private Property, and the State*. Harmondsworth, Middlesex: Penguin.

Engelstein, Laura. 1992. *The Keys to Happiness: Sex and the Modern in Fin-de-Siècle Russia*. Ithaca: Cornell University Press.

Esherick, Joseph W. 1987. *The Origins of the Boxer Uprising*. Berkeley and Los Angeles: University of California Press.

———. 1994. "Deconstructing the Construction of the Party-State: Gulin County in the Shaan-Gan-Ning Border Region." *China Quarterly*, no. 140:1052–79.

Esherick, Joseph W., and Jeffrey N. Wasserstrom. 1992. "Acting Out Democracy: Political Theater in Modern China." In Jeffrey N. Wasserstrom and Elizabeth J. Perry, eds., *Popular Protest and Political Culture in Modern China: Learning from 1989*. Boulder: Westview Press.

Esherick, Joseph W., and Mary Rankin, eds. 1990. *Chinese Local Elites and Patterns of Dominance*. Berkeley and Los Angeles: University of California Press.

Evans, Peter. 1992. "The State as Problem and Solution: Predation, Embedded Autonomy, and Structural Change." In Stephen Haggard and Robert Kaufmann, eds., *The Politics of Economic Adjustment: International Constraints, Distributional Conflicts, and the State*. Princeton: Princeton University Press.

Farnsworth, Beatrice. 1985. "Village Women Experience the Revolution." In Abbott

Gleason, Peter Kenez, and Richard Stites, eds., *Bolshevik Culture.* Bloomington: Indiana University Press.

————. 1986. "The Litigious Daughter-in-Law: Family Relations in Rural Russia in the Second Half of the Nineteenth Century." *Slavic Review* 45, no. 1:49–64.

Fei, Hsiao-tung, and Chang Chih-i. 1945. *Earthbound China: A Study of Rural Economy in Yunnan.* Chicago: University of Chicago Press.

Felstiner, William. 1974. "Influences of Social Organization on Dispute Processing." *Law and Society Review* 9, no. 1:63–94.

Feng, Jicai 1991. *Voices from the Whirlwind: An Oral History of the Chinese Cultural Revolution.* New York: Pantheon.

Fitzpatrick, Sheila. 1978. "Sex and Revolution: An Examination of the Literary and Statistical Data on the Mores of Soviet Students in the 1920s." *Journal of Modern History* 50, no. 2 (June): 252–78.

————. 1994. *Stalin's Peasants: Resistance and Survival in the Russian Village after Collectivization.* New York and Oxford: Oxford University Press.

Ford, Joseph. 1977. *The Local Histories of Yunnan.* China Society Occasional Papers, no. 19. London: China Society.

Friedman, Edward, Paul Pickowicz, and Mark Selden. 1991. *Chinese Village, Socialist State.* New Haven: Yale University Press.

Friedman, Lawrence. 1977. *Law and Society.* Englewood Cliffs, N.J.: Prentice Hall.

Frolic, B. Michael. 1980. *Mao's People: Sixteen Portraits of Life in Revolutionary China.* Cambridge: Harvard University Press.

Fudan University Sociology Students. 1983–1984. "Why Can They Not Remain Devoted Couples to the End of Their Lives: An Investigation of Conditions of Divorces in Hongkou District, Shanghai." *Chinese Sociology and Anthropology* 16, nos. 1–2 (fall-winter): 99–104

Galanter, Marc. 1983. "The Radiating Effect of Courts." In Keith O. Boyum and Lynn Mather, eds., *Empirical Theories about Courts.* New York: Longman.

————. 1989. *Law and Society in Modern India.* New Delhi: Oxford University Press.

Gamble, Sidney. 1921. *Peking: A Social Survey.* New York: Doran.

Gao, Yuan. 1987. *Born Red: A Chronicle of the Cultural Revolution.* Stanford: Stanford University Press.

Gardner, John. 1969. "The Wu-fan Campaign in Shanghai: A Study of the Consolidation of Urban Control." In A. Doak Barnett, ed., *Chinese Communist Politics in Action.* Seattle: University of Washington Press.

Geiger, H. Kent. 1968. *The Family in Soviet Russia.* Cambridge: Harvard University Press.

Giddens, Anthony. 1965. "The Suicide Problem in French Sociology." *British Journal of Sociology* 16:3–18.

Gilmartin, Christina. 1990. "Violence against Women in Contemporary China." In Stevan Harrell and Jonathan Lipman, eds., *Violence in China: Essays in Culture and Counterculture.* Albany: State University of New York Press.

Gladney, Dru. 1994. "Representing Nationality in China: Reconfiguring Majority/Minority Identities." *Journal of Asian Studies* 53, no. 1:92–123.

Goffman, Erving. 1959. *The Presentation of Self in Everyday Life.* New York: Anchor.

Goldman, Merle. 1967. *Literary Dissent in Modern China.* Cambridge: Harvard University Press.

————. 1981. *China's Intellectuals: Advice and Dissent.* Cambridge: Harvard University Press.

————. 1987. "The Party and the Intellectuals." In Roderick MacFarquhar and John K. Fairbank, eds., *The Cambridge History of China,* vol. 14. Cambridge: Cambridge University Press.

Goode, William. 1970. *World Revolution and Family Patterns.* New York: Free Press.

Goodman, Bryna. 1995. *Native Place, City, and Nation: Regional Networks and Identities in Shanghai, 1853–1937.* Berkeley and Los Angeles: University of California Press.

Goodman, David. 1986. *Centre and Province in the PRC: Sichuan and Guizhou, 1955–1965.* Cambridge: Cambridge University Press.

Greenhalgh, Susan, and Jiali Li. 1995. "Engendering Reproductive Policy and Practice in Peasant China: For a Feminist Demography of Reproduction." *Signs: Journal of Women in Culture and Society* 20, no. 3:601–41.

Gulliver, P. H. 1979. *Disputes and Negotiations: A Cross-Cultural Perspective.* New York: Academic Press.

Haley, John O. 1978. "The Myth of the Reluctant Litigant." *Journal of Japanese Studies* 4, no. 2:359–89.

Hammick, James. 1873. *The Marriage Law of England.* London: Shaw and Sons.

Hanan, Patrick. 1995. Introduction to his translation of *The Sea of Regret: Two Turn-of-the-Century Chinese Romantic Novels,* by Wu Jianren. Honolulu: University of Hawai'i Press.

Hane, Mikiso. 1982. *Peasants, Rebels, and Outcastes: The Underside of Modern Japan.* New York: Pantheon.

Hanson, Stephen E. 1997. *Time and Revolution: Marxism and the Design of Soviet Institutions.* Chapel Hill and London: University of North Carolina Press.

Harrell, Stevan, ed. 1995. *Cultural Encounters on China's Ethnic Frontiers.* Seattle: University of Washington Press.

Harrell, Stevan, and Deborah Davis, eds. 1993. *Chinese Families in the Post-Mao Era.* Berkeley and Los Angleles: University of California Press.

Hartmann, Susan M. 1982. *The Home Front and Beyond: American Women in the 1940s.* Boston: Twayne.

Hassan, Riaz. 1983. *A Way of Dying: Suicide in Singapore.* Singapore: Oxford University Press.

Havel, Václav. 1986. *Living in Truth.* Ed. Jan Vladislav. London: Faber and Faber.

Heng, Liang, and Judith Shapiro. 1984. *Son of the Revolution.* New York: Viking.

Herman, John. 1997. "Empire in the Southwest: Early Qing Reforms to the Native Chieftain System." *Journal of Asian Studies* 56, no. 1:47–74.

Hexter, J. H. 1979. *On Historians.* Cambridge: Harvard University Press.

Hill, Enid. 1979. *Mahkama! Studies in the Egyptian Legal System.* London: Ithaca Press.

Hinton, William. 1966. *Fanshen: A Documentary of Revolution in a Chinese Village.* New York: Vintage.

————. 1983. *Shenfan: The Continuing Revolution in a Chinese Village.* London: Seeker and Warburg.

Hobsbawm, Eric. 1978. "Man and Woman in Socialist Iconography." *History Workshop,* no. 6 (autumn): 121–38.

Hohenberg, Paul M., and Lynn H. Lees. 1985. *The Making of Urban Europe, 1000–1950*. Cambridge: Harvard University Press.

Honig, Emily. 1986. *Sisters and Strangers: Women in the Shanghai Cotton Mills, 1919–1949*. Stanford: Stanford University Press.

———. 1992. *Creating Chinese Ethnicity: Subei People in Shanghai, 1850–1980*. New Haven: Yale University Press.

Honig, Emily, and Gail Hershatter. 1988. *Personal Voices: Chinese Women in the 1980s*. Stanford: Stanford University Press.

Hosie, Alexander. 1897. *Three Years in Western China: A Narrative of Three Journeys in Ssu-ch'uan, Kuei-chow, and Yun-nan*. London: George Philip and Son.

Howe, Irving. 1976. *World of Our Fathers: The Journey of East European Jews to America and the Life They Found and Made*. New York: Touchstone Books.

Hsieh, Shih-chung. 1995. "On the Dynamics of Tai/Dai-Lue Ethnicity: An Ethnohistorical Analysis." In Stevan Harrell, ed., *Cultural Encounters on China's Ethnic Frontiers*. Seattle: University of Washington Press.

Huang, Philip C. C. 1985. *The Peasant Economy and Social Change in North China*. Stanford: Stanford University Press.

———. 1990. *The Peasant Family and Rural Development in the Yangzi Delta, 1350–1988*. Stanford: Stanford University Press.

———. 1994. "Codifed Law and Magisterial Adjudication in the Qing." In Kathryn Bernhardt and Philip C. C. Huang, eds., *Civil Law in Qing and Republican China*. Stanford: Stanford University Press.

———. 1996. *Civil Justice in China: Representation and Practice in the Qing*. Stanford: Stanford University Press.

Huang, Yasheng. 1994. "Information, Bureaucracy, and Economic Reforms in China and the Soviet Union." *World Politics* 47:102–34.

Hunt, Lynn. 1984. *Politics, Culture, and Class in the French Revolution*. Berkeley and Los Angeles: University of California Press.

———. 1992. *The Family Romance of the French Revolution*. Berkeley and Los Angeles: University of California Press.

Jaros, Dean, Herbert Hirsch, and Dennis Chong. 1968. "The Malevolent Leader: Political Socialization in an American Subculture." *American Political Science Review* 62:564–75.

Johnson, Chalmers. 1962. *Peasant Nationalism and Communist Power*. Stanford: Stanford University Press.

———. 1982. *MITI and the Japanese Miracle: The Emergence of Japanese Industrial Policy, 1925–1975*. Stanford: Stanford University Press.

Johnson, Kay Ann. 1983. *Women, the Family, and Peasant Revolution in China*. Chicago: University of Chicago Press.

Jordan, David K., and Daniel Overmeyer. 1986. *The Flying Phoenix: Aspects of Chinese Sectarianism in Taiwan*. Princeton: Princeton University Press.

Judd, Ellen R. 1989. "*Niangjia*: Chinese Women and Their Natal Families." *Journal of Asian Studies* 48, no. 3:525–44.

Kaffman, Mordecai, Sheryl Shoham, Michal Palgi, and Menachem Rosner. 1986. "Divorce in the Kibbutz: Past and Present." *Contemporary Family Therapy* 8, no. 4 (winter): 301–15.

Kazuko, Ono. 1989. *Chinese Women in a Century of Revolution, 1850–1950.* Stanford: Stanford University Press.

Ko, Dorothy. 1996. "Thinking about Copulating: An Early-Qing Confucian Thinker's Problem with Emotion and Words." In Gail Hershatter et al., eds., *Remapping China: Fissures in Historical Terrain.* Stanford: Stanford University Press.

Koenker, Diane. 1978. "Urban Families, Working Class Youth." In David Ransel, ed., *The Family in Imperial Russia: New Lines of Historical Research.* Urbana: University of Illinois Press.

————. 1995. "Men against Women on the Shop Floor in Early Soviet Russia: Gender and Class in the Socialist Workplace." *American Historical Review* 100, no. 5 (December): 1438–64.

Kraus, Richard. 1981. *Class Conflict in Chinese Socialism.* New York: Columbia University Press.

————. 1989. "The Lament of Astrophysicist Fang Lizhi." In Arif Dirlik and Maurice Meisner, eds., *Marxism and the Chinese Experience.* Armonk, N.Y.: M. E. Sharpe.

Kuhn, Philip. 1970. *Rebellion and Its Enemies in Late Imperial China: Militarization and Social Structure, 1769–1864.* Cambridge: Harvard University Press.

————. 1984. "Chinese Views of Social Classification." In James L. Watson, ed., *Class and Social Stratification in Post-Revolution China.* Cambridge: Cambridge University Press.

Kushner, Howard. 1989. *Self-Destruction in the Promised Land: A Psychocultural Biology of American Suicide.* New Brunswick, N.J.: Rutgers University Press.

Lakoff, George. 1996. *Moral Politics: What Conservatives Know That Liberals Don't.* Chicago: University of Chicago Press.

Landes, David S. 1983. *Revolution in Time: Clocks and the Making of the Modern World.* Cambridge: Belknap Press of Harvard University Press.

Lardy, Nicholas R. 1987. "The Chinese Economy under Stress, 1958–1965." In Roderick MacFarquhar and John K. Fairbank, eds., *The Cambridge History of China,* vol. 14. Cambridge: Cambridge University Press.

Lavely, William. 1991. "Marriage and Mobility under Rural Collectivism." In Rubie S. Watson and Patricia Buckley Ebrey, eds., *Marriage and Inequality in Chinese Society.* Berkeley and Los Angeles: University of California Press.

Lee, Hong Yung. 1978. *The Politics of the Chinese Cultural Revolution: A Case Study.* Berkeley and Los Angeles: University of California Press.

Lee, James. 1982. "Food Supply and Population Growth in Southwest China, 1250–1850." *Journal of Asian Studies* 41, no. 4:711–46.

Levine, Ned. 1982. "Social Change and Family Crises—The Nature of Turkish Divorce." In Ligdem Kagitcibasi, ed., *Sex Roles, Family, and Community in Turkey.* Bloomington: Indiana University Press.

Lewin, Moshe. 1968. *Russian Peasants and Soviet Power: A Study of Collectivization.* New York: Norton.

Li, Victor. 1971. "The Evolution and Development of the Chinese Legal System." In John Lindbeck, ed., *China: Management of a Revolutionary Society.* Seattle: University of Washington Press.

Li, Zhisui. 1994. *The Private Life of Chairman Mao.* Trans. Tai Hung-chao. New York: Random House.

Liang, Ellen Johnston. 1988. *The Winking Owl: Art in the People's Republic of China.* Berkeley and Los Angeles: University of California Press.

Liao, Cailian, and Tim B. Heaton. 1992. "Divorce Trends and Differentials in China." *Journal of Comparative Family Studies* 23, no. 3:413–29.

Lieberthal, Kenneth. 1980. *Revolution and Tradition in Tientsin, 1949–1952.* Stanford: Stanford University Press.

———. 1987. "The Great Leap Forward and the Split in the Yenan Leadership." In Roderick MacFarquhar and John K. Fairbank, eds., *The Cambridge History of China,* vol. 14. Cambridge: Cambridge University Press.

Lifton, Robert Jay. 1961. *Thought Reform and the Psychology of Totalism: A Study of Brainwashing in China.* New York: Norton.

———. 1968. *Revolutionary Immortality.* New York: Random House.

Ling, Ken [pseud.]. 1972. *The Revenge of Heaven: Journal of a Young Chinese.* New York: Ballantine.

Link, Perry. 1992. *Evening Chats in Beijing: Probing China's Predicament.* New York: W. W. Norton.

Liu Binyan. 1983. *People or Monsters? and Other Stories and Reportage from China after Mao.* Bloomington: University of Indiana Press.

———. 1990. *A Higher Kind of Loyalty.* New York: Pantheon.

———. 1996. "Jiang Zemin's 'Stressing Politics.'" *China Focus* 4, no. 4 (1 April): 1, 7.

Lu, Hanchao. 1991. "The Workers and Neighborhoods of Modern Shanghai, 1911–1949." Ph.D. diss., Dept. of History, University of California, Los Angeles.

Luo, Zi-ping. 1990. *A Generation Lost: China under the Cultural Revolution.* New York: Henry Holt.

Lynn (Lin), Jermyn Chi-hung. 1928. *Social Life of the Chinese (in Peking).* Peking: China Booksellers.

MacCauley, Melissa. 1994. "Civil and Uncivil Disputes in Southeastern Coastal China, 1723–1820." In Kathryn Bernhardt and Philip C. C. Huang, eds., *Civil Law in Qing and Republican China.* Stanford: Stanford University Press.

MacFarquhar, Roderick. 1974, 1983, 1997. *Origins of the Chinese Cultural Revolution,* vols. 1–3. New York: Columbia University Press.

MacFarquhar, Roderick, Timothy Cheek, and Eugene Wu, eds. 1989. *The Secret Speeches of Chairman Mao.* Cambridge: Council of East Asian Studies, Harvard University.

MacFarquhar, Roderick, and John K. Fairbank, eds. 1987. *The Cambridge History of China.* Vol. 14. Cambridge: Cambridge University Press.

MacKinnon, Catherine A. 1987. *Feminism Unmodified: Discourses on Life and Law.* Cambridge: Harvard University Press.

———. 1989. *Towards a Feminist Theory of the State.* Cambridge: Harvard University Press.

———. 1993. "Reflections on Law in the Everyday Life of Women." In Austin Sarat and Thomas R. Kearns, eds., *Law in Everyday Life.* Ann Arbor: University of Michigan Press.

MacKinnon, Stephen. 1975. "Police Reform in Late Ch'ing China." *Ch'ing-shih wen t'i* 3, no. 4:82–99.

Madsen, Bernice. 1977. "Social Services for Women: Problems and Priorities." In

Dorothy Atkinson, Alexander Dallin, and Gail Lapidus, eds., *Women in Russia.* Stanford: Stanford University Press.

Madsen, Richard. 1984. *Morality and Power in a Chinese Village.* Berkeley and Los Angeles: University of California Press.

—. 1990. "The Politics of Revenge in Rural China." In Stevan Harrell and Jonathan Lipman, eds., *Violence in China: Essays in Culture and Counterculture.* Albany: State University of New York Press.

Mann, Susan. 1987. "Widows in the Kinship, Class, and Community Structures of Qing Dynasty China." *Journal of Asian Studies* 46, no. 1 (February): 37–56.

—. 1991. "Grooming a Daughter for Marriage: Brides and Wives in the Mid-Ch'ing Period." In Rubie S. Watson and Patricia Buckley Ebrey, eds., *Marriage and Inequality in Chinese Society.* Berkeley and Los Angeles: University of California Press.

Mao Zedong [Mao Tse-tung]. 1963. "China Is Poor and Blank" and "The Question of Agricultural Cooperation." In Stuart Schram, ed., *The Political Thought of Mao Tse-tung.* New York: Praeger.

—. 1963. "An Investigation into the Peasant Movement in Hunan." In Stuart Schram, ed., *The Political Thought of Mao Tse-tung.* New York: Praeger.

—. 1963. "On the Correct Handling of Contradictions among the People." In Stuart Schram, ed., *The Political Thought of Mao Tse-tung.* New York: Praeger.

—. 1974. *Mao Tse-tung Unrehearsed.* Ed. Stuart Schram. Middlesex, England: Penguin Books.

—. 1974. "On the Ten Great Relationships." In Stuart Schram, ed., *Chairman Mao Talks to the People: Talks and Letters: 1956–1971.* New York: Pantheon.

—. 1974. "Talk to Leaders of the Centre." In Stuart Schram, ed., *Chairman Mao Talks to the People: Talks and Letters, 1956–1971.* New York: Pantheon.

—. 1977. "Report to the Second Plenary Session of the Seventh Central Committee of the Communist Party of China" (March 1949). In *Selected Works,* vol. 4. Peking: Foreign Languages Press.

—. 1990. *Report from Xunwu.* Trans. Roger Thompson. Stanford: Stanford University Press.

Marx, Karl. 1978. "The German Ideology." In Robert Tucker, ed., *The Marx-Engels Reader,* 2d ed. New York: Norton.

McAdam, Doug. *The Political Process and the Development of Black Insurgency, 1930–1970.* Chicago: University of Chicago Press.

McCann, Michael W. 1994. *Rights at Work: Pay Equity Reform and the Politics of Legal Mobilization.* Chicago: University of Chicago Press.

McCarthey, J. 1879. "Across China from Chin-kiang to Bhamo, 1877." *Proceedings of the Royal Geographical Society* 1, no. 8 (August): 489–509.

McCord, Edward. 1990. "Local Military Power and Elite Formation: The Liu Family of Xingyi County, Guizhou." In Joseph Esherick and Mary B. Rankin, eds., *Chinese Local Elites and Patterns of Dominance.* Berkeley and Los Angeles: University of California Press.

Mehta, Rama. 1975. *Divorced Hindu Women.* New Delhi: Vikas.

Meijer, Jan. 1968. "Town and Country in the Civil War." In Richard Pipes, ed., *Revolutionary Russia.* Cambridge: Harvard University Press.

Meijer, M. J. 1971. *Marriage Law and Policy in the Chinese People's Republic.* Hong Kong: Hong Kong University Press.

Meisner, Maurice. 1982. *Marxism, Maoism, and Utopianism: Eight Essays.* Madison: University of Wisconsin Press.

Merry, Sally Engle. 1990. *Getting Justice and Getting Even: Legal Consciousness among Working-Class Americans.* Chicago: University of Chicago Press.

Michael, Franz. 1962. "The Role of Law in Traditional, Nationalist, and Communist China." *China Quarterly,* no. 9: 124–48.

Migdal, Joel. 1988. *Strong Societies and Weak States: State-Society Relations and Capabilities in the Third World.* Princeton: Princeton University Press.

———. 1994. "The State in Society: An Approach to Struggles for Domination." In Joel Migdal, Atul Kohli, and Vivienne Shue, eds., *State Power and Social Forces: Domination and Transformation in the Third World.* Cambridge: Cambridge University Press.

Mitchell, Timothy. 1991. "The Limits of the State: Beyond Statist Approaches and Their Critics." *American Political Science Review* 85, no. 1: 77–96.

Mosse, George. 1978. *Toward the Final Solution: A History of European Racism.* New York: Howard Fertig.

———. 1985. *Nationalism and Sexuality: Middle-Class Morality and Sexual Norms in Modern Europe.* Madison: University of Wisconsin Press.

Mote, F. W. 1977. "The Transformation of Nanking." In G.William Skinner, ed., *The City in Late Imperial China.* Stanford: Stanford University Press.

Muller-Freienfels, W. 1978. "Soviet Family Law and Comparative Chinese Developments." In David Buxbaum, ed., *Chinese Family Law and Social Change in Historical and Comparative Perspective.* Seattle: University of Washington Press.

Murphy, Rhoads. 1972. "City and Countryside as Ideological Issues: India and China." *Comparative Studies in Society and History* 14, no. 3: 250–67.

National Center for Health Statistics. 1966. *Marriage and Divorce Registration in the United States.* Washington: National Center for Health Statistics.

O'Brien, Kevin, and Lianjiang Li. 1995. "The Politics of Lodging Complaints in Rural China." *China Quarterly,* no. 143 (September): 756–83.

Okin, Susan Moller. 1982. "Philosopher Queens and Private Wives: Plato on Women and the Family." In Jean Bethke Elshtain, ed., *The Family in Political Thought.* Amherst: University of Massachusetts Press.

Orwell, George. 1958. *The Road to Wigan Pier.* New York: Harcourt Brace.

Osgood, Cornelius. 1963. *Village Life in Old China: A Community Study of Kao Yao, Yunnan.* New York: Ronald Press.

Ozouf, Mona. 1988. *Festivals and the French Revolution.* Trans. Alan Sheridan. Cambridge: Harvard University Press.

Parish, William L., and Martin K. Whyte. 1978. *Village and Family in Contemporary China.* Chicago: University of Chicago Press.

Park, Nancy. 1997. "Corruption in Eighteenth Century China." *Journal of Asian Studies* 56, no. 4: 967–99.

Peh-t'i Wei, Betty. 1993. *Old Shanghai.* Oxford: Oxford University Press.

Pepper, Suzanne. 1978. *Civil War in China: The Political Struggle, 1945–1949.* Berkeley and Los Angeles: University of California Press.

Perrot, Michelle, ed. 1990. *A History of Private Life: From the Fires of Revolution to the Great War.* Trans. Arthur Goldhammer. Cambridge: Harvard University Press.

Perry, Elizabeth J. 1980. *Rebels and Revolutionaries in North China, 1845–1945.* Stanford: Stanford University Press.

———. 1992. "Casting a 'Democracy' Movement: The Role of Students, Workers, and Entrepreneurs." In Jeffrey Wasserstrom and Elizabeth Perry, eds., *Popular Protest and Political Culture in Modern China: Learning from 1989.* Boulder: Westview Press.

———. 1992. "Introduction." In Jeffrey Wasserstrom and Elizabeth Perry, eds., *Popular Protest and Political Culture in Modern China: Learning from 1989.* Boulder: Westview Press.

———. 1994. *Shanghai on Strike: The Politics of Chinese Labor.* Stanford: Stanford University Press.

———. 1994. "Shanghai's Strike Wave of 1957." *China Quarterly,* no. 137 (March): 1–27.

Perry, Elizabeth J., and Li Xun. 1997. *Proletarian Power: Shanghai in the Cultural Revolution.* Boulder: Westview Press.

Philips, Roderick. 1980. *Family Breakdown in Late Eighteenth Century France: Divorces in Rouen, 1792–1803.* Oxford: Clarendon Press.

Pipes, Richard. 1993. *Russia under the Bolshevik Regime.* New York: Knopf.

Posner, Richard. 1992. *Sex and Reason.* Cambridge: Harvard University Press.

Potter, Sulamith Heins, and Jack Potter. 1990. *China's Peasants: The Anthropology of a Revolution.* Cambridge: Cambridge University Press.

Pruitt, Ida. 1945. *A Daughter of Han: The Autobiography of a Chinese Working Woman.* Stanford: Stanford University Press.

Quaife, G. R. 1979. *Wanton Wenches and Wayward Wives: Peasants and Illicit Sex in Early Seventeenth Century England.* London: Croom Helm.

Ramu, G. N. 1989. *Women, Work, and Marriage in Urban India.* New Delhi: Sage.

Richardson, H. L. 1940. "Soil and Man in Western China." *Journal of the West China Border Research Society* 12:102–33.

Rosen, Stanley. 1982. *Red Guard Factionalism and the Cultural Revolution in Guangzhou (Canton).* Boulder: Westview Press.

Rosenberg, Tina. 1995. *The Haunted Land: Facing Europe's Ghosts after Communism.* New York: Random House.

Rosenthal, Bernice Glazer. 1977. "Love on the Tractor: Women in the Russian Revolution and After." In Renate Bridenthal and Claudia Koonz, eds., *Becoming Visible: Women in European History.* Boston: Houghton Mifflin.

Rowe, William. 1984. *Hankow: Commerce and Society in a Chinese City, 1796–1889.* Stanford: Stanford University Press.

Rueschemeyer, Dietrich, and Peter Evans. 1985. "The State and Economic Transformation: Toward an Analysis of the Conditions Underlying Effective Intervention." In Peter Evans, Dietrich Rueschemeyer, and Theda Skocpol, eds., *Bringing the State Back In.* Cambridge: Cambridge University Press.

Ryan, Mary. 1989. "The American Parade." In Lynn Hunt, ed., *The New Cultural History.* Berkeley and Los Angeles: University of California Press.

Sargeant, Margie. 1971. "The Cultural Revolution in Heilongkiang." In *The Cul-*

tural Revolution in the Provinces. Cambridge: East Asia Research Institute, Harvard University.

Schama, Simon. 1984. *Citizens: A Chronicle of the French Revolution.* New York: Vintage.

Schlereth, Thomas J. 1977. *The Cosmopolitan Ideal in Enlightenment Thought: Its Form and Function in the Ideas of Franklin, Hume, and Voltaire, 1694–1790.* Notre Dame, Ind.: University of Notre Dame Press.

Schoenhals, Michael. 1996. "The Central Case Examination Group, 1966–1979." *China Quarterly,* no. 145 (March): 87–111.

Schoppa, R. Keith. 1995. *Blood Road: The Mystery of Shen Dingyi in Revolutionary China.* Berkeley and Los Angeles: University of California Press.

Schram, Stuart, ed. 1963. *The Political Thought of Mao Tse-tung.* New York: Praeger.

———. 1974. *Chairman Mao Talks to the People: Talks and Letters: 1956–1971.* New York: Pantheon.

Schurmann, Franz. 1968. *Ideology and Organization in Communist China.* Berkeley and Los Angeles: University of California Press.

Schwarcz, Vera. 1986. *The Chinese Enlightenment: Intellectuals and the Legacy of the May Fourth Movement of 1919.* Berkeley and Los Angeles: University of California Press.

Scott, James C. 1998. *Seeing Like a State: How Certain Schemes to Improve the Human Condition Have Failed.* New Haven: Yale University Press.

Scott, Joan Wallach. 1988. *Gender and the Politics of History.* New York: Columbia University Press.

Segalen, Martine. 1983. *Love and Power in the Peasant Family: Rural France in the Nineteenth Century.* Trans. Sarah Matthews. Oxford and Chicago: Basil Blackwell and University of Chicago Presses.

Shanley, Mary Lyndon, and Peter Stillman. 1982. "Political and Marital Despotism: Montesquieu's *Persian Letters.*" In Jean Elshtain, ed., *The Family in Political Thought.* Amherst: University of Massachusetts Press.

She, Colleen. 1991. "Toward Ideology: Views of the May Fourth Intelligentsia on Love, Marriage, and Divorce." *Issues and Studies* 27, no. 2:104–32.

Shirk, Susan. 1982. *Competitive Comrades: Career Incentives and Student Strategies in China.* Berkeley and Los Angeles: University of California Press.

Shorter, Edward. 1975. *The Making of the Modern Family.* New York: Basic Books.

Shue, Vivienne. 1980. *Peasant China in Transition: The Dynamics of Development toward Socialism, 1949–1956.* Berkeley and Los Angeles: University of California Press.

———. 1988. *The Reach of the State: Sketches of the Chinese Body Politic.* Stanford: Stanford University Press.

Skinner, G. William. 1951. "Aftermath of Communist Liberation in the Chengtu Plain." *Pacific Affairs* 24, no. 1 (March): 61–76.

———. 1977. "Cities and the Hierarchy of Local System." In G. William Skinner, ed., *The City in Late Imperial China.* Stanford: Stanford University Press.

———. 1977. "Introduction: Urban Development in Imperial China." In G. William Skinner, ed., *The City in Late Imperial China.* Stanford: Stanford University Press.

———. 1977. "Regional Urbanization in Nineteenth Century China." In G. William Skinner, ed., *The City in Late Imperial China.* Stanford: Stanford University Press.

Skocpol, Theda. 1979. *States and Social Revolution: A Comparative Analysis of France, Russia, and China.* Cambridge: Cambridge University Press.

Skowronek, Stephen. 1982. *Building a New American State: The Expansion of National Administrative Capacities, 1877–1920.* Cambridge: Cambridge University Press.

Smith, Robert J. 1981. "Japanese Village Women: Suye-mura, 1935–1936." *Journal of Japanese Studies* 7, no. 2:259–84.

Solinger, Dorothy. 1977. *Regional Government and Political Integration in Southwest China, 1949–1954.* Berkeley and Los Angeles: University of California Press.

Stacey, Judith. 1983. *Patriarchy and Socialist Revolution in China.* Berkeley and Los Angeles: University of California Press.

Starr, June. 1989. "The Role of Turkish Secular Law in Changing the Lives of Rural Muslim Women, 1950–1970." *Law and Society Review* 23, no. 3:497–523.

Steiner, H. Arthur. 1950. "Chinese Communist Urban Policy." *American Political Science Review* 44:47–53.

Stone, Lawrence. 1990. *The Road to Divorce: England, 1530–1987.* Oxford: Oxford University Press.

———. 1993. *Broken Lives: Separation and Divorce in England, 1660–1857.* Oxford: Oxford University Press.

Strand, David. 1989. *Rickshaw Beijing: City People and Politics in the 1920s.* Berkeley: University of California Press.

Thompson, E. P. 1963. *The Making of the English Working Class.* New York: Vintage.

———. 1967. "Time, Work-Discipline, and Industrial Capitalism." *Past and Present* 38:56–97.

Thurston, Anne. 1988. *Enemies of the People: The Ordeal of Intellectuals in China's Great Cultural Revolution.* Cambridge: Harvard University Press.

———. 1990. "Urban Violence during the Cultural Revolution: Who Is to Blame?" In Jonathan Lipman and Stevan Harrell, eds., *Violence in China: Essays in Culture and Counterculture.* Albany: State University of New York Press.

Tilly, Charles. 1973. "Does Modernization Breed Revolution?" *Comparative Politics* 5, no. 3 (April): 425–47.

———. 1986. *The Contentious French.* Cambridge: Belknap Press of Harvard University Press.

Traer, James. 1980. *Marriage and the Family in Eighteenth-Century France.* Ithaca: Cornell University Press.

"The Tribes of North-Western Se-chuan." 1908. *Geographical Journal* 32, no. 6 (December): 594–97.

Trotman, Fiennes. 1837. *An Address on the New Marriage Registration Acts.* London: L. and G. Seeley.

Union Research Institute. 1968. *The Case of P'eng Teh-huai.* Hong Kong: Union Research Institute.

———. 1971. *Documents of the Chinese Communist Party Central Committee, September 1956–April 1969.* Hong Kong: Union Research Institute.

Upham, Frank K. 1987. *Law and Social Change in Postwar Japan.* Cambridge: Harvard University Press.

U.S. Consul General, Hong Kong. *Current Background* (= *CB*).

———. *Selections from Chinese Mainland Magazines* (= *SCMM*).

———. *Selections from Chinese Mainland Press* (= *SCMP*).

Vassal, Gabrielle M. 1922. *In and Round Yunnan Fou.* London: William Heinemann.

Vogel, Ezra F. 1965. "From Friendship to Comradeship: The Change in Personal Relations in Communist China." *China Quarterly*, no. 21 (January–March 1965): 46–60.

———. 1969. *Canton under Communism: Programs and Politics in a Provincial Capital, 1949–1968.* New York: Harper.

Wakeman, Frederic, Jr. 1985. *The Great Enterprise: The Manchu Reconstruction of Imperial Order in Seventeenth-Century China.* Berkeley and Los Angeles: University of California Press.

Wakeman, Frederic, Jr., and Wen-hsin Yeh. 1992. "Introduction." In Frederic Wakeman Jr. and Wen-hsin Yeh, eds., *Shanghai Sojourners.* Berkeley: Institute for East Asian Studies.

Walder, Andrew. 1986. *Communist Neotraditionalism: Work and Authority in Chinese Industry.* Berkeley and Los Angeles: University of California Press.

Wall, James, and Michael Blum. 1991. "Community Mediation in the People's Republic of China." *Journal of Conflict Resolution* 35, no. 1:3–20.

Walzer, Michael. 1994. "A Day in the Life of a Socialist Citizen." In Nicolaus Mills, ed., *Legacy of Dissent: 40 Years of Writing from "Dissent" Magazine.* New York: Touchstone.

Wang, Shaoguang. 1995. "The Politics of Private Time: Changing Leisure Patterns in Urban China." In Deborah Davis, Richard Kraus, Barry Naughton, and Elizabeth J. Perry, eds., *Urban Spaces in Contemporary China: The Potential for Autonomy and Community in Post-Mao China.* Washington, D.C., and Cambridge: Woodrow Wilson Center Press and Cambridge University Press.

Wasserstrom, Jeffrey. 1991. *Student Protest in Twentieth Century China: The View from Shanghai.* Stanford: Stanford University Press.

Watson, James L. 1984. "Introduction." In James Watson, ed., *Class and Social Stratification in Post-Revolution China.* Cambridge: Cambridge University Press.

———. 1992. "The Renegotiation of Chinese Cultural Identity in the Post-Mao Era." In Jeffrey N. Wasserstrom and Elizabeth J. Perry, eds., *Popular Protest and Political Culture in Modern China: Learning from 1989.* Boulder: Westview Press.

Watt, John. 1972. *The District Magistrate in Late Imperial China.* New York: Columbia University Press.

Weber, Eugen. 1976. *Peasants into Frenchmen: The Modernization of Rural France, 1870–1914.* Stanford: Stanford University Press.

Weston, Timothy. 1996. "Beijing University and Chinese Political Culture, 1905–1923." Ph.D. diss., Dept. of History, University of California, Berkeley.

White, Lynn T., III. 1981. "Shanghai-Suburb Relations, 1949–1966." In Christopher Howe, ed., *Shanghai: Revolution and Development in an Asian Metropolis.* Cambridge: Cambridge University Press.

———. 1989. *Policies of Chaos: The Organizational Roots of Violence in China's Cultural Revolution.* Princeton: Princeton University Press.

White, Morton, and Lucia White. 1962. *The Intellectual versus the City, from Thomas Jefferson to Frank Lloyd Wright.* Cambridge: Harvard University Press and M.I.T. Press.

Whitehead, Barbara Dafoe. 1993. "Dan Quayle Was Right." *Atlantic Monthly*, April, 47–84.

Wilde, Oscar. 1950. "The Soul of Man under Socialism." In Hesketh Pearson, ed., *Essays by Oscar Wilde*. London: Methuen.

Witke, Roxane. 1967. "Mao Tse-tung, Women, and Suicide in the May Fourth Era." *China Quarterly*, no. 31:128–47.

Wolf, Margery. 1972. *Women and the Family in Rural Taiwan*. Stanford: Stanford University Press.

———. 1975. "Women and Suicide in China." In Margery Wolf and Roxane Witke, eds., *Women in Chinese Society*. Stanford: Stanford University Press.

———. 1985. *Revolution Postponed: Women in Contemporary China*. Stanford: Stanford University Press.

Wood, Gordon. 1972. *The Creation of the American Republic, 1776–1787*. Chapel Hill: University of North Carolina Press.

Worobec, Christine D. 1991. *Peasant Russia: Family and Community in the Post-Emancipation Period*. Princeton: Princeton University Press.

Wou, Odoric. 1994. *Mobilizing the Masses: Building Revolution in Henan*. Stanford: Stanford University Press.

Wright, Robert. 1994. *The Moral Animal: Evolutionary Psychology and Everyday Life*. New York: Pantheon.

Wu, Harry Xiaoying. 1994. "Rural to Urban Migration in the People's Republic of China." *China Quarterly*, no. 139:669–98.

Xiaobu Lü and Elizabeth J. Perry, eds. 1997. *Danwei: The Changing Chinese Workplace in Historical and Comparative Perspective*. Armonk, N.Y.: M. E. Sharpe.

Xu Yao. 1996. "Education in Civilized Divorce." *Beijing Review*, 23–29 December.

Xue Suzhen et al. 1983–1984. "An Investigation of Some Marriage Cases in Urban Shanghai." *Chinese Sociology and Anthropology* 16, nos. 1–2:82–99.

Yan, Yunxiang. 1996. *The Flow of Gifts: Reciprocity and Social Networks in a Chinese Village*. Stanford: Stanford University Press.

Yang, C. K. 1959. *The Chinese Family in the Communist Revolution*. Cambridge, Mass.: Technology Press.

Yang, Rae. 1997. *Spider Eaters: A Memoir*. Berkeley and Los Angeles: University of California Press.

Yeh, Wen-hsin. 1990. *The Alienated Academy: Culture and Politics in Republican China, 1919–1937*. Cambridge: Council on East Asian Studies, Harvard University.

———. 1992. "Progressive Journalism and Shanghai's Petty Urbanites: Zou Taofen and the Shenghuo Enterprise, 1926–1945." In Frederic Wakeman Jr. and Wen-hsin Yeh, eds., *Shanghai Sojourners*. Berkeley: Institute of East Asian Studies.

———. 1995. "Corporate Space, Communal Time: Everyday Life in Shanghai's Bank of China." *American Historical Review* 100, no. 1:97–122.

Yen, Chia-chi, and Kao Kao. 1988. *The Ten Year History of the Chinese Cultural Revolution*. Taipei: Institute of Current China Studies.

Young, Crawford. 1994. *The African Colonial State in Comparative Perspective*. New Haven: Yale University Press.

Young, Ernest. 1992. "Imagining the Ancien Régime in the Deng Era." In Jeffrey N. Wasserstrom and Elizabeth J. Perry, eds., *Popular Protest and Political Culture in Modern China: Learning from 1989*. Boulder: Westview Press.

Young, Marilyn. 1989. "Chicken Little in China: Some Reflections on Women." In

Arif Dirlik and Maurice Meisner, eds., *Marxism and the Chinese Experience: Issues in Contemporary Chinese Marxism*. Armonk, N.Y.: M. E. Sharpe.

Yue Daiyun. 1988. *Intellectuals in Chinese Fiction*. Berkeley: Institute for East Asian Studies.

Yue Daiyun with Carolyn Wakeman. 1985. *To the Storm: The Odyssey of a Revolutionary Chinese Woman*. Berkeley and Los Angeles: University of California Press.

Zerubavel, Eviatar. 1981. *Hidden Rhythms: Schedules and Calendars in Social Life*. Chicago: University of Chicago Press.

Zha, Jianying. 1995. *China Pop: How Soap Operas, Tabloids, and Bestsellers Are Transforming a Culture*. New York: New Press.

Zhen, Zhaihua. 1992. *Red Flower of China*. New York: Soho Books.

Zheng, Yi. 1996. *A Scarlet Memorial: Tales of Cannibalism in Modern China*. Trans. T. P. Sym. Boulder: Westview Press.

INDEX

Text: Baskerville
Display: Baskerville
Composition: G&S Typesetters, Inc.
Printing and binding: Edwards Brothers